Turner
TR
303
12:30

10/18 first case due - 10/17 - A
12/8 pre case due -

POLICY FORMULATION AND ADMINISTRATION

Cases due:
Prelude Corp chapter 1 – 10/20
Blow-Mold Packers Inc – 12/8
Ch. 6

POLICY FORMULATION AND ADMINISTRATION

A Casebook of Top-Management Problems in Business

C. ROLAND CHRISTENSEN, A.B., D.C.S.
*George Fisher Baker, Jr. Professor of
Business Administration*

NORMAN A. BERG, S.B., D.B.A.
Professor of Business Administration

MALCOLM S. SALTER, A.B., D.B.A.
Associate Professor of Business Administration

All of the
*Graduate School of Business Administration
Harvard University*

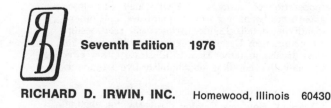

Seventh Edition   1976

RICHARD D. IRWIN, INC.   Homewood, Illinois   60430

Irwin-Dorsey Limited   Georgetown, Ontario   L7G 4B3

Seventh Edition

First Printing, January 1976
Second Printing, November 1976
Third Printing, February 1977

Case material of the Harvard Graduate School of Business Administration is made possible by the cooperation of business firms who may wish to remain anonymous by having names, quantities, and other identifying details disguised while basic relationships are maintained. Cases are prepared as the basis for class discussion rather than to illustrate either effective or ineffective handling of administrative situations.

ISBN 0-256-01820-0
Library of Congress Catalog Card No. 75–28946
Printed in the United States of America

To
GEORGE ALBERT SMITH, JR. (1905–1969)
Friend
Colleague
Teacher to all

Acknowledgments

As HAS BEEN our tradition, we wish to acknowledge again our thanks to all of the people who have helped make possible this seventh edition of *Policy Formulation and Administration*. We are indebted to our colleagues here at the Harvard Business School, to our colleagues in other schools of business administration and in management development institutes, and to the directors of management development activities in private and public organizations in this country and throughout the world. They have been generous in helping us with the improvement of course concepts and case developments, and in sharing their teaching experiences with the previous editions of our book. Many of the changes in this seventh edition reflect their suggestions. We are indebted also to the leaders of the organizations and their associates who have contributed so generously of their time and experience to these case studies. They have shared their failures as well as their successes with all of us who study, learn, and teach in the policy area.

Case research and writing is a demanding discipline—a blend of rigorous research method and artistry of presentation. We are especially indebted to the men and women who researched and developed these case studies. Some of these cases are the products of individual efforts; others grew out of collective efforts. Some of them we have written or supervised ourselves. Others have been written by our associates here and at other schools of business. We congratulate them for their work well done and extend them our gratitude for their cooperation in making this book possible.

Specifically we would like to thank the following associates for their development of the indicated cases: Albert Booth—Merlin-Microwave; Robert F. Bruner—The Real Paper; Ram Charan—Hawaii Best Company; Norman Fast—Lincoln Electric Company and Allied Security, Inc.; T. Gearreald—Tensor Corporation; R. Hamermesh—Fuqua Industries; Hassell H. McClellan—Sturm, Ruger, and Co., Inc., Note on the

Security Service and Equipment Industry and American District Telegraph Co. (ADT); R. A. Pitts—Sybron Corporation and CML Group, Inc.; Elisabeth Lyman Rachal—Note on the Mechanical Writing Industry, Bic Pen Corporation, Scripto, Inc., and Kampgrounds of America; T. C. Raymond—Consolidated Drugs; Charles B. Weigle—Prelude Corporation; Bruce Scott—Midway D-R; George Albert Smith, Jr.— Albert Manufacturing; Mrs. A. T. Sproat—Corporate Performance and Private Criticism—Campaign G. M. Rounds I and II; Thomas D. Steiner and Jeanne Deschamps—Boston Symphony Orchestra; Howard H. Stevenson—Blow Mold Packers, Inc.; Eoin Trevelyan—Proprietary Health Systems, Inc.

We are also grateful to the administrative officers of the Harvard Graduate School of Business Administration for their continuing encouragement of this effort. Lawrence Fouraker, Walter Salmon, A. R. Towl, and Charles Gebhard have been most supportive. Juliet Muenchen has been "administrative director" of the countless tasks involved in the publication of this book; she has handled her assignment with competence.

We wish again to pay tribute and acknowledge our great debt to George Albert Smith, Jr., who passed away October 12, 1969. Professor Smith was "the pioneer" in the development of the Policy area. His influence continues in the thousands of students with whom he worked, in the countless teachers and researchers developed under his personal supervision, and in the concepts and ideas expressed and used in this edition. He personally influenced and taught each of the present authorship group. We hope to honor him by the continuing development of his ideas and by this book.

December 1975   C. ROLAND CHRISTENSEN
                                          NORMAN A. BERG
                                          MALCOLM S. SALTER

Contents

Section Four. *Managing the Overall Organization*

Part Three
Policy Formulation and Administration in Diversified Firms

Part Four
Corporate Response to Social Change

° Denotes non-Harvard cases

Introduction

THE PURPOSES of this seventh edition of *Policy Formulation and Administration* are essentially the same as those of the previous editions. The book provides both text and a selection of cases that can assist men and women preparing for a career in business administration to become acquainted with the opportunities and challenges confronting the top manager of a firm. This material also provides significant opportunities for learning for middle managers and senior managers enrolled in university or corporate management development programs.

The educational objectives of this edition are the same as for earlier editions. Its orientation is managerial. It seeks to encourage the development of leadership skills. Men and women who can "take charge" of organizations are a scarce resource. The hope of the authors is that the study of these situations may encourage interest in general management skills and may provide an opportunity for academic practice of skills requisite to this organization position via discussion of selected case problems.

Specifically, the study and discussion of these cases, and the accompanying text, offers opportunities:

1. To learn about the functions, roles, and skills of top management; the perspective of top management.
2. To develop skill in envisaging goals; to delineate the functions and activities that must be performed to achieve the goals; and to determine what functional strategies are needed for goal achievement.
3. To become familiar with "risk" and its place in top-management thinking.
4. To learn to identify—and to attract to a business—personnel with the requisite technical and emotional abilities and to build them into a thinking, living, acting organization.
5. To develop the ability to divide the work of a firm into logical and understandable assignments, with limitations of authority and, at

the same time, provisions for individual decision-making powers and opportunities for cooperation.

6. To learn to set standards for measuring performance.
7. To understand how to provide motivation for the members of the management group so they will apply their skills (which the organization needs) and in doing so find nutriment for their own needs—both economic and ethical.
8. To gain insight, self-confidence, imagination, and the ability to furnish leadership to the organization. Coupled with leadership is the willingness to take ultimate responsibility not only for the results of one's own decisions but also for the results of the decisions and actions of all to whom the leader has delegated authority.
9. To anticipate and accept the responsibilities of the leader and those of the organization to the various sectors of society that are affected by the organization's actions: the investor, the worker, the supplier, the community, and the country.

This casebook invites both instructor and student to enter into a process of policy formulation and administration. This process, as will become apparent from class discussion, depends upon a melding of intellectual and administrative skills. For example, identifying problems that affect the long-term position of the firm calls for the ability to select and relate disparate bits of information so that an inclusive statement of key problems can be made. Making such a statement requires, however, more than the intellectual skill of analyzing environmental trends and data on internal corporate operations. It also requires the ability to articulate problems in such a way that suggests actionable alternatives that can be submitted to careful evaluation. This ability reflects what we can call an administrative sense. Similarly, setting objectives and formulating a plan of action require both the sense of what is needed and what will work.

The cases presented in this book are not meant to stand alone. They are not traditional research documents which describe important aspects of policy formulation and administration. Nor are they studies which suggest how policy should be formulated and administered by top corporate executives. Rather the cases have been designed to provide the raw material for students to work out for themselves, under the guidance of a trained instructor, what business policies are appropriate for particular firms. It is intended that a course based upon these cases will help the student develop an analytical approach to broad business policy problems.

Each case in this book describes an actual situation as of the time the case was written. To preserve confidences, fictitious names have been used in some instances, and sometimes the geographical locations have been changed. Only on rare occasions has the industry been changed or the size of the company materially altered. Almost always the case contains information about the industry and its competitive conditions; some historical background about the company itself; financial and statistical data; information about products and production, and marketing methods and facilities; the organization plan; and executive personnel. These cases are the raw materials that permit simulation in the classroom of the actual discussions carried on informally among managers and in board and committee rooms.

In the tradition of earlier editions, this volume contains a selection of "seasoned" cases used in previous editions as well as a selection of new cases not heretofore published. We have also selected cases from a wide variety of corporate organizations, ranging in size from the small, new enterprise to the large and very complex conglomerate organization. In addition to cases covering problems of the overall enterprises, we have included, in this edition, some cases focusing on the problems of the individual manager as he attempts to survive and to influence his organization.

It has been our experience and the experience of many other instructors that, by using cases such as these, a teacher and his students can together create "ways of thinking," "ways of feeling," and "ways of doing" that accelerate tremendously both intellectual growth and emotional development.

The Questions or Problems in the Cases and Their Solutions

At the top level, an executive does not have any "all-wise" adviser to identify what problem or problems he or she should be watching or working on at a particular time—that must be decided personally. And there is no reference book to look into, no infallible aid to give *the* solution. The executive must, nevertheless, find *some* solution, some workable solution. This is done by the use of experience and the exercise of judgment, usually after discussion and consultation with others. And neither before a decision is made, nor after, can the executive be absolutely sure what action is *right* or *best.*

The administrator must be willing and able to work in a climate of uncertainty, which is often uncomfortable. He or she must accept the responsibility for reaching decisions under time pressure, on the basis of limited facts, and in the face of many unknowns. Imperfect, the administrator must work with people who also are imperfect. Almost always, some associates or other parties involved will disagree, and their disagreement and their views should be taken into account. The administrator is in the usually lonesome situation of being the possessor of ultimate responsibility. He or she inevitably will make some mistakes.

If experienced and mature, the administrator will expect this and will allow for it, but will hope to reach wise decisions most of the time. The administrator who succeeds in doing that is a successful business leader.

This clearly suggests that the cases do not include any "official" or "demonstrably correct" answers. We do not have either "official" questions or "approved" solutions. It is part of the student's task, as it is part of an executive's task, to discover questions and to distinguish the important from the unimportant. In some instances, we do not agree among ourselves as to exactly what the most fundamental problems or opportunities are; and in still more instances we do not agree on the best possible course of action. If we did, we would question the reality of our cases and perhaps also the quality and integrity of our own views. Complicated business situations such as are presented here are episodes taken out of business life. Since we are all different people, with our own special backgrounds and experiences, we will attach to these problems at least somewhat differing interpretations and envision somewhat differing or substantially differing solutions or courses of action.

We do have our own ideas about each of the cases we are offering; so do our colleagues who use them. In some instances, we hold our views with strong conviction. In others, we are much less sure of what we think. And we change our views from time to time. So we certainly do not feel that we *know* what should be done in each of the situations presented. The value of the cases in the classroom lies in their discussion, not in the giving or finding of an "authoritative" answer.

Organization and Philosophy of the Book

This edition contains the basic organizational features of its predecessor efforts with some modifications. We have divided the book into four major subsections, on Policy Formulation; Policy Administration; Policy Formulation and Administration in Diversified Firms; and Corporate Response to Social Change.

This plan with its selected distribution of cases can give you as students a sense of the atmosphere in which top-level executives work and can make real to you the individuals in top management, with their range of human frailties and strengths. It also will make clear to you that managers must work through and depend on other people; that they must engage in much routine work; that virtually all they can be sure of is "change" and the "unexpected." You will learn also that policy formulation is not always a formal process; that there often is a discrepancy between "stated" policy and policy as "practiced"; that much policy making is done (and should be done) at fairly low levels in organizations; and that effective authority or leadership is not conferred from above but is earned and awarded from below.

As you progress in your study of the cases, many other important things will become clear. For example, you will be disabused of any idea that the executive discovers and solves one problem at a time. On the contrary, he or she deals with many problems concurrently, each at a different stage of development. Furthermore, the route of travel from sizeup, through planning, organizing, putting plans into action and control, to reappraisal, is not a straight line. The route is much more like a circle. Even in dealing with one problem, the administrator goes around the circle many times: and, as we have said, is busy with many circles. The executive's job is never really finished.

Preparing a Case for Class

The question of how students should prepare a case for class has been put to us many times by our own students and also by people studying and teaching these cases elsewhere. Actually, the question is often phrased: "What is the *best* way to prepare a case?" That one we cannot answer, inasmuch as we do not think there is any *best* way. There are, no doubt, many good and useful ways. Each of us must develop the methods that serve us best. Moreover, we all must change our approach somewhat to deal with each new situation. And each case is a new situation. So there is no formula, no basic pattern that we can pass on. We can, at most, make a few overall observations and then try to detail some specific suggestions.

We recommend, with the qualifications just stated, the following to the student: we suggest you first read the case through to get a general impression of what it is about, how it seems to come out, and what kinds of information it contains. We think there is a real advantage in doing this first reading a day or two before the time when you must do your thorough and final preparation. There is a value in having the general situation in mind in time to mull it over, both consciously and subconsciously, for a while. That is true of any important problem one has to deal with—in school, in business, anywhere.

For the second reading, we suggest you take the time to proceed slowly and carefully, studying the tables and exhibits and making notes as you go. Perhaps some headings will occur to you under which you want to summarize what you believe are especially pertinent factors. Perhaps, however, when you feel you are about at the end of your preparation, it will be well to ask: "Have I worked this thing through to the point where, if I really had a chance to talk to the persons responsible for this company, I could (1) talk intelligently with them about their company and their job in managing it; (2) show them why the main issues I have distilled out as a result of my analysis are really of first importance; and (3) give them a coordinated program of action that would be practical and would have a reasonable chance to succeed?"

Specifically, Part I of this book contains cases that require the student to define and assess corporatewide problems affecting a firm's long-run performance. The most important long-run problems are not necessarily obvious after a first reading of the case. Nor do the statements of managers quoted in the cases always reveal the scope of issues to be faced. Given this realistic setting, developing the ability to identify the critical or strategic problems facing a general manager constitutes a major objective of Section 1. The cases are broad and require the student to "size up situations" from the top manager's perspective and to understand the critical functions he or she carries out.

The "size-up," as we like to call it, starts with an identification of the nature of the company's business; its economic goals; its key operating policies; its organizational structure; its economic, social, and political environment; and the values and administrative procedures used by top management. This process of identification is a kind of intelligence operation which should lead to a general status report on the company in question. This process relies heavily upon the skills and knowledge developed in functional courses in finance, marketing, manufacturing policy, organizational behavior, and the like. The added challenge presented by the first cases of this book is the need to relate and to synthesize disparate bits of information in an overall assessment of a company's current position.

In preparing the cases in Section 1 for class discussion, each student should consider as a start the following kinds of questions: What kind of company is this? Is there an identifiable strategy? What are the environmental factors affecting the company today, and what can we foresee as potential changes in the company's environment? What are the company's greatest opportunities and risks? What are the company's strengths and weaknesses in light of the industry trends and apparent opportunities and risks? What is your size-up of the general manager— his understanding of his company's situation and the manner in which he is dealing with company problems and opportunities?

A complete and well-thought-out status report on a company will inevitably suggest future alternatives or courses of action. While the first cases provide ample opportunity for the exploration of such alternatives, the cases presented in Section 2 are cast in such a light that particular attention must be paid to establishing objectives and formulating future plans of action. Moving to this aspect of the general manager's job requires that the student develop criteria for establishing meaningful goals and evaluating alternative strategies. The development of such criteria is a major goal of Section 2.

Each class should aim at developing such criteria for itself. In addition, each class should be able to develop a feel for when specific criteria are most relevant. There is no checklist which can be usefully applied to every company situation. This feel can be developed through the process of informed discussion in the classroom. In preparing for this discussion, each student should start by doing the kind of overall corporate assessment suggested above for the cases in Section 1. On the basis of this broad-gauged assessment, major strategic alternatives should be identified. In addition, each student should come to class with a recommended course of action based on his analysis of the company's principal alternatives. The following questions may be a useful point of departure for individual preparation: What constitutes a reasonable set of goals for this company? Given these goals, what are the company's existing strengths? Under which alternatives are profit opportunities best exploited and risks properly hedged? Which alternatives fit most closely with existing corporate values? If selected, what are the implications of each alternative for the company, and can the company accommodate these new demands?

The cases in Part II of this book focus more directly on the problems of designing and managing an administrative organization than do the cases presented in Part I. Consequently, the educational objective of the sections in this part is to extend the range of skills stressed in Part I by presenting case problems which focus class discussion on (1) those instruments of management that a general manager can use in implementing a plan of action, (2) the alternate ways of structuring decision-making within administrative subunits, and (3) administrative problems at the level of the individual manager which result from attempts to effect change.

In Section 3, for example, the principal issue raised is how best to gear a firm's organizational structure and systems of measurement and reward to overall corporate strategy. The student is asked to confront such basic questions as: How many administrative subunits should a given company have? How should these subunits be structured internally? How should their performance be measured and their managers rewarded? How should the various parts of the company be related as a whole?

The cases in Section 4 present situations which for the most part assume both corporate strategy and structure as given. These cases focus, therefore, upon the total general management process of formulating and administering policy. Part III carries that process into the realm of diversified firms. Part IV highlights the increasingly critical task of the general manager in responding to major social change.

We urge students, if possible, to discuss the cases with one another while preparing them. Managers in business discuss their problems with other key people. But be sure you do your own independent work and independent thinking. Do not be too stubborn to recognize a better idea than your own, but be sure you really understand and believe in it before you adopt it.

One more observation. Not infrequently, students express the wish for more information than is in a case; they feel they cannot make a decision without more facts. Do not hide behind that bogeyman. For one thing, business leaders never have all the facts they would like to have. And, as far as the cases are concerned, they all contain enough information to enable you to decide and recommend something sensible. Be sure you learn how to use, and do use, all the information you have.

Outside Reading

While the text and cases in this book make up the subject matter of a complete course, an instructor may wish to assign outside readings which reinforce the concepts brought out in class discussion. Several works, in particular, are relevant to the cases presented in this book:

> Andrews, Kenneth R.   *The Concept of Corporate Strategy*. Homewood, Ill.: Dow Jones-Irwin, 1971.
>
> Ansoff, H. Igor.   *Corporate Strategy*. New York: McGraw-Hill Book Co., 1965.
>
> Chandler, Alfred D. *Strategy and Structure*. Cambridge, Mass.: The M.I.T. Press, 1962.
>
> Levinson, Harry.   *The Great Jackass Fallacy*. Boston: Division of Research, Harvard Business School, 1973.
>
> Selekman, Benjamin.   *Power and Morality in a Business Society*. New York: McGraw-Hill Book Co., 1956.
>
> Sloan, Alfred P.   *My Years at General Motors*. Garden City, N.Y.: Doubleday & Co., Inc., 1963.
>
> Zaleznik, Abraham.   *Human Dilemmas of Leadership*. New York: Harper & Row, Publishers, 1966.

The work by Andrews provides a good overview of the range of policy problems which will be addressed in this casebook. Zaleznik's book complements Andrews by shedding light on the human problems of top-level decision-makers. The works of Ansoff, Zaleznik, and Sloan are particularly relevant to Part I of the book, while the Chandler study will provide an important perspective for looking at the cases presented in Section 3. Professor Levinson's study is of primary value in relationship to the issues raised in Section 4. Finally, Selekman will provide the kind of viewpoint which can usefully be discussed in connection with the cases appearing in Part IV.

Each instructor, of course, will be able to add to this list. In doing so, the relevant criteria for selection should be whether a given work sharpens the focus of policy problems or helps students of administration broaden their perspective in analyzing the cases presented for study.

Quite apart from "course specific" readings, there is a world of literature relevant to the study of policy formulation and administration. Biographies and autobiographies offer a rich account of policy formulation and decision-making. Similarly, history and political science present innumerable opportunities to study the evolution of policy and organization. Accounts as diverse as those on the administrative organization set up in France by Napoleon in the 18th century, the development of the railroads in the 19th century, and the path of the social revolutions in the 20th century all offer clues about how organizational leaders manage their affairs.

Introduction
The Tasks and Tools of General Management—An Overview

Since most managers—in contrast to doctors, lawyers, engineers, or architects—need no license to practice, many people are surprised to hear the practice of management referred to as both the oldest of the arts *and* the newest of the professions. This surprise is not shared, however, by experienced managers and educators who believe that managers, like members of other professions, need to be trained to focus their skills upon "the solutions of certain classes of recurring practical problems that are not amenable to amateur, uniformed, irresponsible, or fortuitous solutions."[1]

While there are many incentives to "professionalize" management through training, one of the most compelling is the desire of managers themselves to cope more effectively with the complexity and the ambiguities of the general management task. C. Roland Christensen, who has spent over 25 years studying the job of the general manager, has captured the essence of this task. He writes, "The uniqueness of a good general manager lies in his ability to lead effectively organizations whose complexities he can never fully understand, where his capacity to control directly the human and physical forces comprising that organization is severely limited, and where he must make or review and assume ultimate responsibility for present decisions which commit concretely major resources for a fluid and unknown future."[2]

---

[1] Kenneth R. Andrews, "The Progress of Professional Education for Business" (Remarks presented for discussion at the Centennial Convocation on Graduate Professional Education at the Episcopal Theological School, Cambridge, Massachusetts, January 27–29, 1967).

[2] C. Roland Christensen, "Education for the General Manager" (Harvard Business School case number 4–375–241).

The following discussion of general management is directed at those students of administration interested in grappling with the complexity and the ambiguities of the general manager's task which Christensen has highlighted. While the ideas and concepts presented do not add up to a rigorous theory of general management, they can provide a useful analytical framework for those aspiring to enter into a process of policy formulation and administration at the level of the chief executive, divisional general management, or the management of multifunctional profit centers or other kinds of semiautonomous units.

DIMENSIONS OF THE GENERAL MANAGER'S JOB

The inevitable shock of assuming one's first general management position is tied to the realization that the general manager must assess on a continuing basis what constitutes an effective balance between conflicting aspects of his job. To what extent, for example, should he concentrate on supervising and coordinating current operations in contrast to planning for future operations? What balance should there be between direct personal intervention in establishing policy as opposed to less directive management of a policy-making process that is widely shared throughout the organization? How much attention and time should be spent on purely corporate operations in contrast to industry matters and public service? What should be the relative responsibilities of developing a rich personal life and concentrating on the heavy stewardship responsibilities which general managers carry for the company's shareholders and employees?

The puzzling nature of these questions, inevitably a part of the general manager's role, is complicated by the fact that general managers do not have the luxury of cost-free time to learn their jobs, and few organizations have significant absorption power for costly mistakes of an economic or organizational nature. Nevertheless, recognizing the breadth of the tensions and conflicting pressures facing the general manager is the first step in understanding the job's critical dimensions.

The most immediate concern of the general manager is supervising current operations. This normally involves setting goals and targets for various functional departments and product divisions, and periodically reviewing performance against preestablished goals. Sometimes operating goals and policies need to be modified by the general manager (and his associates) as changes in the environment suggest courses of action different from those currently being followed by various parts of the organization. Both the review of current performance and the reassessment of current operating goals and policies require a flow of relevant, reliable, and timely information. Overseeing this activity is an important aspect of the general manager's operating concerns.

Perhaps the most critical aspect of supervising current operations is the occasional need to intervene in disputes over operating problems where those closest to the situation cannot reach agreement on appropriate courses of action. Here the task of the general manager is to identify or "extract" the relevant policy issues and suggest action that reflects his view of appropriate policy. This intervention must be done selectively and in ways which do not permanently upset established methods for resolving problems at lower levels of management. If every crisis were to be brought to the general manager's desk for resolution, most of his time would be taken up with managing a myriad of small crises which would detract from careful attention to other important general management tasks, such as planning for future operations.

Planning for future operations is more often paid lip service than practiced. In part, this is due to the fact that many general managers perceive the payoff of comprehensive forward planning as being quite low. For those who are guiding companies which have dominant positions in relatively stable, low growth markets, there is the tendency to accept projections of past experience as solid bases for estimating future resource needs. General managers of relatively weak companies, occupying subordinate roles in either growing or stable markets, also tend to invest lightly in future-oriented planning since their tendency is to "wait for the breaks" and scramble as fast as possible when opportunities present themselves. The greatest incentive to invest heavily in comprehensive forward planning is for general managers of companies with dominant positions in dynamic growth markets. Here the costs of losing that position of dominance can be very high. However, it is companies without dominant market positions which can often profit the most from comprehensive forward planning since it is the principal means of organizing the development of competitive strength over time. A large majority of companies fall into this category.

Planning for future operations involves making informed judgments about what opportunities and risks will face the company in the future, and identifying alternate means of either exploiting these opportunities or accommodating these risks. For the general manager this process first requires an identification of the current objectives and policies of his company or operating unit. It also involves grappling with a deceptively simple cluster of questions: What are the company's strengths and weaknesses? Where, in the company's perceived industry, are profit and service opportunities? And, how can those corporate capacities and industry opportunities be effectively related?

This framework of questions helps the general manager give order to the chaos that often surrounds planning future courses of action. It also focuses attention on selecting and ordering data relevant to the formulation or ratification of corporate purpose. It is thus an exercise in both logic and nonlogical thinking. Feelings, sentiment, and judgment are—and, indeed, need to be—mixed with the discipline of systematic enquiry and argument. All this takes time, commitment, and a certain amount of nerve.

In addition to supervising current operations and planning future strategies, every general manager inevitably becomes preoccupied with forging an organizational structure that fits the company's needs and unique characteristics. In its most basic sense, this structure is primarily a decision-making apparatus. Differences among organization structures result from different ways of allocating decision-making authority and responsibility to administrative subunits and to individuals within these subunits. An organization structure thus defines the locus of decision-making responsibilities and identifies who will make which decisions under normal conditions. At operating levels of management, departmental or product-oriented structures typically provide the basic models for each company's organizational format. At the top policy levels of management, collectives of executives from key operating posts are often asked to review recommendations and approve decisions made at the departmental or product division levels.

General managers must determine which decision-making structure best suits their current and future needs. They must also reinforce its effectiveness by communicating clearly and directly what is expected from each decision-maker. Performance measurement and reward systems typically have an important role to play in this effort. Designing and administering these systems is thus another important aspect of the general manager's job.

An additional responsibility of general management is the development of human capabilities and resources appropriate to the organization's present and future needs. The general manager must analyze both current operations and future plans in order to judge how many persons with what kinds of experience and competences are required. Once these needs are identified, the general manager must ensure that realistic plans are implemented to provide adequate human resources at all organizational levels when they are needed.

As straightforward as this sounds, there is perhaps no aspect of general management that is left so much to chance as manpower planning. Recruitment, staffing, job rotation, and training are often handled on an *ad hoc* basis rather than studied in advance. A common result of this practice is an unsystematic scramble for people, on the one hand, and career blockages, on the other, as companies experience shifting manpower needs. For general managers who proclaim that their organizations' past successes are due to the high quality of personnel, there can be no greater irony than finding that their organizations are equipped with inadequate personnel resources for the future or staffed with persons who face few opportunities for increased growth and development.

Apart from the administrative aspects of manpower planning, the development of an organization's human capabilities rests in large measure on the commitment of individuals to stretch themselves beyond their known limits. The reinforcement of this commitment (and morale) is the most subtle task of general management. While each successful general manager develops his own approach, a common characteristic shared by many organization leaders is the ability to institutionalize those values and articulate those objectives critical to the organization's success. Few groups of individuals—either inside or outside of the business world —have been able to maintain their effectiveness without the leadership of those who can both represent and guide the development of the group's goals and values. This requirement is virtually universal; fulfilling this requirement is unquestionably the general manager's most difficult responsibility.

A final responsibility of general managers is representing their organizations to the world at large. One way of describing the external environment of companies and other purposive organizations is in terms of evolving coalitions of interests and power. These coalitions can be semi-permanent alliances, as in the case of joint ventures between companies. They can also be extremely fluid coalitions which have coherence around certain issues and little coherence around other issues. A company's relations with labor unions and industry associations are cases in point. In these coalitions there are elements of both cooperation and controversy, and relations between parties are typically fluid and sometimes volatile. Relations between companies and various levels of government can have these characteristics as well. In this context the general manager has a dual responsibility. First, he must defend the integrity of his organization in these shifting coalitions and lobby for its interests. Second, where contracts, government regulation, and other aspects of law are evolved, he must be cognizant of the rules of law and take personal responsibility for ensuring compliance with these rules. Recent scandals involving large corporations show how vulnerable some general managers are on this count.

In summary, the basic dimensions of the general manager's job are five in number:

1. Supervising current operations.
2. Planning for future operations.
3. Designing and administering decision-making structures.
4. Developing human resources and capabilities.
5. Representing and holding responsible an organization to its various constituencies.

The basic dilemma of the general manager concerns what emphasis to give these tasks and responsibilities at any point in time. Pushing hard on all fronts at once is plainly a Herculean task. Yet no part of the general manager's job can be ignored for long without jeopardizing the viability of his organization. The challenge is therefore one of developing conceptual frameworks which "force" attention to as many of the general manager's concerns as possible.

This challenge has provided ample incentive to practitioners and theorists to develop concepts useful to the general manager. Some of the most original thinking was reflected in the development of Du Pont and General Motors during the 1920s and 1930s. The conceptual contributions of the Du Pont family in the development of their company and Alfred Sloan in the conversion of General Motors from a weak agglomerate of automotive companies to an industry leader provided other companies and several important management writers with standards for comparison and bases for the development of explicit concepts relating to general management.[3] The flourish of important publications in the 1950s by such unusual practitioners as Chester Barnard and such widely read academics as Peter Drucker and Herbert Simon was followed in the 1960s by a growing list of writers—including Edmund P. Learned, Philip Selznick, Alfred Chandler, and Kenneth Andrews—all of whom shared a common interest in the problems of the generalist.[4] In particular, their interest centered around the formulation of corporate purpose and the structural vehicles available for implementing purpose once it had been articulated. During the same decade, a group of writers and teachers of general management, including the present authors and some of their colleagues at Harvard, were exploring ways in which administrative practices and systems could support both corporate purpose and formal organizational arrangements.[5]

The principal utility of this literature, taken as an entirety, is that it has given rise to a cluster of concepts which can aid the general manager in dealing with the breadth of the tasks and responsibilities outlined above. Two of these concepts will be discussed in the following section.

---

[3] Alfred D. Chandler, Jr., and Stephen Salsbury, *Pierre S. DuPont and the Making of the Modern Corporation* (New York: Harper & Row, 1971); and Alfred P. Sloan, Jr., *My Years at General Motors* (New York: Doubleday & Company, 1963).

[4] Edmund P. Learned, David N. Ulrich, and Donald R. Booz, *Executive Action* (Boston: Division of Research, Harvard Business School, 1950); Philip Selznick, *Leadership in Administration* (New York: Harper & Row, 1957); Alfred D. Chandler, Jr., *Strategy and Structure* (Cambridge: The MIT Press, 1962); and Kenneth R. Andrews, *The Concept of Corporate Strategy* (Homewood, Ill.: Dow Jones–Irwin, Inc., 1971).

[5] Bruce R. Scott, "An Open System Model of the Firm" (Unpublished doctoral dissertation, Harvard University, 1963); Norman A. Berg, "The Allocation of Strategic Funds in a Diversified Firm" (Unpublished doctoral dissertation, Harvard University, 1963) and "Strategic Planning in Conglomerate Companies," *Harvard Business Review*, May–June 1965; Malcolm S. Salter, "Stages of Corporate Development: Implications for Management Control" (Unpublished doctoral dissertation, Harvard University, 1967); and Joseph L. Bower, *Managing the Resource Allocation Process* (Boston: Division of Research, Harvard Business School, 1969).

TWO BASIC CONCEPTS OF GENERAL MANAGEMENT

When the general manager promotes strategic planning within his organization and develops effective means of strategic control, he is in a strong position to influence the substance of decisions made at all levels of management which affect the long-run position of the enterprise. Strategic planning is one way of ensuring that corporate objectives and key operating policies are systematically developed. Strategic control is the means by which the general manager can create a decision-making environment that facilitates the allocation and the management of resources required by a particular corporate strategy.

Strategic Planning. Decision-making practices reflect a variety of assumptions about what constitutes an appropriate approach to planning and action. According to one approach, emphasis is placed on·evaluating a wide range of alternate means of achieving an organization's existing goals. If the specific decision issue is critical to the long-run position of the organization, the organization's long-run goals may be reviewed before a final decision on that specific issue is agreed upon. According to a contrasting approach, rather than evaluating multiple ways of achieving an organization's goals and reviewing the appropriateness of the goals themselves, emphasis is placed on evaluating only those possible courses of action which represent as little departure as possible from existing practices or states of being.

A basic assumption of many policy experts is that the *strategic mode* of planning and action, described in the first example, is often a more constructive influence on an organization's performance than the *incremental mode* of planning, described in the second example. This assumption is based on what is perceived to be the risks of incrementalism in coping with the various aspects of the general manager's job.

Before commenting on the risks of incrementalism, it is useful to contrast the incremental and the strategic modes of planning. The strategic mode of planning is based upon two propositions about policy and the policymaker:

1. The aims of policy should be clearly formulated *in advance* of choosing among alternative policies.
2. The policymaker should attempt a *comprehensive* overview of policy problems and of alternate policies.[6]

Businessmen and academicians who share these assumptions have developed scores of conceptual frameworks to help organize the planning

---

[6] David Braybrooke and Charles E. Lindblom, *A Strategy of Decision* (New York: The Free Press, 1963), p. 40.

task for such top-level policy makers as general managers. The best of these share a sequence of steps comparable to the following.[7]

1. *Preparation of Strategic Intelligence.* This intelligence operation involves the gathering of information—questions, insights, hypotheses, evidence—relevant to policy. As a minimum, this intelligence should be based on three data gathering efforts: (a) a detailed description of what the company does and how it defines its sphere of operations; (b) a prediction of future environmental opportunities and risks and their likely impact on the company's competitive position; and (c) an identification of corporate strengths and weaknesses and resources required to cope with future opportunities and risks.

2. *Definition of Purpose.* Based upon an analysis of this strategic intelligence, an appropriate "concept of the business" needs to be defined. For business firms, this concept can serve as a generalized model of how to compete in a specific industrial environment. An example of such a model is Alfred P. Sloan, Jr.'s, notion of first developing a "mass-class automobile" to compete against Henry Ford's basic Model T in the 1920s, and then bringing the consumer up the price ladder by offering an automobile in every segment of the market above Ford's cheapest model. In addition to such a conceptual idea, purpose needs to be defined in terms of relevant baselines for measuring performance and desired performance targets. If, for example, a firm is interested in rapid sales growth, the relevant baseline may be total industry expansion, and the target may be to grow at the industry growth rate plus 5 percent. As in the selection of an appropriate concept of the business, the selection of appropriate baselines for measuring performance and specific targets needs to be based upon an analysis of a firm's opportunities and risks, its available resources, and the preferences of its various constituencies.

3. *Policy Analysis.* Once objectives and a generalized model of how to compete have been selected, alternate operating policies need to be identified and analyzed. This step is central to the task of making a strategic idea operational. Thus, a comprehensive list of policy alternatives needs to be generated, the probabilities of the consequences of each alternative need to be assessed, and the consequences themselves need to be evaluated in terms of satisfying corporate objectives.

4. *Strategic Choice.* The selection of consistent operating policies which, in the judgment of top management, best fit available resources and best serve the organization's purpose, provides the basic guidelines for executive action. The establishment of specific policy represents the most visible evidence of a strategic commitment.

5. *Time Sequencing.* The final step in the initial formulation of strategy

---

[7] See for example, Andrews, *The Concept of Corporate Strategy;* and Hugo E. R. Uyterhoeven *et al., Strategy and Organization* (Homewood, Ill.: Richard D. Irwin, Inc., 1973).

involves the designation of a timed sequence of conditional moves based upon prior analysis of possible competitive responses and counterattacks.

6. *Strategy Review.* The strategic planning process also involves a periodic reexamination of the assumptions underlying current strategy, and an evaluation of organizational performance to date.

In the context of this conceptual framework, the key components of "strategy" include: (a) a concept of the business or a generalized model of how to compete; (b) objectives, principally economic in nature; (c) operating policies; and (d) a timed sequence of conditional moves. Exhibit 1 presents a summary of the strategic planning process in chart form.

There are several distinguishing features of this approach to planning. First, there is the attempt to define objectives *before* the final analysis of policy alternatives are considered. This provides an important set of criteria for evaluating alternate ways of exploiting environmental opportunities and reducing risks.

While such criteria help to structure the analytical process, the consideration of policy alternatives remains comprehensive in nature. This is a second distinguishing feature of the strategic mode of planning. Specifically, evaluating policy alternatives involves assessing the strengths and weaknesses of a wide range of alternatives which could be followed under a large number of environmental conditions.

Another characteristic of this mode of planning is the presumption on the part of the policy maker that major changes in strategy can and will be made if the comprehensive, analytical process indicates that major change is required. Great confidence is placed in the ability of the organization to change course when the imperative to do so is logically laid out and supported by detailed analysis and a sequenced plan of action. Change is thus considered a necessity rather than an insurmountable

EXHIBIT 1

Strategic Planning Mode

I	II	III	IV	V	VI
Strategic Intelligence*	Definition of Purpose	Policy Analysis	Strategic Choice	Time Sequencing	Strategy Review
Organizational profile	Concept of the business	Generation of a comprehensive list of policy alternatives	Selection of an internally consistent set of policies which best fits corporate resources and best serves corporate purposes	Designation of a timed sequence of conditional moves	
Environmental analysis	Objectives				
Strategic forecasts		Assessment of the probabilities of the consequences of each alternative		Action step 1	
				Etc.	
		Evaluate each set of consequences for corporate objectives			

* Information—questions, insights, hypotheses, evidence—relevant to polic

organizational problem by practitioners of the strategic mode of planning.

While major change is considered a feasible alternative by the strategic planner, comprehensive strategic planning often tends to limit the frequency of major policy changes in large organizations. Strategic planning in the modern corporation requires that top-level policy makers devise and administer a complex process for capturing the detailed knowledge of opportunities and risks that exists at lower levels in the organization.[8] Once this elaborate and time consuming process leads to a major strategic decision and steps are taken toward implementing that decision, the need and the incentive to modify key goals and policies is often minimal over the short run.[9] Thus, another hallmark of strategic planning is that it tends to result in "discontinuous policy-making" rather than in continual modifications of policy.

The assumptions underlying the strategic mode of planning differ radically from those underlying the incremental approach to planning and action. Incremental planners will argue that the effectiveness of strategic analysis is severely constrained by man's limited intellectual capabilities, and that there often is not sufficient time for evaluating the full range of alternative strategies and ranking them according to some set of preferences and utilities.[10]

Incrementalists also believe that nonincremental alternatives usually do not lie within the range of choice possible in complex organizations. They claim that complex structures can only avoid intolerable dislocation by meeting certain preconditions, among them that major changes of a political nature are admissible only if they occur slowly.[11] Since most decisions leading to a departure from current strategy affect internal coalitions of interests and power, incrementalists see wisdom in proceeding through a sequence of approximations. Rather than undertake both a comprehensive review of the external environment and internal resources and an assessment of major strategic alternatives when faced with a specific problem, attention is focused by incrementalists at that problem (or opportunity). The first satisfactory policy alternative is tried, altered, tried in its altered form, altered again, and so forth.[12]

Thus, the critical feature of the incremental approach to planning is that the analysis accompanying decisions proceeds through comparative analysis of marginal or incremental differences in states of being rather than through attempts at more comprehensive analysis of broadly con-

---

[8] For a full treatment if this idea see Norman A. Berg, "Allocation of Strategic Funds," and Joseph L. Bower, "Managing the Resource Allocation Process."

[9] The corporate histories presented by Chandler, in *Strategy and Structure*, provide evidence on this point.

[10] Braybrooke and Lindblom, *A Strategy of Decision*, pp. 48–57.

[11] Ibid., p. 73.

[12] Ibid., p. 73.

ceived alternatives.[13] A related feature of this planning mode is that while the policy maker contemplates means, he continues to contemplate objectives as well, unlike the strategic planner who ideally must stabilize his objectives at some point and then select the proper strategic alternative.[14] Exhibit 2 presents a generalized view of the incremental planning process.

It would be foolish, of course, to overdraw this dichotomy in planning behavior. Seldom do organizations practice one mode to the total exclusion of the other. However, we can realistically view planning practices as being arrayed across a spectrum, similar to the one depicted in Exhibit 3. A position at either end of this spectrum reflects a dominant *tendency* towards one of the two modes of planning. Pure forms of strategic or incremental planning behavior probably exist only in the mind of the theorist.

EXHIBIT 2

Incremental Planning Mode

I	II	III	IV	V	VI
Problem Recognition	Sequential Consideration of Policy Alternatives	New Policy Tested	New Policy Revised	New Policy Tried in Altered Form	Revision of Objectives
Unexpected external shock to the organization	Search for policy alternatives focused on specific problem at hand				Continual revision of objectives as more is learned about environment and policy alternatives
Sudden recognition of new opportunities and risks	Marginal changes in policy considered first				
Other kinds of feedback from the environment creating uncertainty	The first satisfactory alternative is accepted; other alternatives ignored				

Despite the difficulties inherent in the strategic mode of planning and action, the risks of incrementalism to the general manager can be high. The principal risk of such planning behavior is the risk of misallocating resources. Without systematic strategic planning, financial and management resources will most likely be allocated in an *ad hoc* manner. Without a broad assessment of corporate resources and opportunities, and a precise statement of objectives and priorities, the vast expenditure of time and money typically devoted to new programs and activities cannot be judged in terms of the benefits and costs involved. Strategic planning serves to reduce this risk. While it cannot guarantee future success, a general

---

[13] Ibid., p. 86.
[14] Ibid., p. 93.

EXHIBIT 3

A Spectrum of Planning Modes

Strategic Planning	Incremental Planning
More comprehensive analysis	More incremental analysis
Objectives defined prior to evaluation of major policy alternatives	Continual revision of objectives as more is learned about environment and policy alternatives
Major changes in goals and policies considered feasible	Only marginal moves considered feasible at any one point in time
Intermittent changes in policy	Continual modification of policy

manager who emphasizes the strategic mode of planning can increase the probability that timely revisions of goals, standards, and administrative mechanisms will take place. He will also ensure that his organization develops adequate programs to meet *emerging* needs.

The output of the strategic planning process is a series of decisions which, when taken together, comprise a company's strategy. The general manager's ability to manage this planning process and direct the development of a specific corporate strategy is his greatest source of influence within his organization. With paramount control over both the definition of objectives and the development of basic business policies, the general manager can establish a practical framework for analyzing all subsequent decisions which relate to corporate strategy.

Strategic Control. Complementing the general manager's ability to influence decision-making through the promotion of certain planning practices is his ability to influence decision-making and, indirectly, performance, by establishing a pattern of strategic control consistent with the needs of his company. Top management's control over the development of corporate strategy, the allocation of corporate resources, and the perceptions of those who initiate new business plans and projects depends to a great degree upon the structure of authority and responsibilities in the organization and the design of administrative systems used to monitor and control ongoing operations.[15] The structure of authority and responsibilities typically reflects the company's past and current growth strategy, its so-called administrative inheritance, and the patterns of

---

[15] This is a major theme in Bower's work on managing the resource allocation process, pp. 320–48.

operating performance and risk associated with the company. The same factors often influence the design of resource allocation measurement and reward systems.

While there is little widely accepted theory to guide the general manager in developing a proper pattern of strategic control for his company, the general manager can usefully consider the three factors mentioned above in designing an appropriate structure and set of administrative systems for the organization as a whole. Consider how these factors can influence the organization structure of a company.

The allocation of tasks (that is, decision-making authority and responsibility) between a headquarters office and various organizational subunits is the foundation of organization structure. Every growing organization is continually splitting up or redefining the mission of these subunits. The relationships among these units and the chief executive's office are also being reviewed and revised on a continuing basis. A company's past and current growth strategy will affect the interim set of operating relationships in several important ways. First, size and growth goals will necessarily raise the issue of span of control. As has been pointed out in a diverse array of organizational studies, the ability of any one executive to oversee the activities of a group of subordinates is inversely proportional to the size of that group. Thus, the larger the organizational unit, the greater the probability that it will need to be restructured into multiple units in the future.

More important than size, however, is the product-market diversity of a company. This is another aspect of strategy that directly affects the structure of authority and responsibility within a company. Generally speaking, the more a company diversifies into different product-market areas, the more likely it is that decentralized management structures will appear. In fact, recent research suggests a certain inevitability to the impact of corporate diversification upon organization structure.[16] As companies enter markets which are unrelated in terms of technology or consumers to the traditional core of the business, semiautonomous product divisions are bound to appear. The diversification of companies into technologically related product-market areas (concentric diversification) or into manufacturing and service operations which support the core business (vertical integration) creates more complex structural problems; but even in these situations, the inevitable drift toward increasing amounts of subunit independence is often apparent.

The impact of product-market diversity upon organization is not limited to the definition of semiautonomous divisions with the organization;

---

[16] Bruce R. Scott, "The Industrial Estate: Old Myths and New Realities," *Harvard Business Review*, March–April 1973.

it also concerns how these divisions relate to the organization as a whole. Here the role of the headquarters office is a key consideration. How directly should this office supervise and intervene in departmental or divisional affairs? What functions should the headquarters office perform? These questions can only be answered by closely examining the structural implications of specific product-market strategies. Typically, the more related a company's product-market commitments, the more the headquarters office will find occasions to promote interdivisional cooperation in areas of research, manufacturing, and marketing.

The balance between internal growth and acquisition also has important implications for headquarters-subunit relationships. In a company like Hewlett-Packard, which has grown and diversified internally from a core technology based on electronic instrumentation and minicomputers, staff at the corporate headquarters plays a very important role in supervising research and marketing activities on a corporate-wide basis. In contrast, a widely diversified company such as Textron, which participates in many different industrial and consumer markets by virtue of numerous acquisitions made during the 1960s, maintains no functionally oriented staff at the corporate level to oversee research, marketing, or manufacturing activities. Thus, little substantive contribution is made by headquarters staff to the so-called functional operations of the divisions. While these two cases do not suggest an invariably uniform pattern, they do suggest that acquired divisions often remain more independent from direct headquarters involvement in functional operations than do internally developed divisions, especially when these divisions operate in product-market areas unrelated to those of other divisions.

In addition to the past and current growth strategy of the company, patterns of operating performance and risk and the administrative inheritance of the organization can and should influence the characteristics of organization structure. Where either corporate performance or a specific division's performance has been poor, the headquarters office will often need to intervene directly in the affairs of functional department and operating divisions. High stakes coupled with deteriorating performance and increasing risks often lead to a recentralization of operating authority. This process is typically filled with tension since no operating manager cherishes the thought of having some of his independence taken away. There is also tension associated with the fact that many persons at the headquarters level do not understand the operations of organizational subunits sufficiently to intervene in subunit affairs on a continuing basis.[17]

Traditional bureaucratic practices and the distinctive character of a company's personnel, which we have referred to as the company's ad-

---

[17] Victor A. Thompson, *Modern Organization* (New York: Alfred A. Knopf, 1965).

ministrative inheritance, are also factors to be considered in designing or revising a company's structure of authority and responsibility. The old aphorism, "You can lead a horse to water but can't make it drink," has some special relevance here. If, for example, the founder-chairman of a company has reviewed and debated all capital requests above a certain amount for 15 years, the chances are slim that he will be easily convinced to give up control over the purse strings to a finance committee with members drawn from key parts of the company. In this situation, the broadening of authority and responsibility for resource allocation will necessarily be constrained. Similarly, if a company's bureaucratic traditions are rooted in colleagial decision-making, the manager who wants "to play his own chips and live by the results" may find himself under suspicion and criticism by his peers and superiors for his apparent attempts to assert his independent authority. This can be a serious matter if the traditions of colleagial decision-making are rooted in the character of the company's personnel. Where, for example, a young company is led by engineers with equivalent training and recognized competences, attempts will often be made to minimize highly centralized decision-making authority and to encourage group consensus before important decisions are taken.

Meaningful generalizations about the relationship between bureaucratic traditions and the character of a company's personnel, on the one hand, and the structure of decision-making authority and responsibility within the company, on the other, are difficult to make. But everyday experience suggests that this set of factors must be given serious attention when developing a structure that fits an organization's idiosyncratic needs. How much weight to give these factors in relation to past and current growth strategy and patterns of operating performance and risk is, of course, a matter for the general manager's judgment.

Effective strategic control depends as much upon the workings of various administrative systems as it does upon the structure of decision-making authority and responsibility. As corporate strategy, patterns of performance and risk, and administrative inheritances affect the decision-making structure, so too do these same factors affect the design and administration of resource allocation, measurement, and reward systems. For better or for worse, bureaucratic traditions will tend to influence the choices of what investment criteria to stress in allocating resources (such as a "four-year payback" rule of thumb) and what measures to use in monitoring the performance of new and long-standing projects (such as market share). These traditions and habits are often difficult to change. Similarly, the degree of diversity and uncertainty in a company's environment—or, in other words, its pattern of risk—can influence how the general manager designs his administrative systems. In a company facing a highly diverse and uncertain environment, the general manager might want to design administrative systems which stress different goals, different time horizons, different degrees of formality, and, indeed, different interpersonal orientations (such as task orientation versus cooperation with peers) for different departments or divisions. The logic here is that since each of these departments or divisions operates in quite diverse subenvironments, different behavior patterns on the part of managers may be required. Conversely, in a less diverse, more stable environment, the general manager may want more uniform measurement and reward systems which would tend to minimize differences along these behavioral dimensions. In this situation, the appropriate degree of subunit differentiation may be quite low since each group of managers interacts with a common and relatively predictable external environment.[18]

While these concepts may appear straightforward in the abstract, developing an appropriate fit between a company's environment and its administrative systems can be extremely troublesome in practice. So, too, can developing an appropriate relationship between corporate strategy and the design of administrative systems, a process that shares many similarities with the preceding line of thought.

The selection of appropriate measurement criteria for monitoring performance and rewarding executives provides the most dramatic case of how strategy can affect the design of administrative systems. Consider, for example, the most logical strategies for companies falling into the "strategic quadrants" identified in Exhibit 4. These quadrants are defined according to two factors: the rate of growth of a company's market and the competitive position which a company has in that market.[19]

Quadrant 1 companies are in the most enviable situation. With a dominant position in a growth market (say, 10 percent to 20 percent annually) their prospects are excellent. So, too, in many cases, is their level of profits. The proper strategy for companies in this strategic cluster is to gain or maintain relative share of market and to invest for continued dominance of the market. The proper performance objectives are relative growth in revenue (they cannot afford to lose market share) and increases in net worth.

Quadrant 2 companies provide the opportunity to harvest cash flow. With a dominant position in a low growth market (say, less than 5 percent annually), there is little reason to invest heavily in market share or relative growth. Rather, the proper strategy is to minimize new invest-

---

[18] Paul R. Lawrence and Jay Lorsch, *Organization and Environment* (Boston: Division of Research, Harvard Business School, 1967).

[19] In contrast to the framework developed and publicized by the Boston Consulting Group, this framework recognizes market share as only one of several possible indicators of a company's competitive strength or weakness in the market. Other indicators include technological leadership, financial strength, manufacturing competences, and marketing skills.

EXHIBIT 4

Framework for Identifying Strategic Clusters of Companies

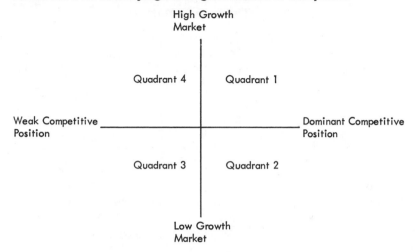

ment in this business and to use excess cash to finance new operations or other businesses if the company is already diversified. The proper performance objective for companies in this strategic cluster is therefore to maximize cash throw-off within the constraints of maintaining a respectable industry position.

Quadrant 3 companies are usually problem companies. With a weak competitive position in a low growth market, their prospects are dim. Reinvesting cash in these companies is most likely foolhardy. The appropriate strategy for this cluster of companies is liquidation or divestiture if they are part of larger diversified companies. One aspect of liquidation would be abandoning market share. An appropriate set of performance objectives for these companies is to maximize cash flow over the short run.

Quadrant 4 companies are excellent candidates for liquidation or heavy support by new infusions of capital. If the decision is made to invest in the weak company competing in a growth market and transform it into a relatively strong competitor, the performance objectives will have to change over time. Exhibit 5 shows what profit and cash flow expectations are reasonable as businesses in this strategic cluster develop.[20]

---

[20] This pattern of profit and cash flow is similar, of course, to the underlying product life cycle. Many new products and new ventures will tend to show negative cash flow and profits as they move through early stages of fast growth. When product maturity is associated with a high market share, the cash flow and profits will tend to increase. For a discussion of the relationship between market share and profitability, see Sidney Schoeffler, Robert D. Buzzell, and Donald F. Heany, "Impact of Strategic Planning on Profit Performance," *Harvard Business Review*, March–April 1974.

EXHIBIT 5

Profit and Cash Flow Expectations for Developing Quadrant 4 Companies

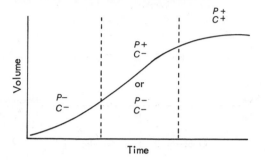

What the "strategic cluster" framework dramatizes is that companies can be shown to have radically different financial characteristics and strategic requirements. More to the point, it demonstrates that for companies in different strategic clusters, different combinations of profit, cash flow, and investment objectives should form the basis of performance measurement systems. For multibusiness companies it suggests that performance objectives and measures should not be uniformly applied across all subsidiaries, regardless of superficial characteristics of product-market relatedness or diversity. A similar logic suggests that incentive compensation systems for executives should also reflect the strategy of the company in question.

In the context of actual operations, the general manager needs to work out the logic of strategic control in greater detail than what is presented in this short summary. However, at this point the logic should be quite clear. Through the design of organization structure and such administrative systems as measurement and reward systems, the general manager can establish a pattern of authority relationships and decision premises consistent with the needs of a specific corporate strategy. This pattern of control, referred to here as "strategic control" since it reflects to a great extent the needs of corporate strategy, is the primary means by which the general manager can direct the allocation and management of resources within his organization. Together with strategic planning, the concept of strategic control can also help the general manager understand the important relationships among his key tasks and responsibilities.

GENERAL MANAGEMENT AND THE EXERCISE OF POWER

When a general manager uses the concepts and tools of strategic planning and control, it represents in a very fundamental sense an attempt on his part to influence individual and group action towards the achievement of some desired and explicit objectives. The strategic plan, the capital allocation procedures, and the measurement and reward system all provide an organization's membership with a common set of decision premises or a shared rationale for action. When these tools are carefully managed by a general manager, they become his basic instruments of power.

A general manager's power, derived from his position, competence, and personal charisma, serves several important purposes. Power is required to influence individuals and groups within the organization to modify their behavior and attitudes so that a different form of adaptation to the environment can be secured. An executive will also want to use his power to bring about a change in the environment that conforms more closely to the skills and resources within his organization. Occasionally, power is required to maintain an organization's internal stability in the face of potential internal disruptions.[21]

As appropriate as a general manager's use of power may be, there are limits to what the basic instruments of power can do for him. It is not likely, for example, that every individual decision-maker in the organization will share a common conception of corporate purpose. Even if loyalty to the organization is high, each decision-maker possesses his own unique values and habits which influence his decisions in unique ways. No set of administrative tools can completely dominate these individual characteristics. Nor is it clear that such domination should be the goal of most managers.

Sufficient attention has been given in recent years to the study of the unconscious motives of individual decision-makers to suggest that the most powerful motivating force for any decision-maker is his wish to attain his ego ideal or, in other words, his vision of himself at his ideal future best. As Dr. Harry Levinson, a noted psychologist, has pointed out, "In the course of growing up, out of our identifications with our parents, out of our wish to emulate them, out of the encouragement and affection of our teachers and other people who are important to us, out of the refinement of our skills and competences, we evolve a picture of ourselves of how we should be at our ideal best. When we work toward our ideal best we like ourselves; when we come close we are elated. When we do not, we become extremely angry with ourselves."[22] When persons are angry with themselves, or when their self-esteem is low due to a widening gap between their ego ideal and current self-images, rigid authority relationships and motivational concepts based on rewards and punishments

---

[21] Abraham Zaleznik and Anne Jardim, "Management" in Paul F. Lazarsfeld, William H. Sewell, and Harold L. Wilensky, eds., *The Uses of Sociology* (New York: Basic Books, Inc., 1967), pp. 217 and 222.

[22] Harry Levinson, *The Great Jackass Fallacy* (Boston: Division of Research, Harvard Business School, 1973), p. 29.

can trigger individuals to fight back at the organization, even at the risk of hurting themselves.[23] From a purely practical point of view, every general manager naturally wants to limit this possibility. From a humanistic point of view, the desire to avoid such problems is no less compelling.

Thus, while the use of strategic planning and control techniques may well be a necessary condition for effective general management, it is not a sufficient one by itself. In exercising his power the general manager must also come to understand the psychological needs of his organization's members, and to think about the development of work environments in behavioral terms. He must make attempts to delineate the kinds of work styles, values, skills, and personality characteristics required to carry on successfully the work of various departments or divisions, so that the chances of developing a good fit between the individual and the work organization will be increased.

In the final analysis, effective strategic planning and control requires a willingness of others to cooperate with the general manager. While the social psychologists will undoubtedly have much to contribute in the future to a better understanding of how executives develop and maintain "cooperative systems," most general managers will have to rely for the time being on their own sense of what personal competences and administrative practices are required to lead the process of policy formulation and administration within their organizations with at least the tacit approval of its membership. This intuitive sense can be strengthened by a willingness to study critically not only the purposes toward which their power and influence should be directed, but also their own ability to generate organizational commitment to these purposes. When a general manager perceives a weakness or gap in his own resources, he must have the foresight and courage to surround himself with senior colleagues who possess the requisite skills. In many instances the path to effective general management may well involve the sharing of power, rather than the monopolizing of power.

Careful observation shows that organizations rely upon various forms of executive leadership at top levels of management: the single "patriarch" or dominant leader, the system of pairs (an inside and an outside man), and a system of equals.[24] Choosing which constellation of executive leadership best serves an organization's needs and best fits the personalities and competences of that organization's top-level executives is an art which only the sensitive and self-aware general manager can hope to perfect. Only from self-knowledge and a deep understanding of others will the general manager be able to build a power structure, acceptable to the

---

[23] Ibid., p. 30.
[24] Zaleznik and Jardim, "Management," p. 228.

organization's membership, which can help him direct the critical management processes of strategic planning and control.

FROM CONCEPTS TO CASES

As suggested in the Introduction, the case material presented in Part One of this book lends itself to the application of strategic planning concepts. The case material in Part Two poses problems to which the concepts of strategic control can be readily applied. Part Three challenges students to use both sets of concepts in dealing with the problems of diversified companies. The material in Part Four highlights social issues which cannot be resolved by any one set of general management concepts. Thus, Part Four challenges students to move beyond the concepts discussed in this overview of the general manager's job.

Part One

Policy Formulation

Section One

The Job of the General Manager: Perspective, Function, Role, and Skills

1   *Prelude Corporation*

In June 1972, Prelude Corporation could look back on 12 years of pioneering in the newly developed offshore segment of the Northern Lobster fishing industry. (See Appendix.) Having accounted for 16 percent of the offshore poundage landed in 1971, this Massachusetts company ranked as the largest single lobster producer in North America. Mr. Joseph S. Gaziano, president since 1969, looked forward to a still more dominant position and, in the long run, to further vertical integration beyond what he had already introduced:

> Basically, we're trying to revolutionize the lobster industry by applying management and technology to what has been an 18th century cottage industry heretofore. Other companies have become giants by restructuring such commodity businesses as crab, tuna, avocados, celery, and chicken; we want to become the Procter & Gamble of the lobster business. Until we opened up the offshore resource there was no way to bring about this revolution, but now the chance is there. Furthermore, the technology and money required to fish offshore are so great that the little guy can't make out; the risks are too great. The fishing industry now is just like the automobile industry was 60 years ago; 100 companies are going to come and go, but we'll be the General Motors.
>
> We have toyed with the idea of establishing a restaurant chain featuring the Prelude lobster, similar to Black Angus or Red Coach [local chains which offer only a small selection of beef as their fare], but have never really gotten serious about it. We find we have enough to manage now. The Deep Deep and Wickford distribution systems, which we purchased in the past fiscal year, have given us some vertical integration.

As Mr. Gaziano voiced these expectations, Prelude hopefully saw itself as starting to recover from a recent precipitous and unexplained decline in its per trip catch (Exhibit 1). This decline had plunged the company

EXHIBIT 1

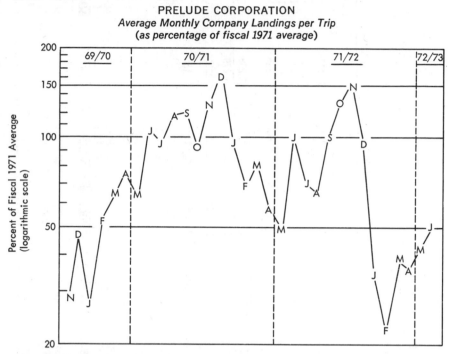

PRELUDE CORPORATION
Average Monthly Company Landings per Trip
(as percentage of fiscal 1971 average)

back into the red for the fiscal year ending in April (Exhibit 2) and had raised the specter of depletion of the offshore lobster population by pollution or overfishing. Mr. Gaziano viewed these possibilities as bleak, but discounted them:

> The vessels we have are especially designed and constructed for our lobster gear and couldn't be used for any other purpose without costly refitting. I suppose we could go south into the Caribbean for crawfish or go after finfish that are amenable to the long line techniques. We could even use the vessels for research, laying cables, or as oil-survey ships. Practically speaking, if someone said tomorrow that we couldn't sell lobsters due to mercury content or some other reason, I guess we would be forced to close the doors. However, I foresee this risk as minimal. Certainly it is possible, but there are no studies or indications that this is at all a likely occurrence.[1]

---

[1] In support of his belief that depletion of the resource was unlikely, Mr. Gaziano employed a widely used argument—namely, that the average weight of offshore lobsters caught was holding steady at about 2½ pounds (with a range of 1–11 pounds or more), a fact taken to indicate that the more mature lobsters were not being fished at a rate higher than their natural replacement.

EXHIBIT 2

PRELUDE CORPORATION
Statement of Operations and Accumulated Deficit, 1967–72
(dollars in thousands)

			Year Ended April 30			
	1967	1968	1969	1970	1971	1972 (consolidated)*
Net sales	$ 128	$ 176	$ 152	$ 371	$1,511	$ 3,064
Costs and expenses:						
Cost of vessel operations	$ 108	$ 161	$ 225	$ 445	$ 832	$ 1,175
Cost of purchased seafood	—	—	—	—	—	1,062
Depreciation	22	23	21	68	135	253
Selling, general and administrative†	53	90	193	249	271	265
	$ 183	$ 274	$ 439	$ 762	$1,238	$ 3,055
Income (loss) from operations	$(55)	$(98)	$(287)	$(391)	$ 273	$ 9
Other income (expense)	—	(1)	(69)	(21)	(107)	(157)
Income (loss) before income taxes and extraordinary items	$(55)	$(99)	$(356)	$(412)	$ 166	$(148)
Provision for income taxes	—	—	—	—	84	—
Income (loss) before extraordinary items	$(55)	$(99)	$(356)	$(412)	$ 82	$(148)
Extraordinary items:						
Write-down of vessels	—	—	—	(133)	—	—
Credit arising from carryforward of operating loses	—	—	—	—	72	—
Net income (loss)	$(55)	$(99)	$(356)	$(545)	$ 154	$(148)
Accumulated deficit at beginning of year	—	(55)	(154)	(510)	1,055	(901)
Accumulated deficit at end of year	$(55)	$(154)	$(510)	$(1,055)	$ (901)	$(1,049)
Income (loss) per share of common stock assuming full dilution	$(0.23)	$(0.41)	$(1.25)	$(1.15)	$ 0.28	$(0.27)
Shares assumed outstanding	240	240	285	474	550	550

* Includes the results of subsidiary operations from November 1, 1971, on.
† Includes all operating costs incurred after landing such as vehicle operations, salaries of delivery and restaurant personnel, and tank maintenance as well as executive salaries and general overhead.
Source: Company records.

HISTORY

Prelude's predecessor company had been organized in 1960 to develop techniques for deep-sea lobster fishing. Its founder was an ordained minister, the Reverend William D. Whipple, and its name reflected Mrs. Whipple's profession—music. In the course of raising money for a company that was never in the black until 1971, Rev. Whipple had incorporated in 1966 and had arranged a private placement of 140,000 shares (58 percent of the total). This brought in $350,000, which was supplemented by debt. Late in 1968, when Rev. Whipple felt ready to start commercial operations, prospects for growth plus creditor pressure led to additional financing (Exhibit 3), some of it completed before the ending of the go-go market in 1969:

[handwritten: 2.50 a share]

Date	Financing	Amount
February 1969.......	250,000 common shares at $8.50	$2,125,000 gross
September 1969*....	10% senior notes (John Hancock Insurance Co.)	500,000
September 1969.....	40,000 rights at $6.75 (John Hancock)	
June 1970..........	50,000 common shares at $3.00 (private placement)	150,000

* This financing became necessary when an expected government subsidy for fishing fleets failed to materialize.

Also during 1969, Rev. Whipple agreed to bring in Mr. Gaziano as president, and to have him put together a professional management team. The purchase of two 101–foot trawlers for $1,585,000 completed Prelude's makeready, and the year ending April 30, 1971, brought operating earnings of $273,000 from a lobster catch of 1.1 million pounds.

Spurred by this success, Prelude purchased two more ships of 96 feet and 125 feet for $1,118,000 and acquired two nearby subsidiaries in the lobster distribution business. The latter were the Wickford Shellfish Company and the distribution segment of Deep Deep Ocean Products; these would, it was hoped, reduce price fluctuations and raise margins by reducing Prelude's dependence on independent wholesalers. In the three fiscal years prior to their purchase, Wickford had had two nominal profits and one nominal loss. Deep Deep had suffered significant losses, but these were laid by management chiefly to Deep Deep's operation of three ships[2] which Prelude did not buy—although it agreed to market their catch. Prelude saw both firms as competently managed, but beset by inability to raise enough capital to finance their rapidly expanding sales:

	Dollars in Thousands			
	1969	1970	1971	1972
Wickford (years ending February 28)..........	—	$ 870	$1,000	$1,600
Deep Deep (years ending December 31)......	$950	1,623	1,414	—

[2] By June 1972, one of these ships had been sold.

[handwritten: sales have decreased]

EXHIBIT 3

PRELUDE CORPORATION
Balance Sheet
(dollars in thousands)

	April 30	
	1971	*1972*
Assets		*(consolidated)*
Current assets:		
Cash and marketable securities............	$ 460	$ 253
Accounts receivable......................	22	243
Lobster and seafood inventories...........	13	62
Trapping supplies........................	158	323
Prepaid expenses.........................	55	108
Total current Assets...................	$ 708	$ 989
Fixed assets................................	$2,743	$3,471
Less—accumulated depreciation...........	189	420
	$2,554	$3,051
Goodwill....................................	—	315
Total Assets........................	$3,262	$4,355
Liabilities and Stockholders' Equity		
Current Liabilities:		
Notes payable............................	$ —	$ 350
Current portion of long-term debt..........	79	270
Accounts payable.........................	107	257
Accrued taxes and expenses...............	46	75
Total Current Liabilities................	$ 232	$ 952
Long-term debt.............................	$1,616	$1,857
Stockholders' equity:		
Common stock		
Authorized—1,100,000 shares		
Issued and outstanding—569,985		
shares in 1972, 530,000 shares		
in 1971................................	$ 265	$ 285
Additional paid-in capital................	2,065	2,325
Accumulated deficit.....................	(901)	(1,049)
	$1,429	$1,561
Less—6,200 treasury shares............	15	15
	$1,414	$1,546
Total Liabilities......................	$3,262	$4,355

Source: Company records.

Both Prelude's new ships (which began fishing in July 1971 and January 1972) and its acquisitions (effected in December and January) led to *raising expansion funds by issuing new shares.* additional financing:

Date	Financing	Amount
April 1971.	Two ships mortgages consolidated at 1 percent above prime	$1,200,000
December 1971.	Paid 17,500 common shares, valued at $7.00* for Wickford, plus cash	122,000
		170,000
January 1972.	Paid 22,845 common shares valued at $7 for Deep Deep distribution, plus assumption of certain liabilities	—

* According to the terms of sale, if the former owner should sell his stock at less than $6.50 a share, the company would pay the difference.

Still another episode in Prelude's history deserves mention because of the worldwide attention it received. In the spring of 1971, Prelude became the focus of a well-publicized international incident involving the United States and Russia. Early in the year, ships of the Russian commercial fishing fleet had caused the loss of more than $70,000 of Prelude's gear by dragging fishing nets over the bottom on which Prelude's traps were resting, clearly marked by buoys and radar reflectors. Such fixed gear had legal right-of-way, so Mr. Gaziano not only sued the Russian Government for $177,000 in actual damages plus $266,000 in punitive damages, but also caused a Soviet merchant ship to be attached in San Francisco. The actual out-of-court settlement was for only $89,000 but it was hailed as a precedent in commercial relations between the two countries.

PRELUDE IN 1972

In mid-1972, Prelude was organized primarily along functional lines, with departments for operations, engineering, research, and finance and administration. Distribution functions were divided among the Deep Deep and Wickford subsidiaries (Exhibits 4 and 5).

Operations

Fishing. Fishing operations and the logistics involved in landing and distributing the lobster catch were under the direction of Robert E. (Gene) White, age 33, vice president, operations. Prelude's four ships operated year-round on a two-week cycle, ten days fishing and four days in port for unloading and resupply. Each ship carried a crew of ten: captain, mate, engineer, cook, and six deckhands. After a 12-hour steam to the offshore lobster grounds, the crew would begin "hauling pots" 12

EXHIBIT 4

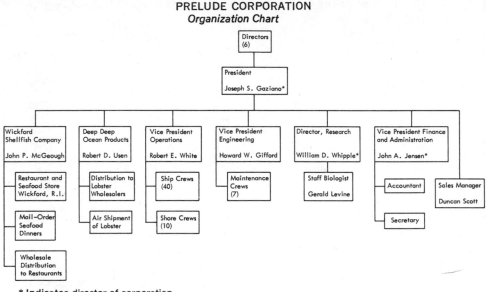

PRELUDE CORPORATION
Organization Chart

* Indicates director of corporation.
( ) Indicates number of personnel involved.
Source: Company records.

hours a day. (See Appendix.) When the lobsters were brought up and removed from the pots, their claws would be pegged with a red plastic peg which displayed the Prelude brand, and then they would be stored in the hold. The empty trap would be rebaited and stacked until the line was ready to be played out again for three days of fishing.

Whether the trawl was relaid where it had been, or in another location, 'was a decision made by the captain, depending very much on how the catch was running. In any event, the captain was charged with bringing in as many pounds of lobster as possible on each trip, an amount which could vary tremendously. Although Prelude's ships averaged about 20,000 pounds per trip, the results of a single trip could range from 4,000 to 40,000 pounds. (An indication of the variation in the size of the catch can be obtained from Exhibit 1.) In Mr. Gaziano's words:

> The biggest problem in the production process is the variability in the size of the catch. It is not like a manufacturing business. The size of the catch is uncertain. There is no proven way of forecasting where the lobsters will be on a given day. Mating habits, weather, etc., are some of the many variables which determine the size of the catch. Black magic is used by the captains to find lobsters. Presently, it is an art, not a science. Actually it is on a trial and error basis. If one canyon is not producing, the skipper moves to another location.

Workforce. Along with dispatching and supplying the vessels, Mr. White was responsible for staffing both the ships and Prelude's truck fleet and storage facility. These operations used 50 people who were engaged in manning the ships or moving lobster. Because Prelude was located in Westport Point, these workers were nonunion. In nearby New Bedford, where the larger portion of the fishing industry was located, unions were a predominant force. Unlike most others in the fishing industry, who were required by the union to pay their crews a straight percentage of the catch, Prelude paid a base salary plus a sum of 20 cents a pound on everything over 25,000 pounds, to be divided among the crew in a pro rata basis. Mr. White commented on some of the problems with people:

> The fisherman is an independent worker. He is always in demand and has a job waiting at his beck and call. His reputation stays with him, although references are not easy to evaluate. Since there is "always a ship leaving" he does not hesitate to tell his boss to "get screwed" if he is unhappy about something. How do you get a reference on somebody who has told his last three bosses to "get screwed?" So we end up hiring them and taking a chance based on their informal reputation, which I get from my sources in the industry. We spin our wheels on quite a few. We attempt to hire experienced fishermen but 20 percent of our crews are bank tellers and "potato farmers" who want to try something more exciting and more financially rewarding. We start the experienced fishermen at $225 per week and the layman at $150. If the latter pans out after two or three trips he goes to $225, also.
>
> The cook is one of the most important men on the ship. If I get a bad cook, morale goes to hell. Most ship cooks are drunks—it is just a question of whether they are good drunks or bad drunks. I try to have at least one crewman on each ship to have welding expertise. This avoids having to return to shore to make minor repairs. Engineers are hard to get—their education allows them to earn good money on shore and avoid the hard sea duty. Lobstering is a hard and demanding job. Guys over 40 break up after several trips.

Logistics. Since the inlet leading to Prelude's headquarters in Westport Point was not deep enough for the draft of the four ships, the company rented 225 feet of pier space at the State Pier in Fall River, about 15 miles away. Here the vessels tied up for unloading, maintenance, and resupply. The company owned and maintained a fleet of refrigerated trucks with which to transport the catch. After a returning ship had docked, the mesh baskets of pegged lobsters were lifted out of the hold and into these trucks. If the catch had already been sold, the truck, driven by a member of the shore crew, began its delivery rounds immediately.

If there was an excess, however, or if it was desired to hold the catch for better prices, then the truck would make the 20-minute run to West-

EXHIBIT 5

PRELUDE CORPORATION
Personal Data on Officers and Management Personnel

	Joseph S. Gaziano	*John A. Jensen*	*W. D. Whipple*
Title(s)...............	Director, President, CEO	Director, VP Finance and Administration	Director, Director of Research
Age...................	36	33	41
Education............	MIT, BSEE, 1956 AMP programs: Harbridge House Sloan School	Babson Institute BS/BA, 1962 MBA, 1963	Princeton, BA 1953, Boston Univ. School of Theology, STB *cum laude,* 1958
Previous experience...	Raytheon Co., 1962–67, rising to manager, Major Space Systems Allied Research Associates, Engineering and Systems Div. 1967–69, VP and GM	U.S. Army, Sept., 1963–Feb. 1964 Price, Waterhouse, & Co., 1964–June 1968.	Owner of a charter yacht business, 1954–58 Inventor and innovator in the area of fishing equipment, especially for deep-water lobster fishing, 1958–59.
Date of entry..........	January 1969 Exec. VP	June 1968	Founded predecessor company, 1960.
Office(s) held.........	President	VP, June 1970, Director, Sept. 1971	President, 1960–69

port Point, where the lobsters would be transferred to the Prelude holding tank. This tank, built during 1968 and 1969 at a cost of $250,000, was capabable of holding 125,000 pounds of lobster in seawater cooled to 42°F. The tank was designed around an experimental system aimed at reducing handling costs by keeping the lobster in mesh baskets aboard ship and stacking these baskets in the storage tank. The system had not worked out well in practice, however, since one dead lobster could cause the loss of 10 percent to 15 percent of its tankmates with a 24-hour period. As a result, the baskets had to be hauled out and culled regularly. Prelude management felt that if they did expand their holding capacity it would be with conventional three-tier tanks which, even though they required more space and lobster handling, could be culled more efficiently and could be built for only $1 per pound of storage capacity. Security measures, both at the holding tank and on the trucks, were important since lobster was a readily marketable commodity at any roadside stand.

Howard W. Gifford	Robert E. White	John P. McGeough	Robert D. Usen
Vice President Engineering	Vice President Operations	President, Wickford Shell-fish Co., Inc.	President, Deep Deep Ocean Products, Inc.
37	33	31	42
New Bedford Institute of Technology, B.S.	U.S. Navy Nuclear Sub School.	Providence College BS, 1962	Tufts University, BA
Electric Boat Division of General Dynamics, rising to supervisor in the Mechanical Engineering Dept.	U.S. Navy, 1960–69, rising to 1/C Engineman. Held technical assignments, including mechanical inspection, systems and machinery testing.	Former Professional football player. Increased sales of Wickford almost tenfold in the five years prior to its acquisition.	Over 15 years' experience in several family-owned seafood businesses, including the Tabby Cat Food Company. As president, Mr. Usen had expanded this to $25 million sales volume prior to its sale. Founded Deep Deep in 1968.
May 1969	March 1969	December 1971	January 1972
VP, Sept. 1971	Vice President	President of subsidiary	President of subsidiary

Note: The three outside directors were: Chester A. Barrett, Chairman, Merchants National Bank of New Bedford; Joshua M. Berman, Partner, Goodwin, Proctor and Hoar; Robert F. Goldhamer, Vice President and Vice Chairman of the Executive Committee, Kidder, Peabody and Co.
Source: Company data.

Engineering

Engineering activities at Prelude were under the direction of Howard W. Gifford, age 37, vice president, engineering. These activities included the maintenance and procurement of vessels and equipment, as well as the development of gear, and so on.

Maintenance. With each ship representing an investment of over $500,000 and subject to continual stress at sea, maintenance was an important and continual activity. This work was carried out by a seven-person maintenance department located at the pier in Fall River. Availa-

should the bill be the responsibility of personnel (eng. dept.)

ble there were complete facilities for the welding and machinery necessary to overhaul and repair a ship's engines, life-support equipment, and trap-handling gear. Additionally, this crew performed periodic preventative maintenance on the holding tank at Westport Point. This life-support system was particularly important since its failure, if full, would result in the loss of 125,000 pounds of lobster. Mr. Gifford was responsible for the hiring and firing of the maintenance personnel. Also, even though the ship's engineers were under the operational command of Mr. White, Mr. Gifford was responsible for their technical direction.

Purchase of Ships and Gear.   Mr. Gifford was responsible for evaluating potential vessels for use as fishing platforms; writing the specifications for their conversion; and initiating, supervising, and approving their fitting out. In all these activities Mr. Gifford worked closely with Rev. Whipple in improving designs. Mr. Gifford also spent considerable time working with manufacturers' representatives on developing improved refrigeration technology for the life-support systems. The corrosive nature of the seawater, coupled with the lobster's sensitivity to trace amounts of certain metals which were traditionally used for refrigeration systems, made this a difficult area.

Research

Rev. Whipple, age 41, held the title of director of research. Since 1958 he had devoted a major portion of his time to commercial fishing and to developing a number of improvements and innovations in its equipment. Among these were an hydraulic power block and various rigging and hauling devices related to high-speed handling of deep-water lobster trapping systems.[3] Rev. Whipple was constantly evaluating the operational design of the ship's fishing gear and experimenting with ways to improve it. A qualified captain himself, Rev. Whipple would often take a ship out when a captain was sick or missing for some reason. In any case, he was generally at sea whenever there was a new idea to be tried out, a frequent occurrence.

In an effort to enhance their knowledge about the habits of the lobster, Prelude's management had recently hired a marine biologist. Mr. Gaziano remarked, regarding research on the "product":

> We knew a lot about management and lobster fishing when we started, but we didn't know a damn thing about the lobster. We hired Jerry [a marine biologist] to give us some expertise in this area. He started with the task of accumulating all the data he could find on the lobster. It turned out nobody really knows a heck of a lot about them.

---

[3] Although the company held design patents on certain of these mechanisms, management stated that the patents were no protection against competitors using similar but not identical equipment.

[margin handwriting: permently set up a rearing facility]

He has three current projects. One is to set up a lobster rearing facility downstairs [corporate headquarters] and see what we can learn from that. The second project is to help us figure out what to do with the crabs we catch in our traps along with the lobsters. They are highly perishable and only bring 25 cents per pound. There is not much market for them, but, since we haul them in from the sea in quantities equal to or greater than the lobsters, we would like to exploit the resource. And lastly, we've chartered a little research sub. Jerry's going to spend five days on the bottom seeing what really goes on down there. It's going to cost us $25,000, but we will have information that no one else has.

[margin handwriting: why]

Marketing

Prior to the acquisition of Wickford and Deep Deep late in fiscal 1971, Prelude sold most of its catch directly to wholesale lobster dealers in large lots, usually an entire shipload. As a result, the number of transactions was limited, and Mr. Gaziano was able to handle the telephone negotiations himself. He commented on the bargaining process as follows:

> The distributor knows when you have a large catch. He may say, "You have 30,000 pounds—well, we don't really want any today," and thereby drive down the price. Even with our large holding capacity we have been caught in this situation. There are no long-term, fixed-price contracts. It is cutthroat haggling to a great degree. We are really in the commodity trading business—buy and then sell at a profit; there is very little value added.

With the acquisition of Wickford and Deep Deep, each of which owned a variety of trucks and sorting tanks of 50,000 pounds capacity, marketing arrangements had changed. The original plan was for the two acquisitions combined to handle some three-fourths of Prelude's catch, although, in line with the intent to treat all three entities as profit centers, each could sell or buy where it got the best price. In any event, the Wickford and Deep Deep acquisitions happened to coincide with the precipitous drop in lobster catches, so all of Prelude's lobsters were sold "inside" during the first half of 1972.

Wickford, located in North Kingston, Rhode Island, had brought Prelude a business in live lobsters (about 70 percent of sales) and in other types of seafood, including other shellfish and frozen-fish products. It distributed in various ways: Thus, it had a combined retail seafood store and restaurant located in its home town, which accounted for 30 percent of its sales; it had a mail-order business in prepackaged clam and lobster dinners; and it operated a wholesale business in a market area that extended along the Eastern seaboard south to Pennsylvania. Customers were restaurants and small dealers, whom it reached by making four delivery runs a week, locally, and to Pennsylvania, Connecticut, New York, and New Jersey.

Deep Deep, located in Boston, Massachusetts, brought Prelude a business that consisted of distributing lobsters to dealers and restaurants in New England, New York, the Midwest, West, and South, the latter three markets being served by air shipments. Deep Deep's major accounts, however, were wholesalers serving restaurants in New York City. Shipments to these accounts had to be made by common carrier, since Prelude's nonunion drivers could not gain safe access to the city's highly organized Fulton Fish market.

Critical to selling all accounts of both companies was knowing who wanted to buy what, where, when, and at what offered price. "Contacts" were a marketer's paramount asset in the lobster trade. Prelude's management believed that Mr. John P. McGeough, former owner of Wickford, and Mr. Robert D. Usen, founder and ex-president of Deep Deep, were highly qualified in this regard, basing this opinion partly on a three-week cross-country trip that the financial vice president had made with Mr. Usen prior to the Deep Deep acquisition.

Both Messrs. Usen and McGeough had agreed to follow their companies into Prelude, where they continued to serve as presidents of the two subsidiaries. Here the compensation of each would be based primarily on the total profit of his unit. Although the decline in the lobster catch had prevented a full-scale testing of the two companies' performance, Prelude management indicated that their expectations had been largely fulfilled to date.

Besides bringing in Mr. Usen and Mr. McGeough, Mr. Gaziano had staffed marketing with a new sales manager, hired in November 1971. This was Mr. Duncan Scott, who had been on the road since his arrival, "cold calling" potential new distributor and restaurant accounts, and visiting old ones. Any business Mr. Scott turned up was referred to either Wickford or Deep Deep.

In still another marketing move in the spring of 1971, $15,000 had been invested in advertising on two Boston radio stations, WBZ and WHDH. This advertising was aimed at raising the ultimate consumer's awareness of Prelude's offshore lobster. Mr. Gaziano outlined the rationale behind this program:

> We are trying to establish brand identification for the Prelude lobster. We want people to ask for Prelude lobster—not just lobster—similar to the Chiquita Banana strategy. Toward this end we have used radio advertising and promotional devices in the form of handouts and red plastic lobster pegs with the Prelude name etched on them. The handouts are put in our lobster shipping boxes, and Scott leaves them wherever he goes. We plant to start direct mailings. But our radio advertising was ill-timed in that we didn't follow up soon enough with sales calls, and our catches were not large enough to satisfy the demand we created.

EXHIBIT 6

PRELUDE CORPORATION
Projected Statement of Operations
(dollars in thousands)

	For Years Ending April 30		
	Actual 1972	Projected 1973	Projected 1974
Sales*			
Prelude.....................................	$n.a.§	$2,656	$3,990
Wickford†..................................	n.a.	1,250	1,360
Deep Deep†...............................	n.a.	850	840
Total.................................	$3,064	$4,756	$6,190
Costs and expenses			
Vessel operations..........................	$1,175	$1,464	$2,146
Purchases.................................	1,062	1,420	1,316
Depreciation..............................	253	312	362
S, G & A..................................	565	780	1,014
Total.................................	$3,055	$3,976	$5,108
Operating income (loss)......................	9	780	1,082
Other income (expense)‡.....................	(157)	(123)	(180)
Income (loss) before taxes...................	$ (148)	$ 657	$ 902
Provision for income taxes...................	—	338	464
Income (loss) before extraordinary credit.....	$ (148)	$ 319	$ 438
Extraordinary credit from operating loss carryforward...............................	—	272	347
Net income.................................	$ (148)	$ 591	$ 785

* Assumes that fishing conditions parallel those of May 1970–January 1972; that two new ships for a total of six begin fishing in fiscal 1974; that sales of the subsidiaries continue at mid–1972 levels; and that Prelude receives a price per pound of $1.33, with 25 percent of its sales to outsiders.
  † Assumes that the subsidiaries will handle 75 percent of sales reported by the parent.
  ‡ Primarily interest expense.
  § n.a. = not available.

Sources and Uses of Funds
(dollars in thousands)

	For Years Ending April 30	
	1973	1974
Uses of funds:		
Increase in fixed assets (new vessels)..............	$ 300	$ —
Increase in current assets (32% of sales)............	531	460
Reduction in note payable.........................	350	—
Reduction in long-term debt.......................	370	270
Total Uses of Funds...........................	$1,451	$ 730
Sources of funds:		
Increase in accounts payable (11% of sales)........	$ 191	$ 157
Net operating income..............................	319	438
Anticipated operating loss carryforward.............	272	347
Depreciation......................................	312	362
Total sources of funds........................	$1,094	$1,304
Funds needed (surplus).............................	$ 357	$ (574)

Source: Company records.

Finance and Administration

Mr. John A. Jensen, age 33, was in charge of the financial affairs of the company. In the past he had been responsible for shepherding the financial transactions required to raise needed capital. Mr. Jensen kept close tabs on the day-to-day state of affairs, maintaining an eight-week cash flow projection which he revised weekly, monitoring the daily transactions of the subsidiaries, and monitoring accounts receivable. (Restaurants and their suppliers were notoriously slow payers.)

His most current concern was centered around providing the funds needed to finance the two new ships which were planned for 1973. Exhibit 6 shows the projected income statement assuming the two new ships were added. The cost of the two vessels was estimated at $1.3 million, of which all but $300,000 could be mortgaged. Additionally, Mr. Jensen and Mr. Gaziano were concerned about the impact of interest charges on net income, interest being the main component of the fairly substantial figure carried in the operating statement as "other" income and expense (Exhibits 2 and 6). They felt that they needed a reduction in short-term debt of between $200,000 and $450,000 to "clean up" their balance sheet and reduce interest charges.

The company's underwriter had prepared a prospectus proposing a private placement of 100,000 to 150,000 shares of stock at $5 per share in order to secure the needed funds. Unfortunately, the release of the prospectus in March 1972 coincided with the drop in the catch and the issue had had to be withdrawn.

THE OUTLOOK FOR THE FUTURE

By the summer of 1972, Prelude had weathered the downturn of fishing catches which had so far occurred that year. The company's boats had been able to bring in enough lobster to meet its $190,000 per month cash flow breakeven (including the subsidiaries).

Breakeven costs were divided as follows:

Vessel operations..........	$120,000	S,G&A......................	$23,000
Selling....................	42,000	Taxes, interest..............	13,000

In terms of breakeven per trip, this monthly $190,000 (which excluded depreciation of about $25,000), worked out to about $22,000. The breakeven catch in pounds varied, of course, with the price attainable in the market. In the spring of 1972 it ran about 8,000 pounds a trip, since the wholesale price of "select" lobster had risen to more than $3 per pound during some of this period.

Although the lobster catch had recently risen (Exhibit 1), no one knew when or whether it would return to normal. On the one hand, industry optimists argued that the scare condition was only a transient event and that there were still "plenty of lobsters out there for everybody." On the other hand, industry pessimists, championed by federal fishery officials, raised doubts about the long-term viability of the resource, and were calling for some form of management to <u>sustain</u> the yields.

Competition

Even under "managed" conditions, Prelude's leaders expected the company to survive if not to prosper—barring total disappearance of the offshore lobster. They felt that they had the staying power to outlast the one-boat competitors who had come in on a shoestring, and, further, that they had an edge of experience and success which would enable them to outdistance the newer and better capitalized multiboat competitors. Chief among these had been Deep Deep; Mr. Usen had had three new boats fishing out of Boston since 1968, but had not been able to make them pay. He was presently operating two of these boats under a separate company, but selling his catch at market price to Prelude and attempting to dispose of the fleet. A second established competitor, MATCO, which fished five boats off the Virginia coast, was also reported to be in financial trouble, having been dragged under by its allegedly overextended parent, Marine International Corporation. Although three other firms were putting three to five boats each out to sea, Mr. Gaziano was not particularly worried about the threat they presented. He summed up his feelings as follows:

> This is going to be one hell of an interesting summer [1972]. We're going to have some new boats out there, each backed by some rich Johnny who is fascinated by the sex appeal of lobstering. They're going to find out the hard way how much it really costs to pot fish offshore. We have got a real shakeout coming.

In management's eyes a more real threat was that Prelude itself would be "taken over" by a larger company. Although there were no blocks of stock large enough to make for an easy takeover, the depressed state of Prelude's stock made a tender bid not unlikely.[4] For example, Mr. Jensen had heard a speech in which a spokesman for a West Coast seafood firm with 1971 sales of $25 million had stated:

> We are, then, a seafood company. And we want to remain a seafood company. The potential in utilizing the rich harvest of the sea is enough to keep any company of our size busy for as long into the future as we care to look.

---

[4] In June 1972, the bid price of Prelude's stock was in the range of $2¼–$3. Five brokers made an over-the-counter market in the 530,000 shares outstanding. Of these, Rev. Whipple held 92,400; a prominent Boston family, 70,000; Mr. Usen, 22,845, and Mr. McGeough, 17,500. The balance of the holdings were widely fragmented, with no individual or institution owning more than 15,000 shares. No other officer or employee held more than a few thousand shares, although this group as a whole held qualified options granted at prices of $6.50 to $9 on 53,500 shares.

Already we are expanding from a solid base in the Pacific salmon industry into a much broader segment of the total spectrum of Alaskan and Northwestern fisheries. But we do not see ourselves as confined to Alaska and the Pacific Northwest. Rather we are interested in fisheries virtually anywhere on the globe if we can find a way to enter them in a sound and profitable manner. And, yes, we are constantly looking for acquisitions which could expand and compliment our activities in the seafood industry.[5]

Expansion and Diversification

With the acquisition of Wickford and Deep Deep, Prelude had achieved integration all the way through to the consumer, and management was considering expanding this chain in several ways. One way would be to develop more restaurant/lobster stores similar to the one in Wickford. Another way would be to enlarge on the branding program already underway. One California firm, Foster Farms, Inc., had been very successful with branding its fresh chickens and placing them in supermarkets.

A third alternative entailed broadening the product base by marketing other types of seafood that could be purchased outside and then resold through the company's distribution system. Flounder, trout, clams, oysters were among the types of gourmet seafood products bought by restaurants in much the same way as lobster was.

Processing and marketing crab meat was another possibility, but somewhat remote. Canning crab meat required a multimillion dollar investment in centrifuging equipment and a continuous supply of crab meat. Although Prelude did catch a lot of crabs, they could not be stored together with lobsters, and furthermore, the catch was sporadic. There was, however, a minority small business company in New Bedford which was using government funds to develop a crab processing plant, and Prelude was watching this development with interest.

Nor were Mr. Gaziano's interests entirely confined to seafood. Previously, the company had looked at the possibility of acquiring a manufacturer of small boats, but had been beaten out by the CML Group, Inc. In any event, Mr. Gaziano did feel that any future expansion or acquisition efforts should be seaward-oriented, once the present difficulties were resolved.

---

[5] Larry M. Kaner, Vice President, Whitney-Fidalgo Seafoods, Inc. Speech to Boston Security Analysts, February 9, 1971.

Appendix on the Lobster Industry

Having graced the Pilgrims' first Thanksgiving, the Northern lobster remained a U.S. gourmet delicacy, demand for which was growing abroad. Supply had not kept pace, however, even though the U.S. market drew 80 percent to 90 percent of the Canada-landed catch, thereby roughly doubling poundage available for domestic consumption and export.

From a 1960 peak of 73.2 million pounds live weight, supply had dropped to 56.5 million pounds in 1967, but rose again thereafter, partly owing to the success of new techniques of offshore fishing:

Total U.S. Supplies of Northern Lobster (live weight in millions of pounds)

	1968	1969	1970	1971
U.S.-landed	32.6	33.8	34.2	33.3
Imports*	31.3	31.6	30.2	34.5
Total	63.9	65.4	64.3	67.9

* Converted to live weight equivalent.
† Includes exports (about 1 percent in 1968, and growing).
Source: National Marine Fisheries Service.

Shortage had sent prices rising even faster than general inflation, and in 1971 the 33.3 million-pound, U.S.-landed catch brought fishermen $35.1 million in sales, making lobsters the second most valuable single species (after Gulf shrimp) in the $643 million fishing industry.

The Resource

The Northern lobster inhabited the chilly waters of the North Atlantic from Newfoundland to North Carolina. Two populations had been observed, one in the shallow water from Canada's Maritimes south to New Jersey, the other further out, usually in the deep, cold canyons of the continental shelf from Massachusetts to the Carolinas. During the spring and fall the latter population migrated, and could thus sometimes be found crawling across the flats of the shelf. Estimated weights and numbers for "legal sized" (legally fishable) lobsters in the two populations were as follows:

Population	Total Weight (millions of lbs.)	Annual Replenishment (millions of lbs.)	Number (millions)	Weight Average (lbs.)
Inshore...............	25–31	15–20 est.	20–25	1¼
Offshore..............	100–120	25 est.	25–30	4

Besides fluctuating from year to year, lobster catch rates were seasonal, being lowest in the winter when lobsters and fishermen were least active, and highest in October and May. Since demand was highest in mid-summer (shore-dinner time) prices rose then, giving dealers a motive to buy and hold lobsters in enclosed tidal pools until values increased.

Harvesting the Resource

Inshore Fishing. Inshore and offshore lobster fishing differed in technique, the inshore method being much the same in the 1970s as in the 1840s. A 30-foot boat, manned by its owner and a relative, could manage 300–800 lathe traps or "pots," sinking each at depths of less than 30 fathoms, and hauling it up with a power winch to empty, bait, and toss overboard again.

By 1971 some 8,000 individuals were engaged in inshore lobster fishing, and a million pots were being used. Fishing was so intensive that government sources estimated that 90 percent of the legal-sized inshore lobster population was caught every year. Of this total, some 70 percent was delivered to ports in Maine. Optimum investment for entering this trade was estimated at $8,000–$10,000, but anyone could enter who had a few used traps, an outboard motorboat, and a license.

Offshore Fishing. Only after World War II were feasible methods devised for fishing the offshore lobster population, and only in the late 1950s did the industry start significant growth. By 1968, two techniques were being used: trawling, and potting on long lines.

Trawling involved scooping up migrating lobsters from the offshore flats by dragging weighted nets along the bottom. With the government pointing the way on methods, catches rose quickly, fluctuating around 5.5 million pounds a year in 1965–71, but ranging between 3.9 million in 1966 and 7.1 million in 1970.

Attractive features of offshore trawling included the absence of competition from Canada and Maine (where it was illegal to land the catch), relatively modest manning requirements compared with other types of fishing, and the low investment needed to equip a boat for switching back and forth from ground fish to lobsters. Increasingly unattractive features included overcrowding, loss of expensive gear when nets were dragged across the rising number of offshore pots, and injuries to the catch which might render 50–70 percent of it unsalable. Thus, government sources believed that this industry segment would level off at 100–130 boats.

Offshore lobster potting started with experiments to develop gear for trapping lobsters in the deep canyons of the continental shelf, where government researchers reported a year-round abundance. Prominent among the first experimenters was Prelude's Rev. Whipple, who finally settled on a method that entailed a mile-long line, buoyed and anchored at each end, to which 50–75 weighted traps were attached by four-foot wires. Keys to his system were gears strong enough to haul the heavy line, and also a special clip to permit the automatic attachment and detachment of the traps as the ship steamed along.

In 1970 this technique proved its worth when Prelude landed nearly all of the 1.5 million pounds attributed to offshore potting in the first statistics to segregate this figure. In 1971 the offshore potting catch rose to 2.3 million pounds, but this was shared by a growing number of competitors, lured in part by Prelude's success. By mid-1972, 92 vessels were fishing 50,000 offshore pots, nearly half of which had come into service during the previous six months.

Such an influx brought technical problems. These included loss of gear when one's boat line was laid across another's, or when the lines were cut by boats pursuing fin fish. Crowding, too, was a problem in the canyons, with the result that some pot lines had been set upon the flats, where they ruined the offshore trawlers' nets and motivated trawlers to retaliate.

Costs varied widely for putting a vessel into offshore lobster potting, some vessels having been converted from dragging to potting for as little as $50,000, whereas Prelude's fourth ship came to almost $600,000, including both cost of the hull and conversion. *sub contract with the small boat fishermen*

Regulation

Lobstering was a regulated trade, the regulations being set by the states, the federal government, and international conventions. Thus, to protect the resource, all states except North Carolina and Virginia set a minimum size for a landable lobster, and most states forbade the harvesting of egg-bearing females. To protect the consumer, the federal government required all lobsters to be alive when sold, and forbade U.S. ships to process them at sea. To govern fishing rights, nations had agreed not to fish within 12 miles of one another's coasts, and most had signed an international convention establishing a court-enforced code of conduct for vessels.

One clause in this code, of special interest to lobstermen, gave right-of-way to "fixed" equipment, such as pot lines. This requirement tended, however, to be ignored by ships in "hot pursuit" of fin fish, particularly, lobstermen believed, by foreign ships. In any event, losses were frequent and significant: One incident alone could damage or destroy several trap lines costing about $7,000 each and thereby put a one-boat operation out of business. Lobstermen vociferously complained, but the U.S. Coast Guard lacked enough patrol boats for adequate policing. New England congressmen, however, had been persuaded to sponsor a bill to reimburse fishermen for cumulative gear losses of about $500,000.

In other future plans, the federal government was pressing the states to enact uniform and more stringent laws for resource protection within the three-mile limit, which was the area of state jurisdiction. To protect the resource further out, the federal government might take several steps, from imposing a federal license requirement to extending the 12-mile limit to a highly controversial 200 miles. What fishermen favored was bringing foreign as well as domestic deep-sea lobstermen under federal control, an objective that could be accomplished by officially declaring lobsters to be "creatures of the shelf" as opposed to "free-swimming" fish.

How urgent it might be to take protective action on the offshore resource was not clear. Reported removal of 14 million pounds[6] by all takers was well below the 25 million pounds a year that government biologists estimated could be removed without depleting the resource, but no one knew how many pounds were being taken out unreported or how many were maimed and killed through fishing operations. One highly placed official admitted, "It would not be at all unreasonable to speculate that as much as 25 million pounds might be being removed."

Handling and Transport

Unlike inshore lobstermen, offshore lobstermen making 10-day runs required refrigerated tanks to hold their catch, not just barrels and some seaweed for moisture. Once delivered to the dock, most lobsters again went into holding: perhaps for a few days in a dockside "car" or floating tank, then for a few months in a "pound" or tidal pool, and then for a few more days in a dealer's sorting and culling tank. In total, cars, pounds, and dealers' tanks in the northeast could accommodate an estimated 7 million pounds.

With the advent of refrigeration and lightweight packing containers, shipments by rail or truck posed no problem, and shipment by air could carry Northern lobsters to far-distant points.

Over the years, consumers had come to expect their lobsters live. Weak and dying lobsters could be culled and cooked, then canned and frozen,

---

[6] In 1972, U.S. offshore trawling and potting reported 5.7 million and 2.3 million pounds; foreign lobstermen about 5 million, and U.S. ground fish fishermen about 1 million.

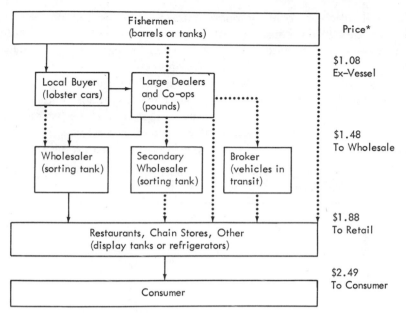

* Casewriter's estimate, typical 1971 price per pound.

but despite high prices these operations barely recovered their costs, so dealers pressed suppliers for a high-quality catch.

Aquaculture

Although worked on for some time, techniques to supplement lobster fishing by "farming" remained undeveloped in 1972. Progress has been made, however, especially on the biological side: Lobsters had been developed to breed in captivity, and experiments had been started to breed selectively for fast growth, bright color, two crusher claws, and high meat content. Already, lobsters had been grown to one-pound size in two years, compared with six years in the wild. And lobsters had been grown to half-pound size in six to seven months, with tails bigger than any commercially available shrimp.

The big problem lay with engineering the life-support system. Depending on investment in development and plant, the start of commercial operations was put at two to five years away by the best-known authority in lobster hatchery.

Marketing the Resource

Channels. As indicated by solid lines on the diagram, lobsters typically moved from the fishermen's barrel or tank to a local buyer with a lobster car or so, who then sold to a larger dealer operating a lobster pound. From there, the lobsters passed to a primary wholesaler, who sold to a retail outlet—most likely to a restaurant, since about 80 percent of all lobsters reached the consumer that way. Lobsters could pass to the retailer in several alternate ways, however, as indicated by dotted lines. These could either add or eliminate a step.

Price. As indicated by the price data on the diagram, prices more than doubled between the fisherman and the consumer, with retailers (largely restaurants) accounting for the biggest rise. The estimated price figures shown conceal wide seasonal variations, as well as variations for different weights of lobsters, and a steep year-to-year uptrend:

Live weight Wholesale Prices per Pound, Fulton Fish Market, New York City

	"Chix" 1⅛ lbs.	"Quarters" 1¼ lbs.	"Duces" 2 lbs.
1970			
High...................	$1.85	$1.88	$1.89
Low...................	1.24	1.34	1.36
1971			
High...................	2.06	2.14	2.66
Low...................	1.45	1.46	1.47

Source: National Marine Fisheries Service, *Shellfish Situation and Outlook, Annual Review, 1971.*

Two major market segments combined to yield these aggregate statistics. Restaurants and fancy seafood stores, which favored "select" (1½–2½ pound lobsters), had a relatively constant demand, so that prices sometimes reached astronomical levels. Supermarkets and volume restaurants had a price-sensitive demand and tended to drop out of the picture when prices went above a certain level. When prices were low, however, chains tended to buy for promotions, thus helping to stabilize the market.

Competition Among Distributors. Companies of varying types and sizes were engaged in lobster distribution, and they competed fiercely to handle the limited supply on a price basis favorable to themselves.

Two of the largest entities in the business were J. Hook and Bay State, both of Boston, who together handled an estimated 30 million pounds a year. Despite their size, they might find themselves outbid by "small lotters," who were able to sell crate lots in Europe for twice what their large competitors were getting from a high-volume restaurant account.

Hook and Bay State operated quite differently, thus illustrating the wide variety of ways that entities in lobster distribution could be linked together or combined. Bay State specialized in furnishing the restaurant trade with sorted lobster at a stable year-round price, which might be above or below the current market. While it had preferred to confine itself to a wholesale function, it had recently been forced to enter the dealer function of running a pound in order to secure its sources of supply. In contrast, Hook maintained only a skeleton staff year-round, but geared up when the market was good to provide tremendous quantities of case lots of unsorted lobsters to secondary wholesalers. Hook also brokered a large volume to chains.

Weighted Average Annual Price per Pound Paid to Maine Fishermen

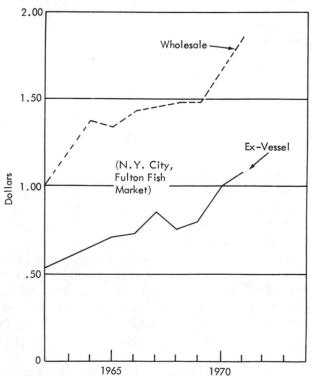

2

Merlin-Microwave, Inc.

In February, 1970, Merlin-Microwave, Inc., of Bridgeport, Connecticut, reported that its first two years in business had ended with cumulative losses in excess of cumulative sales, which in 1969 had totaled just over $100,000. Nevertheless, management had been able to increase MM's initial capitalization (under $55,000 in cash, mostly from relatives and business associates) by a successful public offering. Early in 1969, 50,000 shares of common had been marketed at $6 per share, with proceeds to the company of $225,000. (See Exhibits 1 and 2 for financial statements.) Furthermore, MM's management believed that they had devised a strategy capable of making their company a viable competitor in the $161 million microwave tube market, which was seen as headed toward rapid expansion.

As an early major step toward its objective, management had decided to try to obtain a substantial military contract. The thinking on this matter was described as follows by Mr. Albert Olsen, marketing vice president and (along with Dr. Edwin Merlino, president, and Mr. Harold Rhodes, treasurer) one of the company's three co-founders:

> We see many favorable things about the military market. The procurement rules are well established; on sales of replacement tubes, for example, the low bidder will win as long as he can demonstrate financial and technical capability. Various government circulars make it easy to find what bids are outstanding. Finally, the market is large and it is possible to strike at certain tubes where prices are high and there is a good chance of winning a contract.
>
> In the long term, we see the primary benefit of the military market as a springboard. If we can win a large contract and deliver, we will prove

EXHIBIT 1

MERLIN-MICROWAVE, INC.
Balance Sheets
As of January 31, 1969–70

	1969	1970
Current assets:		
Cash..	$23,386	$ 18,571
Accounts receivable............................	504	33,488
Inventories.....................................	8,891	71,468
Other..	2,879	1,541
Total......................................	$35,660	$125,068
Fixed assets, net:		
Machinery and equipment......................	9,874	40,425
Other..	1,639	3,990
Total......................................	$11,513	$ 44,415
Capitalized research and development*...........		56,884
Other assets...................................	250	450
Total assets...........................	$47,423	$226,817
Current liabilities:		
Accounts payable, trade.......................	$ 5,840	$ 44,071
Accrued payroll and expenses..................	1,066	7,520
Other..	1,352	4,317
Total......................................	$ 8,258	$ 55,908
4% Notes, convertible at $2 per share, due 1973......	25,000	25,000
Capital:		
Common stock ($0.01 par value).................	981	1,481
Paid-in capital in excess of par†.................	76,413	375,913
Accumulated deficit...........................	(63,229)	(231,485)
Total......................................	$14,165	$145,909
Total liabilities and capital...............	$47,423	$226,817

* R&D costs incurred in 1970 were to be amortized over five years.
† Included $52,312 received from exchange of stock for cash and $24,101 received.
from exchange of stock for salary in 1969. The increase in the following year mainly
represented proceeds from the public issue of 50,000 shares of common at $6 per
share.
Source: Company records.

that MM is a real company. We will develop a product history and a good name for commercial and government contracts. We will also very importantly be building up a technology base with government money. By producing tubes we will be gaining invaluabe R&D experience and knowledge of tricky vacuum and brazing technologies. With this base we can move naturally into commercial areas with a minimum of investment on MM's part.

We feel that if we concentrate on the military replacement market we can win contracts and build a reputation. Then we can offer new services such as refurbishing other companies' tubes. By ths process we can earn a profit in the short term and build expertise to make successful bids on other military and commercial contracts.

EXHIBIT 2

MERLIN-MICROWAVE, INC.
Operative Statements, 1969, 1970

	Eleven Months to January 31, 1969	Twelve Months to January 31, 1970
Gross sales	—	$ 98,980
Returns	—	474
Net sales	$ 3,591	$ 98,506
Cost of goods sold:		
Materials used	5,041	10,929
Direct labor	8,735	50,858
Factory overhead*	31,462	44,305
Total	$45,238	$106,092
Gross loss	$41,647	$ 7,586
Operating expenses:		
Selling	—	57,835
General and administrative	—	60,251
Total	21,542	$118,086
Loss from operations	$63,189	$125,672
Interest and other income	60	7,550
Total loss	$63,129	$118,122
Provision for state taxes	100	642
Net loss for period	$63,229	$118,764

*Included expensed research and development costs of an undisclosed amount for 1969 and of $1,966 for 1970.
Source: Company records.

THE MICROWAVE TUBE INDUSTRY

In their 1969 stock *Prospectus,* MM's management defined their company's business and industry as follows:

> The Company's business is the design, development, manufacture, and sale of tubes for the generation and amplification of microwave power.
>
> Microwaves are waves of electromagnetic energy. . . . They fall in the spectrum between the long waves used in radio communication and the very short waves of visible light. Although the term "microwave" [does not define] an exact frequency range, the frequencies most commonly associated with this term are between 1 billion and 100 billion cycles a second. Due to the unique properties of waves in this frequency range, they are useful for radar, communications, and, more recently, for rapid cooking and special industrial [heating] processes.

Products and Applications, R&D, Production

Microwave tubes fell into three generic types: magnetrons, klystrons, and traveling wave tubes (TWTs). Although more than one of these types might be used in some applications, each type had certain properties which normally gave it an advantage for a particular purpose. Thus, the magnetron was characterized by high efficiency and low weight per unit of power output; these properties gave it an advantage in the application of airborne radar. The magnetron was also relatively low-cost, which gave it an advantage in heating. The klystron was characterized by extreme stability of operation; that is, it could receive a signal, amplify it, and send it without distortion. This property gave it an advantage in ground-based, high-power radar and in many types of communications. The TWT was characterized by its ability to carry signals over a broad band width; this property gave it an advantage in communication systems like cross-country telephone transmission, since thousands of conversations could be simultaneously sent through one tube.

By 1970 all three types of microwave tubes had been long established, though magnetrons had been the first to achieve importance. Invented in England in 1939 and further developed at MIT, they had performed an invaluable service in radar during World War II. Early in the war, Raytheon became the top producer, and in 1945 a Raytheon scientist was credited with discovering the cooking application of the magnetron. The klystron, like the magnetron, had first appeared in 1939; it was an invention of Dr. Russell H. Varian of Stanford. The market for this type of tube did not open up until after the war, however, when high-powered versions were developed. The TWT was a postwar creation of the Bell Laboratories; it had come into use by 1948.

In line with this long history, MM's management said that future advances in the state of the art for microwave tubes were not expected. Development rather than research would be required to create new tubes capable of meeting new specifications. Another change predicted was lower unit costs. Eventually, microwave tubes might be coupled with solid-state devices, but MM's management saw this change as occurring in the distant future and thus as posing no present competitive threat.

In terms of production, intraclass differences among tubes could be at least as significant as differences among different tube categories, since tubes within each major type might differ greatly in complexity and size. To some extent this variety was reflected in the wide range of prices at which tubes in each category were sold (Exhibit 3). The very high prices of some tubes, however, could only be interpreted as reflecting the inclusion of substantial development work.

According to MM's management, the production of microwave tubes, regardless of generic type, had been likened to "black magic." Many complicated technologies were necessary, and extremely close tolerances were required in most applications. Several types of exotic metals and brazing alloys were used, and many scientific disciplines were required. While the formulae involved in the creation of the desired power, frequency, etc., could be calculated at the drawing-board stage with considerable accuracy, the number of relevant variables was so great that

EXHIBIT 3

MERLIN-MICROWAVE, INC.
Tube Price Data

Tube Type	Price Range	Average Price Range	Comments
Klystrons:			
Reflex.........	$ 70–$500	$ 300–$400	Tubes in the $400–$500 price range were for specialized uses.
Power.........	$500–$250,000	$1,000–$1,200	Tubes in the higher price ranges were for specialized uses and included high development costs.
Magnetrons......	$100–$4,000	$600–$700	Tubes in the lower price range were for heating purposes. The majority of tubes were used in radar.
TWTs...........	$700–$50,000	$1,500	Tubes in the higher price range included high development costs.

Source: MM management estimates.

finalization of the design could usually be accomplished only after varying degrees of "tinkering" or experimentation. Even if the design was right, management had further found that failure to perform as expected might be due to such production "bugs" as minute differences in cavity size or contamination by miniscule particles of cigarette ash or dust. In addition, tube assembly had a "learning curve" as technicians became more proficient in putting together intricate components. Therefore, the larger the quantity of a given tube produced, the faster and more efficient production became.

Markets and Competition

In 1970 the three main markets for microwave tubes continued to be radar, the original use; communications, to which the tubes had spread from radar; and heating, including cooking. Markets could be further subdivided into military and civilian, and the civilian heating market could be broken down into industrial, commercial, and home use.

In one market estimate for 1969, the total market size was put at $161 million, of which radar (using all three types of tubes) accounted for $88 million; communications (using klystrons and TWTs) accounted for $66 million; and heating (using lower-priced magnetrons almost exclusively) accounted for $7 million (Exhibit 4). Growth rates were available only for tube types rather than for markets (Exhibits 5 and 6), but these figures showed that volume as a whole had grown 9.5 percent in units and 2.9 percent in dollars from 1968 to 1969. Commenting on the

EXHIBIT 4

MERLIN-MICROWAVE, INC.
The Microwave Tube Market in 1969
(dollars in millions)

Market Segment	Estimated Application Breakdown			Reported Total*
	Klystrons	*Magnetrons*	*TWTs*	
Communications.........	$19	—	$47	$ 66
Radar....................	19	$36	33	88
Heating:				
Industrial.............	1	1	—	2
Domestic..............	—	3	—	3
Commercial...........	—	2	—	2
Total..............	$39	$42	$80	$161

* Not projected to total industry figures. Represents factory sales data from reporting firms.
    Source: Aggregate tube sales by class are Electronic Industries Association figures from *Electronic News,* May 6, 1970, p. 2. Sales breakdown by market segment based on management estimates.

2.9 percent dollar growth, MM's management suggested that it reflected the general economic downturn. For future years they estimated that a realistic growth rate would be 7 percent.

MM's management further believed that the radar and communication markets were not only the oldest and largest, but the most mature in terms of potential expansion, new applications, established competition, and market shares. On the other hand, management saw the heating market as very young, with a large growth potential and with competition not yet firmly established.

Overall, management believed that 90 percent of the tube market was shared among the three top suppliers: Varian Associates with 50 percent, Raytheon with 25 percent, and Litton Industries with 15 percent. Other suppliers included Hughes Aircraft, Sperry Rand, Ampex (of Holland),

EXHIBIT 5

MERLIN-MICROWAVE, INC.
Factory Sales in Units and Dollars, 1968–69*
(units and dollars in thousands)

Tube Type	1968 Units	1969 Units	Percent Change	1968 Dollars	1969 Dollars	Percent Change
Klystron............	153.0	142.6	(6.8)	$ 41,413	$ 39,107	(5.6)
Magnetron.........	94.3	135.4	43.6	38,440	42,004	9.3
TWT................	49.6	47.0	(5.2)	76,512	79,758	4.2
Total.........	296.9	325.0	9.5	$156,364	$160,870	2.9

Note: Failure of figures to add is due to rounding.
* Not projected to total industry data. Represents data from reporting firms.
Source: Electronic Industries Association figures in *Electronic News,* May 6, 1970, p. 2.

EXHIBIT 6

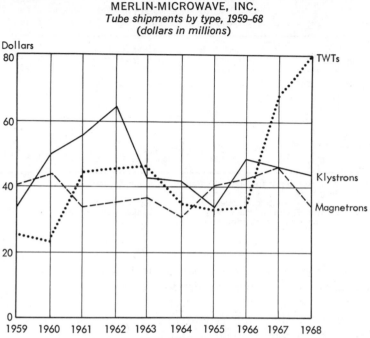

MERLIN-MICROWAVE, INC.
Tube shipments by type, 1959–68
(dollars in millions)

Source: Electronics Industries Association figures in *EIA Yearbook, 1969*, p. 60.

Microwave Associates, and Microwave Electronics Co. Most of these companies were very large (see Exhibit 7) and had been making tubes for up to 25 years.

Although the three major competitors were in all three generic tube types and in all three basic markets, no company blanketed the market for all subtypes and applications. Most kinds of military tubes, for example, were manufactured by only one supplier. In the commercial area, tubes made by different manufacturers were not interchangeable within systems. Thus, once a buyer had designed his equipment around a particular supplier's tube, he could not easily switch his source, since he could not purchase an alternate tube off some other supplier's shelf. As a result, the market tended to be monopolistic and prices and profit margins were high. MM's management saw in this situation an opportunity for a small company to make a profit for itself by attacking the flanks of large companies with substitutable designs at lower prices. Alternatively, it might try to get its tubes selected for new or "second-generation" systems.

Management further believed that competition was restricted by the difficulty of changing from one tube field to another with very different requirements. For example, Hughes made sophisticated radar tubes

EXHIBIT 7

MERLIN-MICROWAVE, INC.

Size and Product Data for Companies Competing in the Microwave Tube Market, 1969 (dollars in thousands)

Company	Total Sales and Ending Date of Fiscal Year	Net Income	Microwave Sales/ Total Sales*	Major Product Lines
Amperex (Holland)	—	—	—	—
Hughes Aircraft Co.	—	—	—	Weapons systems, equipment and controls, missiles, space vehicles, communications and guidance systems, electronic components, etc.
Litton Industries, Inc.	$2,176,598 (7/31)	$82,258	1 + %	Computers and controls, automatic guidance systems, data processing, radar, communications, business machines, electronic and other components, shipbuilding including nuclear submarines, etc.
Microwave Associates, Inc.	27,756 (9/27)	839	—	Microwave energy components, semiconductors, solid state devices, transmission line devices, subassemblies, TV relay equipment, etc.
Microwave Electronics Co., Inc. Division of Teledyne, Inc.	1,294,755 (10/31)	60,103	—	Electronic control systems and components, electrical products, services for the oil industry and oceanographic service, specialty metals, metal working machinery, etc.
Raytheon Co.	1,285,134 (12/31)	35,232	3 + %	Electronic systems, subsystems, equipment, and components; heating, cooking, and cooling appliances, etc.
Sperry Rand Corp.	1,607,340 (3/31)	77,036	—	Information handling and retrieval systems; aerospace products; industrial, agricultural, construction, and materials-handling equipment, office machines, consumer and marine technology products, etc.
Varian Associates	186,172 (9/30)	7,004	43 + %	Microwave tubes and other electronic equipment and solid-state devices.
Miscellaneous "uni-tube" companies	—	—	—	—

* Based on management's assumption that Varian had 50% of the 1969 market, or $80.5 million; Raytheon had 25%, or $40.3 million; and Litton had 15%, or $24.2 million.

† Believed by MM management to be undercapitalized as well as narrowly based.

Source: Standard & Poor's Corporation Records and Poor's Register of Corporations, Directors and Executives, 1970.

where very close tolerances were required to meet power and frequency specifications. It would not have been easy to switch this production to the manufacture of heating magnetrons where tolerances and the pride of craftsmanship were not as critical. Therefore, management believed that, although Litton, Raytheon, and Varian were large, they did not represent as formidable competition as appeared. Transfer of talents did occur, however, from military contracts to commercial activities within related tube classes.

Military and Civilian Markets for Radar and Communications

Looked at in another way, the market for microwave tubes could be divided into military and civilian segments. MM's management stated that the military was by far the largest buyer of all three types of tube, although its proportion was expected to decline, as is shown in Table 1.

TABLE 1

Tube Type	Volume 1969 (millions)	Estimated Military Share		Estimated Commercial Share	
		1970	1973	1970	1973
Magnetron............	$42	80%	50%	20%	50%
Klystron...............	39	90	90	10	10
TWT...................	80	70	50	30	50

Source: Exhibit 4 and MM management estimates.

Based on these estimates and a total dollar volume of $161 million in 1969, the military was spending $34 million for magnetrons, $35 million for klystrons, and $56 million for TWTs, for an overall total of $125 and an 80 percent combined market share.

Of the three applications for microwave tubes—radar, communications, and heating—the first two were predominantly military; only the third had no specific military importance.

So far as radar applications were concerned, the market was almost wholly military, since the major use for radar was in defense systems— in the air; on the ground, including landing fields; and on ships. Military demand for a particular type of tube was relatively easy to assess. Essentially, each defense system required a set number of tubes (for example, each B–52 airborne radar system used one particular coaxial magnetron), and the number of systems in use was fairly constant, as was the rate at which tubes were replaced. (For example, tubes for the B–52 radar system were replaced every four months, and 1,200 tubes were purchased each year.) How long military demand could continue to be confidently predicted was, however, doubtful, owing to changing defense needs and to budgetary constraints.

Nonmilitary uses of tubes for radar included weather reconnaissance, surveillance of commercial airports and air traffic control, airport landing systems, and navigation systems for ships and small boats. These commercial uses had come into being as military needs were satisfied and as engineers were freed to investigate nondefense applications. New segments were appearing and growth was accelerating, so demand was not easy to predict—except that the small boat market was expected to show the fastest gains. Overall, however, the radar market was expected to expand at a slow pace.

So far as communications applications for microwave tubes were concerned, the military market was believed to account for 65 percent to 70 percent of sales. Here the major use was long-distance voice and ground-to-air communications.

The principal nonmilitary use of microwaves for communications was in telephone and television relay links. Microwaves performed 90 percent of all TV transmission and two-thirds of all long-distance communication, including telephone data transmission and facsimile. The principal purchasers were Bell Telephone, Western Union, Microwave Communications, Inc., and the UHF–TV stations. Annual sales ran approximately $20 million.

For military and nonmilitary uses combined, MM's management predicted that the communications market would be growing at 7 percent, the industry average. Over the long run, microwaves might encounter some competition from lasers, which had an even greater capability for carrying information. So far, however, technical difficulties with laser systems had prevented their extensive use. For the foreseeable future management believed it probable that the bulk of communication transmissions would continue to be carried out at microwave frequencies. Microwave systems were finding greatly expanded use in satellites for transcontinental communications.

Selling the Military Market

Sales to the military might be direct—i.e., to military procurement offices, or indirect—i.e., to manufacturers who made defense systems incorporating tubes. Indirect sales, MM's management believed, were the more difficult type to make. Not only did some major systems manufacturers produce their own tubes (e.g., Raytheon, Hughes, Microwave Associates, and Sperry), but key sales factors in this area were long-standing intercompany relations, reputation, and past performance.

Direct military sales were made to user agencies which employed two methods of procurement: Invitations for Bids (IFBs), and Requests for

Proposals (RFPs). At the government's option, a bidder might be required to have previously qualified his product as acceptable by meeting standards contained in a Qualified Product List (QPL) for the item. By qualifying a tube at a cost of approximately $30,000 for development and testing expenses, a company could always bid on the tube without having to meet test standards to insure that the tube was acceptable.

If an IFB was used, all terms of the contract were final as bid, and the low bidder won, provided he passed certain tests as a "reliable" supplier. Under a RFP, terms and prices were negotiated both before and after the award, and the low bidder did not always win. If a QPL was stipulated, a non-QPL vendor could not bid. Contracts could be let with or without a QPL stipulation.

Direct military sales broke down into sales of tubes for new equipment, for replacement, or for R&D. Each of these segments varied in terms of procurement methods used, ease of entry, market effort required to win the business, and potential profit payoff. The least difficult segment to enter, MM's management believed, was the replacement segment. Here the purchaser stated the specifications, followed well-established procurement regulations, and purchased on the basis of price. In this segment, QPLs were often but not always used. Profits, however, were generally lowest. As one moved into military sales for original equipment and R&D, contracts became harder to obtain since factors such as new design and innovation were important. Profits increased, but so did costs and capital investment.

As previously noted, MM was interested in entering the military market, especially the replacement sector, not only as an end in itself, but also as a "springboard" to greater visibility for the company and to more business elsewhere.

Besides these advantages, company management also saw some problems in the military market. These were identified by Mr. Olsen as follows:

> There are some drawbacks, too, in the military market. First, there is the cyclicality of defense spending. Second, there is the risk of choosing a line of tubes for qualification on QPLs and then not receiving a bid for the tubes. Third, the profits are generally not as high as in the commercial market. They are high in some areas now, but if we enter the market, we will be forced to underbid the competition to win.

The Heating Market

Unlike radar and communications, the $7 million heating market for microwave tubes was civilian. In this market purchasers used the product for heating nonmetallic materials, including food. The advantage in this technique arose from the ability of microwaves to dissipate energy uniformly throughout the mass of the substance being heated. In conventional heating, energy was applied only to the outside surface of the material and was carried to the inside by conduction. This process limited the amount of energy that could be applied without burning the outer surface of the material. The microwave tube, though, could supply energy at a sufficient rate to heat a nonmetallic substance without burning in a fraction of the time required by conventional methods.

The ability to heat rapidly was the principal promise of microwave heating. Mainly because of this feature, microwave heating had three basic applications: industrial, domestic, and commercial. Of these, both of the last two featured the heating or cooking of food. In this application, as in others, speed was a prime consideration: For example, a microwave oven could cook eight strips of bacon in three minutes or bake a cake in four minutes. In addition, a secondary value of the process was the ability to cook food in its own juices without drying it out. Lastly, since no conventional heat was used, grease would not burn onto the side of the oven and therefore could be wiped off easily with a sponge.

Industrial Heating Applications. The industrial segment of the heating market used microwave systems to produce rapid drying and curing of products. These applications were practically endless. Microwave heating had been used to dry paper, leather, baseball bats, tobacco, glue, and foundry sand cores. In the field of medicine it had been used for diathermy treatments where deep heat penetration was required. Experiments were being performed by several industries to determine the usefulness of microwave heating. For example, Kodak was attempting to dry film and PPG Industries was looking into microwave heat to dry fiberglass.

MM's management believed that no clear-cut competition had yet appeared in the industrial segment. Varian, as the largest tube producer with 1969 tube sales of approximately $80 million, appeared to be the most likely leader. Raytheon was known to have a small share of the market with one of its tubes (they had shipped a potato chip dryer to Frito-Lay). Litton might be a source for some end-users, but MM's management believed that Litton's heating tubes were mostly geared to the commercial and domestic oven markets and that Litton probably had no extant working tubes that would be especially efficient if transferred to the industrial scene.

Summing up MM's assessment of the industrial heating market segment, President Merlino spoke as follows:

> The primary advantage of microwave heating is its time saving. General Motors, for example, has found that foundry sand cores can be dried in five minutes with a microwave oven versus over an hour with a

conventional oven. Additional benefits are a saving of floor space, greatly improved consistency since the cores dry at the same rate all the way through, and lower capital investment and operating expenses.

The industrial market has been an enigma for years. Since 1945 technicians and scientists have recognized the vast potential savings and have been attempting to adapt microwave power to industrial uses. Yet sales of tubes for these purposes increase only slightly each year. Everyone wants to know what the magic word is to open this potentially enormous market.

There are two keys to the market. First, tubes must cost less. One system being designed to dry a single type of fiber will use 150 tubes and require four replacements a year. The system will be used on 20 lines. Therefore, 12,000 tubes a year will be needed. A tube today costs approximately $300 in this quantity; the user, though, looks to a $100 tube, or savings of nearly $2.4 million.

Second, a systems approach must be taken in developing a heating process. The microwave engineer cannot design a system without a good knowledge of the nature of the product being heated. Each product has particular characteristics that alter cavity size, heating time, and the power frequency required. The heating system must also be capable of being incorporated without disruption into the overall production process. Therefore, the microwave specialist must work very closely with the product technicians and the mechanical engineers.

In spite of these problems, some facts are obvious about this market. Its potential is tremendous, if just *one* application for *one* company requires 12,000 tubes a year. Thus, a supplier must have a sufficient amount of automated equipment and capital to produce tubes in the quantity and at prices required by customers. Finally, a company like us with microwave expertise must find people to provide a "systems approach" to the market.

Domestic Oven Applications. Of all the uses for microwave tubes, the domestic oven market appeared to have the greatest growth potential, since domestic ovens were used in the home for daily cooking. Table 2 shows the tremendous projected growth of this market.

For comparison, past growth in unit sales of some other appliances are reported in Table 3.

Several tube manufacturers were already in the domestic oven market, and others were planning to enter. Some produced the total system (ovens plus tubes), though in different divisions or subsidiaries (e.g., Raytheon); others sold their tubes to independent oven manufacturers (e.g., Amperex), while others handled oven tubes both ways (e.g., Litton). Management's knowledge of competition is summarized in Table 4.

Any plans which other large appliance manufacturers might have for marketing a domestic oven were not known to MM's management team, nor were the plans of foreign manufacturers.

In at least one foreign country—Japan—microwave ovens had made much greater progress than in the United States. Unit sales were already

TABLE 2

Year	Units Sold (thousands)	Estimated Oven Sales Price*	Estimated Total Sales (thousands)
1966	2	$1,000	$ 2,000
1967	4–5	700	3,000
1968	15–20	500	8,000
1969	30	500	15,000
1970 est.†	80	475	38,000
1971 est	200	375	75,000
1972 est	375	300	112,500
1973 est	600	275	165,000

* The tube was approximately 15 percent of the selling price in 1969.
† Raytheon and Litton both said they were building 50,000 ovens apiece for 1970.
Source: For units sold, *Appliance Magazine*, February, 1970, p. 62; for estimated prices, MM management.

250,000 by 1969, with 500,000 to 750,000 predicted for 1970. Several Japanese suppliers were already established, the principal ones being Toshiba, Sharpe (Hayakawa), and Matsushita.

The rapid acceptance of microwave ovens in Japan was deemed due to some local market factors. Thus, Japanese food was readily adaptable to microwave cooking—vegetables, rice, and fish being more easily cooked than roasts. Japanese homes were traditionally small, so a microwave oven fitted better into the kitchen than a large stove with oven. Urban husbands and wives in Japan usually worked, so an oven became important as a time-saving device. By nature the Japanese also loved

TABLE 3

	1960 (thousands of units)	1969 (thousands of units)	Percent Change 1968–69
Dishwashers	555	2,157	10
Food waste disposers	760	1,880	8
Electric ranges	1,495	2,468	7
Gas ranges	1,814	2,499	10
Electric refrigerators	3,475	5,485	1
Washing machines	3,364	4,482	2
Dryers	1,260	3,120	9
Electric irons	6,410	10,000	
Vacuum cleaners	3,313	7,144	10
Electric fans	4,687	9,257	1
Freezers	1,045	1,135	1
Wholesale price index (1957–59 = 100)	97.0	94.1	2

Source: Bureau of the Census, Bureau of Labor Statistics, and *Merchandising Week*, in Business and Defense Services Administration, *U.S. Industrial Outlook*, 1970, p. 109.

TABLE 4

Oven Source	Tube Source	Date of Entry	Estimated Annual Sales
Tappan Co.*	—	1954	About 2,000 (until 1968)
Amana Division of Raytheon Co.	Raytheon	1967	2,000–3,000 in 1967; 15,000 in 1968. Objective of 50,000 in 1970.
Litton Industries, Inc.	Litton	Late 1969	Planned to sell through Montgomery Ward under the "Signature" label. Objective of 50,000 in 1970.
Norris Industries, Inc. "Thermador" ranges†	—	March 1970 (planned)	—
General Electric Co.	—	—	—
Roper Corp.	Litton	—	Five-year exclusive agreement to use Litton tubes in an oven to be sold through Sears, Roebuck.
Husqvarna Corp.‡ (Sweden)	—	Planned to enter U.S. market after 1970	

* Microwave and regular oven combination.
† Microwave in combination with an infrared unit to brown food, at a price of $680, or $1,200 with a self-cleaning feature.
‡ Round-shaped oven, which some industry observers believed would be particularly appealing to housewives.
Source: MM management.

gadgets. Finally, very few of the older generation in Japan had possessed stoves. Therefore, in contrast to the United States, none of the younger Japanese had been taught by mother to cook on a conventional appliance, so they had no reluctance to cook with microwave.

Summing up MM's assessment of the U.S. domestic oven market, President Merlino spoke as follows:

First of all, the demand for microwave ovens is increasing rapidly as TV shows give them away as prizes and as full-page ads are run in large magazines like *Ladies' Home Journal* and *Life* [September 19, 1969, Amana oven]. This publicity, of course, works in our favor, since it develops a market for us to enter.

Second, the conventional appliance companies are very interested in the microwave oven market. There are a lot of these companies: Hotpoint, Whirlpool, Frigidaire, Corning Glass Works, Hamilton Beach, Hupp Corp., and others. They will not be satisfied to see their markets taken away by microwave ovens, nor will they be happy to see these oven manufacturers making a very healthy profit in areas where they consider they have expertise. Many are not sure exactly what product to sell: Should it be an oven, a sandwich grill, or a unique device for the kitchen? It is certain, though, that several of them will enter the market.

The major tube producer, though, may not as yet have appeared. Litton and Raytheon are working at capacity for their own needs, and the other tube companies either show little interest or have little expertise in this area. Therefore, a supplier must come forth to meet the demand.

On the negative side, four factors have restricted growth in this market. First, there is the tendency for all girls to prefer to cook the way their mothers did. We are dealing here with personal tastes, and some people are reluctant to eat food prepared by a fantastic machine that shoots electricity into food and cooks it in a few minutes.

There is also the basic problem of selling the oven, a radically new product, to the public. A particular problem here is the recent HEW allegation of radiation leakage from ovens. Its statement that radiation above certain levels can cause cataracts and chromosome damage and that oven leakage is not being properly controlled has significantly cut sales in the first few months of 1970. We feel that by the time we are in the market, firm regulations will be in effect and we will take them into account in our designs. [See the Appendix for a more complete discussion of this problem.]

Third, the microwave oven, by the nature of its heating process, does not brown food. A steak is cooked the same all the way through and does not have the conventional "charcoal-broiled" look. Finally, there is the problem of packaging food for use in the oven. Not all food can be cooked in the oven and each type and amount of food requires different cooking times. When you speak of baking a potato in four minutes, it is critical that food not be left in the oven too long. This problem is being solved with the planned introduction by frozen food companies [Stouffer] of food packaged for microwave ovens, with cooking times on the package.

MM feels that the combination of these factors leads to a basic conclusion: The domestic microwave heating market has come of age and is ready to explode. The lead time in developing, testing, and getting approval of an oven is about two years. Therefore, the time to act is today before another tube manufacturer appears and before the market matures around the existing oven manufacturers.

Commercial Oven Applications. The commercial market for microwave ovens was mainly composed of a restaurant segment, with some demand also from a fast growing automatic food-vendor segment. Since the primary advantage continued to lie in the saving of time, restaurant users tended to be those that prided themselves on fast service. Such customers included some important franchise chains, e.g., Howard Johnson's Sizzlebord, and Pewter Pot. These used the ovens to reheat precooked foods.

Besides speed, a secondary advantage of microwave heating for commercial use lay in the fact that the ovens gave off no grease, thereby eliminating the need for exhaust hoods and easing sanitary problems with boards of health. Additionally, the consistent cooking time in an oven allowed for better planning, more extensive menus, and more consistent tasting food.

Litton was the principal producer of ovens for restaurants and cafe-terias. It had been in this market since 1965, and, according to MM's management, Litton had been able to prove itself as a source of dependable, quality ovens. The original market entrant had been Raytheon, which had started this business in 1945. After putting millions into its "Radarange" venture, however, Raytheon dropped out in 1968. Increased competition from Litton plus a desire to concentrate on the domestic market potential of its own Amana oven were the factors that reportedly led to its decision. More recently, the restaurant market had been invaded by Magic Chef with an oven similar to Litton's and using Litton tubes. In addition, two small companies sold commercial restaurant ovens: Welbilt Corp. and Thermo Kinetics, Inc. Welbilt (Garland Oven) used an oven manufactured by Husqvarna (Sweden) and was believed to have a problem in obtaining replacement tubes. Therefore, it was selling the oven to restaurants only in the northeast United States and had not sold over 500. Thermo Kinetics sold a large oven that was used for bulk processing of food. They had sold only about 20 ovens, and MM's management believed that there was no real market for the product. It used an Amperex tube.

In the vending segment of the commercial market, the microwave oven was used to heat sandwiches and other foods. For example, an oven could cook a frozen hot dog or it could thaw (yet not heat up) a frozen milk shake. Since cooking was accomplished in a matter of seconds, machines could be used in many types of location: gasoline stations, airports, or even special microwave areas on a turnpike.

So far, microwave cooking for vending machines was accomplished by separate vending mechanisms and ovens rather than by an integrated system. Although the technology for the latter had been available for many years, no one had yet placed it on the market.

Each of the three principal competitors in the food-vending business had made an exclusive agreement with a microwave oven supplier. Thus, Rowe International Co., the largest, had an exclusive agreement with Litton to place Litton's oven next to Rowe's vendor; Vendo, the second largest, had a similar agreement with International Crystal Manufacturing Co.; and National Vendors, the third largest, had a similar agreement with Sage Laboratories, Inc., of Natick, Massachusetts. Of these oven suppliers, Litton and Sage used the Litton tube, while Crystal used the Amperex from Holland.

Although Rowe, Vendo, and National were the only vending machine companies that had national coverage, many other smaller competitors (for example, the Cornelius Company) were anxious to enter the market with microwave equipment and were looking for a microwave oven supplier. In addition, Vendo was reportedly interested in an integrated vending-oven arrangement. Its present oven supplier, Crystal, was con-

EXHIBIT 8

MERLIN-MICROWAVE, INC.

Major Firms in the U.S. Market for Microwave Cooking Capability, 1969*
(dollars in thousands)

Company	Current Participation in the Microwave Oven Market	Total Sales and Ending Date of Fiscal Year	Net Income
Amana Division of Raytheon Co.......	√	$ 1,285,134 (12/31)	$ 35,232
Automatic Vendors of America, Inc....	√	32,016 (9/30)	129
Cornelius Co..........................	—	39,309 (12/31)	d(989)
Corning Glass Works..................	—	350,568 (12/28)	50,029
Crystal Mfg. Co.......................	√	—	—
Frigidaire Division of General Motors Corp...............................	—	24,295,141 (12/31)	1,710,695
Hamilton Beach Division of Scovill Mfg. Co.............................	—	444,490 (12/31)	15,616
Hotpoint Division of General Electric Co..................................	√	8,447,967 (12/31)	278,015
Hobart Mfg. Co.......................	—	201,016 (12/31)	13,102
Hupp Division of White Consolidated Industries, Inc......................	—	767,601 (12/31)	29,853
Litton Industries, Inc.................	√	2,176,589 (7/31)	82,258
Magic Chef, Inc.......................	—	90,067 (6/30)	3,018
National Vendors Division of UMC Industries, Inc......................	√	136,469 (12/31)	7,284
Roper Corp...........................	√	205,412	4,972
Rowe International, Inc., Division of Triangle Industries, Inc..........	√	67,237 (12/31)	2,844
Seeburg Corp. of Delaware...........	—	—	—
Sage Laboratories, Inc...............	√	3,763 (6/30)	200
Tappan Co............................	√	133,877 (12/31)	3,441
Norris Industries, Inc................. (planned) (7/31)		281,800	14,400
Thermo-Kinetics, Inc.................	√	—	—
Vendo Co.............................	√	99,326 (12/31)	2,408
Welbuilt Corp........................	√	56,842 (12/21)	882
Whirlpool Corp.......................	—	1,153,530 (12/31)	45,943

* Excludes a Swedish firm with a microwave oven in the U.S. market (Husqvarna) and three Japanese suppliers (Sharpe-Hayakawa, Matsushita, and Toshiba).

Source: MM management and Standard & Poor's *Corporation Records.*

sidered too small to develop such a product, and consequently Vendo was seeking another source to develop and produce this equipment.

Commenting on prospects in the commercial market, Mr. Rhodes, MM's treasurer, expressed himself as follows:

> There is a great range of possible customers to consider in this area. We can sell our microwave expertise to vending machine companies, food-processing equipment manufacturers, food processors, or conventional appliance makers. Likewise, the variety of food that can be heated is enormous, and each type requires a different oven configuration.
>
> We must be careful in this market, though, because some of these ideas for dispensing food are novel and require sizable capital to develop machinery and back-up systems. Also we cannot design an oven to heat, say, cheeseburgers without ensuring that the cheeseburger has a uniform size and consistency [fat and meat content]. Because of the nature of the heating process, the set machine time, and the automation of the machinery, cheeseburgers of differing sizes would have very uneven quality and would not sell. This "systems" aspect goes one step further in a situation like, say, McDonald's, which has uniform kitchens at each location. While a microwave oven might work well, installing an oven would necessitate a change in the rest of the kitchen and therefore would not be worth its savings.
>
> The systems approach requires coordination with food suppliers, but this is not an insurmountable problem. Large and small frozen-food companies are producing food for microwave ovens. We feel that since the system is being attacked by others and the technology and desire are here, microwave heating in the commercial area has finally come of age. [See Exhibit 8 for data on the potential market for microwave cooking capability.]

MERLIN-MICROWAVE IN 1970

Management and Key Personnel

In 1970, MM's management and key personnel included the company's three co-founders and three outside members of the board (see Exhibit 9 for details on their experience and education). Dr. Merlino, as president, was responsible for overall administration. In reality, he indicated, all decisions were made on a consensus basis by the three principals, with no individual attempting to sway the others to his own opinions. The group worked very closely as a team and rarely made a decision, other than one of a minor administrative nature, without agreement.

Like Dr. Merlino, Mr. Rhodes, the treasurer, and Mr. Olsen, the marketing vice president, both had engineering backgrounds. Dr. Merlino, who was a listed inventor on several patents in the field of high-power microwave tubes, was considered the company's expert in klystrons. Mr. Rhodes was considered its microwave heating specialist. Mr. Olsen

EXHIBIT 9

MERLIN-MICROWAVE, INC.
Background Data on Founder-Managers and Key Board Members

Name	Office	Age	Holdings of MM Shares*	Education	Previous Positions
Dr. Edwin Merlino........	President	36	25,000	BS (engineering) Pennsylvania State MS (electrical engineering) Stanford PhD Northeastern	Microwave engineer, Varian Associates, 1957–61 Manager of Advanced Tube Development, Microwave Associates, 1961–67
Mr. Albert Olsen.........	Marketing Vice President	45	18,525		Chief Engineer, Joseph Pollak Corporation,† 1959–62 Manager of Engineering, Waters Manufacturing,† 1962–65 National Radio Co., 1965–67 Consultant 1967–68
Mr. Harold Rhodes......	Treasurer	38	10,000	BS (physics) Geneva College MS (physics) MIT	Engineer, Raytheon Microwave Power Tube Division Engineer, Microwave Associates Director of R & D, Contek, Inc.,† 1963–68
Professor———.........	Head of the Department of Electrical Engineering, ———University since 1966	—	1,000		
Mr.———............	Treasurer and Director, [snack chain] Management Corp.; Director, [pizza] Management Corp.	—	1,000		International Vice President [Snack-bar chain]

Note: The only available information on Mr.———, the lawyer, is on p. 25.
* Out of 148, 129 common shares outstanding.
† Small companies in the Bridgeport area.
Source: Interviews with company management.

was relied upon for his knowledge of machinery, material, mechanical engineering, and drafting. Ten patents in various fields had been granted to Mr. Olsen, and he had others pending.

Outside members of the board also had specialized expertise. Thus Professor ———, the head of the electrical engineering department in a local Ivy League university, acted as technical advisor; Mr. ———, the treasurer of a successful restaurant franchise chain, was the financial individual on the board; and Mr. ———, a recent graduate of the Harvard Law School, was an associate of MM's firm of legal advisors.

Production and Sales Organization

After raising some $225,000 through its public issue, MM increased the number of people employed from six to 21. By early 1970, the production group included four experienced tube technicians, a test engineer with an associate in engineering degree, a factory superintendent, a senior engineer with a BS degree and 12 years of experience in microwave tube development, and a physicist with an SM degree from MIT and 12 years of experience in electrical and mechanical engineering and particle physics.

The selling group included a retired Army procurement colonel who consulted on government procurement, a Washington representative, and a national network of 18 sales offices (manufacturers' representatives).

Although management noted that MM lacked sufficient assets to step into large-scale tube production, management believed that the company had established a nucleus of capable people and administrative and control systems.

Product Line and Sales to Date

At the time of MM's stock offering, the *Prospectus* told investors that management had had experience in the design, development, and production of all three generic types of microwave tubes and that the company intended to develop products in each of these fields. Products already developed included a line of heating magnetrons for home and restaurant ovens, plus other models having direct application in industrial processing. Of the proceeds to be raised by the public offering, about $50,000 was intended for "tooling and cost reduction engineering" relating to these heating tubes.

Besides its magnetrons, the company reported that it had also developed a klystron for use in the receiver portion of an airport radar system; this klystron was also believed to be potentially useful in transmitting and receiving communications.

By the end of its second year, MM had been involved in two major contracts, both of which had been successfully completed. One of these was with the Federal Aviation Agency (FAA) and involved a $65,000 order for 185 reflex klystrons of a type on which the company had had little previous experience. This contract had lasted 12 months, during the last of which the yield had been 85 percent of all tubes put into production, while shipments totaled 64 tubes during the last month MM had had no rejects from the FAA.

The second major contract had been a $21,500 order from Westinghouse for two magnetrons. Also, under contract, the company had developed three industrial heating tubes for Bechtel Corporation, and it was working on an integrated hot dog oven-vendor for a major machinery manufacturer which was contemplating this product as a possible diversification.

As of February 1970, MM had no contracts for commercial products, but it had spent approximately $45,000 on travel and communication in order to get in touch with potential microwave tube users, especially those interested in heating applications. To demonstrate the workability of its heating tubes, the company had put them into several Litton and Raytheon ovens. Management believed that the company had made many valuable contacts with potential customers.

The DESC Order

Early in 1970 management indicated that the most significant event in MM's immediate future would be the outcome of a $222,500 military order from the Defense Electronics Supply Corps (DESC), obtained in October 1969. This order involved 310 coaxial magnetrons to be used in an air force airborne radar system.

The decision to go after this contract stemmed directly from management's strategy of penetrating the military market as a way to get established in the tube industry. The contract thus successfully pursued had been one for a replacement tube, though not for a type of tube which MM had so far produced. The contract had involved an Invitation for Bid (IFB) rather than a Request for Proposal (RFP), so management was sure that the low bidder would be successful. Also, the contract had not stipulated that the tube must be purchased from the Qualified Product List (QPL), and thus a non-QPL vendor could bid. Instead, the contract terms had required a First-Article Test and a Systems-Compatibility Test.

At the time of bidding on this contract (August 1969), management had known that both Raytheon and Varian would also bid. Moreover, both had previously won awards for this same tube, though Raytheon's version had not yet passed its First-Article Test. On these earlier occasions, Varian's price had been $1,200 a tube and Raytheon's $1,250 (the latter set on a negotiated basis).

To insure that MM would win, management bid a price of $750, or enough to cover estimated variable costs of $730 per tube and to make a minor contribution toward estimated allocated unit costs of $225 for selling and administration. Thus, MM's management decided to accept a $60,000 loss as a necessary "investment" to enter the military market. As it turned out, the company's bid was just a few dollars a tube below Raytheon's at the 310 volume level.

Before the final award, MM had to pass a pre-award survey to determine its productive, financial, and technical capability. By September all phases of the survey had been completed and a favorable report had been sent by the New York Region of the Defense Contract Administration Services (the contract administrator) to DESC, which had the final contract authority.

According to MM's management, DESC was very unhappy with the favorable report, since they wanted a known tube company as the supplier. They had never expected MM to win and were not anxious to nurse the company through financial and technical problems. Furthermore, the head of procurement at DESC was about to be promoted and he did not want MM to damage his chances. Nonetheless, MM could not be disqualified, and the award was made on October 31, 1969.

The contract had the following schedule:

Date: 1970	Event
April 9	Completion of First Article Test
April 30	Completion of Systems Compatibility Test
April 30	Shipment of 50 tubes
May 30	Shipment of 100 tubes
June 30	Shipment of 100 tubes
July 30	Shipment of 60 tubes

The contract also had a 50 percent "follow-on" option for another 155 tubes, exercisable by the supplier until April 15, 1970. Given the "learning curve" on tube production, management believed this would be very profitable.

Future Plans

Having implemented the first major step in its strategy by obtaining the DESC contract, MM's management had to turn its attention to planning its succeeding steps. By this time it had already been decided that the heating tube business would be the next area on which to concentrate, and MM had already got in touch with several possible clients in this field. Early in 1970, the company was engaged in active negotiations with one supplier of domestic ovens (Corning Glass Works) and with several sources in the commercial field (Vendo, Cornelius, Sage Laboratories, and Crystal Manufacturing Co.). (See Exhibit 8 for data on the potential oven market.)

In addition, several tubes had been sold to a company (Bechtel Corporation) active in industrial heating tubes.

Management said that while "military sales were bringing in profits and a reputation," all segments of the heating market would be attacked by means of cooperative ventures with nationally known companies. All companies that might have an interest in microwave heating would be contacted, and MM would work with as many partners as it could to reach the home-oven and industrial heating markets. In the commercial market, in contrast, what seemed needed was a single partner who could provide a distribution system, marketing ability, and a willingness to invest. MM's executives indicated that their company, by itself, did not have the capital and expertise to compete with the extensive marketing organization of Litton, Raytheon, G.E., etc.

As for product and production plans, MM's market entry would occur in two phases. First, the company would continue to refine its current heating tube designs, and it would build prototypes. Also in this phase, designs of ovens, electronic packages, and heating systems would be accomplished. Whether the company would eventually move forward into actual production of such electronic packages or total systems or both, remained an open point to be decided. In the second phase of its market entry, MM would create automated equipment capable of producing up to 100,000 tubes a year. The development of such equipment was seen as being within the "state of the art," although none had actually been constructed.

Besides working out their marketing and product approach to heating tubes, MM's management had some financial planning done for these and other longer-range objectives. To implement the company's goals, an estimated $2 million would be needed: $500,000 in 1970, $800,000 in 1971, and $700,000 in 1972. Applications would be as follows:

Domestic and Commercial Heating

$350,000	Tooling and product development
150,000	Automated production line
100,000	Marketing

Industrial Heating

$150,000	Product development
70,000	Control circuitry and power supply modules
85,000	Marketing

Military

$250,000	TWT development
150,000	Magnetron development
100,000	Marketing
250,000	Working capital

Special Products

$150,000	Solid-state coupling of tube devices
250,000	Oven electronics, transformers

Management's Long-Range Personal Goals

Over the longer run, each of the three founder-managers had in mind a picture of what kind of company he wanted MM to become and what personal satisfactions he expected to derive from working for this kind of firm. Dr. Merlino, the president, expressed himself as follows:

> I had three reasons for starting MM. First, I have a particular personality trait of being unable to work for someone else. I have always been in trouble with my bosses, and in fact that was the reason I parted from my previous employer, Microwave Associates. Second, my wife is a biology professor and has a good salary. Therefore, 30 to 40 percent of any money I make goes to the government in taxes. In order to make my time worthwhile, I must have either a high salary to get sufficient take-home pay or a capital gains situation. MM offers the latter alternative. Third, I desire to be independently wealthy by 40, and I am 36 now.
>
> Besides these personal goals, I have certain corporate objectives. First, MM must be a profit-making device. Second, I want to make a profit without exploiting employees. In fact, if there is anything unique about the company, I want it to be a feeling of responsibility toward the employees. Varian, for example, shows real respect for its employees and they in turn work hard for the company. Most of the employees have considerable longevity; they are rarely laid off because management anticipates the market and does not overhire so that it will not have to release people. I hope to do the same within the constraint of survival and profits. If MM has to, we'll reduce profits to keep employees.
>
> I also want to apply my knowledge of microwave tubes and physics in a company. I feel that there is great potential in the microwave heating market and that we can make a contribution to it. MM should use this area as a springboard to make contributions elsewhere, probably in the technological areas, since our expertise lies there. Essentially, we hope to be a technical company that is trying to sell products in the commercial world.
>
> I do not want MM to be a very small company. It is not difficult to be a $1 million tube firm, and such a company could operate well until I retire. But this is not my goal. I want a large business that grows as fast as it can. One problem we might have is wanting to grow too fast, in the sense that we are not sufficiently aware of the outside world to realize that our goals are not realistic.

Mr. Rhodes, treasurer, described his desires for MM as follows:

> As for my personal objectives, I want to build a successful small company out of nothing. A small company has great interest to me. First, there are very few experts in small companies because either these companies fail or get large. Second, I am interested in the total process of building and managing a company. If one can manage a small company well, there is satisfaction from having done a successful job. Third, I am looking forward to drawing together all aspects of business—finance,

psychology, marketing—within a technical area and making a success. Expertise to me is not science or business but the ability to join the two together.

Mr. Olsen, marketing vice president, described as follows what he hoped to achieve through MM:

> In relation to the company, I am interested in seeing it have a significant and profitable place in a market with a product that does something for people. I am not interested in the aerospace or military market. These areas do advance technology faster than would normally occur, but I am not sure whether all their product spin-offs are worth the expense. Some of the output, though, is very helpful in the commercial market, and we plan to take our share of these advances. I would like to take these advances and turn them into something that makes people's lives easier and more significant.
>
> This country is in need of a new industrial revolution based on the last 20 years of technology. Scientists and engineers today are too interested in advancing the state of the art, and not in giving people products they want and need. In the microwave heating area we have seen an evolution in the last 25 years based on advances in material technology. I would like to see MM extend this evolution by producing better products for microwave heating.
>
> Eventually we should expand into related areas, e.g., all aspects of microwave heating and producing better power supplies. But the microwave heating area is so large that MM could spend all its life in the field and not even make a big dent.
>
> Personally, I enjoy making products better and/or cheaper by manufacturing or application engineering. I also enjoy finding new uses for products. I should like to be able to motivate people along these lines so that there would be a group of people to make better products and not just myself. We must, though, find people that are interested in this type of work.
>
> There are many ways to approach making a better product: working on the product itself, using better tooling, or making more investment in tooling. We must be careful, though, to relate our manufacturing effort to marketing feedback and find out how good a product we can make based on what people want. Only after we know what to make can we finance it.
>
> I expect to make a profit for myself and the company if we go about our product development correctly. Profit should be a natural evolution from this process. If we have good marketing and production, everything else will fall into place.

Immediate Prospects as Assessed by MM's President

In looking to the near-term future, Dr. Merlino assessed MM's prospects as follows:

In spite of the size of Litton, Raytheon, Varian, and other tube companies, we feel that we have certain assets we can sell. Litton and Raytheon have Japanese subsidiaries they originally hoped would make tubes for the U.S. market. But with Japanese sales increasing dramatically, the subsidiaries cannot export tubes. They are working at capacity making tubes for their own use. On the other hand, MM has the necessary talent, capability, and desire to produce tubes for appliance and vending machine companies. We can move very quickly in contrast to the long time it takes a large company to act. We also can underprice the large companies in a market where price is important. Finally, our tubes have a ceramic seal rather than a conventional glass one and can therefore be baked at higher temperatures, which leads to a longer life and quicker, less costly production.

A final asset is the fact that there is a limited pool of talented microwave tube engineers. For many years this area has not been a glamor field like solid-state physics, and there have been few new engineers. Additionally, few people in the universities have been interested in microwave tubes. With normal attrition, then, the pool has shrunk, and nearly all qualified people are tied in with present companies. To enter the field from scratch would require hiring engineers away from other companies, which is difficult, since they are needed in their present jobs. The fact that we have three qualified microwave people and have no capacity constraints makes us an important entity.

We have been purposefully open-minded about our entry into the market. Our expertise is the design of tubes, but a microwave system requires, in addition, a power supply, transformer, miscellaneous elec-

Normal Product Life Cycle

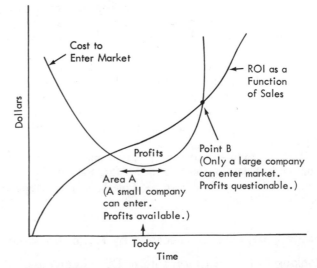

Source: MM management and casewriter.

tronic equipment, and the oven itself. Therefore, we are not limiting our entry to microwave tubes only.

When you look at the market [Exhibit 8], it is evident that a certain amount of stratification has occurred. Three vending machine companies are set with tube sources. Varian has stated that if they get any portion of the microwave heating market it will be the industrial segment; Raytheon is already entrenched in the domestic oven market; Litton has contracted with Montgomery Ward to sell domestic ovens, and they also have a strong reputation in the commercial oven market. Therefore, time is a very precious commodity to us. If you look at the picture of a normal product life cycle [see graph], we feel that we are not too far into it yet to be hurt. For example, on the ROI curve of the graph we are probably in Area A, where we can still invest a small amount and make good profits. But Point B, where the costs of entry will be very high and profits questionable, is only nine months to one year from now.

We are now faced with the question of whether it was wise to bid on a large contract with the prospect of a $60,000 investment. We have never made these tubes before. Going after the commercial market will take a lot of money, and we are not positive that we can raise capital. If we do not, it will be difficult to finance delivery of the government tubes. We also wonder whether we have guessed correctly that the microwave heating market is ready to take off. Does everyone else believe this, too, or are the well-heeled "partners" we are looking for still not ready to move ahead?

Appendix: Merlin-Microwave, Inc.

Problems of Radiation Leakage in Domestic Microwave Oven*

One of the more serious problems facing microwave oven producers in early 1970, particularly producers of domestic ovens, was the recent allegation that microwave ovens were releasing harmful amounts of radiation.

The problem had two aspects: one political, the other biological. The political aspect centered around a disagreement in the Bureau of Radiological Health of HEW as to how strict rules for products under

---

* Sources: Edward Gross, "Microwaves and Health Effects," *The World,* February 18, 1970. (Reprinted from *Science News*); Association of Home Appliance Manufacturers, *Newsletter,* December, 1969; *Wall Street Journal,* March 3, 1970; *Microwave News,* February, 1970, pp. 17–24.

BRH's jurisdiction should be. With the appearance of Ralph Nader, who had effectively publicized the ineffectiveness of certain regulatory federal agencies, plus the revelation of some disturbing facts on certain ovens, the proponents of more stringent requirements found the perfect time to proselytize for their position. As a result, HEW tested some ovens in the field and found that in fact some of the ovens (one-third of 155 tested) had leakage of ten percent to 20 percent above the commonly accepted 10 milliwatt-per-square-centimeter (MW/CM^2) level. (This standard had been set by the Department of Defense for radar, based on Atomic Energy Commission research.) HEW, however, admitted that these results did not reflect the nationwide picture because of sampling inaccuracies.

In essence, the industry (that is, the Association of Home Appliance Manufacturers) claimed that they had been monitoring all their ovens and that they were all within the accepted limits. Furthermore, the association claimed in testimony in Washington on October 1, 1969, that these appliances were "not unreasonable hazards to health and safety." The testimony continued, "However, if the Commission [National Commission on Product Safety] concludes some products are unreasonably hazardous, requiring mandatory safety standards, AHAM suggests the expertise in industry, and in nationally recognized standards-setting organizations, be used to initiate and develop them. . . ."

The biological side of the argument was not clear-cut. It had been known for a long time that microwaves in *sufficient* amounts and over a *long enough* period could cause harmful heating in human systems, particularly in eyes, testes, gall and urinary bladders, and in the digestive tract. But these harmful effects stemmed from large doses of microwaves, and scientists were uncertain about the effects—either short-term or cumulative—of low-level doses. Scientists were not even certain if all effects were thermal: Russian scientists claimed that microwaves caused changes in heart rhythm and neurological activity in the brain. Western scientists variously agreed and disagreed with the Russian theories. Apparently, the Russian experiments were conducted on a different basis from similar studies elsewhere. One problem with the studies underlying the HEW allegations was that scientists considered them "ancient," and therefore questionable—given today's more sophisticated testing procedures and consumer concerns.

Against this backdrop, discussion had shifted to what the maximum permissible level of microwave leakage should be. Early in 1970, HEW was expected to release a new standard under the authority of the Radiation Control for Health and Safety Act (1968). It was expected to say that not over one milliwatt per square centimeter of leakage could exist when the oven was shipped, and that no oven could *ever* remain in service with over five. The manufacturers (AHAM) suggested on October 31,

1969, that a 10 MW/CM² level was "reasonable, conservative, and completely adequate to protect the public health and safety." The crux of the problem was seen as being that no manufacturer could guarantee a 5 MW/CM² level for life. For example, what happens if the oven is dropped by the owner?

The problem facing manufacturers at this point was more serious than simply meeting a government requirement. While manufacturers had 30 days to comment on the standard after it was published in the *Federal Register,* they would also have to test their ovens in the field and change their design specifications. Sales dropped off, and, as one industry expert stated, "Any publicity is bad publicity." Once a standard was agreed upon, there was still a question as to whether the product environment would have changed so as to make selling the ovens an unprofitable venture.

3   Sturm, Ruger & Company, Inc.*

Founded in 1949, Sturm, Ruger & Company, Inc., had sales of $19.5 million in 1973 and was an acknowledged leader in the design and manufacture of quality target shooting and hunting firearms. At its headquarters in Southport, Connecticut, and a manufacturing facility in Newport, New Hampshire, the company produced both handguns and long-guns for consumers in the United States, Canada, and some foreign countries. Over the period 1968–73, sales and earnings had increased at compound rates of 16.6 percent and 13.8 percent, respectively, and net profit margins had averaged 14.7 percent for the same period. (For additional financial information, see Exhibits 1, 2, and 3.)

In September 1974, as he assessed the future for his company, Mr. William Ruger, president and chairman of the board, reflected on the performance of Sturm, Ruger & Company:

> I think of this company as a composite whole, or picture, which includes design, customers, employees, engineering, and manufacturing. It is a picture that I have painted and I think it's a perfect picture of a model company. It has made money honestly, provided for its employees, advanced the technology of the industry, and continued to grow and be profitable. If anything, these are the standards by which a company should be judged. The most important of all these criteria is that we have been profitable, and that's been a plus for everyone involved. But deep down inside, it also makes me feel very good to know that we've designed some damn beautiful firearms.

Even as Mr. Ruger reflected on the past performance of Sturm, Ruger, he was concerned with developing and implementing the appropriate strategy to insure the continued viability of his company in the face of

---

* This case was made possible by the cooperation of Sturm, Ruger & Company, Inc.

EXHIBIT 1

STURM, RUGER & COMPANY, INC.
P&L Data for the years 1949–73

Year	Net Sales Amount	Net Sales %	Cost of Goods Sold Amount	Cost of Goods Sold %	Gross Profit Amount	Gross Profit %	Selling Amount	G&A Amount	Total Amount	Total %	Other Inc. (Exp.)	Profit Bef. Taxes Amount	Profit Bef. Taxes %	Taxes Amount	Taxes %	Net Profit Amount	Net Profit %
1949	$ 29	100	$ 35	—	$ (6)	—	$ 7	$ 9	$ 16	—	(1)	$ (22)	—	$ —	—	$ (23)	—
1950	206	100	125	60.7	81	39.3	13	23	36	17.5	(1)	44	21.4	6	3.0	38	18.4
1951	368	100	214	58.2	154	41.8	33	39	72	19.5	(3)	79	21.5	42	11.4	37	10.1
1952	427	100	240	56.3	187	43.7	45	42	87	20.4	1	101	23.6	59	13.8	41	9.8
1953	535	100	303	56.6	232	43.4	51	44	95	17.9	—	137	25.5	87	16.3	49	9.2
1954	802	100	460	57.4	342	42.6	60	46	106	13.2	—	236	29.4	122	15.2	114	14.2
1955	1,297	100	786	60.6	511	39.4	83	73	156	12.0	(2)	353	27.2	188	14.5	165	12.7
1956	1,849	100	960	51.9	889	48.1	107	79	186	10.1	(2)	701	37.9	374	20.1	327	17.7
1957	2,509	100	1,293	51.5	1,216	48.5	144	92	236	9.4	5	985	39.2	525	20.9	460	18.3
1958	2,562	100	1,341	52.3	1,221	47.7	167	101	268	10.4	4	957	37.4	509	19.9	448	17.5
1959	2,938	100	1,493	50.8	1,445	49.2	182	141	323	11.0	8	1,130	38.4	602	20.5	527	17.9
1960	2,742	100	1,536	56.0	1,206	44.0	215	162	377	13.8	10	839	30.6	446	16.3	393	14.3
1961	2,581	100	1,491	57.8	1,090	42.2	298	97	395	15.3	(33)	662	25.6	357	13.8	305	11.8
1962	3,474	100	2,098	60.4	1,376	39.6	286	87	373	10.7	(29)	974	28.0	526	15.1	448	12.9
1963	3,713	100	2,176	58.6	1,536	41.4	312	112	424	11.4	(12)	1,100	29.7	591	15.9	509	13.7
1964	4,121	100	2,478	60.1	1,643	39.9	343	107	450	10.9	(54)	1,139	27.6	587	14.2	551	13.4
1965	5,797	100	3,319	57.2	2,478	42.8	354	183	534	9.2	(36)	1,980	34.2	980	16.9	1,001	17.3
1966	6,023	100	3,490	57.9	2,533	41.1	370	196	566	9.4	63	2,030	33.7	997	16.5	1,003	17.2
1967	7,595	100	4,359	57.4	3,236	42.6	447	228	675	8.9	69	2,630	34.6	1,268	16.7	1,362	17.9
1968	9,068	100	5,364	59.1	3,704	40.9	515	283	798	8.8	63	2,969	32.7	1,568	17.3	1,401	15.4
1969	11,090	100	5,968	53.8	5,122	46.2	631	315	946	8.5	30	4,206	37.9	2,246	20.2	1,960	17.7
1970	12,789	100	6,956	54.4	5,833	45.6	886	296	1,182	9.2	27	4,678	36.6	2,452	19.2	2,226	17.4
1971	13,318	100	9,064	68.1	4,254	31.9	1,050	347	1,397	10.4	45	2,902	21.8	1,440	10.8	1,462	11.0
1972	16,183	100	10,510	65.0	5,673	35.0	1,151	407	1,558	9.6	107	4,222	26.1	2,093	12.9	2,129	13.2
1973	19,542	100	12,643	64.7	6,899	35.3	1,325	490	1,815	9.3	343	5,426	27.8	2,752	14.1	2,674	13.7

Source: Company reports.

EXHIBIT 2

STURM, RUGER & COMPANY, INC.
Consolidated Balance Sheets

	December 31	
	1973	1972
Assets		
Current assets:		
Cash and certificates of deposit (1973–$4,300,000; 1972–$4,025,000).....................	$ 6,315,337	$ 5,565,565
Trade receivables, less allowance (1973–$25,000; 1972–$5,000)...........................	1,050,576	1,228,826
Inventories:		
Finished products.....................................	709,981	435,105
Materials, supplies and products in process............	5,314,740	4,548,979
	6,024,721	4,984,084
Prepaid expenses......................................	110,294	56,340
Total Current Assets...............................	13,500,928	11,834,815
Property, plant, and equipment:		
Land and improvements...............................	405,298	319,583
Buildings..	2,479,145	2,092,641
Machinery and equipment.............................	3,413,030	2,806,755
Dies and tools..	1,689,500	1,403,350
	7,986,973	6,622,329
Less allowances for depreciation......................	3,595,523	2,996,907
	4,391,450	3,625,422
Other assets:		
Deferred federal income taxes.........................		216,600
Cash value of life insurance...........................	115,175	108,359
Miscellaneous accounts...............................	158,045	136,161
	273,220	461,120
	$18,165,598	$15,921,357
Liabilities and Stockholders' Equity		
Current liabilities:		
Trade accounts payable...............................	$ 390,506	$ 252,463
Employee compensation..............................	276,883	220,674
Taxes, other than income taxes.......................	100,134	99,433
Pension plan...	92,400	93,900
Federal and state income taxes.......................	971,603	983,357
Total Current Liabilities...........................	1,831,526	1,649,827
Deferred federal income taxes.........................	48,700	—
Stockholders' Equity		
Common Stock, par value $1 a share:		
Authorized—3,500,000 shares		
Issued and outstanding—1,651,320 shares—Note B......	1,651,320	1,651,320
Retained earnings.....................................	14,634,052	12,620,210
	16,285,372	14,271,530
	$18,165,598	$15,921,357

Source: Company annual reports.

EXHIBIT 3

STURM, RUGER & COMPANY, INC.
Financial and Statistical Highlights

Highlights	1950	1955	1960	1965	1970	1973
Net sales (dollars in thousands)	$ 206	$ 1,297	$ 2,742	$ 5,797	$ 12,789	$ 19,542
Net income after taxes ($ in 000s)	38	165	393	1,001	2,226	2,674
Net income as a percent of sales	18.4%	12.7%	14.3%	17.3%	17.4%	13.7%
Return on total assets	53.5%	39.4%	19.3%	23.2%	19.6%	14.7%
Number of units sold	9,147	42,589	71,111	157,827	271,040	391,863
Average sales price/unit	22.52	30.45	38.56	36.73	47.18	49.87
Average profit/unit	4.15	3.87	5.53	6.34	8.21	6.82
Total number of employees	27	62	104	153	380	694
Square feet of manufacturing space	2,220	6,844	23,192	58,129	96,714	134,000

Supplemental Data

Growth rates:	Sales	Gross Profit	Total Selling, G&A	Profit Before Taxes	Net Profit
1959–1969	13.8%	13.5%	11.4%	13.8%	13.8%
1969–1973	15.2%	7.7%	13.9%	6.6%	8.1%
1972–1973	20.8%	21.6%	16.5%	28.5%	25.6%

Per Share Data

	Earnings	Dividends	Price Range
1969	$1.19	$0.18	$15½–10½
1970	$1.35	0.20	15 – 8¾
1971	$0.89	0.20	23¼–10
1972	$1.29	0.225	18¼–10¼
1973	$1.62	0.30	12 – 6½

Source: Company reports.

potentially adverse legislation and economic circumstances. As the company's product mix was approximately two-thirds handguns, Mr. Ruger believed enactment of handgun control legislation could have a significant impact on the company's future. Although he had not completely rejected the possibility of diversifying outside of the gun industry, he had tentatively decided to prepare the company for the impact of potential handgun control laws by adding police handguns and army rifles to his product line, and shifting the product mix toward long-guns.[1]

As Mr. Ruger pondered the appropriateness of this strategy, he was also concerned with questions of greater utilization of the company's overall skills and resources, its organizational strengths and needs, and his future role in the company.

THE GUN INDUSTRY

Structure and Competition

The firearms industry was one of the oldest industries in the United States, dating back to 1798. The industry consisted of four major segments: handguns, long-arms, ammunition, and accessories. Firearms were usually divided into three categories: handguns, rifles, and shotguns.

Until fairly recently, public data on the U.S. gun industry were extremely scarce as there was no central reporting agency and many of the producing companies were privately owned.

Approximate figures for firearms sales in millions in 1973, however, were reported by the Bureau of Alcohol, Tobacco and Firearms as follows:

TABLE 1

Wholesale Shipments of Firearms and Ammunitions

	1973		1972	
	Millions	*% of Total*	*Millions*	*% Total*
Pistols and Revolvers.............	$ 86.6	21.5	$ 75.8	21
Rifles and Shotguns..............	142.4	35.4	122.6	33.9
Ammunition......................	173.5	43.1	162.8	45.1
Total......................	$402.5	100%	$361.2	100%

Source: Tax Records of U.S. Treasury Department—Bureau of Alcohol, Tax and Firearms.

---

[1] Handguns, rifles, and shotguns were the three common types of civilian small arms. Handguns included both revolvers (cartridge chambers in a rotating cylinder separate from the barrel) and pistols (single chamber contiguous with the barrel) designed to be fired with one hand. Shotguns and rifles were classified as "long-guns" because of their longer barrels.

In the handgun segment of the industry, the Colt Firearms Division of Colt Industries, Smith and Wesson (a division of Bangor Punta), and Sturm, Ruger & Company were the acknowledged leaders in sales. In long-guns, Remington Arms and the Winchester–Western Division of Olin Corporation were generally acknowledged as the industry leaders, followed by Savage Arms and Marlin Firearms; Winchester–Western and Remington were believed to each have approximately 24 percent of the total market share.[2]

In ammunition sales, an estimated 90 percent of the market was thought to be controlled by Winchester, Remington, and Federal Cartridge Company, a privately held company.[3]

Markets and User

The primary uses for sporting firearms were for hunting and target shooting. However, many recent sales were believed to have been motivated by fear, generally of possible burglaries, assaults, and other people with guns.

Some industry observers estimated the number of firearms in civilian hands in the United States to be in excess of 90 million.[4] Studies done for the National Commission on Violence in the late 1960s also indicated that nearly 50 percent of the approximately 60 million U.S. households owned one or more firearms. (See Exhibits 4 and 5.) Production by domestic manufacturers for private sale in the United States had shown a growth trend which reflected the rising demand for guns. For fiscal year 1973, domestic and foreign gun makers produced approximately 5.7 million firearms for nonmilitary U.S. consumption; of this amount, roughly 38 percent were handguns.

TABLE 2

Annual Growth of Domestic Firearm Production

	Handguns (percent)	Rifles (percent)	Shotguns (percent)	Total All Firearms (percent)
1960–65	7	11.0	9.8	9.3
1965–68	23	11.8	8.7	14.3
1960–68	13	11.2	9.4	11.2

Source: Staff Report to National Commission on Causes and Prevention of Violence.

---

[2] Source: Industry data and Sporting Arms and Ammunition Manufacturers' Institute.

[3] Source: Sporting Arms and Ammunition Manufacturers' Institute.

[4] Source: Staff Report to National Commission on Causes and Prevention of Violence, 1969.

TABLE 3

Firearms Available for U.S. Domestic Consumption in 1973* (number of units)

	Total Domestic Production	less	Exports	plus	Imports	=	Total Available for U.S. Consumption
	(000s)		(000s)		(000s)		(000s)
Pistols and revolvers..........	1,734		95		559		2,198
Rifles...............	1,830		124		195		1,901
Shotguns...........	1,280		60		420		1,640
Total..........	4,844		279		1,174		5,739

* Based on fiscal year July 1, 1972–June 30, 1973.
Source: U.S. Treasury Department—Bureau of Alcohol, Tobacco and Firearms.

EXHIBIT 4

STURM, RUGER & COMPANY, INC.
Firearms Introduced into the U.S. Civilian Market (1899–1968)
(in millions for every ten-year period)

Period	Rifles	Shotguns	Handguns	Total
1899–1948 (average)............	4.7	3.2	2.7	10.6
1849–1958.......................	6.4	9.4	4.2	20.0
1859–1968.......................	9.6	9.4	10.2	29.2
Accumulated total.......	39.5	34.9	27.9	102.3

Source: Staff Report to National Commission on Causes and Prevention of Violence.

EXHIBIT 5

STURM, RUGER & COMPANY, INC.

A. *Percent of Households with Firearms, by City Size*

	Rural	Towns	Suburbs	Large Cities
Handguns............	19 %	22 %	16 %	21 %
Rifles.................	42	29	25	21
Shotguns.............	53	36	26	18

B. *Percent of U.S. Households Owning Firearms, by Region*

	East	South	Midwest	West	Total U.S.
Handguns............	15 %	18 %	20 %	29 %	20 %
Rifles.................	22	35	26	36	29
Shotguns.............	18	42	40	29	33
Any firearms*........	33	59	51	49	49

* Any firearm = households having any firearm at all.
Source: 1968 Harris Poll.

In addition to hunting and target shooting, law enforcement officers and collectors constituted a significant market for guns.

Despite its growth, many observers believed the industry faced an extremely paradoxical and potentially restrictive set of environmental conditions. As described by Mr. David Gumpert of the *Wall Street Journal:*

> On the one hand, there's growing pressure to limit or outlaw entirely the private ownership of firearms. And even without legal restrictions, gun makers fear that a growing public aversion to hunting—derisively attributed by some in the industry as a "Bambi complex"—is undermining a major source of their business. At the same time, population pressures are reducing the amount of hunting land available, discouraging hunters.[5]

Gun Control Legislation

The question of gun control was one which evoked considerable emotional debate from both opponents and proponents of gun control laws. It involved such prominent individuals and organizations as Senator Edward Kennedy and Mayor Richard Daley of Chicago, on one side, and the National Rifle Association and the National Shooting Sports Foundation on the side opposing gun controls.

Although some proposed legislation was aimed at controlling all firearms, the majority was geared to curtailing the sale and dissemination of so-called "Saturday Night Specials," small, concealable handguns costing $10 to $25. Many established gun manufacturers felt that these cheap handguns should be controlled as they gave the industry a bad name and were thought to be of no use for other than killing or wounding a human being. Mr. William Ruger noted:

> Often the handguns made abroad are contemptible contraptions and are unreliable and dangerous. It's the importation and assembly of these guns that has caused such adverse public reaction and led to enactment of some of the existing gun control laws.

Opponents of gun control laws stressed the constitutional right of individuals to own firearms for hunting and sporting purposes. Led by the National Rifle Association, with about one million members, opponents of gun controls consisted of a vocal and well-disciplined group of gun manufacturers, sellers, and sportsmen who used their weapons for hunting and target shooting, not for killing people.

Still, the relationship of guns and violence in the United States had provided considerable fuel for the actions of those who pushed for strong federal and state control of firearms. Many of the most outspoken

---

[5] *Wall Street Journal,* May 1, 1972.

proponents of gun control laws attempted to substantiate their views with data which cited the role of firearms in criminal activity.

In spite of the controversy over gun control legislation, gun sales were expected to continue to grow. These expectations, combined with the profitability of the industry, led some public officials to make statements that many in the industry felt were rather radical and emotional. For example, Representative John M. Murphy of New York was quoted as saying:

> Manufacturers and sellers who consider only profit divorce themselves completely from the final results of their activity. There's just no conscience on the part of these people.[6]

TABLE 4

Crime and Firearms Data

Type of Crime	Number of Crimes	Percent Involving Firearms
Murder............................	19,510	67*
Armed robbery......................	252,570	63
Aggravated assault.................	416,270	26

* The data also indicated that approximately 6,928 murders, or 35.5 percent of the total murders, involved handguns.
Source: 1973 Uniform Crime Reports—FBI, September 6, 1974; Crime Index Totals—Year of 1973.

HISTORY OF STURM, RUGER & COMPANY, INC.

Beginnings

Founded in 1949, Sturm, Ruger & Company, Inc., owed its existence principally to the gun designs, engineering skills, and interests of Mr. William B. Ruger, Sr. In his early childhood, Mr. Ruger had developed an interest in guns which led to the eventual founding of Sturm, Ruger. As described by Mr. Ruger:

> My interest in firearms actually began when my father taught me to hold a rifle to my shoulder when I was eight or nine years old. He had a duck hunters' lodge out on Long Island and many times he would take me out and let me shoot. These experiences stimulated my initial interest in guns. For my eleventh birthday, I received a .22 rifle of my own. Mechanically, the rifle was particularly appealing to me; the fact that it could fire a bullet so fast, and hit a target so far off, was fascinating.
>
> Also, one of the reasons I eventually went into the firearms business was because I liked the life style the gun seemed to symbolize: the rugged, early western frontier and the outdoor sportsman. In combination with that was a driving interest in machinery and design.

---

[6] *Wall Street Journal*, May 19, 1972.

As a boy, I used to go to the library and look at a book on steamboat designs and dream of making one myself. I hung around gun stores and I gained an insight into the design, mechanisms and engineering of guns. This led me to try to design one of my own. This was a tremendous challenge for me. In view of all the limitations, finding a way of making things you want is perhaps the greatest of challenges.

You know, there are two kinds of boys: those that like baseball, and those that like guns; I liked guns. When I was about 14 years old, I saw an article in a magazine about a machine gun and I was awed by the simplicity of the technology, although the machine gun was really a leap forward in technology. A machine gun design played a very important role in my later life.

Although his childhood experiences laid the foundation, Mr. Ruger did not become actively involved in the gun industry until 1937. After attending the University of North Carolina for two years, Mr. Ruger took a job with the War Department as a draftsman in the Springfield Armory. Although he had developed several gun designs, Mr. Ruger had had no formal training as a draftsman. He explained:

At the time, I was 22 and really wasn't a very good draftsman. In fact, until the War Department job, I had never been inside a real drafting room. I worked there for a while but didn't stay long. When the War Department made an invitation for drawings for a new machine gun, I submitted one I had done. On the strength of that design, I got a job with the Auto Ordnance Corporation, for whom I worked all during the war. Auto Ordnance, now McGuire Industries, was famous for the Thompson submachine gun. While working for Auto Ordnance, I was one of the youngest people working and developing a real perspective on gun design.

Mr. Ruger went on to describe the events leading to the founding of Sturm, Ruger & Company, Inc.:

I left Auto Ordnance Corporation in 1945 and was still interested in a company of my own. For about three years, I tried to make a go of a little machine shop making small parts. It began losing money and finally went into receivership in 1948. Later that same year, Alexander Sturm came to me and offered to finance me in a new company to manufacture an automatic target pistol I had designed. This .22 pistol looked something like the German Luger. The design of the gun led to low production costs, which enabled us to have a cost advantage of about 20 percent less than the then competitive models of Colt and High Standard. With the $50,000 provided by Alex Sturm, we went into production. Although this gun had some technical improvements, we would not have survived if we had not had a price advantage, since we didn't have the reputation that Colt and other gun makers had.

Another important factor was timing. People had suddenly begun to become involved in hobbies and specialty interests. The war was over, the depression was over, and it was an entirely new atmosphere. In effect, the company's start couldn't have occurred at a more opportune time economically.

Priced at $37.50 (retail), this target pistol proved to be a tremendous success. In 1950, the company had net sales of $206,000 and net profits of $38,000 for a net return on sales of 18.4 percent. The company sold approximately 9,147 of the guns in 1950.

1950–60

With the death of Alexander Sturm in 1951, complete responsibility for the business fell on Mr. Ruger. Over the next ten years, Mr. Ruger continued to add new handguns to his product mix. By 1961, the Sturm, Ruger product line consisted of a few small arms: the original automatic pistol, still at $37.50; a single-action .22 Western style six-gun at $54.50 to $75.50; a Blackhawk line single-action revolver introduced in 1955 for big caliber cartridges, at $87.50 to $116; and the Bearcat .22 single-action revolver, at $49.50. By 1960, sales had risen to $2.7 million and net income totalled $393,000. Mr. Ruger commented:

> After the first target pistol, our next product was a single-action Western style six-gun. This gun was the kind that the shooter had to cock the hammer after each shot. For some reason, Colt had abandoned this product although there was a demand for it. They saw their primary market as the police and law enforcement. I thought they were out of touch with the market. I was a gun and shooting enthusiast, however, and was completely familiar with the market. I knew this gun would sell.

Mr. Ruger's calibration of the market potential proved accurate and the company sold thousands of the handguns. According to the vice president of marketing, Mr. Edward P. Nolan, "Some were even bought by people who buckled on a six-gun to watch television Westerns."

Growth and Product Line Expansion

In 1961, with sales of its handguns approximating $2.6 million, Mr. Ruger broadened the company's product line by introducing a hunting rifle called the Deerstalker. Mr. Ruger described the development of this rifle:

> We had developed the Blackhawk revolver for the .44 magnum cartridge, which is the most powerful handgun cartridge made. As a result of the revolver, we had acquired a reputation for having the best revolver for the .44 magnum. As a hunter, I thought the .44 cartridge would make an excellent deer rifle and would appeal to hunters. There was no

market research, just a gut feel that it would sell and that selling only handguns would limit the company's growth.

Enjoying considerable success with this long-gun, Sturm, Ruger added additional rifles to its product line. By 1971, the company manufactured four rifles, priced from $56.50 to $265, and six handguns, priced from $47.50 to $125.[7] Most of the company's success during this period was attributed to the intuitive approach and design skills of Mr. Ruger. One writer in *Outdoor Life*, a leading magazine for hunters and fishermen, wrote:

> Bill Ruger, the president of the Sturm, Ruger Company which manufactures the Ruger firearms, has a number of things going for him. Among them he is a gun-nut of the first order, a guy with a sentimental love of guns for their own sake. He is also a firearms designer who can look at a blueprint of a gun mechanism, visualize the gun, see how it works, and know how it should be manufactured.
>
> He is attuned to the same wave-length as a considerable part of the gun-loving, gun-buying public, and he has always felt that if he was interested in and liked a certain design that enough gun buyers would feel the same way to make the manufacture profitable. He is also fortunate in that he is for all practical purposes the Sturm, Ruger Company and he has no board of directors on his neck to second-guess him.
>
> Ruger's initial success, the one that put him in business and financed other ventures in the field, was the .22 automatic pistol, which was shrewdly designed for reliable functioning, simple manufacture, and eye appeal. His next success was a single-action .22 rimfire caliber revolver. In outward appearance it was the spitting image of the old Colt Frontier revolver.
>
> At the time Ruger began manufacture of his single action it was generally believed in the trade that the single-action revolver was dead beyond recall. When Ruger showed me the prototype of his .22 single action and asked me how I thought it would go I told him I thought it would sell like mad. Some straws were then in the wind. One was that a single-action Colt in good condition was bringing from four to six times the price it had brought new before the war.
>
> Another was that movies and the infant TV were leaning heavily on horse operas and that in such exciting dramas the single-action revolver is a prop of prime importance.
>
> Like many a gun nut Ruger had always admired the appearance of the . . . single action. I'm quite sure that Ruger made no consumer surveys, didn't consult his dealers and failed to test the market. If Ruger has a genius with a Ph.D. from the Harvard School of Business Administration doing market research and chained to a desk in a back room somewhere, I am sure the guy fainted when Ruger told him what he had in mind.[8]

---

[7] Retail price.
[8] Mr. Jack O'Connor, *Outdoor Life*, 1967.

Diversification Effort

Again reflecting Mr. Ruger's interests and skills as an engineer, the company in 1965 initiated an attempt to diversify into the automobile business. At Mr. Ruger's direction, the company undertook to design and build a working prototype of a luxury sportscar similar to the British-made 1929, 4.5 litre Bentley. The intent was to sell these cars on a limited basis, at a price of approximately $12,000–$13,000 per car.

The "Ruger Tourer" was designed to be a sports-touring car with a soft-top and body styling of the 1929 vintage Bentley, but with a modern power plant and structural mechanics. The car was to be equipped with a 427 V–8 Ford racer motor, sophisticated Monroe shocks, Bendix brakes, and a double-walled fiberglass body.

In interviews with the casewriter, Mr. Ruger and Mr. Nolan, vice president, marketing, described the rationale and events leading to the company's efforts in this area. Mr. Ruger explained:

> I've always been interested in cars and motorcycles since I was young. I've tinkered around with a number of cars, including Jaguars, Rolls Royces, and Ferraris. In the process, I noticed that there was a lot of overlap between guns and cars among purchasers. I felt that a well-known reputation for quality and engineering design in guns would be useful in selling a particular type of car; hopefully, the name Ruger would correlate the two. I also felt I had some insight into what people would like to have in cars. I thought we could come up with a beautifully engineered car that we could sell at a profit.

Mr. Nolan indicated the automotive project was in line with Mr. Ruger's skills and interests in engineering and design which had made the company successful in guns.

> Bill has a love for engineering and design in everything, particularly cars. When we used to go to lunch, and I would stop for gas, Bill would get out and look underneath the cars on the racks. After he bought one Bentley, I remember he set up a guy in a garage to work on it. We would go to lunch and then stop by the garage afterwards; Cal always kept a second slide board and before you knew it, Bill had his coat off and was banging around underneath the car and talking about it for hours with Cal. I started taking work with me to lunch because I knew we would wind up at the garage.

Two prototypes of the Ruger Tourer were built at a cost of approximately $400,000 for design and development. These prototypes were displayed at various auto shows, including the New York Automobile Show, and received the attention of several widely read car magazines. In the December 1970 issue of *Motor Trend,* a feature article discussed the Ruger car and the man behind it:

> Bill Ruger won't fit on anybody's bar-chart, nor will his car jibe with any bean-counter's forecast of what's happening in the world of personal

EXHIBIT 6

Strum, Ruger & Company, Inc.

REPRINTED FROM
DECEMBER 1970
MOTOR TREND

". . . when cars and car makers seem to be tumbling off assembly-lines with a desperate dreary sameness, a kind of cookie-cutter uniformity, a little outrageous automotive non-conformity may be just what the doctor ordered."

It was a Bentley Vanden Plas that provided the inspiration for the Ruger Tourer. The body is double-walled fiberglass reinforced at stress and attachment points with bonded-in steel pieces. The floor, battery box are molded in as well.

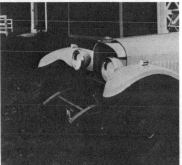

Source: Reprinted from December 1970 Motor Trend.

transportation. He's made a fortune designing and building firearms that combine the elements of nostalgia, classical good taste and faultless function with reasonable price—and he's flown in the face of doubting "experts" and conventional wisdom at every stage of his upward climb. Therefore, it's no surprise that he's decided to build and sell a car that

combines these same principles, despite the doubts and chuckling dis-
approval of entrenched automotive nay-sayers.

Bill Ruger, then, is not of the common herd. He is the product of
another time, a different environment. He is more like the merchant-
princes of the Italian Renaissance or the go-getter nobility of Victoria's
reign than today's interchangeable captains of industry. His collections
of art and antique arms are remarkable, and he has steeped himself in
history and the classical lore of the gentle folk.

It's been remarked that nothing of redeeming social value has ever
been devised in committee, and Ruger's success would seem to bear this
out. His firm, Sturm, Ruger & Company recently went public and now
has a proper board of directors and all the other trappings of a modern
manufacturing concern. What's more, there are a number of Ruger heirs
and relations scattered through the company's hierarchy. Yet one cannot
visit either of his two factories—one in Southport, Connecticut and the
other in Newport, New Hampshire—without the feeling that the company and all its products are cast exclusively in the image of William B.
Ruger himself. Ayn Rand would have loved him.

In this sense, one is reminded forcefully of other, similar business
enterprises headed by the likes of Ettore Bugatti and Enzo Ferrari.
Ruger resembles Bugatti in the way his products are so profoundly influenced by his personal tastes and enthusiasms, and he's like Ferrari in
that he's been able to make it pay handsomely.

He has owned a fair fleet of exotic automobiles over the years, and
though his automotive buying habits have been quite catholic—spanning
the distance from a Pontiac GTO or a Plymouth Hemi to classic Bentley
and Rolls-Royces, salted liberally with Jaguars and MGs and God knows
what else—his true loves are more sharply defined. For instance, right
now he owns three Ferraris, a Land Rover, a Mercedes–Benz 6.3 sedan
(for his wife) and a 4.5 liter Bentley Vanden Plas tourer built in 1929.

Over the eight-year period from 1965–73, the company attempted to
assess the realistic potential for the Ruger car. These efforts included the
preparation of an extremely comprehensive and detailed production and
financial plan by Ernst and Ernst.[9] However, in 1974, the following
statement appeared in the company's 1973 annual report:

> In previous reports, I have mentioned the company's automotive
> project with great pride and enthusiasm. During the past year we have
> been reassessing our position in connection with this project. After
> weighing all the alternatives, in view particularly of the current stringent
> requirements for anti-pollution devices and the marked trend for com-
> pact, high mileage per gallon automobiles, it was reluctantly decided to
> abandon this project. This is a substantial disappointment in view of the
> time and money expended, but our decision is undoubtedly correct.

---

[9] This plan projected required sales of approximately 180 cars per year in order
for the company to show a profit on automobile business.

Mr. Ruger commented to the casewriter:

> I really felt this car would sell but unfortunately we got a very ambiguous market reception. Then there was also a mechanical problem in the steering which caused the car to drift. This blasted some confidence in the car. We finally decided to abandon the program in 1973.

STURM, RUGER & COMPANY, INC., IN 1974

Product Policy

In 1974, Sturm, Ruger manufactured several basic models of pistols, revolvers, and rifles for a variety of sporting purposes. In addition to its sporting guns, police revolvers were added to the company's product line in 1969. A program was also underway to develop and manufacture shotguns and a carbine for law enforcement and military use.

The keynotes of Mr. Ruger's product policy were design quality and purchaser utility. Mr. Ruger emphasized that his guns "appealed primarily to hunters and sportsmen who demand exceptional performance." In the 1973 annual report to stockholders, Mr. Ruger elaborated on this subject:

> The demand for our entire range of firearms continues to be highly gratifying. Those products which have achieved market leadership continue to grow in popularity, while our newer products appear to be rapidly gaining the recognition we hoped for.
>
> Our products are engineered and produced to the highest possible standards of quality and performance. It is, therefore, not surprising that we have a growing share of the market for firearms, and that we have enthusiastic supporters among all categories of users. Our identification with quality manufacturing and unique engineering capability is the result of 20 years of constant effort.

All of the company's guns were sold under the name "Ruger," and while they were not subject to annual design change, the company's policy was to strive for product improvements. Many of the guns were available in varying models for different cartridge calibers, ranging from .22 caliber to .44 magnum and .458 magnum. Some were also manufactured in such special finishes as stainless steel to appeal to particular market segments or geographic areas, e.g., gun collectors, performers and/or to individuals in areas where heat and humidity were a problem.

Handguns

Pistols and revolvers accounted for approximately 62 percent of the company's sales in 1973. (See Exhibit 7.) In total, 248,337 units were sold for an average manufacturer's price of $48.85 in 1973. Distributor

EXHIBIT 7

STURM, RUGER & COMPANY, INC.
Product Breakdown

	1969 ($000s)	1970 ($000s)	1971 ($000s)	1972 ($000s)	1973 ($000s)
Handgun:					
Sales......................	$7,768	$9,375	$8,813	$10,621	$12,132
% Total sales..............	70%	73%	66%	66%	62%
Income before taxes........	$3,464	$4,002	$3,283	$ 3,501	$ 3,995
% Total IBT...........	82%	86%	113%	83%	74%
Rifles:					
Sales......................	$3,062	$3,074	$3,896	$ 4,913	$ 6,618
% Total sales..............	28%	24%	29%	30%	34%
Income before taxes........	$ 611	$ 527	($ 538)	$ 431	$ 1,058
% Total IBT...........	15%	11%	(19%)	10%	19%
Parts and Service:					
Sales......................	$ 260	$ 340	$ 609	$ 649	$ 791
% Total sales..............	2%	3%	5%	4%	4%
Income before taxes........	$ 132	$ 149	$ 158	$ 290	$ 382
% Total IBT...........	3%	3%	6%	7%	7%

STURM, RUGER & COMPANY, INC.
Pine Tree Division
Profit and Loss Statement

	Six Months Ended June 30, 1973	Six Months Ended June 30, 1974
Net sales...........................	$2,101,459	$2,304,409
Cost of goods sold.................	930,513	1,104,264
Operating profit....................	$1,170,946	$1,200,145
Expenses:		
Selling...........................	$ 10,938	$ 16,611
General and administrative.......	11,460	13,542
Total.......................	$ 22,398	$ 30,153
Income (loss) before taxes........	$1,148,548	$1,169,992

pricing ranged from $34.80 to $84.95. The basic retail prices ranged from $61.75 for a standard target pistol to $152.50 for a Security Six Stainless Steel Magnum.

Rifles

Rifles and carbines accounted for roughly 34 percent of the company's 1973 sales. The company sold 143,526 of the five basic models in 1973. Prices to distributors ranged from $40.93 to $148.02. The basic retail price ranged from $66 for a .22 rifle to $265 for a Number One Single Shot Rifle. (See Exhibit 8.)

In addition to guns, Sturm, Ruger also sold component parts and accessories for and with its guns. These included extra revolver cylinders,

EXHIBIT 8

STURM, RUGER & COMPANY, INC.
Models and Prices of Ruger Firearms*

	Suggested Retail Price List	Dealer Price (tax inc.)	Net Distributor Price	Distributor Price (fed. tax inc.)
Pistols				
(1) *Standard Model:* This was the company's original product and was designed for target shooting and small game hunting.				
Lowest priced model	$61.75	$46.93	$34.80	$38.28
Highest priced model	66.90	50.84	37.70	41.47
(2) *Mark 1 Target Model:* A refined version of the standard model and was intended for formal, competitive target shooting.				
Lowest priced model	$78.50	$59.66	$44.24	$48.66
Highest priced model	83.45	63.42	47.03	51.73
Revolvers				
(3) *New Model Super Single-Six:* Designed in 1952, it was modeled after the .45 caliber Colt Army model of 1873 and was intended to capture the flavor of the "Old West." Intended for use as an informal target or hunting gun, the Single-Six was the most expensive single-action .22 on the market. When sold with an extra cylinder for the use of .22 magnum cartridge, it was called the Single-Six Convertible.				
Lowest priced model	$ 92.25	$ 71.30	$53.34	$58.55
Highest priced model	143.85	111.20	83.00	91.30
(4) *New Model Blackhawk:* Blackhawk revolvers were essentially enlarged "Single-Six revolvers" and were made for the most powerful handgun cartridge available, such as the .357 magnum, the .44 magnum, .41 magnum and the .30 caliber cartridge. These guns were intended for informal target shooting and hunting.				
Lowest priced model	$119.75	$ 91.01	$ 67.49	$ 74.24
Highest priced model	148.50	112.86	83.69	92.06
(5) *Security Six-Double Action:* These weapons were designed for police and law enforcement use.				
Lowest priced model	$102.00	$ 77.52	$ 57.49	$ 63.24
Highest priced model	152.50	115.90	85.95	94.55
(6) *Speed-Six-Double Action:* A smaller, lighter revolver, the Speed-Six was intended for use in police work.				
Lowest priced model	$102.00	$ 77.52	$ 57.49	$ 63.24
Highest priced model	120.00	91.20	67.63	74.39
(7) *Old Army (Cap & Ball):* This firearm was intended for target shooting and hunting.				
Lowest priced model	$125.00	$ 95.00	$ 70.45	$ 77.50
Highest priced model	140.00	106.40	78.90	86.79
Rifles				
(8) *Model 10/22:* Purported to be one of the most popular .22 rifles on the market, the 10/22 was intended for use in informal target shooting and small game hunting.				
Lowest priced model	$ 66.00	$ 49.50	$ 36.87	$ 40.93
Highest priced model	77.50	56.58	42.18	46.82
(9) *Model .44 Carbine:* A short, light self-loading firearm, the .44 magnum carbine was designed particularly for deer hunting in heavily wooded areas.				
Lowest priced model	$131.56	$ 99.94	$ 73.44	$ 81.52
Highest priced model	134.50	102.22	75.12	83.38

EXHIBIT 8 (*continued*)

	Suggested Retail Price List	Dealer Price (tax inc.)	Net Distributor Price	Distributor Price (fed. tax inc.)
(10) *M77 Bolt Action:* The M77 was designed primarily for large game hunting.				
Lowest priced model	$193.00	$144.75	$107.79	$119.65
Highest priced model	278.30	208.73	155.43	172.53
(11) *Single-Shot Rifle:* Conceived as a luxury product, the single shot was a high-powered rifle meeting a wide range of requirements including hunting and target shooting.				
Lowest priced model	$165.00	$123.75	$ 92.16	$102.30
Highest priced model	265.00	198.75	148.02	164.30

* Prices shown are for highest priced and lowest priced guns of each model. Other models with variations such as longer barrels, walnut panels, or stainless steel were available at prices within the two price limits.
Source: Company's distributor price list.

magazines for selected rifles and pistols, telescope mounting rings, and panels for handguns. Sales of these accessories and related services accounted for approximately four percent of total revenues and amounted to $791,128 in 1973.

Marketing

Sturm, Ruger competed, through one or more of its various models, with the active domestic and foreign arms industry. Most of its competitors, such as Colt, Remington, Savage, and Winchester, were older, larger, and better known, but Mr. Ruger stressed that his company sought to compete by concentrating on limited lines of high-quality products and building in unique qualities into his guns. Although Mr. Ruger believed that pricing was often competitive, he indicated that price was not a major factor for many of his guns:

> Some of our models are price competitive, but many have unique qualities which enable us to get a premium price. For example, in our single-shot rifle, we have no major competitors, so competitive pricing is not a prime factor and we peg the price up considerably more than we do with a high volume product like our 10/22.

The company sold its products throughout the United States, Canada, and several other countries. Management, however, estimated that foreign sales represented less than ten percent of the company's business. According to Mr. Ruger, foreign sales had considerable potential in spite of the company's relatively small share of foreign sales. As he explained:

> In foreign markets, we are almost unknown, although foreign governments and law enforcement groups prefer American revolvers. To my

knowledge, there is no quality revolver made in Europe, so there is little foreign competition. Primary competition in foreign markets would come from Smith and Wesson, which is selling a lot of revolvers abroad and is quite well known.

Sales of the company's products were promoted by advertising in national magazines and assorted firearms specialty magazines, e.g., *Outdoor Life,* the *Rifleman,* and *Field and Stream.* Mr. Nolan, vice president, marketing, indicated that approximately $250,000 was spent on advertising in 1973 to keep the ultimate consumer familiar with Ruger guns.

Because the company's firearms were used primarily for hunting and target shooting, sales records indicated that sales tended to be highest in nonurban areas and in the Southeast and Southwest. Rifle sales were greatest in the period from July to November in anticipation of the fall hunting seasons, while handgun sales were fairly constant throughout the year. A one-year warranty against defective materials and workmanship was extended to retail purchasers of all its products. Through 1973, Sturm, Ruger had not been required to expend material amounts of money as a result of warranty claims. Mr. Nolan commented:

> We emphasize service and quality, and there is a place in this industry for a company with good service. We also make a better product, and at a better price than the competition.

Mr. Nolan, who had joined the company in 1956 when the company's sales approximated $1.8 million, went on to state:

> Year in and year out, the market for guns is pretty static. I would estimate that the total market for guns is about 15 million people. If we are to grow in this static market, we have to win some market share away from competition.
>
> Because of this static market, I think our future is definitely in long-guns. In fact, our sales ratio has begun to change slightly; for the first six months of 1974 ending in June, our sales mix was roughly 54 percent handguns versus 46 percent for rifles, compared to a ratio of about 64 percent for handguns the previous year. That's a major shift. Keep in mind our total sales were up.

Distribution and Sales

Distribution of the company's products was accomplished through a group of approximately 160 wholesale distributors in 43 states. These distributors varied in size from an organization with one salesman in the field to an organization with over 300 salesmen calling on retailers. Approximately 48 percent of the distributors were hardware specialists, 26 percent were sporting goods distributors, and the remaining 26 percent were composed of firearms specialty distributors and chain stores.

EXHIBIT 9

Sturm, Ruger & Company, Inc.

RUGER® SECURITY-SIX®
DOUBLE ACTION REVOLVER

FRONT SIGHT CROSS PIN
FRONT SIGHT BLADE
BARREL
FRONT LATCH SPRING
FRONT LATCH CROSS PIN
FRONT LATCH

CYLINDER CENTER PIN SPRING
CYLINDER CENTER PIN ROD
EJECTOR ROD
CYLINDER CENTER LOCK PIN
CYLINDER
FRAME
EJECTOR SPRING
EJECTOR ROD WASHER
CRANEVRANE PIVOT ASSEMBLY
CYLINDER LATCH SPRING

REAR SIGHT ASSEMBLY
RECOIL PLATE CROSS PIN
RECOIL PLATE
HAMMER
FIRING PIN
FIRING PIN REBOUND SPRING
CYLINDER RELEASE BUTTON
TRANSFER BAR
HAMMER DOG PIVOT PIN
HAMMER DOG SPRING
HAMMER DOG SPRING PLUNGER
HAMMER PIVOT ASSEMBLY
HAMMER DOG
HAMMER STRUT
MAINSPRING

CYLINDER LATCH PLUNGER
EJECTOR
CYLINDER LATCH
TRIGGER BUSHING
TRIGGER PIVOT PIN
TRIGGER SPRING
PAWL SPRING
TRIGGER
TRIGGER GUARD
PAWL PLUNGER
PAWL

GRIP PANEL BOSS
TRIGGER GUARD PLUNGER CROSS PIN
TRIGGER GUARD PLUNGER
TRIGGER GUARD PLUNGER SPRING
MAINSPRING SEAT
GRIP PANEL SCREW
GRIP PANEL
GRIP PANEL DOWEL
FRAME

CROSS SECTION VIEW

FIELD-STRIPPED VIEW

STURM, RUGER & CO., INC.
Southport, Connecticut, U.S.A.

© 1972 - STURM, RUGER & CO., INC.

These distributors supplied several thousand retailers. The company did not sell directly to retailers nor to the ultimate user, directly or by mail order. No salesmen or field representatives were employed by the company. Contact with the distributors was maintained by correspondence, telephone, and personal visits by company executives.

At the beginning of each year, Sturm, Ruger requested "firm" annual orders from its distributors, although the company usually allowed them to reasonably adjust their orders throughout the year. At the end of the year, Sturm, Ruger cancelled all outstanding unfilled orders and asked the distributors to place new orders. The company's outstanding unfilled orders from dealers/distributors on March 1, 1974, were $37,651,-000 as compared to approximately $21,599,000 on March 1, 1973. Management indicated that the company would be able to produce and ship a large part of these orders during 1974, but not all. It was also management's belief that ten percent to 15 percent of these orders were inflated as customers wanted to insure receiving an adequate supply of Ruger guns.

New Markets

Mr. Ruger had decided to develop several new products for new markets in light of several environmental and market trends. In 1969, the company had introduced a revolver designed for law enforcement use. Development and marketing of a shotgun and a police/military firearm was also underway, with the latter two products scheduled for introduction in 1974. The shotgun was expected to retail at about $400, with roughly 60 percent going to Sturm, Ruger. Mr. John Kingsley, executive vice president, indicated that the company had high hopes for its shotgun and that as many as 50,000 units might be sold over a two- to three-year period after initial introduction. Mr. Ruger indicated that the marketing of the police revolver posed some new problems for the company. He stated:

> We put out our first police revolver in the late 1960s. Ed Nolan had come to me and said "Let's put out one." We did so, but it's just starting to become a significant contributor to our sales. The cost of the product is high so that the product is less profitable. The police revolver line presently constitutes less than ten percent of our business.
>
> We have to approach the law enforcement market and government market differently than we do the consumer market. With consumers, you are involved with many buyers, with many different tastes, often looking for unique and new products. In the law enforcement and government market, we have to deal with purchasing agents who want items they are familiar with. They are not interested in new and innovative products. These markets, however, can produce large sales. Our strategy will have to be to seek an opportunity to see technical pur-

chasers and attempt to familiarize them with our guns before bids are given out. Then when we submit a bid, our products won't be new to the purchasing agent.

Development of these products had also been influenced by some concern with the possible threat of gun control legislation. Mr. Ruger discussed his concerns:

> There is a lot of talk about gun controls, but the real question is whether laws will make it more difficult for individuals to own firearms. Unfortunately, the trend is for people to be more and more supervised by government, which is a personal abbreviation of personal liberties. There's an old saying that "a country that would pass a law like Prohibition can't be trusted." Democracy, I'm afraid, is an unpredictable beast. All of this has given rise to a slight fear on my part that we might be legislated out of business. Enactment of laws like those *requiring* people to fasten seat belts before they can drive their cars suggests that a bureaucratic process might develop a restriction on firearms.
>
> I still regard firearms legislation as remote. People do want the right to defend themselves and they have a right, a God-given right, to do so. Still, we have begun to diversify our product line so that the focus of gun control will not completely dominate our sales. We have moved rather quickly but carefully to develop the shotgun and the Mini 14, which is a Ruger version of the Army M14 rifle. What we want to do is have our long-guns successful but have our handguns continue to grow. Therefore, if our handgun business were lost, it would cause some problem to shrink this company, but we would still have a strong position in long-guns.

Mr. Nolan also commented on this issue:

> Legislation would have a definite impact on our industry, but as long as we continue to make a quality product, the world will still want our guns.
>
> Overall, I am very optimistic and realistic about our future growth and rate of growth. We are still young and unknown by millions of people who buy guns. We're young and ambitious, and we make decisions our large and lethargic competitors can't make because of committees. They also don't innovate or have a Bill Ruger.
>
> We can march into areas that companies already make guns for, because if Bill Ruger makes it, everyone knows it will be good. We're presently making a film about Bill because when Bill has finished designing, he will have contributed more to the state of the art and exceeded the productivity of John Browning or any other gun designer.

Mr. Ruger also stated:

> We have done nothing to frustrate gun control laws other than to testify against some which purported to control guns but also abbreviated the right of citizens to own guns. Unfortunately, most of these proposals

don't have an effective screening mechanism to differentiate between the criminal and the responsible citizen. As a shooter, I also oppose proposals that would give local police chiefs discretionary authority on the issuance of firearm permits; they are simply not trained to do this and end up denying permits to everyone.

Research and Development

During fiscal 1973, Sturm, Ruger spent approximately $146,664 on material research activities relating to the development of new products and the improvements of existing products. Approximately four employees engaged in research and development activities, but it was generally acknowledged that Mr. Ruger was an integral part of the company's design, engineering, and research activities. All work was conducted under his personal supervision. Research expenditures were charged to expense in the year incurred. Mr. Kingsley, executive vice president, indicated "that R&D had generally been less than 2 percent of sales."

Primarily through Mr. Ruger's efforts, the company owned approximately 20 patents and trademarks. Management indicated that none of these patents was considered basic to any important product or manufacturing process of the company.

Production and Manufacturing

Manufacturing of the company's guns took place in its plant facilities in Southport, Connecticut, and Newport, New Hampshire. The Southport plant contained approximately 33,000 square feet on the ground floor, of which approximately 26,000 square feet was devoted to manufacturing operations and the balance was used for office, shipping, and warehousing facilities. The plant was located on a two and one-third acre site near the Connecticut Turnpike. During 1970 a second story was added, giving approximately 2,200 square feet of office and design space.

In a tour of the Southport headquarters and plant, the casewriter observed that the plant appeared to be fully utilized. Many offices looked out onto the shop floor, which was clean, well-organized, and crowded. There appeared to be little room for expansion unless the employee parking lot was eliminated.

The Newport plant, located on eight and one-half acres of land, contained approximately 114,000 square feet, of which approximately 6,000 square feet was office, shipping, and warehouse space. Approximately 40,000 square feet of the building was occupied by the company's Pine Tree Castings Division which manufactured steel investment castings. Approximately 4 acres of land had been acquired in the rear of the plant for expansion, and an additional 60,000 square foot manufacturing plant was scheduled for completion by the end of 1974 to handle expected demand for the shotgun and other new products.

Many of the parts used in the company's products were readily available from several outside suppliers. The company purchased a great majority of its rifle barrels, but equipment to produce a portion of this requirement had been installed at the Newport plant, and some barrels were produced there. The company produced its own walnut and other wood stocks in its woodshop in the New Hampshire plant. The wood used was purchased from several domestic suppliers.

Mr. Ruger indicated that the company's production methods and facilities were probably the equal of any in the industry. He was supported in this assertion by an article in the *Wall Street Journal* which described Sturm, Ruger's manufacturing operation:

> Production methods have also changed relatively little over the years, remaining highly dependent on hand labor with little automation. The gun industry "has tended to be a little slower than other industries to change," says William Ruger, President of Sturm, Ruger.
>
> Indeed, there isn't even a moving assembly line in Ruger's Southport plant. In one area, machinists and other technicians turn out gun frames and other parts. Elsewhere, men seated at tables spread out batches of parts and assemble them into complete revolvers. In a small room off to one side, the weapons are test-fired on a miniature target range by two men wearing soundproof earmuffs.[10]

The Pine Tree Castings division, formerly a subsidiary, produced high-quality steel investment castings for use in the firm's guns. Although 90 percent of the division's output was consumed by Sturm, Ruger, management felt that Pine Tree had the capability to develop substantial outside business. One view was expressed by Mr. Kingsley:

> Our Pine Tree operation is an excellent opportunity for diversification. This operation makes plumbing valves, firearms components, and metal pieces of all sizes and shapes. Although only ten percent of Pine Tree's output presently goes to the outside, I would like to see Pine Tree do 50 percent of its sales with outside customers.
>
> Although coordination and integration is somewhat of a current problem, I don't think a major management restructuring will be required to expand Pine Tree's operation. However, our management structure is pretty thin now. Bill's philosophy has always been to have as low overhead as possible and try to put as much manpower as possible on the production side.

Mr. Ruger also commented:

---

[10] *Wall Street Journal,* May 31, 1972.

Our Pine Tree division offers a range of diversification possibilities. It can manufacture plumbing valves, high-strength metal parts, bits for bridles, and hardware for saddles. Boats, for example, also have created a demand for equipment made of stainless steel and investment castings.

The big question with our Pine Tree situation is the need to develop a strong marketing and sales organization. We currently use sales reps, and our outside orders are rather informal. In fact, it's basically a New England market. In the long run we are going to have to develop a national sales force if we are going to build a substantial outside market for Pine Tree. We might even have local sales offices or even go the route of having multiple plants.

Finance

The initial financing of Sturm, Ruger & Company, Inc., had been $50,000 provided by Alexander Sturm. By year-end fiscal 1973, retained earnings accumulated throughout the years had built the net worth to $16,285,372.

In September 1974, Sturm, Ruger had approximately 900 stockholders as a result of a public offering in 1969. This public offering resulted in the sale of a total of 330,264 shares to the public at a price of $14 per share, with net proceeds to the selling stockholders of $13.05 per share. Mr. Ruger sold 264,000 shares, and the daughter of his deceased partner sold 66,264 shares. As explained by Mr. Ruger, the decision to make a public offering in 1969 was influenced by other alternatives.

> In 1968, I was approached by a major conglomerate who offered me $28 million for the company. At that time I owned 1,320,000 shares, or about 80 percent of the outstanding shares; the other 20 percent was owned by Joanna Sturm. I considered this offer, which was basically a stock deal, and would have been based on bottom line and volumes performance for a specified period, but the alternative was to go public. I chose the latter alternative since it enabled me personally to diversify my assets. After the public offering, I didn't have all my own eggs in one basket and I was still free to operate the company with my own philosophy.

As of September 18, 1974, the company's stock was traded in the over-the-counter (OTC) market at a selling price of 6-¾ bid, 7-¾ asked.[11] Mr. Ruger owned approximately 906,000 shares out of a total of 1,651,320 shares outstanding; an additional 50,000 shares were owned by William Ruger, Jr.

Commenting on the company's financial posture, Mr. Kingsley noted:

> We've been fortunate to not have to use any outside financing, and in the future we plan to finance our expansion internally. A key to this

---

[11] *Wall Street Journal*, September 19, 1974.

will be our ability to manage our inventories more judiciously. I think, however, we can grow and still maintain our net profit margins at about 15 percent of sales.

Personnel

In 1973, the company employed approximately 250 persons in its Southport plant, 356 in the Newport plant, and 88 in its Pine Tree division. Approximately six of the individuals at the Southport headquarters and three at the Newport facility were listed as "executive."

None of the employees of the company or of Pine Tree were represented by a labor union, although a union drive had been attempted during the summer of 1974. The scheduled elections were never held. Mr. Ruger commented on the company's labor relations policies:

> On three occasions, unions have tried to organize our shop. I must admit, I've always felt that if a union came in, I would take it personally, as it would mean I had been a little foolish and had done something wrong. I've always felt that men should work hard and be paid well without the need for a union.
>
> We just had a union drive, but the union backed down before the election. Our campaign against the union was not really a campaign; it was sort of a review of our labor relations in the past. We basically argued that we have a proven record.

Management and Organization

Although no organization chart existed, the casewriter learned that the key managers and executives at the Southport headquarters reported directly to Mr. Ruger; these included the executive vice president, the vice president of marketing, and the vice president of manufacturing of the Southport operation. Also reporting directly to Mr. Ruger were the vice presidents of sales for the Pine Tree division and of manufacturing at the Newport plant. Mr. Ruger and other members of management indicated that he deeply involved himself in all aspects of the company's operations.

The executive vice president, Mr. John Kingsley, had joined the company in 1971 after serving as a consultant to Mr. Ruger. Mr. Ruger indicated that Mr. Kingsley, a Harvard MBA, and former investment banker and a CPA, was brought in to help bolster the company's management structure, particularly in finance and planning. He added:

> John came in at a particularly necessary time as Walter Berger, our secretary and controller, was retiring. However, we were also a public company by then, and we needed to do things a little more openly and improve our reporting to the public. In addition to his title of executive vice president, John is primarily responsible for financial matters.

Other members of management included Mr. Edward Nolan, vice president of marketing, who had joined the company in 1956. Prior to coming to Sturm, Ruger, Mr. Nolan had been a district sales manager with Winchester. Mr. William B. Ruger, Jr., was also employed in the firm. He had formerly been the vice president of manufacturing at the Southport plant, and Mr. Ruger, Jr., was now involved in other areas of the company. Mr. Ruger commented:

> Bill, Jr., now has more of a planning function in the company. This gives him an overview which he should have as he may eventually be president. My son-in-law, Steve Vogel, is also with us, and is responsible for developing government sales.

Mr. Kingsley, 42 years old, and Mr. William Ruger, Jr., 34, were both directors of the company. Other directors included: Mr. William B. Ruger, Sr.; Mr. Townsend Hornor, first vice president of White, Weld and Co., Inc.; Mr. Frank L. McCann, president of Mohawk Aluminum Corporation; Mr. Norman K. Parsells, a senior partner of Marsh, Day & Calhoun; Mr. Richard Kilcullen, member of Bathe, Fowler, Lidstone, Jaffin, Pierie & Kheel; Mr. Lester A. Casler, partner of Little & Casler; and Mr. Hale Seagraves, former partner of Pennie, Edmonds, Morton, Taylor & Adams.

A VIEW TOWARD THE FUTURE

As Mr. Ruger articulated the future opportunities and potential problems for his company in 1974, he commented on the start of the company and his philosophy. When the casewriter asked what had contributed to the success of his company, Mr. Ruger replied as follows:

> I think my being extremely familiar and identifying with gun enthusiasts, hunters, and sportsmen has been one very important factor. This was our market and I have been fortunate to design guns that appealed to their technical and esthetic needs. But I've often thought about another very important factor over the years. At the time I started this company, my confidence was shaken. Everything I had tried had failed. I wasn't sure I had the qualities to be an entrepreneur. As I look back, I was perfectly qualified. I had a mix of interest, experience, and health. In my first business, I think I failed because I didn't think everything through. I had focused on the creative side of the business and not enough on the management side; both have to be of interest if you want to succeed.
>
> You've also got to love money to be an entrepreneur. My uncle, who was on the wealthy side of my family, used to say: "The way you keep score is by how much money you make. When you see a successful company, making money, it means they are making something that people want."

Mr. Ruger indicated, however, that environmental and market circumstances posed entirely new and different problems than had been encountered by the company in the past. The most immediate threat to the company's principal business appeared to be the various pending gun laws. Mr. Ruger voiced his views and concerns:

> Unfortunately, politicians and newspapers who are talking about this issue don't have any knowledge of what they are talking about. Of course I think there should be some controls of maniacs and irresponsible people getting guns, but as I told the governor of New Hampshire, people should be licensed, not guns. Unfortunately, you have people like some of the editors on the *Boston Globe* who have personal biases; but their views are not universal beliefs. I and quite a few other people believe that there is some truth in those bumper stickers that say, "If guns are outlawed, only outlaws will have guns." Besides, if people didn't have guns, they would use sticks, stones, or some other instrument to injure others.

In light of these concerns, Mr. Ruger felt that broadening the company's base of products and achieving some measure of diversification was in order. Diversification, however, as seen by both Mr. Ruger and Mr. Kingsley, required some relationship to the company's skills and resources. Mr. Kingsley commented:

> We have looked at a few acquisitions, for example, we recently looked at an instrument company with sales of a little over $1 million and net profits at about 10 percent. We decided not to follow through, however. If we eventually do purchase another company, it will have to have a sound and strong management team. I don't rule out some potential acquisitions, but I don't see us becoming a mini conglomerate.
>
> Still, diversification is an issue for us. Bill considers the new Mini 14 and shotguns to be a part of our diversification. I think he's right, but I don't think the marketplace will ever change the multiple on our stock because we develop a new gun. I would basically like to see us with an earnings tripod: (1) guns, (2) castings from Pine Tree, and (3) some other type of operations, preferably metal manufacturing. I don't, for example, see us in fast foods.

Mr. Ruger also discussed the issue of acquisitions:

> We have taken a concentrated look at a few companies, but have never seen one that would be perfect for us. Our drive to diversify has been compromised by our need to exploit the businesses that we are in. It dawned on me during the car project that we needed to spend more time on the gun industry.

In looking at the company's future organizational needs, Mr. Kingsley made the following observations:

A key question is whether this company can be transformed from an extension of a man to a professionally managed company. Bill has been 100 percent responsible for the success of the company, and whether the company will ever reach the point where Bill Ruger is not the most important factor is an open question. With our new guns, Bill thinks that our sales will exceed $40 million in the near future. The biggest problem thus will be to take a step up the growth curve, and do so profitably.

Mr. Ruger, in speaking of the future, expressed the following thoughts:

Although we've done extremely well in guns, the gun industry won't grow dramatically. Hunting never was a mass sport. One man needs a lot of land to wander over and that land is getting pretty scarce. Technology won't influence the industry much, either, as technical innovations in this industry are few. Our own growth in guns will have to result from continually seeking increased market share, but that becomes more difficult as you get larger.

Over the long run, however, I would like to bring the company up to a point where it's well established in all areas of the gun business, including government business. I would also like to see Pine Tree with an established outside market and a good management structure. If we get much bigger, I would also like to see a little more vertical integration.

Overall, I would like to remain essentially the same company, but with twice our present sales. There might be a unique event, such as a merger with a big company, but I like my job and am proud of what I'm doing. I'm proud of this company. I think a job or career should always have a tie-in with your interests. I could never understand how anyone could make a career of working for Procter and Gamble selling soap. With this company, I feel like an artist or writer; just because you've painted a good picture or written a good book you don't stop. It's the interest that counts. However (pointing to a picture on the wall behind him, which showed barrels overflowing with dollar bills), when I get too involved in my work, that picture is there to remind me of what I'm here for.

Section Two

Establishing Objectives and Formulating Strategies for Accomplishment

1　Note on the Mechanical Writing Instrument Industry

Competition in this industry is fierce. Materials and labor costs keep rising, and prices keep falling. The situation is a terrible headache, but new companies keep appearing because it's a high-growth market. They're willing to take the risk. As long as there is one firm making it, they think they can, too.

Mr. Frank King
Executive Vice President,
Writing Instrument Manufacturers Association

The mechanical writing instrument industry involved the manufacture and sale of four basic product types: fountain pens, ball point pens, soft tip pens,[1] and mechanical pencils; and their component parts.[2] Each product was introduced in the marketplace to meet a new and specific writing need, rather than to replace an existing product. The fountain pen, for example, was traditionally used in signing documents and letters, while the ball point pen was used in making carbon copies, the soft tip pen in marking and underlining, and the mechanical pencils in working with figures.

In 1973, approximately 200 companies were engaged in the manufacture and sale of mechanical writing instruments, of which 131 made refillable ball point pens, 102 nonrefillable ball point pens, 22 ordinary fountain pens, 16 cartridge-filled fountain pens, 78 thick line markers, 99 fine line porous pens, and 85 mechanical pencils. It was uncommon for firms to manufacture all of the four basic product types. Most firms competed selectively in the industry on the basis of: (1) product type: fountain pen, ball point pen, soft tip pen, and mechanical pencil; (2) price range: low ($<\$0.50$), medium ($\$0.50–\$1.00$), and high ($>\$1.00$);

---

[1] *Soft tip pens* were defined as broad line felt tip markers and fine line porous point pens.

[2] Wooden pencils were customarily considered as a separate industry, the nonmechanical writing instrument industry. The 1973 annual growth rate in manufacturers' dollar sales was 2%.

and (3) market: retail, commercial, advertising/specialty, premium, export, government, and military.

HISTORY OF MECHANICAL WRITING INSTRUMENTS

Product Evolution

The first writing instruments had their origins lost in antiquity, but could be traced through drawings and crude messages smeared with natural colored ore by a finger or scratched by a sharpened stone fragment onto cave walls. The first known instrument, the stylus, appeared around 3400 B.C., and was used to make impressions on wax and clay tablets. About 300 B.C., the Egyptians invented papyrus, the forerunner of modern paper and the standard medium for carrying the written word, which marked the beginning of the development of more sophisticated writing tools. Graphite, the main ingredient in the modern-day pencil, was introduced around 1400 A.D., the first fountain pen around 1650 A.D., and the mechanical pencil at the turn of the 20th century. The ball point pen was introduced in 1945, the soft tip pen in the mid-1960s, and the combination pen[3] in 1969. Proposed future writing instrument products are presented in the Appendix.

Product Life Cycle

Mechanical writing instrument product types tended to follow similar life cycle patterns in the marketplace:

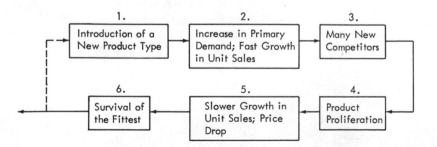

The one exception to this pattern was the fountain pen, whose average price increased relative to a decline in unit sales. As industry prices began to polarize into the high and low price ranges, the low price/high

---

[3] The combination pen had a rotating carbide ball point, which wrote with the flow of a marker using water-based ink, had the hard feel and carbon-making feature of a ball point pen, and the overall feel and writing effect of a fountain pen.

volume manufacturers tended to drop their fountain pen lines, which left only the high price/low volume manufacturers competing in that market.

Exhibits 1–4 present information on manufacturers' dollar sales, unit sales, and average prices by product from 1954 through 1973. During that period, total dollar sales increased from $117.1 million to $353.3 million; total unit sales from 261.7 million to 2,342.4 million, and the average writing instrument price decreased from $0.45 to $0.15.

The Price War

The price war in the mechanical writing instrument industry began in the early 1960s with the overwhelming success of the BIC 19¢ stick pen. It was BIC Pen Corporation's objective "to place a generic name

EXHIBIT 1

Manufacturer's Sales in Dollars—By Product

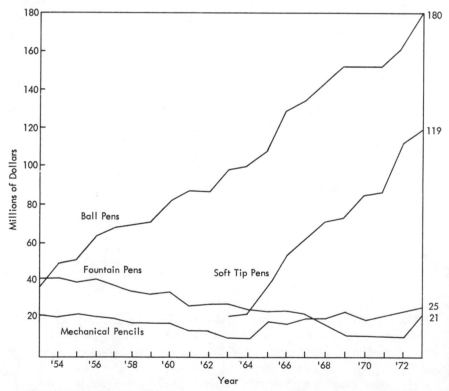

* Desk and pen sets not included.
Source: Writing Instrument Manufacturers Association.

EXHIBIT 2

Unit Sales—By Product

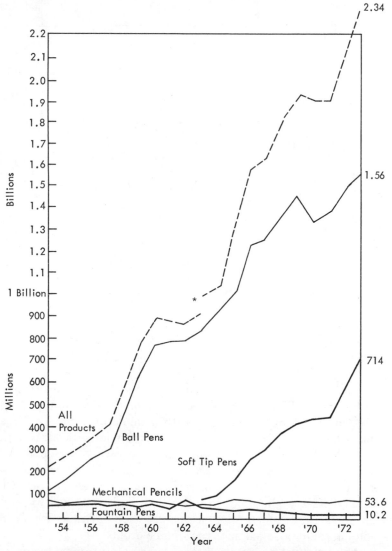

* Unit sales line for "All Products" adjusted in 1963 to include soft tip pens.
Source: Writing Instrument Manufacturers Association.

EXHIBIT 3

Average Price—By Product

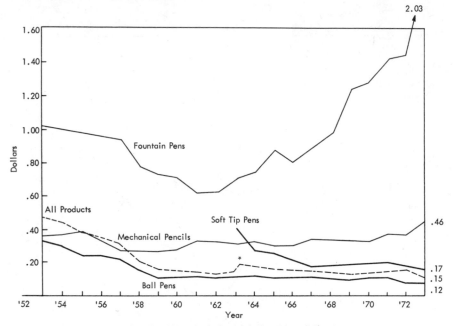

* All-product line adjusted in 1963 to include calulation for soft tip pens.
Source: Writing Instrument Manufacturers Association.

(BIC) on all the cheap "no-name"[4] ball point pens in the industry." Using heavy advertising, BIC created the concept of the "disposable pen" as well as quantity selling in multipacks. By stimulating primary demand, BIC encouraged many other firms to enter the low-priced ball point pen market, which represented the fastest growing segment of the mechanical writing instrument industry at the time. Several well-established writing instrument manufacturers, namely A. T. Cross, Sheaffer, and Parker, chose not to follow suit and continued to position their products in the high-price segment, where margins rather than sheer volume could be relied upon to produce profits.

The price war history repeated itself with soft tip pens in the early 1970s. By 1973, industry officials believed that ball point pen prices had fallen as far as they would go, although soft tip pen prices were still dropping. The price wars were thought to be manufacturer imposed, particularly by high volume producers such as BIC, rather than consumer influenced, which accounted for the fact that prices in the low

---

[4] No-name products were those which were not advertised and were marketed at retail prices far below the comparable, inexpensive, nationally advertised products.

1954–1958

	1954 Units	1954 Value	1955 Units	1955 Value	1956 Units	1956 Value	1957 Units	1957 Value	1958 Units	1958 Value
	Estimated Number of Units Shipped	Estimated Total $ Value at Factory Prices (exclusive of tax)	Estimated Number of Units Shipped	Estimated Total $ Value at Factory Prices (exclusive of tax)	Estimated Number of Units Shipped	Estimated Total $ Value at Factory Prices (exclusive of tax)	Estimated Number of Units Shipped	Estimated Total $ Value at Factory Prices (exclusive of tax)	Estimated Number of Units Shipped	Estimated Total $ Value at Factory Prices (exclusive of tax)
Fountain pens	40.3	$ 41.7	40.8	$ 40.2	42.8	$ 41.5	40.9	$ 38.2	44.9	$ 35.0
Ball point pens	162.0	48.9	210.7	50.6	265.9	63.5	300.5	67.7	485.6	65.0
Mechanical pencils	57.6	22.0	55.8	22.5	64.0	21.8	67.8	20.7	64.6	18.9
Desk and dip pen sets	1.8	4.5	2.3	4.8	3.2	6.2	2.9	6.5	2.5	4.1
	261.7	$117.1	309.6	$118.1	375.9	$133.0	412.1	$133.1	597.6	$123.0

1959–1963

	1959 Units	1959 Value	1960 Units	1960 Value	1961 Units	1961 Value	1962 Units	1962 Value	1963 Units	1963 Value
Fountain pens	44.3	$ 33.5	48.7	$ 35.1	43.9	$ 28.1	46.4	$ 29.6	37.7	$ 27.8
Ball point pens	657.2	71.0	761.9	81.6	775.2	86.1	779.3	85.7	846.2	97.8
Soft tip pens*									55.0	21.7
Mechanical pencils	63.8	18.8	60.1	18.7	45.1	15.1	45.1	15.0	50.7	15.5
Desk and dip pen sets	8.1	5.0	4.1	3.7	3.2	2.6	2.9	3.0	1.3	2.8
	773.5	$128.3	874.8	$139.1	867.4	$131.9	873.7	$133.3	990.9	$165.6

1964–1968

	1964 Units	1964 Value	1965 Units	1965 Value	1966 Units	1966 Value	1967 Units	1967 Value	1968 Units	1968 Value
Fountain pens	33.1	$ 25.4	27.8	$ 24.2	29.7	$ 24.2	25.7	$ 22.9	17.6	$ 17.4
Ball point pens†	914.7	100.7	1,051.5	106.8	1,217.2	126.4				
Refillable							662.2	80.6	725.0	89.6
Nonrefillable							577.4	52.0	623.6	53.4
Soft tip pens*	86.5	22.8								
Markers (thick line)			75.2	22.1	79.6	24.2	103.0	26.2	123.5	28.8
Porous point pens			82.5	15.2	169.6	28.8	195.0	34.9	253.4	41.9
Mechanical pencils	47.2	16.0	64.0	18.9	61.4	18.2	56.4	20.4	55.9	20.1
Desk and dip pen sets	2.2	3.3	10.7	5.0	3.0	4.6	3.3	4.4	6.1	9.7
	1,083.7	$168.2	1,311.7	$192.2	1,560.5	$226.4	1,623.0	$241.4	1,805.1	$260.9

1969–1973

	1969 Units	1969 Value	1970 Units	1970 Value	1971 Units	1971 Value	1972 Units	1972 Value	1973 Units	1973 Value
Fountain pens	12.3	$ 16.0	10.2	$ 15.2	10.1	$ 14.7	9.8	$ 15.3	10.2	$ 20.8
Ball point pens										
Refillable	761.3	94.1	685.5	92.7	670.3	90.9	729.8	99.2	738.6	110.5
Nonrefillable	686.3	58.7	700.3	59.8	720.4	61.4	760.3	64.6	821.8	69.8
Markers (thick line)	116.8	26.8	105.1	25.4	102.2	25.0	120.3	29.5	209.4	33.7
Porous point pens	304.1	50.3	334.5	58.9	344.5	60.7	475.9	80.8	504.5	85.7
Mechanical pencils	65.5	22.3	57.8	20.1	55.7	21.5	59.5	22.9	53.6	24.9
Desk and dip pen sets	7.2	10.3	5.6	7.0	3.7	6.5	4.1	7.1	4.3	7.9
	1,953.5	$278.5	1,899.0	$279.1	1,906.9	$280.7	2,159.7	$319.4	2,342.4	$353.3

* No sales breakdown until 1965.
† No sales breakdown until 1967.
Source: *Annual estimates compiled by Writing Instrument Manufactures Association, Inc.*

TABLE 1

Annual Growth Rate (Percent)

Product Line	1969	1970	1971	1972	1973	5-Yr Average	1973*		
							Unit Sales	$ Sales	Average Price
Fountain pens..............	(29.8)%	(17.8)%	(0.6)%	(3.1)%	4.7%	(9.3)%	0.4%	6.2%	$2.03
Mechanical pencils.............	17.2	(11.8)	(3.6)	6.8	(9.9)	(0.3)	2.3	7.2	0.46
Ball point pens.............	7.3	(4.3)	0.3	7.1	4.7	3.8	66.7	52.3	0.12
Refillables.............	5.0	(10.0)	(2.2)	8.9	1.2	1.0	31.5	32.0	0.15
Nonrefillables.............	10.0	2.0	2.9	5.5	8.1	6.8	35.2	20.3	0.09
Soft tip pens.............	11.7	4.5	1.6	33.5	19.7	14.2	30.6	34.3	0.17
Broad line markers.............	(5.4)	(10.0)	(2.7)	17.7	74.0	14.7	9.0	9.8	0.16
Porous point pens.............	20.0	10.0	3.0	38.1	6.0	15.4	21.6	24.5	0.17
Total industry.............	10.8%	(2.7)%	1.0%	13.3%	8.4%	6.2%	100.0%	100.0%	$0.15

* Excludes desk and dip pen sets.
Source: Writing Instrument Manufacturers Association.

price market segment were never raised despite inflation. Almost all porous point pens and 93% of all ball point pens retailed for less than $1 each in 1973.

The Competition

No single manufacturer dominated the mechanical writing instrument industry in 1973. Rather, individual manufacturers dominated specific industry segments, which were identified by product type, price range, and market. In most cases, purchases were made on the basis of individual products, rather than on the basis of a manufacturer's complete product line.

Industry market shares were subject to wide fluctuation. Those innovative firms which had made an early entry into newly discovered markets, and had subsequently supported their new products with heavy national advertising, tended to become the dominant forces in those markets. BIC Pen, for example, dominated all markets in low-priced ball point pens, as did Gillette in fine line porous point pens. Exhibit 5 presents the 1973 primary corporate focus of major writing instrument competitors, with respect to product line, market, product price range, advertising program, and new products.

Manufacturers felt that success depended heavily upon the strength of their financial resources, which was reflected in their marketing and distribution programs as well as upon their ability to be innovative. Advertising, packaging, and distribution costs combined were estimated to average close to 100 percent of the manufacturer's unit cost of low-priced products. Manufacturers unable to sustain those costs in all markets tended either to position their products in the retail market as no-name brands or to concentrate the bulk of their resources in specific market segments.

INDUSTRY STRUCTURE

Manufacturers

There were two types of writing instrument firms: assemblers (70%) and producers (30%).

The *assemblers* were typically small, privately held, product specialists which sold their products by direct mail on a special order basis to the three most price-sensitive markets: commercial, advertising/specialty, and premium. To become an assembler required very little capital investment, manufacturing expertise, or marketing know-how, which accounted for the large number of assemblers and the fact that they tended to come and go. Assemblers bought writing instrument components from

EXHIBIT 5

1973 Primary Corporate Focus

Writing Instrument Firms	Product Line	Market	Price Range	Ad Program	Newest Product
BIC	bp, pp	All	Low	Consumer (TV)	Disposable lighter
Berol	wp, bp	Commercial	Middle, low	Trade	Combination pen
Cross (A.T.)	mp, bp	Retail	High	Consumer (mag's)	Luxury pp
Gillette	bp, pp	All	High, low	75%–consumer (TV) 25%–trade	Disposable lighter
Lindy	bp	Retail	Low	Consumer (mag's); formerly trade	Disposable lighter
Magic Marker	bp, pp, bm	All	Low	Consumer (all media) trade	pp
Pentel	pp, bm	All	Low, middle	Consumer (TV); formerly trade	Combination pen
Parker	fp	Retail	High	Consumer (mag's)	Luxury pp
Scripto	mp, bp, pp	Retail, ad/ specialty	Low	Consumer (TV, mag's); formerly trade	Disposable lighter
Sheaffer	fp	Retail	High	Consumer (mag's)	Luxury pp
Venus Esterbrook	Full line	All	Low, Middle	60%–trade 40%–consumer (mag's)	Technical drafting products

Abbreviations:
 bp = ball point pens.
 bm = broad tip markers.
 fp = fountain pens.
 mp = mechanical pencils.
 pp = fine line porous point pens.
 wp = wooden pencils.
Source: case researcher's interviews with the corporate marketing personnel.

suppliers which were then assembled and packaged for sale. Competition was based heavily on price, and product promotions were common.

Producers tended to be larger firms, some publicly held, which sold their products to all markets with special emphasis on the retail. Competition centered around the strength of their distribution networks (number of outlets reached and distributor loyalties) and national advertising programs. Producers manufactured most of their own component parts before assembling and packaging products. Their operations were characterized as capital-intensive and precision-oriented. It was not uncommon for some producers to manufacture certain products and to import others.

Distribution

Company Sales Forces. A typical producer used three types of sales forces: regular, specialized, and detail (optional).

The *regular sales force* made direct sales to large retail chains and discount houses, and indirect sales through specialized distributors to smaller retail stores and commercial supply outlets.

The *specialized sales force* made direct sales to the government, military, export, and premium markets, and indirect sales through advertising/specialty distributors to the ad/specialty market.

Some firms added a *detail sales force* to work at the retail level, taking orders and arranging displays. Smaller firms relied more heavily on indirect selling than did the larger firms, which could afford to cover the cost of direct selling to large accounts.

Specialized Distributors. Specialized distributors (wholesalers) first appeared in the writing instrument industry when manufacturers came to realize that they could no longer handle an enormous number of accounts on their own. They carried a multitude of products, and were not captive to any one manufacturer. Their sales function was one of showing promotional items and order taking, for which they received a 15% margin off the retail price. In most cases, they assumed ownership of inventories. Along with the percentage markup, their own sales forces often received promotional monies ("p.m.'s"), which were tied to major manufacturers' promotions at the retail level.

Distributors assisted dealers and retailers by providing an inventory management service, which guaranteed replacement of faulty merchandise, better product selection, and faster inventory turnover.[5] "A better return on investment" became their key selling tool, which was supported by fair and attractive margins (40% off retail price) and frequent sales calls.

---

[5] Dealers were office products stationers in the commercial market. Retailers were over-the-counter marketers in the retail market.

The late 1960s marked the beginning of an industry shift in distribution patterns in the retail market (largest market)—away from indirect selling via specialized distributors to small, independent retail outlets, towards direct selling to large national chains and discount houses. The turn sparked embitterment on the part of distributors, who felt that they were not only being abandoned by the very firms which had influenced their creation, but were also being victimized by manufacturers' price-cutting actions affecting margins on the business which they still had. By 1973, approximately 60% of the dollar volume in the retail market represented direct sales from the manufacturers to mass-merchandise outlets.

Markets

In 1973, manufacturers' dollar shipments by market segment were estimated by industry sources to be: retail (50%), commercial (20%), ad/specialty (16%), export (9%), premium (4%), and military and government (1%).

Retail Market. The retail market represented by far the highest concentration of manufacturers' dollar sales (50%) in the mechanical writing instrument industry in 1973. The only instrument which was selling better in another market was the fountain pen, of which 63.6% of its dollar volume was sold overseas. Drug stores were the highest volume retail outlet for writing instruments, capturing over 33% of the industry's total dollar retail sales, and one out of every two ball point pen sales. Grocery stores were the smallest with 3% of the retail sales. Specialized distributors (tobacco, drug, and sundries) sold products to small chains and independent stores, while large chains and discount houses bought writing instruments direct from manufacturers.

Retailers selected product lines based primarily on product quality and reputation of the manufacturer. National advertising support was believed to be important for boosting retail sales, particularly in the low-priced items.

A survey of retail customers conducted by the researcher indicated the following consumer purchase priorities: 1) function, 2) quality, 3) price, 4) style, and 5) packaging. It was generally felt that:

Products were selected for specific purposes,

Low-priced items tended to be impulse purchases often bought in quantities, while higher-priced instruments were planned purchases bought individually,

prices which varied (a few cents in the low-price range) among fairly undifferentiated products *did not* sway selection of a preferred brand,

Consumers associated generic names with particular products which had been heavily advertised: such as Flair for porous point pens, and Cross for mechanical pencils.

Commercial Market.   The commercial market represented 20% of the total manufacturers' dollar shipments in 1973. Manufacturers' sales were made primarily through office supply distributors to dealers (commercial stationers), whose customers were corporate purchasing agents and students. Distributor/dealer loyalties were common in the commercial market, and were built up over the years on the basis of good account service, good quality merchandise, and attractive product offerings (at least one type at each price point). Commercial sales were heavily concentrated in the low-price range (<$0.50).

As in the retail market, quality was considered the most important factor affecting a purchase decision by the dealer in the commercial market. However, price was more critical to the dealer than to the retailer, because companies were interested in obtaining cost savings through bulk buying, whereas retail customers took personal pride in selecting their merchandise and were often willing to pay a premium for the products of their choice.

Advertising/Specialty Market.   Sales in the advertising/specialty market represented 16 percent of manufacturers' dollar shipments in 1973. Purchasers tended to be organizations requesting inexpensive products on which to stamp advertisements. Price was the most important factor affecting a purchase decision. Orders were placed through ad/specialty distributors and filled by a specialized company sales force. Approximately 70% of the 200 writing instrument firms were engaged in the ad/specialty business, many of whom were assemblers.

Premium Market.   The premium market represented approximately 4% of manufacturers' total sales in 1973. Competitors included non-writing instrument firms, as well as writing instrument companies, which: 1) could meet the price objectives of the purchaser, and 2) could offer products acceptable as give-away promotional items for other products.

Other Markets.   In 1973, export sales represented 9% of the total manufacturers' sales. The rising trend in export sales was attributed to: 1) the lowering of tariffs on imported products in foreign countries, and 2) the increased activities of firms which held licenses or ran operations abroad. The average prices of writing instruments sold abroad were markedly lower than the average retail prices in the United States since so much of the cost in the domestic market was tied up in distribution, advertising, and packaging. Heavy U.S. import taxes (about 2¢/unit) on writing instruments continued to bar entry of low-priced foreign-made products into the United States on a large scale.

The military and government markets combined represented only 1% of manufacturers' unit sales in 1973.

CIGARETTE LIGHTERS

By 1973, many mechanical writing instrument companies had entered the cigarette lighter business as a means of product line diversification and yet another way to capitalize on their production expertise and market contacts. Although the two classes of products were functionally unrelated, their manufacturing processes, distribution patterns, and product life cycles bore striking similarities. The only major differences centered around market appeal, susceptibility to government regulation, and import trends.

Lighter/Writer Similarities

Product Life Cycle. Cigarette lighter product and price patterns almost exactly paralleled those of mechanical writing instruments—only a decade later. Until the late 1960s, competition among dominant cigarette lighter companies was concentrated almost exclusively in regular refillable lighter products selling in the middle price range ($2–$12). Following the introduction of an inexpensive disposable lighter by Garrity Industries in 1967, and an expensive electronic lighter by Maruman in 1970, sales of cigarette lighters began to polarize by price and product: disposables at <$2 and electronics at >$12, leaving the backbone of the business, regular refillable lighters, in a vulnerable position with respect to sales prospects.

Distribution Patterns. Cigarette lighters were sold direct from the manufacturer, or indirect through specialized distributors, to writing instrument markets. In 1973 there were 175,000 retail outlets in the United States marketing cigarette lighters. Grocery stores represented the largest number (45%–50%) of lighter sales. Of all cigarette lighters retailed, 75%–80% were for less than $6.95. Like writing instruments, lighter sales were slightly seasonal, with the heaviest concentration occurring around the holidays. Distributors' margins off retail price generally ran between 15%–25%, increasing proportionately with the price of the product. Retailer margins were 40% off retail price.

Manufacturing Process. Cigarette lighter production required the same basic technology as that of mechanical writing instruments: plastics injection molding of parts, followed by a precision assembly process. The average mechanical writing instrument consisted of seven parts and could be produced in a matter of minutes, whereas the average lighter had 21 parts and required a three-day production schedule because of "cure time" (a 24-hour wait between lamination of the subassemblies and filling the fuel reservoir).

The porous point pen and liquid fuel lighter operated on the same basic principle: The tank of the porous point pen held ink; the tank of the lighter held lighter fluid. The nib of the porous point pen was analogous to the wick of the lighter. Both drew the fluid out of their respective tanks by capillary action.

Lighter/Writer Differences

Import Trends.   Unlike mechanical writing instruments, many cigarette lighters, particularly the disposables (70%), were imported into the United States for sale by domestic firms, which felt that the 25% duty fee on a foreign manufacturer's product was less than the additional amount required for direct labor costs in the United States. An added attraction was the quick access gained to a fast-growth market opportunity. In 1972, 45% of the lighters sold in the United States represented foreign imports, versus 36% in 1965. Japan was by far the largest supplier in every class of imported lighters (54.5% overall), with the exception of disposable butane lighters, 71% of which were imported by France.

Government Regulation.   Until 1973, most cigarette lighter regulation related to the transportation of lighters containing flammable fuel. However, in 1973 the Consumer Products Safety Commission was given the authority to evaluate the quality of consumer products and enforce stringent safety standards. Cigarette lighters, particularly the inexpensive imports, were likely to be subject to CPSC attack if they lacked a flame adjuster (controlled height) or constant flame length regulator (controlled duration).[6] Although they were ranked 38th on the CPSC list in terms of severity of accidents, mechanical writing instruments were considered less hazardous. They were represented in Washington, D.C., by an industry trade association, the Writing Instrument Manufacturers Association, while lighters were not.

Market Appeal.   Writing instruments appealed to a much broader consumer base than cigarette lighters did. All persons of all age groups were considered potential users of writing instruments, whereas cigarette lighter users were mostly smokers or campers.

Industry Trends

Cigarette Smoking.   During 1972, domestic consumption of cigarettes rose slightly from the previous year's level, which had reversed a four-year downtrend. Americans, including those at home and those abroad in the armed forces, consumed 565 billion cigarettes, or 2% above the prior year's level. Annual consumption per adult of 4,040 cigarettes

---

[6] The $1.29 disposable lighter by Rogers was the first disposable lighter to be recalled because of a flame adjuster problem (fall 1973).

(202 packs) remained about the same, which was 7% below the 1963 peak.

There were three principal reasons for the rise in cigarette consumption in 1972:

> Increased concentration of the American population in the heaviest smokers' age group (25–39), which was 18.4% in 1972 and forecast to be 20% by 1975 and 22.9% by 1980.

> Minimal cigarette price boosts, which had not affected the demand for cigarettes.

> A decrease in the influence of anti-smoking campaigns after medical research evidence linking cigarette smoking to serious disease was termed inconclusive.

Cigarette Lighter Sales. Cigarette lighter dollar sales in the United States were estimated to be $153 million in 1973. Compared to a 5.1% drop in per capita cigarette consumption, lighter sales had nearly doubled since 1965. Industry sources attributed the sudden sales surge to: (1) the advent of disposable lighters, and (2) an increased consumer awareness of cigarette lighters as the result of new and vigorous advertising campaigns.

TABLE 2

Cigarette Lighter Retail Dollar Sales (dollars in millions)

	1965	1966	1967	1968	1969	1970	1971	1972	1973 (est.
Total lighters...........	$72.6	$85.9	$90.2	$94.3	$94.9	$98.1	$106.9	$115.0	$153.0

Source: Case researcher's estimates based on trade and company interviews and unpublished figures from the *Drug Topics* magazine research group (1972).

Product Types

There were three basic lighter product types: (1) disposable, (2) regular refillable, and (3) electronic. These types could be further differentiated by: (1) price range: low (<$2), medium ($2–$12) and high (>$12); 2) style: compact, pocket, or table; 3) fuel type: butane gas or naphtha liquid fuel; 4) consumer purpose: refillable or disposable; and 5) starter mechanism: wick, flint, quartz crystals, or battery.

Disposable Lighters. Disposable butane lighters represented the faster growing segment in the cigarette lighter industry, accounting for 35% of total lighter unit sales in 1973.

Disposable lighters were introduced in the United States in 1967 by Garrity Industries, Inc. They earned immediate consumer acceptance due to their low price and no reflint/no refill feature. They appealed for

TABLE 3

Cigarette Lighter Differentiation

Product Type	Price Range	Starter Mechanism	Fuel	Style	Consumer Purpose
Disposable.......	> $2	Flint	Butane gas	Compact	Disposable
Regular refillable.......	Mostly $2–$12	Flint	Butane gas (90%)	Compact Table Pocket	Refillable
	Some > $12	Wick	Naphtha (10%)		
Electronic........	> $12	Quartz crystals Battery	Butane gas	Pocket Table	Refillable

the most part to match users, an untapped end-user market within the lighter industry, and to regular refillable lighter users who were tired of losing pesonal lighters and wished to trade down to the inexpensive line. Like inexpensive mechanical writing instruments, disposable lighters were considered impulse purchase items, which had to be backed with heavy consumer advertising support and sold in mass-merchandise channels.

The success of the disposable lighter in the American market caused a chain reaction among mechanical writing instrument firms which had been seeking to diversify into related product lines. Most firms entered the cigarette lighter business as distributors of foreign-made models. Some intended to eventually set up domestic manufacturing operations of their own.

In 1973, there were three clear contenders for industry dominance in the disposable butane lighter business: Gillette, BIC, and Garrity Industries, with Scripto running a distant fourth. Gillette introduced a $1.49 French-made product called "Cricket," in 1972, through mass merchandise channels, and used heavy consumer advertising. It planned to manufacture lighters domestically by 1973. BIC followed a similar plan one year hence with its $1.49 "BIC Butane." Garrity Industries distributed its $1.49 "Dispoz-a-lite" in smoke shops, hotel stands, and drug stores, and used trade advertising. Scripto introduced its 98¢ Japanese-made "Catch 98" in 1973 through independent retailers and

TABLE 4

Disposable Lighter Retail Sales (dollars in millions)

	1971	1972	1973	1975 (est.)
Dollar sales...............	$18	$36	$50	$120
Unit sales................	13	21	40	100

Source: Trade estimates.

used no consumer advertising. It planned to introduce a family of disposable lighters in 1974.

Regular Refillable Lighters. By 1973, cigarette lighter sales had grown rapidly at the inexpensive and luxury price ends of the market. Victimized by this trend was the regular refillable lighter, the mainstay of the lighter business, 95% of whose sales were concentrated in the middle price range. Industry sources attributed the slow decay of the middle price segment to three factors.[7]

1. Style changes in lighters, which reflected the growing consumer interest in either more decoration (luxury lighters) or more functionally (disposables);
2. A trade-down to disposable lighters by the former purchaser of the refillable butane lighter, who became tired of losing refilling lighters;
3. The trend towards distribution through mass merchandise outlets, where profitability depended upon high volume turnover of inexpensive products away from independent retail outlets, where most regular refillable lighters were sold.

For years three companies had dominated the regular refillable lighter market: Ronson, Zippo, and Scripto. Together they produced two-thirds of the 1973 sales in that product segment. Industry sources believed that, of the three, Zippo would be the least affected by the product/price polarization trend, as Zippo had developed long-time customer loyalties with its high quality product, which held a life-time guarantee. Ronson had lost market share by moving to higher-priced regular refillable lighters and decreasing its advertising support of its products. Scripto lacked the advertising and marketing strength necessary to support its lower-priced regular refillable lighters against the competition from disposable lighters.

Electronic Lighters. Electronic lighters represented less than 2% of the total cigarette lighter unit sales in 1973. They required no flint or wick, as their flames were produced, electronically, by the striking together of ceramic quartz crystals, or with a battery. As luxury gift items, they were sold exclusively in department and jewelry stores and were priced above $12. Electronic lighters were new to the American market in 1973, and had not yet earned wide consumer acceptance—due in part to a lack of consumer awareness of their existence, and in part to the fact that consumers had traditionally thought of lighters as functional, rather than as highly decorative jewel-like products.

The leading distributors of electronic lighters in 1973 were Maruman, Dunhill, Colibri, Crown, and Consul. All electronic lighters were im-

---

[7] Industry sources believed that sales patterns for regular refillables would have been much worse, had it not been for the support of the ad/specialty market in the middle-price range.

ported either from Europe or from the Far East. As was the case with disposables, a number of companies, such as Scripto and Ronson, had introduced electronic lighters in order to expand their product lines and to take advantage of sales opportunities in a high growth segment of the cigarette lighter market.

Appendix

The Mechanical Writing Instrument Industry

Mechanical Writing Instruments of the Future

Multicolor Blending. A pen that will provide many colors, shades, and hues with a simple push of a button or twist of the cap to blend inks. Colors can be darkened, lightened, changed by interaction of inks—an artist's palette within a pen barrel.

Variable Tip Marker. For the Jekyll and Hyde writer who must switch from the fine lines used for underlining to the bold strokes of a package address, he will have to go no further than this soft tip pen. Three point sizes—fine, medium, broad—can be included in the barrel and are as easily interchangeable as a push on the cap top.

Computerized Writing. Enables the most modern businesses to keep the personal touch alive in the computer age. Personalized notes will be produced on a large scale by programming individual handwriting into the memory. It will write any message fed into the computer in exact duplication of the handwriting.

Dictating Pen. "What you say is what you get." A pen that is able to translate spoken messages into your own style of handwriting.

The Permanent Writer. Pen carries its own 100-year ink supply and never needs replacement.

Multitip Pen. A ball point, soft tip, marker, and fountain pen—all in the same writing instrument. For the worker with four jobs at once, and no time to hunt up or change his writing instrument.

Multipointed Mechanical Pencil. Soft, medium, and hard pencil points all encased in one unit for ease in switching from one job to another—without searching through pencil boxes or desk drawers.

Self-destruct Ink. For keeping those hush-hush secrets really secret. This ink disappears after 48 hours, leaving no trace of important information that is written "For Your Eyes Only."

Radio Transmitting Writing Instruments. Write down your message at one location and it is transmitted to another miles away and written down—without connection.

Homing Device. This device will transmit a short sound beam so that you can keep tabs on your mislaid writing instruments. Great for big offices with absent-minded "borrowers."

Power Writing. The conversion of atomic power into a writing ink. Lines will be burned into paper by converting light, neutrons, or other power sources in the barrel of the writing instrument.

Source: *Office Products,* May 22, 1972.

2   *BIC Pen Corporation (A)*

Described by an economic observer as "one of the classic success stories in American business," the BIC Pen Corporation was widely acknowledged as a leader in the mechanical writing instrument industry in 1973. "The success was dramatic," the observer had said, "because it was achieved from the residue of a deficit-ridden predecessor company, over a short period . . . , in the extremely competitive, low price sector of the industry. "BIC" had become a generic name for inexpensive ball point pens."

Mr. Robert Adler, president of BIC, was extremely proud of the firm's success, which he attributed to "numerous and good management decisions based 40% on science and 60% on intuition." BIC had reported its first profit in 1964 based on net sales of $6.2 million. Over the following nine years, net sales increased at a compounded rate of 28.2% and the weighted average after-tax profit as a percentage of net sales was 13.2%. (See Exhibits 1–3 for a summary of financial data from 1964–73.)

Until 1972, BIC concentrated exclusively on the design, manufacture, and distribution of a complete line of inexpensive ball point pen products. The most successful pen was the 19¢ Crystal, which accounted for over 40% of BIC's unit sales in ball point pens and about 15% of industry unit sales in ball point pens in 1972. That same year, BIC expanded its writing instrument product line to include a fine line porous point pen. In 1973 it added a disposable cigarette lighter.

COMPANY HISTORY

The name "Waterman" meant a writing instrument since Mr. Louis Waterman invented the first practical fountain pen in 1875. For many

EXHIBIT 1

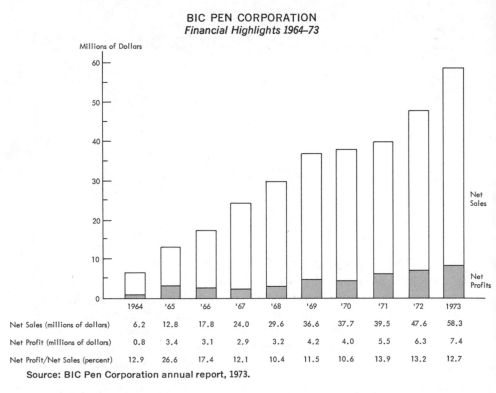

BIC PEN CORPORATION
Financial Highlights 1964–73

	1964	'65	'66	'67	'68	'69	'70	'71	'72	1973
Net Sales (millions of dollars)	6.2	12.8	17.8	24.0	29.6	36.6	37.7	39.5	47.6	58.3
Net Profit (millions of dollars)	0.8	3.4	3.1	2.9	3.2	4.2	4.0	5.5	6.3	7.4
Net Profit/Net Sales (percent)	12.9	26.6	17.4	12.1	10.4	11.5	10.6	13.9	13.2	12.7

Source: BIC Pen Corporation annual report, 1973.

years, the Waterman Pen company led the world in the manufacture of fountain pens. But in the late 1950s, when the shift to ball point pens swept the United States, the Waterman Company continued to concentrate on its fountain pen line, and its performance slipped substantially.

In 1958 M. Marcel Bich, a French businessman well established as a leading European pen maker, bought the facilities, trademark, and patent rights of the ailing Waterman Company, which then became the Waterman-Bic Pen Company. Believing strongly that the ball point pen was the writing instrument of the future, M. Bich established the objective of becoming the leading firm in the low-price disposable ball point pen industry. To obtain that position, management proposed the use of forceful consumer advertising and mass distribution policies.

At the time of M. Bich's purchase of Waterman, ball point pens constituted only 8% of Waterman's unit sales. By 1964, however, all fountain pen and ink products had been eliminated, and most sales came from the 19¢ stick-type ball point pen. The conversion process was costly, as reflected in the five years of deficits (1959–63). BIC reached its

EXHIBIT 2

BIC PEN CORPORATION
Consolidated Financial Statements
For the years ended December 31, 1973 and 1972
(in $1,000)
Consolidated Statement Of Income

	1973	1972
Net sales.....................................	$58,326	$47,571
Cost of goods sold...........................	26,564	19,892
Gross Profit..................................	31,762	27,679
Selling, advertising, and general and administrative expenses.....................	17,191	15,248
Profit from operations........................	14,570	12,431
Other income................................	589	269
Total..................................	15,159	12,700
Other deductions............................	327	196
Income before income taxes..................	14,787	12,504
Provision for income taxes....................	7,357	6,240
Net income..................................	$ 7,430	$ 6,264
Earnings per share...........................	$ 1.15	$ 1.00

Consolidated Statement Of Retained Earnings

	1973	1972
Balance—beginning of year....................	$11,683	$10,262
Net Income.................................	7,430	6,264
Total..................................	19,113	16,526
Dividends:		
Cash:		
Common shares..........................	1,750	1,603
Preferred shares.........................		
Total Cash...........................	1,750	1,603
Common shares...........................		3,240
Total Dividends......................	1,750	4,843
Balance—end of year........................	$17,363	$11,683

Source: BIC Pen Corporation annual report, 1973.

turning point in 1964, marked by the national success of its Crystal pen.

From 1964 through 1973, the company expanded its ball point pen line to include 12 models of retractable and nonretractable pens offered in varying point sizes, ink colors, and barrel colors at retail prices between 19¢ and $1. A 29¢ fine line porous point pen was added in 1972 and a $1.49 disposable butane cigarette lighter in 1973. In addition to product line expansion, BIC established a 100%-owned operation in Canada (1967), joint ventures in Japan (1972) and Mexico (1973), and a distributor arrangement with a firm in Panama (1973).

On May 1, 1971, the company changed its name to the BIC Pen Corporation. The Waterman trademark was subsequently sold to a Zurich

EXHIBIT 3

BIC PEN CORPORATION
Consolidated Financial Statements
December 31, 1973 and 1972
(in $1,000)
Consolidated Balance Sheet

	1973	1972
Assets		
Current Assets:		
Cash...	$ 683	$ 919
Certificates of deposit and short-term investments—at cost, which approximates market..	8,955	10,000
Receivables—trade and other (net of allowance for doubtful accounts, 1973—$143,000, 1972—$102,000)......................................	9,445	8,042
Inventories.......................................	9,787	6,299
Deposits and prepaid expenses..................	644	633
Total current assets..........................	29,514	25,893
Property, Plant, and Equipment—at cost (net of accumulated depreciation, 1973—$9,687,000, 1972—$7,091,000)..................................	15,156	9,687
Investments and other assets.....................	1,790	1,329
Total..	$46,460	$36,909

Liabilities and Shareholder's Equity

	1973	1972
Current Liabilities:		
Notes payable—banks...........................	21	—
Construction loan payable (due March 21, 1974)...	560	—
Accounts payable—trade........................	3,872	$ 1,245
Mortgage payable..............................	62	58
Accrued liabilities:		
Federal and state income taxes.................	1,231	815
Pension plan..................................	306	265
Other...	488	402
Total Current Liabilities.....................	6,540	2,785
Deferred liabilities................................	361	275
Mortgage payable.................................	459	520
Minority interest*................................	91	—
Shareholders' equity:		
Common shares................................	6,480	6,480
Capital surplus................................	15,166	15,166
Retained earnings.............................	17,363	11,683
Total Shareholders' Equity..................	39,009	33,329
Total.....................................	$46,460	$36,909

* Mexican subsidiary is 80%–owned.
Source: BIC Pen Corporation annual report, 1973.

firm, and BIC went public with an offering of 655,000 shares of common stock listed at $25 per share on the American Stock Exchange. In 1973, BIC's parent company, Société Bic, S.A., held 62% of the BIC stock.

MEN OF INFLUENCE

M. Marcel Bich

M. Marcel Bich has been described as having done for ball point pens what Henry Ford did for cars: produce a cheap but serviceable model.

> In 1945, Bich and his friend Edouard Buffard pooled their wealth— all of $1,000—and started making ball point refills in an old factory near Paris. Soon it occurred to Bich that a disposable pen that needed no refills would be more to the point. What his country needed, as Bich saw it, was a good 10¢ pen. Today the cheapest throwaway Bic sells for close to that in France—about 7¢. In the United States the same pen retails for 19¢, and it is the biggest seller on the market. . . .
>
> Marcel Bich is a stubborn, opinionated entrepreneur who inherited his title from his forebears in the predominantly French-speaking Val D'Aoste region of northern Italy. He abhors technocrats, computers, and borrowing money. At 58, he attributes his business successes to his refusal to listen to almost anyone's advice but his own. Bich says that his philosophy has been to "concentrate on one product, used by everyone every day." Now, however, he is moving toward diversification. A disposable Bic cigarette lighter that gives 3,000 lights is being test marketed in Sweden; if it proves out, Bich plans to sell it for less than 90¢. . . .
>
> In the United States, Bich is best known for his fiasco in the 1970 America's Cup Race: His sloop *France,* which he captained, got lost in the fog off Newport. He speaks in aquatic terms even when describing his company: "We just try to stick close to reality, like a surfer to his board. We don't lean forward or backward too far or too fast. We ride the wave at the right moment."[1]

Société Bic, S.A., was known as a "one-man empire" which in 1972 accounted for a third of the ball point pen sales worldwide and included full operations in 19 countries. M. Bich's personal holdings were estimated to be worth about $200 million. "The only way he could control his empire," BIC's Treasurer Mr. Alexander Alexiades had said, "was to have certain rules and guidelines. All Société Bic companies were quite autonomous once they had become consistent with his philosophies."

BIC Pen Corporation had been characterized as the "jewel in M. Bich's crown." In the firm's early years, M. Bich had provided much of the machinery, production techniques, and supplies from the French parent

---

[1] "Going Bananas over BIC," *Time,* December 18, 1972, p. 93.

company. By 1973, the only substantial business exchange which still remained between the two firms was in research and development. One of the few visible signs of the American company's European heritage was the Renaissance artwork which M. Bich had hung in BIC's reception and board rooms.

Mr. Robert Adler

In 1955, the day after Connecticut's Naugatuck River raged out of control and flooded the countryside, Mr. Adler reported to work at the old Waterman Pen Company as a newly hired junior accountant fresh out of Pennsylvania's Wharton School of Finance. Instead of being shown to his desk and calculating machine, he was handed a shovel and ordered to help clean out the mud which had collected in the plant during the flood. Nine years later, at the age of 31, he became president of the Waterman-Bic Pen Corporation, which under his leadership became the largest ball point pen manufacturer and distributor in North America.

Mr. Adler was described by a business associate as "a president who liked to be totally familiar with and completely immersed in every area of his company's operations, one who felt that he should never quash his instincts with an over-dependency on numbers and facts alone . . . a shirt-sleeved president who made it his personal concern to know intimately every facet of the BIC marketing and manufacturing process, including highly technical matters involving complex moulding equipment, advanced production techniques, merchandising, advertising, and sales . . . a do-it-yourself investigator-president who regularly made the rounds of the plant, keeping himself available at all times."

Mr. Adler had stated that he personally selected his colleagues on the basis that they demonstrated aggressiveness and an unswerving belief and conviction that they were serving a company that produced the world's finest writing instruments—products of exceptional quality and value. "A businessman is born, not made," he said, "and education can only enhance and refine what already exists." He attributed much of BIC's success to the fact that in the firm's early years he had consciously hired persons who were unfamiliar with the industry and who therefore did not question BIC's ability to succeed by selling an inexpensive ball point pen via extensive advertising. He emphasized the importance of his own role in determining BIC's performance by stating:

> A lot of decisions are easy because there is only one way to go. Sometimes you're lucky and sometimes, no matter what, you'll get the same outcome. A president gets paid to make decisions. That's his big job. What's important is once a decision is made is to make sure that it comes out right. The decision is not so important; it's the outcome. A president must say to himself: "I will now make my decision successful."

WRITING INSTRUMENT PRODUCT LINE

The BIC Pen Corporation manufactured and sold inexpensive writing instruments in a variety of shapes: stick or pocket pen; ink colors, 1–10; point sizes, medium or fine; and retail prices, 19¢–$1. All retractable pens were produced in a pocket pen shape; all nonretractables in a stick shape.

The most successful product, the Crystal, accounted for over 40% of all ball point pen units sold in North America. Its sister product, the 25¢ Fine Point Pen, which differed from the Crystal only in point size, accounted for over 15% of all ball point pen units sold.

In 1973, writing instruments accounted for approximately 90% of BIC's consolidated net sales. Nonretractable pens accounted for 80% of the writing instrument unit sales, retractable pens for 6%, fine line porous point pens for 12% and refills for 2%.

Table 1 presents the 1973 BIC writing instrument product line.

TABLE 1

BIC PEN CORPORATION
1973 Writing Instrument Product Line

Product Name	Ink Colors	Point Sizes	Retail Price
Ball Point Pens			
Nonretractable/Nonrefillable:			
Crystal............................	4	m	$0.19
Fine Point........................	4	f	.25
Reproduction....................	4	m	.25
Eraser.............................	4	m,f	.25
Deluxe Eraser...................	4	m,f	.29
Deluxe.............................	4	m	.39
Accountant.......................	4	f	.49
Retractable/Refillable:			
Clic.................................	4	m,f	0.49
2-Color Pen......................	2	m,f	.69
4-Color Pen......................	4	m,f	.98
Citation...........................	1	m	1.00
Retractable/Nonrefillable:			
Pocket Pen.......................	3	m	0.29
Fine Line Porous Point Pen			
BIC Banana.......................	10	m,f	0.29

Source: Corporate records.

Nonretractable Ball Point Pens

The Crystal, a nonretractable/nonrefillable ball point pen, was introduced on the market in 1959 at a retail price of 29¢. As the first product of the newly formed Waterman-Bic Corporation, the BIC Crystal was intended to become a "brand name replacement for all no-name,[2] disposable pens in a market where no dominant competitor existed." Its retail price was dropped to 19¢ in 1961. In commenting on the success of the Crystal, Mr. Jack Paige, vice president of marketing, remarked:

> We built this company on the 19¢ pen. In 1961 it was selling for 19¢, and in 1973 it is still 19¢. One-third of all retail sales are from the 19¢ stick. It's a highly profitable business. We've found ways to become more efficient and still maintain our profitability.

Between 1961 and 1968, BIC expanded its nonretractable ball point pen line to include six other models of varying point sizes, ink colors, and usages. Nonretractables were priced from 19¢ to 49¢.

Retractable Ball Point Pens

In 1968, BIC introduced its first retractable/refillable ball point pen, the 49¢ Clic.[3] Management felt that the Clic would (1) improve the overall corporate profit margin, (2) enable the company to sell merchandise in multipacks (quantity selling in one package), such as for school specials, and (3) increase distribution—as some retail outlets, particularly those not dependent on BIC for their profits—had been reluctant to sell the 19¢ and 25¢ pens.

Following the Clic, four other retractable ball point pens were added to the BIC product line. Three imported French pens: the 98¢ 4-Color Pen (1971), the 69¢ 2-Color Pen (1972), and $1 Citation Pen (1973) were introduced to "upgrade ball point pen sales." The 29¢ Pocket Pen, the only nonrefillable pen in the retractable line, was added to "expand primary demand for ball point pens."[4]

Fine Line Porous Point Pens

In April of 1972, BIC introduced its first nonball point pen product, the 29¢ BIC Banana, which was a fine line porous point pen produced in a stick shape. Mr. Paige commented on the Banana decision:

> The development of the concept of entering the porous point pen market was not a sudden decision. Our philosophy was simply that as soon as we had a porous point pen that would reflect BIC quality and

---

[2] No-name products were those which were not advertised and were marketed at retail prices far below the comparable, inexpensive, national advertised products.

[3] In retractable pens, industry sales volume in dollars was concentrated in the high-priced products and in units in the no-name brands.

[4] Despite a major introductory campaign ($1.5 million spent on advertising), sales in the Pocket Pen were "disappointing," according to one company spokesman. He attributed the poor results to styling problems and a lack of room for new products in a market with a declining sales growth rate.

could be mass marketed at a popular price that anybody could afford, we would then move into that business.

For openers, we were faced with a couple of major problems. First we were a late entry and the market was dominated by a 49¢ strong brand name of good quality that had a 50% market share. Maybe for some companies that stark statistic would have been enough not to enter. However, at BIC there is an aggressive attitude about marketing. That attitude manifested itself a year and one-half ago when we began plotting our sales course for the introduction of this new product. (BIC spent $3 million on advertising the BIC Banana in 1972.) We took the attitude that we weren't going to be squeezed into that remaining 50% share that the leading brand left for the rest of the field. Our plan was to expand the consumer market for this type of writing instrument—to make it grow. In a larger market, we felt we would have the opportunity to build a franchise that would give us a substantial share.

In reviewing the same product decision, Mr. Alexiades said:

In 1966 we saw the product opportunity for the soft tip pen, but Marcel Bich owned 90% of the company, and we had a difficult time convincing him that this was the right approach. He thought that the soft tip pen was a passing thing and that it was impractical because it wouldn't write through carbon. But we're in a carbon society and there's no logical explanation for the consumer. However, M. Bich's philosophy changed. Years ago, he only wanted to sell ball point pens. He's now interested in inexpensive, disposable, mass-produced items. He has the marketing know-how, the distribution, the name.

We saw that the porous point pen was not a fad so we got in, perhaps a little late, but at least we entered an expanding portion of the market. The growth rate of ball point pen sales had leveled off. If we didn't enter the porous pen market, it would have been difficult to grow since we're so dominant in the industry. We knew that the only way to grow was through product line diversification or acquisition.

Our objective is to become the largest producer of fine line porous point pens. We are in ball point pens. It might be difficult because Gillette's Flair has been there for five years. Papermate brand is not a no-name brand with no resources like those which we initially attacked in the ball point pen market.

A competitor commented on the market entry of the BIC Banana:

Many people associated BIC with the ball point pen. BIC had a difficult time because people thought that the Banana was a ball point. It's a stick shape and looks like a ball point. They don't have that problem with the lighter (1973) because it is a different looking product altogether. BIC hasn't done well with the Banana against the Flair. After all, who could enter the stick pen market now and do well against BIC? But at least BIC broke the price point (49¢) with its 29¢ point which softened the retail and commercial markets. Maybe they'll get smart and get out.

THE MARKETS

Mr. Adler's philosophy had always been "to sell BIC products wherever there was a doorknob." Consistent with that view, marketing efforts had been focused on all writing instrument markets, with special emphasis placed on the "four key sales volume opportunities": the retail, commercial, ad/specialty, and premium markets, which represented about 90% of the dollar sales volume in the writing instrument industry in 1973. The other three markets, government, military, and export, accounted for the remaining 10%. In 1973, the Writing Instrument Manufacturers Association estimated total industry sales at $353.3 million.

Retail Market

The retail market, or over-the-counter market, was the largest mechanical writing instrument market, accounting for over 50%, or $176.6 million, of the total industry dollar sales in 1973. Of significance in the retail market was the growing trend away from indirect selling through retail distributors to independent stores towards direct selling from the manufacturers to mass merchandise outlets.

Since the national success of the 19¢ Crystal pen in 1964, BIC had completely dominated the ball point pen segment of the retail market. By the end of 1973, BIC held a 66% share of that segment, followed by Gillette with 15% and Lindy with 5%. In fine line porous point pens, Gillette was the front runner with a 35% share followed by BIC with 22%, Magic Marker with 8%, and Pentel with 5%.

Management attributed BIC's successful penetration of the retail market to its aggressive marketing and distribution policies, as well as to the low price and high quality of its products.

Commercial Market

The commercial market, or office supply market, was the second largest mechanical writing instrument market, accounting for about 20%, or $70.6 million, of total industry sales in 1973. Selling in the commercial market was primarily handled through commercial distributors, who channeled products from the manufacturers to office supply dealers, who in turn sold to commercial customers. Large office supply dealers bought directly from manufacturers and used distributors to fill in inventory gaps.

At the end of 1973, management estimated that the leading market shareholders in ball point pens in the commercial market were BIC with 50%, followed by Berol with 18%, and Gillette with 5%. In fine line porous point pens, it was estimated that Gillette held a 40% share, Berol 25%, Pentel 10%, and BIC 4.5%.

In commenting on BIC's 4.5% market share in fine line porous point pens, Mr. Adler said:

> We have had difficulty in the commercial market because that market is conditioned to something like the Flair, Pentel, or Berol porous pens which sell for 49¢ and allow good margins to the distributors. The model which BIC manufactures does not compete head on with is the Flair. Ours is a stick model; theirs is a pocket model. Because of the design of the product, it's difficult to get a certain percentage of the market. The Flair product costs twice as much to manufacture (has a clip, etc.). The 29¢ Write-Brothers also has a clip. For us, we're a long way from being Number 1. To get into the porous pen business, we had to use the stick model. Our problem is that the distributors do not want to push the Banana because they have a 49¢ market. Naturally, they make less on a 29¢ model. It will take time.

Advertising/Specialty and Premium Markets

The ad/specialty and premium markets together accounted for approximately 20% or $70.6 million of the total industry dollar sales volume in 1973.

Ad/specialty sales referred to special orders made through specialized distributors for products imprinted with a slogan or organization name. Competition in the ad/specialty market was based heavily on price which accounted for the strength of the no-name brands in that market. BIC held close to a 5% share in the ad/specialty market in 1973.

A "premium" was defined as a free promotional item which was attached to another product in order to promote the sale of that product. Premium sales were made through distributors or direct from the manufacturer to customer. As in the ad/specialty market, competition was based upon price. Unlike in that market, it was also based upon brand recognition and included a broader base of product types, not just writing instruments. Although it was a small market, management considered BIC's participation in the premium market as important in "reinforcing the firm's dominant position in the pen business." BIC held close to a 100% market share among writing instrument firms in the premium market in 1973.

THE COMPETITION

In 1973, approximately 200 firms were engaged in the manufacture and sale of mechanical writing instruments in the United States. Most firms competed selectively in the industry on the basis of (1) product type: fountain pen, mechanical pencil, ball point pen, or soft tip pen; (2) price range: high (>$1), medium ($0.50–$1.00), and low (<$0.50);

and (3) market: retail, commercial, ad/specialty, premium, military, government, and export. Strong advertising programs and mass-distribution networks were considered critical for national success.

In management's view, BIC had four major writing instrument competitors: Berol, Gillette, Lindy, and Pentel.[5] The five firms competed at the following price points with similar products.

TABLE 2

1973 Selected Product Lines

| | | | Gillette | | | |
Product Type	BIC	Berol	Paper-mate	Write-Bros.	Lindy	Pentel
Ball Point Pens						
Retractable:						
Refillable...........	$0.49	$0.29	$0.98	$ —	$1.00	$2.98
	0.69	0.39	1.50			5.00
	0.98	0.49	1.98			7.00
	1.00	0.59	3.95			8.50
		1.49	5.00			
			5.95			
Nonrefillable.......	0.29			0.39		0.79
Nonretractable.......	0.19	0.19		0.19	0.19–	
	0.25	0.25			0.59	
		0.29			(0.20)	
		0.39				
Fine Line						
Porous Point Pens	0.29	0.29	0.49	0.29	0.59	0.29
		0.49	0.98			0.35
			1.95			0.49

Source: Corporate records.

The Berol, Lindy, and Pentel corporations were well known for product innovation. In 1973, the Berol Corporation, best known for its drafting products, particularly for its Eagle brand pencils, was the second firm to introduce the rolling writer combination pen, a pen which performed like a regular fountain pen, yet could write through carbons. Lindy Pen Corporation had earned its reputation as an early entrant into new markets, yet lacked the advertising strength to back the sale of its new products. Lindy introduced a 39¢ stick pen prior to the introduction of the BIC Crystal in 1959, a fine line porous point pen in 1969, and a disposable

---

[5] The Magic Marker Corporation was considered a strong competitor in fine line porous point pens with 4 models selling from $0.19–0.49 and comprising an estimated 8% share of the retail market. However, Magic Marker was best known for its broad tip markers (ten models, from 39¢ to $1.29). Its ball point pen products were sold strictly as no-name brands.

lighter in 1970. Pentel Corporation had earned the reputation of "revolutionizing the U.S. mechanical writing instrument industry" with the introduction of the soft tip pen in 1964 and the rolling writer combination pen in 1969. Like Lindy, it lacked the resources to support heavy advertising and mass distribution programs.

Gillette

The Gillette Company was considered BIC's major competitor in all writing instrument products. The comparative performance in writing instruments for the two firms from 1968–73 is shown in Table 3.

TABLE 3

Comparative Performance in Writing Instruments (consolidated statements)

	1968	1969	1970	1971	1972	1973
BIC						
Net sales ($ millions)	$29.6	$36.6	$37.7	$39.5	$47.6	$52.4
Net income ($ millions)	3.2	4.3	4.0	5.5	6.3	7.3 (est.)
Net income/Sales	10.8%	11.7%	10.6%	13.9%	13.2%	14.0% (est.)
Net sales/Total Assets*	—	—	1.6	1.4	1.3	1.3
Total assets/Total Equity	—	—	1.3	1.2	1.1	1.2
Gillette (Papermate Division)						
Net sales ($ millions)	$33.2	$36.5	$47.0	$51.1	$60.9	$74.5
Net income ($ millions)	2.5	3.3	3.3	2.5	3.0	4.3
Net income/Sales	4.5%	9.0%	7.0%	4.9%	4.9%	5.8%
Net sales/Total Assets*	1.4	1.4	1.3	1.3	1.3	1.3
Total assets/Total Equity	1.8	1.8	1.8	1.9	2.0	2.1

* Estimated total assets allocated to writing instruments.
† Total corporate assets and equity.
Source: Corporate 10-K reports.

In 1973, Gillette competed in the high-price market with its Papermate products and in the low-price market with its Write-Brothers products. The Papermate ball point pens had been the mainstay of its writing instrument business since the early 1950s. In the late 1960s, management at Gillette "recognized the potential of Pentel's new soft tip pens." Backed by a large research and development capability, a well-known corporate name, and advertising and distribution strength, Gillette set out to capture that market with a fine line porous point pen called "Flair," which retailed in three models from 40¢ to $1.95. In 1972 Gillette created the Write-Brothers products: a 39¢ retractable ball point pen, a 29¢ fine line porous point pen, and a 19¢ nonretractable ball point pen, in order "to take advantage of growth opportunities in the low-price end of the mechanical writing instrument market." The Write-Brothers name was selected to prevent confusion on the part of consumers who had associated

TABLE 4
Bi-Monthly Retail Market Share Patterns (units)

	JF '72	MA	MJ	JA	SO	ND	JF '73	MA	MJ	JA	SO	ND
Ball Point Pens												
Total Bic	66%	67%	65%	65%	66%	65%	67%	66%	65%	66%	68%	66%
$0.19 Crystal	36	35	34	33	31	31	32	32	31	31	31	31
.25 Fine Point	12	14	13	13	11	13	13	12	13	13	11	12
.29 Pocket Pen	—	1	2	2	3	3	3	3	3	2	2	2
.49 Accountant	8	7	7	8	9	7	8	7	7	8	10	9
.49 Clic	8	8	7	7	9	8	8	8	7	8	9	7
Other	2	2	2	2	3	3	3	4	3	4	5	5
Total Gillette	8	8	9	13	13	13	13	15	15	14	14	15
$0.19 W-B	—	—	—	3	3	3	4	6	5	5	5	5
.39 W-B	—	—	1	2	2	2	2	2	2	2	2	2
.98 Retractable	4	4	4	4	4	4	4	4	4	4	4	4
Other	4	7	4	4	4	4	3	3	4	3	3	4
Lindy	7	7	8	7	6	7	6	6	6	5	5	5
Other	19	18	18	15	15	15	14	13	14	15	13	14
Total	100%	100	100	100	100	100	100	100	100	100	100	100
Fine Line Porous Point Pens												
BIC	—	—	5	11	15	16	16	19	19	20	23	22
Total Gillette	49	46	45	43	43	40	39	37	36	37	35	35
$0.49 Flair	45	43	41	36	34	33	32	30	30	30	28	29
.49 Hotliner	2	2	1	1	1	1	1	1	1	1	1	1
.29 W-B	—	—	2	5	7	5	5	5	5	5	5	4
Other	2	1	1	1	1	1	1	1	—	1	1	1
Lindy	5	5	4	4	4	4	3	3	2	2	2	2
Magic Marker	—	—	—	—	—	—	6	6	7	8	9	8
Pentel	9	9	9	7	7	7	7	6	6	5	4	5
Other	37	40	37	35	31	33	29	29	30	28	27	28
Total	100%	100%	100%	100%	100%	100%	100%	100%	100%	100%	100%	100%

Source: Corporate records.

the Papermate name with high-priced ball point pen products and middle- to high-priced Flair products.

Retail market share patterns for BIC and Gillette are shown in Table 4. (The BIC Banana was introduced in May of 1972 and the Write-Brothers products in July of 1972.)

Over the five-year period 1969–73, BIC and Gillette made the following advertising expenditures on writing instruments:

TABLE 5

Writing Instrument Advertising Budget Estimates (dollars in millions)

	1969	1970	1971	1972	1973
Gillette............	$1.9	$4.0	$6.0	$8.5	$9.0
BIC...............	3.6	4.0	4.3	7.0	6.8

Source: Case researcher's estimates derived from corporate records, interviews with company officials, and journal articles.

In commenting on advertising programs and the BIC/Gillette competition in general, Mr. David Furman, advertising director at BIC, said:

> Our strategy has been to emphasize profit, and therefore look for the mass market. Gillette has said: "Let's make the most money and not worry about the size of the market." Gillette had a nice profitable business with Flair. It kept Papermate alive. But they can't stay alive with one-dollar-plus pens. We expanded the market so now their unit sales are up. The philosophy of Gillette has been to spend heavily to develop the product, then let the products decay and spend on new product development. Their unit sales continue to go up but their loss of market share is considerable.

COMPANY POLICIES AND STRUCTURE

Mr. Adler had sometimes described his company as a car with four equally important wheels: sales, manufacturing, finance, and advertising, all of which had to be synchronized in order for the car to accelerate and sustain itself at high speed. That car, he claimed, had equal responsibility to its stockholders, employees, and customers. It followed, therefore, that management's attention should be focused on achieving a good return on investment, which Mr. Adler felt was derived by improving: (1) productivity (unit production per hour), (2) efficiency in production (cost savings methods), and (3) quality control standards and checks.

Finance

In the spring of 1971, BIC Pen effected a recapitalization which resulted in an aggregate number of 3.03 million outstanding common shares,

87% of which were owned by Société Bic, S.A., 3% by M. Bich, 9% by Mr. Adler, and 1% by other officers and directors (stock bonuses).[6] On September 15 of that year, 655,000 of those common shares were offered to the public at $25 per share, resulting in a new capital structure of 67% of the shares owned by Société Bic, S.A., 3% by M. Bich, 7% by Mr. Adler, 1% by other officers, and 22% by the public. Proceeds from the public offering after underwriting discounts and commissions amounted to $15.4 million. On July 27, 1972, M. Bich exercised his warrants for the purchase of 210,000 shares of common stock at $25 per share, totaling $5.25 million, which BIC received in cash. That same day, the company declared a 2-for-1 share split in the form of a 100% share dividend of 3.24 million shares, $1 par value, which resulted in the transference of $3.24 million from retained earnings to common stock. At the end of 1972, 6.48 million shares were outstanding of the ten million shares authorized in June of 1972; none of the one million authorized shares of preferred stock had been issued.

Since 1967, the company paid the following cash dividends:

TABLE 6

Bic Pen Corporation Dividend Payment History

	1967	1968	1969	1970	1971	1972	1973
Consolidated net income (dollars in millions)	$2.862	$3.231	$4.233	$4.033	$5.546	$6.264	$7.430
Dividends (dollars in millions)	2.591	—	1.175	1.166	1.319	1.603	1.750
Adjusted net dividend/ share*	0.43	—	0.19	0.19	0.22	0.26	0.27
Stock price range*	—	—	—	—	12¼–18	16¼–37	11⅝–32½

* After giving retroactive effect to a 2-for-1 share split in 1972.
Source: BIC Pen Corporation annual report, 1973.

Regarding dividend policy, Mr. Alexiades said:

> When we were a private firm, there was no dividend policy. Dividends were only given when declared by M. Bich. In 1969 when we knew that we would be going public, we tried to establish a policy, to find the proper relationship between earnings and dividends. 20%–25% of earnings seemed like a good target policy. Now we're having trouble increasing our dividends, due to government guidelines, although we would like to increase the payout in accordance with our rise in earnings.

The purchase of the original BIC plant from the Norden Company in 1963 was financed with a 5¾% mortgage loan from Connecticut General,

---

[6] Four million common shares were authorized.

payable in monthly installments of $7,749 (principal and interest) until January 1, 1981.[7] The three plant expansions—$1 million for 110,000 square feet in 1965, $1.8 million for 100,000 square feet in 1969, and $5–$6 million for 275,000 square feet in 1973—were financed through short-term loans and cash on hand. Regarding the 1973 expansion, Mr. Alexiades said: "We decided to use our own cash so that if something develops in 1974 or 1975, such as an acquisition or new product opportunity, we can always fall back on our credit rating."[8]

In keeping with BIC's informal organizational structure, management used no formalized budgets. "We use goals, not budgets. We just keep surprising ourselves with our performance," said Mr. Alexiades, "although perhaps as we mature, we will need a more structured arrangement."

BIC was known in the New Haven area for its attractive compensation plan. It was Mr. Adler's belief that good people would be attracted by good pay. Plant workers received the highest hourly rates in the area ($4.53 base rate for the average grade level of work). All employees were invited to participate in a stock purchase plan whereby up to 10% of their salaries could be used to purchase stock at a 10% discount from the market price, with BIC assuming the brokerage commission cost. Executives participated in a bonus plan which Mr. Adler described as follows:

> We have a unique bonus system which I'm sure the Harvard Business School would think is crazy. Each year I take a percentage of profits before tax and give 40% to sales, 40% to manufacturing, and 20% to the treasurer to be divided up among executives in each area. Each department head keeps some for himself and gives the rest away. We never want bonuses to be thought of as salaries because they would lose their effect. So we change the bonus day each year so that it always comes as a pleasant surprise, something to look forward to.

Manufacturing

Manufacturing had emphasized the development over the years of a totally integrated, highly automated production process capable of mass producing high-quality units at a very low cost. Except for the metal clips, rings, and plungers, all components—even the ink—were produced in the Milford plant. Société Bic had supplied the basic production technology, machinery, and research and development.[9] Some raw materials, particularly the brass, were still imported from France.

---

[7] The loan had not been paid off by 1973, because of its low interest rate.

[8] BIC borrowed on a seasonal basis to meet working capital needs, using bank lines of credit ($15.5 million available; maximum borrowed was $10.6 million in 1970).

[9] BIC Pen Corporation spent $30,368, $15,254, and $128,553 on R&D in 1971, 1972, and 1973, respectively.

The U.S. energy crisis posed a major threat to BIC inj 1973. Polystyrene, the key raw material used in making pens, was a petroleum-derivative. Mr. Adler commented on the shortage of plastic:

> We've reached a point in our economy where it's become more difficult to produce than sell. I mean I have this big new plant out there [pointing to the new $5–$6 million addition] and I may not be able to produce any products. I have to worry about the overhead. I'm reluctant to substitute materials.
>
> I predict that in 1974 polystyrene will cost more than double what it costs in 1973, which is 15 cents per pound. It represents about ten percent of the manufacturing cost of the ball point stick pen.

The production process consisted of three stages: (1) manufacture of parts, (2) assembly of parts, and (3) packaging. Porous pens (four parts) were the simplest instrument to manufacture followed by ball point pens (seven parts) and lighters (21 parts). Some parts, such as nonretractable pen barrels, were interchangeable, which built flexibility into the production process. Production rates were steady throughout the year, while inventory build-ups were seasonal. In mid-1973 BIC was producing on average about 2.5 million ball point pen units per day and 0.5 million porous pens per day, which was close to plant capacity.

Management felt that production costs were substantially controlled by the strict enforcement of a quality control system. One-fourth of the plant's employees participated in quality control checks at each stage of the production process, which was precision-oriented, involving tolerances as close as $0.0002\pm$. Mr. Charles Matjouranis, director of manufacturing, had stated that it was his job to search for cost-savings programs which would protect profit margins on products. He said:

> We are in the automation business. Because of our large volume, one-tenth of one cent in savings turns out to be enormous. Labor and raw materials costs keep increasing, but we buy supplies in volume and manufacture products in volume. One advantage of the high volume business is that you can get the best equipment and amortize it entirely over a short period of time (four to five months). I'm always looking for new equipment. If I see a cost-savings machine, I can buy it. I'm not constrained by money.

In 1973, there were 700 persons working at BIC in Milford, of which 625 were production personnel represented by the United Rubber Workers Union under a three-year contract. Management considered its relations with employees as excellent and maintained that BIC offered the best hourly rates, fringe benefits, and work environment in the area. Weekly meetings between supervisors and factory workers were held to air grievances. Workers were treated on a first-name basis, and were encouraged to develop pride in their jobs by understanding production technicalities and participating in the quality control program and production shift competition. Most assembly line workers were women. At least 40% of the factory workers had been with BIC for over ten years, and 60%–65% for over five years. Despite increased automation, very few layoffs had occurred because workers were able to be retained for other positions to compensate for the increase in production unit volume. Over 50% of the workers had performed more than one job.

Marketing and Sales

In admiring his BIC ring studded with six diamonds, each representing an achieved sales goal, Mr. Ron Shaw, national sales manager, remarked:

> It's almost a dream story here. When I started with the company in 1961 as an assistant zone manager, we were selling eight million units a year. We now sell 2.5 million units a day. Everyone said that: One, we couldn't sell 5,000 feet of writing in one unit and succeed; two, we couldn't have the biggest sales force in the writing instrument industry and make money; and three, we couldn't advertise a 19-cent pen on TV and make money. Well, we did and we're Number One!

Distribution. The BIC products were sold in the retail and commercial markets by 120 company salesmen who called on approximately 10,000 accounts. Those accounts represented large retailers, such as chains, as well as wholesale distributors. Through those 10,000 accounts, BIC achieved distribution for its products in approximately 200,000 retail outlets, of which 12,000 were commercial supply stores. In addition, the salesmen called on 20,000 independent retail accounts which were considered important in the marketplace. In the case of those accounts, the BIC salesmen merely filled orders for the distributors. A specialized BIC sales force sold ad/specialty orders to ad/specialty distributors and most premium orders directly to corporate customers.

The backbone of BIC's customer business had originally been the mom and pop stores. They had initially resisted selling BIC pens, but were later forced to trade up from the no-name products once BIC had become a popular selling brand. As product distribution patterns moved away from indirect selling towards more direct selling to large chains and discount houses, the mass merchandisers became eager to carry BIC products, which had earned a reputation for fast turnover, heavy advertising support, and brand recognition. In 1973, BIC did 60% of its sales volume through distributors and 40% through direct sales channels.

Pricing Policy. BIC had never raised the original retail prices of any of its products. Management, therefore, placed a great deal of importance on retail price selection and product cost management. Advertising expenses generally ran 15% of the manufacturer's selling price; the combined costs of packaging and distribution approximated 20%–30% of the manufacturer's selling price. The distributor's profit margin was 15% off the listed retail price; the indirect retail buyer's was 40%; and the direct retail buyer's was 55%. Regarding pricing policy, Mr. Adler said:

> If I increase my price, I help my competition. The marketplace, not ourselves, dictates the price. We must see what people are willing to pay. You must sell as cheaply as possible to get the volume.

Customary Marketing Tools.   In a speech made before the Dallas Athletic Club in September of 1972, Mr. Paige remarked: "We're in the *idea* business. Selling is an idea. Many people have products but we have ideas."

BIC used four basic marketing tools to sell its "ideas": (1) advertising, (2) point-of-purchase displays, (3) packaging forms, and (4) trade and consumer promotions. Management felt that the only way to enter a new market was to be innovative either by: (1) introducing a new product, (2) creating a new market segment, or (3) using unique merchandising techniques designed specifically for that market. The BIC salesmen were known to be aggressive.[10] Products were always introduced on a regional roll-out basis with the entry into each new region attempted only after market saturation had been achieved successfully in the prior region.

Advertising was considered the most important element of the BIC marketing program. Company research had shown that seven out of ten writing instruments sold were impulse purchase items. With that knowledge, management felt that widespread distribution of a generic name product line was essential for success. It was further felt that retailers and commercial stationers preferred to carry nationally advertised brands.

BIC used TV advertising, "the cheapest medium when counting heads," almost exclusively. In 1973, BIC added advertising in *T.V. Guide* and the Sunday supplements "in order to reach more women, the biggest purchasers of writing instruments."

In keeping with the belief that merchandising techniques should be designed differently for each product and market, BIC varied its TV commercials substantially, depending upon the intended product usage, time of entry into the market, and demographic interest. Each advertising message was designed to be simple and to communicate *one* idea at a time. Exhibit 4 presents examples of four different themes: (1) BIC has a lighter (BIC Butane); (2) BIC's products are durable (Crystal); (3) BIC has coloring instruments for children (Ink Crayons[11]); and (4) BIC offers a "new and fun way to write" (BIC Banana).

---

[10] On average, assistant zone managers earned $12,000 and zone managers earned $22,000 a year. Compensation consisted of a base salary plus commission.

[11] Ink Crayons consisted of multipack of BIC Banana pens in an array of ink colors.

Another marketing tool was the *point-of-purchase display*. Mr. Paige remarked:

> Mercandise well displayed is half sold, particularly on a low consumer interest item. Displays must be designed to fit every retail requirement because, for example, what's good for Woolworth's may not be good for the corner drug store.

Packaging was considered another form of advertising. "We want to make the 19-cent pen look like a one-dollar pen," Mr. Paige had said. BIC was one of the first firms to use the concept of multipacks. Packaging forms were changed as much as six times a year. Regarding packaging and *promotions*, Mr. Alexiades commented:

> We've created a demand for constant innovation, excitement in the marketplace. Many people say that's the reason for BIC's success. We change the manner in which we sell (blister packs,[12] multipacks, gift packages), which makes our merchandise turn and keeps our name in front of the wholesaler and retailer all of the time. The consumer remembers us because we offer a true value. The retailer and dealer remember us because they receive special incentive offers, free merchandise, and promotional monies, plus their merchandise turns.

Oganizational Structure

Throughout its 15-year history, the BIC organizational structure had remained small and simple. (See Exhibit 5 for the 1973 organizational chart.) In 1973 the average tenure (since 1958) of the six key executive officers was 13 years. At least 40% of the factory workers had been at BIC for over ten years. Several of the managers commented on the BIC environment:

> We try to run this company as a family organization. We don't try to run it as a General Motors. We've been very successful with this concept. It's a closely knit management group—very informal. Decisions are made immediately. A young guy comes here. He sees that we (management) exist. We understand him. He gets his decisions immediately. We try to get him to join the family. Inside of two to three years, if he's not in the family, he won't work out.
>
> Mr. Robert Adler
president

> Part of the success of management is our ability to communicate with one another. We're trying to remain the same. It's one of the regrets that growth has to bring in departments and department heads, but we're trying to maintain a minimum.
>
> Mr. Alexander Alexiades,
Treasurer

---

[12] Blister packs were product packages which were designed to be displayed on peg boards.

EXHIBIT 4

BIC PEN CORPORATION
Television Advertising Themes

BIC BUTANE / BIC CRYSTAL / BIC INK CRAYONS / BIC BANANA

"For $1.49 and thousands of lights, it's a Pretty Good Lighter. BIC Butane."

"Dear BIC . . . You're probably not going to believe this but...."

"You can't write with blueberries, but you can write with a BIC Banana, the new porous tip pen."

"BIC Banana Ink Crayons. In ten bright colors. The only fruit you can draw with."

Source: BIC Pen Corporation annual report, 1972.

EXHIBIT 5

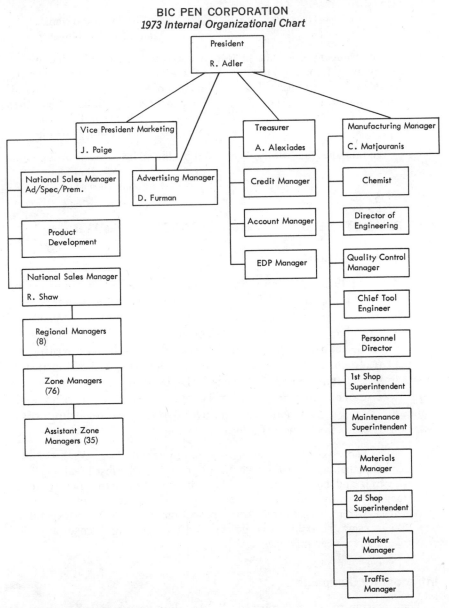

BIC PEN CORPORATION
1973 Internal Organizational Chart

Source: Corporate records.

We have few managers, but the best. One real good one is better than two average.

Mr. Charles Matjouranis,
Manufacturing Director

This company does not believe in assistants. Philosophically, we try to stay away from any bureaucracy. There are no politics involved here, no knifing, no backbiting. Part is a function of size. Everybody knows his place and area of responsibility. We don't want to break from that.

Mr. David Furman,
Advertising Director

We promote from within. We recognize the abilities of our own people.

Mr. Ron Shaw,
National Sales Manager

THE BIC BUTANE DISPOSABLE CIGARETTE LIGHTER

The Lighter Decision

In March of 1973, BIC Pen Corporation introduced its first nonwriting instrument product, the BIC Butane disposable lighter, at a retail price of $1.49. Management viewed the BIC Butane as a logical extension of its current product line as it was inexpensive, disposable, of high quality, and able to be mass-produced and distributed through most writing instrument trade channels, especially retail. It differed from writing instruments in that it required 21 rather than the basic seven assembly parts, more precise manufacturing, and was subject to strict governmental standards. Mr. Furman made the following statement regarding BIC's decision to enter the disposable lighter business:

> For years we were in the high-level, profitability trap. We had had it as far as that market would go. The Banana was the first break out from the trap and now the lighter. We utilize our strengths, but we're no longer a writing instrument company. We're in the expansion stage where writing instruments are a base from which we are expanding. We're using the skills we've gained and are applying them to any kind of mass-produced product.

Introductory Campaign

The decision to sell a disposable lighter dated back to 1971 when M. Marcel Bich purchased Flaminaire, a French lighter company, with the objective of marketing a substitute for matches in Europe. Matches had never been free in Europe, and for that reason disposable lighter sales had been very successful there far before they caught on in the United States. The BIC Butant was imported from Flaminaire, but was scheduled to be produced at the Milford plant on a highly automated production line by March of 1974.

The BIC Butane was introduced first in the Southwest, where management claimed it had captured a 32% retail market share by year's end. Management expected its national retail market share of 16% to rise to 25% when the product reached full national distribution in February of 1974. The regional roll-out was backed with a $1 million advertising campaign. A $3 million campaign was planned for 1974. Lighter sales approximated 10% of BIC's consolidated net sales in 1973. An industry source estimated their pre-tax margin at 15%–21%.

The Cigarette Lighter Industry

Lighters were categorized in three basic product classes: disposables, regular refillables, and electronics. Disposable lighters contained butane gas; electronic lighters contained butane gas or a battery; regular refillable lighters contained either butane gas (90%) or liquid fuel (10%). There were three basic price categories: <$2 (all disposables), $2–$12 (most regular refillables), and >$12 (all electronics and fancy regular refillables). It was estimated that 75%–80% of all cigarette lighters sold in 1972 were priced below $6.95 at retail.

Cigarette lighter sales in the middle price range had begun to fall off in the early 1970s. As a replacement for matches, disposable lighters had expanded the primary demand for lighters and represented the major growth opportunity in the U.S. lighter industry.

TABLE 7

U.S. Cigarette Lighter Retail Sales (dollars and units in millions)

	1969	1970	1971	1972	1973 (est.)
Total lighters ($)..........	$94.9	$98.1	$106.9	$115.0	$153.0
Disposables ($)..........	n.a.*	8.5	18.0	36.0	50.0
Units (#)...............	—	—	13	21	40

* Note: n.a. = not available.
Source: Case researcher's estimates based on trade and company interviews and unpublished figures from the *Drug Topics* magazine research group (1972).

Major Competitors

By 1973 many firms, particularly manufacturers of writing instruments, had entered the disposable lighter business. Most firms served as distributors of foreign-made products, many of which were reputed by trade sources to be of questionable quality. As with writing instruments, BIC's management believed that industry success was heavily dependent on the strength of a firm's advertising program and distribution network, although most firms did well initially due to the excessive demand for disposable lighters relative to the available supply.

There were three clear contenders for industry dominance in the disposable lighter business: Gilette, Garrity Industries, and BIC, with Scripto a distant fourth. Gillette's Cricket lighter was the leading market share holder, accounting for one-third of all disposable lighter sales in 1973.

TABLE 8

1973 Major Competitors in Disposable Lighters

	BIC	Gillette	Garrity	Scripto*
Market entry (year).......	1973	1972	1967	1972
Product...................	BIC Butane	Cricket	Dispoz-a-lite	Catch 98
Price.....................	$1.49	$1.49	$1.49	$0.98
Product produced in......	France (→'73); U.S. (after)	France (→mid '73); Puerto Rico (after)	France	Japan
Ad $ strategy (1973).......	Consumer	Consumer (3/4) Trade (1/4)	Trade	None
Distribution emphasis*....	Mass/chains	Mass/chains	Smoke shops, hotel stands, drug stores	Independent retailers

Source: Casewriter's interviews with corporate marketing managers.
  * In 1974, Scripto planned to raise the price of the Catch 98 to $1.19, add another Japanese disposable lighter at the $1.39 price point, and produce a $1.69 disposable lighter in its Atlanta plant.

In speculating on the future of the BIC Butain lighter, Mr. Paige stated:

> We think that the disposable butane will cannibalize every low-priced lighter. BIC, Dispoz-a-lite and Cricket will do 90% of the business in 1973. Cricket advertises extensively. BIC will compete with Cricket at the $1.49 price point. BIC and Cricket will dominate the industry in the future. The cheaper disposables of lesser quality will only sustain themselves.

3   BIC Pen Corporation (B)

News Release: January 11, 1974

BIC Pen Corporation, which has specialized successfully in mass marketing consumer products, soon will introduce a new product which it will distribute in the $1.3 billion retail pantyhose market, Robert P. Adler, president, disclosed today.

"The sale of pantyhose is for BIC a further expansion into other mass-produced disposable consumer products," Mr. Adler said. "Because of BIC's strong reputation for value, and our ability to merchandise successfully to the consumer through more than 200,000 retail outlets, we believe our new pantyhose product will be well received in this market-place."

THE WOMEN'S HOSIERY INDUSTRY

Hosiery had always been the most rapidly consumable apparel item in a woman's wardrobe. For years the women's hosiery industry had been stable in unit sales and repetitive in product offerings. Many low-profile brands were sold in a wide range of sizes and typical colors. The business "kicked up its heels" in the late 60s with the advent of the convenience product pantyhose and miniskirts. Hosiery became a fashion item, costing as much as $10 a pair, depending upon style, texture, color, and brand name. Prosperity did not last, however, and by 1973 the $2 billion women's hosiery business was characterized as "having to run faster to stay in the same place." The market had become plagued by an uncertainty in consumer demand, sagging profits, price battles, distribution changes, and the rising fashion trend of women's pants. Hosiery

157

TABLE 1

U.S. Women's Hosiery Industry Trends

	1964	*1965*	*1966*	*1967*	*1968*	*1969*	*1970*	*1971*	*1972*	*1973*
Numbers of:										
Companies..............	645	609	576	579	574	530	502	471	457	390
Plants..................	828	782	750	746	741	734	699	665	604	521
Annual per capita consumption:										
Pantyhose............	—	—	—	—	2.3	9.0	13.3	11.0	12.7	11.7
Stockings.............	14.8	15.7	17.3	19.5	18.1	12.7	6.3	4.2	3.1	2.5
Knee-highs, Anklets...............	0.1	0.1	0.1	0.1	0.1	0.1	0.1	0.3	0.6	1.2
Total Consumption	14.9	15.8	17.4	19.6	20.5	21.8	19.7	15.5	16.4	15.5

Source: National Association of Hosiery Manufacturers.

makers claimed that women had begun to go without hose or to wear ripped stockings under pants.

The Pantyhose Market

As an attempt to interject some life into the stable pantyhose market, the three big hosiery makers: Hanes Corporation, Kayser-Roth Corporation, and Burlington Industries, launched an unprecedented $33 million promotional campaign in 1973. They cast aside their established merchandising techniques and began pushing new, low-priced pantyhose in supermarkets. The firms adopted catchy brand names and used dramatic advertising campaigns centering around "trendy" packaging. Their assumption was that women would buy more pantyhose if the products were cheaper, more accessible, and more attractively displayed than before. No longer were branded products available exclusively in department or specialty stores at $3 a pair; rather they could be purchased at every corner market for 99¢ to $1.39. As a result, pantyhose sales in food outlets rose from 5% in 1968 to 28% of the industry pantyhose sales in 1973, with analysts predicting a 50% share by 1975. Despite the surge in supermarket buying, sales of pantyhose declined by 7% in 1973.

The private label business represented 50% of the hosiery sales in food stores in 1973, with some labels selling as low as 39¢ a pair. The supermarket invasion by known brands—"L'eggs" by Hanes, "Activ" by Burlington, and "No-Nonsense" by Kayser-Roth—resulted in a general upgrading in the quality of the private label brands, and an expansion of the branded lines to cover additional market segments, such as pantyhose in large sizes for heavier women, and pantyhose for less than $1 for price-conscious women.

In describing pantyhose purchase behavior, one industry source said:

Generally, all women are interested in quality, price, fit, and availability, but purchasers do tend to fall into three basic categories: (1) women who think that all hosiery is the same and therefore look for the lowest price; (2) women who feel that an extremely low price implies inferior quality; and (3) women who switch off between high and low prices, depending upon their needs.

L'eggs was the largest selling brand name in 1973 with a 9% dollar volume share of the total hosiery market. The idea for L'eggs was born out of the recognition that no high-quality name brand dominated the highly fractionated pantyhose market; nor was one available at a reasonable price (<$2) at convenience locations (supermarkets). The L'eggs integrated marketing program centered around the theme, "Our L'eggs fit your legs," and the distinctive egg-shaped package. The L'eggs direct selling approach leaned heavily on a platoon of 1,000 young delivery women clad in hot pants and traveling their appointed routes in distinctive white vans. Their task was to restock flashy "L'eggs Boutiques" in supermarkets and drug chains. L'eggs retail sales rose from $9 million in 1970 to $110 million in 1973. Hanes spent $20 million on their promotion in 1972 and $13 million in 1973.

Activ and No-Nonsense pantyhose were priced at 99¢ a pair, in contrast with L'eggs at $1.39.[1] Both brands were backed by $10 million promotional campaigns in 1973. The "Activ Girls" competed with the "L'eggs Ladies." Similarly clad and driving red vans, they also sold products on consignment. Besides supermarkets, Activ pantyhose appeared in outlets serviced by tobacco distributors, thus supporting Burlington's motto: "Activs are everywhere." Kayser-Roth shunned the distribution system favored by the other two hosiery makers and delivered its No-Nonsense brand-name pantyhose to food brokers at supermarket warehouses. The No-Nonsense approach—without vans, hot pants, and comely delivery women—allowed the retailers a 45% profit margin, compared with the 35% return guaranteed by Hanes and Burlington.

THE PANTYHOSE DECISION

Mr. David Furman, advertising director, commented on BIC's entry into the pantyhose business:

> The hosiery industry used to be dominated by manufacturing, not marketing, companies. L'eggs was the first attempt to change that. The success of L'eggs and other industry leaders has depended on an extremely expensive direct selling distribution system which is good for large volume outlets but is not feasible for smaller stores or local advertising. BIC intends to use its usual jobbers and make it profitable for them to act as middlemen and garner the independent stores.

---

[1] Hanes introduced First-to-Last pantyhose at 99¢ a pair to counter the price competition from Activ and No-Nonsense pantyhose.

Nearly all companies deal primarily with pantyhose as a fashion item. The market is moving away from the fashion emphasis, which cannot be successful in food stores. BIC will address the fit problem by using the slogan: "It fits there, it fits everywhere"; hence the name—Fannyhose. Ours is a utility story as it was with ball point pens.

In introducing Fannyhose to the trade, management used the theme of "taking a simple idea and making it pay off." The quality product was priced at $1.39, came in two sizes and three colors, and was packaged in a compact little can with a see-through top. The advertising program centered around the "better fit" concept, as was illustrated in animated television commercials and Sunday supplements. Product promotions included cents-off coupons and free samples.

In contrast with its major competitors, BIC planned to act as a distributor of pantyhose, rather than as a manufacturer/distributor, and to establish a specialized sales force to sell the product direct or through distributors to its wide variety of writing instrument retail accounts. BIC's supplier was DIM, S.A., one of France's largest hosiery makers ($100 million in sales), which M. Bich bought control of in 1973. Mr. Furman called the BIC plan "a brilliant stroke around L'eggs. Theirs is a fixed system—low profits, no risk, fixed price. We add promotional profits by passing on to the trade the money we've saved by avoiding the need for our own service crews."

BIC's Investors React

An article appearing in the February 4, 1974, edition of the *Wall Street Journal* described the reaction of the investment community to BIC's entry into the pantyhose business. One analyst cited several obstacles which BIC faced in its new venture, namely: (1) the limited pricing flexibility which BIC would have because of import duty costs[2]; and (2) the fact that BIC had not been particularly strong in supermarkets. Another analyst took a more positive view, citing the recent market price decline in the BIC stock to "investors' questions over the competitive nature of the pantyhose business without understanding the philosophy of BIC: to produce inexpensive disposable consumer products once there is an established market for them and to use its widespread marketing system to become a powerful force in the industry." A third analyst predicted a bright future for BIC in the pantyhose business because of its "access to materials through Société Bic, its reputation for high-quality products, its well-developed distribution system, and its commitment to marketing, rather than to manufacturing, pantyhose."

---

[2] Duty fees averaged 33% per unit. One analyst speculated that the pre-tax margin on Fannyhose was 15%.

4   *Scripto, Inc.*

In January of 1974, Mr. Herbert "Bo" Sams, president of Scripto, Inc., an Atlanta-based mechanical writing instrument and cigarette lighter company, was reviewing the performance of the Atlanta Division which accounted for 64 percent of the firm's total revenues in 1973. Mr. Sams was conducting his review with an awareness of his decision made in 1971 to rebuild Scripto's writing instrument business. Regarding that decision, he had stated:

> Sometimes I wake up at three o'clock in the morning wondering if that was the right decision. Would it have been better to get out of the writing instrument business and consolidate the cigarette lighter operation? All the numbers said to get out of writing instruments, and we were certainly more profitable in lighters. But people had always thought of us as a writing instrument company. They associated the Scripto name with pens and mechanical pencils. Our name was our biggest strength. So we decided to reestablish Scripto as a meaningful factor in the mechanical writing instrument industry.

This case study traces the history of Scripto, Inc., by presidential era from its inception in 1923 through 1973. It focuses on the operations and decision problems of the Atlanta Division which manufactured and/or distributed mechanical pencils, fine line porous point pens, ball point pens, and three types of cigarette lighters, disposable, regular refillable, and electronic, in the domestic and foreign markets. Exhibits 1 and 2 present the consolidated financial statements by presidential era from 1963 to 1973.

EXHIBIT 1

SCRIPTO, INC.
Consolidated Balance Sheets by Presidential Eras

	Carmichael		Singer	
	1963	1964	1965	1966
Net Sales				
Dollars.........................	$26,344,306	$25,237,265	$36,664,054	$33,494,076
Percent........................	100.0%	100.0%	100.0%	100.0%
Cost of goods sold................	54.4	58.8	63.8	57.7
Gross profit......................	45.6	41.2	36.2	42.3
Expenses				
Selling and Administrative.......	32.3	34.4	28.0	30.4
Interest (net)....................	0.4	0.4	0.7	0.4
Other (net)......................	0.9	0.6	0.2	0.8
Profit before tax..................	12.0	5.8	7.3	10.7
Provision for income tax..........	6.2	2.7	3.1	4.9
Net income (loss) before				
extraordinary item..............	5.8	3.1	4.2	5.8
Extraordinary item................	—	—	—	(2.4)*
Net income.................	5.8%	3.1%	4.2%	3.4%
Ratio Analysis				
Net sales/total assets............	1.5	1.5	1.5	1.5
Net income (before extraordi-				
nary items)/total assets.........	8.7	5.7	6.9	8.6
Net income (before				
extraordinary items)/net				
worth..........................	12.4	6.5	12.6	14.3
Depreciation/net sales.............	3.7	3.4	3.3	2.9
Dividend payout...................	51.2	98.0	48.3	41.8
Investment in plant and				
equipment/net sales...........	3.7	5.2	5.7	8.7

* $793,000 lost on discontinued carpet operations.
† Losses: (1) start-up costs for Canadian subsidiary ($264,000); (2) losses on product lines, abandonment of properties.
   Gains: (1) reevaluation of currencies ($55,000); (2) sale of properties ($730,000); (3) tax-loss carryforward credit ($170,000).
‡ Losses: Sale of product lines, abandonment of properties ($105,000).
   Gains: (1) sale of properties ($105,000; (2) tax-loss carryforward credit ($60,000).
§ Gains: Tax-loss carryforward ($89,000).
Source: Scripto, Inc., annual reports.

CORPORATE HISTORY BY PRESIDENTIAL ERAS

Harold Hirsch (1923–39)

Scripto, Inc. was established as a manufacturer of mechanical pencils in Atlanta, Georgia, in 1923. The idea for Scripto was conceived by the then only independent pencil lead manufacturer in the United States, Mr. Monie Ferst, who wanted to prevent the Germans from recapturing the U.S. lead and eraser market which they had held before World War I. Rather than seek government aid to restrict German imports, Mr. Ferst decided to create his own market for leads and erasers by mass producing a quality mechanical pencil which would sell for 25¢ or less and thus

| Ferst | | Harris | | Sams | | |
1967	1968	1969	1970	1971	1972	1973
$30,462,424	$30,914,857	$31,229,304	$31,928,975	$30,979,108	$28,378,819	$31,154,608
100.0%	100.0%	100.0%	100.0%	100.0%	100.0%	100.0%
60.7	65.9	72.1	71.0	72.8	71.2	70.6
39.3	34.1	27.9	29.0	27.2	28.8	29.4
34.0	31.7	32.9	31.9	25.4	25.4	23.1
0.6	0.6	0.8	1.3	1.3	0.9	1.0
0.3	1.3	0.2	—	0.4	0.4	1.4
4.4	0.5	(6.0)	(4.2)	0.1	2.1	3.9
2.1	1.1	(2.2)	(0.8)	1.5	1.5	2.5
2.3	(0.6)	(3.8)	(3.4)	(1.4)	0.6	1.4
—	—	—	—	1.5†	0.2‡	0.3§
2.3%	(0.6%)	(3.8%)	(3.4%)	0.1%	0.8%	1.7%
1.4	1.5	1.3	1.3	1.4	1.5	1.4
3.2	(0.8)	(5.0)	(4.2)	(3.1)	1.0	2.0
5.3	(1.3)	(9.7)	(9.6)	(6.2)	1.6	3.6
3.0	3.0	3.5	2.9	3.1	2.3	2.2
114.0	—	—	—	—	—	—
4.7	3.2	3.1	3.9	2.7	3.2	2.7

appeal to the American mass market.[1] The product earned immediate market acceptance and industry dominance in its product class, although thousands of pencils had to be given away to distributors and retailers initially to overcome the disbelief that a quality mechanical pencil could be produced and sold so inexpensively. Under the leadership of its first president, Mr. Harold Hirsch, Scripto reached its breakeven point in sales in 1930, whereupon the price of the mechanical pencil was dropped from 25¢ to 10¢ and maintained at that level through the War.

Eugene Stern and E. P. Rogers (1940–46)

During World War II, two interim presidents, Mr. Eugene Stern and Mr. E. P. Rogers, managed the firm. Scripto remained a one-product firm relying heavily upon M. A. Ferst, Ltd., Mr. Ferst's company, for its lead

---

[1] Mechanical pencils on the market at the time were only of fair quality and were sold exclusively as gift items priced well over $1.

EXHIBIT 2

SCRIPTO, INC.
Consolidated Balance Sheets by Presidential Eras

	Carmichael		Singer	
	1963	1964	1965	1966
Total assets ($).....................	$17,570,967	$17,168,506	$24,155,764	$22,700,251
Assets (%).........................	100.0%	100.0%	100.0%	100.0%
Current assets:				
Cash............................	5.5	6.0	4.3	5.3
Accounts receivable.............	32.8	29.4	30.0	32.6
Inventory.......................	27.9	27.6	34.3	26.3
Total Current Assets.........	66.2	63.0	68.6	64.2
Property, plant, and equipment....				
(net)...........................	31.1	34.4	29.4	30.0
Investments in affiliates...........	—	—	—	4.2*
Prepaid expenses.................				0.8
	2.7	2.6	2.0	
Other assets......................				0.8
Liabilities (%).....................	100.0%	100.0%	100.0%	100.0%
Current liabilities:				
Notes payable...................	1.7	1.5	8.3	2.2
Accounts payable...............	4.5	6.5	7.5	6.4
Accrued taxes..................	4.0	3.4	3.3	2.7
Accrued liabilities...............	6.0	4.8	4.7	5.6
Total Current Liabilities......	16.2	16.2	23.8	16.9
Long-term debt...................	13.2	11.3	20.8	22.2
Deferred income taxes............	—	—	0.9	1.2
Minority interest..................	—	—	—	—
Stockholders' equity:				
Common stock..................	7.5	7.6	5.7	6.1
Paid-in surplus.................	18.3	18.7	14.4	15.3
Retained earnings..............	44.8	46.0	36.2	40.0
(Treasury stock)................	—	—	(1.8)	(1.7)

* Acquisition of Modern Carpet Industries, pooling of interests.
† 7½% cumulative preferred stock issued by the Irish subsidiary to a bank ($316,000).
‡ Joint ventures between: (1) Wilkinson Sword and Scripto, Inc., in Scripto (Eng), Ltd., and Scripto Industries (Shannon, Ireland), Ltd.; and (2) Scripto, Inc., and Scripto de Mexico.
Source: Scripto, Inc., annual reports.

and eraser supply. The manufacture of mechanical pencils was halted only temporarily during the war when Scripto adapted its precision manufacturing operation to the production of ordnance materials for the U.S. government.

James Carmichael (1947–63)

In 1947, Mr. Jimmy Carmichael, following an unsuccessful bid for the Georgia governorship against Mr. Eugene Talmadge, was selected by Mr. Ferst as the new president of Scripto, Inc. His stated objectives were twofold: (1) to develop Scripto into a full-line mechanical writing instrument manufacturing firm, and (2) to make Scripto the largest manu-

Ferst		Harris		Sams		
1967	1968	1969	1970	1971	1972	1973
$22,556,707	$21,180,588	$23,428,666	$25,210,155	$22,295,681	$18,946,674	$21,705,004
100.0%	100.0%	100.0%	100.0%	100.0%	100.0%	100.0%
5.5	6.4	4.3	8.6	5.7	5.0	2.0
26.7	27.1	31.5	27.6	30.7	31.2	30.9
30.6	28.3	31.3	31.5	29.1	28.8	37.8
62.8	61.8	67.1	67.7	67.6	65.0	70.7
31.4	31.4	27.1	25.8	24.5	22.9	22.0
3.2	5.5	4.2	4.1	4.4	8.5‡	5.5
1.5	0.7	0.7	1.1	1.2	1.0	1.4
1.1	0.6	0.9	1.3	4.4	2.6	0.4
100.0%	100.0%	100.0%	100.0%	100.0%	100.0%	100.0%
5.5	2.8	14.8	23.4	15.0	16.1	23.7
6.0	6.6	8.3	9.2	8.3	3.9	7.6
1.9	1.0					
		6.3	7.2	9.7	9.8	8.0
4.7	5.0					
18.1	15.4	29.4	39.8	38.0	29.8	39.3
20.7	20.2	16.9	14.0	14.1	8.3	4.5
1.5	1.7	1.5	0.3	1.0	1.2	0.8
—	—	—	1.2†	1.4	—	—
6.1	6.5	6.1	5.6	6.5	7.6	6.7
15.4	16.4	15.3	14.2	16.6	19.2	17.0
39.9	41.6	32.6	26.0	29.5	36.0	33.8
(1.7)	(1.8)	(1.8)	(1.1)	(2.1)	(2.1)	(2.1)

facturer of mechanical writing instruments in the world. Over his 17 years as president, Scripto in fact achieved the first objective, but not the second.

A Full Line of Mechanical Writing Instruments.   Mr. Carmichael's principal objective was to expand the Scripto product line by adding other mechanical writing instruments. His first step was to take advantage of the demand in the U.S. market for the new ball point pen which had been introduced by Reynolds in 1946 at a retail price of $15. As it had successfully done with the mechanical pencil, Scripto set out to prove that a quality ball point pen could be produced and sold inexpensively. The ball point pen was introduced on the market in 1947 at a retail price of 25¢ and, like the mechanical pencil, earned immediate market acceptance.

By 1952, Scripto was known as a full-line writing instrument manufacturer in the low price market. Fountain pens had been introduced at retail prices of $1.00 and $3.50; the ball point pen line was expanded to include models retailing at $0.29, $0.39, and $1.00; a $1.00 mechanical pencil was added, as well as a matching fountain pen and pencil set retailing for $5.00. All products were supported by heavy consumer advertising and dealer promotion programs.

Cigarette Lighters: A New Business.   In 1957 Scripto introduced its first nonwriting instrument product, a naphtha fuel lighter called the "Vu-lighter" which derived its name from the fact that its liquid fuel supply was visible. Although it was well known that Mr. Ferst, founder of Scripto and then chairman of the board, had always wanted to add a cigarette lighter to the product line, Scripto had not been consciously seeking product line diversification into nonwriting instruments. Rather, it came across an available opportunity in 1954 to rescue a small cigarette lighter firm in Missouri which was experiencing production and quality control problems. At the time, Scripto was selling its writing instrument products exclusively to the retail and ad/specialty markets, both of which were well suited for the distribution of the Vu-lighter because the same sales force and distributors could be used. The company was purchased in 1954 for a nominal price. The lighter was subsequently redesigned at an investment of $1 million and then reintroduced on the market in 1957 selling at $3.95 for the regular size; and in 1960, $4.50 and $5.00 for the compact models.

International Expansion.   Mr. Carmichael's second objective was to develop Scripto, Inc., into the largest mechanical writing instrument manufacturing firm in the world. In the early 1950s, he felt that the growth of Scripto's business outside of the United States was being curtailed by high tariffs imposed on U.S.-made products and a shortage of dollars abroad. He concluded, therefore, that owning and operating manufacturing subsidiaries abroad was more desirable than exporting American-made products to foreign countries. In 1957 Scripto was reorganized into a corporate group, which managed all domestic and foreign subsidiaries, and a domestic group, which managed the Atlantic operation. By the time that Mr. Carmichael resigned for health reasons in 1963, Scripto had either established or purchased foreign operations in Canada (1950), the United Kingdom (1955), Southern Rhodesia (1955), Australia (1957), Mexico (1959), New Zealand (1959), and Colombia (1959). All were 100%–owned by Scripto with the exception of Colombia, which became a licensing agreement. The purchases and operation of the foreign subsidiaries were funded in three ways: through internally generated funds, long-term debt, and a $2.5 million common stock issue in 1956 at $7.00 per share.

Scripto's Response to a Changing Market.   In 1957 domestic sales began to slip for the first time in Scripto's history. Mr. Carmichael attributed the performance setback to two factors: (1) an oncoming recession in the United States, and (2) the gradual shift from an overdemand to an oversupply of products in the mechanical writing instrument market. From that year on to the end of his presidential term (1963), Mr. Carmichael responded to the squeeze on Scripto's profit margins by:

—implementing a stringent across-the-board cost-cutting program;
—upgrading the Scripto product line to higher-priced writing instruments (>$1) with the objective of eventual dominance in the higher-priced gift item field. (Ball pens retailing at $1.98 and $2.95 were added plus an innovative Tilt-tip pen ($1.95) which featured accurate performance when held at any angle);
—acquiring three domestic subsidiaries (Burnham Products Corporation, Broadway Pen Corporation, and Austin Metal Products, Inc.) in 1959 in order to strengthen Scripto's position in the advertising/specialty market where very inexpensive, unbranded pens were sold;
—revamping the foreign manufacturing operations, particularly in the United Kingdom, with the objective of improving Scripto's competitive position in the Common Market countries where the price war had become even more severe than in the United States;
—making heavy expenditures in the research and development of new markets and products.

During Mr. Carmichael's final six years at Scripto, the firm's market share in writing instruments slipped from 16 percent (ranked second to Paper Mate) to less than ten percent (ranked fifth behind Paper Mate, Waterman–BIC, Parker Pen, and Sheaffer). Performance results were:

TABLE 1

SCRIPTO, INC.
Financial Performance (1958–63)
(dollars in thousands)

	1958	1959	1960	1961	1962	1963
Consolidated net sales.......	$22,369	$23,106	$21,001	$21,156	$25,750	$26,344
Consolidated PAT...........	1,433	1,080	653	1,150	1,706	1,536
PAT/sales (%)...............	6.5%	4.7%	3.1%	5.4%	6.6%	5.8%

Source: Scripto, Inc., annual reports, 1958–63.

Mr. Carmichael retired in 1963. Despite his own assessment of the factors affecting Scripto's performance during his final years, some company officials believed that those factors were not entirely of external origin. Both Mr. Ferst and Mr. Carmichael had had serious health problems. Mr. Carmichael had been seriously injured in a car accident in his early teens and had been on crutches or in a wheel chair ever since. Scripto had assumed the cost of his medical expenses. In addition to his disability, Mr. Carmichael had held many civic obligations which kept him away from the day-to-day operation of the company. In an article appearing in *Business Week* magazine, one company executive remarked:

> The most dangerous time in a company's existence is when things are going well. Lax habits and bad decision-making are hidden by the success of the moment. Jimmy (Carmichael) was paternalistic, so that jobs that were poorly done and decisions that were poorly made tended to be overlooked and condoned. What happened was that an organization was allowed to build up over a period of years that was lax in work habits and in accepting the necessity of getting the job done.[2]

Carl Singer (September 1964–July 1967)

In September of 1964, Mr. Carl Singer, former president of the Chicago-based Sealy Mattress Company, became president of Scripto, Inc. Found by an executive search firm and representing the first top management change at Scripto in 17 years, Mr. Singer was described by his colleagues as "a man of action from a marketing background who saw Scripto's problems with a sense of urgency." Assessing the morale at Scripto as very low, Mr. Singer described his task as one of "complete changeover and repositioning," which he planned to carry out in two stages: Stage I was to focus on cost-cutting measures to improve profit margins which had been Mr. Carmichael's objective; and Stage II was to focus on revenue-generating activities, primarily in foreign markets.

Stage I: Cost-Cutting (1964–66). Mr. Singer felt that Scripto's most immediate problem was the inadequacy of its production facilities. The decline in profit margins, he felt, underscored the need to trim costs by modernizing manufacturing facilities, both in Atlanta and overseas. Scripto's Atlanta plant had fallen into a state of disrepair. A plan was developed to rehabilitate the existing manufacturing facilities (a group of three-story buildings near downtown Atlanta) as well as to build a new plant on newly acquired land outside of Atlanta which would double production capacity. Production improvements were also made on existing facilities in Mexico, Canada, and the United Kingdom, as it was Mr. Singer's objective to continue the worldwide expansion envisioned by Mr. Ferst, Scripto's founder, who had died in 1965.

In 1965, $2.1 million was spent on plant and equipment improvements, and in 1966, another $2.9 million. To finance the improvements and to provide additional working capital, Mr. Singer negotiated a $5 million, 15-year loan at 5.45 percent interest with the Metropolitan Life Insurance Company. A portion of the proceeds was used to retire a $2.3 million balance in previous long-term Metropolitan loans. The new agreement

---

[2] "Rewriting the Script for Scripto," *Business Week*, December 17, 1966, p. 171.

allowed Scripto to take revolving short-term bank loans, providing the total did not exceed $2 million in any 60-day period each year.

A second problem which Mr. Singer faced was how to deal with the low morale of Scripto's employees. He increased the size of the total employee work force from 2,500 to 2,900 to prepare for the expected increase in unit production in Atlanta; he drew the control of subsidiary operations more closely to management in the Atlanta division; and he made substantial reassignments and redefined responsibilities at the top-management level. As the result of a six-week labor dispute, factory workers became unionized (International Chemical Workers Union), much to the opposition of a number of Scripto's managers, some of whom subsequently resigned or were replaced.

In keeping with his "repositioning" theme, Mr. Singer took steps during Stage I to move Scripto in two product directions: (1) to higher-priced writing instruments, and (2) to wholly new product areas unrelated to writing instruments. This objective was to increase profit margins and to lessen the risk of concentration in one or two industries. At the time when Mr. Singer became president of Scripto, the company was in the process of installing highly automated equipment in its manufacturing facilities, which would enable high volume production of low-priced products. Mr. Singer reversed that process in the belief that "low margin products were uneconomical to produce and sell." He began phasing out products such as inexpensive ball point pens and fountain pens. Two "dramatically new" product lines were introduced: (1) butane (gas) lighters retailing at $4.95, and (2) fiber tip pens retailing at $0.39.

Aside from the move to higher-priced writing instruments and lighters, Mr. Singer set in gear a large-scale product diversification program which he carried out either through internally generated research and development or through company acquisitions. Three new products were under internal development: a thermo-fax copier machine, a wide-angle lens camera, and a special butane lighter ("Vu-tane"). The copier machine was intended to gain a better foothold in the commercial (office supply) market where Scripto's sales had been practically nonexistent. The copier made transparencies to be used as audio-visual aids and was to be marketed at a retail price of $250 by a separate sales force through a separate distribution network (A. B. Dick and Heyer Corporation). The wide-angle lens camera was a personal research interest of a long-time Scripto employee, for which he had received between $1–$1.5 million in R & D funds. While no suitable direct application had been found during the lengthy time of its development, management believed that the camera would be of interest to the U.S. military in reconnaissance missions or for underwater photography. The Vu-tane lighter was to become Scripto's first entry into the plastic-encased butane lighter field at a price point of well under $5.

Two acquisitions were made during Stage I. In 1965, Scripto issued 143,000 shares of its stock in exchange for all of the stock of Modern Carpet Industries, a leading privately owned carpet manufacturing firm. The carpet line was compatible with Mr. Singer's background in home furnishings, and he was attracted by "its outstanding organization and position in the fast-growing tufted carpet industry, which was considered to be the most volatile segment of the multibillion home furnishings field." Following the acquisition, management devoted a great deal of time and money to enlarging, modernizing, and adding equipment to MCI. The second acquisition was Florence Ceramics Company, a Pasadena-based firm which produced imprinted ceramic products, such as ash trays. Mr. Singer described the ceramic products "as naturals for Scripto's retail outlets and ad/specialty activities."

Stage II: Revenue Generation (1966–67). Mr. Singer's master "repositioning" plan proved a little too grandiose, and Stage II, which dealt with his long-range objective of revenue growth, hardly met with implementation before his departure from Scripto in July of 1967. During his final months with the firm, Mr. Singer continued to introduce higher-priced writing instruments ($1.00 and $1.95 ball point pens and a $1.00 refillable fiber tip pen) as he had intended, but his visions for the production area and his favorite project, Modern Carpet Industries, fell flat. Construction was delayed on the new Atlanta plant "for economic reasons." MCI was sold in 1966 because "it no longer fit into the re-defined long-range growth projections for Scripto."[3] The employee base was reduced in number from 2,900 to 2,700.

Robert H. Ferst (August 1967–March 1968)

In August of 1967, Mr. Robert Ferst, president of M. A. Ferst, Scripto's graphite and eraser subsidiary, replaced Mr. Singer as an interim president of Scripto, Inc. Company sales revenues had slumped to $30.46 million by the end of that year, returning $716,000 in net profits. Mr. Ferst attributed the poor performance to necessary write-offs of obsolete and excess inventories which had accumulated because of major product changeovers, as well as to currency devaluations on foreign markets.

While only at the helm for eight months, Mr. Ferst saw his mission as twofold: (1) to continue the cost-cutting program which dated back to the Carmichael days, and (2) to focus his attention on marketing the Scripto products aggressively, with specific aim at consumer acceptance, an area which he felt had been neglected over the years. New systems of inventory controls were implemented. Drastic cost-control measures were enforced. Dividend payments were halted for the first time since Scripto's

---

[3] Scripto retained a 35 percent investment in the acquiring company, Modern Carpet Mills, Inc. The sale represented a $793,000 loss to Scripto, Inc.

public offering in 1956, in order to conserve working capital for development and promotion of new and diversified products. Plans to proceed on the construction of a new Atlanta plant were again postponed. Higher-priced butane lighters ($7.95–$16.95) were added to the cigarette lighter product line to follow the continuing emphasis on higher-priced products with sizeable profit margins. Independent design consultants were employed to restyle all products as an attempt to attract new consumers, particularly the younger generation and the adult gift buyers. Mr. Ferst resigned in March of 1968. *too much emphasis on high priced products*

Arthur Harris (April 1968–March 1971)

In April of 1968, Mr. Arthur Harris signed a five-year contract to become president of Scripto, Inc., with the option to terminate after three years. Mr. Harris came to Scripto from the Mead Paper Company where he had been head of its packaging division for many years. He was a fellow Atlantan and personal friend of the Ferst family who owned approximately 43 percent of the Scripto stock and controlled the executive committee of Scripto's board of directors.

Mr. Harris' three-year term as head of Scripto was characterized by change on all fronts: in organizational structure, international activities, maketing and sales programs, and product policies, with the overall objective "to reposition Scripto at the point-of-sale." One Scripto executive described Mr. Harris as "brilliant, strong-willed, and even dictatorial" in his attempt to turn the company around.

should not make every program a new one and never reduce change

1968: Corporate Overhaul. In 1968, Mr. Harris introduced substantial changes is the areas of: (1) corporate organization, (2) marketing programs, and (3) product policies. His first step involved a complete overhaul of both domestic and foreign organizations. In Atlanta, he reassigned existing personnel and added new personnel to develop second echelon depth. Attempts were made to revitalize foreign subsidiaries: in Mexico, new top management was added; in Canada, top management was also changed as well as the entire organizational structure; and in the United Kingdom, plans were made to relocate the plant in Ireland. A second step was to revamp marketing and sales programs which involved:

Complete realignment of sales territories in the United States.

Implementation of a new incentive method of compensation.

Installation of a sophisticated electronic data system for market research and forecasting.

Introduction of a new advertising scheme to tie merchandising more closely to point-of-purchase displays.

Addition of a special detail sales force at the retail level.

Development of an entirely new approach to marketing for the subsidiaries in South Africa, Rhodesia, New Zealand, and Modern Carpet Mills, Inc.

The third step was to "reevaluate all Scripto products." Many old products reappeared in new designs and colors. Three new products: the thermal copier, wide-angle lens camera, and Vu-tane lighter, all of which had been under development since 1964, were given deadlines for launching. A network of distributors and dealers was formed to sell the copier, an appropriate market for the wide-angle lens camera was still being sought, and the Vu-tane lighter was scheduled to be introduced on the market in 1969.

Despite his efforts, Scripto reported a net loss of $173,000 in 1968 based on net sales of $30.915 million. Mr. Harris summed up the performance results by calling the year one of "evaluation and appraisal." He attributed the losses to tax-loss carrybacks which could no longer be applied for tax purposes against foreign losses ($364,000 in 1968) as well as to inventory write-offs.[4]

1969: A Wave of New Products. Mr. Harris looked to 1969 as a year to "capitalize on conclusions drawn in 1968 and to continue to reposition Scripto at the point-of-sale." However, despite an increase in sales revenues to $31.2 million, Scripto reported an even greater net loss ($1.183 million) than the year before. Management attributed the losses to the costs and expenses related to the introduction of new products and the elimination of other products, all of which exceeded $1.6 million before tax credits. In that year, the Vu-tane lighter ($3.95), Scripto-fax copier ($250), a thin line mechanical pencil (49¢) and fiber tip ink crayons (in England), along with many new packages, particularly blister cards,[5] were introduced. In a letter to stockholders, Mr. Harris emphasized the importance of "keeping Scripto's identity as the only nationally advertised company with a *complete* line of writing instruments to meet almost any writing need in price ranges to fit anyone's budget."

Scripto acquired the Butane Match Corporation of America in 1969, which added a 98¢ refillable butane lighter ("Butane Match") to its product line. The net assets of BMC were acquired in a pooling of interests transaction for an exchange of 66,000 shares of restricted Scripto stock at $1.23 per share for accounting purposes, and an additional 62,500 shares contingent upon BMC's future earnings.

In contrast to his predecessors, Mr. Harris began to shift the corporate focus in 1969 from international activities to those centered around the U.S. operation. The Mexican operation, upon its reorganization in 1968,

---

[4] Inventories were reduced by approximately $900,000 during that year.

[5] Blister cards were product packages which could be hung on a peg board for display purposes, and were designed to protect the retailer against pilferage.

was turned into a joint venture with Novaro, publishers of *Time* magazine in Mexico. The South African and Rhodesian operations were turned into licensing agreements, and the English plant was moved to Ireland where its operations would be free from British taxation.

1970: Demise of a Vision. Mr. Harris' third and final year at Scripto, Inc., again produced a substantial earnings loss ($1.075 million) to the condition of the economy and to heavy advertising and promotion commitments. Sales of the Scripto copier were minimal, and Florence Ceramics once again proved unprofitable. Renewed plans to relocate the Atlanta facilities were again termed financially infeasible and were finally abandoned. Scripto exchanged its 35 percent common stock investment and all previous advances to Modern Carpet Mills, Inc., for convertible preferred stock ($436,000 liquidation preference) in a newly formed parent company, Modern Holdings, Inc., and for an unsecured note receivable ($464,000) payable over five years. The New Zealand subsidiary was turned into a licensing arrangement.

Mr. Harris resigned in March of 1971. In his statement to stockholders, he remarked that he had met his principal objectives—"to form an aggressive and capable management team, eliminate unnecessary costs, and streamline operations in general." His future intention was to reside in Europe and spend a portion of his time as a special consultant to Scripto on the sale of Scripto products in the Common Market countries and on new product development.

Herbert "Bo" Sams (April 1971———)

On April 1, 1971, Mr. Herbert "Bo" Sams was elevated to the presidency of Scripto, Inc., from the position of vice president and general manager of the Atlanta division which he had held since 1969. A veteran of Scripto for 35 years, most time of which was spent in the manufacturing area, Mr. Sams had known Scripto in its heyday as well as at the depths of poor performance.[6] It was at the latter point that he found himself in 1971. With that recognition, he set out to rebuild a company which had digressed far from its original business at the expense of an overall declining market share in writing instruments and fluctuating operating results.

Mr. Sams envisioned his mission as twofold: (1) to stop the company-wide losses which implied a "disciplined" approach to cost cutting in the European, Atlanta, and Canadian operations, and (2) to develop a long-range plan for the Atlanta division which would clearly define the corporate business and eliminate those products and activities which were

---

[6] Mr. Sams had worked at Scripto, Inc., during his college days and had joined the firm upon his graduation from Georgia Institute of Technology in textile engineering in 1936.

not consistent with that plan. It was the latter decision which, in part, was unclear to "Bo" Sams. He considered two courses of action: (1) to abandon the writing instrument business altogether, and rebuild Scripto–Atlanta solely as a cigarette lighter company, or (2) to reestablish Scripto–Atlanta as a viable competitor in the U.S. writing instrument business, as well as to continue in cigarette lighters. He chose the latter.

Stage I: A Short-Range Profitability Plan

In the 1970 annual report, Mr. Sams named profitability as his immediate goal, with special attention to be given to the three greatest loss-producing areas: the Atlanta division and the Canadian and English subsidiaries.

Atlanta Division. When Mr. Sams became general manager of the Atlanta division in 1969, the division had reported a net loss of $1.5–$2.0 million for that year.[7] Mr. John Tucker, vice president of finance,[8] assessed the problems in Atlanta:

> Scripto's performance in the early 1970s could not be blamed upon current decisions because it had its roots a decade before. The company had felt that the writing instrument market was locked up in the United States so we had decided to look elsewhere. We had illusions of grandeur which marked the beginning of problems because the U.S. market had not been developed properly. BIC came along and Scripto's attitude was to laugh. Whoever thought that people would buy such a cheap and ugly stick pen? So we chose to go international and later learned that we were not powerful enough. All that time, the Atlanta Division was neglected. The company grew fat with people, and sales did not justify the advertising dollars spent. We didn't have the marketing capability to see if our products were right. And it seemed that every time there were problems, we cut out our research effort and capital expenditures program.

To eliminate the losses in Atlanta, Mr. Sams outlined a six-point program aimed at creating "a leaner organization with a new disciplined approach to marketing." His objectives were:

To build an aggressive, sound, and talented management team (see Exhibit 5).

To eliminate several unprofitable product variations.

To place a new emphasis on accurate sales forecasting.

To orient Scripto's market research towards better identification of consumer needs.

To improve the computerized accounting procedures to give faster, more accurate accounting and better inventory control.

---

[7] The Atlanta Division reported a $404,925 before-tax loss in 1972.

[8] Mr. Tucker was described by a colleague as "Mr. Sams' right-hand man. He adds front office continuity to the team."

To reduce costs by lowering overhead and streamlining the manufacturing process.

Canada and the United Kingdom. Aside from the Atlanta division, the Canadian and British operations represented the major sources of losses to Scripto in the late 1960s. Over the five-year period 1966–71, the Canadian operation produced roughly $500,000 in cumulative net losses. In 1972, Scripto entered a business partnership with the John A. Huston Company in Canada, in which the latter contracted to manufacture and market Scripto products while Scripto, Inc., supplied component parts and the Scripto name. The Canadian operation broke even in 1972 on revenues of $600,000 and was expected to break even again in 1973.

The British operation faced a crunch in 1970. Scripto sold its run-down English plant and moved its facilities to Ireland where income from operations was tax free and government grants were readily available for equipment purchases. Despite those benefits, however, the English skilled labor refused to move to Ireland. The subsidiary reported a $1 million net loss in 1971. In 1972, Scripto, Inc., sold 55 percent of its equity in Scripto Pens, Ltd. (England), and Scripto Industries (Shannon), Ltd., to Wilkinson Sword, Ltd., for which it received $1.1 million and the option to return to a 50–50 deal after five years. Scripto, Inc., continued to supervise the British manufacturing operation while Wilkinson assumed the

EXHIBIT 3

SCRIPTO, INC ·
Consolidated Income Statement

	1973	1972
Income:		
Net sales..	$31,154,608	$28,378,819
Costs and Expenses:		
Cost of sales...	22,006,870	20,192,819
Selling and administrative expenses....................	7,202,628	7,004,770
Interest expense, net..................................	301,075	241,562
Equity in loss of foreign companies.....................	192,267	157,971
Provision for losses on investments and long-term		
notes receivable.....................................	219,751	200,000
Other (income) expense, net...........................	19,441	(18,943)
	29,942,032	27,777,653
Income before income taxes and extra-ordinary items.....	1,212,576	601,160
Provision for income taxes..............................	779,000	420,000
Income before extraordinary items......................	433,576	181,166
Extraordinary items, net of applicable income taxes.......	89,648	58,301
Net income...	$ 523,224	$ 239,467
Per Share:		
Income before extraordinary items......................	$0.15	$0.06
Extraordinary items...................................	0.03	0.02
Net Income...	$0.18	$0.08

Source: Scripto, Inc., annual report, 1973.

marketing responsibility. By year's end, the British operation had cut its net losses to $0.5 million; in 1973, to $175,000, and a small profit was predicted for 1974.

Butane Match Corporation of America. In 1972, Scripto, Inc., arranged to sell the business of its wholly owned subsidiary, Butane Match Corporation of America, and certain related patent rights. Contrary to management's expectations, sales of the 98¢ refillable butane lighter ($644,000 in 1972) had been minimal. Due to the buyer's subsequent inability to meet the financial requirements of the sale, Scripto chose to reacquire Butane Match in September of 1973.

Atlanta Property. During 1971, the holder of the 5.45 percent long-term note agreed to purchase Scripto's undeveloped property in Atlanta for a specified amount, subject to a third party's option to acquire the property at a higher price. The sale was recorded in 1971, and an extraordinary gain of $407,000, net of applicable income taxes, was included. In 1972 the third party exercised its option to purchase the property; an additional $104,768 net gain was included in the 1972 extraordinary item.

Further Eliminations. In 1971, Scripto sold its ceramic products firm, the French operation, and the thermal copier product rights, whose combined contribution to profits had been only marginal. The decline of $1 million in sales revenues for that year was attributed to the elimination of those three revenue-generating activities, as well as to limited production at the new Irish plant facility.

Stage II: A Return to the Basic Business in Atlanta

Management shifted its attention and allocation of resources in 1972 to the task of achieving its long-range objective: the realization of prominence by Scripto in the U.S. mechanical writing instrument industry. Over the previous 15 years and five presidential terms, profitability achieved through cost reduction, particularly in the manufacturing operation, had been the primary concern. The new focus in 1972 became the generation of revenues through the use of aggressive marketing programs, and product line positioning, in the fastest-growth segments of the writing instrument and lighter industries.

Product Line. In 1973, management described Scripto, Inc., as "a full-line manufacturing company in mechanical writing instruments and cigarette lighters." The company reported 0.62 percent of the industry's dollar sales in ball point pens, 0.34 percent in markers, 13.2 percent in mechanical pencils, 2.4 percent in porous point pens, and 10.7 percent in cigarette lighters. Table 2 presents the major consumer products which were manufactured and/or distributed by the Atlanta division from 1965–1973. Exhibit 4 presents a sales breakdown by product line in the Atlanta division from 1965–1973.

TABLE 2

Atlanta Division
1973 Major Consumer Product Line*

	Price	No. of Models	Production Location	Production Capacity (millions of units/year)	1973 Production Rate (Percent capacity)
Writing Instruments					
Ball point pens					
Retractable............	$0.39, $0.98	2	Atlanta	15	28
Nonretractable					
(nonrefillables).......	0.19, 0.25	2	Burnham	>50	60–70
Porous point pens........	0.19, 0.49	6	Atlanta	40–50	About 100%
Mechanical pencils					
Regular................	0.39, 0.49, 1.29	5	Atlanta	25	75
Marking...............	0.49	2	Atlanta	15–20	75
Cigarette Lighters					
Disposables (butane).....	0.98	1	Japan	Purchased	—
Regular refillables					
Butane................	0.98	1	Butane Match	4.5	50
	3.95–14.95	10	Atlanta	6	90
Naphtha...............	4.95, 5.95	2	Atlanta	6–7	100
Electronic..............	17.95–29.95	10	Japan	Purchased	—

* Ball point pen refills, leads, erasers, lighter fuel, and no-name brand pens were manufactured and distributed by other U.S. subsidiaries.

Mechanical Writing Instruments. In 1972, Scripto introduced two inexpensive writing instruments: the 19¢ "Superpen" (a stick model ball point pen), and the "19¢er" (a disposable fiber tip pen). It was management's hope that the Superpen would provide a reentry point for Scripto in the commercial market and that the 19¢er, as a price competitor and quality instrument, would revitalize Scripto's overall position in the mechanical writing instrument industry. Scripto's competitive action was explained in an article appearing in *Distribution Executive,* as follows[9]:

> Scripto, Inc., back in the black last year after three years in the red, is taking an aggressive new posture in writing instruments to increase its profitability.
>
> The Atlanta-based manufacturer, always a factor in writing instruments, has for some time given primary emphasis to its cigarette lighters.
>
> "With the growth of our lighter business, which is substantial, we tended to neglect our writing instruments somewhat," says Marketing Vice President George L. Curran. "It was an easy thing to do. We were making money on lighters and the company in general was profiting.

[9] "Scripto Taking on the Giants," *Distribution Executive,* March 1972, p. 12.

EXHIBIT 4

SCRIPTO, INC.
Consolidated Balance Sheet

Assets	1973	1972
Current Assets:		
Cash...	$ 432,354	$ 941,659
Receivables, less reserves of $545,963 in 1973 and		
$418,649 in 1972..	6,704,883	5,902,845
Inventories:		
Raw materials and supplies...........................	3,585,031	2,029,475
Work in process.......................................	3,720,943	2,627,531
Finished goods..	895,120	791,571
	8,201,094	5,448,577
Prepaid expenses.......................................	318,633	184,554
Total current assets................................	15,656,964	12,477,635
Property, plant, and equipment, at cost:		
Land..	633,220	633,220
Buildings...	2,246,016	2,216,530
Machinery and equipment.............................	9,972,760	8,995,502
	12,851,996	11,845,252
Less accumulated depreciation.........................	8,086,531	7,511,753
	4,765,465	4,333,499
Investments:		
Equity in net assets of and advances to jointly-owned		
foreign companies.....................:...............	1,199,666	1,408,247
Modern Holdings, Inc.:		
Investment in preferred stock less reserve of $436,000....	—	—
Note receivable.......................................	—	200,000
	1,199,666	1,608,247
Other assets...	82,909	527,293
	$21,705,004	$18,946,674

Liabilities and Stockholders' Investment	1973	1972
Current liabilities:		
Notes payable...	$ 4,520,000	$ 2,447,154
Accounts payable......................................	1,659,834	734,555
Accrued liabilities....................................	1,613,978	1,534,213
Income taxes payable..................................	131,934	331,659
Long-term debt due within one year......................	611,776	605,440
Total current liabilities...............................	8,537,522	5,653,021
Long-term debt due after one year:		
5.45% term loan.......................................	965,620	1,565,620
Other...	9,485	10,880
	975,105	1,576,500
Deferred income taxes..................................	179,000	227,000
Commitments and contingent liabilities		
Stockholders' investment		
Common stock, 50¢ par value; authorized 5,000,000 shares,		
issued 2,891,200 shares...............................	1,445,600	1,445,600
Paid-in surplus..	3,693,459	3,693,459
Retained earnings.....................................	7,342,453	6,819,229
	12,481,512	11,958,288
Less:		
Treasury stock, at cost (42,520 shares).................	320,935	320,935
Notes receivable from officers and employees for		
stock issued..	147,200	147,200
	468,135	468,135
Total Stockholders' Investment...................	12,013,377	11,490,153
	$21,705,004	$18,946,674

Source: 1973 Scripto, Inc., annual report.

Then we suddenly awakened to the fact that, though we had both a name and adequate production facilities for writing instruments, we had not been active in this field for a long time."

To regain its former position of prominence in writing instruments, Scripto is going after BIC's market with its new 19¢ Superpen and it's challenging Paper Mate's 49¢ Flair with a new 19¢ fiber tip pen.

Scripto, though it has had entries in both these markets, hasn't been a real contender in either. Of the two, the one it's most interested in developing is the fiber tip. In fact, its objective seems to be to become to the fiber tip business what BIC has become to the ball point business.

"Basically," says Curran, "the fiber tip has been a 49¢ market. What we're doing is positioning ourselves as the BIC of the fiber tip line."

In explaining why Scripto is marketing a fiber tip that's 30¢ lower than the popular price level, Curran mentions that the growth of the ball point market coincided with the gradual price reduction from the initial $12.50 to the present 19¢. The market, which had been a few hundred thousand units in the early Fifties, is now something like 1.8 billion units.

"As late at ten years ago," he says, "everybody felt that $1.00 was the popular pen and 49¢ was the inexpensive pen. Then BIC proved that 19¢ was a lot more popular.

"So, we're trying to repeat this phenomenon in fiber tips. We're bringing the fiber tip into line for more purchases, for an ultimately higher volume of sales.". . .

. . ."Frankly," Sam says, "we're challenging our major competition head on.". . .

At the end of 1973, the three competitors: BIC, Gillette, and Scripto, held the following retail market shares:

TABLE 3

1973 Comparative Retail Market Shares (units)

	Gillette	BIC	Scripto
19¢ nonretractable ball point pen			
price ($)..........................	$0.19	$0.19	$0.19
market share (%).................	5%	31%	<1%
Fine line porous pens			
price ($)..........................	$0.29, $0.49	$0.29	$0.19, $0.49
market share (%).................	35%	22%	3%
All ball point pens			
price ($)..........................	$0.19–$0.98	$0.19–$1.00	$0.19–$0.98
market share (%).................	15%	66%	2%

Source: Corporate records.

During 1962–73, the three firms made the following consumer advertising expenditures on writing instruments:

TABLE 4

Consumer Advertising Expenditures on Writing Instruments*
(dollars in thousands)

	BIC	Gillette	Scripto		BIC	Gillette	Scripto
1962.........	$ —	$ 146	$ 634	1968.........	$4,194	$3,346	$ 209
1963.........	132	165	736	1969.........	3,626	1,900	56
1964.........	285	126	413	1970.........	3,968	4,033	153
1965.........	654	61	536	1971.........	5,000	6,000	1,800
1966.........	943	61	1,449	1972.........	6,900	8,500	650
1967.........	3,071	2,720	766	1973.........	7,000	9,000	545

* Network TV, spot TV, consumer magazines.
Source: Corporate records.

Cigarette Lighters. For years, three companies: Ronson, Scripto, and Zippo, dominated the regular refillable lighter market, which represented ⅔ of the total industry sales in lighters in 1973.

In 1973 cigarette lighter sales were rapidly increasing in the disposable (<$2) and electronic (>$12) lighter market segments. Sales in the regular refillable ($2–$12) segment had begun to level off. Industry sources believed that Zippo would be the least affected by the polarization trend. Zippo had built up long-time customer loyalties based on the high quality of its metal lighters, which held a life-time guarantee. Ronson had lost market share to Scripto and Zippo when it moved to higher-priced regular refillable lighters in the early 1970s and simultaneously cut back on its advertising support. It was felt that Scripto lacked advertising and marketing strength, and its lower-priced regular refillable lighters faced keen competition from the inexpensive disposable lighters which were new to the marketplace. Additions to its regular refillable product line were largely responsible for its dramatic growth (32 percent) in lighter sales in 1972.

TABLE 5

1973 Regular Refillable Lighter Retail Sales (dollars in thousands)

	Estimated Lighter Sales	Percent of Share	Estimated Fuel and Accessory Sales	Percent of Share	Estimated Total Sales	Percent of Share
Ronson............	$ 16,672	16.5%	$26,676	78.0%	$ 43,348	32.1%
Scripto............	18,339	18.2	3,335	9.7	21,674	16.1
Zippo..............	31,678	31.4	1,667	4.9	33,345	24.7
Estimated total market......	$100,809	100%	$34,235	100%	$135,044	100%

Source: Corporate records.

Scripto became a full-line cigarette lighter firm during 1973 upon the introduction of its "Catch 98" disposable lighter and its series of "Piezo" electronic lighters. The Japanese-made Catch 98 retailed at 98¢. Management stated that the Catch 98 had captured a ten percent share of the disposable lighter market and represented 24 percent of Scripto's dollar sales in cigarette lighters in 1973. A tobacco distributor commented on the Catch 98:

> Disposable lighters are not a perfect product yet. In the expansion stage of the market, lighters of questionable quality can be sold when they can't be sold in later stages. The Catch 98 is not the same quality as the Cricket, BIC Butane, or Dispoz-a-lite, which sell at $1.49. It has a smaller fuel reservoir and no pressure wick.

The Japanese-made Piezo series lighters ranged between $17.95–$29.95 in retail price and were sold in jewelry outlets. Their sales were minimal in 1973.

TABLE 6

Consumer Advertising Expenditures on Cigarette Lighters
(dollars in thousands)

	Ronson	Scripto	Zippo		Ronson	Scripto	Zippo
1966	$432.7	$ 8.6	$729.0	1970	$378.0	$1,006.0	$692.7
1967	634.8	533.3	799.6	1971	164.0	175.3	409.8
1968	554.0	312.0	804.7	1972	419.2	8.2	470.9
1969	422.8	317.3	709.6	1973	261.7	0.0	480.5

Source: Leading National Advertisers, Inc.

Problems Facing Scripto

In an interview with the case researcher in October of 1973, Mr. Sams stated that there were four major problems facing Scripto at that time:

1. Potential embitterment on the part of independent distributors who felt that Scripto was going to abandon them in favor of direct selling to mass-merchandise outlets.
2. Uncertainty as to the availability and price of plastic because of the current worldwide energy shortage.
3. Limitation of financial resources due in part to loan covenant restrictions placed on future borrowing and, in part, to a shortage of internally generated cash.
4. Rising vocalism and absenteeism among the labor force in the Atlanta plant.

Disgruntled Distributors. Management's intention to emphasize direct selling to mass-merchandise outlets added to the frustrations of distributors who had relied heavily on the Scripto business over the years and who had already become disenchanted with the firm's marketing and sales programs in recent years. In a survey conducted by Scripto in 1971, distributors complained that the company salesmen were unaggressive and made infrequent sales calls, that deals and promotions were unattractive because they required high minimum orders to get full discounts, that the product line was too broad, and that the products received very little advertising support. Generally, they felt that Scripto was a me-too company which had concentrated too long on cigarette lighters and had neglected its writing instrument business.[10]

In 1973, approximately 58 percent of Scripto's dollar sales in writing instruments and 81 percent in lighters were concentrated in the retail market, 16 percent and 1 percent, respectively, in the commercial market, and 10 percent and 7 percent, respectively, in the ad/specialty market. The remaining sales were distributed among the firm's minor markets. Despite the direct selling trend, Scripto had continued to rely on indirect selling through its distributors.

TABLE 7

Atlanta Division
Dollar Shipments (percentages)

	Writing Instruments 1972	Writing Instruments 1973	Cigarette Lighters 1972	Cigarette Lighters 1973
Regular sales*				
Direct........................	11%	15%	21%	26%
Indirect.......................	60	71	66	66
Specialized sales†				
Direct........................	12	5	5	2
Indirect.......................	17	9	8	6
Total sales................	100%	100%	100%	100%

* Retail and commercial sales.
† Ad/specialty, premium, government sales, etc.
Source: Corporate records.

Mr. Sams commented on Scripto's position:

> Scripto had been devoted to the drug and tobacco distributors for many years and did not change as the market did because we were protecting those distributors. Now we must change, and the specialized distributors whose businesses are rapidly declining feel that they may be jilted.

The Increasing Price of Plastic. Due to a serious worldwide fuel shortage in 1973, industries which relied heavily on oil-based supplies

---

[10] One manager stated that the salesmen were responsible for the shift to lighters because the sales commissions were more attractive on cigarette lighters than on writing instruments in years past.

were predicting a rise in the price of plastics in 1974 and possible production cutbacks in the event of plastics shortages. Cigarette lighter and writing instrument firms, which used metal rather than plastic as their primary raw material, owned their own refineries, or imported products from countries that were looked upon with favor by the Arabs, were likely to be less directly affected by the energy crisis. Scripto, whose products were made primarily from plastic, was predicting at worst a 20 percent production cutback in its Atlanta plant.

Financial Limitations. At the end of 1973, approximately $1.6 million remained outstanding on the original 5.45 percent long-term loan of $5 million negotiated in 1965 with Metropolitan Life Insurance Company. The loan agreement, amended in 1972, required a $600,000 principal plus interest payment at the end of 1974 and 1975 with a balloon payment of $366,000 in 1976. Provisions under the loan agreement required the U.S. and Canadian companies to maintain a minimum net working capital balance of $6.5 million, limited short-term borrowings to $3 million until April of 1974, and prevented dividend payments to stockholders or additional advances to foreign subsidiaries. During 1972, Scripto applied $959,380 from the sale of certain properties to payment of loan principal.

In 1973, there were approximately 2.8 million shares of Scripto common stock outstanding of which 43 percent was controlled by the Ferst family. No dividends had been paid on outstanding stock since 1967.

Work Force Attitudes. In 1973 the absenteeism rate of plant workers ran as high as 7 percent. Mr. Sams had said, "Morale is improving. It was at ground zero in 1971." Absenteeism had never forced an operations shutdown, but production efficiency was always severely damaged.

Management attributed the labor problems primarily to a "change in social attitudes in the United States" but also to the available work force pool within Atlanta itself. About 60 percent of the work force had been with Scripto for over ten years, and it was felt that those workers felt a sense of loyalty to the company and to their jobs. Absenteeism problems prevailed among the remaining 40 percent who in management's judgment tended to be the younger workers, many of whom were hired from the small group of unemployed persons (2.8 percent of the total work force) in Atlanta in 1973.

The work force was composed primarily of black women. About 60%–70% of the male workers were black. Management stated that racial tension existed among black assembly line workers and white foremen, but tension was greater between black foremen and black assembly line workers who resented the foremen for their professional advancement. Base salaries ranged from $2.25–$2.60 per hour (unskilled work) to $4.00 (skilled work).

Factory conditions were felt by some managers to contribute to worker dissatisfaction on the job. The plant facility consisted of a group of old three-story buildings five minutes from downtown Atlanta. The manufacturing areas were noisy (workers were supplied with ear plugs and eye glasses for protection against noise levels above 85 decibels, flying debris, and sparks), dirty and hot (no air conditioning). Production rates were machine-paced. The work was seasonal and lay offs were a common occurrence.

MR. SAMS LOOKS TO THE FUTURE

Mr. Sams viewed his role as that of a major policy maker. Consistent with that view, he had great faith in the capabilities of his management team to oversee the day-to-day operation of the business and to implement his decisions. As president, he felt that he had made three key decisions: (1) to cut the losses in Atlanta, Canada, and Britain; (2) to reemphasize the writing instrument business; and (3) to introduce such products as the 19¢er porous point pen and the Catch 98 disposable lighter, which would compete in the high-growth areas of the market.

Management outlined the 1974 sales objectives for the Atlanta division:

To increase dollar sales in writing instruments by 10 percent and cigarette lighters by 5 percent using proven promotions and programs.

To increase distribution of the basic product line with current chain customers, and to develop new chain customers, with special emphasis placed on writing instruments.

To concentrate sales attention on the products with the greatest potential, that is, disposable lighters, broad tip markers, and porous point pens.

Sales Objectives. Plans to achieve the 1974 sales growth objectives for writing instruments and cigarette lighters centered around a reorganization of the sales organization in the Atlanta division. Specifically, the commercial stationery division was to become a specialized sales operation in which all sales would be handled through 11 manufacturer's representatives in lieu of the 2,000 distributors which it had used in the past. Direct retail sales would be handled by a national accounts manager working with 75–100 large chain accounts, and by 17 company salesmen and 14 manufacturer's representatives working with the 150 small chain accounts in the northeast, central, southern and western divisions. Indirect retail sales would be made through 4,500 specialized retail distributors and 40 food brokers. Scripto would use its five specialized company salesmen to sell to the 1,344 ad/specialty distributors and would sell direct to the other markets. A detail force of 35 women would be used at the retail level. Exhibit 5 presents the new organizational chart.

Chain Store Expansion. In 1973, Scripto sold 15 percent of its writing instruments and 26 percent of its cigarette lighters direct to chain store accounts. Management hoped to increase chain store sales by at least 10 percent and 5 percent, respectively, in 1974, by assigning district managers and detail salespersons to handle all national and regional

EXHIBIT 5

SCRIPTO, INC.
1973 Top Management—Atlanta Division

Name	Title	Years at Scripto	Job(s) Prior to Scripto	Expertise
"Bo" Sams............	President	37	—	Manufacturing
John Tucker..........	Executive vice president	4	Controller (Kelsey–Hayes Tools); accountant, Touche Ross	Accounting
Jack Bozarth..........	Vice president, marketing	½	Marketing manager, consumer Products division of Gulf & Western	Marketing
Morton Chaber	Vice president, manufacturing	4	Vice president of manufacturing at Ronson; vice president of manufacturing at Revlon	Manufacturing
George Dinnerman.....	Vice president, sales	3	Vice president of marketing at Ronson	Sales
Bill Black..............	Vice president, national accounts	8	Sales director at Timex	Sales
Roberta Haynes........	Assistant vice president, sales and marketing	10	Army Services	Administration
John Dolan............	Controller	1	Accountant at Price Waterhouse	Accounting

chain accounts and divisional sales managers to coordinate those activities.

New Products. Management planned to concentrate on rapidly growing segments of the writing instrument and cigarette lighter markets in 1974. A family of disposable lighters selling at retail prices of $1.19, $1.39 and $1.69 would be introduced. The $1.69 lighter would be manufactured at full capacity (10 million units/year) in the Atlanta plant. The $1.39 lighter would be imported from Japan. The $1.19 product was the former Catch 98 at 98¢. The 19¢er porous point pen would be repositioned at the point-of-sale to "provoke greater impulse purchases." The 49¢ porous point pen would be aggressively marketed in the commercial market. Scripto was testing a finer point porous pen with a harder tip which would write through carbons. Scripto planned to introduce a "better cannister marker" in 1974, which management claimed could be differentiated from competitors' products.

An allocation of $1.6 million was planned for the 1974 advertising program which was to cover all products at the trade and consumer levels. Scripto intended to use two themes: (1) Scripto (products) works; and (2) Scripto (company) is alive and well.

Mr. Jack Bozarth, vice president of marketing and sales, summed up Scripto's position in 1974:

Scripto is in a different position than anyone else in the industry. We're the only full-line writing instrument supplier left. Whether they know it or not, BIC is the stick, Papermate is the Flair, Magic Marker is the cannister marker.

For the first time, Scripto is going with the industry. We're competing in the growth areas but are protected by our full line. Right or wrong, it will be interesting to see how the industry goes.

EXHIBIT 6

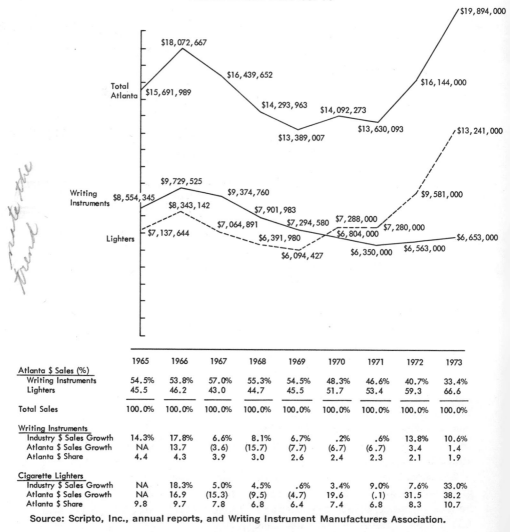

SCRIPTO, INC.

Atlanta Division Sales 1965–73

	1965	1966	1967	1968	1969	1970	1971	1972	1973
Atlanta $ Sales (%)									
Writing Instruments	54.5%	53.8%	57.0%	55.3%	54.5%	48.3%	46.6%	40.7%	33.4%
Lighters	45.5	46.2	43.0	44.7	45.5	51.7	53.4	59.3	66.6
Total Sales	100.0%	100.0%	100.0%	100.0%	100.0%	100.0%	100.0%	100.0%	100.0%
Writing Instruments									
Industry $ Sales Growth	14.3%	17.8%	6.6%	8.1%	6.7%	.2%	.6%	13.8%	10.6%
Atlanta $ Sales Growth	NA	13.7	(3.6)	(15.7)	(7.7)	(6.7)	(6.7)	3.4	1.4
Atlanta $ Share	4.4	4.3	3.9	3.0	2.6	2.4	2.3	2.1	1.9
Cigarette Lighters									
Industry $ Sales Growth	NA	18.3%	5.0%	4.5%	.6%	3.4%	9.0%	7.6%	33.0%
Atlanta $ Sales Growth	NA	16.9	(15.3)	(9.5)	(4.7)	19.6	(.1)	31.5	38.2
Atlanta $ Share	9.8	9.7	7.8	6.8	6.4	7.4	6.8	8.3	10.7

Source: Scripto, Inc., annual reports, and Writing Instrument Manufacturers Association.

EXHIBIT 7

SCRIPTO, INC.
1974 Organizational Chart—Atlanta Division

President

- Vice President Manufacturing
  - Industrial Relations Director
  - Production Control Director
  - Quality Assurance Manager
  - Industrial Engineering Director
  - Traffic Manager
  - Engineering Director
  - Production Director
  - Purchasing Director
  - Customer Relations Director
  - Research

- Vice President Corporate Marketing
  - Vice President Sales
    - Vice President Sales Operations
      - National Accounts Group
      - 4 Divisional Managers
      - Specialty Sales Operations Manager
        - Premium Sales Manager
        - Government Sales Manager
        - Commercial Sales Manager
        - Ad/Specialty Sales Manager
  - Domestic Marketing Director
    - Product Manager
    - Product Manager
    - Marketing EDP Manager
    - Advertising Manager
    - Creative Service Manager
    - Sales Promotion Manager

- Vice President Finance
  - Data Processing Manager
  - Controller
  - Payroll and Cost Account Manager
  - Credit Manager
  - General Account Manager

Source: Company records.

5 Note on the Security Services and Equipment Industry

By 1973, sales of private security services and equipment constituted a $4.1 billion dollar industry.[1] While total industry sales had grown at better than 10 percent over the five-year period 1968–73, industry observers generally agreed that some segments would increase by as much as 25 percent annually over the next five years. The prospects for the industry had led one company president to say:

> I'm sorry to say crime is on the rise, but what's bad for the country is good for us.[2]

However, many industry members felt that the rate and direction of future growth would be affected by a variety of important environmental, legal, and technological factors which had recently emerged.

The following note presents data on the security services and equipment industry, as of 1973. Attention will first be focused on the factors contributing to and affecting the demand for security services and equipment; then the market characteristics, structure, trends, and future of the protective services and security equipment industry will be explored.

FACTORS AFFECTING DEMAND FOR SECURITY

While several factors had been instrumental in the surge in demand for security services and equipment, five were relatively more evident:

---

[1] Estimate made by Quantum Science Corporation in a 1973 study, *Security Systems: Electronics to the Rescue.*

[2] *Barron's*, April 27, 1970.

(1) increasing crime, (2) inducements from insurance companies, (3) insulation from recessionary pressures, (4) the focus of the Justice Department, and (5) improvements in technology.

Increasing Crime

The Federal Bureau of Investigation (FBI) had indicated that over the period 1966–72 the number of crimes committed had increased by over 75%.[3] Significant, and often overlooked, was the fact that a major portion of the crimes committed were increasingly property related, as opposed to crimes against individuals. For example, in 1972, business-

TABLE 1

Cost of Property Crimes to Business (1971)

Industry Category	Dollars in Billions
Retailing...............................	$ 4.8
Manufacturing..........................	1.8
Wholesaling...........................	1.4
Services...............................	2.7
Transportation........................	1.5
Total*...........................	$12.2

*In addition, it was estimated by a congressional (Senate) committee that over $500 million in securities had been stolen from brokerage firms and banks in 1971.
Source: Bureau of Domestic Commerce.

men's losses to property crimes had approximated $12.2 billion.[4] At the same time, most of the public expenditures to combat crime had been used to fight crime against persons. This focus was demonstrated by the number of crimes involving property versus crimes against individuals for which arrests were made and solved. In 1971, FBI statistics had indicated that crimes involving murder were cleared 84 percent of the time, rape 55 percent, and aggravated assault 66 percent; on the other hand, property crimes, such as robbery, burglary, and larceny, were solved only 27 percent, 19 percent and 19 percent of the time, respectively.[5] Combined with an increasing public awareness of rising crime, this disparity helped to create a favorable market condition for private security firms. This was particularly true for industry and business, where property losses had been substantial.[6] (See Table 1.)

[3] Source: FBI Reports.
[4] *Security Systems,* p. 18, see footnote 1 above.
[5] Ibid., p. 17.
[6] "Protective Services," an industry study by Hallgarten & Co., 1973.

EXHIBIT 1

Index of Crime, United States, 1961–71

Year	Total Crime Index	Violent Crime	Property Crime	Figures in Thousands						
				Murder	Forcible Rape	Robbery	Aggravated Assault	Burglary	Larceny $50 and Over	Auto Theft
1971	5,995,000	810,030	5,185,000	18	42	386	365	2,368	1,875	942
1970	5,582,000	732,950	4,849,000	16	38	348	331	2,177	1,750	922
1969	4,990,000	655,100	4,335,000	15	36	298	306	1,950	1,513	872
1968	4,467,000	588,800	3,878,000	14	31	262	282	1,829	1,271	778
1967	3,802,000	494,600	3,308,000	12	27	202	253	1,606	1,047	655
1966	3,264,000	425,400	2,839,000	11	25	157	232	1,387	895	557
1965	2,930,000	383,100	2,547,000	10	23	138	212	1,262	792	493
1964	2,755,000	360,100	2,395,000	9	21	130	200	1,194	732	469
1963	2,436,000	313,400	2,093,000	9	17	116	172	1,069	649	405
1962	2,214,000	298,200	1,915,000	8	17	110	162	978	573	364
1961	2,082,000	286,100	1,796,000	9	17	106	154	934	529	334
Compound growth rate:										
1961–71	11.1%	11.0%	11.2%	7.2%	9.5%	13.8%	9.0%	9.8%	12.9%	10.9%

Source: Compiled from FBI data by Hallgarten & Co.

Insurance Inducements

As the loss of and damage to insured properties increased, insurance companies had begun to take an active role in encouraging firms to purchase protective security services and equipment or systems, or both. In some cases, insurance companies had either denied availability of insurance or given premium reductions as a means of forcing or inducing companies to procure some form of security. In a few instances, premium reductions were estimated to be as much as 40 percent.

Recession Resistance

The steady growth of the industry had also demonstrated a general immunity to business down-turns. Unlike the case in most other industries, the demand for protective services and security could actually increase when economic adversity occurred. Cutbacks in the number of work shifts utilized, or the closing of a plant or facility, for example, often resulted in greater use of guards or protective devices, or both, for greater periods.[7]

Focus of Justice Department Efforts

Through its Law Enforcement Assistance Administration (LEAA), the Justice Department had actively sponsored anti-crime programs. Established in 1968, LEAA's budget in 1973 had approximated $850,000 and had focused on coordination with local law enforcement agencies. However, the state and local agencies had tended to ignore the protection of physical property as political and public attention had focused on the problems of personal safety and street crime.[8]

Technological Improvements

Largely through research and development by both security and non-security companies, many new products had found their way into the protective security industry. Non-security related lighting systems and signal transmission and detection devices were found to have security applications which were highly marketable.

SECURITY SERVICES AND EQUIPMENT MARKETS

Product Definitions

While the range of security services and devices available in 1973 was somewhat broad, they could be classified into the two basic categories

---

[7] Ibid., p. 1.
[8] *Security Systems*, p. 67.

of services and equipment. Finer breakdowns or segments could be identified within each major group, particularly in the equipment class, which could be easily divided into hardware and systems subsegments.

Equipment

Security equipment ranged from simple one-dollar locks and/or latching devices to integrated security protection and environmental control systems costing more than $1 million.

Hardware usually consisted of deterrent devices designed to deter or prevent the intrusion of unauthorized persons. For example, hardware equipment consisted of electronically controlled doors, vaults, safes, teller windows, locks, bank drive-in windows, and other bank equipment. Deterrent hardware also included lighting equipment, such as high-intensity lamps, area floodlighting systems, and accessory items.

Security systems to monitor and detect given events offered integrated sensoring devices, closed-circuit television (CCTV), cable television (CATV), and/or detection and surveillance devices. While many different types of systems were in use, four basic systems had been defined by Underwriters Laboratory (UL) for fire alarm, burglar, and industrial monitoring protection: local alarm systems, central station systems, proprietary systems, and direct-connect systems.[9]

1. *Local Alarm System:* Protective alarm sensors were connected to weather-resistant and tamper-proof bells, gongs, lights, and/or sirens attached to an outside wall of the protected premises.
2. *Central Station:* Detection or monitoring elements were attached to an appropriate communications channel (telephone lines, CATV, etc.) which carried alarm signals to a central station maintained by trained guards and operators present at all times. These systems were usually independently owned, controlled, and operated by firms which had no direct interest in the protected property, but simply furnished supervised protection signaling services. The owning service company designed, installed, and maintained the system, and notified the police or fire department or dispatched its own private guard force to the scene of an emergency.
3. *Proprietary System:* This system was comprised of sensor and monitoring equipment similar to that of central stations. However, it was owned or leased by the facility owner or tenant, and equipment

---

[9] System certification by UL usually carried the benefit of insurance credits, with attendant premium reductions for burglary and fire insurance.

location, supervision, maintenance and alarm response was provided on site by the facility's own force.

4. *Direct-Connect Systems:* A signal was generated at a protected premise and transmitted directly to a municipal fire or police headquarters.

The equipment used in systems often integrated computers, sensors, and manpower. The basic types of intrusion detectors or sensors included ultrasonic, magnetic, photoelectric, foil, resonance, and infrared devices, as well as closed-circuit television.

Services

Security services offered were principally guard and investigative, armored car, courier, and central station protection. Generally better known to the public, guard and investigative services was the oldest and largest group of security services. This segment included both private contract guards and in-house guards. In-house guards usually were full time employees of the company being guarded; in this situation, the company was responsible for recruiting, training, supervising and compensating the guards. Private contract guard services were provided under contract by firms responsible for all aspects of guard performance. Contract guards were estimated to account for roughly 25 to 30 percent (250,000) of private guards in the United States.[10] Guards performed a variety of tasks, including entry control, patrolling premises, monitoring, and crowd control.

Central station services combined sensing devices with off-premise monitored stations. Upon receipt of an alarm, this service company (central station) sent its own guards and/or notified the appropriate force.

The third major service available was armored car and courier services. These services generally provided for the movement of cash and negotiable securities and items of unusually high value. The means of transportation included armored trucks, cars, armed messengers, and planes.

Markets and Trends

Markets for security services and equipment generally fell into four major categories: (1) commercial (including financial and retail), (2) industrial, (3) consumer (residential), and (4) institutional and other. Table 2 summarizes the historical sales to these major markets, and the projected sales by 1978.

---

[10] "Protective Services," p. 27.

TABLE 2

User* Markets for Private Security Services and Equipment

	Millions of Dollars				
Market:	1958	1963	1968	1973	1978
Commercial, financial, retail,					
and transportation...........	$190	$274	$ 468	$ 779	$1,208
Industrial.....................	249	393	729	1,223	1,913
Consumer/residential..........	10	15	23	40	67
Institutions and other..........	62	98	175	298	482
Total.....................	$511	$780	$1,395	$2,340	$3,670

* Excludes in-home guard and investigative services.
Source: "The Private Policy Industry": study by U.S. Department of Justice.

Each of these markets exhibited different use patterns of services versus equipment. As shown in Table 3, some market segments, notably industrial and institutional, had relied more on protective services than equipment.

TABLE 3

Comparative Use of Services Versus Equipment by Market

	Market Percentages			
	Industrial	Commercial	Residential	Institutional
Product:				
Services......................	80	25	25	65
Equipment...................	20	75	75	35
Total....................	100%	100%	100%	100%
Market segment:				
Sales as percent of total......	52.3%	33.3%	1.7%	12.7%

Source: Quantum Science Corporation and industry estimates.

Industrial Markets

The industrial segment was by far the largest market for security in 1973. Accounting for over 50 percent of all private security sales, the market had demonstrated a rapid growth trend, almost doubling between 1968 and 1973. Approximately 80 percent of purchases had been for guard services, with equipment sales accounting for the remaining 20 percent (see Table 3). The smaller industrial firms had traditionally been purchasers of fire and intrusion devices, central station services, and some guard services.

In the face of rising losses, industrial firms had begun to accept security as a cost of doing business. With facilities and plants worth billions of dollars, security expenditures of $100,000 to $2 million for systems at a single location had come to be regarded as necessary to protect machinery, trade secrets, and plants. While services had traditionally retained the largest market share, many medium and large industrial businesses had increasingly resorted to computer based systems to provide integrated functions of security, process and environmental control, and monitoring.[11] In the lower end of the market (firms under $10 million in sales) economics had generally precluded substantial sales of proprietary or computer based systems.

Commercial Markets

The commercial market, which approximated $250 million[12] in 1973, consisted of retail stores, office buildings, banks, financial institutions, and computer facilities. A special subsegment consisted of firms involved in

TABLE 4

Cargo Security Losses (*dollars in millions*)
Carrier Type

	Truck	Maritime	Rail	Air	Total
Losses	$850	$86	$55	$16	$1,007
Percent of Total	84.4	8.5	5.5	1.6	100

Source: Quantum Science Corporation.

the transportation of cargo and people. Growing at about 10 percent annually, this market had been favorably affected by a surge in high-rise construction, more stringent bank security requirements, and rising transportation related crimes. Given a desire to protect million-dollar investments and the economics of automated building control, building owners had spent as much as 1 percent of building costs to provide integrated security and control systems for high-rise office and apartment buildings.[13]

Increasing sales to all sectors of the transportation industry had also given a boost to demand for security services by the commercial sector. This increase in demand had been motivated by the rise in total losses by firms in the transportation industry. In 1972, total losses were estimated to total more than $1 billion annually. (See Table 4 for breakdown.)

Although hijackings and major thefts from loaded cargo containers received much publicity, 85 percent of stolen cargo was believed to go through the door of transportation facilities through persons and vehicles with management authorized access, during normal business hours.[14]

[11] *Securitiy Systems*, p. 101.

[12] Does not include $529 million for transportation security, as shown in Table 2; the sources for this discussion included transportation security in "Industrial Markets."

[13] *Security Systems*, pp. 43–38.

[14] Ibid., pp. 96–99.

Thus the primary method of preventing cargo thefts had utilized a mix of private guards enforcing stricter access control procedures, augmented by such surveillance hardware as CCTV and proprietary systems connected to remote sensors. Other methods utilized included security lighting, security fencing, alarm systems, motion sensors, and helicopters. Other new areas in transportation had also given rise to increased demand for security services and products. For example, the airline industry had developed a new $16–$20 million-a-year market when the federal government began in 1973 to require that all airline passengers and carry-on baggage had to be inspected prior to boarding.[15] Further, protection of such vital transmission facilities as the Alaskan oil pipeline had opened "new" markets. As a result of these factors, the commercial market was projected to be the fastest growing market segment in the future. From $250 million in 1973, the commercial market was projected to grow at an annual rate of 15 percent and reach $600 million by 1980.[16,17]

Institutional Markets

Institutional markets consisted of schools, hospitals, churches, colleges, museums, and other similar type facilities. Sales in this market had grown at about 11 percent per year, with a major surge in the three to four years prior to 1973. However, sales to this market through 1978 were projected to grow at a 15–20 percent rate as hospitals and schools in urban areas increased security expenditures.[18]

Residential Markets

The residential market had for years been an elusive target for security equipment and service companies. Accounting for $40 million, or less than 2 percent, of total industry sales, this segment had been difficult to penetrate due to several market and industry characteristics:

1. A highly fragmented structure, consisting of 75 million individual homes and residences in 1973;
2. High direct sales costs required by door-to-door selling;
3. Apathy toward home safety in "low-crime" areas (suburban) and inability to pay for security in high-crime areas;
4. Security system and equipment suppliers concentrating on developing suitable equipment for more profitable institutional, industrial, and commercial businesses; and

---

[15] Ibid.

[16] Retailers also had increased their purchases of security equipment and services in the face of shoplifting and pilferage losses running at about $4 billion per year.

[17] *Security Systems,* p. 47.

[18] Ibid., pp. 56–58.

5. A poor industry image due to "fly-by-night" operators providing un-
reliable equipment and service.[19]

As a result of these factors, the residential and/or consumer market
had experienced only a 5–7 percent growth through 1970. Approximately
75 percent of the sales in this market had been dominated by local builders
and dealers who provided locks, gates, pressure-sensitive doormats, local
alarm systems, and window locks. The remaining 25 percent of sales had
been generated primarily by central station and guard service companies
in high-rise buildings and upper income suburban communities.[20]

However, between 1970 and 1973, the residential market had experienced a 50 percent growth. Estimates of the future size of this market
ranged from $150 million by 1977 (Quantum Science Corporation) to
$67 million by 1978 (U.S. Department of Justice).[21,22] Several factors
were believed by the industry to have stimulated sales to this market:

1. Increased residential burglaries in both urban and suburban areas:
   In 1973, these losses had approximated $500 million. With increased
   awareness of vulnerability, residential homeowner's apathy toward
   security had diminished rapidly.
2. Increased consumer affluence had elevated home security to a
   "status" equivalent, with pools, air-conditioning, intercoms, and other
   amenities.
3. Major, reliable companies had begun to enter the market.
4. Increased consolidation and stabilization of industrial and commercial
   market shares had caused many companies to begin to seek ways to
   penetrate this relatively untapped market.
5. New products were being developed which could offset the pricing
   problems. For example, cable television, with two-way potential, was
   expected by industry members to play a major role in serving this
   market.[23]

A major difficulty in penetrating the residential market had been the
unavailability of an effective security system priced within the average
homeowner's budget. Most systems offered were versions of industrial
systems that were priced between $5,000–$20,000.[24] Several companies
had begun to develop and offer less expensive systems that were at-
tractively priced for the residential market. These systems were priced be-

---

[19] Ibid., pp. 7–8.

[20] *Security Systems,* pp. 7–8.

[21] The Quantum Science Corporation estimate was made in 1973; the Justice
Department estimate in 1972.

[22] "Private Police Industry," study published by U.S. Department of Justice.

[23] *Security Systems,* pp. 47–48.

[24] Ibid.

tween $400–$1,200 for apartments and condominiums, and between $700–$2,000 for private homes. To these installation costs were added an additional $10–$30 per month telephone line leasing charge for systems connected to central stations. With the leased line system, sensors in the home signaled a remote alarm console or the appropriate authority directly when a fire, intrusion, or other abnormal condition was sensed. An alternative to the leased line was an automatic telephone dialer costing $200–$700.[25] Some companies were experimenting with wireless communication as a way of reducing costs.

In addition to these relatively sophisticated systems, there were a large number of individual, "do-it-yourself" security components and kits. These included locks and alarm switches, costing several dollars, to ultrasonic space detectors priced in the $100–dollar range. Thus one of the major marketing problems facing companies attacking this segment had been to convince the homeowner to pay $500–$2,000 for a system, instead of purchasing a $49.95 security kit at the local hardware store. The traditional industry approach, according to one study, had been to emphasize component quality, low false alarm rates, comprehensive area coverage, plus 24-hour central station monitoring.[26]

THE SECURITY SERVICES AND EQUIPMENT INDUSTRY

In 1973, the security equipment and services industry exhibited considerable diversity. Highly fragmented, the industry consisted of thousands of companies of varying sizes, ages, and degrees of sophistication and reliability. Similar to the market designations, the industry could be divided into service companies and equipment producers, with the latter segment split into hardware and systems. The service companies consisted of guard and investigative services, armored car and courier services, and central stations. Equipment segment producers were more diverse than service companies, with suppliers offering a considerable number of products. Historically, the equipment segment had accounted for a relatively smaller share of total industry revenues. Both segments will be discussed in the following section, with concentration on the key companies and the trends and characteristics of each segment and the industry in general.

Industry Structure

In 1973, the service segment was by far the largest portion of the industry; as shown in Exhibit 2, services accounted for approximately 75

---

[25] Ibid.
[26] Ibid.

EXHIBIT 2

Sales of Security Services and Systems (all dollar figures in millions)

	1973	%	Projected 1978	%	1980	%	Historical and Projected Growth Rates 1968–73	1973–78
Industry Totals:								
Services	$3,000	73.2%	$4,829	68 %	$5,890	63.3%	11.3%	10.0%
Equipment	1,100	26.8	2,295	32	3,410	36.7	10.2	15.8
Total	$4,100	100.0%	$7,124	100.0%	$9,300	100.0%	10.8%	11.7%
Industry Segments:								
Services								
Private contract guards and investigation	$ 875	29.2%	$1,750	36.2%	$2,350	39.9%	11.5%	14.9%
In-house guard and investigative	1,600	53.3	1,800	37.3	1,700	28.9	n.a.*	2.4
Armored car and courier services	250	8.3	440	9.1	540	9.2	10.5	12.0
Central station services	275	9.2	839	17.4	1,300	22.0	17.0	25.0
Total services	$3,000	100.0%	$4,829	100.0%	$5,890	100.0%	11.3%	10.0%
Equipment								
Safes, vaults, and fixed hardware	$ 290	26.4%	$ 565	24.6%			} 8.3%	14.2%
Locks	210	19	340	14.8				10.1
Lighting, computers, dealers, miscellaneous	75	6.8	260	11.3			n.a.*	28.0
Central station equipment	150	13.6	375	16.4			6.4	20.0
Sensors	325	29.5	665	29.0			17.2	14.9
Closed-circuit television	50	4.6	90	3.9			14.5	12.5
Total equipment	$1,100	100.0%	$2,295	100.0%			10.4	15.8

* n.a. = not available.
Source: U.S. Department of Justice and Quantum Science Corporation industry study.

percent of total protective security industry sales. Within the service sector, guard and investigative services accounted for the major share (82.5 percent), with private contract guards contributing $875 million or 29 percent of the total service sector revenues. The balance of service company revenues, $525 million, was derived from courier, central station, and armored car services.[27]

In the equipment segment, companies producing sensing and detection devices and deterrent equipment, such as safes, vaults, and locks, accounted for the bulk of sales; together these companies had generated roughly 68 percent of the total equipment sector sales. (See Exhibit 2.) However, many new market entrants, providing integrated systems utilizing sensors, central station equipment, dialers, and computers, had increased the significance of other areas of the equipment segment.

While there were thousands of firms competing in the security services and equipment industry, the industry was fairly concentrated, with fewer than 15 firms accounting for more than 50 percent of total 1973 industry revenues. This was particularly true for the service segment. For example, over 50 percent of all private guard service sales were accounted for by four firms: Pinkerton's, Inc., Burns International Security Services, Wackenhut Corporation, and Globe Security. Approximately 45 percent of all central station service revenues were accounted for by American District Telegraph Company, with another 20–30 percent spread among Burns, AFA Protective Services, Honeywell, and Baker Industries (Wells Fargo). Brinks, Inc., a subsidiary of the Pittston Co., had long possessed the largest market share of the armored car and courier market; in 1973, Brinks accounted for approximately 40–45 percent of the market, with an additional 40 percent of the market divided between Wells Fargo of Baker Industries and American Air Courier Division of Purolator.[28]

The equipment sector also exhibited a relatively high degree of concentration, despite the presence of thousands of small firms, often producing only one product. A few major companies tended to dominate each subsegment. Some of the more evident examples were: locks (Yale Division of Eaton Corp.); vaults and safes (Diebold, Mosler Safe, Walter Kidde); sensors and detectors (Honeywell, ADT); cable television (Tele-Prompter); integrated systems (IBM, Honeywell, RCA); transmission and cable television equipment (RCA, Motorola, G.E., and Westinghouse). In some segments, a few smaller companies had been able to establish a dominant position; for example, it was estimated that Systron Donner had as much as 50 percent of the market for ultrasonic devices.[29]

---

[27] Ibid., pp. 142–146.

[28] Ibid.

[29] Based on industry data.

SERVICE SEGMENTS AND TRENDS

Guard Services

In 1973, guards and investigative services accounted for approximately 60 percent ($2.5 billion) of the security industry. In-house guards and investigative services in turn accounted for 65 percent, or $1.6 billion of this $2.5 billion guard and investigative sector. Private guard services, as mentioned earlier, were dominated by four firms: Pinkerton's ($174.8 million), Burns International ($153.6 million), Wackenhut Corporation ($90.5 million), and Globe Security ($51.4 million). The balance of the guard/investigative revenues were spread among a few other medium-size firms and thousands of small and local guard companies. It was estimated that there were over 4,000 guard companies in the United States.[30]

Private contract guard companies typically earned lower profit margins on sales than the equipment companies. (See Exhibit 3.) These companies were highly labor intensive, with labor costs absorbing 80 percent or more of sales.[31] Given the labor intensity of the business, knowledge of local wage rates was extremely important in bidding for contracts by the large national firms. Typically, guards were paid $1.60 to $2.50 per hour.[32]

Guard companies had often come under fire for the quality of their personnel. According to the Pennsylvania Attorney General, Mr. J. Shane Creamer:

> The typical private guard is an aging white male, poorly educated, usually untrained, and very poorly paid. He averages between 40 and 55 years of age; he has had little education beyond the ninth grade, and has had a few years of experience in private security. Contract guards earn a marginal wage (between $1.60 and $2.75 per hour, with premium-quality contract guard earning $2.75 per hour). Both often work a 48-hour or 56-hour week to make ends meet.[33]

Mr. Creamer added:

> Part-timers account for 20 percent to 50 percent of the total guards at some large contract firms. Annual turnover rates range from less than 10 percent in some in-house employment to over 200 percent in some contract agencies.

Training of guard employees posed a problem for guard companies as the cost had to be carefully controlled because of the high turnover rate

---

[30] "Private Police," pp. 38–45.

[31] Source: Company annual reports.

[32] "Protective Services," p. 16.

[33] "Private Police in the United States: Funding and Recommendations," *Security World*, 1973.

EXHIBIT 3

Comparative Statistical Data on Selected Security Companies*

| | American District Telegraph (ADT) | Baker Industries | Primarily Guard Companies | | | Diebold | Johnson Service |
			Burns International	Pinkerton's	Wackenhut		
Revenues (millions)							
1973	$148.3	$107.7	$153.6	$174.8	$ 90.5	$189.4	$251.2
1972	128.2	94.6	139.3	162.2	66.9	157.0	231.4
1971	114.9	84.9	128.0	149.8	55.8	139.2	209.5
1970	105.1	68.5	115.9	135.0	52.1	135.9	178.8
1969	97.1	54.7	97.1	120.3	48.5	118.0	169.8
1968	92.5	40.9	82.8	99.6	36.7	100.5	155.0
1967	78.7	22.4	66.5	82.9	29.0	87.1	141.9
Net income (millions)							
1973	$ 10.7	$ 6.7	$ 3.0	$ 6.2	$ 2.1	$ 11.8	$ 9.1
1972	9.6	5.8	2.4	5.5	1.8	9.4	10.2
1971	8.6	4.2	1.0	5.5	1.7	8.8	9.7
1970	7.7	2.8	3.0	4.9	1.7	8.8	8.9
1969	6.5	2.5	2.5	4.2	1.5	6.8	7.8
1968	6.2	2.0	2.6	3.3	.8	4.8	6.9
1967	6.1	1.7	2.1	2.8	.7	2.8	6.5
Net income margins (%)							
1973	7.2%	6.3%	2.0%	3.6%	2.3%	6.2%	3.6%
1972	7.4	6.1	1.8	3.4	2.6	6.0	4.4
1971	7.5	4.9	.8	3.7	3.0	6.3	4.6
1970	7.3	4.1	2.6	3.6	3.2	6.5	5.0
1969	6.7	4.6	2.5	3.5	3.0	5.8	4.6
1968	6.7	5.0	3.1	3.3	2.2	4.8	4.4
1967	7.7	7.5	3.2	3.4	2.5	3.2	4.6
Long-term debt (millions)							
1973	—	$ 20.6	$ 5.0	—	$ 10.7	$ 15.8	$ 16.9
1972	—	18.0	5.0	—	9.2	16.5	16.3
1971	—	19.2	—	—	5.3	17.1	17.4
1970	—	21.7	—	—	4.1	11.7	18.0

	1969	—	13.4	—	—	4.1	14.6	14.1
	1968	—	11.6	—	—	3.6	15.3	12.4
	1967	—	1.4	—	—	2.7	10.5	10.3
Net worth (millions)	1973	$ 88.5	$ 34.9	$ 23.0	$ 31.8	$ 8.1	$ 76.0	$ 63.1
	1972	78.8	29.1	21.5	27.6	6.6	66.7	57.6
	1971	70.9	24.1	20.9	24.1	5.6	58.9	50.0
	1970	66.5	19.7	16.5	20.3	5.8	51.7	43.0
	1969	60.8	18.2	14.8	16.7	4.7	43.8	36.1
	1968	56.5	16.6	13.9	13.6	3.8	37.8	31.0
	1967	50.2	6.0	8.3	11.0	3.6	34.0	27.2
Percent earned net worth	1973	12.1%	19.3%	13.0%	19.7%	26.5%	15.5	14.4%
	1972	12.1	19.8	11.4	19.9	26.9	14.1	17.7
	1971	12.2	17.3	5.0	22.7	30.3	14.9	19.4
	1970	11.6	14.4	18.2	24.1	28.8	17.0	20.7
	1969	10.6	13.9	16.6	25.0	30.7	15.5	21.6
	1968	11.0	12.2	18.6	24.4	21.6	12.7	22.3
	1967	12.1	27.9	25.6	25.3	19.6	8.2	23.9
AVC annual P/E	1973	23.5%	22.2%	12.4%	14.3%	9.2%	20.0%	12.0%
	1972	31.5	34.8	21.9	37.8	21.3	23.5	15.0
	1971	28.4	26.0	69.5	37.4	24.8	27.0	14.5
	1970	17.4	24.8	27.2	34.9	23.7	21	13.5
	1969	21.9	33.7	42.1	39.7	27.2	23	15.0
	1968	27.5	32.8	31.8	33.4	36.5	23	16.0
	1967	17.0	22.8	14.8	22.4	21.4	26.5	15.5
Price range: High-low	1973	61.9–	39.0–	20.8–	69.8–	8.9–	54¾–	16¾–
		35.4	12.3	7.5	16.0	6.1	33⅝	13½
	1972	68.3–	39.6–	29.3–	85.8–	16.3–	50⅝–	37⅜–
		43.0	22.4	12.1	49.5	4.6	30¾	13⅝
	1971	59.1	26.5	35.0	79.0	24.1	50–	38⅜–
		28.8	14.0	15.0	69.5	12.8	38⅜	27¾

* See Exhibit 4 for background on company and product mix.
Source: Company reports and researcher's analysis.

and difficulty in passing nondirect hourly costs on to clients. Mr. Creamer also made the following observations:

> The training . . . is typically no more than eight to 12 hours, and many guards, including some who are armed, receive less than two hours of training.
> . . . a survey of 275 security employees showed that most guard personnel do not know their legal powers and authority. . . .
> . . . over 97 percent of the security employees made serious errors that could lead to civil suits or criminal charges.
> . . . many of the smaller guard forces . . . have essentially no training program.[34]

Reflecting this rising concern for the quality of guards, many states had moved to enact legislation which would mandate greater investment in guard training.

Two growing problems for guard companies had been increased efforts at unionization and minimum wage legislation. The United Plant Guard Workers of America, the largest private guard union, had approximately 20,000 members, which represented about 8 percent of all private contract guards.[35] One industry estimate placed the total number of unionized guards in the United States at 27,000–30,000. Approximately 90 percent of all unionized guards were inhouse guards. Because guard contracts and bidding were extremely competitive, guard companies tended to resist unionization strongly; if a contract guard firm became unionized at a given site, and the union pushed for higher wages and fringe benefits, the client could simply change to a non-unionized firm.[36]

Minimum wage legislation posed a particular management problem for guard companies. Any rise in wages due to minimum wage laws had to be passed on to the client in order to maintain profitability. If clients were unwilling to accept price increases, contracts could be lost.

Expansion of guard revenues and operations could occur without large capital outlays as there were few major investments in fixed assets. Conversely, due to the high labor intensity, there was little operating leverage for guard companies. As a result, in order to increase profits, guard companies had to continually seek to expand or generate new revenue.

Relative to in-house guards, private contract guard companies held a small market share. However, contract guards were expected to expand rapidly and increase their market share from 35 percent in 1973 to 49 percent by 1980.[37] The erosion of in-house guard market share by private contract guards was projected for several reasons:

---

[34] Ibid.
[35] "Protective Services," p. 27.
[36] Ibid., p. 16.
[37] *Security Systems,* p. 27.

(1) *Cost*—contract firms generally had lower costs than in-house guard operations with respect to wages, training costs, fringe benefits, and unionization. It was estimated by the industry that in-house guard costs were $0.50 to $1.00 higher than private contract firms because of the relative economies of scale that private contract firms had in hiring, training, insurance, equipment purchasing, and administration.[38]

(2) *Administration*—with private contract guards, the client did not have to recruit, train, or supervise personnel. Usually, contract firms also possessed a higher degree of security expertise.

(3) *Unions*—While the majority of the in-house guards were unionized, only 10–20 percent of the guards employed by the major contract firms were unionized. As nonunion guards were less apt to strike, there was greater stability.[39]

(4) *Objectivity*—contract guards could avoid establishing close relationships with employees as they were not employees of the client.

Despite these factors favorable to the future of private contract firms, many companies continued to use in-house guards. Their rationale stressed the feeling that in-house guards were of higher quality due to higher pay and fringe benefits. In addition, in-house guards were thought by some security people to have the advantage of being better and more easily controlled, possessing greater company loyalty, and affording the company some "prestige."[40]

Central Station Services

In 1973, central station services accounted for roughly $275 million, or 9 percent of service revenues. More importantly, this industry was projected to be one of the fastest growing segments of the security industry. By 1980, this segment was expected to quadruple to reach $1.3 billion, or 22 percent, of the total security industry.[41]

In 1973, as in the past, the central station service industry was dominated by less than five firms: American District Telegraph Company's 1973 revenues alone represented 40–50 percent of total central station revenues. While there were over 100 central station companies serving this market, ADT's coverage of the market was demonstrated by the fact that in 1972 ADT owned approximately 139 of the total central stations in operation, while the next largest competitor, Burns International,

---

[38] Ibid., p. 30.
[39] "Protective Services."
[40] Ibid., p. 17.
[41] *Security Systems*, p. 4.

TABLE 5

Major Central Station Operators (1973)

Company	Number of Central Stations
American District Telegraph Co.	139
Burns International Security Services	30
Holmes Protection, Inc.	12
Baker Industries (Wells Fargo)	15
Honeywell, Inc.	8
Wackenhut Corporation	5
Total*	209

* Together, these six firms accounted for approximately 75–80 percent of total central station company revenues.
Source: Quantum Science Corporation, and industry data.

owned only 27. Many of the companies, including Burns and Honeywell, had entered the market only after ADT had been successfully prosecuted for antitrust violations; as a result of a divestiture order, ADT had sold some of its central stations to Burns and other firms.

Annual charges for central station services varied over a wide range, averaging $1,000–$2,000 for commercial installation. In addition, there was a line leasing charge. A typical contract for service and installation covered a period of five years. Subscribers were required to pay for the cost of installing the equipment on their premises as well as a monthly fee for being connected to the system. The installation fee, which could be a few hundred to a few thousand dollars, was thought to reduce the cancellation rate of contracts. The average contract life for some firms was 18–20 years.

In providing protection, central stations were considered to have several advantages over guard companies:

(1)   Blanket security—unlike guards, central stations could provide continuous coverage of the complete premise

(2)   Cost—central stations provided wide protection at an estimated 7 percent lower total cost.[42]

For central station owners, the attractiveness of a central station lay in its operational leverage, which allowed profits to increase at a greater rate than sales. Being capital intensive, economies of scale were available. If a central station was operating with 100 customers, for example, the cost of adding the 101st customer was minimal. Further, the larger the number of contract subscribers, the lower were the labor requirements as a percent of revenues and the higher was the contribution to net profits.

---

[42] Ibid., p. 39.

Some central stations could handle as many as 4,000–6,000 subscribers, with breakeven volume approximating $200,000 per year.

Established central station operators had also enjoyed some measure of protection from new competition. New central stations generally had to incur substantial start-up costs in the area of $200,000 and sustained negative operating cash flows until break-even, which generally occurred in the third year.[43]

Insurance companies had also provided a boost to the growth of central station operations. With premium discounts of up to 40–50 percent for belonging to a central station system, many businesses had moved from guard to central station service. These factors, combined with suitable central station services for residential users, were expected to provide a major stimulus to the growth of the central station industry.

Penetration of the residential market by central stations was expected due to continuing efforts to develop lower cost service and transmission facilities. By 1978, the annual charge for residential market central station protection was projected to be in the $100–$150 range instead of the $700–$1,500 range, largely due to the use of cable television as the transmission media rather than the more expensive telephone lines and sensors.[44]

EQUIPMENT SEGMENTS AND TRENDS

Over the period 1968–73, security equipment company revenues had grown at an annual rate of 10.4 percent, and accounted for 25 percent of all security industry revenues. Competing companies ranged from small firms producing a single product to corporate giants such as IBM marketing its System 7 computer for access control applications. The largest and most rapidly growing equipment segments were sensors and detectors and central station equipment.

Sensors and Intrusion Detectors

The largest of the equipment sectors, sensor and detector industry sales amounted to $325 million in 1973, and were projected to grow at a compound rate of 15 percent through 1978. Most industry sources felt that this sector would reach $665 million by 1978.[45]

Most of the sensing devices available in 1973 operated on well-defined physical principles, e.g., ultrasonics, microwave, or photoelectric beams.

---

[43] Estimates of breakeven volume provided to research by two central station operators.

[44] *Security Systems*, pp. 45–47.

[45] Ibid.

It was generally felt in the industry that product differences were more imaginary than real.[46] Thus development and marketing efforts in this segment of the industry had been geared toward improving detector discrimination performance, while reducing the production price in order to appeal to the residential market, which had been virtually ignored. However, some of the major industry competitors had undertaken efforts to produce detection devices to sell for less than $50 to sell to the home market; these firms included ADT, Walter Kidde, Kodak, and Honeywell.

Central Station and System Equipment

Industry sales of central station and proprietary alarm equipment, including remote controls, displays, control centers, and monitoring equipment, amounted to $150 million in 1973. With such firms as IBM, Honeywell, ADT, and Johnson Services becoming major factors, this part of the security industry was projected to grow at a 20 percent annual rate through 1978. Revenues and growth of firms in this segment had been stimulated by several market and technological factors. Substantial sales had resulted from the conversion of over 300 older central stations to modern and automated hardware. Another principal cause had been the increasing use of proprietary and integrated security systems in high-rise apartment and office buildings.

While there were numerous manufacturers of systems and central station equipment, the emerging leaders tended to be those firms that had integrated system expertise and skill in developing computer-based systems, with features capable of monitoring environmental conditions, building access, sensor, and alarm function. Industry leaders had been RCA, ADT, Honeywell, IBM, and Johnson Service Co.

INDUSTRY TRENDS

Along with the overall industry growth, several trends had surfaced which had ramifications for the strategy of security industry firms.

Integration of Services and Equipment. Equipment and services were increasingly being utilized in combination to reduce the problems of rising labor costs and equipment failures. Further, the move to a total system approach was thought to provide better overall security protection.[47]

Increasing Equipment Share. Equipment sales had accounted for a larger and larger share of the total security market. From $1.1 billion

---

[46] Ibid.
[47] Ibid., p. 142.

in 1973 (25 percent of total security industry sales), equipment sales were projected to reach $3.4 billion or 36 percent of total industry revenues by 1980. New entrants into the equipment segment were expected to capitalize on their ability to develop and provide total systems utilizing sensors, monitoring equipment, and guards in an integrated fashion. In fact, central stations were estimated to be the fastest growing segment, with revenues projected to grow from $275 million in 1973 to $1.3 billion in 1980, an increase of 25 percent annually.[48]

Consolidation of the Industry. The 1973 security industry was dominated by a small number of firms. Further consolidation was expected as smaller and regional competitors in all industry segments were acquired by larger firms or forced out of business due to higher operating costs, more stringent regulation, minimum wage legislation, and lack of technological capability.[49]

Little Foreign Competition. Despite the attractiveness of the growth of the security industry, foreign competition had been minimal in both the United States and abroad. Several U.S. firms had made substantial investments in foreign operations, however.[50]

Marketing Strategies. As equipment producers and systems companies gained a relatively larger market share, a shift in the marketing strategies of the total industry was forecast. Historically, all of the service firms had employed direct sales techniques on a local or regional basis to maintain growth. Many of the personnel were ex-military or federal, state, or local law enforcement officials. Relying on direct sales techniques, many advertising budgets of the older security service firms had been relatively small, ranging from zero in the case of several major firms to a maximum of 1.5 percent of the sales dollar. Equipment and hardware companies, however, tended to devote a larger share of their revenue dollar to advertising. Reasons for lack of attention to advertising by service companies had ranged from answers like "Why should I advertise when I already have 50 percent of the market" to "We've got all the business we can handle right now." It was felt by industry analysts that this attitude would change as companies offering integrated security systems, with sophisticated marketing skills, penetrated the industry.[51]

THE FUTURE

Reflecting the surge in demand for security and protection, most industry observers and participants predicted an optimistic future for the

---

48 Ibid.
49 Ibid., p. 146.
50 Ibid., pp. 59–60.
51 Ibid., p. 25.

security equipment and services industry. From $4.1 billion in 1973, the market was projected to reach $9.3 billion by 1980, an increase of better than 12 percent annually.[52] Most observers were agreed that the most dramatic increase would occur in the equipment segment, reflecting a growing demand for total systems, lower costs, and more effective products. After extensive research on the industry, Mr. S. F. Kaufman, of the Quantum Science Corporation, observed in a trade journal:

> The security systems industry, consisting of hardware and services to protect property, is entering a period of rapid growth primarily due to the increasing volume of crime in the United States and the inability of the criminal justice system to significantly reduce the incidence of crime. The application of new electronic technology to the problem of crime will not only benefit society by decreasing the crime rate, but will also provide a profitable new opportunity for private enterprise.[53]

One potential problem that had drawn the attention of the Alarm Industry Committee for Combating Crime (AICCC)—an industry group —had been an initial test project in which alarm system detection devices on private premises were owned by government.[54] Sponsored by the Law Enforcement Assistance Administration, a study in Cedar Rapids, Iowa, had tested a relatively unsophisticated low-cost alarm system wired directly to police headquarters and maintained and owned by the city. Direct connection of residential alarms to police and fire stations had been allowed in many cities. However, high false-alarm rates had led many municipalities to ban direct connections. Much of the cause for the high false-alarm rates was attributed to homeowner negligence and poor equipment.

The AICCC was particularly troubled as its members felt that if this trend were extended, private security services would not be able to compete with a tax-subsidized service. In general, the industry viewed these experiments with mixed feelings; while they liked receiving the benefits of government test findings, they were concerned about government interference in their business. It was felt that as property crime became more and more of a problem, the government could become more of a factor in the future of the industry.[55]

---

[52] *Security World*, October 1973.

[53] *Security Systems*, pp. 77–80.

[54] AICCC consisted of the National Burglar and Fire Alarm Association, American District Telegraph, Burns International, Diebold, Holmes Protection, Inc., Mosler Safe Company, Wells Fargo Alarm Services, and the Central Station Electrical Protection Association.

[55] *Security Systems*, pp. 77–80.

EXHIBIT 4

A Note on the Security Services and Equipment Industry
Selected Company Profiles

Security Services

1. *American District Telegraph Co. (ADT):* 1973 revenues $148.3 million; company designed, manufactured, installed, and maintained electrical protection systems through central stations, direct connection to fire or police headquarters, on-site systems, and local alarms. Central station services accounted for more than 80% of revenues. Company had 6,667 employees and 7,600 stockholders. Founded in 1901. Listed on American Stock Exchange.

2. *Baker Industries:* 1973 revenues $107.7 million; armored transport and courier, security guard, and alarm services were provided under the *Wells Fargo* name; also sold products for fire protection. Revenue mix: armored and courier transport, 33%; security guard services, 21%; alarm service (central station), 23%; pyrotronics (fire), 16%; facility services, 5%; chemicals, 2%. Had over 7,700 employees; 2,189 stockholders; insiders owned about 13% of common stock. Listed on New York Stock Exchange.

3. *Brink's Inc. (83% owned by the Pittston Company):* 1973 revenues $102.4 million* net income $5.6*; the largest armored car company in the United States; also furnished armored car services through subsidiaries and affiliates in 15 foreign countries. Parent company listed on New York Stock Exchange.

4. *Burns International Security Services, Inc.:* 1973 revenues $153.6 million; the second largest company providing uniformed guard services, company was founded in 1909. Revenue mix: guard services, 90%; investigation, 2%; central station, 8%. Company had 107 offices and 27 central stations serving 15,900 guard and 18,600 electronic clients. Insiders owned about 16% of Class A and 81% of class B stock. Had offices in Canada, Latin America, and England. Listed on American Stock Exchange.

5. *Pinkerton's, Inc.:* 1973 revenues $174.8 million; the oldest and largest company in the private contract guard business, with over 105 offices and 12,000 clients. Revenue mix: guard services, 87%; investigation, 7%; electronic surveillance devices, 1%; other 0.5%. Labor costs approximated 85% of revenues. Founded in 1850. Company had over 36,000 employees and 1,500 stockholders. Insiders owned about 32% of Class B and 92% of Class A stock. Listed over-the-counter.

6. *Wackenhut Corporation:* 1973 revenues $90.5 million; the third largest private contract guard company. Wackenhut had been formed in 1954; guards and investigative service accounted for

---

* Standard & Poor's, estimates for Brink's only. Total Pittston Company sales in 1973 were $682.6 million.

Exhibit 4 (continued)

90% of revenues; company had five central stations; had 12,000 clients, 107 offices, and operated in 38 states, Puerto Rico, Dominican Republic, Guam, Canada, Latin America, and three European countries. In 1973, company had 15,000 employees and 1,250 stockholders; insiders owned about 56% of common stock. Listed on American Stock Exchange.

Security Hardware

1. *Walter Kidde & Co.:* 1973 revenues $977.8 million, of which safety, security, and protection sales accounted for 34% of 1973 sales and 25% of operating profit, $332.4 million and $25.8 million, respectively. Company manufactured fire extinguishing and detection equipment, furnished private contract guards through 80% owned Globe Security Systems subsidiary (the fourth largest guard company in the U.S.); made locks and a variety of security equipment for banks and financial institutions. Revenue mix: safety, security, and protection, 34%; consumer and commercial products (incandescent lighting, clocks, electric appliances), 33%; industrial equipment (truck trailers, cargo containers, cranes), 33%. Listed on New York Stock Exchange.

2. *Rusco Industries:* 1973 revenues $50.5 million; operating through 14 manufacturing facilities, company manufactured and distributed window, door, and related building products. Revenue mix: building and architectural accessories, 80%; bed frames, 14%; security control devices, 5%; precision machining of metal parts, 1%. Company had developed a security card-operated electronic access control system that could activate locking and access devices using an encoded card instead of a key. Had 1,650 employees and 8,500 stockholders. Listed on American Stock Exchange.

Security Systems

1. *Diebold, Inc.:* 1973 revenues $189.4 million. Diebold was generally considered to be the leading manufacturer of bank security equipment and systems. Security systems included bank vault doors and linings, safe deposit boxes, teller's lockers, vault ventilators, alarm systems, photographic surveillance systems, and teller windows. Revenue mix: security and record storage equipment, 87%; pneumatic airtube systems, 12%; and check printing and package check plans, 1%. Company had 175 sales offices. New services offered by the company included a computer controlled security and surveillance system for high-rise office buildings and banks; was also developing an alarm system for the commercial market. Had 6,820 employees and 5,932 shareholders. Listed on New York Stock Exchange.

2. *Johnson Service Company:* 1973 revenues $251.2 million; net income $9.1 million. Company designed, manufactured, installed,

Exhibit 4 (concluded)

---

and serviced automatic environmental and other control systems for a variety of building functions including air conditioning, ventilating, heating, security surveillance, fire and smoke detection. Revenue mix: environmental control systems, 79%; Penn Controls (automatic residential and nonresidential heating and air conditioning), 13%; other products, 7%. Had 9,200 employees and 4,394 shareholders. Listed on New York Stock Exchange.

3. *Honeywell, Inc.:* 1973 revenues $2.4 billion; company manufactured a variety of computer systems and industrial control systems. Automatic controls for residences and commercial buildings accounted for 19% of 1973 sales. Honeywell was the largest producer of controls for residential heating and air conditioning systems, and was a major supplier of environmental controls, security systems, and fire protection systems for commercial buildings. Controls and instrumentation for industry, including computer directed systems, represented 14% of 1973 sales. Company also owned eight central stations. Listed on New York Stock Exchange.

4. *RCA:* 1973 revenues $4.2 billion. Through its Government and Commercial Systems Group, the company manufactured and marketed a computer controlled system to direct the functions of both security and environmental systems of large businesses.

5. *Esterline Corp.:* 1973 revenues $108.9 million. Founded in 1967, Esterline was a diversified, multinational, high technology company. Through its Data Acquisition and Control Products Group, the company had developed a minicomputer-based security system, utilizing sequential scanning of a sensor network and visual and/or audible alarms. The Data Acquisitions and Control Products Group accounted for 41% of revenues.

Other Systems Companies

Other major companies producing security systems included IBM, Eaton Corp., Westinghouse, and Motorola.

Cable Television (CATV)

1. *TelePrompTer Corporation:* 1973 revenues $76.7 million. The largest operator of CATV systems, TelePrompTer owned or had substantial interest in about 144 cable systems in 33 states and one Canadian province. In 1974, the number of subscribers totaled 1,022,500; CATV divisions accounted for 70% of revenues; 15% was provided by the Muzak division which supplied functional background music to offices, factories, hotels, etc. Listed on New York Stock Exchange.

Source: Company reports and industry studies.

6

Allied Security, Inc.

Allied Security, Inc., was the seventh largest guard company in the United States in terms of revenues, and the sixth most profitable. In 1974, Allied's net income was $290,000 on revenues of $6.9 million. In the five years from 1969 to 1974, sales had grown at a compounded annual rate of more than 35 percent and profits had almost tripled. (See Exhibits 1, 2, and 3.)

About 98 percent of Allied's revenues were from uniformed guard services, although the company also provided investigative services, detection equipment, and surveillance systems. Its customers were mainly industrial, commercial, and retail firms. (See Exhibit 4.)

Allied, like several of its major competitors, was a young company, founded in the late 50s. It was headquartered in Pittsburgh, where it had first begun operations. Between 1970 and 1975, Allied had expanded into ten other cities, first in the Midwest, then the East and Far West. Of its ten offices operating in 1975, six were profitable, two were hovering around breakeven, and two were in the red. (See Exhibits 5 and 6.)

Neal Holmes, the president and founder of Allied, described his company's strategy:

> We're a security company. More than 90 percent of our business is guarding property, mainly against fire, theft, and vandalism. Fire is the most serious threat to a business. If someone steals equipment, a company can still operate, but if the building burns, it has to close.
>
> Fewer than one percent of our guards carry sidearms. It would be dangerous to arm the others since they are generally unskilled and in some cases have a low level of intelligence. They are hired as firewatch guards and

EXHIBIT 1

ALLIED SECURITY, INC.
Detailed Income Statement 1972–74

	1974		1973		1972	
	$	%	$	%	$	%
Income..........................	6,937	100.0	5,231	100.0	4,175	100.0
Expenses:						
Salaries and Wages						
Guards........................	4,306	62.1	3,139	60.0	2,421	58.0
Investigative.................	3	—	5	—	16	—
Supervisory and administrative.....	871	12.9	769	14.7	685	16.4
Payroll taxes.....................	424	6.1	296	5.7	226	5.4
Profit sharing and pension..........	36	0.5	38	0.7	35	0.8
Depreciation......................	61	0.8	57	1.1	52	1.2
Advertising and selling.............	28	−0.4	39	0.7	40	0.1
Rent.............................	32	−0.5	29	0.6	28	0.7
Guard supplies....................	30	−0.4	14	0.3	26	0.6
Bad debts........................	25	−0.4	7	0.1	16	0.4
Interest..........................	—	—	—	—	1	—
Other............................	488	7.0	339	6.5	350	8.4
Total.......................	6,304	90.8	4,732	90.5	3,896	93.3
Earnings before income taxes and						
minority interest.................	633	9.1	499	9.5	279	6.7
Income taxes.....................	320	4.6	247	4.7	149	3.6
Minority interest in subsidiary*.....	23	—	18	0.3	12	0.3
Net income....................	290	4.2	234	4.5	32	0.8
Earnings per share................	$0.40		$0.34		$0.05	
Guard hours (in thousands)..........	1,987		1,569		1,300	
Average guard fees/hour...........	$3.42		$3.25		$3.13	
Average guard wages/hour..........	$2.17		$2.00		$1.86	
Average wages as % of fees.........	63.5%		61.5%		59.4%	

not policemen. We try to match the mentality of the man to the requirements of the job. We can't use highly skilled people on menial firewatch guard work.

We're not like some of the other guard companies with ex-FBI and ex-CIA men. We don't spend our time tracking the Mafia, Communists, or unfaithful wives. We're oriented toward property protection and our main goal is to make money.

EXHIBIT 2

ALLIED SECURITY, INC.
Summary Income Statement 1965–74

	1965	1966	1967	1968	1969	1970	1971	1972	1973	1974
Income.............	765	945	1,139	1,328	1,369	2,076	2,760	4,175	5,231	6,937
Expenses...........	731	879	1,030	1,188	1,417	1,725	2,283	3,896	4,732	6,304
Income										
before taxes......	34	66	110	139	212	350	477	279	499	633
Net income.........	22	38	62	76	106	163	231	32	234	290
% of income......	2.9%	4%	5.4%	5.7%	7.7%	7.9%	8.4%	0.8%	4.5%	4.2%
E.P.S..............	$0.04	$0.07	$0.11	$0.14	$0.19	$0.28	$0.35	$0.05	$0.34	$0.40

EXHIBIT 3

ALLIED SECURITY, INC.
Balance Sheet—June 30, 1974

Assets

	1974
Current assets:	
Cash..	$ 73,668
Cash—savings...	40,077
Short-term marketable securities—at cost (which approximates market)..	408,668
Accounts receivable—trade (Less allowance for doubtful accounts of $15,000).....................................	1,132,828
Other current assets....................................	26,365
Total current assets................................	1,681,606
Other assets:	
Investments in preferred stock (quoted market $173,500)....	225,173
Deferred income taxes..................................	23,384
Cash value of life insurance...........................	10,600
	259,157
Property and equipment—at cost:	
Land and land improvements............................	51,727
Buildings and building improvements....................	197,754
Furniture and equipment...............................	175,454
Guard uniforms..	89,360
	514,295
Less accumulated depreciation..........................	(134,986)
	379,309
	$2,320,072

Liabilities and Stockholders' Equity

	1974
Current liabilities:	
Accounts payable......................................	$ 82,013
Accrued salaries and wages............................	162,843
Accrued and withheld payroll taxes....................	105,414
Taxes on income......................................	79,940
Accrued expenses—other...............................	36,343
Total current liabilities...........................	466,553
Minority interest in subsidiary stockholders' equity:	72,185
Common stock—par value $0.05 authorized, 2,000,000 shares; issued, 732,833 shares........................	36,642
Additional paid-in capital.............................	805,663
Retained earnings.....................................	985,529
	1,827,834
Less treasury stock—17,088 shares.....................	(46,500)
	1,781,334
	$2,320,072

Allied attempted to maintain above-average profitability by being selective in taking on new accounts, bidding for contracts at levels that would give reasonable profits, keeping tight control over costs, and minimizing overhead. For example, the corporate office was staffed by only six individuals: president—Mr. Holmes; treasurer and controller

EXHIBIT 4

ALLIED SECURITY, INC.
5 Largest Accounts
Annual Billings

	1970	1975
#1	$117,000	$ 520,000
#2	108,000	432,000
#3	88,000	161,000
#4	66,000	155,000
#5	53,000	130,000
Total	$498,000	$1,398,000
% Total income	24.0%	15.8% (est.)

—Ralph Prior; assistant controller—Steve Stein; and three secretaries.

Neal Holmes had set a minimum goal of 20 percent annual growth in profits and felt that this could be achieved through growth in Allied's guard business alone:

> So far, we have not entered the equipment or central station segments of the industry. If an attractive acquisition came along, we'd make it. But meanwhile, there's plenty of room to grow as a guard company and we can meet our goals through internal growth alone.

COMPANY HISTORY

Allied bore the clear imprint of its president, Neal Holmes. His background and experience contrasted with that of his competitors and served to differentiate his company as well. Most of the newer guard companies had been founded by individuals involved in police or investigative work. For example, Wackenhut, the third largest company in the industry, was started by an ex-FBI agent. At least four of its top officers

EXHIBIT 5

ALLIED SECURITY, INC.
Branch Offices

Location	Date Opened	
Cleveland	June	1970
Philadelphia	July	1970
Cincinnati	September	1970
Chicago	October	1970
Los Angeles	November	1970
Trenton, N.J.*	December	1970
Albany, N.Y.	February	1971
New York	July	1971
Newark, N.J.	September	1971
San Francisco	July	1973

* Consolidated with Newark office in December 1971.

EXHIBIT 6

Sales and Profits by Office and Changes in Branch Management 1973–75 (estimate)

Office		1975 Estimate* (7/1/74–6/30/75)	1974 (7/1/73–6/30/74)	1973 (7/1/72–6/30/73)
#1	Revenues	$ 544	$ 494	$ 517
	Profit†	8	3	15
	Management change‡	1/75	2/74	6/73
#2	Revenues	368	376	245
	Profit†	(1)	5	(5)
	Management change‡	7/74	4/74	3/73
#3	Revenues	474	511	394
	Profit†	(1)	13	—
	Management change‡	—	12/73	—
#4	Revenues	459	315	175
	Profit†	8	1	(15)
	Management change‡	5/75	—	6/73
#5	Revenues	3,667	2,894	2,484
	Profit†	276	237	214
	Management change‡	—	11/73	—
#6	Revenues	206	55	—
	Profit†	(8)	(25)	—
	Management change‡	—	2/74	—
#7	Revenues	1,252	831	218
	Profit†	28	19	(11)
	Management change‡	10/74	7/13	—
#8	Revenues	523	381	302
	Profit†	10	3	(1)
	Management change‡	—	—	—
#9	Revenues	1,060	778	572
	Profit†	100	47	37
	Management change‡	—	—	—
#10	Revenues	306	368	359
	Profit†	(7)	10	20
	Management change‡	—	9/73 1/74	—

* Based on 11 months actual.

† After-tax profit includes allocation of regional managers' expenses but not corporate overhead. Management's targets for branch office profitability were:

Revenues (000)	Profit as a Percent of Revenues
350	0%
500	3½
1,000	5

‡ Branch manager replaced.

were formerly with the FBI, and its board of directors included a former director of the C.I.A., and a former director of Defense Intelligence. Even Pinkerton, the oldest and largest guard company, was started by President Lincoln's ex-bodyguard. Neal Holmes saw himself as fundamentally different:

> I'm not an ex-policeman. I have an excellent education, a four-year degree in psychology, which I earned selling encyclopedias door to door.

Sitting in his plush office, with his feet resting comfortably on his desk, Neal Holmes reflected on his "Horatio Alger" past:

> I was born in 1930 in the east end of Pittsburgh. I grew up in a depressed area during the Depression. I never knew it, because everyone else I knew was as poor as we were. When I was 15, I became bored with school and left. I lied about my age and joined the paratroopers. I spent three years in the South Pacific in Japan, Guam, Iwo Jima, the Philippines, and China. In the 11th Airborne Division, I was assigned to the criminal investigation unit where I received my experience in investigative work. When I was 18, my tour of duty was finished and I left the service. I wanted a government police job, but I could not qualify because of my lack of formal education. So, I went to work selling encyclopedias door to door. At each of the three companies I worked for I became their top salesman. In fact, I was making $300 a week before I was 20, when everyone else I knew was making $60.

In 1955, Mr. Holmes and another encyclopedia salesman, John Brown, formed Tab Burglar Alarm Company to sell burglar alarms to churches.

> We sold a lot of burglar alarms, but after two years, we felt like we hadn't built anything. We didn't want to wake up at 40 still selling door to door. So, we each invested $1,000, formed Allied Security Company, and began a patrol service. We signed up customers for a one-year contract and asked them to pay the first six months in advance. For a while, we were robbing Peter to pay Paul, and that gave us our working capital. John and I would go out and sell during the day. Then at night I would put on a guard's uniform and John would chauffeur me around. I covered the first shift, from six to eleven, plus weekends and holidays. Then we hired F. X. Collins, who is now our director of operations, to do the second shift from eleven to seven.
>
> As Allied grew, I discovered that there was more to learn about security. So, I interviewed for a job at three of our largest competitors to meet their managers. Then I hired the best of the three, from Pinkerton, to run Allied. A while later, I hired a competitor's salesman. Our philosophy is that if we need expertise, we hire the best people available and pay them more than they were making previously.
>
> Allied was successful from the start. John and I were both good salesmen and this was coupled with close control over finances. The keys were attention to detail and hard work. We each did three or four different jobs to keep costs down and only drew 40 dollars a week. When we first

hired a manager and a salesman, they each were making more than John and I combined.

In 1970, a third of Allied's shares (220,000) were sold to the public at $5.75 per share[1] and the company launched an expansion program. Five branch offices were opened in 1970 and three more were opened in 1971. When the expansion program began, Allied management adopted a policy of capitalizing the first 12 months' start-up costs of new offices, and amortizing them over the next 30 months. Ralph Prior explained:

> The thing that brought this idea to our attention was that other companies were doing it, particularly Guardsmark, which is most comparable to us. It made sense, since we expected new offices to break even within 12 months. Unfortunately, that didn't necessarily happen. For example, Cincinnati was in the red for more than two years.

After continuous growth in profits, in 1972 Allied's earnings dropped precipitously from $0.35 per share to $0.05. Of this $0.30 drop, $0.18 was attributable to an accounting change. The earlier policy was revised and it was decided to expense start-up costs as incurred.

More significant than the write-off of deferred start-up costs was the poor performance of several branch offices. Ken Slutsky, Allied's eastern regional manager and corporate personnel director, explained what went wrong with the company's expansion:

> Neal had no experience in operating a national company. His outlook was optimistic, to say the least. He thought that there were a great number of people like himself around the country, people who were capable and eager to go into business for themselves, but just lacked the opportunity. He didn't realize that there aren't many people who could do what he did in Pittsburgh.
>
> We advertised in national journals, and we put into business whoever convinced Neal he could succeed. We sent him back to his city, told him to open an office. The help we gave him was long-distance guidance and not very effective.
>
> The former manager in Albany was typical. He was a fast talker and was able to get a lot of business right away. But he couldn't keep it. He was a policeman at heart, and not a manager. He couldn't supervise people or deliver the service that he promised.
>
> Neal tried to counteract this with more and more guidance from corporate, and by replacing our branch managers. In four years, we had more than 20 managers in six of our branch offices, including at least five in Chicago alone. Despite these problems, we've had a satisfactory record of growth in both sales and profits.
>
> Our problems were not unusual for this industry. In my opinion, the guard industry is filled with incompetents to a large extent. Allied has at

---

[1] In 1975, Neal Holmes and John Brown each controlled one-third of the outstanding shares. John Brown had retired from the company in 1973.

least recognized our problems and made some fundamental changes to deal with them.

Operations

Each of Allied's offices was organized in a standard hierarchical structure as shown in the accompanying chart.

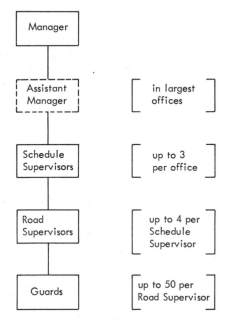

Each office had from one to three schedule supervisors. They in turn had up to four road supervisors reporting to them. Road supervisors were given the titles sergeant, lieutenant, or captain, depending on their length of service in the company and their performance. Each road supervisor had as many as 50 guards reporting to him.

Dick Schwab, the manager of the Pittsburgh office, explained what was involved in meeting a customer's need for guards:

> The first step is to determine the requirements for the job: how many hours and the number of guards. We always have a number of part-time men available as well as full-time men who are on call on their days off or holidays, on a rotating basis.[2] If we need to hire additional men for a big job, we put a newspaper ad in. Of course, we then have to train the new men before they can go out on a job.[3]

---

[2] It was estimated that 75 percent of Allied's guards were full-time employees.

[3] The length of training varied according to the nature of the assignment and the state's legal requirements, if any. It was generally from four to 20 hours per guard.

We have to be careful about who we pick for a particular client. All guards can't work at all facilities. We try to pick clean looking men for public exposure jobs.

The road supervisor is responsible for setting the guard up at a site. He evaluates the property, sets up the rounds, and instructs the guard. Sometimes it's fairly complicated. The guard has to know how often to make the rounds, what to look for, where the telephones and fire equipment are, which people are authorized to be let in, who to contact in emergencies, and where the gas, electric, and water turnoffs are.

Once the guard is on the job, we have to make sure the customer stays satisfied. All sorts of problems can arise—guards may be late, sloppy, drunk, or sleeping. When these problems come up, we have to respond properly. There's no margin of error in this business. If I find a guard sleeping or drinking, I'll fire him on the spot and stay there myself until a relief man arrives.

Branch Management

Allied management had gradually come to the realization that a lack of capable and qualified branch managers was a critical constraint on the company's future expansion and could hurt the performance of existing offices. Two major changes had been made in attempting to deal with this problem:

—An additional level of managers was added to the organization with the creation of regional manager positions between the branch offices and the corporate office (see organization chart in Exhibit 7);

—An entire new set of criteria was established for hiring management personnel.

In 1972, Allied's management made an organizational change that created regional manager positions between the branch managers and the corporate office. Ken Slutzky, who was eastern regional manager (in addition to being corporate personnel director) described his regional manager's job:

I supervise the management of three offices—Chicago, Albany, and New York. In theory, I have two main functions. The first is to act as a line of communication, transferring good ideas between the branch offices and also serving as a buffer between Neal and the branch managers. The second is to placate clients who are upset. Clients feel important if a branch manager says he's bringing in an expert from out of town to solve their problems. To most clients, being from more than 50 miles away makes you an expert.

The way things really work, I'm more involved in boosting up weak branch managers than I should be. I have to keep on top of all aspects of what's going on in each of the three offices. I keep close watch on their financial performance and accounts receivable collections, do most

EXHIBIT 7
Organizational Chart

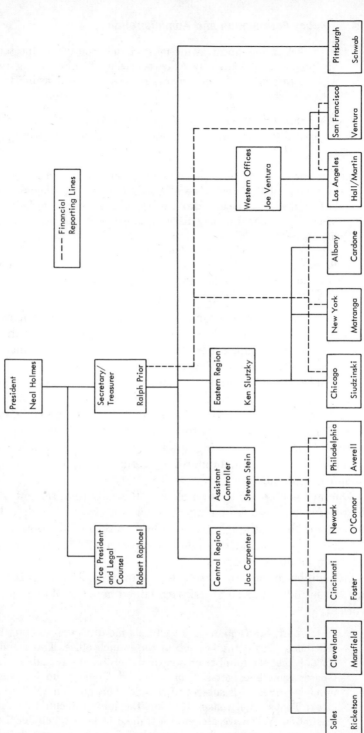

of the key hiring, and provide most of the expertise in the security field. My involvement varies by office according to how strong the manager is. I try to give my branch managers as much responsibility as possible, if they're competent. But, developing good managers is a slow process.

Ralph Prior felt that the regional managers gave the company an added capability for turning around offices which were performing poorly:

> The corporate office is dependent on the regional managers for timely evaluation of the branches and working out their problems. For example, last summer, in Newark, profit margins had dropped to half their normal level. The regional manager spent six weeks in that office. It was a training exercise for the staff. He showed them how to properly run the office, and the margins returned to the expected level.
>
> Before we had regional managers all we could do was make periodic visits to the offices. When there were problems, we usually ended up replacing the office manager.

In January 1975, Allied's management adopted new policies for hiring management personnel, which represented a 180° turn for the company. Formerly, Allied's branch managers were either ex-police officers, security specialists, or former employees of competing guard companies. The main criteria were whether they impressed Neal Holmes and whether he believed they could do the job. Under the new policy, Allied decided to hire only individuals who were educated in management or had supervisory experience. They then attempted to train them in the security industry. Rather than relying solely on gut feelings in selecting among applicants, they used a standardized formal procedure developed by an outside consultant.

One major point of contention was the new requirement of a college degree for all branch managers. Ken Slutzky and Ralph Prior both pushed for this, although Neal Holmes was initially opposed to it. In the end, it was included in the requirements, with the understanding that there could be exceptions.

In addition to the stricter selection standards, a new approach to training was introduced. Ken Slutzky explained how the old training program worked:

> In the past, future managers spent six months in an existing branch as a scheduler. This is the key job in the branch office. The scheduler has to see to it that the number of guards requested are available when needed. Guards sometimes get sick or simply don't show up for work, and the number requested is subject to change. This goes on 24 hours around the clock. That's what makes this job the most difficult in terms of petty frustration. When we assigned a trainee to be a scheduler, he learned a lot about the business, but it was also an endurance test, to see if he had the guts and will to stick with the job.

With the new training procedure for branch managers, trainees spent from four to six months learning all facets of a branch operation. They carried out the scheduling function but also learned the details of every other function performed in a branch office.

Branch managers were paid a base salary of approximately $15,000–$18,000 per year, plus a possible annual bonus of up to about $3,000.

Corporate Staff

During the past few years, Neal Holmes had attempted to build a strong, young management team at the corporate level. He had delegated almost all responsibility for day-to-day decisions to Ralph Prior. A management advisory board, consisting of Ralph, Steve Stein, and the eastern and central regional managers, had taken a more active role in corporate policy decisions. Neal Holmes explained:

> In 1969, I hired Ralph as controller. He was working for our accounting firm and knew our business well. Our philosophy is that everybody should have a back-up man, so in 1972, Ralph hired Steve and moved up to treasurer. Although Ralph is only 28 and Steve is two years younger, those two really coordinate the entire operation for me. They are both CPAs and stay right on top of the numbers.
>
> I delegate anything they are capable of doing. In fact, the most difficult part of my job is finding new challenges for them.

Five of Allied's nine branches outside of Pittsburgh reported on a dotted line to Ralph while the other four reported to Steve. The branch offices sent detailed monthly reports to the regions. These were consolidated, and abbreviated reports were sent to corporate. Then a summary report was prepared and sent to the branches to compare their relative performance.

In the past, the reporting relationship of the branch offices had been informal, but it had gradually become more standardized as the number of branches increased. Ralph Prior had developed a new format, which was to begin in May, 1975. It required the branches to report in seven key areas:

New accounts for the month.

Terminated accounts for the month.

Training costs.

Overtime costs.

Uniforms outstanding.

Accounts receivable past due.

Personnel changes.

In addition, each month Steve and Ralph compared monthly hours billed for guards to hours on payroll for guards. Where these differed by more than one-half hour they were investigated. All of Allied's accounting was centralized and done on the company's computer in the corporate office. Invoices were paid through the corporate office and had to be approved by either Steve or Ralph. All salary increases had to be approved by them as well, and even petty cash slips were sent to the corporate office for their review.

Branch managers were informed of unwarranted or unwise expenditures. In the few cases where these continued, they were deducted from the manager's paycheck. Managers could also be personally responsible for bad debts when these resulted from an incomplete credit check. These were deducted from their bonuses, but not from their regular pay. Ralph Prior commented on these practices:

> We rarely resort to making the managers pay out of their own pockets, and even then the amounts involved are relatively small. But this potential threat keeps them honest and paying attention to what they are spending money on.

Marketing

Allied management felt that the main area in which the company could effectively compete for customers was in service, mainly professionalism in setting up the guard and in responsiveness to customer complaints. Neal Holmes commented:

> The whole thing revolves around maintaining a personal interest in the client and properly supervising the guards. Price is a factor, but in most cases it's not the most important.

Allied's experience had demonstrated that demand for guards was relatively inelastic with respect to changes in price. In 1972, in an attempt to increase market penetration, Allied had lowered its rates in Albany. Demand increased only slightly and profits dropped sharply. In Cleveland, Allied had taken the opposite tack and priced their guards at the high end of the scale. They had done this for several years with excellent results. In that market, Allied was recognized for high-quality service and the higher rates were expected. In fact, in the past, clients had at times expressed surprise when lower rates were quoted.

It was believed that the industry would eventually move in the direction of cost-plus bidding. Clients were becoming more sophisticated, and recognizing that they were getting what they paid for. As Ken Slutzky explained:

> Clients have seen the $2.10 guard and are not happy with him. He's not what was promised.

Mr. Slutzky saw an increasing client awareness of this and a willingness to pay more for better quality services. Recently, Allied had put more emphasis on a security survey for customers as a means of expanding demand for their guards, and to make more explicit the role and functions of the guard. In some cases, when it appeared likely that they would get the account, they provided this service free of charge.

Management believed that high market share in a local area offered several important advantages. These included:

1. Better exposure in the marketplace, which attracted new business and tended to further increase share.
2. Higher profitability due to economies of scale. These were most significant up to approximately $1,000,000 in revenues per year, and resulted from absorption of overhead over a greater number of guards and increased flexibility in the utilization of personnel.

In most cities, the largest guard company had well below 50 percent of the market and there were several strong competitors. Allied held its strongest position in Pittsburgh where it was the largest guard company with 35–40 percent of the market. In contrast, most of Allied's branch offices had 10 percent or less market share.

Allied was not in enough cities to effectively compete for most national contracts, but management felt that these were not a major factor in the industry. Generally, clients recognized that a given company's offices varied widely, and thus used the best guard company in each of their locations.

THE FUTURE

Allied's top officers all saw a promising future for the company, and felt that whatever threats the company faced were not imminent. Ken Slutzky commented:

> We're most heavily dependent on firewatch, and there's no way that equipment will replace the guard in this function. Equipment will only detect a fire, it won't find the source or do anything about it. Sprinklers are not the answer, since they can do more damage than the fire they put out. The insurance companies know the value of a guard—they knock ten to 20 percent off fire insurance rates for having one. Our real threats are internal and from the government. We have to clean house, which we're already doing, and try to fight restrictive legislation, like mandatory training requirements. If that's enacted, it will add to outside guard company costs but won't apply to in-house guards.

Ralph Prior felt that a long-term technological threat existed, but there was no need to act on it now:

There's going to come a day when guard services are the horse and buggy of the security industry, and right now we're totally unprepared for it. At some future time we'll have to get into equipment and systems, and when that time comes we'll hire experts or make an acquisition. But now, we have room to grow in our area of expertise.

Neal Holmes also saw a promising future for Allied, with little trouble on the horizon:

The only business growing faster than ours is crime. Ten years ago, no one ever thought of guards in restaurants, motels, or retail stores, but in the cities you now need them. Today, every home is a fortress. We're the caretakers of a sick society and until society changes, we're going to grow. But, long term, I'd like to get into three new areas: armored cars, electronic systems coordinated with guard service, and building maintainance and janitorial services.

We're going to have to get into electronics eventually. The only question is the timing. In the last few years, the equipment companies have been sought after and bid up to unrealistic prices. Most of these companies are people working out of the back of their car. The big companies like Honeywell, IBM, and Westinghouse are moving cautiously in this field. I think we'll move in after the shakeout.

Janitorial services is a natural for us. It's a lot like the guard business, and we would be selling to the same people who purchase our guard services. We have over a million dollars in cash and securities. We are considering acquisitions and would like to make several a year, but most of what we see is junk. Several large companies have wanted to acquire us. When they ask if we're interested, I respond by saying "for the right price." Our business has appeal to a large company. We are in a growth industry. When the economy gets bad, and plants shut down, our business gets better because they need guards to watch the property. When the economy improves, our business also gets better.

Last week we were offered eight dollars a share in cash for our stock which is selling for less than four dollars. I turned it down because I think we're worth more.

What we'll probably do is just continue in the guard business and expand into new markets. We're considering licensing our name and management procedures in secondary markets, and we'll continue to open our own new branches in major cities.

7 American District Telegraph Company (ADT)

Founded in 1874, American District Telegraph Company (ADT) was by 1974 a major supplier of electronic security, fire detection, monitoring, and central station services. With 1973 revenues of $148.3 million derived largely from the operation of central stations, ADT dominated the domestic central station segment of the protective services industry. As fiscal 1973 ended, Mr. Raymond Carey, the president and chairman of ADT, was attempting to assess the environmental and industry trends affecting the demand for security services, particularly central station services.

Mr. Carey had been President of ADT for three years and was attempting to develop a strategy to broaden the company's operations outside of its traditional institutional and commercial central station markets. Operating under the constraints imposed by a 1967 antitrust judgment, Mr. Carey wanted to utilize the company's strong market position, financial strength, and technological expertise to expand the sales and earnings of his company.

While the financial implications were significant, Mr. Carey was also greatly concerned with the broader issues the company faced as he moved to develop a strategy for the future. As he summarized in the fall of 1973:

> ADT is undergoing a one-generation technological leap. We're trying to develop an organization and company which had certain of the characteristics and problems of a monopoly into a more aggressive and well-managed company. In doing so, the problems of structure, market segmentation, and product development are the areas which will be the most important for our future.
>
> Part of our strategy calls for penetration of the residential market for

for security. None of the major security companies have really tapped this market. With our technology and creative selling, we think we have a good chance to take advantage of an excellent opportunity.

In this case, a description of the history, growth, and operations of ADT is presented. Attention will be focused on the nature of the company's business, its operating characteristics, and issues posed by changing market trends.

Description of Central Station Alarm Services

In 1973, central station alarm services represented a growing segment of the $4.1 billion protective services industry. It was estimated that central station revenues accounted for 9 percent ($275 billion) of the $3 billion service segment of the security industry. This segment was projected to grow at a compound rate of 25 percent per year and reach $1.3 billion by 1980. This level of growth would increase the central station segment's market share to 22 percent of total service revenues.[1]

Central stations, from off-premises locations, provided continuous monitoring of a subscriber's premises to detect burglary or fire, water pressure failure, or other problems on the monitored premises. Monitoring was done by means of various electronic and electromechanical sensor devices which, in turn, communicated with the central station by means of telephone lines or other communications media. Alerted at the central station by a ringing alarm or flashing light, the attendant immediately notified the police, fire department, and/or sent guards, subscriber technicians, or other appropriate personnel to the protected site.

Geographically, a central station was limited to a range of about 25 miles, with the primary constraints being the cost of leasing telephone lines, signal weakness, and the practicality and cost of maintaining each subscriber's system. While industry averages indicated that the cost of leasing telephone lines ranged from $10–$50 a month, one official of a security company indicated the cost could run as high as $150 a month.[2]

A recent innovation aimed at reducing the problem of line leasing costs had been the use of "satellite" stations. Satellites were unmanned and acted as relay stations between the subscriber's premises and the central station. In this manner, the effective radius of operation was expanded, enabling outlying areas to receive this service. The absence of additional manpower also enabled the satellite to operate at a lower cost than a central station, which required supervisory personnel. Satellite stations could also be operated manually in emergencies. Various other

---

[1] Quantum Science Corporation estimates.

[2] Moore, Schley, Cameron and Co.

means of transmission, including radio, were being researched by ADT.

Central station services were purchased principally by commercial, industrial, and institutional users. Residential users were estimated to account for no more than about 3–5 percent of the total market.[3] There were five basic types of central station services:

1. *Watchman's Supervisory Service:* client guards made a scheduled plant tour "check in" at designated locations at specified time. Failure to do so, and the absence of the signal or a manually operated signal, was supposed to bring a response from central station personnel.

2. *Burglary Alarm Service:* detection devices transmitted warning signals to alert the central station personnel.

3. *Fire Protection:* sprinkler supervisory and water-flow alarm service to monitor automatic sprinkler system operations, smoke detectors, etc.

4. *Monitoring Industrial Processes:* typical applications included machinery stoppage, temperature or humidity deviation, loss of air pressure or vacuum, valve closing, and power failure.

5. *Security Alarm Notification Service:* geared to small businesses, this service notified the policy and subscriber of an emergency condition without either guard response and/or opening and closing of signals.

Compared with other types of security services, central stations and direct connection were thought to have several advantages:

1. Total area security.
2. Quick response time.
3. Lower cost than guards—it was estimated that guard coverage was priced at $12,000–$15,000 per man-year, while equivalent central station coverage could be as low as $2,000 per year.
4. Reduced insurance premiums.[4]

HISTORY OF AMERICAN DISTRICT TELEGRAPH COMPANY

Beginnings

Founded in 1874 in Baltimore, the predecessor of American District Telegraph Company (ADT) originally had been a simple messenger service. Operating from district offices, the company received subscriber signals transmitted by telegraph and then notified the messengers to contact the police, fire department, doctor, or the appropriate service. After a merger with 56 other independent companies in 1901, ADT gradually expanded its services and geographical coverage both by acquiring other companies and by internal growth. Establishing new production and

---

[3] Estimate by management of ADT.

[4] Industry estimates.

service facilities continually, ADT concentrated on the technological part of the protective services and security industry and maintained a low profile relative to some of its more well-known competitors in the security business, i.e., Wells Fargo, Pinkerton's, and Burns International.

Development Years

From 1901 to 1967, ADT continued to expand and develop new services. The company initiated sprinkler services and began the development of its off-premises burglary and intrusion detection services. Consisting primarily of door and window protection, this service became the foundation of the company's central station business.

Until 1953, ADT was controlled by Western Union (62 percent); in that year, Western Union sold its interest to the Grinnell Corporation, a major manufacturer of fire protection equipment. Later Grinnell Corporation increased its ownership to 80 percent.

In addition to the 1953 acquisition of ADT, the Grinnell Corporation earlier acquired Holmes Electric Protection Company and Automatic Fire Alarm Company (AFA). Through these and other acquisitions via ADT, Grinnell by 1964 accounted for over 75 percent of the Central Station Alarm revenues. By 1966, ADT's earnings had expanded to $6.7 million on revenues of $82.8 million, from 1961 earnings of $4.6 million on revenues of $63.2 million.

Over this record of growth, however, the government cast a dark shadow by filing an antitrust suit. This suit charged ADT, Grinnell Corporation, Holmes Electric Protection Company, and AFA with alleged "unlawful combination and conspiracy in restraint and monopolization of interstate trade." The companies denied these allegations and began a seven-year legal contest that was to be a losing battle.

Antitrust Judgment

In 1967, the final judgment in the antitrust suit was delivered. Finding that ADT, along with the other defendants, had violated the Sherman Act, the judgment contained "certain injunctions against the company applicable to its furnishing of Central Station Protection Services." Grinnell Corporation was ordered to divest itself of ADT, Holmes, and AFA; in addition, ADT was required to divest itself of $3.1 million in annual service contract revenues, together with the equipment in place on subscriber premises in 26 cities. Further, ADT was prohibited from buying existing accredited central stations, and consented to abrogate certain agreements with Grinnell, which resulted in cash payments to Grinnell in excess of $3.6 million.

1968–1972

Over the period following the antitrust settlement, ADT continued to increase its volume and earnings, and also added to its product mix of services and equipment through increasingly larger investments in R&D and manufacturing capability. Over this period, ADT's annual revenues increased at a compound rate of 8.3 percent, reaching $129 million in 1972. Record earnings were also seen in 1972, with income growing at a rate of 11.5 percent since 1968. During the same period, revenues for the central station market as a whole grew at a compound rate of 10.7 percent.[5]

Despite some pressure on profit margins and earnings immediately following the antitrust action, ADT sustained its level of profitability. Pre-tax income margins increased from 11.1 percent in 1968 to over 14 percent in 1971 and 1972.

ADT's performance continued to be one of the industry's best during the period 1968–73. As described by one analyst, the company did experience some pressure on profit margins and earnings due to:

Heavy legal and related expenses stemming from the antitrust case, largely charged to 1967 earnings.

Diversion of management effort and the consequent disruption of ongoing operations because of the protracted litigation.

Erosion of part of the historical business base at ADT was required to divest itself of $3.1 million in annual revenues.

Increased operating costs, especially for labor and leased telephone lines.

Disruption of operations and added expenses . . . due to a strike of certain field personnel.[6]

By 1969, the company was on the way to recovering due to several factors:

1. Less managerial and financial pressure associated with legal problems.
2. Institution of price increases.
3. More aggressive expansion and broadening of operations and market share of new products.
4. Upgrading of products, personnel, and marketing effort.
5. Investment in new technology and systems.

ADT IN 1973

By 1973, ADT was still a major factor in the market for central station protective services. In spite of the antitrust action, the company had main-

---

[5] Quantum Science Corporation.

[6] From company reports.

tained a fairly stable pattern of growth; from $71.4 million in 1963, revenues had expanded at a rate of 7.5 percent annually to $148.3 million in 1973. Earnings for the same period grew from $5 to $10.7 million at a rate of 7.9 percent compounded annually.

The following sections will examine ADT's product/service mix, marketing policies and operations, and management. Finally, attention will be focused on the strategic issues as seen by the company.

Services

ADT had traditionally supplied its services through four methods: central stations, direct connection to police and fire headquarters, local alarm systems, and on-site proprietary systems. In 1973 central station services, including burglar and sprinkler alarms, accounted for about 58 percent of total revenues.

TABLE 1

Percentage of Composition of Annual Sales, 1968–72

	(%) 1973	(%) 1972	(%) 1971	(%) 1970	(%) 1969	(%) 1968
Central station burglar alarm......	40	42	44	43	42	40
Central station sprinkler alarm.....	18	20	22	23	24	24
Subtotal: Central Station....	58	62	66	66	66	64
Local alarms*.....................	11	14	15	14	14	14
Advance charges..................	11	11	—	—	—	—
Others*...........................	20	13	19	20	20	22
	100%	100%	100%	100%	100%	100%

* Includes sales of equipment and hardware.
Source: Company data.

Outright sales had recently become more significant. While ADT had emphasized the sale of services, outright sales of equipment had increased as shown below:

TABLE 2

Outright Sales (millions)

	1973	1972	1971
Commercial...........	$6,837	$4,730	$1,538
Residential............	2,868	2,172	720

Source: Company data.

In addition to its central station services for commercial and industrial uses, ADT had added other relatively new services and products. Mr. Carey indicated that these new services were part of the company's intent "to build a rapidly growing position in all technological aspects of security." Some of the company's other services were:

1. *Residential Protection Service.* Similar to industrial customers, residential homeowners could avail themselves of intrusion and alarm devices. These devices were wired directly to an ADT central station, the police and/or fire departments. They could also be used to activate local on-site alarms, and smoke and/or fire alarms. However, as will be discussed later, sales of residential products had been a major focus of the company only since 1971. In 1972 and 1973, it was estimated that residential revenues accounted for less than 3 percent of the company's revenues.[7]

2. *Sound Services.* Introduced in 1964, this consisted of background music, public address, and tone signalling systems. This service provided on-site music, FM broadcasts, sound tones to signal fire drills/alarms, evacuation warnings, and/or other emergency signals.

3. *Central Building Control Systems.* Made possible through development of new multiplex technology, this most recent development in commercial security provided for the integration of multiple monitoring functions into a single on-site coordinated protection system. Integrating fire, security, and sound services with the monitoring of temperature, humidity, steam, and water pressure, this provided a full building control system that was increasingly necessary and economically feasible for large office buildings, plants, and major industrial facilities. First introduced in 1970, these systems had enjoyed rapid acceptance.

Prices for ADT control systems ranged from a few thousand dollars to $200,000. In 1973, ADT had sold several of the 7300 Series systems.

Through selective acquisition ADT had also expanded its product line to include a mobile radio and communications company with U.S. rights to certain pagers, two-way band and mobile radios of a Japanese manufacturer, two locksmith and safe businesses, and a company which had developed a new concept combining electronic keyless door control for hotels and motels with room occupancy reservation status systems. These acquisitions, plus entrance into the CCTV field, reflected management's desire to obtain operations that would complete its existing base of services, strategically enhance its product/service range, and provide opportunities for penetrating new or related markets.

Markets

By 1973, ADT had over 125,000 contracts of varying size. Its services were sold primarily to six segments:

1. *Industrial*—Allied Chemical, General Motors, etc.
2. *Commercial/retail*—Tiffany, Abraham and Strauss, etc.
3. *Government*—U.S. Treasury, Virginia State Legislature, etc.

---

[7] Hallgarten and Company.

4. *Special properties*—Smithsonian Institution, churches, etc.
5. *Residential*—individual homeowners.
6. *Banks*—Chase, etc.

ADT derived 90 percent of its revenues from the commercial and industrial markets.[8] The residential market was relatively untapped, but penetration of the residential market was perceived to be difficult because of high marketing costs and the cost of central station service and equipment to the homeowner. Mr. Carey commented on this market.

> We think the U.S. market for residential systems of all types is about $60 million and is growing at about 10 to 15 percent per year. Predictions on our growth in this market are mixed, however, we feel the central station growing base supports our predictions of 20 percent growth for ADT and average levels of profitability.

ADT's management also indicated that the Canadian market would be comparable to the U.S. market in terms of percentage growth. By 1974, ADT had a substantial subscriber position in Montreal and Toronto, with about 90 percent taking central station service.

ADT's Position in the Industry

As indicated earlier, ADT, with about 35–40 percent of estimated industry revenues, had a substantial market share of the central station industry. Further, this $275 million dollar segment of the security industry was highly concentrated; together, ADT, Burns, Baker Industries, Holmes, AFA, and Honeywell controlled over 70 percent of the market. Although major companies, such as Honeywell and 3M, had entered the field, new entrants were faced with two major hurdles.

1. *High Capital Requirements.* Industry estimates indicated that at least $200,000 was required to start a central station. This was necessary to cover the cost of a fireproof building, fixed equipment, and start-up personnel.

2. *Need to Absorb Initial Operating Losses.* Initially, a central station had to absorb operating losses associated with the cost of marketing, promotion, making new installations, and waiting for breakeven. Breakeven was usually reached within five years. Breakeven volume on a typical station was estimated to be in the area of $200,000 per year. During the period prior to breakeven, subscribers had to be generated. For each additional subscriber, it was estimated 50–70 percent of installation costs ($400–$500) was recovered at the time of installation. The balance was recovered over the ensuing months of operation as a part of the monthly service charge.

---

[8] Estimates provided by management of several central station operators.

Despite these competitive barriers, ADT was faced with greater competition than ever. As expressed by Mr. Carey:

> Within the basic central station business, ADT has absorbed nearly $3 million in divestiture and is faced with about 200 certified competitors compared to 30 ten years ago. Despite this, the company is growing in the traditional business at close to the rate of the industry. Overseas, we are growing faster.

Most of the company's competition came into being after 1967. However, the large companies entering the field were acquiring existing local operations in spite of high selling prices. As observed by ADT's management:

> There are major companies competing with us now in the central station business. Honeywell is moving rapidly into total building systems and IBM, with its computers, into the area of access and entry monitoring. For ADT, the problem is sorting out industry trends—proprietary systems versus greater automation.

In 1956, ADT had internationalized its operations by entering the Canadian and European markets through acquisitions. Since that initial entry, ADT had continued to expand its foreign operations. In 1973, ADT had derived approximately 13 percent of its gross revenues and 26 percent of total annual income from its foreign operations. Performance of the foreign operations had outpaced domestic results in terms of gains over 1972 as foreign revenues rose 14.5 percent compared to 11.8 percent for the company as a whole. Management pointed out that "part of the disparity was due to application of a greater percentage of overload to U.S. operations."

Foreign net income increased by 44.3 percent versus 8.6 percent on a company-wide basis. Net assets of the foreign operations amounted to $18.3 million and accounted for about 9 percent of total company assets.

Of all revenues generated outside the United States, approximately 60 percent ($10 million) were contributed by the Canadian operation. However, growth in this market was considered by some industry analysts

TABLE 3

Performance of Foreign Operations

Year	Gross Revenues	Net Income	Post-Tax Profit Margin
1973.............	$18,762,000	$2,778,000	14.8%
1972.............	$16,387,000	$1,924,000	11.7%
1971.............	$14,043,000	$1,198,000	8.5%

Source: Company reports.

to be limited because of "the vastness of the country and the limited number of densely populated cities that might feasibly be served by central stations."

European operations were still relatively small, although profits were high. Management indicated:

> Central stations have been in England, France, Belgium and Holland for up to 10 years, but the coverage is now being greatly expanded by use of satellite stations. Part of the problem has been the lack of and non-compatibility of European transmission and telephone equipment.
>
> Canada, particularly with central stations, has been an extremely profitable venture for years and continues to grow and remain highly profitable.

Marketing Policies

Pricing of ADT's services was of critical concern to the company. Historically, the firm's contracts covered a period of five years with a guaranteed price. But after the antitrust judgment, this was reduced to two years. During the period 1964–68, the company generally froze its prices on contracts up for renewal. This was primarily in deference to the on-going litigation. In 1968, many contracts were renewed at higher prices. The contracts written between 1968 and 1970 were expected to be renewed between 1973 and 1975 at prices up to 20 percent above the original price. In 1970, ADT put a clause in their contracts allowing for renegotiation of rates after two years. In 1971, this was stepped up to one year.

Prices for the company's services were spread over a fairly wide range. Typically, a normal central station contract included a nonrecurring advance service charge and an advance payment toward the first year's service charge. The one-time advance service charge covered the expense of labor and nonrecoverable materials installed on the customers' premises. The advance service charge was deferred and credited to income as earned. ADT also had to absorb the marketing and start-up costs. However, when breakeven had been reached, the follow-on revenues contributed incremental profits. As a capital intensive operation, the variable cost component was less crucial. The variable costs for servicing an additional subscriber were principally the incremental labor costs and telephone line leasing costs, which were paid by the client.

However, according to one industry source:

> . . . in our opinion, the typical initial installation fee recovers from 50 percent to 75 percent of the total installation cost, and the balance is recovered in the ensuing 24 months from the recurring monthly service charges. Hence, on a typical new installation, a company would expect to recover all cost and to break-even during the third year of operation.[9]

---

[9] Moore, Schley, Cameron and Company.

To provide ample service and market coverage, ADT maintained a field organization of several thousand service and sales representatives. Over 2,000 servicemen were available to perform installations, inspections, and repairs; another 2,000 plus operations personnel manned the network of central stations. Supporting these field forces was a centralized administrative, engineering, manufacturing, and supply organization that established practices for all ADT operations.

Residential Market Penetration

Although ADT had provided central station services for the residential market, this end of the company's activities had remained a small portion of the company's business. However, in 1972, ADT had embarked on a program to aggressively pursue this market. As stated by Mr. Carey:

> With the threat of burglary and fire to residences, the potential for protection of homes appears to be great, particularly in the $50,000 to $100,000 range. However, we have had to be extremely careful. The merchandising techniques for the residential market are different from our traditional products. By developing a marketing posture in the residential phase of our business, we think it will rub off on other parts of the company.

The development of an effective marketing program and the appropriate technical equipment was a key concern of management. Since the residential market had different requirements from the commercial and industrial markets, management felt that many new problems would confront the company as it attempted to move in this direction. In spite of the problem potential of moving into residential sales, the company felt that the environment, market conditions, and ADT's technological capabilities justified a major move. ADT's view and approach to this market was summarized by the financial vice president:

> For decades, ADT has provided its residential alarm services to the affluent and to persons in public life who were concerned because their prominence caused susceptibility to burglary, kidnapping, and vandalism. With the sociological upheavals in the 60s, and the increase of domicile-directed crime, market opportunities for residential alarm systems have increased sharply. Since 1970 our revenues have increased to the point where, by the end of 1974, recurring revenues and annual outright sales will exceed several million dollars.
>
> We designed special systems for the homeowner—as uncomplicated, aesthetic, and convenient as possible—yet having features demanded by good security and fire protection. With the introduction of new systems, we make available options to the homeowner; he could buy the system outright, as he is accustomed to doing with other household purchases, or he could "lease" it; in both instances he could also contract with us for central station connections, and for periodic inspection and maintenance

services. Additionally, we provide our sales representatives with other security-related items for sale to the homeowner—escape ladders, fire extinguishers, and low-priced but effective standby emergency lighting devices.

Selling the system with associated service is important. The success of our commercial business has been built upon the operating dependability that well-maintained installations provide. This concept of maintenance can be critical to the homeowner, whose family safety and property preservation depend on an installation that works when emergency strikes. The recurring service relationship with the client helps safeguard our reputation for high-quality alarm service, and, most importantly, provides us with an on-going revenue flow which has been a proven ingredient in our commercial success over the years. It is this so-called "razor blade" portion of the residential business that will really assist ADT's earnings in the long run. Currently over 50 percent of residential sales take central station service.

In the last few years we have developed improved techniques in penetrating the residential market, which unlike much of the commercial market, purchases protection services for the sake of the security that they provide, not because of significant reductions in insurance premium rates, or elimination or reduction in costly guard forces, or because of other business-based influences. Despite growing concern with crime by the average homeowner, investment in a residential alarm system does not normally seem as important to him as the purchase of, say, wall-to-wall carpeting, although, of course, it could be the most vital buying decision a homeowner can make.

Our residential sales representatives have found that this is a reaction market, often emotional in nature; a large portion of our sales are consummated with those who have experienced a burglary or a fire, or who have seen a sharp upsurge of crime in their neighborhoods. Consistent with our reputation as a reputable company, we assiduously avoid capitalizing on fear tactics in selling, instead stressing the peace of mind that a well-designed and well-maintained alarm system can provide. The fact that we can demonstrate stability and responsibility because of our nationwide service presence, and our long list of satisfied commercial and industrial customers, weighs heavily in our favor in competitive situations.

Our merchandising efforts have included almost all of the commonly accepted techniques, such as media, spot radio, direct mail, billboard advertising, and publicity releases. So far, we've discovered that our greatest source of sales leads come from customers—those who utilize our commercial services, or residential clients who refer ADT to their relatives, friends, and neighbors. There is synergistic interaction between the commercial and residential markets; often the commercial user is a prime prospect for a residential system and vice versa.

The majority of our sales to date have been for private homes ranging in value between $50,000 to $100,000, and our typical system sale ranges from $1,200 to $1,500. Better than 50 percent of our residential cus-

tomers contract for connection to our central station or a service maintenance contract. For this type of installation, connection and service
charges average between $20 and $25 per month.

Broadening our effort to sell a price-sensitive mass market, including
apartments and other multi-occupancy premises, and more modestly
priced single-family homes, is the phase in which we are currently engaged, utilizing low-cost control and sensor devices, as well as economies
in the labor expended to install systems, and lower-cost transmission
techniques, so that it will be economically possible for lower-income users
to be connected into our central stations, despite the rising costs of telephone wire facilities.[10]

To this market, we currently offer a table-top-type burglary system
which in its simplest form sells for about $500. To this package can be
added fire protection, a basic system being priced at approximately $250.
Connection and service contracts for these systems are priced at $15 to
$20 per month.

Our efforts so far have been fairly well on target, and we plan to
continue our innovative technology, as well as developing research, both
technological and psychographic, which will help us capture a larger
share of a growing market.

Some of the challenges we've encountered: ADT is not well known
to the consumer, because for generations we've dedicated our sales and
advertising efforts to the commercial, industrial, and institutional buyers
of protection systems. Through recent advertising in media such as *Time*,
we've successfully created more homeowner awareness of ADT as THE
security company, but more needs to be done. We have intense interest in
developing awareness of our stature as responsible experts in the alarm
industry, primarily because of the fact that many sales of residential
systems are of the reaction type, triggered by a personal experience; when
the prospect convinces himself that he needs a system, we want him to
think of ADT first.

Another area of concentration is convincing our prospects that a
balanced home alarm system should include fire protection, as fire is a
far greater threat to life and property than burglary. Yet despite the most
recently published statistics on U.S. residential fires (700,000 annually,
with $864 million in property losses, and loss of life totaling 8,400), there
is a built-in buyer apathy, sharply demonstrated by our own sales
records: only 20 percent of our sales included fire alarm service, despite
heavy emphasis on the need for such detection systems.

Most important of all, in analyzing the future, we must devise means
of convincing a huge market that the decision to buy a residential alarm
system must be made *before* the fire or intrusion, and of making available
efficient, reasonably priced, well-maintained systems that are accepted as

---

[10] Westinghouse, Honeywell, and other major security firms were negotiating with
the insurance industry to establish discounts on rates of insurance for UL-approved
home security equipment. According to one insurance company, these discounts
averaged from 10–20 percent of the annual premium. Thus, for a suburban $50,000
brick 30-year-old house, the customer's savings would approximate $24–$48 annually.

being as necessary to the welfare of the homeowner as life insurance or central heating.

Manufacturing

ADT manufactured most of its own equipment and apparatus in company-owned plants in New Jersey, Arkansas, and Toronto, Canada. The two U.S. plants were equipped with a full range of machinery necessary for manufacturing electrical security equipment, and had a total of 165,000 square feet of floor space. Management indicated that as new products were introduced as a result of research and development on proprietary systems, additional manufacturing facilities would be needed.

Research and Development

Through its own in-house research, ADT developed its own electronic protective systems and devices. The company had also invested in programs of modernization, research, and development. According to management, "most of these were of a long-ranged nature and were essential to the company's objectives of maintaining its prominence in the industry and ensuring the long-term growth and profitability of the business."

In 1973, ADT had expended about $2.8 million for research and development, versus $1.75 million in 1972. Most of the company's R&D efforts had been focused on those areas which management felt would "play an important role in the future of the company":

Multiplex transmission.
Computerization and automation of central stations.
Residential security systems.

Approximately 100 employees were engaged in research and development activities, of whom roughly 75 were professional employees with advanced training and experience.

Management felt that ADT's research and technological capabilities would be crucial to the future of the company. According to the president, this was a major factor in the company's decision to acquire Boston-based Aerospace Research, Inc. Aerospace specialized in ultrasonic motion detectors, and had been formed by a group of researchers formerly associated with MIT's Lincoln Laboratory. Mr. Carey described this acquisition:

> We're quite happy about acquiring Aerospace. We recognized some time ago a need for investment in technology. In Aerospace, I think we've found a technological partner. In one acquisition, we brought in a whole new generation of research people.

We could have built up our research capability internally, but getting a research team of Aerospace's quality would have been difficult to do at one time. In addition, our offices here on lower Sixth Avenue don't quite have the same appeal to research types as Cambridge, Massachusetts, does.

Management

As the litigation of the middle 1960s decreased in relative importance, the managerial emphasis of the company shifted. The main focus of the company became the desire to improve profitability, engineering, research, and marketing; this was in part stimulated by sluggish growth in sales and earnings in 1969. Thus in 1970, Mr. Carey was brought into ADT by the then chairman and chief executive officer, Mr. Lawrence O'Brien. As chairman and chief executive officer, Mr. O'Brien had been responsible for many innovations and decisions ADT had made.

In 1971, Mr. Carey ascended to the presidency, and also became chairman upon the retirement of Mr. O'Brien in 1973. Prior to coming to ADT, Mr. Carey had been president and general manager of the Electro Dynamic Division of the General Dynamics Corporation. He had also been chief operation executive and group vice president of Robert Morse, Ltd.

Organization

Mr. Carey indicated that one of the company's major tasks was to structure itself for "growing a good deal faster." Thus, in 1971, the company reorganized its field forces in order to decentralize authority and place greater responsibility in the regional districts. Formerly, each district had its own separate sales, servicing, and operations manager, each of whom reported to a vice president at headquarters. According to Mr. Carey:

> In restructuring the company, we have reorganized domestically into districts, with a general manager responsible for operations and marketing. Abroad, we have super districts with general managers. While the general managers have product-oriented marketing people and service people working for them on a decentralized basis, some activities and expenses are centrally handled and accounted for; for example, all the systems salesmen have been trained centrally, and then sent out into the field. By absorbing certain costs centrally, we hope to simultaneously emphasize greater profit center responsibility and innovation on the part of general managers. Hopefully, the general managers can be more decisive and improve customer service.

Mr. Carey also commented:

The company has been restructured in all departments. For the first two years of my time here this restructuring was done with people from within the company. One objective was to shift the company towards more of a sales orientation. As the necessity indicated, we have steadily added to the management talent by bringing in good people from outside, e.g., vice president–operations, treasurer, director of manufacturing, general manager of R&D, systems sales specialists, and financial analysts. The melding of the continuity of experienced people with the skills of the new talent has progressed very well.

Financial

ADT's financial position in 1973 was relatively strong, with no long-term debt, and stockholder equity of $97.5 million, a net working capital position of $11.6 million, and a current ratio of 1.6 to 1.

Capitalization

Long-term debt:	None
Common stock:	5,460,000 shares outstanding (NYSE)
Shareholder's equity:	$97.5 million

	Working Capital	
	12/31/73	*12/31/72*
Working capital.....................	$11.6 million	$15.2 million
Current ratio........................	1.6 to 1	1.9 to 1
Cash and marketable securities.....	$14.3 million	$20.3 million

Although capital expenditures had approximated $28 million annually, management felt the company had the capacity to maintain this level of capital investment from internally generated funds. In 1973 and 1972, the company had generated cash flows of $28.2 million and $27 million, respectively.[11]

Over the five-year period since 1968, EPS had increased at a compound annual rate of about 10.9 percent. Net income per share in 1973 was $1.96 versus $1.81 in 1972. Management indicated that ADT had the second longest dividend paying record of any company on the New York Exchange. Dividends currently averaged about 25 percent of net income.

In discussing the company's financial picture, the president had these remarks:

Our financial strategy is based primarily on exploiting our opportunities for profitable expansion. Lack of debt encourages a reasonably aggressive expansion plan. But it is now clear that our growth rate, working capital requirements, plus the capital investment in automation and new transmission will place heavy demands on capital. One of our criteria has been the existence of a relationship to our fundamental business. We be-

---

[11] Cash flows equal to net income plus depreciation.

lieve that our growth emphasis should have a real logic relative to our base business and base technology. For example, we are considering making a major capital investment into the development of a capability in communications since that fits with our expertise.

The absorption level in any company, even well-structured ones, is a critical consideration. The span of control problems in various companies due to too broad diversification are very clear and are ones which we wish to avoid.

ADT AND THE FUTURE

Industry Trends

As a dominant company in the fastest growing segment of the protective services industry, ADT's management felt that the company faced excellent opportunities for growth. This view was reinforced by various industry reports:

> The electronics and technology phase of the protective services industry is becoming more and more important. ADT's manufacturing capability enables the company to introduce more advanced devices, which gives the company a competitive advantage over other central station operations. Its strong industry position as an operator of central stations also gives it an advantage over new entrants in the equipment phase such as Honeywell, RCA, and IBM.

Management also felt that relative to other industry segments, ADT appeared to be strategically placed. As crime increased, they felt the demand for the company's services followed. Further, while guard and investigative services, the largest segment of the industry, were projected to grow at better than 10 percent rate, this growth was not expected to be at the expense of central station business. Guard services were labor intensive, and management felt that wage increases and inevitable price pressures, together with the development of improved electronics and other surveillance systems, would retard the growth of the guard services. To some extent guard and central stations were considered to be complementary rather than directly competitive. As rising labor costs increased the spread between the cost of guard services and central station operations, management felt many companies would shift to the central station service as the latter provided for the monitoring of a variety of events at a lower cost.

Management also believed ADT to be well insulated from new competition of any consequence:

> Anyone entering the central station business will have some problems. This business requires a sizeable capital investment for equipment and installation. There is also a need for a high degree of technical and

service skills and a national field force to market and service the product. In remote areas, the need to have a local force is very important. Financial viability is also crucial as there must exist the capacity in any newcomer to absorb the initial operating losses associated with the high start-up costs of marketing, promotion, and installation of a new central station.

The prosperity brought about by a rise in crime was also accompanied by potential problems, however:

> With the increase in crime in the inner city, there will be a continuing exodus of industrial and commercial business from inner-city locations to newer suburban facilities. This shift in market location means a potential erosion of business and profitability in our existing central stations and higher marketing and start-up costs associated with new central stations. To counteract this, ADT is spending large engineering dollars in researching alternate methods of transmission, including radio.

Future

While Mr. Carey felt that a total strategy for the company could not be articulated until the completion of a current and major planning program, he summarized the company's approach to the future:

> Our basic philosophy can be summarized as primarily doing more of what we are already good at. Even as we expand in this basic direction— internationally with conventional business, residentially, and into new products—we expect and hope our growth and development will not stray too far from this philosophy. With our technological skills, I hope we can take advantage of some real opportunities in fields outside of security. For example, the field of communications is one which is compatible with our skills. Five to ten years from now, ADT may be more known as a communications company than a security company. The technology of transmission, monitoring, and automation are all areas in which we are developing expertise. Many things we monitor now have nothing to do with security; I think this trend will continue in the future.

EXHIBIT 1

AMERICAN DISTRICT TELEGRAPH CO.
Consolidated Statement of Income and Retained Earning*

	1973	1972	1971	1970	1969	1968
Income:						
Service charges..................	$133,427	$124,105	$114,296	$104,774	$96,872	$92,475
Sales...........................	13,234	7,423	1,465	837	686	—
Other..........................	1,617	1,102	746	310	529	790
	$148,278	$132,630	$116,507	$105,921	$98,087	$93,265
Costs and Expenses:						
Cost of service, other than those below...................	$ 53,716	$ 49,978	$ 44,518	$ 41,026	$39,401	$35,421
Depreciation....................	17,422	17,138	16,101	15,672	15,420	16,101
Maintenance of signal plants.....	16,996	15,597	14,285	12,968	11,224	11,510
Research, selling, general, and administrative.................	24,347	21,211	19,734	18,422	16,852	16,154
Cost of sales....................	9,238	5,032	902	478	429	—
Taxes other than taxes on income.......................	6,568	5,097	4,407	4,185	3,351	3,599
	$128,287	$114,053	$ 99,947	$ 92,751	$86,677	$82,785
Income before income taxes.....	$ 19,991	$ 18,577	$ 16,560	$ 13,170	$11,410	10,480
Income tax......................	9,256	8,690	7,923	5,444	4,962	4,290
Net income.....................	$ 10,735	$ 9,887	$ 8,637	$ 7,726	$ 6,448	$ 6,190
Net income per share......	$ 1.96	$ 1.81	$ 1.62	$ 1.47	$ 1.22	$ 1.17

* All figures in thousands, except per share earnings.
Source: Company records.

EXHIBIT 2

AMERICAN DISTRICT TELEGRAPH CO.
Consolidated Balance Sheet
(dollars in thousands)

Assets	1973	1972	1971	1970	1969	1968
Current assets:						
Cash...............................	$ 3,526	$ 4,326	$ 3,117	$ 4,030	$ 4,140	$ 3,274
Short-term investments.............	10,792	16,090	10,871	3,017	1,809	2,157
Receivables........................	16,129	9,737	7,368	6,708	6,373	4,309
Inventory (other than materials).....	1,632	627	—	—	—	—
Recoverable federal income tax.....	—	2,203	—	—	—	—
Prepaid expenses...................	425	648	1,026	1,121	809	660
	$ 32,504	$ 33,631	$ 22,382	$ 14,876	$ 13,131	$ 10,400
Other assets:						
Materials and supplies (for construction)......................	$ 17,021	$ 10,842	$ 11,349	$ 15,301	$ 12,974	$ 10,468
Other miscellaneous...............	2,377	434	406	827	895	1,215
	$ 19,398	$ 11,276	$ 11,755	$ 16,128	$ 13,869	$ 11,683
Plant, property, and equipment:						
Land and buildings.................	$ 5,973	$ 5,511	$ 5,000	$ 4,913	$ 4,762	$ 4,734
Factory and office equipment.......	8,409	7,567	7,703	7,536	7,326	7,148
Central station signal equipment....	23,177	20,754	18,673	17,098	16,065	12,666
Signal equipment on-site...........	235,721	224,214	209,501	191,689	176,406	167,492
Construction in progress...........	12,988	8,799	9,141	11,565	9,311	6,298
	$286,268	$266,845	$250,018	$232,801	$213,870	$198,338
Less depreciation..................	147,377	141,065	134,360	129,800	122,908	112,064
	$138,891	$125,780	$115,658	$103,001	$ 90,962	$ 86,274
**Franchises, contracts, and intangibles.......................	9,130	8,496	8,350	8,350	8,350	8,350
	$199,923	$179,183	$158,145	$142,355	$126,312	$116,707
Liabilities						
Current liabilities:						
Accounts payable..................	$ 14,443	$ 11,936	$ 8,980	$ 8,475	$ 8,019	$ 6,390
Notes payable.....................	110	373	350	2,257	—	—
Litigation settlement...............	1,971	1,617	1,617	—	—	—
Income taxes payable..............	1,811	1,534	1,969	1,354	973	1,247
Other taxes payable...............	2,503	1,605	972	1,118	997	921
	$ 20,838	$ 17,065	$ 13,888	$ 13,204	$ 9,989	$ 8,558
Long-term liabilities:						
Amount due for actuating device purchase.........................	$ —	$ —	$ —	$ 350	$ 1,750	$ 1,000
Revenue billed and collected in advance.........................	51,123	50,114	49,247	42,825	37,822	36,118
Accruals for employee benefit plans............................	13,961	11,887	9,443	7,395	5,326	3,454
Deferred payments on litigation settlement.......................	3,233	3,097	3,262	4,850	—	—
Investment tax credit deferred......	2,860	2,288	1,870	1,812	2,243	2,735
Deferred income taxes.............	10,318	5,989	1,045	905	—	—
	$ 81,495	$ 73,375	$ 64,867	$ 58,137	$ 47,141	$ 43,307
Stockholder's equity:						
Common stock (payable)...........	$ 5,460	$ 5,445	$ 5,347	$ 5,270	$ 5,270	$ 5,270
Capital in excess of par value.......	4,565	3,994	3,457	1,832	1,832	1,832
Retained earnings..................	87,565	79,304	70,586	63,912	62,080	57,740
Total Shareholder's Equity......	$ 97,590	$ 88,743	$ 79,390	$ 71,014	$ 69,182	$ 64,842
	$199,923	$179,183	$158,145	$142,355	$126,312	$116,707

Source: Company records.

EXHIBIT 3

AMERICAN DISTRICT TELEGRAPH CO.
Supplemental Information and Analysis

	1973	1972	1971	1970	1969	1968
1. *Items as Percent of Revenue:*						
Cost of service..............	36.2%	37.7%	38.2%	38.7%	40.2%	37.7%
Depreciation.................	11.7	12.9	13.8	14.8	15.7	17.7
Maintenance of signal plants.	11.5	11.8	12.3	12.2	11.4	12.3
Research, selling, gen.,						
and admin................	16.4	16.0	16.9	17.4	17.2	17.3
Cost of sales...............	6.2	3.8	0.8	0.5	0.4	0.5
Income before taxes........	13.5	14.0	14.2	12.4	11.6	11.2
Net income.................	7.2	7.5	7.4	7.3	6.6	6.6
2. *Return on AVG. Equity*.........	11.5%	11.8%	11.5%	11.0%	9.6%	9.9%
3. *Return on Total Assets*........	5.4%	5.5%	5.5%	5.4%	5.1%	5.3%
4. *Balance Sheet Analysis*						
Current ratio................	1.6%	2.0%	1.6%	1.1%	1.3%	1.2%
Total debt/equity...........	1.05	1.02	0.99	1.00	0.83	0.80
5. *Shareholder's Equity per Share*...	$17.87	$16.30	$14.85	$13.50	$12.44	$11.61
Average annual P/E ratio....	23.6	31.5	28.4	17.4	21.9	27.5
High-low stock price						
(rounded to nearest dollar).	$62–35	$68–44	$59–29	$31–20	$38–19	$44–23

EXHIBIT 4

AMERICAN DISTRICT TELEGRAPH COMPANY
A.   *Geographical Composition of Revenues and Profits*

Year	Gross Revenues (millions)			Net Income (millions)		
	Foreign	U.S.	Total	Foreign	U.S.	Total
1972...............	$16.4	$116.2	$132.6	$1.9	$8.0	$9.9
1971...............	14.0	102.5	116.5	1.2	7.4	8.6
1970*...............	11.9	94.0	105.9	0.5	7.2	7.7
1969*...............	9.2	88.9	98.1	0.3	6.1	6.4

Percentage Composition of Revenues and Profits

Year	Gross Revenues			Net Income		
	Foreign	U.S.	Total	Foreign	U.S.	Total
1972........	12.7%	87.6	100.0%	20.1%	79.9%	100.0%
1971........	12.0	88.0	100.0	13.9	86.1	100.0
1970*........	11.2	88.8	100.0	7.8	92.2	100.0
1969*........	9.4	90.6	100.0	5.0	95.0	100.0

Source: Company estimates.

Net Post-tax Profit Margins

Year	Foreign	U.S.	Total
1972...............	11.6%	6.9%	7.5%
1971...............	8.6	7.2	7.4
1970*...............	5.0	7.6	7.3
1969*...............	3.3	6.9	6.5

* Estimated.
Source: Company estimates.

B.   *Major Central Station Operators (1973)*

Company	Number of Central Stations*
American District Telegraph Co.......................	139
Burns International Security Services, Inc.............	30
Holmes Protection, Inc...............................	12
Baker Industries (Wells Fargo).......................	15
Honeywell, Inc.......................................	8
Wackenhut...	5

* Includes non-UL certificated stations and foreign operations.
Source: Industry estimates.

8 The Boston Symphony Orche

The Boston Symphony Orchestra (BSO) had existed since 1881 as a major element in Boston's cultural life. Largely supported and attended by the city's most affluent residents, the orchestra had gained both national and international prominence. For many years all subscriptions for the BSO concerts had been sold out. The waiting list for these subscriptions was long, and family tickets were frequently passed on from one generation to another.

Beginning in 1968 there had been a sharp decline in subscription sales. The amount of revenue lost by empty seats increased from $6,000 in the 1968–69 season to over $60,000 in 1969–70. The causes for this decline seemed to be many: People were unwilling to travel into the city in the evenings; the audience for established classical repertoire was decreasing in numbers; the staid format of symphony performances was unsatisfactory for younger people accustomed to rock concerts; and contemporary composers had seemed either unable or unwilling to create exciting new music.

In October of 1970, the Trustees of the BSO appointed a concert activities committee to consider the problem of declining ticket sales. Discussions, subsequently held, yielded suggestions for making symphony attendance more convenient, but the major objective of attracting new subscribers seemed to require a change in the actual content of symphony programs. Therefore, the committee was considering a proposal by Michael Tilson Thomas, 26-year-old associate conductor, for a new series of concerts. These concerts would consist of music of all periods in unusual juxtaposition, to be presented informally with the conductor talking to the audience. The series would be lower priced and intended to attract an entirely new audience.

The Founding and Early Development of the BSO

The Boston Symphony Orchestra was founded in 1881 as a personal creation of a wealthy Boston financier, Major Henry Lee Higginson. Because he personally and singly paid for the operating deficits of the orchestra, Higginson clearly had a free hand in its management. Higginson hired the conductors (music directors) and modelled the Boston Symphony after his conception of the great European orchestras.

It is estimated that Higginson spent about $1 million of his personal fortune on the symphony over nearly 40 years. His crowning achievement was the construction of Symphony Hall in 1900, at a cost of $750,000. With other Bostonians supplying only $40,000, Higginson played the major role in the building's design, which was based upon the German Liepzig Gewandhaus.

After World War I Major Higginson, then in his 80s, relinquished the BSO to a board of trustees composed of several prominent citizens. In 1925, Serge Koussevitzky became music director. He held that position until two years before his death in 1951, and under his leadership the BSO became known as one of the world's finest symphony orchestras. Musically, Koussevitzky augmented the traditional selections by introducing many works by contemporary composers. The power which Higginson conveyed to the managing board of trustees gradually came into Koussevitzky's possession, and he used it to improve the quality of the BSO by hiring the finest musicians and to develop several new musical activities for the BSO. Koussevitzky envisioned himself as above both the board of trustees and the management of the BSO, believing that it was the trustees' function to supply funds for the orchestra's activities, and the management's role to carry out the necessary nonmusical details. In 1970, there was still a faint reflection of Koussevitzky's vision of the supremacy of the music director at the BSO.

Charles Munch was the music director during the 1950s, and he expanded the orchestra's activities further, leading the BSO on tour for the first time both in the United States and in Europe, and introducing open rehearsals on Thursday nights for the benefit of the orchestra pension fund.

In the period from 1962 to 1969, Erich Leinsdorf was music director. The major thrust of Leinsdorf's leadership was in presenting new musical selections. The BSO under Leinsdorf presented many world and American premieres of new works, and, in addition, Leinsdorf restored many forgotten and long neglected works to the orchestra's repertoire.

In 1969, William Steinberg, then near 70, was engaged by the trustees in a three-year contract as music director. However, Steinberg retained the position of music director of the Pittsburgh Symphony Orchestra, dividing his attention between the two orchestras and being in Boston about one-third of his time. Steinberg's dual responsibilities were symptomatic of the desire of contemporary conductors to work with several orchestras, a phenomenon which has produced the guest conductor system, whereby nearly a dozen conductors each lead an orchestra for a few weeks during the symphony season. By 1969 it had become virtually impossible to find a music director willing to conduct for an entire season. Talcott Banks, president of the trustees, acknowledged, "There is little or no likelihood that the BSO or any leading orchestra can return in the near future to the former tradition of one music director who will prepare and conduct almost all of the concerts in both winter and summer seasons." Furthermore, Steinberg's responsibilities extended only to the winter season; Leonard Bernstein was then director for the summer season at Tanglewood.

THE MUSICAL ACTIVITIES OF THE BSO

Each year the BSO undertook a wide range of musical activities, which included, in addition to the formal winter season concerts, the Boston Pops, the Esplanade Concerts, the Berkshire Music Festival, the Berkshire Music Center, and the Boston Symphony Chamber Players. A balance sheet and an income statement for these activities are found in Exhibits 1 and 2.

Boston Symphony Winter Season

The winter season of the BSO began in the last week of September and continued until the end of April. During the 31-week period, the BSO played 22 weeks at Symphony Hall, three weeks in Europe, and five weeks in New York, with a one-week Christmas vacation. In the previous season, 1969–70, the BSO had played 119 concerts, an average of more than three concerts per week. Exhibit 3 shows the BSO concert schedule for the 1969–70 season.

Revenue from the 79 subscription concerts at Symphony Hall in 1969–70 was $1.086 million. The five concert Beethoven festival had produced revenues of $77,000.

The concert schedule for a particular season was quite complex, reflecting a rich mixture of tradition, musical performance constraints, musicians' union contracts, and the preferences of contemporary conductors. During the Higginson era, the BSO presented one concert each week, on Saturday evening. However, a rehearsal was held on Friday afternoon, which became quite popular, especially among wealthy people who were in the habit of leaving Boston for the country on the weekends.

EXHIBIT 1

THE BOSTON SYMPHONY ORCHESTRA
Income Statement, 1966–70

	1966–67	1967–68	1968–69	1969–70
Winter, Pops, etc.				
Concert receipts	$1,709,195	$1,765,124	$1,807,386	$2,035,636
Other receipts	170,000*	175,000*	180,719	175,719
Player compensation	$1,587,712	$1,603,284	$1,880,397	$2,083,695
Other direct concert costs	318,931*	336,615*	336,423	336,818
Direct administrative expense	257,660*	260,939*	263,472	266,818
Net loss	$ 285,108*	$ 260,714*	$ 492,187	$ 475,867
Berkshire Festival				
Concert receipts	$ 453,747	$ 488,697	$ 562,706	$ 487,812
Other receipts	8,842	13,534	12,843	25,792
Player compensation	$ 480,178	$ 478,230	$ 490,862	$ 527,149
Other direct concert costs	88,301	102,677	152,217	156,454
Direct administrative expense	85,610	113,377	162,400	172,399
Net loss	$ 191,500*	$ 192,053*	$ 229,930	$ 342,398
Berkshire Music Center				
Tuition	$ 130,000*	$ 126,847	$ 125,859	$ 141,332
Concert receipts	160,000*	150,000*	158,130	214,578
Other receipts	20,000*	18,073	19,196	83,005
Faculty salary	$ 41,363*	$ 50,276	$ 47,140	$ 68,983
Fellowships	60,000*	66,510	60,475	66,653
Dormitory cost	73,242	96,135	87,093	94,445
Direct concert cost	125,081*	139,073*	132,771	200,695
Direct administrative expense	85,374*	90,312*	95,529	109,989
Net loss	$ 75,060*	$ 147,386*	$ 119,823	$ 101,850

Recording (net)	$ 174,812	$ 243,969	$ 181,490	$ 223,187
Symphony Hall (net)	$ 162,432	$ 187,462	$ 228,930	$ 249,172
Tanglewood property	122,794	142,938	170,385	159,609
Indirect administrative costs	372,000*	463,000*	520,073	570,790
Operating deficit	$1,034,082	$1,149,584	$1,579,838	$1,676,499
Investment income	$ 222,799	$ 297,001	$ 278,540	$ 333,592
Contributions	289,638	336,702	362,098	650,994
Trust income	275,640	223,324	381,759	367,539
Net unearned income	$ 788,077	$ 857,027	$1,022,397	$1,352,125
Deficit (withdrawn from unrestricted funds)	$ 246,005	$ 292,557	$ 557,441	$ 324,374

* Casewriter's estimate.

EXHIBIT 2

THE BOSTON SYMPHONY ORCHESTRA
Balance Sheet
(year ending August 31)

	1967	1968	1969	1970
Assets				
Cash and short-term investments.....	$ 561,008	$ 556,568	$ 708,323	$ 480,058
Accounts receivable and deferred				
exp................................	354,251	525,507	530,971	865,284
Investments (book value)*...........	5,192,058	6,180,451	7,099,927	7,626,689
Land and buildings..................	439,331	439,331	439,331	439,331
	$6,546,648	$7,701,857	$8,778,552	$9,411,362
Liabilities				
Accounts payable and deferred				
income..............................	$1,288,732	$1,214,983	$1,564,027	$1,460,109
Unrestricted funds...................	1,001,583	863,347	913,895	1,341,221
Restricted funds.....................	2,800,538	2,801,136	2,802,210	2,836,359
Ford matching grant..................	1,303,667	2,520,335	3,025,918	3,331,169
Undistributed security gains..........	152,128	302,056	472,502	442,504
	$6,546,648	$7,701,857	$8,778,552	$9,411,362
*Market Value of Investments..........	$6,664,178	$7,881,922	$8,297,246	$7,878,308
Unrestricted Funds:				
Beginning.........................		$1,001,583	$ 863,895	$ 913,895
Less: net deficit..................		292,557	557,441	324,374
		709,026	306,454	589,521
Plus: unrestricted capital				
gifts and bequests†.............		127,321	607,441	751,700
Ending............................		$ 836,347	$ 913,895	$1,341,221
Ford matching grant:				
Beginning.........................		$1,303,667	$2,520,335	$3,025,918
Plus: Gifts to fund†..............		1,216,668	505,583	305,251
Ending............................		$2,520,335	$3,025,918	$3,331,169

† Casewriter's "Plug" figures.

Thus, over the years the Friday afternoon rehearsal, upgraded to a formal concert, became fully as prestigious as the Saturday concerts. Initially, because the Friday afternoon concert was a rehearsal for Saturday night, the programs for these two performances were identical, and following in this tradition, the audience at the Friday series at 2:00 P.M. has invariably heard the music which filled Symphony Hall 30 hours later at the Saturday series at 8:30. The programs for these 24 Friday–Saturday concerts formed the core around which the other BSO concerts were built.

Using essentially these same 24 programs, the BSO presented Tuesday and Thursday evening concerts at Symphony Hall nearly every week during the winter season. The BSO also presented five of the 24 programs twice each at New York's Lincoln Center each season. In effect, the orchestra practiced roughly one program per week, which it performed in concert about four times. Although rehearsal times varied depending on the difficulty of a particular program, it is estimated that four hours

EXHIBIT 3

THE BOSTON SYMPHONY ORCHESTRA
Winter Concert Schedule, 1969–70 Season

Week of:	S	M	T	W	T	F	S
Sept. 21–27						Fri.	Sat.
28–Oct. 4			Tues. A		Thurs. A	Fri.	Sat.
Oct. 5–11			Tues. C		Providence	Fri.	Sat.
12–18			Tues. B		Open Reh.	Fri.	Sat.
19–25				New York		New York	
26–Nov. 1			Tues. A		Open Reh.	Fri.	Sat.
Nov. 2–8			Tues. B		Providence	Fri.	Sat.
9–15			Tues. A		Open Reh.	Fri.	Sat.
16–22			Tues. C		Thurs. A	Fri.	Sat.
23–29			Tues. A			Fri.	Sat.
30–Dec. 6			Tues. B		Open Reh.	Fri.	Sat.
Dec. 7–13				New York		New York	
14–20			Tues. C		Thurs. A	Fri.	Sat.
21–27				Christmas Vacation			
28–Jan. 3			Tues. C			Fri.	Sat.
Jan. 4–10			Tues. A		Thurs. B	Fri.	Sat.
11–17			Tues. B		Providence	Fri.	Sat.
18–24			Tues. C		Open Reh.	Fri.	Sat.
25–31			Tues. A		Thurs. A	Fri.	Sat.
Feb. 1–7				New York		New York	
8–14			Tues. B		Open Reh.	Fri.	Sat.
15–21			Tues. A		Thurs. B	Fri.	Sat.
22–28				New York		New York	
Mar. 1–7			Tues. A		Providence	Fri.	Sat.
8–14			Tues. C		Thurs. A	Fri.	Sat.
15–21			Tues. A		Thurs. B	Fri.	Sat.
22–28					Providence	Fri.	Sat.
29–April 4				New York		New York	
April 5–11				Beethoven Festival			
12–18			Tues. B		Thurs. A	Fri.	Sat.
19–25			Tues. A		Open Reh.	Fri.	Sat.

Note: The BSO presented 119 concerts: 79 regular concerts at Symphony Hall, five concerts in Providence, and ten concerts in New York, 19 other tour concerts, five Beethoven concerts, and one special concert in Boston.

of orchestra rehearsal were required for each hour of finished music. Due to these rehearsal requirements and the repeated performances, the orchestra divided its time about evenly between rehearsals and performances during the winter season.

For the 1969–70 season, William Steinberg, the music director, was scheduled to conduct the orchestra for 12 of the 24 weeks in Boston, and for two of the five weeks in New York. For the remaining weeks, various guest conductors led the orchestra for one- or two-week periods. These guest conductors included Erich Leinsdorf, the former music director; Michael Tilson Thomas, the BSO associate music director; Colin Davis, music director at London's Convent Garden; and Seiji Ozawa, music director of the San Francisco Symphony Orchestra.

Traditionally the selection of programs was the exclusive province of the music director and guest conductor. Programs for the two years prior to 1970 showed that roughly two-thirds of the works selected were by "well-known composers," although they might not be the best-known or most popular works of those composers. The remaining one-third of the programs consisted of works by lesser-known composers, including contemporary Americans. The guest conductor system worked to provide a balance in programming, in that conductors tended to prefer certain periods as well as composers.

Nearly all tickets to BSO concerts were sold to season subscribers who purchased their tickets by mail before the beginning of the winter season. There were ten different subscriptions offered, including two in New York, one in Providence, and an open rehearsal series, which varied in length from three concerts to 24. The two longest concert series were the Friday series at 2:00 P.M. and the Saturday series at 8:30 P.M., which in 1969–70 each included 24 concerts. Ticket prices for either of these series ranged from $60 for a second-balcony seat to $233 for a choice seat in the center of the main floor. On the average, the subscription price was approximately $6 per seat per concert.

The next longest series was the ten-concert Tuesday–A series at 8:30 P.M., for which tickets ranged in price from $29 to $72 for the series, or about $5 per concert on a per-unit basis. A Tuesday–A subscriber heard roughly one out of every two concerts that the Friday–Saturday subscribers heard.

There were two other concert series on Tuesday nights, the Tuesday–B series at 7:30 P.M., and the Tuesday–Cambridge series at 8:30 P.M. Both of these series had six concerts each, with series prices ranging from $13 to $37, or roughly $4 per concert. The Tuesday–B concert was unusual because of its earlier starting time. The Cambridge series concerts were originally held at Sanders Theatre at Harvard, and although they were more recently held at Symphony Hall, they still attracted a Harvard audience. The program for these two Tuesday series was almost invariably the program which had been played for the preceding Friday–Saturday concert.

The Thursday–A series at 8:30 P.M. was a six-concert series with exactly the same prices as the Tuesday six-concert series. The Thursday concert, like the Tuesday one, was often the concert from the preceding Friday and Saturday.

The shortest concert series offered was the three-concert Thursday–B series at 8:30 P.M., which sold for $6.50 to $18.50, or about $4.00 per concert. In addition, there were seven Thursday Open Rehearsals, for which seats were unreserved. Admission tickets for these rehearsals cost $17.50 for the series, or $2.50 per concert. These revenues went to the BSO pension fund. For this low price, one heard the program that was to be played on the following Friday and Saturday. Exhibit 4 shows the rather complex price structure for all the concerts heard at Symphony Hall.

The BSO also played three series of concerts away from Symphony Hall. One was a five-concert series played in Providence on Thursday, for which subscribers paid from $14 to $31, or roughly $4.50 per concert. The programs at these concerts were usually past Friday–Saturday ones. Finally, there were two five-concert series played at New York's Lincoln Center, a Wednesday series and a Friday series. Series prices for these concerts ranged from $17 to $44 or about $6 per concert, roughly the

EXHIBIT 4

THE BOSTON SYMPHONY ORCHESTRA
Ticket Prices for Concert Series at Symphony Hall
1969–70 Season

Friday (24 concerts):
  Floor: $83, $99, $112, $134, $157, $185, and $229
  First balcony: $83, $112, $134, $157, and $203
  Second balcony: $83, $112

Saturday (24 concerts):
  Floor: $84, $104, $116, $132, $138, $148, $152, and $233
  First balcony: $84, $116, $138, $148, $152, and $195
  Second balcony: $60, $84, and $116

Tuesday–A (ten concerts):
  $29, $34, $46, $59, and $72

Tuesday–B, Tuesday–Cambridge, Thursday–A (6 concerts):
  $13, $20, $27, $33, and $37

Thursday–B (three concerts):
  $6.50, $10.00, $13.50, $16.50, and $18.50

Open Rehearsals (seven rehearsals):
  $17.50 (unreserved)

same price as the Friday or Saturday series at Symphony Hall. The programs presented the preceding Fridays and Saturdays in Boston, although they often combined works which had been presented on different past programs. In recent times, the BSO never performed a selection in New York which it had not first performed in Boston in the same season.

The Boston Pops

Higginson had originally intended that the BSO, in addition to classical concerts, also perform somewhat lighter music. In 1885, Wilhelm Gericke, the second conductor of the BSO, concerned that his musicians suffered from inactivity during late spring and summer, decided to implement Higginson's idea. He thus established the tradition that the spring Pops were always conducted by someone other than the music director of the winter symphony season.

The appeal of the Pops is that, although the performances retain the high musical quality of the winter season, they present lighter and more familiar programs. This music combined with beverages, refreshments, gay flowers, green and gold tables and chairs (replacing the symphony seats), and warm spring nights has been successful since its inception.

A distinguishing feature of the Pops is Arthur Fiedler, a musician who joined the BSO in 1915 as a violinist, following in the footsteps of his two brothers and his father. Up to 1930, when Fiedler became conductor of the Pops, there had been 17 Pops conductors, an average of one Pops conductor every three years. Through his showmanship, programming of American music, and ability to adapt popular music to the symphony orchestra, Fiedler in 40 years as conductor has gained an unparalleled national and international reputation for the pops.

The Pops program consists of performances six nights per week, excluding Sunday, for nine weeks beginning at the end of April and ending in early July. For the 1969–70 season, Pops revenues from the 54 concert performances was roughly $470,000; revenues from Pops records were roughly $150,000 for this period.

Fiedler explained his views on Pops programming and its audience appeal as follows:

> My career has been compounded on the theories that listening is a happy experience and that variety is both an essential and desirable part of learning. An illustration of this was a Pops program with Al Hirt in which we achieved a balance between familiar music, and Hirt on a more serious level playing Haydn. His fans listened, respectfully at first, because it was *their* Hirt performing, and then enthusiastically when they discovered that the music of Haydn, which many were possibly hearing for the first time, was pretty listenable in itself. Let them listen

to classical music—they may just like it. Rare is the person who can like something unless he is exposed to it.

The Esplanade Concerts

Originated by Fiedler in 1929, the outdoor concerts on June and July evenings attracted thousands to the banks of the Charles to hear the orchestra perform in the Hatch Shell. In the summer of 1970, the Esplanade Concerts attracted more than 100,000 people to 14 performances. These concerts were performed for the public without charge, and served as a focal point in the BSO drive to raise funds from Boston corporations and foundations.

The Berkshire Musical Festival

In 1936, Mrs. Gorham Brooks and Miss Mary Aspinwall Tappan offered their grandfather's magnificent estate, Tanglewood, with its beautiful 210 acres of woods, lawn, and meadows to Koussevitzky as a permanent summer home for the orchestra. Accepting, Koussevitzky and the orchestra played in a large tent set up on the estate the following summer. However, their first program, commencing with Wagner's "Ride of the Valkyries," was interrupted by a now-famous thunderstorm which, in spite of the tent, drenched the audience and the orchestra and gave the impetus to a drive to build a permanent structure. The 5,000 seat Tanglewood Shed, designed by Gottlieb Eliel Saarinen, was completed the following summer, 1938, and was where the BSO currently performed its eight-week 24-concert summer program. In addition to three weekly symphony concerts on Friday evening, Saturday evening, and Sunday afternoon, the BSO also presented a variety of programs on seven summer Tuesdays featuring the Boston Pops, contemporary music, student performances, and popular guest artists. The revenues from the 24 Berkshire festival concerts for the summer of 1970 were $488,000.

The Berkshire Music Center

In 1940, Koussevitzky established an educational center at Tanglewood for training musicians. The purpose of the program was to provide a meeting ground for young instrumental musicians who had completed their formal training and were employed as active performers. This highly intensive eight-week program gave young musicians an opportunity to perform often in a variety of musical settings: chamber music, orchestra, contemporary music. Because of its educational value and the strong financial support, the school has attracted as pupils some of the world's finest musicians, and the Berkshire Music Center's alumni make up a remarkable 10 percent of the country's major orchestras.

Other BSO Activities

The Boston Symphony Chamber Players consisted of the orchestra's virtuoso principal players (first-desk players), who performed in a wide variety of instrumental combinations, from duos to septets and nonets. Although the Chamber Players presented concerts year-round, most of their performances occurred during the spring Pops season when the first-desk players did not play with the orchestra. Revenues from the Chamber Players concerts were $35,000 in 1970.

Also, the Friday afternoon and Saturday evening winter season concerts were broadcast live over two Boston radio stations, WGBH and WCRB, and also were recorded for rebroadcast by a network of 65 radio stations. Total revenues for radio broadcasts were roughly $150,000 for the 1969–70 season. In addition, at least four concerts were recorded annually for television to be broadcast by WGBH-TV in Boston. A series of Pops programs were produced to be broadcast nationally.

The BSO had been producing records since 1917. For many years the Pops and the Symphony both recorded exclusively for R.C.A. However, in 1970 the Boston Symphony contracted to record for the German company, Deutsche Grammophone Geselleschaft (D.G.G.). Net income from sales of all recordings was $223,000 in 1970.

BOSTON SYMPHONY ORGANIZATION

There were four major organizational components in the BSO organizational structure: (1) the management staff, (2) the board of trustees, (3) the players of the orchestra, and (4) the music director.

Management Staff

Thomas Perry, manager of the BSO, gave his views of the structure, problems and strategic alternatives for the Boston Symphony Orchestra as follows:

> The Music Director makes the artistic decision. It is the role of the management to arrange that these activities can take place. This means earning money and spending money. It is the management which initiates policy. The Trustees have public responsibility, but are not active and guide policy in only a general sort of way. However, I confer frequently with Talcott Banks, president of the Trustees, often several times per week.
>
> The structure of the management follows these general outlines. Tom Morris handles business affairs. This means the non-musical aspects of our activities: food, books, the buildings, housing and budgeting. David Rockefeller, Jr., is our marketer, looking at Symphony from the consumer view, watching ticket sales, and planning what sorts of concerts we

should present. Mary Smith co-ordinates the artistic production. This means she co-ordinates the musical selections of the Music Director and the guest conductors. Finally, Forrester Smith is in charge of fund-raising. What this amounts to is goading the Trustees into giving what is necessary to keep us afloat. These are the supporting functions.

Mr. Perry said that the symphony's problems were divided between maintaining high standards of performance and surviving financially. The symphony was continually faced with cost-quality trade-offs, as those activities which contributed most to the BSO's reputation for high quality —the extensive repertoire featured during the winter season, the Berkshire teaching program—were also the most expensive to execute. The problem of keeping a deficit business alive was the subject of discussion at the frequent management staff meetings. These discussions explored various commercial areas: the possibility of video cassettes, competition of foreign record companies, and the problems of union costs in recording. Mr. Perry commented about the dilemma inherent in using the symphony to make money:

> With respect to the cash generating process, the Pops with its emphasis on entertainment comes closest of all activities to paying for itself. Recording is a good generator, but clearly not so in its own right because it leans on the orchestra's reputation. There are many other activities which we have considered: food at Tanglewood, going into the publishing business, more public service like Esplanade for contributions, and parking cars near Symphony Hall. The problem with these activities is that you must ask yourself at what point do you take your eye off the ball? Once commercialism sets in there is a shift of emphasis and the artistic quality begins to slip. For this reason, financial controls are very difficult.

Mr. Perry said that corporations and the government represented two untapped sources of funds, although he was wary of the commitments the symphony would have to make to gain government support.

> I view government support with mixed feelings. I have seen the financial problems which the European state-supported orchestras suffer. Also, what commitments would the Symphony have to make to gain government support?

Thomas Morris, assistant manager for business affairs, was in charge of the financial side. His original role had been primarily performing the accounting function, but it had evolved beyond that into labor relations and negotiation of television and radio contracts. Mr. Morris, a graduate of Princeton and Wharton, came to the BSO in 1969. He had tried to introduce the concept of control budgeting, which was practically non-existent when he arrived. He described this process as follows:

> In the past with regard to cost, what the conductor said, we did. The idea of putting financial restrictions on the artistic decision was totally

new and, consequently, we've had trouble working the problem out. The problem is essentially that in dealing with a conductor you must steer around the issue of refusing a particular piece—Mahler's Eighth Symphony, for example—which requires eight soloists.

To avoid this confrontation you must apply financial controls within the framework of a season. Once an aggregate amount is determined for a season, a conductor can begin to make financial trade-offs. It is possible to put a dollar figure in particular works; we know what extra players are required and their cost as well as the rehearsal time required.

Mr. Morris' second area of responsibility, labor relations, was quite sensitive. It concerned the paradoxical situation in which highly gifted musical artists were rigidly unionized and their rehearsals and performances were strictly governed by the clock. Mr. Morris described the BSO labor policies as follows:

> Our best approach is to seek close relations with the orchestra members and to avoid incidents. For example, recently there was a controversy in the interpretation of a contract clause governing the compensation of members of the orchestra who performed for only part of a recording session. Because this involved only six or eight players, and because the players felt very strongly that everyone should be paid, we paid everyone even though the recording provision did not strictly require this.

Mary Smith, assistant manager for concerts and artists, was directly involved in all problems related to making the annual schedule for the BSO's winter season of 100 or more performances, the five New York trips, and the 24 Tanglewood concerts. Ms. Smith filled a blank calendar with dates for the various series, starting with 24 Friday and Saturday concerts, then adding the shorter ten, six, and three concert series on Tuesday and Thursday nights. She conferred with the music director regarding which weeks he would conduct to fulfill his contract. Traditionally, this meant at least opening and closing the season. Communicating with the trustees and the music director, she filled the remaining weeks' slots in the winter season with the associate conductor and other guest conductors. Soloists were then selected generally by the conductors with an occasional input from the trustees. Finally, programs were selected by the conductors with the approval of the music director who, with Ms. Smith's assistance, solved problems of program duplication. Although the scheduling was done at least one year in advance, the above functions did not fall into a neat sequence of steps. Instead there was a process of continuous scheduling revision and adjustment.

Ms. Smith commented on this process of negotiation:

> Decision on selections made by guest conductors go to the Music Director and the Board of Trustees, who usually defer to the Music Director. However, our president [Talcott Banks] is very active and involved, and he is the final authority in everything except music direction.

Forrester Smith, the director of development, was in charge of generating "unearned income" for the BSO, i.e., fund-raising. Prior to the recent arrival of Mr. Smith, the BSO relied on an outside firm to handle an annual appeal letter. Under his direction the fund-raising had been increased significantly and the figures reflected his success. The $650,000 he had raised in his first year far exceeded the average of $330,000 for the three years prior to his arrival. The development office was separate from the rest of the BSO management, and Mr. Smith reported to the Trustees directly.

Forrester Smith saw the decline in subscriptions at the BSO and the large operating deficits as problems which complicated the fund-raising functions; he explained his view as follows:

> Boston Symphony has a champagne and caviar image, and this is not totally inaccurate. Consistent with this image, there are unbusinesslike people in the arts. If they see merit in a program, they say "go ahead" without looking at a budget to see if we can afford it. For example, recently the organ was broken and some members of management were ready to spend $50,000 immediately to fix it up. At my urging this expenditure was delayed until we could find a donor who would offer to underwrite the expense. Another perfect example of lack of control concerned a performance in New York by the concertmaster, Joseph Silverstein. Two other members of the Symphony decided to go along for moral support and they charged the whole thing to the BSO.
>
> I believe that budgeting could be done tactfully. The BSO is one of New England's greatest cultural assets, but there would be more respect for the BSO if we were fiscally responsible.

Mr. Smith said that trustee involvement was important to fund-raising. The BSO was at some disadvantage, compared with other cities, because there were relatively few home-based corporations in Boston, and Mr. Smith saw significant government funding as a long-range necessity. He commented,

> The paradox of these last few years is that our capital has been increasing slightly despite the fact that our sizable operating deficits have forced us to invade capital. However, this policy of invading capital has been at the expense of building up our income-producing funds. I believe that our deficits have finally reached the point where our trustees must face up to the fact that we simply are going to run out of money. We must budget so that we stop invading capital; otherwise we will eventually follow those orchestras which have eaten up their endowment funds, such as Chicago.

David Rockefeller, Jr., the assistant manager for audience and public affairs, was in charge of a recently created position, which roughly corresponded to the marketing function at the BSO, including the box office, the subscription office, the press office, and the switchboard. Mr.

Rockefeller saw his role as coordinating these functions and providing feedback and policy advice on the timing and content of the major BSO marketing activities, i.e., Symphony, Pops, and Tanglewood.

Mr. Rockefeller, a graduate of Harvard College and Harvard Law School, came to the BSO in 1969. He described his present role as follows:

> In the past, the stated policy and organizational rule at the BSO was that, after gaining a thorough knowledge of the whole orchestra, all individuals in management did basically what they were good at. I recognized that there were small spheres of influence at the BSO, such as audience research, subscriptions, and the program book department. There had been over the years a proliferation of self-contained service centers, some of which duplicated other BSO functions. I believed there was a need for some office with a general overview, a need for coordination. Thus, in 1970 several marketing functions were grouped into my present department.
>
> I would like to see our organization get on an even keel. We need to be organized first, so that we can be solicitors in the music market, so that we can respond with our programs to the market. Secondly, we need to improve fund-raising. And third, we must be able to interface with government in the future.
>
> I have very little input into the musical decision. The product is already determined and they give it to me to sell.

Board of Trustees

The 20 members of the board of trustees of the Boston Symphony Orchestra represented the most powerful elements of Boston's financial, corporate, legal, political, religious, and social communities. The trustees could be classified into three groups: business leaders, lawyers, and other prominent citizens. The business leaders included the following: Vernon Alden, chairman of the Boston Corporation; Allen Barry, chief executive officer of New England Telephone; Richard Chapman, president of New England Merchants Bank; Abram Collier, senior vice president of New England Mutual Life Insurance Company; and Irving Rabb, vice chairman of Stop and Shop. The lawyers were senior partners in some of Boston's major law firms: Talcott Banks of Palmer & Dodge; John Noonan of Herrick, Smith; and Sidney Stoneman of Singer, Stoneman & Kurkland. Among the prominent citizens were: Edward Kennedy, Sr., U.S. Senator; Hon. Paul Reardon, justice of the Massachusetts Supreme Judicial Court; and Rev. Msgr. Edward Murray, pastor St. Paul's Church, Cambridge. There was one woman on the board: Mrs. James Perkins, daughter of the former president of the trustees, Henry Cabot.

The trustees served life terms and their average age was roughly 60 years old. The trustees met monthly in downtown Boston.

Mr. Perry, the BSO manager, described the trustees' role in the BSO decision-making process as follows:

> First, they have the power to select and appoint the music director. Second, they are responsible for hiring the manager. Mr. Banks, the president of the trustees, is the most active trustee. I know that he spends a great deal of his time on orchestra business because I confer with him so frequently. The other trustees are less active, except for the three officers, Mr. Allen, Mr. Gardiner, and Mr. Thorndike, who form the executive committee. However, the bulk of the work falls on Mr. Banks.

Vacancies on the board of trustees were usually filled by selecting someone from the 60-member board of overseers. Mr. Rockefeller had observed the functions of the trustees at close hand. He described those functions as follows:

> The present relationship of the president of the trustees and the manager is a case of the old style, person-to-person, management. In the past, the president ran a one-man show in which problems were solved by the manager and the president "figuring things out." The manager, in effect, was the double lackey of both the president and the music director. Mr. Banks, whose legal background is suited to a personal administration, has to some degree followed in this tradition.
>
> To some extent, in the past few years we have moved from a triumvirate, of the music director, the manager, and the president of the trustees, to a degree of participatory democracy with more overseers and even more orchestra players being involved in decisions. This is partly a mark of the times.

There were a series of close relationships between the trustees and management. For example, Mr. Allen consulted with Forrester Smith on fund-raising; Mr. Thorndike of Fiduciary Trust was the BSO treasurer and counseled with Mr. Tom Morris on financial matters; as mentioned above, Mr. Banks conferred with Mr. Perry on affairs concerning conductors, programs, and musical policies. David Rockefeller had worked on various separate projects with Mr. Rabb, Mrs. Perkins, Mr. Allen, and Mr. Thorndike.

Talcott Banks, president of the trustees, commented on the functions of the trustees and his own role as follows:

> I participate so far as is possible in the formulation of policy and the making of decisions on every level, including the details of operations. Part of my task is to maintain and strengthen the personal relationship between the players, the administrative staff, and the trustees and overseers, plus other elements of the institution, including concert goers and people who are personally interested in symphony.

By participating in many conferences with players' committees I have acquired a personal friendship with quite a range of players. Now, after many years, there is a basis of strong mutual interest.

To a large extent I work through the manager, Tod Perry. He and I are in almost daily contact. I spend 50 percent or perhaps more of my time on symphony affairs.

The trustees are the body who make decisions with the advice and recommendations of the staff. For example, the decision to send the orchestra on a European tour this coming year was a trustee decision. The selection of a guest conductor is made on the recommendation of the staff with trustee approval. The trustees here are very active. Their decisions here touch on values, on the reason for a symphony orchestra's existence. A corporation's performance can be measured by the profit it makes, but measuring the performance of a symphony is much more complex.

In the world of music, a symphony has almost universal appeal. A symphony orchestra is *sui bonum,* the highest expression of musical art, in its broadest concept. Since 1750, the symphony has been an increasingly dominant contributing factor to civilization and to people who are persuaded of its importance, there is nothing more important, not sports, not health care, nothing.

Players of the Orchestra

The four sections of the orchestra were made up of 106 players: 66 strings, 16 woodwinds, 15 brass, five percussion, two harps, plus two librarians. Vacancies with the orchestra were rare, but clearly there was more likely to be an opening for a violinist (18 first, 16 second) than for any other instrument. Mr. Perry described the hiring process as follows:

> When a vacancy occurs it is published in the *International Musician,* a publication with wide circulation amongst the players in the major orchestras in this country and Europe. Next the applicants are invited to come to Boston for a preliminary audition which is run by members of the orchestra. Those who have been found capable have a final audition with the Music Director and a few members of the orchestra. Once the Music Director has reached a decision upon consultation with the players, I make the business arrangements with the new members of the orchestra.

Once a musician had joined the orchestra his relationship with the management was governed by the contract between the BSO and Local 9 of the Federation of Musicians. Because only 5 percent of the members of Local 9 are symphonic players, the contract was negotiated by a committee of the BSO players who hired their own labor lawyer.

The summer program at Tanglewood enabled the BSO to guarantee year-round employment to the players at a minimum salary of $16,500, which with extras came to more than $20,000. Because this was the minimum, many players made much more, especially the principal players (first-desk players) who were paid more than twice this figure. In addition, upon reaching age 60, players were eligible for a pension of $8,100.

The union contract ran for three years and provided for 79 concerts at Symphony Hall each year. In addition, the contract covered the terms of performance for tours, Tanglewood, and recording sessions. Generally, eight "services" per week were required from the orchestra, a service lasting $2\frac{1}{2}$ hours, and being either a performance or a rehearsal. During the symphony season there were roughly four rehearsals and four performances per week, but during Pops there were only two rehearsals and six performances, the latter being a very fatiguing schedule for the players. Because the BSO was tied to the contract, however, nothing could be saved in expenses by cutting back on the number of programs.

A recent development was the formation of the artistic advisory committee, a group of six representatives elected by the orchestra, which represented the players' views to the music director, management, and the trustees.

Mr. Perry commented on the relationship of this group and the music director:

> Whereas the music director was the conventional high prince in the past, particularly in the days of Koussevitzky, today he is confronted by the players' committee. They consult with the music Director and make their views known. This is a serious threat to the conductor's realm.

Mary Smith related the details of management's contact with the artistic advisory committee:

> Mr. Perry and I meet with this group about once per month. The role of these members of the orchestra is purely advisory. They give musical and artistic advice. Sometimes they withdraw suggestions when they learn more from us. But this is a two-way street and we ask for musical advice from them, especially regarding the necessity to coordinate programs or the difficulty of a work and its required rehearsal time.

Music Director

A conductor's conception of his own position was clearly very personal and varied a great deal with individual styles. The resulting artistic decision was thus a function of the conductor's views of his own role, as well as his insight into the current state of symphonic music.

Leonard Bernstein, musical advisor to Tanglewood, as well as guest conductor of the Boston Symphony, gave his views on the position of music director:

The role of the music director has changed a great deal since Kousse-vitzky's day. You hear that Koussevitzky was always complaining about the trustees. They were upset because there was too much modern music or because the programs were too expensive. Koussevitzky was always in a tizzy.

When I went to New York in 1958 I never had to confront the trustees. In fact, I had to be dragged to only one trustee meeting each year. It was largely a ceremonial meeting; I would tell my plans for the year and for the next three years in general terms. Not once in 12 years was there even a battle with the trustees. Really, the trustees had no impact on the artistic decision. There was no importance at all to my meeting with the trustees. There were no strings on the programs.

I did not consciously follow the subscription sales. But when I came in, the Philharmonic was in bad shape. The prior conductor had some artistic problems and also some problems with the press. My work was primarily a matter of working with the orchestra, and giving them a sense of pride in themselves, in their functions. It was just as basic as getting them to play in tune and developing a pride in the orchestra. And this affects the audience; they began to come back. Later we did touring, recordings, and television, and this added to the financial picture, as well as our pride.

During this time I was not aware of the financial state of the orchestra. I couldn't tell you what the financial problems were. I learned not to go into these details.

Michael Tilson Thomas, the associate music director of the BSO, spoke of one way in which the music director is concerned with the financial affairs:

In programming concerts for an entire season, you are constrained by the relative poverty of the orchestra. One big thing must be paid for by doing less at many other concerts. One big name soloist will be a sure fire success, but then you cannot do as much the rest of the season.

Michael Tilson Thomas also spoke of the relationship of the management to the music director:

The management should do two things. First, they should aid and carry out the plans of the music director. They have physical responsibility for these plans. Second, they should recognize the abilities of the music director and the orchestra and then think of ways to capitalize on these abilities. Looking at the people presently in the BSO management, no one is spending much time on this second function; they are mostly working on the details of concerts. This is unfortunate because they are only thnking about concert-giving as it exists.

WINTER SEASON SUBSCRIPTION CRISIS

Over the past 30 years, all the subscriptions for the BSO concerts had been sold out and there had been a long waiting list. For example, as recently as the 1967–68 season, an average of 2,470 subscriptions were sold for all series in Boston. This was 94 percent of the 2,631 seats available at Symphony Hall, and several dozen of the seats were held as complimentary seats and not for sale. Exhibit 5 contains data on all the Symphony Hall subscription series for the past three years. However, in the two seasons since 1967–68, there had been a sharp falling off in subscription sales which had affected all series. The average subscriptions for all Boston concerts was 2,415 or 92 percent of capacity for the 1968–69 season; 2,295 or 87 percent for the 1969–70 season; and 2,180 or 83 percent for 1970–71 season. In short, there had been about a 12 percent decrease in subscriptions in only three years. As a direct result of this decline in subscriptions, the amount of revenue lost by empty seats increased tenfold, from $6,000 in 1968–69 to over $60,000 in 1969–70 (see Exhibit 6).

Although the decrease had affected all series, it had affected some series much more than others. For example, the Friday afternoon series and the Tuesday–Cambridge series had lost only slightly more than 100 subscribers or about 5 percent loss, while the Tuesday–A, Tuesday–B, and Thursday–B series had lost several hundred subscribers, each series losing at least 20 percent of its 1967–68 subscription level.

Mr. Banks analyzed the decline in subscriptions in the following manner:

> Regarding the decline in subscriptions for symphony, the causes are many. The decline is paralleled in other cities. This is a time of change for symphony orchestra affairs generally.
>
> We are no longer firmly in the classical pattern; there is no longer a

EXHIBIT 5

THE BOSTON SYMPHONY ORCHESTRA
*Winter Season Subscription Sales, Symphony Hall Concerts, by Concert Series
Subscriptions Sold and Percent of Capacity (Total Seats = 2,631)*

Concert Series	1967–68	1968–69	1969–70
Friday (24 concerts)	2,363	2,351	2,343
	(90%)	(89%)	(89%)
Saturday (24)	2,491	2,436	2,288
	(94%)	(92%)	(87%)
Tuesday–A (ten)	2,480	2,450	2,241
	(94%)	(93%)	(85%)
Tuesday–B (six)	2,514	2,474	2,142
	(96%)	(94%)	(81%)
Tuesday–Cambridge (six)	2,546	2,525	2,300
	(97%)	(96%)	(88%)
Thursday–A (six)	2,577	2,596	2,390
	(98%)	(99%)	(91%)
Thursday–B (three)	2,461	2,232	2,054
	(93%)	(88%)	(78%)
All series	2,470	2,415	2,295
(weighted average)	(94%)	(92%)	(87%)

EXHIBIT 6

THE BOSTON SYMPHONY ORCHESTRA
Winter Season Revenues*

		1966–67	1967–68	1968–69	1969–70
(1)	Number of concerts at Symphony Hall.................................	79	79	79	79
(2)	Maximum possible revenue..........	$901,338	$983,129	$983,129	$1,148,150
(3)	Subscription revenue.................	871,284	952,034	941,397	1,031,622
(4)	Single ticket sale revenue............	20,472	22,769	35,910	55,247
(5)	Subscription percent [(3) ÷ (2)].......	96%	97%	95%	90%
(6)	Single ticket percent [(4) ÷ (2)].......	2%	2%	4%	5%
(7)	Percent of capacity [(5) + (6)]........	98%	99%	99%	95%
(8)	Percent of empty seats [100%–(7)]....	2%	1%	1%	5%
(9)	Total revenue [(3) + (4)]..............	$891,756	$974,804	$977,308	$1,086,870
(10)	Revenue lost by empty seats [(2)–(9)]..	9,582	8,325	5,821	61,280

* Includes only concerts at Symphony Hall, not New York or Providence concerts.

classical repertoire with an established audience filling the hall. Boston has been uniquely fortunate to sell out for decades; only recently have subscriptions been for sale. The generations are changing. The newer up-coming generation is no longer one which grew up on symphony. The younger people are initially less interested in music as performed by such a bastion of the establishment as the Boston Symphony.

The broad question is, "how can the symphony orchestra be better attuned to this age?" The pendulum is swinging away from a lot of ele-ments characterized by contemporary composition. It is swinging back toward greater popularity of the classical repertoire and the exploration of relatively unknown aspects of music, even pre-Bach. There is declining interest in exceedingly complicated modern music and a renewal of satis-faction in earlier works. The accompanying opening up of music of the 19th century and earlier is exploring relatively neglected areas of the classical repertoire.

Why should we play contemporary music at all? Unless this music is played, we won't have the art of music. The players have their interest renewed and invigorated; these works are very interesting to perform.

Leonard Bernstein had commented in his *The Infinite Variety of Music* that "it is a scary moment" in the history of music. He believed that the traditional relationship between composer and public had ended about the time of the World War I, when composers of classical music in general tended to produce experimental works less compatible with the public taste. "From then on," according to Bernstein, "it became a hassle: composer versus public." He defined the significance of this conflict as follows:

What this means is that for 50 years the public has not anticipated with excitement the premiere of a single symphonic or operatic work.

And if this is true, it signifies a dramatic qualitative change in our musical society: namely, that for the first time we are living a musical life that is not based on the composition of our time. This is purely a 20th century phenomenon; it has never been true before. . . .

The last great symphony was written by Stravinsky in 1945; I don't know of a great symphony since then. In Koussevitzky's day there was always a great symphony. This was the reason I left the New York Philharmonic, because there were no new pieces to play. The Symphony became like a magnificent museum.

      ✿   ✿   ✿   ✿   ✿

I am a fanatic music lover. And in this role of simple music lover, I confess, freely though unhappily, that at this moment, as of this writing, God forgive me, I have far more pleasure in following the musical adventures of Simon and Garfunkel or of the Association singing "Along Comes May" than I have in most of what is being written now by the whole community of "avant-garde" composers. Pop music seems to be the only area where there is to be found unabashed vitality, the fun of invention, the feeling of fresh air.

Michael Tilson Thomas, like Bernstein, attributed the decline in subscription sales to the current state of music:

The traditional concert series has become very boring. There used to be a value in the repetition of the works of the great composers. This music was not available to the people of a town in any other form than the town symphony because there were no recordings.

Records have done very bad things to music; esthetically, they have done great harm. Part of the point of going to concerts was to see the personalities involved, to see the eccentricity. People would go to hear the great violinist, the great pianist, and on the way out they would say, "Oh, brother did you hear what Horowitz did to that piece?"

Recordings, by making music available, have ended the hierarchal position of classical music. Classical music is no longer the best, the closest to God. Many people think that Janis Joplin and Jimmie Hendrix are the best. Radio stations have contributed to this breakdown of hierarchy by juxtaposing different types of music; they might play in close succession Eastern music, classical music, then Hendrix and Joplin.

Even within the classical world there are many different kinds of audiences. Most people don't really know what is a good performance. They may know how it goes, at least according to their record, which they have heard over and over. But the composer's work exists in an infinite number of ways. There are best performances at different levels. For example, I have often envisioned record stores selling Beethoven's Fifth Symphony by three groupings: "beginning," which would be very clear and pronounced; "intermediate," which would highlight the counter subjects; and "advanced," which would have no interpretation. Because of this tendency of records to cement people's views of musical work, I have often said that all records should self-destruct after five playings.

The problem is that 50 pieces have been repeated, repeated, and repeated. This music has become like Forest Lawn and where you see a copy of Michaelangelo's David, not grained as the original, but perfectly clear and pure, plus a tape cassette which explains it. This is all wrong.

Strangely enough, another serious problem which we run into concerns the space in which we work. We are locked into a proscenium theater which is superb for a particular event, the traditional concert. But if you want more contact with the audience, or if you have visual material, the equipment is not here. We must be satisfied with complicated, awkward, temporary alternatives. The newer halls cannot match the acoustics of Symphony Hall. Philharmonic Hall at Lincoln Center is acoustically terrible, although not as bad as it was. Before alterations, it was a disaster. But it has built-in equipment and projection capability.

The Financial Condition of the BSO

Due to its reporting practices, the financial condition of the BSO could not be easily determined on the basis of examining a single annual report. Over the four seasons from 1966–67 to 1969–70, the BSO reported a total operating deficit of $5.44 million, and a final deficit of $1.42 million, after taking account of annual contributions and investment income. However, despite the fact that the BSO reported that it annually invaded working capital to the extent of at least $250,000, during the period of these four seasons the BSO had actually increased its unrestricted capital by $340,000. This was because the BSO did not report on its annual income statement unrestricted capital gifts and bequests, which ranged from $150,000 to $600,000 each year; however, these items did show up on the balance sheet by increasing the level of unrestricted funds. Thus, although the annual statements indicated that the BSO had been running deficits of 6 percent to 11 percent over the past four years, actually the BSO had increased its net worth.

The slight increase in net worth was quite remarkable because the annual expenditure had been increasing by more than 12 percent per year during this period, growing from $3.8 million in 1966–67 to more than $5.5 million in 1969–70. The bulk of the increase in expenditures came from musicians' salaries. Musicians' salaries increased from $2.07 million to $2.61 million. However, musicians' salaries were increasing by only 8 percent per year compared with the 12 percent per year increase in administration. Thus, in the last three years, administrative costs and musicians' salaries combined had increased by $860,000 or roughly 37 percent.

Earned income, primarily revenue from concerts, had grown by 6 percent annually, more slowly than expenditures. This resulted in roughly a

19 percent increase over the past three years. Because earned income was not keeping pace with expenditures, earned income as a percentage of expenditures decreased from 73 percent to 67 percent during this period, just under the average for the five major orchestras. Partially offsetting this trend was recording income; net recording income, after expenditures actually increased by $50,000. Although only about 5 percent of the other major orchestras' earned income came from recording, the BSO gained about 15 percent of its revenue from records. Much of this revenue could be attributed to the recordings of Arthur Fiedler and the Boston Pops.

In addition to the fact that revenues had not kept pace with expenditures, relatively, the absolute size of both revenues and expenditures was increasing. As a result, the annual operating deficit had increased by 63 percent in only three years, from $1.03 million to $1.68 million. The $642,000 increase in operating deficit from 1966–67 to 1969–70 was distributed as follows: $191,000 for Winter Pops; $27,000 for the Berkshire Music Center; $150,000 for the Berkshire Festival; $199,000 for indirect administration; $87,000 for Symphony Hall; and $37,000 for Tanglewood. This deficit increase was offset by $48,000 increase in net recording income.

Outside income and contributions were growing sufficiently quickly to meet the one-third of the expenditures which were not covered by earned income. In fact, the reported cash flow from unearned sources was growing quite rapidly, with the $1.352 million in investment income and contributions in 1969–70 representing more than a 70 percent increase over the $788,000 raised just three seasons before. With investments at a market value of $7.88 million and returning income of about 3.5 percent, the BSO received about $300,000 in investment income each year. However, with the investment income growing at less than 7 percent per year, and expenditures by more than 12 percent, it was clear that this source of income was not ample to cover the deficit. In fact, the deficit was covered by withdrawals from unrestricted funds, a balance sheet account to which sizable gifts were made each year that were not reported on the income statement. In the past three years, nearly $1.5 million in gifts had been received by this account (see Exhibit 2). This was, in fact, the reason the BSO had been able to meet its rising expenses.

A final source of funds, which increased annual funds only slightly, but which had a significant impact on restricted capital, was the Ford Foundation grant, received in 1967. The $2 million grant, currently held in trust by the Ford Foundation, would become unrestricted capital of the BSO in 1976, provided it was matched two-to-one by other capital gifts by 1971. In short, the BSO had five years to raise $4 million. At the end of the 1969–70 fiscal year $3.33 million of this goal had been raised. The $2 million trust, primarily Ford stock, was returning roughly $90,000.

Mr. Banks described the financial condition of the BSO as follows:

> The accounting for the Symphony is terribly complicated. Even if you know how to read the reports, there is a paradox in our accounting. We are using unrestricted capital every year of necessity; we've got to do it. However, this capital is being replenished, primarily by legacies, so that our total unrestricted capital is increasing.
>
> We evaluate our financial performance on three separate categories: first, operating deficit; second, the income statement plus annual contributions; third, the capital situation, that is the amount of decrease in capital. We also consider what I call the "x factor," the intangible aspects of our financial situation.
>
> We are irrevocably tied by the trade agreement to a full year salary for the players. Therefore, we have to put these services to the most profitable use. We can't save by curtailing our activities because of the enormous fixed cost of paying for these services.
>
> The operating deficit last year was over $1.5 million. There is only one way to deal with the problem. We must look to see where economies can be effected without the loss of quality or the loss of aspects of our program which are important. We are unique in owning our own summer home at Tanglewood; we also have a very high-quality school. Both are expensive but they are great contributions to the world of music.
>
> However, a very large deficit must be reduced. Commercial expedients are unavailable to us, and we are limited by a fixed capacity, although Tanglewood is expandible to some extent. There is a maximum number of concerts permitted by the agreement as well as an intangible maximum on ticket prices. If we raise prices too high there are diminishing returns. But also we are responsible to the public; our prices should not exclude those who are intensely interested in music.
>
> The amount involved here is a mere trifle to the federal government. I see the government taking some kind of interest here; the government should sustain music. Music is an essential ingredient of civilization. The foundations have assisted. For example, there is the needed seed money of the Ford grants. Business and corporate support is another source of funds, but this has been slow to grow.

The Appendix provides a brief overview of the conditions of U.S. orchestras taken as a group.

Concert Activities Committee

In October of 1970, the trustees of the BSO responded to the decline in concert attendance by appointing a concert activities committee to consider broadly the underlying causes of the problem. The committee was composed of several trustees, a few overseers, and many staff members. Mrs. Perkins was the chairman and David Rockefeller served as staff liaison to the committee. In a memo to committee members, Mr. Rockefeller outlined the problem as developing an "audience of the future," i.e., the necessity of attracting "entirely new fans if Symphony Hall is to be filled in the future." Members were also aware of the need to think about finding a new music director, since Steinberg was in his 70s and had been idle for much of the previous season due to ill health.

Mr. Banks explained why the subscription problem was not handled by management without direct trustee intervention:

> The purpose of the Concert Activities Committee is to inquire into why subscriptions were declining, that is, why is the Boston Symphony failing to reach a considerable section of the population?
>
> Theoretically, this problem could be handled by the management staff without the appointment of a special committee. However, this would make inhuman demands on management. Therefore, we look to trustee participation; we look to the Trustees for new ideas and support.
>
> This could be a change in course and the Trustees should know about possible improvements. The relationship of the Boston board to the staff could probably be broadened a good deal by this experience.

Mrs. Perkins opened the first meeting on November 11 summarizing the task of the committee: "To isolate the problem areas related to reduced concert attendance, to investigate the causes of the problems and to recommend solutions before January 1, 1971, the deadline for major changes in the 1971–72 season." The problem areas discussed at the first meeting included parking, social conditions, concert times, transportation to concerts, program content, poll of the audience, ease of ticket purchase, and special audience groups. Although there was a full discussion of these issues, some committee members felt that program content was not a proper subject for anyone beyond the music director. In addition, some members were skeptical of the value of an audience poll.

One month later, on December 8, the concert activities committee met again to consider the problem of declining ticket sales. Present at this meeting were representatives of the orchestra and Michael Tilson Thomas, the young associate conductor of the BSO.

Several suggestions emerged from the second meeting: (1) the possibility of establishing a bar at Symphony Hall, (2) varying the concert format possibly to include smaller ensembles, (3) the possibility of holding BSO concerts in a suburban auditorium, (4) the need for more "stars" at performances, and (5) generally the need to make BSO offerings genuinely exciting in order to overcome the cost of a seat at Symphony Hall. Some members expressed the view that important decisions could not be based upon guesswork and suggested that a fuller study of the market and newer subscribers should be undertaken.

Due to the pressure of the January 1, 1971 deadline, a third meeting of the concert activities committee was scheduled for December 22. Prior to that meeting, David Rockefeller circulated a memo setting forth a list of possible alternatives for changes in the 1971–72 symphony subscription season. These five alternatives were as follows:

1. To create a three- or six-concert series for a weeknight beginning early (5:30) to attract commuters;
2. To change the 20-concert Saturday series to ten concerts on Saturday and ten on Thursday, to allow the subscribers more free Saturday evenings;
3. To create a six-concert Friday night series;
4. To change the weekday series names from "A," "B," etc., to distinctive titles, such as "The Beethoven Series";
5. To increase the number of open Rehearsals and make them more informative, e.g., provide the conductor with a microphone.

The New Concert Series Proposal

At the third meeting of the concert activities committee, Michael Tilson Thomas presented a proposal for a sensational new series of concerts. These concerts, he believed, would draw attention generally to the activities of the orchestra. They would consist of music of all periods in unusual juxtaposition and would be presented informally.

Michael Tilson Thomas stated his proposal as follows:

> I feel it is possible to present a program which will appeal to a different kind of audience, different from our regular subscribers. I think that we can reach the people who don't normally come, people who aren't attracted to our traditional programming. In short, I think we can reach the music freaks.
>
> The series should be lower-priced so that it will not exceed the budget of young people. It should be completely outside the regular subscription series so that we will attract an entirely new audience. These new concerts can be done in a number of different ways. Each year they should become progressively more experimental.
>
> The concerts should be in some way challenging, and we should not let them turn into traditional concerts of the 50 greatest moments of music which the audience knows and memorizes. The most disturbing works, perhaps even the most negatively received pieces, at least by the press, would be the best in my view. The very best concerts should be conceived in unusual ways.
>
> At the end of one of these concerts the audience might sit in a state of shock; as people file out, you might hear, "Man, my head was destroyed at this concert." According to my ideal, it should be impossible for the audience to return to thinking of things in the same way after one of these concerts.
>
> We should be trying to activize the audience; I want to force the audience to form reactions; we need to make the audience make decisions. We should do offstage things, wild stuff. We need to break down

the traditional barriers that separate the audience and the orchestra. The players should dress informally; I should talk to the audience; I even envision having some of the audience on stage for a piece. This can be a very good sort of thing.

Mr. Thomas proposed a total of six concerts, two each to be performed in October, January, and April, on Friday and Saturday evenings. The Friday and Saturday series would be essentially identical, although the January concerts might perhaps be different, but complementary. For example, there might be two separate Stravinsky programs, one on Friday and the other on Saturday.

Because of the unusual nature of the music for these concerts, they would require one and one-half times as much rehearsal time as a regular BSO subscription concert. The price of tickets would be $10 for a three-concert series.

Appendix

The Boston Symphony Orchestra
American Symphony Orchestras in the 1970s

The Financial Condition of U.S. Orchestras

The five major U.S. orchestras (Boston, Chicago, Cleveland, New York, and Philadelphia) as a group had not been able to keep pace with their expenditures in the 1960s. Annual expenditures for these orchestras exceeded their earned income and contributions by an average of 4 percent. These major orchestras had been able to earn, primarily by concert revenues, roughly 68 percent of their expenditures; contributions amounted to another 28 percent. Financial data on American orchestras and other performing arts is found in Exhibits A–1 and A–2. The cumulative effect of the resulting gap was quite serious. For example, during the period of 1964 to 1968 the Chicago Symphony had used up $5 million of its $6.2 million endowment to meet the deficit. This invasion of capital, although necessary to preserve the Chicago Symphony's solvency, unfortunately contributed significantly to the deficit problem because the loss of $5 million endowment meant that investment interest decreased by roughly $350,000 each year, or nearly 10 percent of the orchestra's annual budget. Hence, there was a compounding effect to running deficits successively for several years.

The budgets for the major orchestras were about $1.9 million in 1964, but most of these budgets had doubled by 1970. Artistic personnel was the dominant expenditure, comprising 64 percent of the budgets of the

EXHIBIT A–1

THE BOSTON SYMPHONY ORCHESTRA

Table 1

Median Earned Income, Median Expenditure, and Median Income Gap, by Art Form

	Season or Year (1)	Earned Income (thousands) (2)	Expenditure (thousands) (3)	Net Gap* (thousands) (4)	Gap as Percent of Expenditure (5)
Orchestras					
Major orchestras					
Five largest.................	1963–64	$1,539	$1,873	$ (750)	32
All 25........................	1963–64	415	715	(327)	46
Metropolitan orchestras.......	1963–64	88	182	(83)	48
Opera Companies					
Metropolitan Opera Association.................	1963–64	6,871	8,748	(1,877)	21
Ten other operas.............	1963	65	182	(82)	45
Dance Companies					
New York City Ballet..........	1964–65	1,744	2,289	(545)	24
Two Civic Ballets.............	1963	6–8	9	(14)–(6)	70–40
Theater—14 regional					
companies....................	1964–65	157	250	(40)	15

* Column 4 need not equal column 3 minus column 2, because medians cannot be subtracted from one another.
Source: Baumol and Bowen, *Performing Arts—the Economic Dilemma*, p. 149.

Table 2

Median Income Gap, Median Contributed Income, and Median Surplus or Deficit, by Art Form (thousands)

	Season or Year (1)	Income Gap (2)	Contributed Income (3)	Net Surplus* or Deficit (4)
Orchestras				
Major orchestras				
Five largest.....................	1963–64	$ (750)	$ 703	$ (4)
All 25...........................	1963–64	(327)	294	(4)
Twenty-five metropolitan orchestras......................	1963–64	(83)	86	0
Opera Companies				
Metropolitan Opera..............	1963–64	(1,877)	1,638	(240)
Ten other operas................	1963	(82)	93	(3)
Dance Companies				
New York City Ballet.............	1964–65	(545)	477	(68)
Two Civic Ballets................	1963	(14)–(6)	11–6	0–(3)

* Column 4 need not equal column 3 minus column 2, because medians cannot be subtracted from one another.
Source: Baumol and Bowen, *Performing Arts—the Economic Dilemma*, p. 155.

THE BOSTON SYMPHONY ORCHESTRA
Financial Data on Major Arts Organizations in Boston

Table 1

Operating Budgets of 13 Major Arts Organizations in Greater Boston for 1968[a] (in thousands of dollars)

Organization	Earned Income[b]		Unearned Income[b]		Deficit[b]		Total Expenditure
Museum of Fine Arts..........	$1,267	35%[c]	$1,969	55%[c]	$374	10%[c]	$ 3,610
Boston Symphony Orchestra...	2,420	68	857	24	293	8	3,570
Opera Company of Boston (1966–67).....................	339	45	472	62	0[d]	0	757
Gardner Museum.............	12	3	470	114	0[d]	0	411
Children's Museum (1968–69).....................	110	30	195	53	60	16	365
Boston Ballet Company.......	151	43	114	32	89	25	354
Charles Playhouse............	260	75	54	16	31	9	345
DeCordova Museum..........	218	63	118	34	8	2	344
Theatre Company of Boston...	99	64	57	37	0[d]	0	155
Institute of Contemporary Art..	33	23	108	77	0	0	141
National Center of Afro–American Artists............	2	2	106	93	6	5	114
Boston Philharmonia (1968–69).	24	27	67	76	0[d]	0	88
Handel and Haydn Society.....	26	40	37	57	2	3	65
Total....................	$4,961		$4,624		$863		$10,319
Percent of expenditure..		48%		45%		8%	

Information provided by the arts organizations:
[a] Except as indicated, budgets are for either the 1968 calendar year or the 1967–68 fiscal year.
[b] Because of rounding or unearned income surplus, percentages of total expenditures may not equal 100.
[c] Figures in this column represent percent of each organization's total expenditure.
[d] Organization ended the year with a surplus as a result of contributions or endowment income.
Source: Taper, *The Arts in Boston*, p. 52.

Table 2

Sources of Unearned Income in 1968[a]

Organization	Individuals	Corporations	Foundations	Government	Endowment
Museum of Fine Arts..............	8%	1%	0%	7%	85%
Boston Symphony Orchestra........	65	6	12	0	17
Opera Company of Boston (1966–67)..	57	1	31	11	0
Gardner Museum..................	0	0	0	0	100
Children's Museum (1968–69)........	7	0	18	56	19
Boston Ballet Company.............	12	0	88	0	0
Charles Playhouse.................	60	1	0	39	0
DeCordova Museum...............	14	0	0	0	86
Theatre Company of Boston........	36	1	37	26	0
Institute of Contemporary Art.......	62	1	9	28	0
National Center of Afro–American Artists..........................	53	15	30	2	0
Boston Philharmonia (1968–69)......	66	4	30	0	0
Handel and Haydn Society..........	3	0	0	0	97
Totals, in thousands of dollars.	1,244	88	466	357	2,469

Information provided by the arts organizations:
[a] Because of rounding, percentages may not equal 100.
Source: Taper, *The Arts in Boston*, p. 59.

five orchestras. Musicians' salaries had increased annually by 5.1 percent in the early 1960s and by an even greater percentage since then. Musicians' unions were quite strong in the major orchestras, and thus a continued increase in musicians' salaries was foreseen in the near future. The other 36 percent of the orchestra's expenditures was for advertising, tour expense, concert production, and administration. Because these were all competitive sectors of the economy, there was little room for orchestras to reduce these expenses. The net effect was that although the average 4 percent gap appeared small, over time it could lead to disaster, and it was not possible for orchestras to trim their budgets; instead, unions and competitive pressures continually forced their expenditures to expand.

The financial picture for the 25 next most prominent American orchestras was equally bleak. The budgets of these orchestras were usually under $1 million, on the average less than one-half the size of the budgets of the major orchestras. They were able to cut costs by performing only about 100 concerts per year, compared with about 150 for the five major orchestras. In addition, their artistic personnel were paid less; hence, the highest quality personnel were attracted to the major orchestras. Finally these orchestras performed in larger concert halls with roughly 3,500 seats compared to the 2,500 seats of the major orchestra concert halls. Despite these economical measures, the 25 orchestras were able to earn only about 54 percent of their expenses, 14 percent less than the major orchestras earned. However, the 25 orchestras did better than the five major orchestras in contributions, receiving 42 percent of their expenses from outside sources. The net effect was that the 25 orchestras ran about the same deficit, 4 percent of annual expenditures, as the five major orchestras and hence their financial state was equally critical or perhaps more so because they did not have endowments to the same extent as did the major orchestras.

An article titled "Inflation Comes to the Arts" in the December 30, 1972, issue of the *Economist* stated that the financial state of American orchestras was typical of all institutions in the performing arts:

> A 1970 survey of 187 major institutions . . . which had 20m [20,000] attendances in the 1969–70 season, found that earned income, from subscriptions, box office sales and fees for recordings, etc., was expected to increase to over $90m in the 1970–71 season, $10m more than in the previous year; but costs of operation and staffing in that season would be over $160m. Costs were going up faster than earned income and faster too than income from contributions, grants, and endowments combined; this came to $59, and the 1960–70 season, while the net deficit for the whole group in that year was $6m.[1]

---

[1] "Inflation Comes to The Arts," the *Economist*, December 30, 1972, p. 59.

The *Economist* article explained that although audiences for the arts were increasing, this increase was somewhat due to the current use of the arts "as an answer to some of America's urban ills, a way not only of making the cities more attractive . . . but also of breaking into the isolation of the ghettos." Therefore, "little consideration is given to the possibility of balancing supply and demand by pushing up prices."

There had been two recent responses from the private sector to the plight of the orchestras. First, in 1967 the "Business Committee for the Arts" was formed, motivated primarily by David Rockefeller, Sr. The committee, composed of prominent members of the business community, sought to lend its skills and financial resources to the "enlargement, enrichment, and development of the arts." At the committee's initial meeting David Rockefeller, Sr., set forth broad goals:

> If we, as a committee, can contribute to bringing about in this country a renaissance of beauty and creativity and greatness in culture, we will have made a significant contribution to our country and toward solving the problems that seem in one sense so remote from the arts and in another so close to them.

Corporate giving to the arts rose to $56 million in 1970 and was expected to pass $70 million in 1971.

Second, in 1966 the Ford Foundation pledged $80 million to 61 orchestras throughout the country, granting $1 for every $2 that the orchestras could raise. The purpose of the grants was to bolster the orchestras' resources by stimulating large fund-raising drives.

Direct government support of the arts has been effected through the National Endowment for the Arts, which provided grants in aid to the arts agencies of the various states, to nonprofit-making organizations and to individuals of exceptional talent. In 1972 the funds available totalled almost $40 million. In addition, individuals were able to deduct 50 percent from their incomes for charitable contributions, including contributions to the arts, before assessing taxes; as nonprofit-making bodies, arts organizations were tax exempt.

In Massachusetts both state and the city governments provided funding for the arts, although to a far lesser extent than some other states. (Massachusetts appropriated $280,000 for the arts in 1973, compared with $14.3 million budgeted by New York.) Boston, with its modest tax base, devoted most of its arts fund to Summerthing and the development of the Boston Center for the Arts, both of which were designed to serve a broader and less affluent audience than such traditional institutions as the Boston Symphony Orchestra. In 1973, a bill was before the state legislature to increase the budget of the Massachusetts Council for the Arts to $800,000, as well as to provide special bicentennial funding for those arts activities promoting tourism.

The Economics of the Performing Arts: The Baumol Thesis

A remarkable study of the performing arts in 1966 by two Princeton economists, William J. Baumol and William G. Bowen, concluded that the financial difficulties of organizations in the arts were both inevitable and inherent in a high-technology society. The cornerstone of the Baumol thesis was that from "an engineering point of view, live performances were technologically stagnant." This meant that in a business like that of a symphony orchestra where the product is the labor itself, large amounts of capital would be unlikely to increase productivity. This of course contrasted with a technology-oriented industry in which capital is accumulated in order to provide equipment by which laborers increase their output.

The following example makes this clear. At its first performance at Symphony Hall on October 15, 1900, the BSO presented a Bach chorale and Beethoven's *Missa Solemnis*. With respect to economic productivity, the BSO has made no technological advances in the last 70 years because it would take just as many man-hours to rehearse that program today.

Because there were no collected data on the impact of technology on productivity in the arts, the Baumol thesis was supported in more general terms by showing that productivity had increased at a faster rate in the goods industry (more responsive to capital) than in the service industry (less responsive).[2]

Because relative productivity in the arts was thus actually decreasing with respect to the rest of the economy, it was obviously very difficult for a performer in the arts to maintain his economic position vis-à-vis laborers who were increasing output. For example, automobile technology had developed to the point where an ordinary unskilled laborer on the General Motors assembly line produced $40,000 worth of cars annually, while a highly skilled violinist in the Boston Symphony after years of training and practice could produce only $20,000 worth of concerts.[3] Therefore, if the musician were to maintain his economic position he had to increase continually the price of his product with respect to other products. However, a second tenet in the Baumol thesis was that technology was a limiting factor with respect to the performing arts. The second side of technology was the modern entertainment industry, particularly the movies, radio, and television, which competed with live performances and took advantage of the efficiencies of performing for

---

[2] Productivity increased in the goods sector by 2.5 percent in the period 1929–61, while in the service sector the increase was only 1.6 percent. In the more recent years, 1945–61, this difference was even more pronounced—3.1 percent versus 1.7 percent.

[3] In general terms, General Motors' 600,000 employees produce $24 billion in goods, or $40,000 each, while the 106 BSO players produced just over $2 million in concerts in 1969–70, or $20,000 each.

the mass audience. Thus, the high-technology society not only exerted great pressure on the performing arts to increase wages, but also restricted them from increasing prices because of competitive forces.

The Baumol thesis concluded that the performing arts, caught between these pincers of technology, would inevitably continue to run at increasing deficits in the future.

The Symphony Audience

Symphony managements actually know relatively little about the size and composition of the audience. Phillip Hart cites a study of symphony paid attendance, which showed an increase of about 1.1 percent annually between 1947 to 1964, less than the population as a whole. The increase in free concerts has made audience size difficult to estimate in recent years, but, according to Hart, "In the crucial area of paid symphony attendance during the past generation, it would appear that the so-called 'cultural explosion' has been a myth so far as the orchestras are concerned."[4]

In a study of symphony demographics published in 1966, William J. Baumol and William G. Bowen discovered that more women than men attend symphony concerts.[5]

> In addition they reported that symphony audiences contain a higher proportion of people over 60 than does the performance arts audience or the urban population in general. . . . Among the occupational groups defined in the performance arts audience, symphony patrons and concert-goers in general include a higher proportion of students, teachers, and professionals.[6]

There also seem to be different types of audiences, subdivisions of the general audience, which attend different types of performances. Hart describes these as,

> . . . the ladies who almost literally inherit their subscriptions from generation to generation, the serious music students, the tired businessmen who come with their wives because they do not want the ladies driving home at night alone, the music lovers introduced to the art by recordings, the fans primarily attracted by the charisma, of conductors and soloists, the socially ambitious who need to be seen at events carrying the cachet of responsibility and prestige.[7]

---

[4] *Orpheus in the New World* (New York: W. W. Norton & Company, Inc., 1973), p. 388.

[5] Baumol and Bowen, *Performing Arts—The Economic Dilemma* (New York, 1966), cited in Hart, p. 389.

[6] Ibid., Hart, p. 389.

[7] Ibid., p. 390.

Although the financial support of most orchestras usually comes from the older and more affluent season subscribers, many symphony managements are anxious to attract more young people to performances. Orchestras have tried various means of promoting themselves to new listeners, including various direct mail campaigns and the performance of symphonic music in less traditional settings. An obvious example of an attempt to do some institutional advertising for symphony orchestras was a recent NBC television special called "The Switched-On Symphony." Zubin Mehta and the Los Angeles Philharmonic attempted, with many visual effects, to demonstrate a connection between pop and classical music. Although one critic described the program as "an attempt to hide up our dying symphony orchestras by associating them with the glamour of the rock scene," the program did pose the question of how to impact classical music to today's young audiences.

In a recent issue of the *New York Times*, Erich Leinsdorf, past music director of the BSO, recommended another means of a symphony's attracting young people than by playing rock music, essentially by paying more attention to the *quality* of classical music performed for the young:

> Our symphony and opera associations have entrusted the entire program for young people to their second and third echelons of performers. . . . Specifically, I would do away with the institution of "youth" performances. It seems more effective, much easier for all concerned, and less patronizing to simply reserve 10 to 20 percent of the available places at every public performance for people under 25 . . . at a vastly reduced price.

Orchestra managements have recently been forced to consider the patronage of certain minority groups, such as ethnic groups living in urban ghettos, audiences interested in particular types of music, and suburbanites unwilling to go through the babysitting and transportation arrangements necessary to enjoy an evening at the symphony. In response some orchestras have sacrificed the acoustical excellence of their own halls to perform in suburban school auditoriums. In Cincinnati, "Open Door Concerts" were presented for the benefit of ghetto residents; the Phoenix Center has visited Navajo centers and performed music based on Indian themes.

9   *Tensor Corporation*

TENSOR HISTORY TO 1969

Mr. Jay Monroe, president, summed up the early history of Tensor Corporation as follows:

> I had a considerable amount of mechanical aptitude as a kid and always wanted to be an engineer. But in the 1930s engineering was still a closed field to Jews. Jewish kids just did not grow up to be engineers. Sperry Gyroscope was the largest hirer of engineers in New York City, and they did not hire Jews.
>
> Consequently I decided to be an inventor so that I could be an engineer. I attended Cornell and majored in electrical engineering. At the end of my senior year in 1945 I went to Western Electric to apply for a job. Even though I got a perfect score on the engineering employment qualification test, Western Electric could not figure out what to do with me.
>
> This inability to find a meaningful job at many of the large companies is one of the reasons for the existence of the large number of small companies in the New York City area. Of the ten members of my Cornell Jewish fraternity in my graduating class, all are now presidents of small companies.
>
> Shortly after I got out of school, there was a marked change of attitude in the country in general, and anti-Semitism was no longer condoned or tolerated by most Americans. I took a variety of jobs for short periods to gain experience and in 1949 was a partner with Gerald Starr in the formation of Tensor Electric Development Company.
>
> Tensor Electric Development was solely a government contractor for the first ten years of the company's history. A number of consumer products were tried during that period, but none was successful enough

to justify continued production. The idea remained, however, that the only way to be free to guide your own destiny was through developing and marketing a consumer product. It took ten years to invent that product, but finally in 1959, we thought we had developed the basis for a profitable company from a consumer product: the Tensor lamp.

The Tensor Lamp

High intensity lamps consisted basically of a step-down transformer built into the base of the lamp, an automobile headlight bulb, and a reflecting cone. Mr. Jay Monroe had designed the small transformer in order to power a lamp whose light would be bright enough to compensate for his poor vision and focused enough to keep from disturbing his wife's sleep while he read in bed. The first lamp, which used a tin measuring cup for a reflecting cone, was designed by Mr. Monroe in 1959. The *Lamp Journal* for August, 1964, reviewed the physical characteristics of the high intensity lamp:

> Its chief advantages are: white light, high intensity, and size, perhaps in that order. Each of these three features was available before the advent of high-intensity lamps, although not all at the same time from the same lamp.
>
> The advantages of white light, high intensity, and [small] size in the high-intensity lamps are achieved at the sacrifice of bulb life. The shortest bulb life of a 75-watt bulb in common use is 55 hours. At 25¢ retail per bulb this amounts to ½¢ per hour bulb cost; power cost is ¼¢ per hour. The equivalent conventional lamp, using a 200-watt bulb, would cost approximately ⅟₃₀¢ per hour for the bulb and 1¢ per hour for power. In general, short bulb lives notwithstanding, the miniatures are cheaper to operate than equivalent incandescents, but considerably more expensive than equivalent fluorescents.

When his friends began to ask him to make lamps for them also, Mr. Monroe decided that the new lamp had commercial possibilities. He set up a production line inside the Tensor factory to begin small-scale manufacture. The Tensor lamp encountered rapid success from the start of its commercial introduction in 1960. Table 1 gives sales of Tensor lamps from 1960 through 1965.

TABLE 1

Tensor Lamp Sales, 1960–65

Year	Sales
1960	$ 1,000
1961	50,000
1962	285,000
1963	850,000
1964	3,893,000
1965	6,863,000

EXHIBIT 1

TENSOR CORPORATION
Officers—1970

JAY MONROE
President
b. 1927. Graduated from Cornell in 1945. Majored in electrical engineering. Founded Tensor Electric Company in 1949.

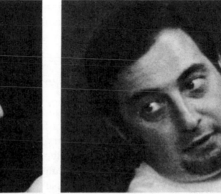

GEORGE SAVITSKY
Vice President—Sales and Marketing
b. 1938. Graduated from Pace College in 1960. Worked as an accountant with a N.Y.C. accounting firm before joining Tensor in 1964.

STANLEY JARET
Treasurer
b. 130. Graduated from City College of New York in 1953. Worked in public accounting with a N.Y.C. accounting firm until joining Tensor in 1964.

WALTER GLOUMAKOFF
Director of Manufacturing
b. 1934. Attended Rutgers University. Concentrated on engineering courses. Worked for Rotobroil. Joined Tensor in 1964.

EDMUND SOVATSKY
Vice President—Engineering
b. 1934. Attended Brooklyn Vocational High School. Joined Tensor in 1950.

During this period of expansion, Tensor was constantly pressed by the necessity for more management personnel and larger facilities. In 1964, Tensor sold off the government contract division to Mr. Gerald Starr and concentrated completely on the Tensor lamp. A December, 1964, article in *Business Week*[1] detailed some of the changes which had taken place at Tensor since the introduction of the high intensity lamp:

> Tensor is showing a growth pattern typical of rapidly growing small companies. Early in their growth they usually rely heavily on outsiders to beef up a slim executive staff. As they grow, they soon find they can afford larger administrative overhead to handle much of the farmed-out work.
>
> Just six months ago Monroe ran Tensor with only four other executives —an executive vice president, two marketing executives, and a treasurer. Ten outsiders helped run the company. Two full-time consultants reshaped production lines to fit Tensor's hodgepodge plant that rambles through eight floors of three adjoining buildings in Brooklyn. Legal counsel handled most business dickering, such as adding new plant space, as well as legal problems. Two advertising agents handled last year's $300,000 advertising campaign and also acted as material purchasing agents. New equipment and design changes were recommended by other consultants.
>
> While most of the outsiders still work with Tensor, many of their extra duties have been turned over to a beefed-up home office executive team. Tensor has recently added a comptroller, a production director, and a troubleshooting presidential assistant.
>
> Still Tensor's shape, like its lamps, is something less than classic, but it seems to be paying off. A consultant-tailored incentive labor plan cut pre-lamp costs in half; bookkeeping and inventory controls are working smoothly; plant security is being tightened—losses so far have been cut in half; and this year Tensor lamps are expected to show a healthy profit.

As sales of Tensor lamps continued to expand in 1965 and 1966, Tensor added to corporate overhead by (1) leasing new executive offices in Great Neck, Long Island, (2) leasing a new one-story manufacturing plant in Brooklyn, which replaced the old manufacturing facility, and (3) investing in new mass-production machinery, which for some operations could handle ten times the company's 1965 lamp volume. The new Great Neck office included a much expanded laboratory for Mr. Monroe, who believed he could turn his attention away from administration and back to inventing.

During the 1965–66 period the company was receiving letters from many of its customers praising the high-intensity lamp for its ability to give sufficient light to allow older persons and persons with poor vision to read and carry on other visually detailed operations.

---

[1] "The Little Lamp that Grew Up," *Business Week,* December 19, 1964, pp. 64–65.

The success of the Tensor lamp did not go unnoticed by other lighting manufacturers. A mid-1965 investment report by du Pasquier & Co., Inc., summarized the competition as follows:

> There are now at least 15 manufacturers of high intensity lamps and this number is expected to increase. Tensor estimates that it had some 50 percent of the market for high intensity lamps in 1964 and that this percentage is currently being maintained (total industry sales of high-intensity lamps in 1964 are estimated to have been $8.0 million).
>
> Tensor feels it is now over the critical period where a competitor could come out with a single design that would capture the bulk of the market. There is considerable speculation of the effect of a large manufacturer such as Westinghouse or G.E. would have entering the market with a major advertising campaign. It is doubtful, however, that a major company will enter the arena until the total market is larger and in the meanwhile Tensor is continuing to achieve broader distribution and the name to provide effective competition. Of incalculable value is the fact that all high-intensity lamps are increasingly becoming known as Tensor lamps regardless of their manufacturer.
>
> Tensor's major competitor is the Lampette, which is manufactured in Japan and Germany for Soss Manufacturing. Some $2.5 million worth of Lampettes were sold in 1964. Lightolier, a leading manufacturer of lighting fixtures, and Rotobroil are shortly expected to introduce high-intensity lamps.

As Tensor faced the future of the high-intensity lamp market at the end of 1965, many uncertainties remained about the eventual size of the industry and Tensor's role in it. The Tensor lamp was the only high-intensity lamp manufactured in the United States. This gave competitors who used foreign suppliers a cost advantage which was reflected by being able to offer a lower price to the consumer or higher margins to the sales and distribution network.

Furthermore, although Tensor had advertised heavily and established a brand name with the consumer, that brand name had been built on the basis of product utility. Recent competition, however, seemed to emphasize styling. Mr. Monroe disdained this attempt to turn the high-intensity lamp into a "fad" item. He believed that the market would respond best to an appeal to utility rather than style. Mr. Monroe therefore continued to emphasize utility, and Tensor was the last major marketer of high-intensity lamps to introduce a telescoping lamp neck into their product line.

Tensor's goal in the high intensity lamp market was to maintain the 50 percent share of market the company held in 1965. In order to assure the financial ability to support a higher forecasted sales level, Tensor sold 100,000 shares of stock at $11\frac{1}{8}$ per share net to the company. This new stock, issued in the summer of 1966, gave Tensor a wide ownership and a listing on the American Stock Exchange. It also gave the company the necessary cash to finance the advertising budget ($100,000 in 1963; $300,000 in 1964; $1,000,000 in 1965 and 1966) and the new building and equipment expenditures.

But 1966 and 1967 did not produce the high level of sales the company had been forecasting. Sales increased slightly in 1966 to $7.4 million, but fell more than 30 percent in 1967. Net income plummeted from earnings of over $0.5 million in 1965 to a deficit of $0.5 million in 1966 and a similar loss in 1967.

Looking back on those two years, Mr. Monroe commented that the stupidest thing he had done was to "lose contact with the plant" and to allow overexpansion:

> It was extremely painful to me and to the company and its employees to undergo the major contractions of late 1966 to early 1967. We closed down the Great Neck offices and moved back to the plant in Brooklyn. Both salaried and hourly employees were cut back drastically in order to allow the company to survive.
>
> The major cause of our misjudging the market size was the erroneous belief that the high-intensity lamp was an all-purpose lamp which would replace many other forms of lighting. We interpreted the letters we were receiving as a sample of the reaction of the general public. Actually the bright light of the high-intensity lamp was not needed by younger people with good eyesight. It was no more useful to them than a good incandescent lamp, and it made their eyes tire more rapidly. One rumor which was current in 1966 and 1967 was that the more rapid tiring of the eyes caused by high-intensity lamps resulted in permanent eye damage. This rumor was subsequently proved to be completely false, but it did nothing to improve our declining sales.
>
> Another problem we had with our demand forecasts is a common problem with any new product area: The boundaries of our forecasts were so wide that the forecasts themselves became almost useless as a planning tool.
>
> Two demand factors contributed significantly to our inability to assess accurately future high-intensity lamp sales. The first factor was our lack of ability to predict sales to the consumer as opposed to factory sales to wholesale and retail outlets. In mid-1966 we ran a trade promotion. Shortly thereafter we received a significant number of reorders, and we concluded that consumer demand was remaining strong. The large number of retail and wholesale outlets that began to carry Tensor in 1964 and 1965 were all well stocked for the mid-1966 demand level. But in late 1966 consumer sales fell off sharply, and our distribution channels were stuck with an inventory appropriate for a much higher demand level. Consequently, factory orders did not recover for some time.
>
> The second factor which affected our forecasts was the extra consumer demand generated by the large amount of advertising and promotion. We "over-advertised" to try to build up our name while the market was still immature, and this contributed to a larger final demand than would have

been experienced in a time of less aggressive promotion. In addition, a number of new competitors entered the market in 1964–65. Each new entrant needed a large promotional campaign in order to carve out an initial market share; promotional campaigns often increased the total market rather than resulting in "conquest" sales from other manufacturers. These campaigns stimulated some demand which was not sustainable when the promotion level became more normal.

Exhibit 2 shows schematically the unsuitable demand on which Tensor based its 1966 and 1967 sales forecasts. Mr. Monroe estimated that the dotted line represented the sustainable demand for high-intensity lamps

EXHIBIT 2

TENSOR CORPORATION

A Comparison of Theoretical Tensor Lamp Sales under Normal Conditions versus Actual Experienced Demand, 1960–68

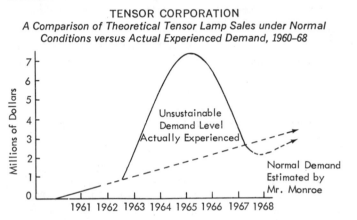

which Tensor would have experienced without unusual pipeline and promotional sales.

The Tensor Tennis Racket and Disposable Flashlight

Mr. Monroe commented on Tensor's expansion into a new product line:

> In late 1967 it was clear to me that the drop in high-intensity lamp sales was not just a temporary phenomenon. Tensor lamps, because of our strong brand name, retained a 50 percent market share. However, total high-intensity lamp sales were contracting to meet a stable level of demand which represented the share of market for high-intensity lamps in the total lamp market. From that point, I expected that high-intensity lamp sales would only increase as fast as population growth.
>
> I did not want to take the risk that stabilized Tensor lamp sales would not be sufficient to support the company's organization. I was also displeased that sales in the high-intensity lamp market were becoming more dependent on product styling than on product utility. This trend empha-

sized fad rather than lighting improvement. Consequently, I began to look around for other new product possibilities. The Tensor lamp had helped the company to build a valuable national name, and I believed that our reputation would be a big help in any new area we entered.

My major source of recreation is playing tennis, and early in 1968 I noticed that the waiting list for metal rackets at pro shops was growing longer and longer. This was an indication to me that metal racket production capacity for the major producers of tennis rackets was lagging behind demand. Metal tennis rackets did not seem to represent any major manufacturing innovation, and by early 1968 the contraction in lamp sales had left us with plenty of spare production capacity.

In February we made the decision to go ahead with the design work on a metal tennis racket, and by May production had begun on a small-scale basis. We priced our racket with the premium models put out by the competition, and evidently our name made the price stick.

The Tensor steel tennis racket sold well from its inception, and by the end of 1968 tennis racket sales were contributing a substantial part of

EXHIBIT 3

TENSOR CORPORATION
Tensor Corporation and Subsidiaries: Income Statements,
Year Ending December 31, 1962–69
(000 omitted except for last three items)

	1962	1963	1964	1965	1966	1967	1968	1969
Net sales...........	$ 757	$1,415	$4,263	$6,863	$7,445	$5,135	$3,262	$3,825
Cost of goods sold..	518	765	2,454	4,137	5,649	4,040	2,259	2,393
Gross profit.....	$ 239	$ 650	$1,809	$2,726	$1,796	$1,095	$1,003	$1,432
Selling, general and administrative expense...........	321	495	1,238	1,711	2,669	1,513	914	1,206
Operating profit (loss)..........	$ (82)	$ 155	$ 571	$1,015	$ (873)	$ (418)	$ 89	$ 226
Interest expense....	—	—	6	41	80	42	29	27
Other income (expense)...........	(31)	5	3	13	(8)	13	43	42
Income before taxes.........	$ (113)	$ 160	$ 568	$ 987	$ (961)	$ (447)	$ 103	$ 241
Taxes (refund)......	(24)	74	270	450	(465)	(200)	45	125
Profit (loss) before extraordinary items....	$ (89)	$ 86	$ 298	$ 537	$ (496)	$ (247)	$ 58	$ 116
Extraordinary income (loss).............	—	—	—	—	—	(195)	45	60
Net income.	$ (89)	$ 86	$ 298	$ 537	$ (496)	$ (442)	$ 103	176
Shares outstanding.	300,000	300,000	313,535	325,200	425,200	425,200	430,200	434,700
Earnings deficit per share*........	$(0.30)	$ 0.29	$ 0.95	$ 1.65	$(1.17)	$(0.58)	$ 0.14	$ 0.27
Return on stockholders' equity*...	(28.1)	21.3	40.2	40.8	(25.7)	(16.7)	3.6	6.4

* All returns based on profit (loss) before extraordinary items.
Source: Annual reports.

EXHIBIT 4

TENSOR CORPORATION
Tensor Corporation and Subsidiaries: Balance Sheets,
Year Ending December 31, 1962–69
(000 omitted except for book value and price)

	1962	1963	1964	1965	1966	1967	1968	1969
Assets								
Cash................................	$ 29	$108	$ 336	$ 79	$ 104	$ 124	$ 329	$ 90
U.S. government securities.........	—	25	—	—	—	344	325	350
Accounts receivable................	127	302	777	1,382	1,177	501	700	743
Inventories.........................	137	159	677	1,383	1,643	649	563	889
Claims for refund of income taxes.....................	35	—	—	—	531	227	21	—
Prepaid expenses...................	2	13	110	19	30	18	43	40
Total Current Assets..........	$330	$607	$1,900	$2,863	$3,485	$1,863	$1,981	$2,112
Machinery and other equipment.......................	78	74	123	419	669	630	529	489
Leasehold improvements...........	5	10	45	128	177	111	112	112
Accumulated depreciation..........	26	29	59	133	234	281	275	288
Total Fixed Assets............	$ 57	$ 55	$ 109	$ 414	$ 612	$ 460	$ 366	$ 313
Other miscellaneous assets and deposits.....................	4	3	64	205	163	118	104	159
Total Assets.................	$391	$665	$2,073	$3,482	$4,260	$2,441	$2,451	$2,584
Liabilities and Stockholders' Equity								
Accounts payable...................	$ 38	$102	$ 751	$ 614	$ 668	$ 385	$ 320	$ 226
Notes payable......................	—	—	—	550	1,000	—	—	—
Current portion of noncurrent liabilities.........................	—	—	15	4	47	43	43	43
Accrued liabilities..................	21	72	151	146	138	126	124	127
Federal income taxes payable.......	15	88	280	350	—	—	—	65
Total Current Liabilities.......	$ 74	$262	$1,197	$1,664	$1,853	$ 554	$ 487	$ 461
6½% promissory note payable......	—	—	135	450	412	375	338	300
Due under contract for purchase of leasehold............	—	—	—	33	28	23	17	12
Deferred federal income taxes......	—	—	—	20	35	—	—	—
Total Noncurrent Liabilities....................	$—	$—	$ 135	$ 503	$ 475	$ 398	$ 355	$ 312
Common stock: Par value 10¢ per share.....................	30	30	31	33	42	42	43	43
Additional paid-in capital...........	253	253	292	327	1,431	1,431	1,447	1,473
Retained earnings..................	34	120	418	955	459	16	119	295
Total Stockholders' Equity.....	$317	$403	$ 741	$1,315	$1,932	$1,489	$1,609	$1,811
Total Liabilities and Stockholders Equity.....	$391	$665	$2,073	$3,482	$4,260	$2,441	$2,451	$2,584
Book value per share..............	$1.06	$1.34	$2.36	$4.04	$4.54	$3.50	$3.74	$4.17
Stock Price Range*								
High.............................	Not	Not	14	18.375	15.75	9.625	10.25	11.25
Low..............................	traded	traded	3.375	10.5	3.75	4.25	4.125	6.0

* Price on March 2, 1970 = $6.875.
Source: Annual reports.

Tensor's sales. The only miscalculation apparent in the introduction of the Tensor tennis racket was the use of a soft gauge of steel in the very early rackets. This caused a large number of customer returns of rackets with snapped handles. Tensor quickly changed to a harder gauge of steel and customer returns subsequently declined to less than 2 percent.

Largely because of the tennis racket, Tensor became profitable in 1968 and 1969—even though 1969 sales remained substantially below the 1964 level. Exhibits 1 and 2 detail Tensor's financial statements from 1962 to 1969.

Tensor had introduced one other new product in 1968—a disposable flashlight retailing for $1.98 and guaranteed to last for at least one year. Mr. Monroe had first seen the product as a French import, but when the French company would not issue Tensor a license to sell the flashlight under the Tensor name, he designed his own version.

Mr. Monroe had not been enthusiastic about the disposable flashlight, but at the time of its introduction in mid-1968, it had helped to fill some of Tensor's excess production capacity. Most of the disposable flashlight sales were "premium sales." Under this arrangement Tensor printed another company's name as well as its own on the product. The other company could then use large quantities of the product in consumer or trade promotions and as prizes in sales contests. Although Tensor continued to make minor design and packaging improvements in disposable flashlights, the specialty nature of the premium market made a stable sales level above $1 million annually extremely unlikely.

TENSOR IN 1969–70

Competition

By 1969 Tensor's competition in the high-intensity lamp market had dwindled to only two other firms with national distribution and a number of smaller firms with regional distribution. The two nationwide competitors were Lightolier—a company with $40 million in annual lamp sales, of which 5–8 percent were high-intensity—and Universal. Universal, a high-intensity lamp company with headquarters in Chicago, had an annual sales of $1 million. George Savitsky, Tensor's vice president of sales and marketing, estimated the high-intensity lamp market, including the regional firms, at about $7 million. Tensor's line of high-intensity lamps sold at retail for prices ranging from $8.95 to $50.00. A major portion of the volume was concentrated at two points in this range—$12.95 and $19.95. By comparison, some of the private-label brands imported from Japan sold for as little as $3.99. The Lightolier price range was $12.95 to $25.00.

The metal tennis racket market was much more difficult to estimate. All manufacturers wished to withhold from competitors possibly helpful information on the size of the market and the unit volume that each manufacturer was selling.

The three brand names in the market were Wilson, Spalding, and Tensor. In 1969 Tensor had introduced a lower-cost model of its metal racket under the brand name of Melbourne. This was an effort to broaden the appeal to new market segments without diluting the Tensor brand name. Tennis rackets which carried the Tensor brand name ranged in price from $34 to $60 at retail. The aluminum racket was the least expensive at $34; the steel racket sold for about $40; a new 24K gold-plated line sold for $50; and the new top-of-the-line stainless steel racket was priced at $60. Tensor's Melbourne brand was produced in both aluminum and steel with selling prices from $19.95 to $29.95. Although the Tensor steel racket at $40 was competitive with Wilson and Spalding, private-label rackets sold as low as $12. A 40–50 percent retail markup on factory price was considered normal in sporting goods distribution.

Although estimates were only approximate, Mr. Savitsky believed that Tensor in mid-1969 was selling 10–20 percent of the market in comparison to 45–70 percent for Wilson, 10–15 percent for Spalding, and 10–20 percent for the combined small private-label manufacturers. He also estimated that Wilson had 60 percent of the wooden racket market, while Spalding had 30 percent, and all others accounted for the remaining 10 percent.

Mr. Monroe had a different estimate for market share based on the metal rackets he observed at country clubs and on some information he had heard about the total market size. Mr. Monroe believed that 4 million tennis rackets were sold annually and that recently 35 percent of tennis racket sales were metal rackets. Combining these figures with his own observations, Mr. Monroe reasoned that Wilson metal rackets were outselling Tensor 10 to 1. Wilson Sporting Goods, Inc., was a $100 million subsidiary of a $3.5 billion conglomerate. Spalding had annual sales of $65 million and had recently been acquired by a $220 million conglomerate.

Marketing

Mr. Monroe saw marketing as the key area in Tensor's recent recovery. He believed that Tensor's quality image had allowed the company to market successfully a second and third consumer product. Exhibits 3 and 4 give sample advertising and pictures of lamps and flashlights; Exhibits 5 and 6 do the same for tennis rackets. George Savitsky commented on Tensor's image:

> We established our image with the customer by advertising and with the dealer by not allowing price cutting. Our advertising was quite heavy

EXHIBIT 5

TENSOR CORPORATION
Sample Lamp Advertising

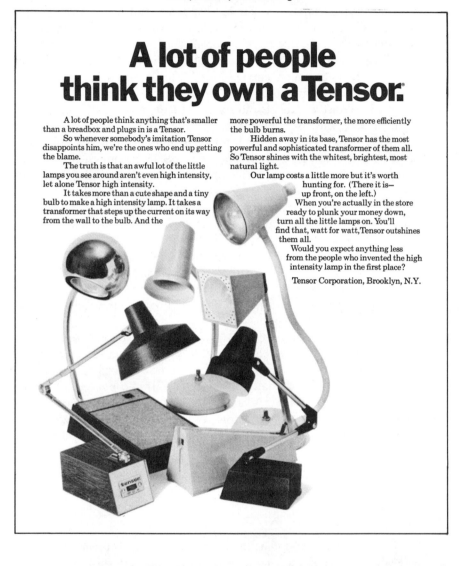

A lot of people think they own a Tensor.

A lot of people think anything that's smaller than a breadbox and plugs in is a Tensor.

So whenever somebody's imitation Tensor disappoints him, we're the ones who end up getting the blame.

The truth is that an awful lot of the little lamps you see around aren't even high intensity, let alone Tensor high intensity.

It takes more than a cute shape and a tiny bulb to make a high intensity lamp. It takes a transformer that steps up the current on its way from the wall to the bulb. And the more powerful the transformer, the more efficiently the bulb burns.

Hidden away in its base, Tensor has the most powerful and sophisticated transformer of them all. So Tensor shines with the whitest, brightest, most natural light.

Our lamp costs a little more but it's worth hunting for. (There it is—up front, on the left.)

When you're actually in the store ready to plunk your money down, turn all the little lamps on. You'll find that, watt for watt, Tensor outshines them all.

Would you expect anything less from the people who invented the high intensity lamp in the first place?

Tensor Corporation, Brooklyn, N.Y.

as a percent of sales, but it helped us maintain our market share in periods of expansion and later contraction. Perhaps we even "over-advertised" on Tensor lamps, but the name we developed gave us an image which we could trade on to our advantage in 1969.

As far as our channels of distribution were concerned, we initially avoided discount stores as much as possible. We didn't want to do business in areas of severe price cutting. Whenever that happens we'll

EXHIBIT 6

TENSOR CORPORATION
Lamp and Flashlight Sample Pictures

| Tensor Model 6500 | Tensor Model 7200 | Tensor Model 100 Disposable Flashlight |

leave the business to others. I believe Tensor was 98 percent effective in stopping price cutting on Tensor lamps. We brought suit under fair-trade laws, cut off distributors who were cutting their prices, coded our lamps so we could determine which distributors were selling to the retail price cutters, and even bought up some of the discounters' lamps to dry up their supply.

We feel we are continuing to enhance our image with tennis rackets. Recently we refused a large order from a major retailer because they wanted us to put our name on the tag and cut the price. This willingness to turn away business that is not on our terms is what establishes a reputation. Perhaps we will soften our stance in tennis rackets after this reputation is firmly established.

Tensor's allocation of margin to the various aspects of its distribution network depended on the product involved. In the lamp business, where Tensor had a narrow margin, most of this margin was allocated to the channel of distribution. The manufacturers' representatives received only a 5 percent commission.

For tennis rackets, on the other hand, Tensor was able to allow more margin to the sales force. At present the tennis rackets were being sold on a 10 percent commission basis.

Tensor's two sales forces consisted solely of manufacturers' representatives. The first group, numbering about 25, sold high-intensity lamps to 30 department stores and chains and to 300–400 wholesalers. Retail out-

EXHIBIT 7

TENSOR CORPORATION
Sample Metal Tennis Racket Advertising

Tensor explains the high price of its metal racquets.

It all began with Jay Monroe, tennis fanatic.

He liked the basic idea of metal tennis racquets. But he realized that there was, ah...room for improvement, shall we say.

Not being like you and me, Jay Monroe, inventor, thereupon sat down and built his very own metal racquet. One with all the advantages of metal over wood, but without the little faults and fumbles of the pioneer efforts.

And then, knowing that there were a lot of fellow tennis nuts who wouldn't mind paying a few dollars more for something better, he thought about having it produced in quantity.

It just so happened that Jay Monroe was also the President of Tensor Corporation...

The idea paid off.

The very first Tensor was the first metal racquet selected by the United States Lawn Tennis Association.

Spend more, get more.

A Tensor racquet has a streamlined, open-throat design. It cuts wind resistance to a minimum so the racquet slices cleanly through the air.

Every square inch of the rounded Tensor face is alive, eliminating the dead spots you find at the top and bottom of oval heads.

The stringing is orthodox, completely without gimmicks or surprises. No contrived suspension system. No trampoline effect. And no special equipment needed for restringing.

Sturdy metal grommets, instead of plastic, are there to protect the strings.

The grip is more comfortable. Unlike the other metal racquets with handles of unyielding plastic, the Tensor has a handle of porous wood to absorb perspiration and impact. And deluxe leather wraps it up.

Steel or aluminum?

Tensor gives you a choice of racquets. Steel is for power—what 8 out of 10 players are looking for. Because steel is springy, more of the energy of impact gets put right back into the ball. It turns a swing into a slam.

Aluminum is a stiff metal. So the aluminum racquet is for the rare player—the very hard hitter—who can afford to give up some power for the extra bit of control the stiffness can give him.

Both are guaranteed for a full year.*

Our philosophy.

At Tensor, we think a metal racquet should be more than just a wood racquet that happens to be made of metal. It costs more to do it this way. So be it.

Tensor Corporation, Brooklyn, New York.

Tensor warrants that the frame will be free of any defect in material or workmanship for one year after date of purchase. If such a defect is found, we will repair or replace the frame. This warranty does not apply to damage arising under normal usage.

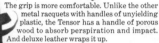

lets serviced by these wholesalers probably averaged 100 per wholesaler. The second sales force, also numbering about 25, sold tennis rackets to sporting goods stores, specialty stores, and pro shops. This sales force serviced about 2,000 accounts.

EXHIBIT 8

TENSOR CORPORATION
Sample Metal Tennis Racket Pictures

Tensor Aluminum Tennis
Racket

Tensor Steel Tennis
Racket

In addition, Tensor was in the process of developing a 25-man "premium" sales force to sell the disposable flashlight and other Tensor products to companies for use in sales contests and promotional campaigns.

As manufacturers' representatives, Tensor's salesmen served the same distribution outlets with non-Tensor products. Mr. Savitsky was uncertain of the extent of the increase in volume on present product lines that Tensor could obtain by raising sales commissions or by developing additional Tensor product lines appropriate for sale by the present sales force.

Finance

Stanley Jaret, the treasurer, outlined the company's 1969 financial position as follows:

> Now that we are back in the black again, our problem is not cash. We had almost $450,000 in cash and marketable securities at the end of

1969. Most of this cash resulted from our failure to expand sales—and therefore inventories and receivables—as fast as we had anticipated when we acquired new equity in the summer of 1966.

Our real problem is to assure that we retail control of the company. Jay owns 26 percent of the stock, but none of the rest of the management owns more than a nominal amount of Tensor's equity. As far as we are able to determine now, the stock is widely distributed with no other party owning any significant percent. We could use our cash to repurchase some of the stock on the open market and virtually assure control, but our stock price doubled with our return to profitable operations, and any significant volume of buying seems to boost the price sharply.

We have made some structural changes to keep Tensor from being taken over. For instance, at our next stockholder meeting we will propose cumulative voting for positions on our expanded nine-man board of directors. Directors will have staggered three-year terms, allowing management to retain control for two years even in the eventuality of a raid. With our large cash position and our deficits for 1966 and 1967, a raid was a distinct possibility. Also, we recently voted an employee stock plan. The employee stock fund buys shares on the open market. This should put more shares in friendly hands. Finally, a management stock bonus plan has been started. The four officers of the company received 5,000 shares of stock (restricted for ten years as to sale) in 1968. Forty-five hundred additional restricted shares were given to management in 1969.

I would say our biggest area for present improvement of financial management is internal control. We should be able to avoid the capital expenditure errors we made in the past, and also to remain more current in our sales projections.

Production

In 1969 Tensor employed approximately 200 persons in its Brooklyn headquarters and plant facility. Most of the production jobs required only short training periods, and manual dexterity was the major requirement for many of them.

The lamp section of the plant consisted of a couple of subassembly lines, a small amount of in-process inventory to smooth the work flow, and finished inventory at the shipping end of the plant.

Tennis racket production started with precut metal rods. These rods were bent, drilled, and finished. A handle and grip then were added at the end, and the racket was strung and stored on a long rack by size and type. As orders were received, they were filled by picking the rackets off the easily accessible storage rack and sending them to shipping.

Walter Gloumakoff, the plant manager, summarized the Tensor production operation as simple and flexible:

> Our strength is in keeping operating costs low and in not sinking resources into production tooling. We have quite experienced toolmakers

who save us time by cooperating in the product design stage. As a product is being designed, they simultaneously create the tools to produce it. That way we don't create any new products we can't produce. Our toolmakers also save us money by designing more economical limited purpose tools instead of general purpose tools which do more than is required. A good example is the $2,000 drill rig made up to drill the string holes for our rackets. A general purpose tool to perform the same task might have cost as much as $10,000.

We are essentially a design and assembly business with low fabrication content. We did bring some of the lamp fabrication in-house when sales dropped off, but that was mainly to fill idle production capacity.

One production decision which was a continuing possibility was the transference of some manufacturing to Japan. This was an alternative available not only for lamp production, but also for any other electromechanical devices which Tensor developed in the future. Because of the original uncertain nature of the lamp market and the need to make the large fixed-volume and design commitment necessary to secure Japanese production at a low cost. Recently, however, design maturation and cost competition had forced a reconsideration of the desirability of lamp importing.

In the area of new products, Mr. Monroe continued to believe that the best course to follow was to retain start-up and initial production in the Brooklyn plant until the design could be stabilized and some estimate of the demand was possible. Using this production strategy, original Tensor selling price would be based on eventual Japanese production costs rather than actual Brooklyn production costs. Tensor would make little or no profit on any new electro-mechanical product until production could be transferred to Japan.

Research and Development

Tensor's research and development was concentrated entirely in the hands of Jay Monroe. He had ten other people working for him on development projects. Every couple of months Monroe made out a list of ideas that were of current interest to him. Then he and the development staff worked on that list until each item was either finished or discarded. The February 1969 list, shown in Table 2, consisted solely of innovations concerned with tennis.

Mr. Monroe believed that Tensor's product development was less fruitful than would be possible if he could find a larger congenial staff to do development work. The general problem was that sophisticated research and development personnel often required the freedom to conceive and independently execute their own ideas, rather than execute engineering details under someone else's direction. Mr. Monroe had found only one

TABLE 2

February, 1969, R&D List

1. Improved tennis ball
2. Nylon tennis string
3. Deep groove in hardened frame
4. Flanged eyelets
5. Fiberglass racket
6. Stainless steel racket
7. "U" channel for aluminum racket
8. Lithographed nameplate
9. Box to hold string

Source: Company document.

tool and model maker (known throughout the company as "Mac") who was a major help to him in his development work. Mr. Monroe stated the personality problem this way:

> I know I don't have the easiest personality to work with, and many qualified applicants will not like development work at Tensor because of the way I run it. I do feel, however, that my talent is being underutilized, and that I could direct much more extensive development work.

By June of 1969 Tensor had completed all the projects on the February list except the "U" channel, which had been dropped, the fiberglass racket, which was waiting for completion of final testing, and the improved tennis ball, which was still pending. The delay on the tennis ball was attributed to the inability to find a molding method which did not require a capital investment of $1 million or more. However, in April of 1970, Tensor finally finished the design of a hairless rubber ball which had the characteristics on a cement or composition court that a regular tennis ball had on a clay court. Mr. Monroe had designed this ball in the belief that tennis had become too fast a game on nonclay courts and that his ball would allow a normal clay court speed on a nonclay court. The new ball could be mass-produced with less than $100,000 in equipment investment.

Tensor was uncertain about the company's ability to market tennis balls with such radical characteristics. Consequently, Tensor planned first to gain experience by introducing under the Tensor name a conventional tennis ball manufactured in Ireland.

Telephone Message Recorder.   During early 1970 Tensor was also planning to announce the introduction of a $200–$250 (a firm price had not yet been decided) telephone message recorder. Jay Monroe had invented the recorder so that he would not have to take messages personally for his children when they were not at home. With his message recorder all he would have to do was turn on the recorder; it was designed so that it could be attached to his children's telephone, which had its own separate number.

EXHIBIT 9

TENSOR CORPORATION
Photograph of Tensor Telephone Message Recorder Unit

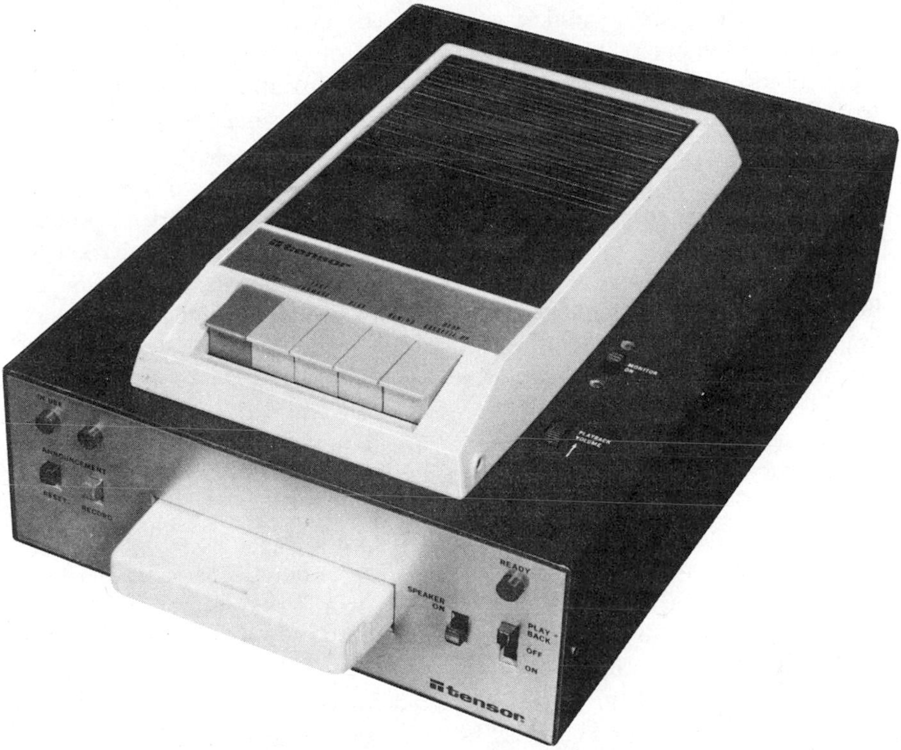

The telephone message recorder consisted of a cassette recorder, a tape to give messages to the caller, a tap on which the caller can leave messages, and an automatic on/off mechanism. The breakthrough in the Tensor product was a low price achieved through simple design and the use of recent advances in the size and capability of cassette recorders. Tensor also planned to market a lower-priced model which would not include its own cassette recorder. Any tape recorder could be attached to this model.

The present message recorder market had four brand entrants. Three of those four were priced far above the Tensor level, and the fourth was a very recent entry priced at $150–$200.[2] Mr. Monroe was hoping that his latest product would have wide acceptance by individual consumers. Previous message recorders were used mainly by businesses. Exhibit 9 shows a photograph of a Tensor message recorder unit.

---

[2] This recent entry was imported from Japan and was roughly competitive with Tensor in its product characteristics.

Mr. Monroe estimated the present message recorder market at $10 to $15 million annually and growing extremely rapidly. One question being debated by Tensor management in late 1969 was how to finance the introduction of the message recorder. Management estimated the capital required at $1 million and was not anxious to jeopardize the existence of the company by risking internal operating capital. One possible solution was to form a majority-owned subsidiary and issue stock to the public. The subsidiary could then develop separate management and production facilities.

This strategy of public capitalization of the message recorder did not seem to Mr. Monroe likely to succeed, however, because of the lackluster state of the U.S. economy and the low level of the stock market in early 1970. An alternative to public capitalization was for Tensor to introduce the recorder over a period of time which would cause less financial risk. A slow product introduction would have less market impact but would allow Tensor to cut its losses earlier if the product was not accepted by the consumer. Under this alternative Tensor planned to manufacture the first recorders at the plant in Brooklyn. If the product were successful, mass production could be shifted to Japan to keep costs down.

Paddle Tennis Racket. In late 1969, Tensor began production on a paddle tennis racket. Tensor management predicted that this market, although only $50,000–$100,000 annually, would be highly profitable. Exhibit 10 is a photograph of the Tensor paddle tennis racket.

Sportsmen Inc. In order to expand into additional sporting goods areas, in February 1970, Tensor acquired Sportsmen Inc., a small Long Island manufacturer of fiberglass billiard cues, archery sets, and fishing

EXHIBIT 10

TENSOR CORPORATION
Photograph of the Tensor Paddle Tennis Racket

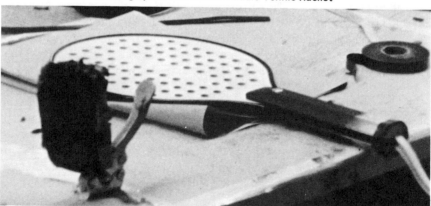

EXHIBIT 11

TENSOR CORPORATION
Photograph of the Sportsmen, Inc., Product Line

PRODUCTS OF SPORTSMEN, INC.

equipment. The Tensor 1969 *Annual Report* stated that Tensor planned "to utilize the sporting goods distribution channels we have established to increase the sales of Sportsmen's existing products while developing new products combining Tensor's technology and Sportsmen's manufacturing facilities." In particular Tensor hoped to employ the fiberglass manufacturing techniques which the president of Sportsmen had developed. Mr. Monroe believed that fiberglass usage in consumer products was expanding and that these techniques might be useful in any number of future Tensor products.

Sportsmen Inc. sales had previously been as high as $1 million, but lack of marketing expertise had resulted in a 90 percent sales decline and in unprofitable operation. Tensor purchased Sportsmen for approximately $15,000 cash and 5,500 shares of stock. Valuing Tensor shares at the closing price of $6.75 recorded on the purchase date, Tensor paid about $30,000 below book value. Exhibit 9 shows the Sportsmen product line.

As opposed to the 1960–67 period, when Tensor seemed content to confine new products to new lamp models, the 1969 approach was spread out in a number of diverse product areas.

Organization

Tensor's organization at the end of 1969 was similar to its pre-expansion organization in 1964. It consisted of Mr. Monroe and one executive each in marketing, finance, manufacturing, and development engineering. Exhibit 12 gives the 1970 Tensor organization chart. These five executives had a five-year contract for compensation totaling $147,000 annually.

The interrelations among the five executives were frequent and informal. The financial job consisted of a preliminary financial profit forecast for the company derived from marketing and production estimates

EXHIBIT 12

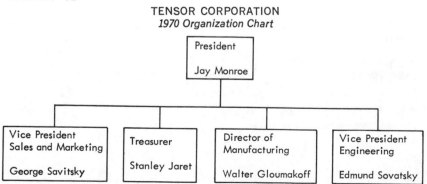

TENSOR CORPORATION
1970 Organization Chart

Note: All five executives served as Tensor directors.

and a monitoring of operations to assure that the company was not below forecast.

Production scheduling was a combined effort of marketing and production. Marketing supplied forecasts and production scheduled on that basis. Marketing forecasts were continually revised on the basis of orders being received. Production, which was not set up to derive economies from long runs, was able to adjust rapidly to changes in demand.

The central coordinating device in the Tensor organization was the daily lunch meeting of the five top executives, which took place in the company conference room. Almost all corporate decisions were made at these meetings. Each executive, including Mr. Monroe, took an active part, and decisions were made by discussion until a consensus was reached. Exhibit 13 is a sample of the topics discussed at one luncheon meeting.

EXHIBIT 13

TENSOR CORPORATION

Topics of Discussion at One Lunch Meeting in February 1970

A recent speech by economist Pierre Rinfret
Tennis racket returns
Logo and printing on Tensor-marketed tennis balls
Sportsmen acquisition
Financing the message recorder introduction
Deciding where to invest development time
Trading-off risk and gain in development decisions
What the executives want to sell regardless of the return

THE FUTURE

Each of Tensor's five executives was asked to express his feelings about his job and his goals for the future of Tensor. Their answers were as follows:

Jay Monroe, President

I think of the whole company as a toy. My motive for establishing and operating Tensor is for the sheer fun of running it. I have no official duties of any kind and feel that management on a day-to-day basis is boring and not worth the time it takes.

I feel it is a tragedy that the present economic system has made my motivations unacceptable. Product decisions in the United States are being made more and more on the basis of return on investment. This means that industrial art and creative technical development suffer. The state of product development of consumer products would be higher if business were willing to make decisions on aesthetic rather than return on investment criteria. The creative guy wants to gamble, but the professional manager stifles him.

From my own point of view, I want to be able to produce a product I like even if it did not show any chance of an acceptable level of return. Above all, I don't want to have to take my ideas to a professional manager and have to convince him economically of the idea's worth. This may not be in the short-term best interest of the other stockholders, but I believe that the company will contribute better and more interesting products.

My goal for new products is to market only "classy" products which contribute to the image of the company. For instance, we could probably profitably expand into tennis clothes, but I am determined to avoid the bad image of the garment industry.

One element of management I don't like is the constant degradation of ethics necessary to restrain a competitive operation. It seems that no matter how low you sink, someone is always more unethical. This cycle is repulsive. For instance, kickbacks to marketing channels and questionable advertising claims may become increasingly necessary to continue to compete. I believe this practical necessity is unethical and very objectionable.

In terms of size, I am happy to have Tensor remain at its present volume. We have four other executives, all roughly the same age, who are content to spend their lives with this company. Perhaps we should grow enough to keep up with expanding wages and overhead, but I've experienced rapid expansion once, and I don't want to go through that again. In addition, any major expansion that required new equity would seriously endanger management control of Tensor's ownership.

Stanley Jaret, Treasurer

My goals from the company are a responsible position, a good living, security, and a job I can enjoy. I would like to see Tensor stabilize at around $6–$7 million sales. Any further increase would probably necessitate a major organizational change. I am content with the present arrangement and do not feel that the company needs to try to cope with an expansion larger than $3–$4 million.

One of my personal goals for the company is to assure that Tensor remains above breakeven. If we can stay profitable, we substantially reduce the threat of takeover or insolvency.

George Savitsky, Vice President—Sales and Marketing

My job is to tear apart everything Jay wants to do and figure out what parts we can do and what parts we can't. The general pattern is his ideas and my exploitation.

As far as new products, I'd like to see more products which fit into our present channels of distribution. We have a fairly meager volume per store, and I would like to increase our worth to our distribution channels.

I would like to see steady growth for Tensor through product diversification. I don't believe I would enjoy the impersonality of a $50 million business, but I would like the excitement of a $20–$30 million company.

Edmund Sovatsky, Vice President—Engineering

My greatest pleasure is to finally put a product into production after fooling with the design for a few months. I like sporting goods as a product area because the time from idea to market is exceptionally short.

My sales goal for the company is $10 million per year or a little over. I dislike emergencies and feel that a company that size is still small enough to be controlled. Also, I like the freedom I have to make decisions, and I believe that freedom would be impaired if the company grew too large.

Walter Gloumakoff, Director of Manufacturing

My objective for Tensor is profitability with a reasonable growth curve which would include diversification in products and in manufacturing assets. I am particularly fond of electro-mechanical consumer products. They represent more of a challenge than strictly mechanical products.

I would like to see Tensor achieve a sales level of $30–$50 million. At that volume production would be a lot more complicated. Production is always a rat race, but I love it.

SUPPLEMENT: TENSOR CORPORATION

The following article appeared in the January 8, 1970, issue of the evening edition of the *Boston Globe*. Additional information relating to the controversy described is included in Exhibits 1–A to 3–A.

Tensor's Friend at Chase too Friendly with Arabs[3]

NEW YORK—An advertisement bearing the headline "Tensor Corporation no longer 'has a friend at Chase Manhattan'" appears in today's edition of *The New York Times*.

Tensor's president, Jay Monroe, said in the quarter-page ad that the company would close out its account at the New York City bank whose slogan is, "You have a friend at Chase Manhattan."

Monroe, president of the company which manufactures high-intensity lamps and tennis rackets, said in the ad the action was being taken as a protest to reported efforts of Chase Manhattan's chairman of the board, David Rockefeller, and a former chairman, John J. McCloy, to induce President Nixon to reshape Middle East policies to mollify the Arab

---

[3] The *Boston Globe*, evening edition, January 8, 1970. Reproduced with permission.

states because of what Monroe said was the bank's "considerable economic interests in the oil-rich region."

When informed of the ad's contents, Rockefeller issued a statement in which he said, "I believe, as I always have, that the United States must do everything it can to safeguard the security and sovereign existence of Israel.

"My sole interest," he added, "is in seeing that hostilities are ended and peace is achieved, a peace taking fully into account the legitimate aspirations of the parties involved."

Monroe, who is of Jewish origin, said in the advertisement: "Now Mr. Rockefeller has apparently decided it is best to put his mouth where his money is. I feel that turnabout is fair play. Accordingly, Tensor's account is being withdrawn from the Chase."

A source close to Tensor said the company maintained an account with the bank that was "in excess of $50,000." He said the cost of the ad was about $2,200.

Monroe said he based his statement about the Rockefeller's advocacy of a new Middle East policy on a story in the Dec. 22 issue of *The New York Times*.

The *Times* article had reported that a group including Rockefeller and McCloy had discussed the Middle East political situation at an unpublicized meeting with President Nixon at the White House Dec. 9.

The article said: "According to officials familiar with the discussion, the consensus in the group was that the United States must act immediately to improve its relations with oil-producing and other Arab states. The group was said to feel this was necessary to deflect what the group feared to be an imminent loss of United States standing in the Middle East that might be reflected politically as well as in terms of American petroleum interests in the area."

EXHIBIT 1A

TENSOR CORPORATION SUPPLEMENT
Article from The New York Times, *December 22, 1969*

U.S. POLICIES IN MIDEAST ARE UNDER FIRE
Industrialists Reported to Warn Nixon on Loss of Influence with Arabs

TAD SZULC
Special to The New York Times

WASHINGTON, Dec. 21—President Nixon is reported to have received warnings from a group of top American industry leaders with oil and other interests in the Middle East that the United States is rapidly losing political and economic influence in the Arab states because of its present policies.

The industrialists' concern over the deterioration of the United States position in the Middle East and over the proportional growth of the Soviet importance there—attributed by them in part to Washington's

EXHIBIT 1A (continued)

past support for Israel—was expressed at an unpublicized meeting at the White House on Dec. 9.

Bankers Attended

A White House spokesman has confirmed that Mr. Nixon had asked the group to discuss with him the "political situation in the Middle East." The members included David Rockefeller, president of the Chase Manhattan Bank; John J. McCloy, former president of Chase Manhattan, and Robert B. Anderson, former Secretary of the Treasury and a director of Dressor Industries Company, which has oil interests in Kuwait and Libya.

Administration officials said that the President had invited them to hear their views on the eve of the Dec. 10 session of the National Security Council, which was dedicated to a review of the United States policy in the Middle East.

Attending the industrialists' meeting with Mr. Nixon was Henry A. Kissinger, the President's special assistant for national security affairs. White House officials emphasized that those conferring with the President were "people with a political knowledge of the Middle East situation and the oil situation in the Middle East."

Action Was Urged

Administration officials declined, however, to disclose what specific advice the industrialists had offered Mr. Nixon and none of the participants were available today for comment.

According to officials familiar with the discussion, the consensus in the group was that the United States must act immediately to improve its relations with oil-producing and other Arab states. The group was said to feel this was necessary to deflect what the group feared to be an imminent loss of United States standing in the Middle East that might be reflected politically as well as in terms of American petroleum interests in the area.

The group was said to feel that United States weapons deliveries to Israel, including the recent shipment of supersonic Phantom jets, and Washington's alleged support of Israeli policies in the Middle East conflict were turning moderate and conservative Arab leaders as well as radical Arabs against the United States.

That basic evaluation was presented to Mr. Nixon early this year by William W. Scranton, former Governor of Pennsylvania, who toured the Middle East on a presidential mission.

But the increase in Middle East hostilities in the intervening period and the aggravation of the over-all situation had led a group of United States oil executives to submit a private memorandum to Mr. Nixon last September urging the preservation of American interests as a basis for the United States policy in the region.

EXHIBIT 1A (concluded)

The September meeting of oil executives was reportedly held in Beirut, Lebanon. Subsequent meetings were held in Beirut in October, informants said, and a session on Oct. 29 was attended by Mr. Rockefeller.

According to authoritative sources, Mr. Rockefeller then met with President Abdel Gamal Nasser of the United Arab Republic in Cairo on Oct. 31, to discuss the Middle East political situation along with some of the Chase Manhattan Bank's projects in Egypt.

Official quarters said that Mr. Rockefeller reported to the Administration at the time that President Nasser hoped the United States, through a change in its policies, could help him to become freer of the growing Soviet influence. The Soviet Union supplies most of the United Arab Republic's military equipment. The United States has had no diplomatic relations with Cairo since the 1967 Middle East war.

Others who conferred with Mr. Nixon on Dec. 9 have had direct communication with Arab leaders as well. Mr. Anderson, for example, talked with President Nasser and King Hussein of Jordan in Cairo last March.

It was this direct experience in the Middle East that, in the judgment of the White House, qualified these industrialists to present their views to Mr. Nixon.

However, officials said that the views expressed by the visiting group to the President were not mentioned directly when the National Security Council met Dec. 10 to debate the Middle East policy.

Authoritative informants said that the United States oil industry is concerned over the danger of Arab terrorist attacks on American petroleum installations and over the possibility that the greater British and French sympathies for the Arab policies may in time result in the erosion of the American oil presence in the Middle East.

EXHIBIT 2A

TENSOR CORPORATION SUPPLEMENT
Advertisement in The New York Times, *January 8, 1970*

TENSOR CORPORATION NO LONGER "HAS A FRIEND
AT CHASE MANHATTAN"

An Open Letter to the American Public:

It would appear that our neighborhood banker, who goes to great pains to tell us that he is our friend, has a rather narrow (mercenary) definition of the word friendship.

As reported in the December 22 issue of The New York Times, David Rockefeller, president of The Chase Manhattan Bank, and John McCloy, its former president, have warned President Nixon that U.S. policies in the Middle East are resulting in a loss of political and economic influence in the Arab world.

EXHIBIT 2A *(continued)*

One must wonder how much Chase Manhattan's considerable economic interests in the oil-rich region figured in the decision to urge a new policy which would mollify the Arabs. Certainly world conditions do not indicate that such a change is in order. Israel is a truly democratic state, a modern oasis surrounded by feudal baronies. With the support of cynical Communists countries, the Arab chieftains have attempted to destroy Israel. With the moral support and material help of Americans, Israel has survived, so far.

Now Mr. Rockefeller has apparently decided it is best to put his mouth where his money is. I feel that turnabout is fair play. Accordingly, Tensor's account is being withdrawn from the Chase.

Ours is not one of the corporate giants, and no doubt Chase Manhattan will carry on very nicely without Tensor's business. But if others—small depositors and giant corporations alike—join in this protest against a "dollar diplomacy" based on oil interests, our former friends at Chase may learn that free men do not live by oil alone.

> Sincerely,
> JAY MONROE
> President
> Tensor Corporation

EXHIBIT 3A

TENSOR CORPORATION SUPPLEMENT
Article from The New York Times, *January 9, 1970*

DAVID ROCKEFELLER SAYS HE SUPPORTS SECURITY OF ISRAEL

David Rockefeller, chairman of the Chase Manhattan Bank, said yesterday that the United States "must do all it can to safeguard the security and sovereign existence of Israel."

Mr. Rockefeller said that his interest in Middle East issues was "in seeing that hostilities are ended and peace is achieved—a peace directly negotiated between the parties involved and taking fully into account their legitimate aspirations."

His statement followed the publication in The New York Times yesterday of an advertisement signed by Jay Monroe, president of the Tensor Corporation, manufacturer of high-intensity lamps, asserting that the corporation "no longer 'has a friend at Chase Manhattan.'" The advertisement cited a dispatch in The New York Times Dec. 22 reporting that Mr. Rockefeller had been among a group of business leaders who met with President Nixon and warned that the United States was losing influence in the Arab states because of policies the Arabs felt favored Israel.

A spokesman for the Chase Manhattan Bank said Mr. Rockefeller's statement was in answer to the dispatch and not to the advertisement.

EXHIBIT 3A (*continued***)**

Mr. Rockefeller said he had been convinced during a recent trip to the Middle East that more and more thoughtful Arabs "appear disposed to explore reasonable compromises."

He said that in the meeting with the President, he intended "merely to suggest that the United States encourage these more positive and conciliatory sentiments."

Reached by telephone, Mr. Monroe said he was not a Zionist but supported Israel's "democratic position in the Middle East." He said he had withdrawn an account with a $250,000 line of credit from the bank.

Part Two

Policy Administration

Section Three

Designing the Overall Organization

1   The Adams Corporation (A)

In January of 1972, the board of directors of The Adams Corporation simultaneously announced the highest sales in the company's history, the lowest after-tax profits (as a percentage of sales) of the World War II era, and the retirement (for personal reasons) of its long-tenure president and chief executive officer.

Founded in St. Louis in 1848, the Adams Brothers Company had long been identified as a family firm both in name and operating philosophy. Writing in a business history journal, a former family senior manager comments: "My grandfather wanted to lead a business organization with ethical standards. He wanted to produce a quality product and a quality working climate for both employees and managers. He thought the Holy Bible and the concept of family stewardship provided him with all the guidelines needed to lead his company. A belief in the fundamental goodness of mankind, in the power of fair play and in the importance of personal and corporate integrity were his trademarks. Those traditions exist today in the nineteen sixties."

In the early 1950s, two significant corporate events occurred. First, the name of the firm was changed to The Adams Corporation. Second, somewhat over 50 percent of the corporation shares were sold by various family groups to the wider public. In 1970, all branches of the family owned or "influenced" less than one-fifth of the outstanding shares of Adams.

The Adams Corporation was widely known and respected as a manufacturer and distributor of quality, branded, and consumer products for the American, Canadian, and European (export) markets. Adams products were processed in four regional plants located near raw material

sources,[1] were stored and distributed in a series of recently constructed
or renovated distribution centers located in key cities throughout North
America, and were sold by a company sales force to thousands of retail
outlets—primarily supermarkets.

In explaining the original long-term financial success of the company,
a former officer commented: "Adams led the industry in the development
of unique production processes that produced a quality product at a very
low cost. The company has always been production-oriented and volume-
oriented and it paid off for a long time. During those decades the Adams
brand was all that was needed to sell our product; we didn't do anything
but a little advertising. Competition was limited and our production efficiency and raw material sources enabled us to outspace the industry in
sales and profit. Our strategy was to make a quality product, distribute it
and sell it cheap.

"But that has all changed in the past 20 years," he continued. "Our
three major competitors have outdistanced us in net profits and market
aggressiveness. One of them—a first-class marketing group—has doubled
sales and profits within the past five years. Our gross sales have increased
to almost $250 million but our net profits have dropped continuously
during that same period. While a consumer action group just designated
us as 'best value,' we have fallen behind in marketing techniques, e.g.,
our packaging is just out of date."

Structurally, Adams was organized into eight major divisions. Seven of
these were regional sales divisions, with responsibility for distribution and
sales of the company's consumer products to retail stores in their area.
Each regional sales division was further divided into organizational units
at the state and county and/or trading area level. Each sales division was
governed by a corporate price list in the selling of company products but
had some leeway to meet the local competitive price developments. Each
sales division was also assigned (by the home office) a quota of salesmen
it could hire and was given the salary ranges within which these men
could be employed. All salesmen were on straight salary and expense reimbursement salary plan, which resulted in compensation under industry
averages.

A small central accounting office accumulated sales and expense information for each of the several sales divisions on a quarterly basis, and
prepared the overall company financial statements. Each sales division received, without commentary, a quarterly statement showing the number
of cases processed and sold for the overall division, sales revenue per case
of the overall division, and local expenses per case for the overall division.

Somewhat similar information was obtained from the manufacturing

---

[1] No single plant processed the full line of Adams products, but each plant processed the main items in the line.

division. Manufacturing division accounting was complicated by variations in the cost of obtaining and processing the basic materials used in Adams products. These variations—particularly in procurement—were largely beyond the control of that division. The accounting office did have, however, one rough external check on manufacturing division effectiveness. A crude market price for case lot goods, sold by smaller firms to some large national chains, did exist.

Once a quarter, the seven senior sales vice presidents met with general management in St. Louis. Typically, management discussion focused on divisional sales results and expense control. The company's objective of being "number one," the largest selling line in its field, directed group attention to sales versus budget. All knew that last year's sales targets had to be exceeded—"no matter what." The manufacturing division vice president sat in on these meetings to explain the product availability situation. Because of his St. Louis office location, he frequently talked with Mr. Jerome Adams about overall manufacturing operations and specifically about large procurement decisions.

The Adams Company, Mr. Millman knew, had a trade reputation for being very conservative with its compensation program. All officers were on a straight salary program. An officer might expect a modest salary increase every two or three years; these increases tended to be in the thousand dollar range regardless of divisional performance or company profit position. Salaries among the seven sales divisional vice presidents ranged from $32,000 to $42,000, with the higher amounts going to more senior officers. Mr. Jerome Adams's salary of $48,000 was the highest in the company. There was no corporate bonus plan. A very limited stock option program was in operation, but the depressed price of Adams stock meant that few officers exercised their options.

Of considerable pride to Mr. Jerome Adams had been the corporate climate at Adams. "We take care of our family" was his oft-repeated phrase at company banquets honoring long-service employees. "We are a team and it is a team spirit that has built Adams into its leading position in this industry." No member of first line, middle or senior management could be discharged (except in cases of moral crime or dishonesty) without a personal review of his case by Mr. Adams. In matter of fact, executive turnover at Adams was very low. Executives at all levels viewed their jobs as a lifetime career. There was no compulsory retirement plan and some managers were still active in their mid–70s.

The operational extension of this organizational philosophy was quite evident to employees and managers. A private family trust, for over 75 years, provided emergency assistance to all members of the Adams organization. Adams led its industry in the granting of educational scholarships, in medical insurance for employees and managers, and in the encouragement of its "members" to give corporate and personal time and effort to community problems and organizations.

Mr. Adams noted two positive aspects of this organizational philosophy. "We have a high percentage of long-term employees—Joe Girly, a guard at East St. Louis, completes 55 years with us this year, and every one of his brothers and sisters has worked here. And it is not uncommon for a vice president to retire with a blue pin—that means 40 years of service. We have led this industry in manufacturing process innovation, quality control and value for low price for decades. I am proud of our accomplishments and this pride is shown by everyone—from janitors to directors." Industry sources noted that there was no question that Adams was "number one" in terms of manufacturing and logistic efficiency.

In December of 1971, the annual Adams management conference gathered over 80 of Adams's senior management in St. Louis. Most expected the usual formal routines—the announcement of 1971 results and 1972 budgets, the award of the "Gold Flag" to the top processing plant and sales division for exceeding targets, and the award of service pins to executives. All expected the usual social good times. It was an opportunity to meet and drink with "old buddies."

After a series of task force meetings, the managers gathered in a banquet room—good naturedly referred to as the "Rib Room" since a local singer "Eve" was to provide entertainment. At the front of the room, in the usual fashion, was a dais with a long, elaborately decorated head table. Sitting at the center of that table was Mr. Jerome Adams. Following tradition, Mr. Adams's vice presidents, in order of seniority with the company, sat on his right. On his left, sat major family shareholders, corporate staff, and—a newcomer—soon to be introduced.

After awarding service pins and the "Gold Flags" of achievement, Mr. Adams announced formally what had been a corporate "secret" for several months. First, a new investing group had assumed a "control" position on the board of Adams. Secondly, that Mr. Price Millman would take over as president and chief executive officer of Adams.

Introducing Mr. Millman, Adams pointed out the outstanding record of the firm's new president. "Price got his MBA in 1958, spent four years in control and marketing, and then was named as the youngest divisional president in the history of the Tenny Corporation. In the past years, he has made his division the most profitable in Tenny and the industry leader in its field. We are fortunate to have him with us. Please give him your complete support."

In a later informal meeting with the divisional vice presidents, Mr. Millman spoke about his respect for past Adams's accomplishments and the pressing need to infuse Adams with "fighting spirit" and "competitiveness." "My personal and organizational philosophy are the same—the name of the game is to fight and win. I almost drowned, but I won my first swimming race at 11 years of age! That philosophy of always winning is what enabled me to build the Ajax division into Tenny's most profitable operation. We are going to do this at Adams."

In conclusion, he commented, "The new owner group wants results. They have advised me to take some time to think through a new format for Adams's operations—to get a corporate design that will improve our effectiveness. Once we get that new format, gentlemen, I have but one goal—each month must be better than the past."

EXHIBIT 1

THE ADAMS CORPORATION (A)

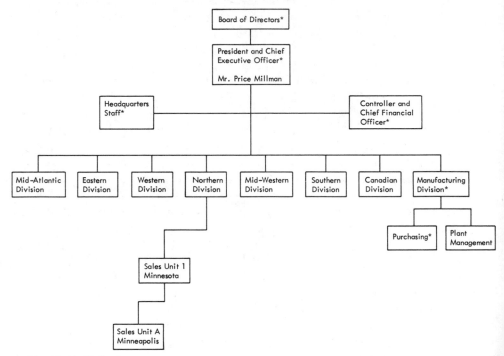

* Located in St. Louis.

2

Barclay, Inc. (A)

In December 1973, Mr. Robert Cannon became the new president and chief operating executive of Barclay, Inc., a firm operating in the electrical equipment field. In 1973, it was estimated, Barclay's sales were $100 million and the enterprise employed over 2,600 people.

Barclay, Inc., had recently been purchased by a group of wealthy investors. In view of their other varied business interests, the investing group planned to operate Barclay as a separate, independent company. Mr. Cannon was given complete responsibility for the direction of Barclay's affairs. He had achieved an excellent reputation among industrialists as a manager capable of dealing with difficult business problems, and the investors had agreed that he was to have a free hand to make whatever changes he thought necessary to improve the company's lackluster profit performance.

Barclay manufactured and sold electrical equipment for industrial and consumer use. Its industrial products included a wide variety of standard and specialty motors. The company had achieved an excellent reputation for engineering design work. Over the years its legal staff had built up an imposing number of patents protecting improvements created by company engineers. In the consumer products line, the firm manufactured and sold a line of small "traffic" household appliances for American markets.

In recent years company sales had increased substantially but profits had gradually declined to a point where only a very small profit was anticipated for 1973. While industrial products had been extremely profitable for many years, the competitive situation had changed substantially in the late 1960s. Consumer appliance operations varied from early losses to small profit contributions in 1970 through 1973. Barclay was encountering increasing competition for its appliances from full-line companies, e.g., Sunbeam. Despite this, Mr. Cannon believed that in the long run the consumer traffic appliance area would become the most important and profitable part of the firm's business. He hoped to add new appliance items as rapidly as production and marketing facilities permitted.

In the manufacture of these products, Barclay purchased substantial quantities of two raw materials (16 million, estimated in 1972). These raw materials were subject to substantial price fluctuations and it was important for Barclay to buy at "the right time and price."

The new owners of Barclay requested that Mr. Cannon prepare salary recommendations, for board consideration, in December 1973. His recommendations were to cover the top 20 executives in the company including himself. Knowing the backgrounds of the new owners, Mr. Cannon knew he would have to be able to defend his assignments of salary to specific jobs. He also knew that the owners had been critical of the "haphazard way" in which salary payments had been made by the former general manager.

To carry out this assignment, Mr. Cannon asked the member of the personnel department in charge of the executive payroll for the amount paid in salaries to the top 20 managers of the firm in the year 1973. This sum amounted to $860,000. He excluded individual bonus payments and incidental privileges, such as company furnished cars. Bonus payments for the Barclay management group had declined steadily during the past years and salary payments were now the important element in the firm's compensation program.

He then prepared to assign funds from this "common pool" to individual jobs in the organization. Mr. Cannon realized that, after he had determined an ideal salary structure, he would have to modify his assignments on the basis of historical precedent as well as other factors. But he believed that the process of allocating the total salary fund to individual jobs, without prejudice of past history, would help him in thinking through his problem.

EXHIBIT 1

BARCLAY, INC. (A)

Board of Directors

President and Chief Operating Executive
Robert Cannon

Legal Counsel*

Director in Charge of Finance

- Accounting Supervisor (64)†
- Economic Information Supervisor (14)
- Financial Supervisor (6)

Director in Charge of Personnel (20)

Director in Charge of Manufacturing

- Supervisor Works A Industrial Products (400)
- Supervisor Works B Consumer Products (1680)
- Supervisor Motor Department (200)
- Supervisor Production Scheduling (10)

Director in Charge of Purchasing

- Raw Materials Buyer (1)
- Finished Parts Buyer (11)

Director in Charge of Sales

- Sales Manager Industrial Products (30)
- Sales Manager Consumer Products (180)
- Manager of Market Services (20)

Director in Charge of Engineering (20)

* Full-time legal counsel.
† Indicates number of staff/or employees, or both.

Westinghouse Electric
Corporation (A)

The Westinghouse Electric Corporation, with headquarters in Pittsburgh, Pennsylvania, had long been one of the largest and most diversified corporations in the United States. In terms of the annual *Fortune* survey of the 500 largest United States industrial corporations, Westinghouse ranked seventeenth in sales ($2.3 billion) and twenty-fourth in total assets employed ($1.6 billion) for 1964. The company had about 64 plant locations in the United States, sales offices throughout the country, and employed about 115,000 people in 1964. In addition to its domestic operations, Westinghouse also had investments in about 35 foreign countries and had over 150 foreign licensees.

Westinghouse was generally classified as an electrical equipment manufacturer, and produced a wide range of industrial and consumer equipment for the generation, transmission, distribution, control, and utilization of electric power. Some measure of the diversity of its operations can be inferred from the following comments in a *Time* article:

> Any company that makes both reactors for nuclear submarines and $1.25 magnets for extracting wire and nails from cows' stomachs has some claim to diversity—and Westinghouse Electric claims to be the world's most diversified company. The oldest electronics firm and the second biggest producer of electrical equipment (after General Electric) in the United States, Westinghouse makes 8,000 different products in 300,000 variations. The company's 59 divisions with their 64 plants spread through 20 states, daily confront almost every American with some Westinghouse product, from 6,000 types of light bulbs to the output of five TV and seven radio stations.[1]

---

[1] *Time*, October 30, 1964, p. 97.

A more complete listing of Westinghouse products and facilities as of 1964 is shown in Exhibit 1. Of the product groups shown, the electric utility group had been the largest in terms of sales, followed by the industrial and the atomic, defense, and space groups.

Single divisions ranged in size from about $5 million to well over $100 million in sales, and had from 500 to 5,000 employees. If listed as independent companies, all of the product groups listed as well as many of the divisions would have been included in the *Fortune* list of the 500 largest U.S. industrial companies.

The great diversity of the products and services offered by Westinghouse is shown in somewhat more detail in Exhibit 2, which is a reproduction of several pages selected from a booklet entitled "The World of Westinghouse." It was stated in the booklet that the list of over 1,300 products was constantly growing and changing, and it was emphasized that multiplying the products listed by "ratings, sizes, styles, enclosures, colors, combinations, and all the other variables which fit them to specific needs" would explode the list into one of thousands and thousands of items.

EXHIBIT 1

WESTINGHOUSE ELECTRIC CORPORATION (A)
Westinghouse Divisions and Products

ATOMIC, DEFENSE, AND SPACE

AEROSPACE ELECTRICAL DIVISION, Lima, Ohio
Electric power systems, generators, motors, control apparatus, thermoelectric devices, power conditioning and conversion equipment, and support equipment for military and commercial aircraft, missiles, and spacecraft.

ASTRONUCLEAR LABORATORY, Large, Pa.
Nuclear power for space and other advanced applications; specialized equipment for space applications.

ATOMIC EQUIPMENT DIVISION, Cheswick, Pa.
Main coolant pumps, valves, control rod drive mechanisms, and other specialized apparatus for nuclear reactors; pumps for controlled circulation boilers; thermoelectric

ATOMIC, DEFENSE AND SPACE (CONTINUED)

cooling devices for military applications.

ATOMIC FUEL DIVISION, Cheswick, Pa.
Nuclear reactor cores and core components for naval applications.

BETTIS ATOMIC POWER LABORATORY, Pittsburgh, Pa.
Government-owned facility operated by Westinghouse for the Atomic Energy Commission. Development of nuclear reactors for naval propulsion and electric power generation under contracts with U.S. government.

DEFENSE AND SPACE CENTER:
Aerospace Division, Baltimore, Md.
Aerospace systems, equipment, and associated support items: re-

EXHIBIT 1 (continued)

ATOMIC, DEFENSE AND SPACE
(CONTINUED)

connaissance; detection, surveillance, and weapon control; navigation; data handling and display; missile launch, guidance, and control; space vehicle guidance and control; communications; command and control; instrumentation; scientific satellites and space vehicles; advanced weapons and electronic warfare.

Surface Division, Baltimore, Md.

Ground, ship and mobile surface systems, equipment, and associated support items: surveillance; detection and weapon control; navigation; data handling and display; command and control; communication; instrumentation; satellite control; tracking and discrimination; antimissile protection; advanced weapons and electronic warfare.

Underseas Division, Baltimore, Md.

Underwater systems, equipment, and associated support items; torpedoes, mines, and advanced weapons; mine, weapon, and CW countermeasures; surveillance; sonar detection; data handling and display; instrumentation; oceanographic systems and equipment; manned submersibles.

Systems Operations, Baltimore, Md.

Management, design, and integration of major defense and space systems and systems involving resources and capabilities of several Westinghouse divisions.

ATOMIC, DEFENSE AND SPACE
(CONTINUED)

PLANT APPARATUS DIVISION, Pittsburgh, Pa.

Procurement of reactor plant equipment for Naval applications.

SUNNYVALE DIVISIONS:

General Products Division, Sunnyvale, Cal.

Electrical, mechanical, and shock mitigation components for missile and rocket programs; missile launching and handling equipment; wind tunnel equipment, including axial-flow compressors; special apparatus, such as telescope drives and mountings, centrifugal machines, shock machines, and large hydraulic valves.

Marine Products Division, Sunnyvale, Cal.

Equipment for marine applications, including propulsion, providing ship service electrical power, ship handling equipment, such as anchor and cargo winch controls, automatic ship and engine room controls, marine condensers, air ejectors, and marine wet winding submersible motors.

CONSTRUCTION

AIR CONDITIONING DIVISION, Staunton, Va.

Packaged air conditioning and heating equipment for residential, commercial, and industrial applications; engineered air conditioning systems; heat pumps and electric heat systems for residential and commercial installations.

BRYANT ELECTRIC DIVISION, Bridgeport, Conn.

EXHIBIT 1 *(continued)*

CONSTRUCTION (CONTINUED)

Wiring devices; lampholders; fluorescent devices; outdoor fixtures for reflector backed lamps; circuit breaker load centers.

ELEVATOR DIVISION, Jersey City, N.J.

Passenger, freight, and shipboard elevators; electric stairways; electric walks; security systems.

ENVIRONMENTAL SYSTEMS DIVISION, Grand Rapids, Mich.

Micarta-clad doors; movable partitions and walls; controlled atmosphere work areas; clean rooms.

LAMP DIVISION, Bloomfield, N.J.

Lamps for all types for all applications: incadescent; fluorescent; mercury; sealed-beam; reflector; miniature; medical; photographic; Christmas tree; flashlight; sun; heat.

LIGHTING DIVISION, Cleveland, Ohio

Commercial, industrial, fluorescent, and incandescent fixtures; fluorescent and mercury ballasts; flood, roadway, and marine lighting; lighting accessories; Sterilamp equipment.

STURTEVANT DIVISION, Hyde Park, Mass.

Air distributing units; fans, blowers—general purpose and heavy duty; heaters; heating and cooling coils, steam, and hot water; Precipitron air cleaners; dehumidifiers.

PRINTING DIVISION, Trafford, Pa.

Nameplates, printed circuits, all forms of printing.

CONSUMER

AUTOMATIC MERCHANDISING DIVISION, East Springfield, Mass.

Automatic beverage coolers for bottlers of Coca-Cola.

CONSUMER (CONTINUED)

COLUMBUS APPLIANCE DIVISIONS:

Dishwasher & Specialty Products Division, Columbus, Ohio

Dishwashers; waste disposers; water coolers; water heaters.

Refrigerator Division, Columbus, Ohio

Refrigerators and freezers.

Room Air Conditioning Division, Columbus, Ohio

Air conditioners.

MANSFIELD APPLIANCE DIVISIONS:

Laundry Equipment Division, Mansfield, Ohio

Laundromat® automatic washers; dryers; dry cleaners.

Portable Appliance Division, Mansfield, Ohio

Electric housewares; bed coverings; fans; floor polishers; vacuum cleaners.

Range Division, Mansfield, Ohio

Ranges and ovens; kitchen cabinets.

THE C. A. OLSEN MANUFACTURING COMPANY, Elyria, Ohio

Residential heating and air conditioning; incinerators; unit heaters.

TELEVISION-RADIO DIVISION, *Metuchen,* N.J.

Television receivers; radios, portable, and consoles; high fidelity and stereo phonographs; tape recorders.

ELECTRIC UTILITY

ATOMIC POWER DIVISION, Pittsburgh, Pa. (Forest Hills)

Advanced concept development programs, atomic fuel, nuclear steam supply systems, turn-key nuclear power plants—for commercial atomic power installations.

EXHIBIT 1 (continued)

ELECTRIC UTILITY (CONTINUED)

EAST PITTSBURGH DIVISIONS:

Distribution Apparatus Division, Bloomington, Ind.

Capacitors; lightning arresters; fuse cutouts; surge protective devices; reclosers; sectionalizers; load pick-up switches.

Large Rotating Apparatus Division, East Pittsburgh, Pa.

Large generators, motors, motor-generator sets; electric couplings; frequency changer sets; synchronous condensers.

Power Circuit Breaker Division, Trafford, Pa.

High voltage power circuit breakers; condenser bushings, insulators; arc heaters.

Power Control Division, Research and Development Center, Pittsburgh, Pa. (Churchill)

Dispatching control; digital datalogers; load-frequency control; printed circuit modules; steam plant automation; steam plant computer systems; turbine control systems.

Switchgear Division, East Pittsburgh, Pa.

Assembled switchgear; high voltage fuses; network protectors; nuclear plant control; regulators; substations; generator synchronizers.

MEASUREMENTS DIVISIONS:

Meter Division, Raleigh, N.C.

Watthour, demand, recording meters, and accessories; sockets and mountings.

Relay-Instrument Division, Newark, N.J.

Electrical measuring instruments of all types; protective relays and relaying systems.

ELECTRIC UTILITY (CONTINUED)

STEAM DIVISIONS:

Heat Transfer Division, Lester, Pa.

Surface condensers, air ejectors, circulating and condensate pumps, priming ejectors, flash evaporators, water conversion plants—for installation on land; nuclear steam generators.

Large Turbine Division, Lester, Pa.

Large steam turbine generators —for installation on land.

Small Steam and Gas Turbine Division, Lester, Pa.

Gas turbines, small steam turbine generators, steam turbines for mechanical drive—for installation on land.

TRANSFORMER DIVISIONS:

Distribution Transformer Division, Sharon, Pa.

Dry and liquid immersed distribution transformers; current and potential instrument transformers; metering units.

Power Transformer Division, Sharon, Pa.

Power transformers; power regulators; reactors; self-contained unit substations.

ELECTRONIC COMPONENTS AND SPECIALTY PRODUCTS

ELECTRONIC TUBE DIVISION, Elmira, N.Y.

Electronic tubes of all kinds; power amplifiers, oscillators, pulse, rectifier, cathode ray tubes; television camera and picture tubes; miscellaneous special tubes—industrial and military.

INDUSTRIAL CERAMICS DIVISION, Derry, Pa.

EXHIBIT 1 (continued)

ELECTRONIC COMPONENTS AND SPECIALTY PRODUCTS (CONTINUED)

Porcelain insulators; industrial ceramics.

MATERIALS MANUFACTURING DIVISION, Blairsville, Pa.

High temperature, permanent, and soft magnetic alloys; nonfuel nuclear and refractory metals.

MICARTA DIVISIONS:

Decorative Micarta Division, Hampton, S.C.

Decorative Micarta sheets.

Industrial Micarta Division, Hampton, S.C.

Laminated fabricated plastics, Micarta shapes, sheets; insulating enamels and materials (Trafford, Pa.).

MOLECULAR ELECTRONICS DIVISION, Baltimore, Md., Newbury Park, Cal.

Epitaxial material; functional electronic blocks; integrated circuits.

NEW PRODUCTS TASK FORCE, Research and Development Center, Pittsburgh, Pa. (Churchill)

Cryogenic systems; scientific equipment (Edgewood Site); electronic capacitors (Irwin, Pa.)

SEMICONDUCTOR DIVISION, Youngwood, Pa.

Transistors; power rectifiers; diodes; solid state relays; thermoelectric devices; specialty devices.

SPECIALTY TRANSFORMER DIVISION, Greenville, Pa.

Cores; charging reactors; transducers; specialty transformers.

X-RAY DIVISION, Baltimore, Md.

Medical and industrial X-ray apparatus, supplies and accessories; electro-medical products.

INDUSTRIAL

MOTOR DIVISIONS:

Motor and Gearing Division, Buffalo, N.Y.

Integral hp. motors for general industry and specific purpose applications; brakes; couplings; motocylinders; drives; gearing and gear motors; speed reducers.

Small Motor Division, Lima, Ohio

Small motors, general and special purpose for all types of domestic, appliance, and industrial purposes.

Copper Wire Division, Buffalo, N.Y.

Copper and aluminum conductors.

CONTROL DIVISIONS:

General Control Division, Buffalo, N.Y.

Motor starters and controllers; special purpose control; control components; static control; pilot devices; power supplies.

Hagan Controls Corporation, Pittsburgh, Pa.

Control components; control devices; control systems for combustion, flow and level, pressure and differential pressure, temperature, and chemical systems.

Low Voltage Distribution Equipment Division, Pittsburgh, Pa.

Control centers; panelboards; switchboards; custom control assemblies; special switchgear; custom power centers; high voltage bus.

Standard Control Division, Beaver, Pa.

Controls for motors; starters, contractors, relays, pushbuttons; bus duct; circuit breakers; safety switches.

EXHIBIT 1 *(concluded)*

Industrial (continued)

INDUSTRIAL EQUIPMENT AND SERVICE DIVISIONS:

Electric Service Division, Pittsburgh, Pa.
Field engineering; technical direction; installation and startup service; inspection and maintenance.

Homewood Division, Homewood, Pa.
Non-current apparatus and parts.

Industrial Electronics Division, Baltimore, Md.
Induction heating equipment; ultrasonic devices for cleaning and process equipment.

Repair Division, Pittsburgh, Pa.
Repair, rewind, rebuild, update, modernize electrical and mechanical apparatus, in the field or in one of 42 repair plants.

Transportation Equipment Division, East Pittsburgh, Pa.
Motors, generators, gearing, and control for transit vehicles; transit expressway vehicles.

Westing-Arc Division, Buffalo, N.Y.
Electric arc welders, electrodes, accessories; brazing alloys.

Industrial (continued)

INDUSTRIAL SYSTEMS DIVISIONS:

Computer Systems Division, Research and Development Center, Pittsburgh, Pa. (Churchill)
Digital computers.

Industry Systems Division, Research and Development Center, Pittsburgh, Pa. (Churchill)
Design and management for large scale systems; includes the Metals Industry Systems Department, the General Industries Systems Department, and the Public Works Systems Department.

Systems Control Division, Buffalo, N.Y.
Mill and marine materials handling control systems; numerical control; packaged drives; power rectifiers; Semitron® rectifier equipment (East Pittsburgh).

THERMO KING CORPORATION, Minneapolis, Minn.
Air conditioning for automobiles, trucks, buses, and other personnel vehicles. Refrigeration-heating for semi-trailers, trucks, van bodies, and other produce carriers.

Source: "The World of Westinghouse," a company publication.

EXHIBIT 2

WESTINGHOUSE ELECTRIC CORPORATION (A)
Sample Listing of Westinghouse Products

Coolers, portable, *Portable Appliance Division, Mansfield, Ohio*
Evaporative
Cores, *Specialty Transformer Division, Greenville, Pa.*
Cubex®
Hipersil®

Wescor®
Corona detectors, *Distribution Apparatus Division, Bloomington, Ind.*
Couplings, electric, *Large Rotating Apparatus Division, East Pittsburgh, Pa.*

EXHIBIT 2 (continued)

Couplings, flexible, *Motor and Gearing Division, Buffalo, N.Y.*

Cryogenic systems, *Cryogenic Systems Department, Research and Development Center, Pittsburgh, Pa. (Churchill)*

Cryptographic equipment, *Aerospace Division, Surface Division, Defense and Space Center, Baltimore, Md.*

Cutouts, fuse, *Distribution Apparatus Division, Bloomington, Ind.*
Enclosed
Open

Data processing and display equipment, ground and shipboard, *Surface Division, Defense and Space Center, Baltimore, Md.*

Data processing equipment, airborne and spaceborne, *Aerospace Division, Defense and Space Center, Baltimore, Md.*

Data processing systems, *Systems Operations, Defense and Space Center, Baltimore, Md.*

Data transmission and reception equipment, ground and shipboard, *Surface Division, Defense and Space Center, Baltimore, Md.*

Decorative Micarta®, *Decorative Micarta Division, Hampton, S.C.*

Degaussing equipment, marine, *Marine Products Division, Sunnyvale, Calif.*

Dehumidifiers, *Dishwasher and Specialty Products Division, Columbus, Ohio*

Dehumidifiers, *Sturtevant Division, Hyde Park, Mass.*
Sprayed coil type

Digital datalogers, *Power Control Division, Research and Development Center, Pittsburgh, Pa. (Churchill)*

Dishwashers, *Dishwasher and Specialty Products Division, Columbus, Ohio*
Built-in
Portable

Doors, Micarta-clad, *Architectural System, Grand Rapids, Mich.*

Drives, *Motor and Gearing Division, Buffalo, N.Y.*
Mechanical adjustable speed (AdjustiFlow℗)
Planer

Drives, packaged, electrical, adjustable speed, *Systems Control Division, Buffalo, N.Y.*

Dry cleaners, commercial, *Laundry Equipment Division, Mansfield, Ohio*

Dryers, *Laundry Equipment Division, Mansfield, Ohio*
Commercial
Domestic

Pushbuttons, *Standard Control Division, Beaver, Pa.*
Heavy duty
Oil tite
Standard duty

Radars, airborne and spaceborne, *Aerospace Division, Defense and Space Center, Baltimore, Md.*

Radars, ground and shipboard, *Surface Division, Defense and Space Center, Baltimore, Md.*

Radios, *Television-Radio Division, Metuchen, N.J.*
Clock
AM, AM/FM, pushbutton
Portable
AM, AM/FM, transistor, shortwave

EXHIBIT 2 (continued)

Table
AM, AM/FM, FM stereo
Transceivers
Ranges, electric, *Range Division,*
Mansfield, Ohio
Built-in
Cooking platforms
Electronic
Ovens
Free standing
Conventional
Eye-level ovens
Reactors, *Power Transformer Divi-*
sion, Sharon, Pa.
Current limiting
CL, oil-immersed and dry
type
MSP, dry type
Shunt, oil-immersed and dry
type
Reactors, charging, *Specialty*
Transformer Division, Green-
ville, Pa.
Reactors, saturable core, *Distribu-*
tion Transformer Division,
Sharon, Pa.
Reclosers, *Distribution Apparatus*
Division, Bloomington, Ind.
Reconnaissance equipment, air-
borne and spaceborne, *Aero-*
space Division, Defense and
Space Center, Baltimore, Md.
Reconnaissance systems, *Systems*
Operations, Defense and
Space Center, Baltimore, Md.
Rectifier assemblies, *Semiconduc-*
tor Division, Youngwood, Pa.
High voltage
Standard
Rectifier diodes, silicon, *Semicon-*
ductor Division, Youngwood,
Pa.
Controlled avalanche
Fast recovery
"O.E.M." line
Standard

Rectifier equipment, Semitron®,
Rectifier Product Group (Sys-
tems Control), East Pitts-
burgh, Pa.

Self-lubricating bearing materials,
Materials Manufacturing Divi-
sion, Blairsville, Pa.
Service, electric, *Electric Service*
Division, Pittsburgh, Pa.
(Available at all Westinghouse
sales locations)
Field engineering services
Inspection, maintenance, and re-
pair service
Starting service on apparatus
and systems
Technical direction and advice
Service, steam, *Steam Divisions*
Service Department, Lester,
Pa.
Complete installation service,
maintenance service, repair
service, and modernization
programs for all products mar-
keted by the Steam divisions,
including generators, exciters,
and regulators sold with tur-
bines and waterwheel genera-
tors marketed by Large Ro-
tating Apparatus Division.
Silicon Rectifier, *Rectifier Product*
Group (Systems Control),
East Pittsburgh, Pa.
Subassemblies for replacing Ig-
nition tubes
Sockets and mountings, meter, *Me-*
ter Division, Raleigh, N.C.
Sonar, *Underseas Division, Defense*
and Space Center, Baltimore,
Md.
Space propulsion concepts, *Astro-*
nuclear Laboratory, Large, Pa.
Space systems, *Systems Operations,*
Defense and Space Center,
Baltimore, Md.

EXHIBIT 2 *(concluded)*

Electrical

Mechanical

Specialty devices, *Semiconductor Division, Youngwood, Pa.*

Speed reducers, *Motor and Gearing Division, Buffalo, N.Y.*

Helical

Moduline®

Shaft

Worm gear

Spot film devices, X-ray, *X-Ray Division, Baltimore, Md.*

Starters, electric motor, *Standard Control Division, Beaver, Pa.*

Magnetic

Manual

Steam generators, marine, *Marine Products Division, Sunnyvale, Calif.*

Steam generators, nuclear, *Heat Transfer Division, Lester, Pa.*

Steam plant automation systems, *Power Control Division, Research and Development Center, Pittsburgh, Pa. (Churchill)*

Steam plant performance computer systems, *Power Control Division, Research and Development Center, Pittsburgh, Pa. (Churchill)*

Steam turbine generators, land, *Large Turbine Division, Lester, Pa.*

20,000 to 1,000,000 kw

Steam turbine generators, land, *Small Steam and Gas Turbine Division, Lester, Pa.*

20 to 15,625 kw

Source: "The World of Westinghouse," a company publication.

4 Westinghouse Electric Corporation (B₁)

Assume that you are the general manager of a product group with total sales of about $400 million in 1964. (See Exhibit 1, Westinghouse (A), for brief descriptions of typical product groups and divisions.)

Assume that each division manager reports directly to you. Profit objectives are established each year by corporate officers for your group as a whole, and by you and your division managers for the divisions in your group. A full set of financial statements is prepared by each division in your group. Your performance, and the performance of the division manager, is evaluated to a considerable extent each year on performance with respect to the objectives established.

While attending a management seminar made up of division managers and group managers from a number of large, diversified companies, you have been asked to indicate the degree of delegation you feel is appropriate in your organization for a number of problem situations. The "Delegation Questionnaire"[1] is reproduced as Exhibit 1, Westinghouse (B₁). In order to facilitate comparisons among companies, you also have been asked to assume, for your company, that:

1. Business conditions have been fairly good, and are expected to continue to be favorable;
2. All of your divisions have been profitable, although generally not as profitable as desired by corporate management;
3. Each division has had at least one major product line that has shown losses, but you stand a fairly good chance of meeting your profit goals for the group this year; and
4. You have held your job for some time, and each of the division managers in your group has been in his job at least three years.

---

[1] Source of delegation questionnaire and problem situation: Mr. William Nesbitt, director, organization planning, Westinghouse Electric Corporation.

EXHIBIT 1

WESTINGHOUSE ELECTRIC CORPORATION (B₁)
Delegation Questionnaire

As a group general manager you would expect your division managers to:		See Legend Below for Detailed Explanation of Headings:					
		Take Action		Advise You		Provide Information	
Problem Requiring Action		A	B	C	D	E	F
1. Hire a replacement for the division manager's secretary who is leaving.		X					
2. Authorize a temporary $50,000 increase in division raw material inventory in anticipation of a possible steel strike.		X					
3. Establish next month's manufacturing schedule for the division, at an increased level which will require the hiring of two additional people in the factory.			X				
4. Establish next month's manufacturing schedule, at a substantially higher level which will require the addition of 50 people in the factory.			X				
5. Pass final approval on the design of a new product, and authorize work to start on production tooling.				X			
6. Postpone the scheduled introduction of a new model by 45 days, and authorize a crash program estimated to cost $100,000 which will modify the design and permit incorporation of a recently developed design feature.					X		
7. Establish the list price of a major product line, which in the aggregate amounts to 30 percent of division volume.				X			
8. Increase the price of an existing product line by 4 percent, to attempt to recover cost increases that have taken place in material and labor; this will place the price above the competitive level.					X		
9. One product line has an extremely seasonal pattern, with all sales occurring in the summer. Authorize the production schedule for the year, which will create a $6 million shipping stock of this product at the time of its peak selling season.				X			
10. Make a change in the division inventory standards, which will reduce field shipping stocks but increase factory work-in-process inventory, maintaining the same total investment.					X		
11. Increase the investment in inventory on a different product by approximately $1 million, because the sales department feels that they can get more sales if they have greater product availability.						X	
12. Initiate a computer activity, estimated to cost $1 million for feasibility study and programming, and which will require a commitment for a computer that will ultimately cost $200,000 per year.							X
13. Introduce a new system into the factory that is recognized to have a 20 percent chance of precipitating strong opposition, possibly leading to a strike on the part of the union.				X			
14. Change advertising program for the division, reducing magazine advertising, increasing direct mail and trade show promotional activities.		X					
15. Authorize the manager of manufacturing to increase the methods and industrial engineering activity and reduce the size of the quality control department, maintaining the same total manufacturing expense.					X		
16. Authorize the marketing manager to increase the number of salespeople in the field, reduce the number of manufacturing engineers by a corresponding amount to maintain the same total cost.		X					
17. Select the replacement for the manufacturing superintendent who will retire soon.		X					
18. Take the superintendent off the job for poor performance; replace with another person now serving as a general foreman.		X					
19. Select the replacement for the general foreman position now open.		X					
20. Increase the number of general foremen positions in the division from four to six. Select the individuals to fill the new positions.		X					
21. Authorize an 8 percent salary increase for the manufacturing superintendent, allowed for in the budget and within the rate range for the job.		X					
22. Authorize an 8 percent salary increase for the division sales manager, allowed for in the budget and within the rate range.		X					
23. Authorize the factory to work overtime two Sundays next month to reduce the backlog of overdue orders.		X					
24. Increase the job classification and rate range for the engineering manager, to reflect the growth of that department and the position's increased responsibility.		X					
25. Authorize a change in job classification for the six general foremen positions, as a result of changes in their responsibility.		X					
26. Cancel two engineering development projects included in this year's program, and concentrate the $250,000 effort on a new development believed to have real commercial potential, identified as a result of research performed in the corporate research center.							X

Explanation of headings

A. Take action without any contact with you.

B. Take action; mention the action taken if division manager happens to see you.

C. Advise you in advance of the action intends to take; act unless you instruct not to.

D. Advise you in advance of the action would like to take; delay action until you give approval.

E. Give you an analysis of the alternative actions possible, with their merits and disadvantages, supporting the choice of the one recommended for your approval.

F. Give you as many facts about the case as possible so you can identify alternatives and select the action you want to be taken.

5 Westinghouse Electric Corporation (B₂)

Assume that you are the manager of a division with total sales of about $60 million in 1964. Your division is a part of a product group which accounted for about $400 million in sales in 1964. (See Exhibit 1 Westinghouse (A) for brief descriptions of typical product groups and divisions.)

Assume that you and all of the other division managers in your group report directly to the group general manager. Profit objectives are established each year by corporate officers for your group as a whole, and by you and your group general manager for your division. A full set of financial statements is prepared by each division in the group. Your performance, and the performance of your group general manager, is evaluated to a considerable extent each year on performance with respect to the objectives established.

While attending a management seminar made up of division managers and group general managers from a number of large, diversified companies, you have been asked to indicate the degree of delegation you feel is appropriate in your organization for a number of problem situations. The "Delegation Questionnaire"[1] is reproduced as Exhibit 1, Westinghouse (B₂). In order to facilitate comparisons among companies, you also have been asked to assume, for your company, that:

1. Business conditions have been fairly good, and are expected to continue to be favorable;
2. All of the divisions in your group have been profitable, although generally not as profitable as desired by corporate management;

---

[1] Source of delegation questionnaire and problem situation: Mr. William Nesbitt, director, organization planning, Westinghouse Electric Corporation.

3. Each division, including yours, has had at least one major product line that has shown losses;
4. You feel that you have a reasonable chance of meeting your division profit goals for the year;
5. Your group general manager has said that the group will probably meet its profit goals for the year "if everyone comes through";
6. You have held your job for some time, and the group general manager as well as the other division managers have all been in their jobs for at least three years.

EXHIBIT 1

WESTINGHOUSE ELECTRIC CORPORATION (B₂)

Delegation Questionnaire

Problem Requiring Action — As a division manager, you would:	Take Action		Advise Group Manager		Inform Group Manager	
	A	B	C	D	E	F
1. Hire a replacement for the division manager's secretary who is leaving.	X					
2. Authorize a temporary $50,000 increase in division raw material inventory in anticipation of a possible steel strike.	X					
3. Establish next month's manufacturing schedule for the division, at an increased level which will require the hiring of two additional people in the factory.		X				
4. Establish next month's manufacturing schedule, at a substantially higher level which will require the addition of 50 people in the factory.		X				
5. Pass final approval on the design of a new product, and authorize work to start on production tooling.				X		
6. Postpone the scheduled introduction of a new model by 45 days, and authorize a crash program estimated to cost $100,000 which will modify the design and permit incorporation of a recently developed design feature.				X		
7. Establish the list price of a major product line, which in the aggregate amounts to 30 percent of division volume.				X		
8. Increase the price of an existing product line by 4 percent, to attempt to recover cost increases that have taken place in material and labor; this will place the price above the competitive level.				X		
9. One product line has an extremely seasonal pattern, with all sales occurring in the summer. Authorize the production schedule for the year, which will create a $6 million shipping stock of this product at the time of its peak selling season.			X			
10. Make a change in the division inventory standards, which will reduce field shipping stocks but increase factory work-in-process inventory, maintaining the same total investment.			X			
11. Increase the investment in inventory on a different product by approximately $1 million, because the sales department feels that they can get more sales if they have greater product availability.					X	
12. Initiate a computer activity, estimated to cost $1 million for feasibility study and programming, and which will require a commitment for a computer that will ultimately cost $200,000 per year.					X	
13. Introduce a new system into the factory that is recognized to have a 20 percent chance of precipitating strong opposition, possibly leading to a strike on the part of the union.		X				
14. Change advertising program for the division, reducing magazine advertising, increasing direct mail and trade show promotional activities.	X					
15. Authorize the manager of manufacturing to increase the methods and industrial engineering activity and reduce the size of the quality control department, maintaining the same total manufacturing expense.				X		
16. Authorize the marketing manager to increase the number of salespeople in the field, reduce the number of manufacturing engineers by a corresponding amount to maintain the same total cost.	X					
17. Select the replacement for the manufacturing superintendent who will retire soon.	X					
18. Take the superintendent off the job for poor performance; replace with another person now serving as a general foreman.	X					
19. Select the replacement for the general foreman position now open.	X					
20. Increase the number of general foremen positions in the division from four to six. Select the individuals to fill the new positions.	X					
21. Authorize an 8 percent salary increase for the manufacturing superintendent, allowed for in the budget and within the rate range for the job.	X					
22. Authorize an 8 percent salary increase for the division sales manager, allowed for in the budget and within the rate range.	X					
23. Authorize the factory to work overtime two Sundays next month to reduce the backlog of overdue orders.	X					
24. Increase the job classification and rate range for the engineering manager, to reflect the growth of that department and the position's increased responsibility.	X					
25. Authorize a change in job classification for the six general foremen positions, as a result of changes in their responsibility.	X					
26. Cancel two engineering development projects included in this year's program, and concentrate the $250,000 effort on a new development believed to have real commercial potential, identified as a result of research performed in the corporate research center.						X

Explanation of Headings:

A. Take action without contacting group general manager.

B. Take action; mention action later if you happen to see the group general manager.

C. Advise group general manager in advance of action you intend to take; act unless told not to.

D. Advise group general manager in advance of action you would like to take; delay action until given approval.

E. Give the group general manager an analysis of the alternative actions possible, with their merits and disadvantages, supporting your choice of the one you recommend for approval.

F. Give the group general manager as many facts about the case as possible so that the manager can identify alternatives and select the action to be taken.

6

The Rose Company

Mr. James Pierce had recently received word of his appointment as plant manager of Plant X, one of the older established units of the Rose Company. As such, Mr. Pierce was to be responsible for the management and administration at Plant X of all functions and personnel except sales.

Both top management and Mr. Pierce realized that there were several unique features about his new assignment. Mr. Pierce decided to assess his new situation and relationships before undertaking his assignment. He was personally acquainted with the home office executives, but had met few of the plant personnel. This case contains some of his reflections regarding the new assignment.

The Rose Company conducted marketing activities throughout the United States and in certain foreign countries. These activities were directed from the home office by a vice president in charge of sales.

Manufacturing operations and certain other departments were under the supervision and control of a senior vice president. These are shown in Exhibit 1. For many years the company had operated a highly centralized functional type of manufacturing organization. There was no general manager at any plant; each of the departments in a plant reported on a line basis to its functional counterpart at the home office. For instance, the industrial relations manager of a particular plant reported to the vice president in charge of industrial relations at the home office, the plant controller to the vice president and controller, and so on.

Mr. Pierce stated that in the opinion of the top management the record of Plant X had not been satisfactory for several years. The board had recently approved the erection of a new plant in a different part of the city and the use of new methods of production. Lower costs of

EXHIBIT 1

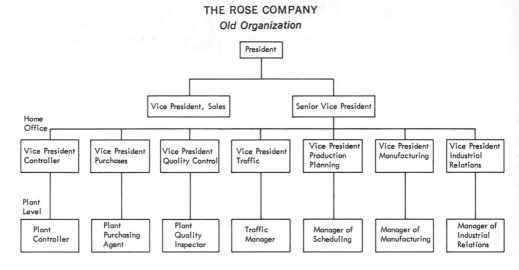

THE ROSE COMPANY
Old Organization

processing and a reduced manpower requirement at the new plant were expected. Reduction of costs and improved quality of products were needed to maintain competitive leadership and gain some slight product advantage. The proposed combination of methods of manufacturing and mixing materials had not been tried elsewhere in the company. Some features would be entirely new to employees.

According to Mr. Pierce the top management of the Rose Company was beginning to question the advisability of the central control of manufacturing operations. The officers decided to test the value of a decentralized operation in connection with Plant X. They apparently believed that a general management representative in Plant X was needed if the new equipment in manufacturing methods and the required rebuilding of the organization were to succeed.

Prior to the new assignment Mr. Pierce had been an accounting executive in the controller's department of the company. From independent sources the case writer learned that Mr. Pierce had demonstrated analytical ability and general administrative capacity. He was generally liked by people. From top management's point of view he had an essential toughness described as an ability to see anything important through. By some he was regarded as the company's efficiency expert. Others thought he was a perfectionist and aggressive in reaching the goals that had been set. Mr. Pierce was aware of these opinions about his personal behavior.

Mr. Pierce summarized his problem in part as follows: "I am going into a situation involving a large number of changes. I will have a new plant—new methods and processes—but most of all I will be dealing with a set of changed relationships. Heretofore all the heads of departments in the plant reported to their functional counterparts in the home office. Now they will report to me. I am a complete stranger and in addition this is my first assignment in a major 'line' job. The men will know this.

"When I was called into the senior vice president's office to be informed of my new assignment he asked me to talk with each of the functional members of his staff. The vice presidents in charge of production planning, manufacturing, and industrial relations said they were going to issue all headquarters instructions to me as plant manager and they were going to cut off their connections with their counterparts in my plant. The other home office executives admitted their functional counterparts would report to me in line capacity. They should obey my orders and I would be responsible for their pay and promotion. But these executives proposed to follow the common practice of many companies of maintaining a dotted line or functional relationship with these men. I realize that these two different patterns of home office—plant relationships will create real administrative problems for me."

Exhibit 2 shows the organization relationships as defined in these conferences.

EXHIBIT 2

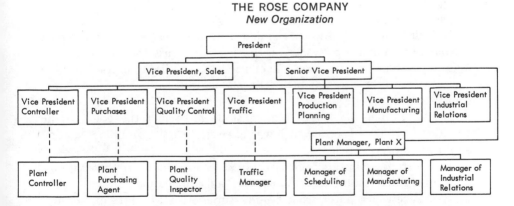

THE ROSE COMPANY
New Organization

7   *The Larger Company (A)*

The phone rang, and highly indignant words blared: "Masters, what do you mean by submitting a report to all the executives without first talking it over with the division manager!"

Masters replied, "My men made every effort to see him. They never got past his secretary. He instructed her to have them talk to the works manager."

"I don't believe a word of it. Vining is up in arms. He says the report is vindictive. What are you trying to do—embarrass the division manager? I don't believe your men ever tried to see Vining and I question the veracity of their statements!" The phone on the other end was hung up with a bang.

Masters said to himself, "Gunn must be hot under the collar or he wouldn't have called me when I was away from my own office, visiting another plant."

The next day Masters' office received Gunn's letter confirming this telephone conversation and demanding an explanation. A week later Masters received a letter from Gunn's superior, a Mr. Jordan, stating: "I have read the aforementioned report and discussed it with Mr. Gunn. He has advised me that the report is essentially untrue, inaccurate, and overstated. I am not satisfied to have such wide differences of opinion and have scheduled a meeting to be held in my office on ———. I would appreciate it if you would be present."

In light of the phone call and the two letters, Mr. Masters decided to reassess all events leading to this climax.

✷   ✷   ✷   ✷   ✷

The cast of characters is as shown in Exhibit 1. The Larger Company had an elaborate organizational structure as a result of its scale of operation. At the headquarters office of the corporation the president had a group of staff vice presidents in charge of functions. Mr. Masters was a staff department head reporting to the vice president, manufacturing. The headquarters staff departments assisted in policy formulation and made staff studies for the operating organization when requested. Members of such departments were encouraged to offer ideas for the good of the company. Their proposals were considered by a management committee consisting of the vice presidents at the headquarters level and the operating vice presidents in charge of product groups. Mr. Jordan of this case was the operating vice president, Product Group "B."

EXHIBIT 1

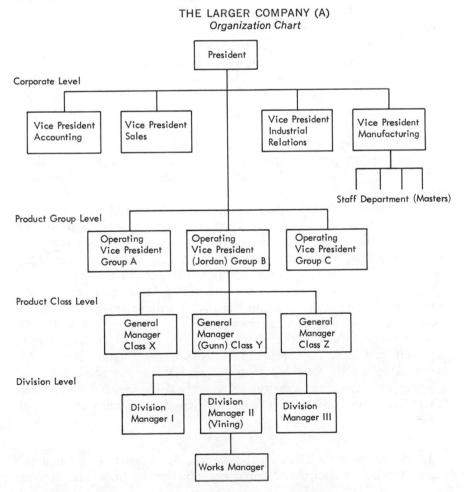

THE LARGER COMPANY (A)
Organization Chart

President

Corporate Level

Vice President Accounting

Vice President Sales

Vice President Industrial Relations

Vice President Manufacturing

Staff Department (Masters)

Product Group Level

Operating Vice President Group A

Operating Vice President (Jordan) Group B

Operating Vice President Group C

Product Class Level

General Manager Class X

General Manager (Gunn) Class Y

General Manager Class Z

Division Level

Division Manager I

Division Manager II (Vining)

Division Manager III

Works Manager

Under the product groups there were general managers of product classes. They supervised the division managers, who were in charge of the sales and manufacturing operations of one or more plants. Mr. Gunn was general manager of Product Class "Y." One of the four division managers under him was Mr. Vining of Division II.

* * * * *

Two years before this incident occurred, Mr. Masters' staff department proposed to the management committee, with the approval of the vice president, manufacturing, that representatives of Mr. Masters' office join wih representatives of the vice president, accounting, to make studies in each plant of the producers for and actual practices regarding expense control. The suggestion was approved and enthusiastically endorsed by the general managers. They sent a letter through channels to each division manager advising that periodically a team of two men would visit each plant to make a comprehensive analysis of expense-control practices and systems.

After a visit these field representatives of headquarters were to prepare a report giving findings and recommendations. They were to discuss it with the appropriate division manager and his staff. Thus they would be able to incorporate any specific plans of action set in motion by division managers. Next, a report was to be submitted to Mr. Masters. Both his department and the accounting office were to make comments. The final document was then to be submitted to the vice president, accounting; the vice president, manufacturing; the operating vice president, product group; the general manager, product class; and the division manager concerned.

This general procedure had worked smoothly within the company until general manager Gunn of Product Class "Y" exploded. In the first plant studied, the two team members spent approximately four weeks examining documents, interviewing line management, interrogating industrial engineers, observing operations, etc. The employees of this plant were very cooperative. Some of the facts revealed by them could have been embarrassing to the division manager. The team was enabled to make specific recommendations for improvement to the division manager. His reception of the report was good. According to him, the study had given an opportunity to review his situation and get his house in order. He intended to implement the recommendations unless they were changed in the review process at the higher level. Sixteen other plants were visited with reasonably good acceptance of the work of the team.

* * * * *

In his review of the Division II situation, Mr. Masters found that the team had observed all the required organization routines. Mr. Sawyer, representing Mr. Masters, had a master's degree in industrial engineering and had 12 years with the company. Mr. Peters, from the accounting office, had served that department for 30 years. Both men had shown ability to gain confidences and to use them discreetly. They were considered straightforward, conscientious, and unobtrusive in their work. In Division II the team obtained from plant personnel considerable information which pointed up a number of practices and procedures requiring improvement. In the opinion of the team members, the operating organization at the lower levels sincerely wanted to make these changes. The team thought that there was some resistance at some level within the division to these suggestions and, in fact, to any from headquarters.

While the study was in process, Mr. Sawyer advised Mr. Masters about the possible impact of the information which was being collected. Mr. Masters emphasized the necessity to report to the division manager, and Mr. Sawyer promised that he and Mr. Peters would do so.

The team made several efforts to see the division manager, but his secretary informed them that he was busy. They questioned the secretary closely to learn if the manager had knowledge of the procedural requirement that he and his staff go over the report with the team. She replied that he knew the requirements, but was too busy to discuss a headquarters program. He would ask his assistant, the works manager, and several staff members to go over it, and what they approved would be all right with him. Eventually this meeting was held.

The members of the local management staff took a very reasonable attitude; they admitted the bad situation portrayed in the analysis and offered their assurances that immediate steps would be taken towards improvement. The team members thought that the local management staff was glad to have their problem brought out in the open, and were delighted to have the suggestions of the headquarters representatives.

          *   *   *   *   *

When Mr. Masters reviewed the report, both team members expressed their complete dissatisfaction with the brush-off they got from the division manager. Masters took this as a cue to question them extensively concerning their findings and recommendations. In view of the sensitive character of the situation and the possible controversy that it might create, he was reluctant to distribute the report. It was the consensus of the remainder of the staff and the representatives of the accounting office that the usual transmittal letter should be prepared, and distribution made. Mr. Masters signed this letter and took no other action until the telephone call came from Mr. Gunn.

8   *The Larger Company (B)*

Mr. Jordan, operating vice president, Product Group "B" of the Larger Company, called a meeting to review the report submitted by Mr. Masters' staff department and the accounting office. Mr. Jordan; Mr. Gunn; Mr. Masters; the vice president, accounting; and the vice president, manufacturing, attended. In a very constructive, two-hour meeting, the report was evaluated and many conclusions were confirmed.

Division manager Vining was not present. Mr. Jordan had not invited him because he wanted to keep "heat" out of the meeting. Mr. Jordan regarded Mr. Vining as an "individual operator" who on more than one occasion had shown definite disrespect for headquarters functions and programs.

There was some heat in the meeting, nevertheless. Mr. Gunn stated that Mr. Masters should have discussed the report with him. Thus he might have had an opportunity to take executive action at his level. When a division manager failed to consider a report the superior should have a chance, even though the formal procedure did not provide for it. Mr. Gunn said that Mr. Masters should have known that. Mr. Gunn also read a letter that had been prepared by Mr. Vining. It generally and categorically denied most of the statements in the report that were unsatisfactory to him. The vice president, accounting, and Mr. Masters, however, had certain information and supplementary reports which seemed to discount the effectiveness of the letter of rebuttal.

Before too much time elapsed, Mr. Jordan turned the discussion into ways of bringing about improvement in the future. "Where there was so much smoke," he observed, "there might be some fire." He suggested that men of higher rank review the work of the two team members;

this would serve either to confirm or modify their findings. This step seemed advisable in order to assuage the feelings of the local division manager.

The meeting ended on a very harmonious note. Mr. Jordan asked Mr. Gunn to see Mr. Vining. "He needs to understand and appreciate that he has a responsibility to find time to review and comment on the type of reports being made by team members."

Mr. Masters was pleased by the results of the meeting and the follow-up actions. Mr. Gunn must have talked with Mr. Vining. Whatever was said may have contributed to better working relationships. Plant cooperation immediately improved. The division manager cleared any obstacles interfering with the success of the program. His influence was particularly noticeable in its effect on the behavior of the line supervisory organization. According to Mr. Masters, cooperation rather than resistance was now encouraged. The home office team became the advisory team it was intended to be.

In reviewing this experience, Mr. Masters said, "There was bound to be some form of blow-up because Vining had the reputation of thinking he did not have to conform to company-wide programs unless it was to his advantage. Further, he was more rugged in nature than Gunn. On many occasions Gunn was inclined to support Vining. There has been a very definite change in this respect during the latter part of this year."

9   The Lincoln Electric Company

We're not a marketing company, we're not an R&D company, and we're not a service company. We're a manufacturing company, and I believe that we are the best manufacturing company in the world.

With these words, George E. Willis, president of the Lincoln Electric Company, described what he saw as his company's distinctive competence. For more than 30 years, Lincoln had been the world's largest manufacturer of arc welding products. (See Exhibit 1.) In 1974, Lincoln Electric was believed to have manufactured more than 40 percent of the arc welding equipment and supplies sold in the United States. In addition to its welding products, Lincoln produced a line of three-phase A.C. industrial electric motors, but these accounted for less than 10 percent of sales and profits.

EXHIBIT 1

THE LINCOLN ELECTRIC COMPANY

Arc welding is a group of joining processes that utilize an electric current produced by a transformer or motor generator (electric or engine powered) to fuse various metals. The temperature at the arc is approximately 10,000° Fahrenheit.

The welding circuit consists of a welding machine, ground clamp and electrode holder. The electrode carries electricity to the metal being welded and the heat from the arc causes the base metals to join together. The electrode may or may not act as a filler metal during the process; however, nearly 60 percent of all arc welding that is done in the United States utilizes a covered electrode that does act as a very high-quality filler metal.

The Lincoln Electric Company manufactures a wide variety of covered electrodes, submerged arc welding wires and fluxes, and a unique self-shielded, flux-cored electrode called "Innershield." The company also manufactures welding machines, wire feeders, and other supplies that are needed for arc welding.

LINCOLN ARC WELDING MACHINES

Lincoln's 1974 domestic net income was $17.5 million on sales of $236 million. (See Exhibit 2.) Perhaps more significant than a single year's results was Lincoln's record of steady growth over the preceding four decades, as shown by the following graph:

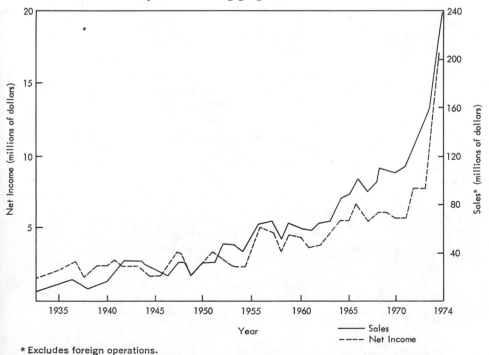

* Excludes foreign operations.

EXHIBIT 2

THE LINCOLN ELECTRIC COMPANY
Statement of Financial Condition
On December 31, 1974
(foreign subsidiaries not included)

Assets	1974	Liabilities	1974
Current assets		Current liabilities	
Cash and certificates of deposit....................	$ 5,691,120	Accounts payable..............	$ 13,658,063
Government securities........	6,073,919	Accrued wages................	1,554,225
Notes and accounts receivable.	29,451,161	Taxes, including income taxes..	13,262,178
Inventories (Lifo basis)........	29,995,694	Dividends payable.............	3,373,524
Deferred taxes and prepaid expenses...................	2,266,409		$ 31,847,990
	$ 73,478,303		
Other assets		Shareholders' equity	
Trustee—notes and interest receivable...................	$ 1,906,871	Common capital stock, stated value........................	$ 281,127
Miscellaneous................	384,572	Additional paid-in capital......	3,374,570
	$ 2,291,443	Retained earnings.............	66,615,762
			$ 70,271,459
Intercompany			
Investment in foreign subsidiaries.................	$ 4,695,610	Total Liabilities and	
Notes receivable..............	—0—	Shareholders' Equity...	$102,119,449
	$ 4,695,610		
Property, plant, and equipment			
Land..........................	$ 825,376		
Buildings*....................	9,555,562		
Machinery, tools and equipment	11,273,155		
(*After depreciation)..........	$ 21,654,093		
Total Assets.............	$102,119,449		

THE LINCOLN ELECTRIC COMPANY
Statements of Income and Retained Earnings
(year ended December 31)

Income	1974
Net sales...	$232,771,475
Interest..	1,048,561
Overhead and development charges to subsidiaries............................	1,452,877
Dividend income..	843,533
Other income...	515,034
	236,631,480
Costs and expenses:	
Cost of products sold......................................	154,752,735
Selling, administrative, and general expenses and freight out...................	20,791,301
Year-end incentive bonus......................................	24,707,297
Pension expense...	2,186,932
	202,438,265
Income before Income Taxes	34,193,215
Provision for income taxes:	
Federal..	14,800,000
State and local...	1,866,000
	16,666,000
Net income..	$ 17,527,215

During this period, after-tax return on equity had ranged between 10 percent and 15 percent. Lincoln's growth had been without benefit of acquisition and had been financed through internally generated funds.

COMPANY HISTORY

Lincoln Electric was founded by John C. Lincoln in 1895 to manufacture electric motors and generators. James F. Lincoln, John's younger brother, joined the company in 1907. The brothers' skills and interests were complementary. John was a technical genius. During his lifetime he was awarded more than 50 patents for inventions as diverse as an apparatus for curing meat, an electric drill, a mine door activating mechanism, and an electric arc lamp. James's skills were in management and administration. He began as a salesman but soon took over as general manager. The Lincoln Electric Company was undeniably built in his image.

In 1911, the company introduced its first arc welding machine. Both brothers were fascinated by welding, which was in its infancy at the time. They recognized it as an alternative use for the motor-generator sets they were already producing to recharge the batteries for electric automobiles. It was becoming apparent from the success of Ford, Buick, and others that the days of the electric auto might be numbered, and the brothers were anxious to find other markets for their skills and products.

John's mechanical talents gave the company a head start in welding machines which it never relinquished. He developed a portable welding machine (a significant improvement over existing stationary models) and incorporated a transformer to allow regulation of the current. As described by a biographer of John C. Lincoln:

> This functional industrial development gave Lincoln Electric a lead in the field that it has always maintained, although the two giants—Westinghouse and General Electric—soon entered the market.[1]

By World War II, Lincoln Electric was the leading American manufacturer of arc welding equipment. Because of the importance of welding to the war effort, the company stopped producing electric motors and devoted its full capacity to welding products. Demand continued to outpace production, and the government asked the welding equipment manufacturers to add capacity. As described by Lincoln President George Willis:

> Mr. Lincoln responded to the government's call by going to Washington and telling them that there was enough manufacturing capacity but it was being used inefficiently by everyone. He offered to share proprie-

---

[1] Raymond Moley, *The American Century of John C. Lincoln* (New York: Duell, Sloan & Pearce, 1962), p. 71.

tary manufacturing methods and equipment designs with the rest of the industry. Washington took him up on it and that solved the problem. As a result of Mr. Lincoln's patriotic decision, our competitors had costs which were close to ours for a short period after the war, but we soon were outperforming them like before.

In 1955, Lincoln once again began manufacturing electric motors, and since then its position in the market had expanded steadily.

Through the years, Lincoln stock had been sold to employees and associates of Mr. Lincoln. In 1975, approximately 48 percent of employees were shareholders. About 80 percent of the outstanding stock was held by employees, the Lincoln family, and their foundations.

In its 80 years to 1975, Lincoln had had only three board chairmen: John C. Lincoln, James F. Lincoln, and William Irrgang, who became chairman in 1972.

Strategy

Lincoln Electric's strategy was simple and unwavering. The company's strength was in manufacturing. Management believed that Lincoln could build quality products at a lower cost than their competitors. Their strategy was to concentrate on reducing costs and passing the savings through to the customer by continuously lowering prices. Management had adhered to this policy even when products were on allocation due to shortage of productive capacity. This had brought an expansion of both market share and primary demand for arc welding equipment and supplies over the past half century. It had also encouraged the exit of several major companies from the industry (including General Electric) and had caused others to seek more specialized market niches.

Management believed its incentive system and the climate it fostered were responsible in large part for the continual increase in productivity upon which this strategy depended. Under the Lincoln incentive system, employees were handsomely rewarded for their productivity, high quality, cost reduction ideas, and individual contribution to the company. Year-end bonuses averaged close to 100 percent of regular compensation, and some workers on the factory floor had earned more than $45,000 in a single year.

Lincoln's strategy had remained virtually unchanged for decades. In a 1947 Harvard Business School case study on Lincoln Electric, James F. Lincoln described his company's stratgey as follows:

> Is is the job of the Lincoln Electric Company to give its customers more and more of a better product at a lower and lower price. This will also make it possible for the company to give to the worker and the stockholder a higher and higher return.

In 1975, Chairman William Irrgang's description was remarkably similar:

> The success of the Lincoln Electric Company has been built on two basic ideas. One is producing more and more of a progressively better product at a lower and lower price for a larger and larger group of customers. The other is that an employee's earnings and promotion are in direct proportion to his individual contribution toward the company's success.[2]

Management felt it had achieved an enviable record in following this strategy faithfully and saw no need to modify it in the future. Lincoln Electric's record of increasing productivity and declining costs and prices is shown in Exhibit 3.

Company Philosophy

Lincoln Electric's corporate strategy was rooted in the management philosophy of James F. Lincoln. James F. Lincoln was a rugged individualist, who believed that through competition and adequate incentives every person could develop to their fullest potential. In one of his numerous books and articles he wrote:

> Competition is the foundation of man's development. It has made the human race what it is. It is the spur that makes progress. Every nation that has eliminated it as the controlling force in its economy has disappeared, or will. We will do the same if we eliminate it by trying to give security, and for the same reason. Competition means that there will be losers as well as winners in the game. Competition will mean the disappearance of the lazy and incompetent, be they workers, industrialists, or distributors. Competition promotes progress. Competition determines who will be the leader. It is the only known way that leadership and progress can be developed if history means anything. It is a hard taskmaster. It is completely necessary for anyone, be he worker, user, distributor, or boss, if he is to grow.
>
> If some way could be found so that competition could be eliminated from life, the result would be disastrous. Any nation and any people disappear if life becomes too easy. There is no danger from a hard life as all history shows. Danger is from a life that is made soft by lack of competition.[3]

Lincoln's faith in the individual was almost unbounded. His personal experience with the success of Lincoln Electric reinforced his faith in

---

[2] *Employee's Handbook*, the Lincoln Electric Company, 1974.

[3] James F. Lincoln, *Incentive Management* (Cleveland, Ohio: The Lincoln Electric Company, 1951), p. 33.

EXHIBIT 3

LINCOLN ELECTRIC COMPANY
Lincoln Electric's Record of Pricing and Productivity

Indexes of annual selling prices of ³⁄₁₆″ diameter electrode in No. 5 and No. 5p in 3,000 pound quantities, by the Lincoln Electric Company, in relation to indexes of wholesale prices of all commodities, intermediate materials, metal and metal products, and iron and steel, 1934–71

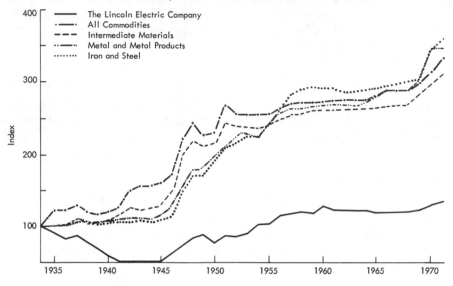

Indexes of average annual prices of specific welders by the Lincoln Electric Company in relation to wholesale prices of machinery and equipment (including electrical) and of electrical machinery and equipment: United States, 1939–71. 1939 = 100.

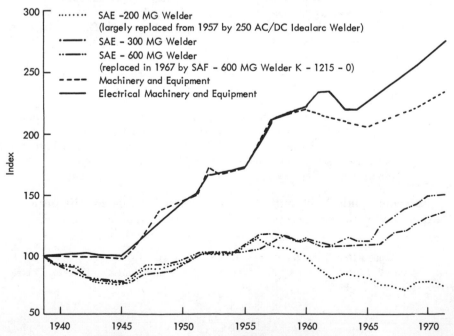

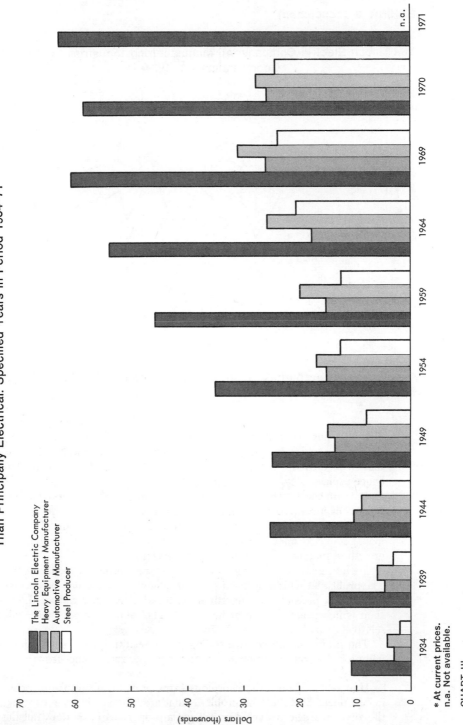

Sales Value* of Products per Employee
The Lincoln Electric Company and Three Prominent Companies Other
Than Principally Electrical. Specified Years in Period 1934–71

The Lincoln Electric Company
Heavy Equipment Manufacturer
Automotive Manufacturer
Steel Producer

Dollars (thousands)

* At current prices.
n.a. Not available.

CHART III
Source: Table 3

EXHIBIT 3 (concluded)

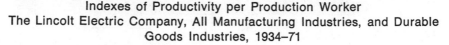

Indexes of Productivity per Production Worker
The Lincolt Electric Company, All Manufacturing Industries, and Durable
Goods Industries, 1934–71

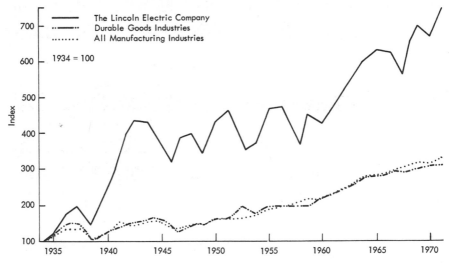

what could be accomplished given the proper conditions. In 1951, he
wrote:

> . . . development in many directions is latent in every person. The
> difficulty has been that few recognize that fact. Fewer still will put
> themselves under the pressure or by chance are put under the pressure
> that will develop them greatly. Their latent abilities remain latent,
> hence useless. . . .
>
> It is of course obvious that the development of man, on which the
> success of incentive management depends, is a progressive process. Any
> results, no matter how good, that come from the application of incentive
> management cannot be considered final. There will always be greater
> growth of man under continued proper incentive. . . .
>
> Such increase of efficiency poses a very real problem to management.
> The profit that will result from such efficiency obviously will be enormous.
> The output per dollar of investment will be many times that of the usual
> shop which practices output limitation. The labor cost per piece will be
> relatively small and the overhead will be still less.
>
> The profits at competitive selling prices resulting from such efficiency
> will be far beyond any possible need for proper return and growth of any
> industry. . . .
>
> How, then, should the enormous extra profit resulting from incentive
> management be split? The problems that are inherent in incentive dictate
> the answer. If the worker does not get a proper share, he does not desire

to develop himself or his skill. Incentive, therefore, would not succeed. The worker must have a reward that he feels is commensurate with his contribution.

If the customer does not have a part of the saving in lower prices, he will not buy the increased output. The size of the market is a decisive factor in costs of products. Therefore, the consumer must get a proper share of the saving.

Management and ownership are usually considered as a unit. This is far from a fact, but in the problem here, they can be considered together. They must get a part of the saving in larger salaries and perhaps larger dividends.

There is no hard and fast rule to cover this division, other than the following. The worker, (which includes management), the customer, the owner and all those involved must be satisfied that they are properly recognized or they will not cooperate, and cooperation is essential to any and all successful applications of incentives.[4]

Additional comments by James F. Lincoln are presented in Exhibit 4.

EXHIBIT 4

THE LINCOLN ELECTRIC COMPANY
James F. Lincoln's Observations on Management

• Some think paying a man more money will produce cooperation. Not true. Many incentives are far more effective than money. Robert McNamara gave up millions to become Secretary of Defense. Status is a much greater incentive.

• If those crying loudest about the inefficiencies of labor were put in the position of the wage earner, they would react as he does. The worker is not a man apart. He has the same needs, aspirations and reactions as the industrialist. A worker will not cooperate on any program that will penalize him. Does any manager?

• The industrial manager is very conscious of his company's need of uninterrupted income. He is completely oblivious, though, to the worker's same need. Management fails—i.e., profits fall off—and gets no punishment. The wage earner does not fail but is fired. Such injustice!

• Higher efficiency means fewer manhours to do a job. If the worker loses his job more quickly, he will oppose higher efficiency.

• There never will be enthusiasm for greater efficiency if the resulting profits are not properly distributed. If we continue to give it to the average stockholder, the worker will not cooperate.

• Most companies are run by hired managers, under the control of stockholders. As a result, the goal of the company has shifted from service to the customer, to making larger dividends for stockholders.

• The public will not yet believe that our standard of living could be doubled immediately if labor and management would cooperate.

---

[4] *Incentive Management*, pp. 7–11.

EXHIBIT 4 *(continued)*

• The manager is dealing with expert workers far more skillful. While you can boss these experts around in the usual lofty way, their eager cooperation will not be won.

• A wage earner is no more interested than a manager in making money for other people. The worker's job doesn't depend on pleasing stockholders, so he has no interest in dividends. Neither is he interested in increasing efficiency if he may lose his job because management has failed to get more orders.

• If a manager received the same treatment in matters of income, security, advancement, and dignity as the hourly worker, he would soon understand the real problem of management.

• The first question management should ask is: What is the company trying to do? In the minds of the average worker the answer is: "The company is trying to make the largest possible profits by any method. Profits go to absentee stockholders and top management."

• There is all the difference imaginable between the grudging, distrustful, half-forced cooperation and the eager whole-hearted vigorous happy cooperation of men working together for a common purpose.

• Continuous employment of workers is essential to industrial efficiency. This is a management responsibility. Laying off workers during slack times is death to efficiency. The worker thrown out is a trained man. To replace him when business picks up will cost much more than the savings of wages during the layoff. Solution? The worker must have a guarantee that if he works properly his income will be continuous.

• Continuous employment is the first step to efficiency. But how? First, during slack periods, manufacture to build up inventory; costs will usually be less because of lower material costs. Second, develop new machines and methods of manufacturing; plans should be waiting on the shelf. Third, reduce prices by getting lower costs. When slack times come, workers are eager to help cut costs. Fourth, explore markets passed over when times are good. Fifth, hours of work can be reduced if the worker is agreeable. Sixth, develop new products. In sum, management should plan for slumps. They are useful.

• The incentives that are most potent when properly offered are:

> Money in proportion to production.
> Status as a reward for achievement.
> Publicity of the worker's contributions and skill.

• The calling of the minister, the doctor, the lawyer, as well as the manager, contains incentive to excel. Excellence bring rewards, self-esteem, respect. Only the hourly worker has no reason to excel.

• Resistence to efficiency is not normal. It is present only when we are hired workers.

• Do unto others as you would have them do unto you. This is not just a Sunday school ideal, but a proper labor-management policy.

EXHIBIT 4 *(continued)*

• An incentive plan should reward a man not only for the number of pieces turned out, but also for the accuracy of his work, his cooperation in improving methods of production, his attendance.

• The progress in industry so far stems from the developed potentialities of managers. Wage earners, who because of their greater numbers have far greater potential, are overlooked. Here is where the manager must look for his greatest progress.

• There should be an overall bonus based on the contribution each person makes to efficiency. If each person is properly rated and paid, there will not only be a fair reward to each worker but friendly and exciting competition.

• The present policy of operating industry for stockholders is unreasonable. The rewards now given to him are far too much. He gets income that should really go to the worker and the management. The usual absentee stockholder contributes nothing to efficiency. He buys a stock today and sells it tomorrow. He often doesn't even know what the company makes. Why should he be rewarded by large dividends?

• There are many forms and degrees of cooperation between the worker and the management. The worker's attitude can vary all the way from passivity to higher imaginative contributions to efficiency and progress.

Source: *Civil Engineering–ASCE*, January 1973.

Compensation Policies

Compensation policies were the key element of James F. Lincoln's philosophy of "incentive management." Lincoln Electric's compensation system had three components:

1. Wages based solely on piecework output for most factory jobs.
2. A year-end bonus which could equal or exceed an individual's full year regular pay.
3. Guaranteed employment for all workers.

The first component of this compensation system was that almost all production workers at Lincoln were paid on a straight piecework plan. They had no base salary or hourly wage, but were paid a set "price" for each item they produced. William Irrgang explained:

Wherever practical, we use the piecework system. This system can be effective, and it can be destructive. The important part of the system is that it is completely fair to the worker. When we set a piecework price, that price cannot be changed just because, in management's opinion, the worker is making too much money. Whether he earns two times or three times his normal amount makes no difference. Piecework prices can only be changed when management has made a change in the method of doing that particular job and under no other conditions. If this is not carried out 100 percent, piecework cannot work.

Today piecework is confined to production operations, although at one time we also used it for work done in our stenographic pool. Each typewriter was equipped with a counter that registered the number of times the typewriter keys were operated. This seemed to work all right for a time until it was noticed that one girl was earning much more than any of the others. This was looked into, and it was found that this young lady ate her lunch at her desk, using one hand for eating purposes and the other for punching the most convenient key on the typewriter as fast as she could; which simply goes to show that no matter how good a program you may have, it still needs careful supervision.[5]

A time-study department established piecework prices which were guaranteed by the company, until there was a methods change or introduction of a new process. An employee could challenge the price if he felt it was unfair. The time-study department would then retime the job and set a new rate. This could be higher or lower but was still open to challenge if the employee remained dissatisfied. Employees were expected to guarantee their own quality. They were not paid for defective work until it had been repaired on their own time.

All of the jobs in the company were rated according to skill, required effort, responsibility, etc., and a base wage rate for the job was assigned. Wage rates were comparable to those in similar jobs in the Cleveland area, and were adjusted annually based on Department of Labor statistics and quarterly to reflect changes in the cost of living. This determined the salary or hourly wage. For piecework jobs the time-study department set piece prices so that an employee could earn the base rate for a job if he produced at a standard rate.

The second element of the compensation system was a year-end bonus. Each year since 1934, Lincoln had paid a year-end bonus to its employees. As explained in the *Employee's Handbook:* "The bonus, paid at the discretion of the company, is not a gift, but rather it is the sharing of the results of efficient operation on the basis of the contribution of each person to the success of the company for that year." In 1974, this totalled $26 million, an average of approximately $10,700 per employee, or 90 percent of pre-bonus wages.

The total amount to be paid out in bonuses each year was determined by the board of directors. The concentration on cost reduction kept costs low enough so that, generally, prices could be set (and not upset by competition), based on costs at the beginning of the year to produce a

---

[5] William Irrgang, "The Lincoln Incentive Management Program," Lincoln Lecture Series, Arizona State University, 1972, p. 13.

target return for stockholders and to give employees a bonus of approximately 100 percent of wages. The variance from the planned profits was usually added to (or subtracted from) the bonus pool to be distributed at year-end. Since 1945, the average bonus had varied from 78 percent to 129 percent of wages. In the past few years, it had been between 40 percent and 55 percent of pre-tax, pre-bonus profit, or as high as twice the net income after taxes.

An individual's share of the bonus was determined by a semiannual "merit rating," which measured individual performance, compared with other members of the department or work group. Ratings for all employees had to average out to 100 on this relative scale. However, if an individual had made an unusual contribution, and deserved a rating above 110, there was a special corporate pool of bonus points that could be awarded so as not to penalize co-workers. Ratings above 110 were thus reviewed by a corporate committee of vice presidents who evaluated the individual's contribution. Merit ratings varied widely from as low as 45 to as high as 160.

In determining an employee's merit rating, four factors were evaluated separately:

Dependability.
Quality.
Output.
Ideas and cooperation.

Foremen were responsible for the rating of all factory workers. They could request help from assistant foremen (dependability), the production control department (output), the inspection department (quality), and methods department (ideas and cooperation). In the office, supervisors rated their people on the same items. At least one executive reviewed all ratings. All employees were urged to discuss their ratings with their department heads if they were dissatisfied or unclear about them.

Lincoln complemented its rating and pay system with a guaranteed continuous employment plan. This plan provided security against lay-offs and assured continuity of employment. The plan guaranteed employment for at least 75 percent of the standard 40-hour week to every full-time employee with the company two or more years. In fact, the company had not had any lay-offs since 1951, when initial trials for the plan were put into effect. It was formally established in 1958.

This was seen by the company as an essential element in the incentive plan. Without it, it was believed that employees would be more likely to resist improved production and efficiency for fear of losing their jobs.

In accepting the guaranteed continuous employment plan, employees agreed to perform any job that was assigned as conditions required, and to work overtime during periods of high activity.

The philosophy and procedures regarding the incentive plan were the same for management and workers, except that Mr. Irrgang and Mr. Willis did not share in the bonus.

Employee Views

To the casewriter, it appeared that employees generally liked working at Lincoln. The employee turnover rate was far below that of most other companies, and once a new employee made it through the first month or so, he rarely left for another company (see Exhibit 5). One employee explained:

> It's like trying out for a high school football team. If you make it through the first few practices, you're usually going to stay the whole season, especially after the games start.

One long-time employee who liked working at Lincoln was John "Tiny" Carrillo, an armature bander on the welding machine line, who had been with the company for 24 years. "Tiny" explained why:

> The thing I like here is that you're pretty much your own boss as long as you do your job. You're responsible for your own work and you even put your stencil on every machine you work on. That way if it breaks down in the field and they have to take it back, they know who's responsible.
>
> Before I came here, I worked at Cadillac as a welder. After two months there I had the top hourly rate. I wasn't allowed to tell anyone because there were guys who still had the starting rate after a year. But, I couldn't go any higher after two months.
>
> I've done well. My rating is usually around 110, but I work hard, right through the smoke breaks. The only time I stop is a half hour for lunch. I make good money. I have two houses, one which I rent out, and four cars. They're all paid for. When I get my bills, I pay them the next day. That's the main thing, I don't owe anyone.
>
> Sure, there are problems. There's sometimes a bind between the guys with low grades and the guys with high ones, like in school. And there are guys who sway everything their way so they'll get the points, but they [management] have good tabs on what's going on. . . .
>
> A lot of new guys come in and leave right away. Most of them are just "mamma's boys" and don't want to do the work. We had a new guy who was a produce manager at a supermarket. He worked a couple of weeks, then quit and went back to his old job.

At the end of the interview, the casewriter thanked "Tiny" for his time. He responded by pointing out that it had cost him $7 in lost time, but that he was glad to be of assistance.

EXHIBIT 5

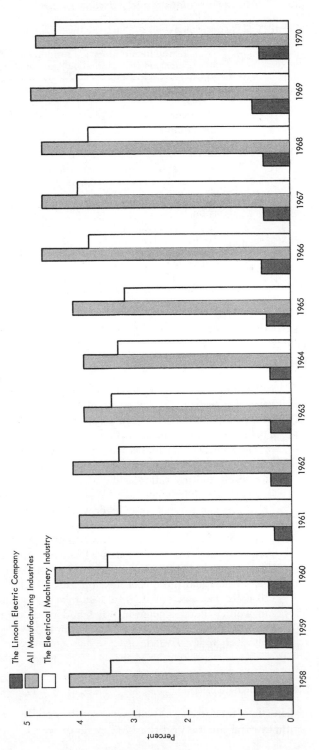

THE LINCOLN ELECTRIC COMPANY

Labor Turnover Rates and Employee's Years of Service

Labor Turnover Rates (total separations)
The Lincoln Electric Company, All Manufacturing Industries, and the
Electrical Machinery, 1958–70
(monthly rate)

EXHIBIT 5 *(continued)*

The Lincoln Electric Company—1975
Employee Distribution by Years of Service

Employees Years of Service	Number of Employees
Less than 1	153
1	311
2	201
3	93
4	34
5	90
6–10	545
11–20	439
21–30	274
31–40	197
41–50	27
51 or more	1
Total	2,365

Another piece worker, Jorge Espinoza, a fine-wire operator in the Electrode division, had been with the company for six years. He explained his feelings:

> I believe in being my own man. I want to use my drive for my own gain. It's worked. I built my family a house and have an acre of land, with a low mortgage. I have a car and an old truck I play around with. The money I get is because I earn it. I don't want anything given to me.
>
> The thing I don't like is having to depend on other people on the line and suppliers. We're getting bad steel occasionally. Our output is down as a result and my rating will suffer.
>
> There are men who have great drive here and can push for a job. They are not leaders and never will be, but they move up. That's a problem. . . .
>
> The first few times around, the ratings were painful for me. But now I stick near 100. You really make what you want. We just had a methods change and our base rate went from 83 to 89 coils a day. The job is tougher now and more complex. But, it's all what you want. If you want 110 coils you can get it. You just take less breaks. Today, I gambled and won. I didn't change my dies and made over a hundred coils. If I had lost, and the die plugged up, it would have cost me at least half an hour. But, today I made it.

Management Style

Lincoln's incentive scheme was reinforced by top management's attitude toward the men on the factory floor. In 1951, James Lincoln wrote:

It becomes perfectly true to anyone who will think this thing through that there is no such thing in an industrial activity as Management and Men having different functions or being two different kinds of people. Why can't we think and why don't we think that all people are Management? Can you imagine any president of any factory or machine shop who can go down and manage a turret lathe as well as the machinist can? Can you imagine any manager of any organization who can go down and manage a broom—let us get down to that—who can manage a broom as well as a sweeper can? Can you imagine any secretary of any company who can go down and fire a furnace and manage that boiler as well as the man who does the job? Obviously, all are Management.[6]

Lincoln's President George Willis stressed the equality in the company:

We try to avoid barriers between management and workers. We're treated equally as much as possible. When I got to work this morning at 7:30, the parking lot was three-quarters full. I parked way out there like anyone else would. I don't have a special reserved spot. The same principle holds true in our cafeteria. There's no executive dining room. We eat with everyone else.[7]

Mr. Willis felt that open and frank communication between management and workers had been a critical factor in Lincoln's success, and he believed that the company's advisory board had played a very important role in achieving this.

An advisory board of elected employee representatives had been established by James F. Lincoln in 1914. It had met twice a month ever since then. The advisory board provided a forum for employees to bring issues of concern to top management's attention, to question company policies, and to make suggestions for their improvement. As described in the *Employee's Handbook:*

Board service is a privilege and responsibility of importance to the entire organization. In discussions or in reaching decisions Board members must be guided by the best interests of the Company. These also serve the best interests of its workers. They should seek at all times to improve the cooperative attitude of all workers and see that all realize they have an important part in our final results.

All advisory board meetings were chaired by either the chairman or president of Lincoln. Usually, both were present. Issues brought up at board meetings were either resolved on the spot or assigned to an executive to be answered by the next meeting. After each meeting, Mr.

---

[6] James F. Lincoln, *What Makes Workers Work?* (Cleveland, Ohio: The Lincoln Electric Company, 1951), pp. 3–4.

[7] The cafeteria had large rectangular and round tables. In general, factory workers gravitated toward the rectangular tables. There were no strict rules, however, and management personnel often sat with factory workers. Toward the center was a square table that seated only four. This was reserved for Mr. Irrgang, Mr. Willis, and their guests when they were having a working lunch.

Irrgang or Mr. Willis would send a memo to the responsible executive for each unanswered question, no matter how trivial, and he was expected to respond by the next meeting, if possible.

Minutes of all board meetings were posted on bulletin boards in each department, and members explained the board's actions to the other workers in their department.

The questions raised in the minutes of a given meeting were usually answered in the next set of minutes. This procedure had not changed significantly since the first meeting in 1914, nor had the types of issues raised changed significantly since then (see Exhibit 6).

EXHIBIT 6

Management Advisory Board Minutes—1944
September 26, 1944

———

Absent: William Dillmuth

A discussion on piecework was again taken up. There was enough detail so it was thought best to appoint a committee to study it and bring a report into the meeting when that study is complete. That committee is composed of Messrs. Gilletly, Semko, Kneen and Steingass. Messrs. Erickson and White will be called in consultation, and the group will meet next Wednesday, October 4th.

The request was made that the members be permitted to bring guests to the meetings. The request was granted. Let's make sure we don't get too many at one time.

The point was made that materials are not being brought to the operation properly and promptly. There is no doubt of this difficulty. The matter was referred to Mr. Kneen for action. It is to be noted that conditions of deliveries from our suppliers have introduced a tremendous problem which has helped to increase this difficulty.

The request was made that over-time penalty be paid with the straight time. This will be done. There are some administrative difficulties which we will discuss at the next meeting but the over-time payment will start with the first pay in October.

Beginning October 1st employees' badges will be discontinued. Please turn them in to the watchmen.

It was requested that piecework prices be put on repair work in Dept. J. This matter was referred to Mr. Kneen for action.

A request was made that a plaque showing the names of those who died in action, separate from the present plaques, be put in the lobby. This was referred to Mr. Davis for action.

The question was asked as to what method for upgrading men is used. The ability of the individual is the sole reason for his progress. It was felt this is proper.

J. F. Lincoln
President

EXHIBIT 6 (continued)

Management Advisory Board Minutes—1974
(excerpts)

September 23, 1974

Members absent: Tom Borkowski
Albert Sinn

Mr. Kupetz had asked about the Christmas and Thanksgiving schedules. These are being reviewed and we will have them available at the next meeting.

Mr. Howell had reported that the time clocks and the bells do not coincide. This is still being checked.

Mr. Sharpe had asked what the possibility would be to have a time clock installed in or near the Clean Room. This is being checked.

Mr. Joosten had raised the question of the pliability of the wrapping material used in the Chemical Department for wrapping slugs. The material we use at the present time is the best we can obtain at this time . . .

Mr. Kostelac asked the question again whether the vacation arrangements could be changed, reducing the fifteen year period to some shorter period. It was pointed out that at the present time, where we have radically changing conditions every day, it is not the time to go into this. We will review this matter at some later date . . .

Mr. Martucci brought out the fact that there was considerable objection by the people involved to having to work on Saturday night to make up for holiday shutdowns. This was referred to Mr. Willis to be taken into consideration in schedule planning . . .

Mr. Joosten reported that in the Chemical Department on the Saturday midnight shift they have a setup where individuals do not have sufficient work so that it is an uneconomical situation. This has been referred to Mr. Willis to be reviewed.

Mr. Joosten asked whether there would be some way to get chest x-rays for people who work in dusty areas. Mr. Loughridge was asked to check a schedule of where chest x-rays are available at various times . . .

Mr. Robinson asked what the procedure is for merit raises. The procedure is that the foreman recommends the individual for a merit raise if by his performance he has shown that he merits the increase . . .

William Irrgang
Chairman

William Irrgang:MW
September 25, 1974

Workers felt that the advisory board provided a way of getting immediate attention for their problems. It was clear, however, that management still made the final decisions.[8] A former member of the advisory board commented:

> There are certain areas which are brought up in the meetings which Mr. Irrgang doesn't want to get into. He's adept at steering the conversation away from these. It's definitely not a negotiating meeting. But, generally, you really get action or an answer on why action isn't being taken.

In addition to the advisory board, there was a 12-member board of middle managers which met with Mr. Irrgang and Mr. Willis once a month. The topics of discussion were broader than those of the advisory board. The primary function of these meetings were for top management to get better acquainted with these individuals and to encourage cooperation between departments.

Lincoln's two top executives, Mr. Irrgang and Mr. Willis, continued the practice of James F. Lincoln in maintaining an open door to all employees. George Willis estimated that at least twice a week factory employees took advantage of this opportunity to talk with him.

Middle managers also felt that communication with Mr. Willis and Mr. Irrgang was open and direct. Often it bypassed intermediate levels of the organization. Most saw this as an advantage but one commented:

> This company is run strictly by the two men at the top. Mr. Lincoln trained Mr. Irrgang in his image. It's very authoritarian and decisions flow top down. It never became a big company. There is very little delegated and top people are making too many small decisions. Mr. Irrgang and Mr. Willis work 80 hours a week, and no one I know in this company can say that his boss doesn't work harder than he does.

Mr. Willis saw management's concern for the worker as an essential ingredient in his company's formula for success. He knew at least 500 employees personally. In leading the casewriter through the plant, he greeted workers by name and paused several times to tell anecdotes about many of them.

At one point, an older man yelled to Mr. Willis, good-naturedly, "Where's my raise?" Mr. Willis explained that this man had worked for 40 years in a job requiring him to lift up to 20 tons of material a day. His earnings had been quite high because of his rapid work pace, but Mr. Willis had been afraid that as he was advancing in age he could injure himself working in that job. After months of Mr. Willis's urging, the man switched to an easier but lower paying job. He was disappointed

---

[8] In some cases, management allowed issues to be decided by a vote of employees. A recent example was when employees voted down a proposal to give them dental benefits paid by the company, recognizing that it would come directly out of their bonus.

in taking the earnings cut, and even after several years let the president know whenever he saw him.

Mr. Willis pointed to another employee and explained that this man's wife had recently died and for several weeks he had been drinking heavily and reporting to work late. Mr. Willis had earlier spent about half an hour discussing the situation with him to console him and see if the company could help in any way. He explained:

> I made a definite point of talking to him on the floor of the plant, near his work station. I wanted to make sure that other employees who knew the situation could see me with him. Speaking to him had symbolic value. It is important for employees to know that the president is interested in their welfare.

Management's philosophy was also reflected in the company's physical facilities. A no-nonsense atmosphere was firmly established at the gate to the parking lot where the only mention of the company name was in a sign reading:

> $1,000 REWARD for information leading to the arrest and conviction of persons stealing from the Lincoln Electric parking lot.

There was a single entrance to the offices and plant for workers, management, and visitors. As one entered, the company motto in large stainless steel letters extending 30 feet across the wall was unavoidable:

THE ACTUAL IS LIMITED
THE POSSIBLE IS IMMENSE

A flight of stairs led down to a tunnel system for pedestrian traffic that ran under the single story plant. At the base of the stairs was a large bronze plaque on which were permanently inscribed the names of the eight employees who had served more than 50 years, and the more than 350 active employees with 25 or more years of service who were in the "Quarter Century Club."

The long tunnel under the plant that led to the offices was clean and well-lit. The executive offices were located in a windowless, two-story cement block office building, which sat like a box in the center of the plant. At the base of the staircase leading up to the offices, a Lincoln automatic welding machine and portraits of J. C. Lincoln and J. F. Lincoln welcomed visitors. The handrail on the staircase was welded into place, as were the ash trays in the tunnel.

In the center of the office building was a simple, undecorated reception room. A switchboard operator/receptionist greeted visitors, between filing and phone calls. The reception room reflected the spartan decor that was evident throughout the building. It was furnished with a metal coat rack, a wooden bookcase, and several plain wooden tables and chairs. All of the available reading material dealt with Lincoln Electric Company or welding.

One could leave the reception room through any of seven doors, which would lead almost directly to the desired office or department. Most of the departments were large open rooms with closely spaced desks. One manager explained that "Mr. Lincoln didn't believe in walls. He felt they interrupted the flow of communications and paperwork." Most of the desks and files were plain, old, and well-worn, and there was a scarcity of modern office equipment. One reason for this was that the same criteria were applied for expenditures on equipment in the office as in the plant. The maintenance department had to certify that the equipment replaced could not be repaired. If acquired for cost reduction, the equipment had to have a one-year payback.[9]

The usually omnipresent Xerox machines were nowhere to be found. The explanation was that copying costs were tightly controlled and only certain individuals could use the Xerox copiers. Customer order forms, for example, which required eight copies, were run on a duplicating machine.

The private offices that existed were small, uncarpeted, and separated by green metal partitions. The president's office was slightly larger than the others, but still retained a spartan appearance. There was only one carpeted office. Mr. Willis explained:

> That office was occupied by Mr. Lincoln until he died in 1965. For the next five years it was left vacant and now it is Mr. Irrgang's office and also the Board of Directors' and Advisory Board meeting room.

Personnel

Lincoln Electric had a strict policy of filling all but entry level positions by promoting from within the company. Whenever an opening occurred, a notice was posted on the 25 bulletin boards in the plant and offices. Any interested employee could apply for an open position. Because of the company's sustained growth and policy of hiring outsiders for entry level jobs only, employees had substantial opportunity for advancement.

An outsider generally could join the company in one of two ways: either taking a factory job working at an hourly or piece rate, or entering Lincoln's training programs in sales or engineering.[10] The company recruited their trainees at colleges and graduate schools, including Harvard

---

[9] Mr. Willis explained that capital projects with paybacks of up to two years were sometimes funded when they involved a product for which demand was growing.

[10] Lincoln's president and chairman both advanced through the ranks in manufacturing. Mr. Irrgang began as a pieceworker in the armature winding department, and Mr. Willis began in plant engineering. (See Exhibit 7 for employment history of Lincoln's top management.)

Business School. Starting salary in 1975 for a trainee with a bachelor's degree was $5.50 an hour, plus a year-end bonus, at an average of 40 percent of the normal rate. Wages for trainees with either a master's degree or several years of relevant experience was 5 percent higher.

Although Lincoln's president, vice president of sales, and personnel director were all Harvard Business School graduates, the company had

EXHIBIT 7

THE LINCOLN ELECTRIC COMPANY
Employment History of Top Executives

Mr. William Irrgang—Board Chairman

1929—Hired, Repair Dept.
1930 Final Inspection
1934 Inspection, Wire Dept.
1946 Director of Factory Engineering
1951 Executive Vice President for
      Manufacturing and Engineering
1954 President and General Manager
1972 Chairman of the Board of Directors

Mr. George E. Willis—President

1947—Hired, Factory Engineering
1951 Superintendent—Electrode
      Division
1959 Vice President
1969 Executive Vice President of Manu-
      facturing and Associated
      Functions
1972 President

Mr. William Miskoe—Vice President—
International

1932—Hired, Chicago Sales Office
1941 President of Australian Plant
1969 To Cleveland as Vice President—
      International

Mr. Edwin M. Miller—Vice President and
Assistant to the President

1923—Hired, Factory Worker
1925 Assistant Foreman
1929 Production Dept.
1940 Assistant Dept. Head—Production
      Dept.
1952 Superintendent—Machine Division
1959 Vice President
1973 Vice President and Assistant to the
      President

Mr. D. Neal Manross—Vice President—
Machine and Motor divisions

1941—Hired, Factory Worker
1942 Welding Inspector
1952 General Foreman, Extruding Dept.,
      and Asst. Plant Superintendent
1953 Foreman—Special Products Dept.,
      Machine Div.
1956 Superintendent—Special Products
      Division
1959 Superintendent—Motor
      Manufacturing
1966 Vice President—Motor Division
1973 Vice President in Charge of Motor
      and Machine Divisions

Mr. Albert S. Patnik—Vice President of
Sales Development

1940—Hired, Sales Student
1940 New London, Conn., as Welder
1941 Los Angeles Office as Junior
      Salesman
1942 Seattle Office as Salesman
1945 To Military Service
1945 Reinstated to Seattle
1951 Cleveland Sales Office as Rural
      Dealer Mgr.
1964 Asst. to the Vice President of Sales
1972 Vice President

Mr. Donald F. Hastings—Vice President and
General Sales Manager

1953—Hired, Sales Trainee
1954 Emeryville, Cal., as Welding
      Engineer
1959 District Manager—Moline Office
1970 To Cleveland as General Sales
      Manager
1972 Vice Pesident and General Sales
      Manager

not hired many recent graduates. Clyde Loughridge, the personnel director, explained:

> We don't offer them fancy staff positions and we don't pretend to. Our starting pay is less than average, probably $17,000–$18,000 including bonus, and the work is harder than average. We start our trainees off by putting them in overalls and they spend up to seven weeks in the welding school. In a lot of ways it's like boot camp. Rather than leading them along by the hand, we like to let the self-starters show themselves.

The policy of promoting from within had rarely been violated, and then only in cases where a specialized skill was required. Mr. Loughridge commented:

> In most cases we've been able to stick to it, even where the required skills are entirely new to the company. Our employees have a lot of varied skills, and usually someone can fit the job. For example, when we recently got our first computer, we needed a programmer and systems analyst. We had 20 employees apply who had experience or training in computers. We chose two, and it really helps that they know the company and understand our business.

The company did not send its employees to outside management development programs, and did not provide tuition grants for educational purposes.

Lincoln Electric had no formal organization chart, and management did not feel that one was necessary (Exhibit 8 shows a chart drawn for the purpose of this case.)

As explained by one executive:

> People retire and their jobs are parcelled out. We are very successful in overloading our overhead departments. We make sure this way that no unnecessary work is done and jobs which are not absolutely essential are eliminated. A disadvantage is that planning may suffer as may outside development to keep up with your field.

Lincoln's organizational hierarchy was flat, with few levels between the bottom and the top. For example, Don Hastings, the vice president of sales, had 37 regional sales managers reporting to him. He commented:

> I have to work hard, there's no question about that. There are only four of us in the home office plus two secretaries. I could easily use three more people. I work every Saturday, at least half a day. Most of our regional men do too, and they like me to know it. You should see the switchboard light up when 37 regional managers call in at five minutes to twelve on Saturday.

The president and chairman kept a tight rein over personnel matters. All changes in status of employees, even at the lowest level, had to be

EXHIBIT 8

THE LINCOLN ELECTRIC COMPANY
Organization Chart

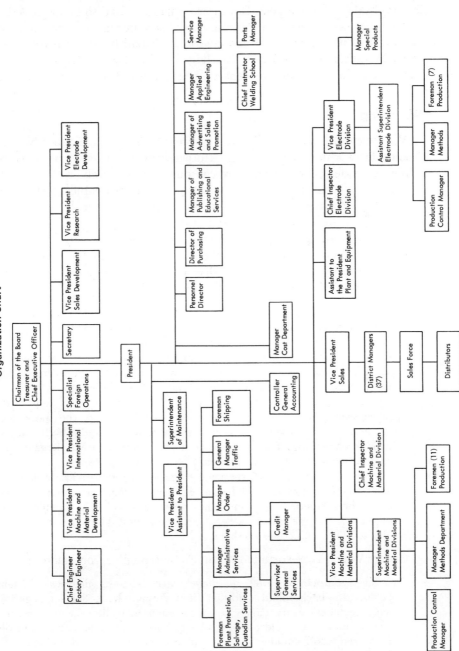

approved by Mr. Willis. Mr. Irrgang also had to give his approval if they involved salaried employees. Raises or promotions had to be approved in advance. An employee could be fired by his supervisor on the spot for cause, but if it was on questionable grounds it had to be approved afterward by either Mr. Willis or Mr. Irrgang. Usually the supervisor was supported, but there had been cases where a firing decision was reversed.

Marketing

Welding machines and electrodes were like "razors and razor blades." A Lincoln welding machine often had a useful life of 30 years or more, while electrodes (and fluxes) were consumed immediately in the welding process. The ratio of machine cost to annual consumables cost varied widely from perhaps 7:1 for a hand welder used in a small shop to 1:5 or more for an automatic welder used in a shipyard.

Although certain competitors might meet their costs and quality in selected products, management believed that no company could match Lincoln on their whole line. Another important competitive edge for Lincoln was its sales force. Al Patnik, vice president of sales development, explained:

> Most competitors operate through distributors. We have our own top field sales force.[11] We start out with engineering graduates and put them through our seven-month training program. They learn how to weld, and we teach them everything we can about equipment, metallurgy, and design. Then they spend time on the rebuild line [where machines brought in from the field are rebuilt] and even spend time in the office seeing how orders are processed. Finally, before the trainees go out into the field, they have to go into our plant and find a better way of making something. Then they make a presentation to Mr. Irrgang, just as if he were one of our customers.
>
> Our approach to the customer is to go in and learn what he is doing and show him how to do it better. For many companies our people become their experts in welding. They go in and talk to a foreman. They might say "let me put on a headshield and show you what I'm talking about." That's how we sell them.

George Ward, a salesman in the San Francisco office, commented:

> The competition hires graduates with business degrees (without engineering background) and that's how they get hurt. This job is getting more technical every day. . . . A customer in California who is using our equipment to weld offshore oil rigs had a problem with one of our new products. I couldn't get the solution for them over the phone, so I flew in to the plant Monday morning and showed it to our engineers.

---

[11] The sales force was supplemented in some areas by distributors. Sales abroad were handled by wholly owned subsidiaries or Armco's International Division.

Mr. Willis said to me, "Don't go back to California until this problem is solved. . . ." We use a "working together to solve your problem" approach. This, plus sticking to published prices, shows you're not interested in taking advantage of them.

I had a boss who used to say: "Once we're in, Lincoln never loses a customer except on delivery." It's basically true. The orders I lost last year were because we couldn't deliver fast enough. Lincoln gets hurt when there are shortages because of our guaranteed employment. We don't hire short-term factory workers when sales take off, and other companies beat us on delivery.

The sales force was paid a salary plus bonus. Mr. Ward believed that Lincoln's sales force was the best paid and hardest working in the industry:

We're aggressive, and want to work and get paid for it. The sales force prides itself on working more hours than anyone else. . . . My wife wonders sometimes if you can work for Lincoln and have a family, too.

Manufacturing

Lincoln's plant was unusual in several respects. The casewriter was struck by how crowded with materials and equipment it was, and how few workers there were. It was obvious that employees worked very fast and efficiently with few breaks. Even during the ten minute "smoke breaks" in the morning and afternoon employees often continued to work.

An innovative plant layout was partly responsible for the crowded appearance. Raw materials entered one side of the plant and finished goods came out the other side. There was no central stockroom for materials or work-in-process. Instead, everything that entered the plant was transported directly to the work station where it would be used. At a work station, a single worker or group operated, in effect, as a "subcontractor." All required materials were piled around the station, allowing visual inventory control, and they were paid a piece "price" for their production. Wherever possible, the work flow followed a straight line through the plant from the side where raw materials entered to the side where finished goods exited. Because there was no union, the company had great flexibility with what could be performed at a work station. For example, foundry work and metal stamping could be carried out together by the same workers when necessary. Thus, work could flow almost directly along a line through the plant. Intermediate material handling was avoided to a great extent. The major exception was where a large or expensive piece of machinery was used by multiple production lines, and the work had to be brought to the machines.

Many of the operations in the plant were automated. Much of the manufacturing equipment was proprietary,[12] designed and built by Lincoln. In some cases, the company had modified machines built by others to run two or three times as fast as when originally delivered.

Close coordination between product design engineers and the methods department from the time a product was originally conceptualized was seen as a key factor in reducing costs and rationalizing manufacturing. William Irrgang explained:

> After we have [an] idea . . . we start thinking about manufacturing costs, before anything leaves the design engineering department. At that point, there is a complete "getting together" of manufacturing and design engineers—and plant engineers, too, if new equipment is involved.
>
> Our tooling, for instance, is going to be looked at carefully while the design of a product is still in process. Obviously, we can increase or decrease the tooling very materially by certain considerations in the design of a product, and we go on the basis of total costs at all times. In fact, as far as total cost is concerned, we even think about such matters as shipping, warehousing, etc. All of these factors are taken into consideration when we're still at the design stage. It's very essential that this be done: otherwise, you can lock yourself out from a lot of potential economies.[13]

In 1974, Lincoln's plant had reached full capacity, operating nearly around the clock. Land bordering its present location was unavailable and management was moving ahead with plans to build a second plant 15 miles away on the same freeway as the present plant.

Over the years, Lincoln had slowly back-integrated by "making" rather than "buying" a larger percentage of their components. For example, even though their unit volume of gasoline engines was only a fraction of their suppliers', Lincoln purchased engine blocks and components and assembled them, rather than purchasing completed engines. Management was continually evaluating opportunities to back integrate and had not arbitrarily ruled out manufacturing any of their components or raw materials.

Administrative Productivity

Lincoln's high productivity was not limited to manufacturing. Clyde Loughridge pointed to the personnel department as an example:

> Normally, for 2,300 employees you would need a personnel department of about 20, but we have only six, and that includes the nurse, and our responsibilities go beyond those of the typical personnel department.

---

[12] Visitors were barred from the electrode division unless they had a pass signed by Mr. Willis or Mr. Irrgang.

[13] "Incentive Management in Action," *Assembly Engineering*, March 1967.

Once a year, Mr. Loughridge had to outline his objectives for the up-coming year for Mr. Willis, but he did not operate on a budget.

> I don't get a budget. There would be no point to it. I just spend as little as possible. I operate this just like my home. I don't spend on anything I don't need.

In the traffic department, workers also seemed very busy. There, a staff of 12 controlled the shipment of 2½ million pounds of material a day. Their task was complex. Delivery was included in the price of their products. They thus could reduce the overall cost to the customer by mixing products in most loads and shipping the most efficient way possible to the company's 39 warehouses. Jim Biek, general traffic manager, explained how they accomplished this:

> For every order, we decide whether it would be cheaper by rail or truck. Then we consolidate orders so that over 90 percent of what goes out of here is full carload or full truckload, as compared to perhaps 50 percent for most companies. We also mix products so that we come in at the top of the weight brackets. For example, if a rate is for 20,000 to 40,000 pounds, we will mix orders to bring the weight right up to that 40,000 limit. All this is computed manually. In fact, my old boss used to say, "We run traffic like a ma and pa grocery store."

As in the rest of Lincoln, the employees in the traffic department worked their way up from entry level positions. Jim Biek had come into his position of general traffic manager after nine years as a purchasing engineer. He had received an MBA degree from Northwestern, after a BS in mechanical engineering from Purdue, started in the engineering training program, and then spent five years in product development and methods before going to purchasing and finally to traffic. Lack of experience in traffic was a disadvantage, but the policy of promoting from within also had its advantages. Mr. Biek explained:

> One of my first tasks was to go to Washington and fight to get welders reclassified as motors to qualify for a lower freight rate. With my engineering experience and knowledge of welders, I was in a better position to argue this than a straight traffic man . . .
>
> Just about everybody in here was new to traffic. One of my assistant traffic managers had worked on the loading platform here for ten years before he came into the department. He had to go to night school to learn about rates, but his experience is invaluable. He knows how to load trucks and rail cars backwards and forward. Who could do a better job of consolidating orders than he does? He can look at an order and think of it as rows of pallets.
>
> Some day we'll outgrow this way of operating, but right now I can't imagine a computer juggling loads like some of our employees do.

Lincoln's order department had recently begun computerizing its operations. It was the first time a computer was used anywhere in Lincoln except in engineering and research, and according to Russell Stauffer, head of the order department, "It was a three-year job for me to sell this to top management."

The computer was expected to replace 12 or 13 employees who would gradually be moved into new jobs. There had been some resistance to the computer, according to Mr. Stauffer.

> It's like anything new. People get scared. Not all the people affected have been here for the two years required to be eligible for guaranteed employment. And even though the others are assured a job, they don't know what it will be and will have to take what's offered.

The computer was expected to produce savings of $100,000 a year, plus allow a greater degree of control. Mr. Stauffer explained:

> We're getting information out of this that we never knew before. The job here is very complex. We're sending out more than two million pounds of consumables a day. Each order might have 30 or 40 items, and each item has a bracket price arrangement based on total order size. A clerk has to remember or determine quickly whether we are out of stock on any items and calculate whether the stock-out brings the order down into another bracket. This means they have to "remember" the prices and items out of stock. This way of operating was okay up to about $200 million in sales, but now we've outgrown the human capability to handle the problem.

Although he had no previous experience in computers, Mr. Stauffer had full responsibility for the conversion.

> I've been here for 35 years. The first day I started, I unloaded coal cars and painted fences. Then I went to the assembly line, first on small parts, then large ones. I've been running the order department for 12 years. Since I've been here, we've had studies on computers every year or two and it always came out that we couldn't save money. Finally, when it looked like we'd make the switch, I took some courses at IBM. Over the last year and a half, they've totaled eight and a half weeks, which is supposed to equal a full semester of college.

To date, the conversion had gone well, but much slower than anticipated. Order pressure had been so high that many mistakes would have been catastrophic. Management pressure, therefore, had been to assure 100 percent quality operation rather than faster conversion.

Lincoln's Future

The 1947 Harvard Business School case study of Lincoln Electric ended with a prediction by a union leader from the Cleveland area:

The real test of Lincoln will come when the going gets tough. The thing Lincoln holds out to the men is high earnings. They work like dogs at Lincoln, but it pays off . . .

I think [Mr. Lincoln] puts too much store by monetary incentives—but then, there's no denying he has attracted people who respond to that type of incentive. But I think that very thing is a danger Lincoln faces. If the day comes when they can't offer those big bonuses, or his people decide there's more to life than killing yourself making money, I predict the Lincoln Electric Company is in for trouble.

Lincoln President George Willis joined the company the year that the above comment was made. Reflecting on his 28 years with the company Mr. Willis observed:

The company hasn't changed very much since I've been here. It's still run pretty much like Mr. Lincoln ran it. But today's workers are different. They're more outspoken and interested in why things are being done, not just how. We have nothing to hide and never did, so we can give them the answers to their questions.

Looking forward, Mr. Willis saw no need to alter Lincoln's strategy or its policies:

My job will continue to be to have everyone in the organization recognize that a common goal all of us can and must support is to give the customer the quality he needs, when he needs it, at the lowest cost. To do this, we have to have everyone's understanding of this goal and their effort to accomplish it. In one way or another, I have to motivate the organization to meet this goal. The basic forms of the motivation have evolved over the last 40 years. However, keeping the system honed so that everyone understands it, agrees with it, and brings out disagreements so improvements can be made or thinking changed becomes my major responsibility.

If our employees did not believe that management was trustworthy, honest and impartial, the system could not operate. We've worked out the mechanics. They are not secret. A good part of my responsibility is to make sure the mechanics are followed. This ties back to a trust and understanding between individuals at all levels of the organization.

I don't see any real limits to our size. Look at a world with a present population of just under four billion now and six and a quarter billion by the year 2000. Those people aren't going to tolerate a low standard of living. So there will be a lot of construction, cars, bridges, oil, and all these things that have got to be to support a population that large.

My job will still be just the traditional things of assuring that we keep up with the technology and have sufficient profit to pay the suppliers of capital. Then, I have to make sure communication can be maintained adequately. That last task may be the biggest and most important part of my job in the years ahead as we grow larger and still more complex.

EXHIBIT 9

THE LINCOLN ELECTRIC COMPANY

After reading the completed case study, Mr. Richard S. Sabo, manager of publicity and educational services, sent the following letter to the casewriter:

July 31, 1975

TO: Mr. Norman Fast

Dear Mr. Fast:

I believe that you have summarized the Incentive Management System of The Lincoln Electric Company very well; however, readers may feel that the success of the Company is due only to the psychological principles included in your presentation.

Please consider adding the efforts of our executives who devote a great deal of time to the following items that are so important to the consistent profit and long range growth of the Company.

I. Management has limited research, development and manufacturing to a standard product line designed to meet the major needs of the welding industry.

II. New products must be reviewed by manufacturing and all production costs verified before being approved by management.

III. Purchasing is challenged to not only procure materials at the lowest cost, but also to work closely with engineering and manufacturing to assure that the latest innovations are implemented.

IV. Manufacturing supervision and all personnel are held accountable for reduction of scrap, energy conservation and maintenance of product quality.

V. Production control, material handling and methods engineering are closely supervised by top management.

VI. Material and finished goods inventory control, accurate cost accounting and attention to sales costs, credit and other financial areas have constantly reduced overhead and led to excellent profitability.

VII. Management has made cost reduction a way of life at Lincoln and definite programs are established in many areas, including traffic and shipping, where tremendous savings can result.

VIII. Management has established a sales department that is technically trained to reduce customer welding cost. This sales technique and other real cusomer services have eliminated nonessential frills and resulted in long term benefits to all concerned.

IX. Management has encouraged education, technical publishing and long range programs that have resulted in industry growth, thereby assuring market potential for The Lincoln Electric Company.

Richard S. Sabo

bjs

Section Four

Managing the Overall
Organization

1   *Kampgrounds of America, Inc.*

Late one evening in January of 1974, Mr. Darrell Booth, chief executive officer of Kampgrounds of America, Inc., was developing the agenda for the annual budget and planning session that he had scheduled with his management group for the following day. In reviewing the company's performance for 1973, he was concerned that franchise sales had fallen off sharply for the first time in company history, that the corporate annual growth-in-earnings objective of 20 percent had not been met, and that the KOA stock was trading at an all-time low of $3. He wondered whether the current energy crisis was primarily to blame or whether it was simply time to move the company in new directions. He felt that it was necessary, therefore, to spend a good portion of the planning session discussing long-term goals for KOA and, in light of those goals, to review the feasibility and progress of KOA's four relatively new activities: (1) merchandising, (2) company-owned campgrounds, (3) overnight lodging, and (4) fast food services.

Kampgrounds of America, Inc. (KOA) was engaged in the business of franchising and developing campgrounds and, through a subsidiary, in the business of manufacturing recreational vehicles (RVs). The company was incorporated in Montana in 1960, entered the campground franchising business in 1963, and acquired its RV subsidiary, Gardner, Inc., in April 1970. KOA and its franchises comprised the largest commercial campground system in North America in 1974, with 707 operating campgrounds located in 47 states, five Canadian provinces, and Mexico. (See Exhibit 1.)

THE CAMPING INDUSTRY

The camping industry in 1974 was defined in a broad sense to include four major segments: (1) public and private campground operations, (2) manufacturers and distributors of RVs, (3) recreation journal publishers, and (4) outdoor equipment manufacturers and suppliers. The primary focus of this case history is on the campground segment.

Industry Trends

Three factors were believed by industry officials to directly influence the level of consumer spending on camping activities: (1) discretionary spending power, (2) availability of leisure time, and (3) recreation preferences. Statistics provided by the U.S. Department of Commerce revealed that consumer expenditures on recreation as a percentage of funds available for discretionary spending rose from 14.0 percent to 16.4 percent over the 60s, and that even in recessionary periods, consumers appeared reluctant to pare expenditures on recreation. People found increasingly more time to spend on recreation, as the average work week declined over the period from 40.5 to 39.6 hours. In the early 70s, the U.S. Department of the Interior projected that camping would become one of the fastest growing outdoor activities of the decade due to its inexpensive nature, the "back-to-nature" movement, the rapid development of new campsites, and the rising interest in RV vacationing.

In 1974, there were approximately 45–50 million campers in the United States, with 10 million tents and 3.826 million RVs in use. Approximately 45 million tents were believed to be owned, and 1.5 million new tents were sold that year. From 1963–72, annual retail sales in RVs grew at a rate of 35 percent, reaching the $2.5 billion level in 1973. Recreation experts estimated that the camping industry (all sales of gear, RVs, and campground revenues) grew at least 500 percent during that period. They attributed the camping boom to the increasing desire of pleasure-seeking families to find a relatively inexpensive way to escape the pressures of everyday life as well as to the reaction of cost-conscious families to the rising hotel and motel rates for food and accommodations.

The dramatic growth in the camping industry resulted in the development of a variety of camping experiences to fit a diversity of needs. No longer was camping a sole means of demonstrating outdoor skills, self-reliance, and thrift. Rather, it had developed from a "fitness test" into a "social experience" requiring comfort and conveniences. Campgrounds had begun to sell the service of recreation in an environment conducive to social interaction, rather than to continue to sell cheap overnight accommodations. As public parks and forests became more and more crowded, private enterprise stepped in to take advantage of the overflow. Many commercial campgrounds offered planned activities, rental trailers

EXHIBIT 1

KAMPGROUNDS OF AMERICA, INC.
Campground Locations

and motel-type units, fast food operations, laundry services, winter RV storage, recreational facilities, year-round camping, and even condominium trailer lots for sale.

The Camper of the 70s

Campers covered a broad spectrum in definition, ranging from those who hiked in the wilderness with packs on their backs to those who vacationed in fancy motor homes in condominium resort camps. Within that range, campers fell into two general categories: RV campers and tenters.

RV campers often referred to themselves as "trailerites" who enjoyed "comfort or easy access auto camping." RV campers tended to prefer private campgrounds adjacent to major highways for overnight stays and public parks for destination stays. Their equipment was of two varieties: towed (camping trailer or travel trailer), or self-propelled (truck camper, pick-up cover, or motor home). The greatest concentration of RV owner/campers fell between the ages of 46 and 65 and belonged to camper clubs.

Tenters often referred to themselves as "lightweight gear campers," who enjoyed a "rough or remote wilderness camping experience." Their basic equipment consisted of a stove, pack, boots, tent, jacket, and sleeping bag. They relished privacy, were generally noncamper club members and preferred to camp in national parks or forests, which provided a more rustic out-of-doors experience than the commercial parks. Lightweight gear camping was common among all age groups, but was particularly popular among the young who could not afford to purchase RVs and who tended to be more caught up in the environmental movement than the older generation.

A survey of over 500 campers conducted in 1971 by the National Advertising Company, a subsidiary of the 3M Company, revealed the growing popularity of private campgrounds, semimodern or modern facilities, RV camping, and year-round camping. An average camping family reported 27.1 days of camping a year. The average trip covered 15.4 days, 6.7 campground locations, and 2,600 miles. The typical camping family averaged 4.1 persons and spent $17.18 in total per day, of which $2.00 represented the campsite fee. The household head was 45 years of age, had completed 13.3 years of schooling, and earned $12,000 a year.

Campgrounds

Camping families had the option of camping in public or in private parks. Statistics from the 3M NAC study showed that 40 percent of all campers preferred camping in state or national parks, 22 percent in state or national forests, 32 percent in private campgrounds, and the remaining 6 percent elsewhere. Despite the preferences for public facilities, campers were increasingly using private parks, which provided 66 percent of all campsites in the United States in 1973. Seventy-four percent of the private campsites, versus 19 percent of the public campsites, had electrical hookups; 61 percent versus 8 percent had water hookups; and 31 percent versus 3 percent had sewer hookups for RVs.[1] The average national occupancy factor for private campgrounds during the 1973 season was 35–40 percent, while it was 75–80 percent for public campgrounds.[2] Campground growth in the public and private sector from 1969–73 is shown in Table 1.

TABLE 1

U.S. Campground Statistics

	Private			Public			Total	
Year	Parks	Sites	Aver. No. Sites	Parks	Sites	Aver. No. Sites	Parks	Sites
1969.......	9,520	372,888	39.2	6,626	205,454	31.0	16,146	578,342
1970.......	9,267	425,616	45.9	6,928	230,395	33.3	16,195	656,011
1971.......	9,513	462,386	48.6	7,566	247,472	32.7	17,079	709,859
1972.......	8,665	534,085	61.6	6,613	285,975	43.2	15,278	820,058
1973.......	9,190	583,679	63.5	6,463	306,063	47.4	15,653	889,742

Source: Woodall Publishing Company.

There were two types of campgrounds: destination and overnight. *Destination campgrounds* were those that attracted visitors for their natural beauty, historical significance, or recreational facilities, where tourists tended to remain for an extended portion of their vacation. *Overnight campgrounds* were generally stop-over spots for cost-conscious families resisting high motel fees, or for families en route to destination parks. The overnight campgrounds offered little in the way of scenic beauty or recreational facilities. They were usually open fields outfitted with RV hookups and were located adjacent to major interstate highways. Public parks were considered destination campgrounds. Private parks were of both varieties.

Public Campgrounds. Public campgrounds were the havens for "campers" in the traditional sense of the word. Overcrowding in the public areas and the simultaneous move of the RV camper towards the use of private facilities resulted from (1) the move by environmentalists to preserve beauty in its natural state, (2) the opposition among government officials to commercialize the public areas to fit the convenience and comfort needs of the new breed of camper, and (3) the reluctance

---

[1] Statistics compiled by Woodall Publishing Company.

[2] Lee Oertle, "Campground Scene," *RV Dealer,* November 1973, pp. 220–226.

on the part of Congressional bodies to allocate enough funds to support operations to accommodate the camping boom.[3] While visitations in public parks increased, overnight stays were on the decline.

Private Campgrounds. The decline of government support for public campgrounds, coupled with the sharply rising interest in camping in the United States, led to an increasing need for private enterprise to provide recreational areas for campers. While independently owned ("unaffiliated") campgrounds preceded the camping boom in their development, franchised ("affiliated") campground systems appeared in the mid-60s as a result of the boom. Owners of the 8,000 unaffiliated campgrounds often found the competition rough against the affiliated campgrounds, which benefited from the established reputation of their franchise systems. The flurry of franchise sales prompted industry complaints against the franchise companies regarding (1) overselling of franchise territories in certain areas, (2) nondevelopment of many sold franchises, which lacked construction financing or zoning clearances, (3) misunderstandings between the franchisee and franchisor over corporate objectives and obligations to the franchisee, and (4) poor campground site selection, based upon improper market analysis of prospective camper usage.

Industry participants classified campground franchises as two types: "passive" and "active." *Passive franchises* were those which were owned by large motel/hotel chains or oil companies for whom each franchise manager worked. *Active franchises*, on the other hand, were those where each franchisee owned his particular franchise. Passive franchises tended to be destination campgrounds, often lavish and large. Active franchises tended to be overnight campgrounds, smaller and more numerous, and suited to the small-time entrepreneur.

In 1974, there were approximately 50 companies engaged in the franchised campgrounds business. Major affiliated companies are presented in Table 2.

KOA was the first, largest, and most successful of the "active franchise" companies. Its nearest active franchise competitors were Safari Campgrounds of America, Inc., Jellystone Campgrounds, Ltd., and Crazy Horse Campgrounds, Inc., which were all developed in the late 60s. Crazy Horse and Jellystone reportedly were having severe financial difficulties in 1973 due to the strain of having to support national promotions on a small economic base. Safari was reported to be undergoing a major management change. Each used a distinctive advertising theme: African (Safari), Crazy Horse (Crazy Horse), and Yogi Bear (Jellystone).

The primary "passive franchise" companies were Holiday Inns, Inc.,

---

[3] In 1973, Congress eliminated overnight camping fees at federally operated campgrounds, and designated a major portion of the national parks as "roadless wilderness areas."

TABLE 2

1974 Major Affiliated Companies

Company	No. Operating Campgrounds	Primary Location
KOA.........................	707	Heavy in all states; Mexico, Canada
Crazy Horse.................	86	28 states, scattered
Safari......................	75	36 states, heavy in the Midwest and Florida
Jellystone..................	32	Midwest, southern California, Florida
Holiday Inn.................	42	17 states, heavy in South, adjacent to motels and cities
Ramada Inn.................	18	South, adjacent to motels and cities

with its Trav-L-Parks and Ramada Inns, Inc., with its Camp Inns. Established in 1970, Holiday Inn Trav-L-Parks typified the big investors' concept of modern-day campgrounds. In contrast to KOA franchises, they were more luxurious, generally higher priced, situated only in proven metropolitan and resort areas, and catered to a more sophisticated RV owner. Trav-L-Parks averaged 100–500 campsites apiece at an investment of $2,000 per site. Established in 1972, the Ramada Camp Inns were extremely similar in concept and size to the Trav-L-Parks. Camper night registration fees averaged between $4–$6 at the Ramada Camp Inns and $3.50–$9.00 at the Holiday Inn Trav-L-Parks.

The 1973–74 Energy Crisis

The gasoline shortage and tight money situation put the brakes on the feverish development of campground facilities across the United States in 1973. Campground owners began to respond by cutting rates and stepping up promotional efforts to offset a drop in business. Rand McNally & Company reported that it listed only 110 new facilities in its *1974 Campground and Trailer Park Guide* over its 1973 listings. Between 1960 and 1973, the guide listed an average of 1,000 new campgrounds each year.

Campgrounds began feeling the pinch in the summer of 1973. Many reported a decrease in visits of 10–20 percent where, in the past, visits had been increasing an average of 5 percent a year. Unit shipments of RVs dropped by 3 percent in 1973, compared with an increase of 36 percent in 1972. RV manufacturers, dealers, and campground operators were adopting the slogan: "Save energy. Turn off your house. Turn to RVacationing." The RV Institute launched a "50/50" campaign to encourage RV users to discover places to camp closer to home, driving at 50 mph for 50 miles. Several franchised campground firms began to build parks closer to metropolitan areas, using the slogan: "If you don't have gas to get to the mountain, we'll bring the mountain to you." RV manufacturers began to diversify by producing minibuses; others added larger gas tanks to their RVs.

KAMPGROUNDS OF AMERICA, INC.

Company History

In an interview with the case researcher, Mr. Darrell Booth, chief executive officer of KOA and former director of the chamber of commerce in Billings, Montana, described the founding and evolution of the company:

> In 1961 there was considerable pressure on the city of Billings to build a public campground for the many travelers passing through en route to the Seattle World's Fair and Rocky Mountain vacation spots. The City Council was reluctant to do so for two reasons: (1) it would be competing with local hotels and motels, and (2) local taxpayers would not look favorably upon building a public campground on city land. Three Billings businessmen of diverse backgrounds and interests believed the need could be met more effectively by private enterprise, so they undertook the construction of a privately owned campground. A fourth man joined them a year later and from there, because of limited resources and the makeup of the principals who were marketers and promoters, the idea of developing a franchised campground system got nurtured.
>
> The KOA founders were busy with their own interests so they asked me to join KOA in 1966 as executive vice president and general manager. I was everything then, although Dave Drum whose orientation was creativeness and promotion had a great deal of influence on the development of the company as he became the central figure in the group.
>
> Our objective in 1966 was to get a deep penetration of what we felt was a captive market—the American camping family, particularly RV owners—and to create a system of clean, sensible campgrounds. We wanted to spread-eagle the country along the highways with campgrounds as fast as we could.[4] We put our efforts into marketing and promotion to the consumer and into selling franchises. We felt that the technical aspects of managing the operating campgrounds were minimal at the time, and the important thing was to make franchises as successful as we could by providing safe, clean, comfortable accommodations. We placed lesser emphasis on the development of campground facilities and more on advertising. After all, if we had built nice facilities that couldn't promote themselves, then we wouldn't have been successful.

---

[4] By 1973, 80 percent of the KOAs were located within a 100-mile radius of population centers with over 50,000 inhabitants.

By 1968 we felt that our franchise concept was working so we began to focus our attention on gaining operating experience. We knew that our franchise sales would run out at some point so we wanted to replace that revenue with a recurring income stream. About that time, franchises had a bad image earned by sales practices. We wanted to change all that.

We began to raise money to make investments and to diversify. First we borrowed $1 million from John Hancock in 1968, but we still needed more so we went public in June of 1969 with a $1 million common stock issue. We started buying land, which gave us a nucleus for operating campgrounds ourselves, particularly in the areas where we couldn't sell franchises. We began to add staff—persons with no experience in franchising but accustomed to the disciplines of corporate life—a different orientation from us as independents, entrepreneurs and marketers. In 1970 we purchased Gardner, Inc., our RV subsidiary.

By 1972 our efforts had all been geared towards making franchises more profitable and getting a handle on the campground business ourselves. The real estate business really chewed up our money in a hurry. We made another stock offering of $4 million in 1972, the money which was all to go towards the acquisition and development of company campgrounds plus strengthening of our organization through the hiring and development of staff.

In reflecting over the past decade, I must say that our original aim was to create overnight campgrounds en route to public parks. The overcrowding of public parks caused us to develop an alternative to those facilities by providing more recreational facilities and activities on our KOAs and by developing more destination campgrounds. For many people, the camping experience in a public park is best, but for others— our market—the preference has been for more conveniences and facilities.

The Campgrounds Business

KOA began granting franchises in 1963. At the end of 1973, KOA reported 707 campgrounds in operation, of which 20 were company-owned. Approximately 40 percent of the 2,269 franchises sold since 1963 were voluntarily terminated or cancelled by KOA for failure to begin campground construction—due primarily to zoning, site selection, or financing difficulties—or for failure to maintain minimum standards under the KOA guidelines for cleanliness and service.[5] Table 3 shows KOA campground development from 1968–73:

---

[5] Since the sale of the first franchise in 1963, ten operating franchisee campgrounds withdrew from the KOA system, franchises of 17 operating campgrounds were cancelled by KOA for failure to maintain minimum standards, and ten campgrounds were converted by their owners to other uses. The remaining 868 cancellations and terminations related to construction problems of nonoperating campgrounds.

TABLE 3

KOA Campground Development

	1968	1969	1970	1971	1972	1973
No. franchises operating...........	160	262	352	492	582	687
No. sites (est.)....................	n.a.*	n.a.*	33,800	49,200	59,900	72,800
No. co-owned parks operating.....	1	1	4	10	14	20
No. sites (est.)...................	100	100	560	1,000	2,500	4,500
Unopened franchises (beginning of year)...............	158	304	546	690	712	704
New franchises sold...............	242	421	383	303	362	233
Completions......................	(68)	(118)	(129)	(123)	(135)	(152)
Cancellations, terminations........	(28)	(61)	(110)	(158)	(235)	(245)
Unopened franchises (end of year)....................	304	546	690	712	704	540

* n.a. = not available.
Source: KOA annual reports.

KOA reported the following financial results for its campgrounds activities from 1968–73:

TABLE 4

Financial Performance—Campground Activities

	1968	1969	1970	1971	1972	1973
Revenues..........	$994,058	$2,071,170	$3,330,867	$4,021,321	$6,068,395	$8,891,637
Gross profit........	604,025	1,163,223	1,828,743	2,441,998	3,627,679	4,441,683
	(60.8%)	(56.2%)	(54.9%)	(60.7%)	(59.8%)	(50.0%)
SG & A and int......	362,487	798,867	1,265,753	1,439,867	1,842,894	2,278,756
	(36.5%)	(38.6%)	(38.0%)	(35.8%)	(30.4%)	(25.6%)
Pre-tax............	241,538	364,356	562,990	1,002,131	1,784,785	2,163,467
	(24.3%)	(17.6%)	(16.9%)	(24.9%)	(29.4%)	(24.3%)

Source: Corporate records.

Franchise Development. KOA franchises were sold in the United States, Canada, and Mexico by eight full-time sales representatives who worked strictly on commission. The size of franchise territories was determined on the basis of travel patterns, population, and competitive accommodations in the area. To generate franchisee prospects, KOA placed ads in local papers and in the *Wall Street Journal*. Mr. Booth had commented:

> There never is a problem getting inquiries. We get about 17,000–18,000 annually, although two years ago [1971], it was 25,000–30,000. The vast majority disqualify themselves. About 1,000 write back and are visited by salesmen. About 250 purchase contracts.
> We investigate the financial resources of a prospective franchise owner

very thoroughly, although we take many marginal risks. We're great believers in the free enterprise system and believe that you can do a lot with a little. We allow this practice because we've had enough successes. However, we keep tightening up due to pressure from franchisees and employees.

The franchise development process began after the consummation of the franchise sale and receipt of the initial fee, and lasted on average 12–18 months. First the new franchise owner was invited to attend a three-day operations course at the KOA–University in Billings. It was then his or her responsibility to select a campground location, get contractors' bids, and develop a *pro forma* cash flow statement and budget to be submitted to the KOA headquarters for approval. Once the financial prospectus was approved, the franchise owner obtained financing from a local bank, which usually amounted to 75–80 percent of the owner's needs. The initial franchise contract lasted for one year but could be extended to 18 months given financing or zoning problems. KOA reserved the right to cancel a contract at the one-year mark. Upon completion of the franchise, the contract became valid for five years.

Campground Facilities and Services. All KOA campgrounds were designed to provide supervised facilities for camping families using RVs or tents. In 1974, approximately 75 percent of the campgrounds were overnight facilities; the remainder, destination parks. Ninety-six percent of the KOA users were RV campers. All KOA campgrounds were required to provide a minimum of 50 campsites, and some provided as many as 600 sites. KOA franchises averaged 106 sites, versus 225 sites for the company-owned KOAs. Rates varied from $2–$7 per site. The average rate for franchises was $4 per camper night registration[6] versus $5 for company-owned KOAs. Electricity, water, and sewage facilities were available at each campsite. Each campground had a central building providing modern rest rooms, hot showers, public telephones, a coin-operated laundry, and convenience store selling groceries, camping supplies, souvenirs, ice, and other items. Many campgrounds provided recreational facilities, such as swimming pools and miniature golf and planned activities, such as RV dealer shows. (See Exhibits 2 and 3.)

KOA sold two other types of franchises: Ranch Kamps and KOA Jr.'s. The Ranch Kamps (RKOA) were franchised campgrounds on existing working or dude ranches and numbered 19 in 1973. The KOA Jr.'s were smaller campgrounds designed for locations with short camping seasons or low traffic density and numbered seven.[7]

KOA Camper Profile. An annual KOA camper survey revealed

---

[6] A *camper night registration* referred to a one-night registration for one campsite. A camper night registration averaged 4.1 persons in 1973.

[7] No new KOA Jr.'s were to be sold after 1973 since the program was termed relatively unsuccessful.

EXHIBIT 2

KAMPGROUNDS OF AMERICA, INC.
Campground Scenes

EXHIBIT 3

KAMPGROUNDS OF AMERICA, INC.
KOA Development Plan

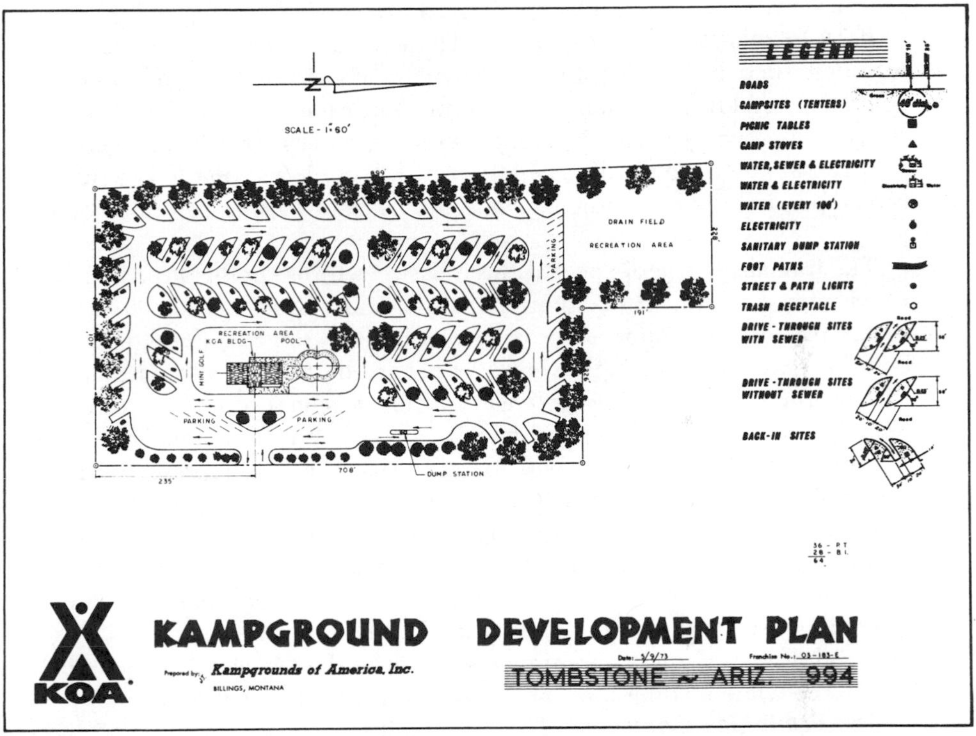

marked differences between the average KOA camper and the typical camper of the 70s, as described in a 3M National Advertising Company survey. In comparison, KOA campers showed stronger preferences for private and modern facilities, and less preference for locations adjacent to bodies of water or interstate highways. KOA campers were more apt to use guidebooks and reservation services. They were more mobile, with the largest concentration (25 percent) reporting using more than 11 different campgrounds on their last vacations. They traveled longer distances, daily averaging 351–400 miles; 50 percent reported trip distances greater than 3,000 miles; and 21 percent, over 5,500 miles. KOA campers showed less preference for wintertime camping and less willingness to use motels when visiting metropolitan areas, unless private camping facilities were unavailable. About 20 percent of both groups reported camping between 1–10 days; 30 percent between 11–20 days; and 25 percent between 21–30 days a year. Close to 50 percent indicated an intention to camp more in the future. KOA camping families were on average younger than the typical camping family; KOA household heads were slightly more educated and represented a higher professional and income level. KOA campers were more willing to incur additional costs for sites, particularly for souvenirs, and were less willing to incur food and auto costs.

KOA Franchise Owner Profile. The average KOA franchise owner was described by Mr. Booth as "married with a family, some college education, middle-class, some supervisory job experience, white, thrifty, not self-employed, extremely independent, free enterprise-oriented, generally conservative politically, ambitious, and hard working." The wife often operated the campground while the husband/owner held a second job.

The franchise owner expected three basic "returns" on his investment: (1) financial return, (2) land appreciation, and (3) a superior life style to his former occupation. The priority of those returns often differed between owners of overnight versus owners of destination campgrounds. The overnight franchise owner was typically a school teacher or retiree who was looking for the opportunity to become an entrepreneur in an out-of-doors activity dealing with people. His franchise represented his first business venture, which sometimes resulted in discouragement at the prospect of zoning or financing difficulties. His objective was to earn a profit on a seasonal activity and to end up owning a piece of land which in all probability would appreciate in value. The destination campground owner, on the other hand, tended to be a businessman who was involved in several real estate projects. He used the franchise to generate an income while holding the land for future residential development.

The Franchise Contract. The form of franchise agreement used by KOA changed considerably from 1963 to 1973. Formerly, a five-year franchise contract cost $7,500 and included a prefab building, tables, and a grill. In 1971, the franchise contract fee was raised to $10,000. In 1973, it had become $12,500 ($7,500 for KOA Jr.'s). The building and tables and grill had been eliminated; and more sophisticated assistance from KOA management had been provided.[8]

The contract required a nonrefundable "initial" fee of 45 percent of the franchise price, with the remaining 55 percent, known as the "completion fee," due upon construction completion of the franchise. All franchises, whether operating or not, were required to pay an annual $300 franchise renewal fee. All operating franchises were required to submit an 8 percent royalty payment weekly to KOA based on gross vehicle registration fees collected. The royalty fee had been changed from 5 percent to 8 percent in 1970.

Franchise Economics. Campground profitability varied widely by franchise, depending mainly upon location and length of season. The

---

[8] The franchise contract was scheduled to be raised to $14,000 in February 1974.

average investment for a 100-site campground was $150,000, but it varied as much as $35,000–$1 million. Management estimated that the land cost represented about one-third of the $150,000 investment. The remaining costs covered the franchise fee, buildings, site development, sewage disposal, water supply, laundry machines, store fixtures and inventory, picnic tables, grills, and miscellaneous equipment. On an average campground, KOA officials estimated that a 50 percent occupancy rate for a 100-day season would retire the investment in 4–5 years; while a 75 percent occupancy rate for the same season would retire the investment in 3–4 years. Exhibit 4 presents actual financial statements of an overnight and a destination campground in their third year of operation. In 1973, KOA campgrounds in total averaged occupancy levels of 35–40 percent of their seasons.

KOA Services Provided to Franchisees. Upon receipt of the initial franchise fee, KOA provided construction and layout plans to its franchisees, and furnished advice and information relating to construction and maintenance, financing, local zoning requirements, sanitation methods, and bookkeeping and accounting systems. This information was received through an elaborate *Operations Manual* and a three-day operations course provided to new franchise owners at the KOA-University in Billings. In addition, franchisees received ongoing assistance as was necessary from three one-man regional development offices, which dealt with local problems, from periodic conventions and regional meetings, and through weekly bulletins and a monthly newsletter issued from Billings. Franchise owners formed their own associations to deal with problems indigenous to their particular regions.

In order to maintain the KOA stringent standards of operation and maintenance, seven full-time inspectors visited each KOA two or three times a year. Random surveillance visits took place to determine whether KOA campgrounds were operating according to recommended procedures and were properly reporting royalties. Inspections for cleanliness and service were conducted against standards of performance. Exceptional performance warranted company-wide recognition. Only 17 franchises had ever been terminated on the basis of failure to meet minimum performance standards.

Aside from the contractual services, franchise owners felt that the affiliation with the KOA system was an invaluable benefit for attracting customers. KOA operated a toll-free reservations system and distributed a *KOA Kampground Directory* twice yearly, which listed each campground with its rates and services and reportedly had over two million readers. Management believed that 80 percent of the KOA business was generated from its directory and reservations system. In addition, KOA sponsored a KOA Kamper Klub of 39,000 members who, for an annual fee of $5, received promotional materials on the KOA system. The com-

EXHIBIT 4

KAMPGROUNDS OF AMERICA, INC.
Franchisee Income Statements—Third Year of Operation

	Overnight Campground	Destination Campground
Data		
No. sites..........................	100	250
Season...........................	180 days	260 days
Average annual occupancy........	54%	46%
Land cost........................	$10,000	$100,000
Facility improvements*...........	$100,000	$375,000
Depreciation on improvements....	10 year, straight line	10 year, straight line
Equity investment................	$44,000	$237,500
Mortgage (7% interest, 25 yrs.).....	$66,000	$237,500
Registration fee..................	$3.05	$4.36
Tax rate..........................	20%	50%
Income		
Registration fees.................	$30,293	$132,087
Merchandise sales................	27,887	51,690
Vending machines, etc............	1,985	4,947
	$60,164	$188,724
Less cost of merchandise........	−22,616	−33,081
Gross Profit........................	$37,548	$155,643
Operating Expenses		
Salaries and wages...............	$ 5,094	$ 20,368
Utilities..........................	1,840	7,596
Operating supplies...............	1,803	8,119
KOA royalty......................	2,423	10,128
Property taxes....................	1,016	6,091
Repairs, maintenance............	397	3,067
Miscellaneous....................	3,637	10,051
Total Operating Expenses............	$16,210	$ 65,421
Net Profit Before Dep., Int., Taxes.....	$21,338	$ 90,222
Less depreciation.................	−10,000	− 37,500
Less interest.....................	− 4,478	− 16,081
Net Profit Before Tax................	$ 6,860	$ 36,641
Net Profit After Tax.................	$ 5,488	$ 18,321
Depreciation.....................	$10,000	$ 37,500
Less principal repayment.........	1,122	4,299
Net Cash Flow to Equity.............	$14,366	$ 51,522
Net After-Tax Return on Equity......	12.5%	7.7%
Net Cash Flow Return on Equity.......	32.7%	21.7%

* Includes franchise fee of $12,500.
Source: Corporate records.

pany also acted as a distributor, selling prefab buildings, swimming pools, supplies, and equipment, such as washers, dryers, packaged food, and souvenirs.

KOA/Franchisee Relations. Mr. Booth summed up KOA's relationship with its franchisees by stating: "We don't do any work for the franchisees. We only offer advice." Problems with the franchisees stemmed from some confusion over the definition of that relationship. Certain franchise owners held greater expectations for assistance from KOA, particularly in the areas of financing, zoning, and operations problems. Older franchises, which had established repeat customers, claimed less dependence upon the KOA system than the fledgling facilities that had tenuous occupancy rates.

Several comments reflecting the frustrations of franchise owners were voiced at a regional conference in December 1973:

> If KOA, Inc., fails, you're (KOA) only out of a job, but this (franchise) is our whole life.
>
> KOA is not in the same business as we are (franchisees). They make money for KOA, Inc., and we make money for us.
>
> It's a two-way street . . . me and you. Why should I (franchisee) put money into a campground if you're (KOA) going to build campgrounds and Leisure Inns next door?
>
> Why should I (franchisee) have to do my own site selection and make arrangements for financing? I don't know anything about the camping business. That's why I came to you (KOA).

In a telephone interview with the case researcher, a destination campground owner expressed his satisfaction with the KOA system:

> I run a 133-site year-round campground in Florida which is 100 percent occupied during the winter months and 80 percent filled in the summer. I benefit from my location and really don't need KOA, although its name is a drawing card. I receive no assistance from KOA. This is my business. I can get my merchandise cheaper from local suppliers.

Campground Competitors. In management's view, KOA occupied the unique position within the industry where public facility competitors enhanced the KOA business, and private firms were deterred because of the strength of the KOA name and size of its campground network. Regarding the competition, Mr. Booth said:

> The national parks and forests plus the desire of the American family to travel are the reasons for our existence. They act as stimulators for our business. Congress has been charged to preserve these areas in their natural state. So we (KOA) provide a place for tourists to stay while enjoying national parks and now with the overcrowding, we have begun to create resort-type parks.
>
> In the private sector, we do not view the independent parks as serious competition because they are undercapitalized, poorly managed, and are unable to benefit from affiliation with a nationally known system. Our small franchise competitors have financial problems, too. And the big motel chains cater to a different market—the top 15 percent of the KOA campers—the guy who arrives with a self-contained RV unit.

They can't build a business and expect to support it on a guy who has a basic reluctance to spend. And second, to build a broad network of luxury-type campgrounds would cost about $100 million. They're finding it difficult to break even on a campground investment of $300,000–$400,000 which requires a huge volume of business. It just doesn't help to have to carry corporate overhead.

In the campground business, market share was extremely difficult to measure, let alone define, since hard data could only be collected on those who registered as campers at campgrounds. The KOA management estimated its market share on the basis of people-nights, that is by multiplying the number of KOA camper night (one-site) registrations (4.5 million in 1973) times the average number of persons per camping family (4.1). The resultant figure of 18.45 million people-nights was estimated to represent 2% of all nights spent by all individuals camping in the United States in 1973. It was management's hope to increase that share to 4 percent in 1974.

The Recreational Vehicles Business

In April 1970, KOA acquired Gardner, Inc., an RV manufacturing firm located in Bristol, Indiana. Mr. Booth commented on the acquisition:

> We bought Gardner because we wanted to diversify. We were running a Stay & Tow program[9] on our campgrounds and couldn't find a decent rental unit and knew what we wanted to build. Acquisitions were in vogue at the time, and Gardner seemed to us to be a well-managed, R&D-oriented company which was creative in its market.

KOA acquired all of the outstanding capital stock of Gardner, Inc., in a pooling of interests transaction in exchange for 86,256 shares of common stock. In accordance with the agreement, Gardner was paid 43,128 shares selling at $20 a share. The remaining shares were held in escrow and would revert to KOA if the earnings of Gardner, determined on a cumulative basis through December 31, 1974, did not equal or exceed specified amounts. Until its loss in 1973, Gardner was on target to receive the shares in escrow.

From 1968–73, Gardner reported the following financial results:

---

[9] The Stay & Tow program was an RV rental program. Renters used the RV at the rental site or drove to another KOA location. The program had two complications. (1) Renting an RV was far more involved than renting a car because it was necessary to understand the sewage system, refrigerator, and electricity hookups. Rental service instruction took 2–4 hours. (2) Franchisees were unwilling to spend the money to purchase RVs for their locations. They did not believe that people drove to KOAs to rent RVs.

TABLE 5

Gardner Financial Performance

	1968	1969	1970	1971	1972	1973
Revenues........	$570,821	$1,062,077	$1,370,276	$2,700,995	$3,405,684	$3,183,847
Gross profit.......	65,373	188,539	226,336	447,998	561,700	409,917
	(11.5%)	(17.8%)	(16.5%)	(16.6%)	(16.5%)	(12.9%)
SG & A, int.......	41,251	107,766	172,940	274,921	363,990	508,146
	(7.2%)	(10.1%)	(12.6%)	(10.2%)	(10.7%)	(16.0%)
Pre-tax...........	24,122	80,773	53,396	173,077	197,710	(98,769)*
	(4.2%)	(7.6%)	(3.9%)	(6.4%)	(5.8%)	(-3.1%)

* Pre-tax loss reflected a one-time charge of $103,606 for plant closing and casualty loss.
Source: Corporate records.

History of Gardner, Inc. Gardner, Inc., was founded in 1968 by the Gardner brothers, both of whom left shortly thereafter, one for health reasons and the other simply to leave corporate life. From the date of purchase, Gardner was plagued with problems. In the fall of 1970, a California plant was opened. It was closed in April of 1973 due to the difficulty of multiplant management, excessive labor turnover, and production and marketing problems. The following June, fire destroyed the truck camper facilities in Bristol. A temporary line was set up almost immediately, which prevented a major down-turn in sales revenues that year. By early 1974, the KOA management was seriously considering closing the Gardner operation, which had been victimized by management problems, the impact of the energy crisis on RV sales, and the competitive nature of the RV industry.[10]

TABLE 6

1973 Gardner Product Line

Product	Length (in feet)	Avg. Price	Avg. Price— Competition	Unit Sales			
				1970	1971	1972	1973
Truck camper............	9½, 11	$3,750	$2,450	476	670	977	893
Travel trailer.............	16	$2,800	$2,000	19	116	190	193

Source: Corporate records.

Product Line. Gardner, Inc., manufactured two models of luxury truck campers called "Amerigo" and a high-styled body travel trailer called the "Amerigo FG-16." A mini motor home was scheduled to be introduced in 1974.

The Gardner products competed at the top of the industry line. The two truck camper models were designed to provide temporary living

[10] There were 700 manufacturers of truck campers and travel trailers in the United States. Gardner was one of the smallest firms.

quarters for sportsmen and traveling families. Their exteriors were constructed of aluminum siding and fiberglass. Their interiors were wood panelled. They were positioned in the marketplace on the basis of quality, floor plan, and style against models by Open Road and Coachman, rather than on the basis of price against the remaining 60–70 competing models. The travel trailer model competed on the basis of size, quality, and its all-fiberglass body. Its sales had been minimal, due primarily to design problems, a limited available supply, and the fact that the model was too small to appeal to the retired family market and too expensive to appeal to the family market.

RV Production. The Bristol plant was primarily a parts assembly operation. The mobile fiberglass roof and front sections were purchased from vendors, as were all appliances, upholstering, curtains, mattresses, cabinets, windows, doors, toilets, fixtures, and optional equipment. All wooden frames were fabricated by Gardner, as well as the exterior aluminum panelling.

RV Sales and Financing. Gardner, Inc., received financial support from KOA and its working capital needs from banks. RVs were sold by 145 independent dealers in the United States, of which 80 percent were exclusively RV dealers carrying a number of lines. All sales to dealers were for cash, although in many cases the company participated in individual dealer's floor plan financing.[11] Gardner never experienced a material loss under those arrangements.

KOA in 1974

Management. In late November of 1973, Mr. Booth announced his plans to withdraw from the daily operation of the business to become the chief executive officer, with his new role to focus on "long-range planning, finance, foreign ventures, and new ventures." He named Mr. Jim Collins, a former divisional vice president of North American Rockwell Corporation and Harvard Business School graduate, as his new chief operations officer. Mr. Collins had joined KOA in late 1972 as president of KOA's Shelter Division.

Mr. Booth had joined KOA in 1966 from his post as director of the chamber of commerce in Billings, Montana. He was described by his colleagues as a "man of great integrity, common sense, and social grace . . . a self-taught businessman with great capability as the day-to-day manager of the business." One officer had said: "His business ethics are above reproach; he has an honest, straightforward approach to business." "Roughing it is my bag," Mr. Booth had once stated, "but as a businessman, I know that if that was all I had to offer, I'd go broke. Most people

---

[11] Floor plan financing was an arrangement whereby a dealer financed his RV purchases with a bank or finance company and pledged the merchandise as security.

nowadays want good facilities. I'll provide them, and meanwhile, I'll do my own camping in my own way."

Mr. Booth described his management group:

> KOA's biggest plus is its management group, although we're lacking in second-level depth. The group is marketing-oriented, receptive to new ideas, young in spirit and in age, highly visible, and always looking for new ways to improve the KOA image. In contrast to the campgrounds business, the RV business requires a less sophisticated management process. Anyone can open a garage and assemble an RV. It's a highly fragmented, labor-intensive business. The Gardner management produces a product which sells itself and therefore has not developed its marketing capability.

In the fall of 1973, KOA was reorganized along functional lines. (See Exhibit 5 for the new organizational structure and the management group profile.) Prior to the reorganization, all KOA franchise activities were included in the camping division headed by Mr. Don Ryan. Mr. Ryan left KOA in September 1973 to join Outdoor Resorts, Inc., a firm which sold condominium trailer lots. Mr. Ryan had joined KOA in 1969 and had been responsible for the development, marketing, and operation of all franchised campgrounds in the United States, and the sales of all KOAs in the United States, Canada, and Mexico. He bore the primary responsibility for franchise relations. Mr. Ryan's departure was considered a real loss at a time when KOA was trying to cement franchisee relations and increase franchisees' marketing effectiveness. In addition to Mr. Ryan, all initial founders of KOA had left KOA by the fall of 1973 and together retained only an 8 percent equity holding in the company.

Marketing. By 1974, KOA had shifted its marketing focus away from franchise sales to expanding its services to franchisees, with the residual objective of getting the campers to stay longer, have more fun, and spend more money at the KOAs. The advertising and promotion allocation for 1974, excluding advertising costs for franchise sales, was $450,000. The *KOA Kampground Directory*, published twice yearly and distributed to 2.1 million readers, was the most expensive promotional item, costing $185,000 net of advertising revenues. Other marketing activities included the KOA Kamper Klub, with its 39,000 members on-site recreational activities, cooperative advertising with RV dealers, discount coupons for KOA camping, a nationwide reservations system, national advertising, a discount supply catalog, international convention, monthly bulletins, weekly newsletters, and KOA-University courses.

Finance. In 1973, KOA reported revenues of $12.075 million and net earnings of $1.072 million, an increase of 28 percent and 10 percent respectively from 1972. For the first time in corporate history, KOA had failed to meet its annual growth objective of 20 percent in earnings. KOA's financial history (1969–73) is summarized in Exhibit 6 and presented in detail (1972–73) in Exhibits 7 and 8.

EXHIBIT 5

KAMPGROUNDS OF AMERICA, INC.
Organizational Structure—December 1973

	Division	Responsibilities
	–Marketing/Merchandising	KOA promotions; sales of merchandise, buildings, and equipment to franchises
	–Operations	Surveillance and inspections of KOA campgrounds; operation of KOA hot line
	–Sales	Franchise contract sales
	–Development/Leisure Inns	Construction phase problems of franchises; development and market testing of motel-type accommodations on KOA campgrounds; KOA University
Chief Executive Officer — Chief Operating Officer —	–Properties	Purchase, development and management of company-owned campgrounds; development of fast food concept
	–Research	New venture research
	–Finance	All financial matters for KOA and franchises
	–West Advertising	KOA advertising (subsidiary)
	–Gardner, Inc.	Manufacture and sale of RVs

Management Group Profile

Name	Age	Joined KOA	Title	Former Job
Darrell Booth	48	1966	Chairman and chief executive officer	Director, Chamber of Commerce in Billings, Montana
Jim Collins	39	1972	Executive vice president and chief operating officer	Divisional marketing vice president, North American Rockwell
William Derrenger	32	1972	Asst. vice president, finance	Loan officer, First National Bank of Boston
Jerome Hanson	32	1969	Vice president, development	District manager, Northwest division of U.S. Chamber of Commerce
Harold Lloyd	46	1970	Vice president, franchise sales	Manager of marketing, Kingsberry West, division of Boise Cascade Corp.
Donald Lowe	33	1972	National merchandise manager	California area store supervisor, S. H. Kress Company
Tom O'Connor	39	1970	Secretary/treasurer	Treasurer of Mule Creek Oil Company, and accountant, Peat, Marwick & Mitchell, Co.
Art Peterson	39	1969	Vice president, properties	Retail store management, S. H. Kress
Homer Staves	35	1967	Vice president, research	Manager, Chamber of Commerce, Huron, South Dakota

EXHIBIT 6

KAMPGROUNDS OF AMERICA, INC.
*Five-Year Financial History**

Operating Results	1973	1972	1971	1970	1969
Sales and operating revenues.....	$12,075,484	$ 9,474,079	$6,722,316	$4,701,143	$3,133,247
Earnings before income taxes.....	2,064,698	1,982,495	1,175,208	616,386	445,129
Net earnings......................	1,071,950	974,860	594,908	315,590	207,560
Earnings per share................	0.98	0.91	0.63	0.35	0.26
Average common and equivalent shares.........................	1,095,668	1,075,862	949,935	902,356	811,002
Depreciation.....................	523,421	243,227	141,245	82,192	31,109
Net additions—property and equipment.....................	5,093,020	3,385,159	1,228,581	1,020,883	164,832
Financial Position (at year end)					
Total assets......................	$13,789,651	$12,380,546	$5,575,089	$4,150,481	$3,185,863
Net working capital (deficit).......	(303,268)	2,326,017	669,927	457,159	625,576
Current ratio......................	0.9	1.8	1.5	1.5	1.8
Net property and equipment......	10,159,289	5,494,647	2,332,770	1,241,138	299,808
Long-term debt...................	2,792,388	1,971,999	2,011,248	1,531,129	632,255
Capital stock.....................	5,557,642	5,557,642	1,256,013	1,256,013	1,259,051
Retained earnings.................	3,162,845	2,090,895	1,116,035	521,127	205,537
Long-term debt/total capitalization...................	24.3%	20.5%	45.9%	46.3%	43.2%
Funds Flow Statement					
Funds Provided					
Net earnings....................	$ 1,071,950	$ 974,860	$ 594,908	$ 315,590	$ 207,560
Noncash charges (credit)					
depreciation..................	523,421	243,227	141,245	82,192	31,109
amortization..................	—	—	36,053	46,863	25,430
deferred taxes................	15,100	(14,200)	173,200	(214,951)	(274,410)
equity in net loss of affiliates..	—	—	26,926	—	—
Total.....................	1,610,471	1,210,355	972,332	229,694	(10,311)
Additions—long-term debt.......	1,266,071	622,176	781,573	968,189	593,781
Proceeds—sale of common shares........................	—	4,301,629	—	—	1,107,451
Warrants issued.................	—	—	—	—	90,000
Other sources...................	504,289	221,512	123,357	28,182	11,600
Decrease in working capital......	2,629,285	—	—	195,417	—
	$ 6,010,116	$ 6,355,672	$1,877,262	$1,421,482	$1,792,521
Funds Used					
Additions—property and equipment.....................	$ 5,398,635	$ 3,893,896	$1,273,347	$1,044,650	$ 435,734
Investment in affiliates............	50,000	40,000	57,881	178,619	—
Reduction—long-term debt........	445,682	584,958	301,454	70,035	25,188
Other uses......................	115,799	180,728	31,812	128,178	163,896
Increase in working capital.......	—	1,656,090	212,768	—	1,167,703
	$ 6,010,116	$ 6,355,672	$1,877,262	$1,421,482	$1,792,521

* Financial statements are restated to reflect 1971 APB ruling on franchise accounting.
Source: KOA annual reports, 1969–73.

In 1971, the accounting principles board adopted a new principle for recording franchise revenues. KOA had previously recorded a total franchise sale and its related costs, including a provision for possible cancel-

EXHIBIT 7

KAMPGROUNDS OF AMERICA, INC.
Consolidated Balance Sheets

	December 31,	
Assets	*1973*	*1972*
Current Assets:		
Cash and short-term deposits (1973—$217,500; 1972—$3,200,000)......................................	$ 330,755	$ 3,789,826
Marketable securities..............................	101,945	—
Accounts and notes receivable.....................	638,350	515,896
Less allowance for doubtful receivables...............	136,638	100,168
Net receivables...................................	501,712	415,728
Inventory of recreational vehicles, merchandise, and supplies...	616,920	532,024
Prepaid expenses and deferred income taxes, current....	422,176	348,449
Total current assets...............................	1,973,508	5,086,027
Land held for future campground development or sale, at cost..	390,753	597,814
Investment in affiliates, at equity........................	286,065	236,719
Property and equipment, at cost*........................	11,089,176	5,996,156
Less allowance for depreciation........................	929,887	501,509
Net property and equipment.......................	10,159,289	5,494,647
Other assets...	980,036	965,339
	$13,789,651	$12,380,546
Liabilities and Stockholders' Equity		
Current Liabilities:		
Notes payable to banks.................................	$ 188,684	$ 370,000
Current instalments of long-term debt....................	375,782	234,946
Accounts payable and accrued expenses.................	830,581	800,324
Income taxes...	203,701	730,705
Unearned revenues.....................................	678,028	624,035
Total Current Liabilities..........................	2,276,776	2,760,010
Long-term debt...	2,792,388	1,971,999
Stockholders' equity:		
Common stock of $0.125 par value per share. Authorized 4 million shares; issued 1,109,046 shares.....	138,631	138,631
Additional paid-in capital...............................	5,419,011	5,419,011
Retained earnings.....................................	3,162,845	2,090,895
Total Stockholders' Equity........................	8,720,487	7,648,537
	$13,789,651	$12,380,546

* Campgrounds investment: (1) land = $1,385,875 (1972) $2,065,017 (1973).
    (2) buildings, sites, equipment = $3,879,666 (1972), $8,038,827 (1973).
Source: KOA annual report, 1973.

lation, at the time the franchise was granted. Under the new ruling, which was applied retroactively to KOA's inception, management recorded the initial fee (45 percent of the total franchise fee) of non-refundable cash as revenue and its related costs as expenses at the time the franchise was granted and initial services performed. The completion fee (55 percent of the total franchise fee) was received and recognized

EXHIBIT 8

KAMPGROUNDS OF AMERICA, INC.
Consolidated Statements of Earnings

	1973	1972
Sales and operating revenues:		
Franchises		
Initial revenue...	$ 1,212,185	$1,439,365
Completion revenue..................................	713,676	630,279
Sales of campground buildings, equipment, and		
supplies...	2,245,584	1,275,828
Sales of manufactured recreational vehicles..............	3,183,847	3,405,684
Annual franchise fees..................................	399,700	430,550
Royalties under franchise agreements....................	1,245,562	876,214
Revenue from company-operated campgrounds..........	2,518,143	1,100,977
Gain on sale of assets net..............................	53,819	—
Other operating revenue................................	502,968	315,182
	12,075,484	9,474,097
Cost and expenses:		
Franchises		
Initial costs...	256,234	325,947
Completion costs......................................	143,172	104,919
Cost of campground buildings, equipment, and supplies..	1,956,441	1,117,117
Cost of manufactured recreational vehicles..............	2,670,864	2,843,984
Expenses of company-operated campgrounds............	2,093,567	891,313
Selling, general, and administrative expenses............	2,736,892	2,206,884
Plant closing and casualty losses.......................	103,606	—
Interest and amortization of debt discount net of interest		
income $178,455 in 1973 and $199,939 in 1972..............	50,010	1,420
	10,010,786	7,491,584
Earnings before income taxes.....................	2,064,698	1,982,495
Federal and state income taxes		
Current..	977,648	1,021,835
Deferred...	15,100	(14,200)
	992,748	1,007,635
Net earnings.......................................	$ 1,071,950	$ 974,860
Weighted average number of common and common		
equivalent shares......................................	1,095,668	1,075,862
Net earnings per common and common equivalent share....	$0.98	$0.91

Source: KOA annual report, 1973.

as revenue upon substantial completion of the campground and performance of all company services. The effect of the change on previously reported net earnings and earnings per share was to reduce net earnings by $78,335; $105,580; $212,134; and $243,735; and earnings per share by $0.12, $0.17, $0.26 and $0.27 in 1967, 1968, 1969, and 1970, respectively. Mr. Booth commented on the change:

I think that it was a good thing for our company in the long run. Out statements became more realistic, and more emphasis was placed on earnings. The change facilitated our borrowing capacity since our statement looked stronger.

In June of 1969, KOA went public with the sale of 170,000 shares of common stock traded over-the-counter at $12.50 a share. Net proceeds to KOA were $1.1 million and to the selling KOA founders, $775,00. The stock was subsequently split three for two. In April of 1972, certain stockholders, mostly KOA officers and directors, sold 180,000 shares and KOA sold 150,000 newly issued shares at $29.50 a share. Net proceeds to KOA were $4.3 million. At the end of 1973, there were 1.096 million shares of KOA common stock outstanding. The KOA stock price reached an all-time high of 30–7/8 in the second quarter of 1972 and fell steadily to its all-time low of 3 in the fourth quarter of 1973.

International Activities.   By 1974, KOA activities outside the United States were still very limited. Management had investigated establishing campgrounds or training foreign nationals in Europe, the Far East, Canada, and Mexico. Entry into Canada, a country with an estimated 1.5 million campers, had been the most successful foreign venture, with 33 KOA franchises operating and 13 under construction in 1973. KOA had established four campgrounds in Mexico, the most difficult market to enter since very few Mexicans camped. In 1973 management sold a license to a partnership of two Japanese firms, Nichimen Co., Ltd. (trading company), and France Bed Company (distributor of mattresses and bedroom furniture) for a total of $200,000 plus a variable royalty computed on the licensee's gross income. KOA planned to train those partners to operate KOAs in Japan, a country that had not yet developed its RV or campgrounds business. Over 300 KOAs were planned, with the first to open in 1975. Australia was being investigated as a business prospect, as well as all of Europe, although travel clubs with their own travel camps were well established in Europe.

THE FUTURE FOR KOA

In contrasting the KOA philosophy of 1964 with that of 1974, one company official stated:

> In the past, we responded to an existing demand. Now our job is to create the demand. Our market used to be campers who traveled, but now it's travelers who camp. Before, we provided a place to park RVs, and now we provide a place to enjoy them. Our motto used to be "clean and friendly"; now it has become "clean, friendly, and fun."

Facing a continued decline in franchise sales plus the negative impact of the energy crisis on RV sales and campground usage, management turned its attention in 1974 to business activities which had the prospect of producing a recurring stream of earnings. Four activities (1) merchandising, (2) company-owned campgrounds, (3) overnight lodging, and (4) fast food services, were under review.

Merchandising. Management considered the merchandise business as a key prospect for earnings growth in the future, as more highly sophisticated KOA campground stores could act as an inducement to greatly increase revenue per camper night. In 1972, KOA added a merchandise manager whose job was to train campground owners in the merchandise business and to manage receivables.

Franchise owners were not obligated to purchase merchandise from KOA, although about 50 percent did because of the attractive price discounts. KOA supplied large capital goods items, such as washing machines, as well as small ticket items like sunglasses and toothpaste. KOA did not inventory the items but rather acted as a jobber operating on low margins by providing the source for equipment and arranging for volume discounts from local suppliers who drop-shipped the merchandise to the KOAs.

A franchisee's investment in a KOA merchandise store cost about $10,000, of which $4,000–$6,000 represented inventory costs. Franchisees set their own margins on merchandise, with ranges suggested by KOA.[12] The GE Credit Corporation agreed to finance the initial store investment for any franchisee whose campground had been operating for more than two years. In 1973, the typical franchise earned $2.00 in merchandise revenues per camper night, whereas the typical company-owned campground earned $4.70 with the goal to double that amount by 1976. Overnight campgrounds reported higher merchandise sales than destination parks where campers tended to arrive with their own supplies.

Company-owned Campgrounds. At the end of 1973, KOA reported an investment (before depreciation) of $10.1 million in 20 company-owned campgrounds. Management felt that the company-owned campgrounds were more profitable than the franchised KOAs due to their better management, larger size (# sites), Southern location, financial strength, bigger merchandise inventories, and pioneering recreational facilities. KOA-owned campgrounds were required to have a minimum of 150 sites expandable to 250, and to be located in a two-season area, such as in the Southwest, Gulf Coast area, and the Southeast. Exhibit 9 presents a discounted cash flow statement of a typical company-owned campground.

Three of the company-owned campgrounds were operated on leased land. Management was searching for other leasing prospects, primarily among independent campgrounds. "We'll lease more in the next few years," Mr. Booth had said. "It's an excellent way for us to generate operating earnings without tying up capital. This is our primary revenue prospect." One leased park required $80,000–$90,000 in initial improvement costs on an escalating lease. Investment in a company-owned camp-

---

[12] KOA suggested an average 30–34 percent markup, although most franchises used on average 15–25 percent markup on merchandise.

EXHIBIT 9

KAMPGROUNDS OF AMERICA, INC.
Cash Flow Analysis—Company-Owned Campground

Data: 242 sites
12-month season
land cost = $131,000
facility improvements = $393,000
depreciation on improvements = 20 years, straight line
equity investment = $262,000
mortgage (9%, 20 years) = $262,000
registration fee = $5
tax rate = 50%

	1970	1971	1972	1973	1974 (est.)
Camper Nights....................	19,572	25,659	28,400	34,450	36,000
Income					
Registrations...................	$ 91,552	$128,791	$140,125	$180,862	$189,000
Other income...................	14,645	32,288	39,908	50,470	52,650
Gross profit........................	$106,197	$161,079	$180,033	$231,332	$241,650
Operating expense.................	46,581	57,659	62,365	69,000	82,800
Net profit before dep., int., Taxes*..	$ 59,616	$103,420	$117,668	$152,332	$158,850
Less depreciation..............	19,650	19,650	19,650	19,650	19,650
Less interest...................	23,580	23,139	22,658	22,134	21,562
Net profit before tax..............	16,386	60,631	75,360	110,548	117,638
Net profit after tax................	$ 8,193	$ 30,316	$ 37,680	$ 55,274	$ 58,819
Depreciation....................	19,650	19,650	19,650	19,650	19,650
Less principal repayment.......	4,902	5,343	5,824	6,348	6,920
Net cash flow to equity............	$ 22,941	$ 44,623	$ 51,506	$ 68,576	$ 71,549
Cumulative net cash flow to equity..	$ 22,941	$ 67,564	$119,070	$187,646	$259,195
Net after-tax return on equity.......	3.1%	11.6%	14.4%	21.1%	22.5%
Net cash flow return on equity......	8.8	17.0	19.7	26.2	27.3

Net present value at 10% = $432,192
Internal Rate of Return = 22%

* Projected to be flat past 1974 at a rate of $158,850 for the purposes of a discounted cash flow analysis.
Source: Corporate records.

ground ranged between $200,000 and $1,750,000, with the average investment being $500,000, of which 20–25 percent represented land cost and 75–80 percent represented buildings, sites, and equipment costs.

Overnight Lodging. In the spring of 1973, KOA tested on six campgrounds in the Southwest 60 cottage-type structures called "Leisure Inns," which were designed to attract traveling families who did not own camping equipment or who did not wish to pay the high cost of motels for overnight accommodations. The Leisure Inn program was the second shelter program which KOA had tried to increase the number of markets served by KOA campgrounds. The first had been the Stay & Tow program, which was designed to attract families who did not own RVs.

Investment in Leisure Inns was available to all franchisees who reported over 5,000 camper nights in 1973. Of the 707 operating franchises, 253 qualified to be able to support the shelters. A minimum purchase of six buildings—two of each style—was required. The units ranged from $6,000–$9,000 apiece, depending upon the style. Purchase arrangements were made through KOA, the distributor for the units, under contract with the manufacturer. KOA's profit per unit averaged $1,500. A leasing program was under consideration. Franchises participating in the program paid an additional $10,000 franchise fee, a $300 annual franchise renewal fee, and 8 percent royalties to KOA on all Leisure Inn night registrations. Exhibit 10 presents a *pro forma* income statement under varying occupancy rates of a franchise in its third year of operation in the Leisure Inn program.

EXHIBIT 10

KAMPGROUNDS OF AMERICA, INC.
Franchisee Leisure Inn Program—Third Year of Operation

Data: 10 Leisure Inns (placed on idle campground land)
    12-month season
    investment/Leisure Inn = $10,000 ($7,000 cost of unit, $1,500 site improvement,
                                  $500 supplies, $1,000 franchisee fee)
    depreciation = 10 years, straight line
    equity investment = $25,000
    mortgage (7 percent, 25 years) = $75,000
    average registration fee = $12.20
    tax rate = 50 percent

	Third Year of Operation			
Occupancy rates..........................	34%	45%	50%	65%
Room nights.............................	125	164	185	237
Registrations............................	1,250	1,642	1,850	2,370
Income				
Registrations.........................	$15,250	$20,000	$22,570	$28,914
Food service (gross profit)............	300	394	444	570
Other income.........................	750	985	1,110	1,422
Gross profit..............................	$16,300	$21,379	$24,124	$30,906
Operating expenses				
Salaries and wages....................	$ 1,875	$ 2,463	$ 2,775	$ 3,555
Utilities..............................	625	821	925	1,185
Supplies..............................	1,600	2,100	2,368	3,033
KOA royalty...........................	1,220	1,600	1,805	2,313
Property taxes........................	1,000	1,000	1,000	1,000
Repairs and maintenance.............	500	500	500	750
Miscellaneous........................	2,400	2,400	2,400	3,150
Total operating expenses................	$ 9,200	$10,884	$11,773	$15,225
Net profit before dep., int., taxes.........	$ 7,080	$10,495	$12,351	$15,681
Less depreciation....................	–10,000	–10,000	–10,000	–10,000
Less interest........................	– 5,078	– 5,078	– 5,078	– 5,078
Net profit before tax....................	($ 7,998)	($ 4,583)	($ 2,727)	$ 603
Tax at 50 percent				
Net profit after tax......................	($ 3,999)	($ 2,292)	($ 1,364)	$ 302
Depreciation.........................	10,000	10,000	10,000	$10,000
Less principal repayment.............	– 1,358	– 1,358	– 1,358	– 1,358
Net cash flow to equity..................	$ 4,643	$ 6,350	$ 7,278	$ 8,944
Net after-tax return on equity...........	(16.0%)	(9.2%)	(5.5%)	1.2%
Net cash flow return on equity..........	18.6%	25.4%	29.1%	35.8%

Source: Corporate records.

EXHIBIT 11

KAMPGROUNDS OF AMERICA, INC.
Leisure Inns

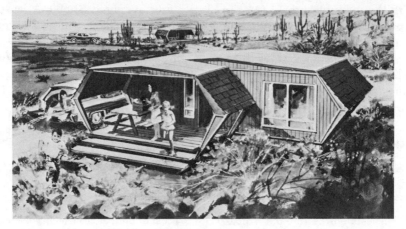

Accommodations to fit every traveler's budget

At Leisure Inns, you have a choice of three, economical accommodations packages.

Hostel $8.00 — sleeps 4   Overnighter $12.00 — sleeps 4   Vacationer $16.50 — sleeps 4

• The *Hostel* handily sleeps four in air conditioned, carpeted comfort. Complete with your own picnic patio and grill.

• The *Overnighter* sleeps four in air conditioned comfort. Complete with your own picnic patio.

• The luxurious *Vacationer* with microwave kitchen, private bath, master bedroom, air conditioning and picnic patio.

Leisure Inns were available in three styles: Hostel, Overnighter, and Vacationer, ranging from spartan to rather luxurious. The Hostel was a dual entry unit and could accommodate two parties of four. The other units accommodated four persons each. The Vacationer was the only unit equipped with kitchen and bath. The charge for each unit per night was $8.00, $12.00, and $16.50 respectively. (See Exhibit 11 for a picture of a Leisure Inn.)

The Leisure Inn modular unit was assembled on a production line and delivered on a trailer to the franchisee. With the addition of three sets of wheels and a towing hitch, the unit became a mobile home, allowing it to be set up at a campground under mobile home zoning and under state mobile home construction codes.

Management viewed budget motels as the chief competition for the KOA Leisure Inns. Budget motels were characterized as "back-to-basics" motels, which offered cost-conscious travelers clean yet modest accommodations at half the rate of the fancy motels that provided all the "extras" (e.g., luxury bathroom fixtures and double curtains for soundproofing).[13] Because of those economies, and especially because budget motel rooms cost less to build than conventional motel rooms $5,000–$7,000, as opposed to $10,000–$15,000 per room), they broke even at a 50 percent occupancy level, as opposed to the Howard Johnson Motel or Holiday Inn that required a 65–70 percent occupancy rate to make money.

Management differentiated the Leisure Inns from budget motels by several factors. Budget motels were located near fancy motels on interstates and were constructed as one unit. One KOA official had said:

> From a price standpoint, ours will be at or below the budget motel level, and from a facilities and environment standpoint, ours will be considered superior by the average traveling family. Unlike the budget motels, we are not focusing on the commercial market. We are focusing on the traveling family who is on vacation. Much of the investment in a budget motel already exists in the campground. Zoning has been accomplished, the utility system is in place, the management is there, and the operating burden is there. So all we really have to put in is the facility itself. Our cost per square foot of rentable space to the traveling family is really significantly below that of a budget motel coming in across the street.

The expected breakeven point for Leisure Inns was estimated at a 34 percent occupancy level on an annualized basis. Another company official stated that budget motels created a "plastic environment. KOA was going to create an experience, an out-of-door environment for children, off the interstates, and in individual units."

Fast Food Services. In 1973, KOA test marketed two fast food operations on its company-owned campground in Billings. While the idea was still very much in the conceptual stage, management felt that a fast food operation could reduce the traveling family's daily expenditure on meals by as much as 60 percent. Furthermore, it had the potential of reaching the local market.

The concept tested was the "Steak Pit," a rustic structure housing an open hearth where campers cooked the meat that they purchased from KOA, a self-service counter offering prepared food, such as salad and bread, and picnic tables. Installation of a Steak Pit cost $6,000. The franchise fee to KOA campground owners was $500 plus royalty payments of 8 percent of the revenues from the fast food operation. Steak Pits were available to non-KOA owners for a franchise fee of $5,000. Gross margins on food items were estimated at 40 percent which was achieved by keeping low inventories, reducing labor requirements, and offering a simple meal. In the test market in Billings, meals averaged $2 apiece and were served to 15 percent of all camper-night registrations (4.1 people per registration) over the season.

---

[13] From 1969–73 the number of low-cost motel rooms in the United States doubled to 28,000. By 1974 there were 20 budget motel chains.

2 Proprietary Health Systems, Inc.

"I think you're quite right, Ed," said Mark French, chairman of Proprietary Health Systems, Inc., to Edward Morgan, the company's president. "We now need to hammer out our future strategy. Let's set aside some time next week to sit down together and talk this over." It was May 1972 and the two executives had been discussing the company's progress to date and alternative strategies for future growth.

The headquarters of Proprietary Health Systems, Inc. (PHS), were in Chicago, Illinois, and the company owned and operated 70 health care facilities (mainly convalescent hospitals) in many parts of the United States. Revenues in 1972 were at an annual level of approximately $35 million.

CHARACTERISTICS OF THE HEALTH SERVICES MARKET

A number of simultaneous trends were increasing the demand for the type of services offered by PHS. National expenditures for all types of health and medical services had been increasing steadily during the past decade. In the period from 1960 to 1970, for instance, total national health expenditures increased from $26.4 billion to $67.2 billion. National health expenditures as a percent of the gross national product increased from 5.3 percent in 1960 to 7 percent in 1970.

In addition to growth in the overall demand for health care services, the demand for the services provided by PHS was growing even faster, due to the fact that utilization of hospital and particularly convalescent facilities increased dramatically with age, and this segment of the population had been increasing. The average number of days of hospital care per 1,000 members of the population was 1,023 days; utilization rates for certain older age groups, however, were higher (see Table 1).

The age groups with the highest utilization had been growing at a much faster rate than the nation's population in general: see Table 2.

TABLE 1

Average Number of Days of Hospital Care

Age	Average Per 1,000 Persons
55–64 years	1,980
65–74 years	2,764
75 years and over	4,674

It was estimated that by 1985, the population of persons over 65 would number at least 25 million.

A characteristic of the health delivery system was its fragmentation—an array of institutions that included intrinsically different types of hospitals, hospital emergency care and outpatient departments, long-term convalescent and rehabilitative facilities, teaching and research institutions, the solo physician in private practice, and the physician group practice.

TABLE 2

Growth in Population Aged 65 and Over

Year	Total U.S. Population (000s)	65 and Over Population (000s)	Percent of Total Population
1930	122,775	6,645	5.4%
1940	131,669	9,036	6.9
1950	150,697	12,294	8.2
1960	178,464	16,560	9.3
1970	203,166	20,050	9.9

In 1970, there were 7,123 short-term and long-term hospitals in the United States with over 1.6 million beds. Of these, 51 percent were non-profit hospitals (also called "voluntary hospitals"), 31 percent were run by state and local governments, 12 percent were proprietary (for-profit) hospitals, and 6 percent were federal institutions. The first three types included a category of hospital termed the "community hospital," which was defined by the American Hospital Association as a "non-federal, short-term, general or non-psychiatric special hospital whose facilities and services [were] available to the entire community." In addition to differences in ownership and length of stay (long-term and short-term), hospitals differed in other ways. Most common among hospital types was the "general" hospital, which did not cater exclusively to a specific disease or clientele as did the specialty hospitals. A partial list of hospital specializations would include tuberculosis and other respiratory diseases, psychiatry, maternity, eye, ear, nose and throat, orthopedics, contagious diseases, children, rehabilitation chronic diseases. Specialty hospitals appeared to be declining as more general hospitals were established and as more general hospitals added special services to their institutions. Illustrative data on services facilities, and programs of community hospitals are shown in Exhibit 1.

Substantive services in hospitals were directed by physicians who were designated members of the hospital's "staff." In 1970, of the 310,000 physicians in the United States, 278,000 were directly engaged in patient care. Within this latter group, approximately 152,000 were in private practice and 40,000 were in group practice (a growing trend among physicians). The remainder were hospital-based and included 11,000 interns, 40,000 residents and fellows, and 35,000 salaried physicians. Except for the major teaching institutions, many hospitals had few full-time senior salaried physicians. Consequently, health care in the various services was the responsibility of independent hospital-affiliated physicians.

Usually the trustees of the hospital granted staff status and hospital privileges (which allowed a physician to treat his patients at the hospital) on the recommendation of the medical staff's executive committee. A key participant in policy making, the trustees held legal responsibility for hospital operations and management; however, the physician staff generally was a key factor in policy decisions.

For the patient, entry into "the health care system" might be through a hospital's emergency room, an outpatient facility, or through a physician. Entering the system through the first two facilities appeared to be the growing practice. In 1970, 95 percent of the community hospitals had emergency service of some kind; and 33 percent reported having outpatient departments. Although the percentage of outpatient departments decreased slightly between 1969 and 1970, the number of outpatient visits grew from 163 million to 181 million. Exhibit 2 illustrates the services of an outpatient department in a 265-bed hospital in New York City.

Another development in the health system during the later part of the 1960s was the appearance of rapidly growing, proprietary companies. Some companies operated nursing homes exclusively; others operated acute-care community hospitals; and others were in a mix of these and other health-related activities. Three examples of larger corporations involved in acute-care hospitals were American Medicorp, American Medical Enterprises, and the Hospital Corporation of America. American Medicorp was established in 1968 and by 1970 operated 30 hospitals,

EXHIBIT 1

PROPRIETARY HEALTH SYSTEMS, INC.
Data on Facilities of U.S. Hospitals: 1970
(Nongovernmental, Not-for-Profit, Community Hospitals)

	Hospital Size (Beds)							
	6–24	25–49	50–99	100–199	200–299	300–399	400–499	500 + over
Expense/Bed........................	$11,818	$13,529	$16,415	$19,964	$23,949	$25,162	$26,821	$29,689
Number of Hospitals Reporting......	120	486	701	829	473	300	155	159
Percentage of Hospitals Having These Facilities								
Postoperative Recovery Room......	15.8%	35.4%	77.0%	95.8%	98.5%	98.7%	100.0%	98.7%
Intensive-Care Unit................	4.2	11.5	32.1	67.9	91.1	98.0	97.4	100.0
Intensive Cardiac Care Unit........	5.8	16.0	30.8	52.1	70.0	79.7	85.8	95.0
Open Heart Surgery...............	0.8	0.0	.9	2.8	9.1	22.3	40.0	63.5
Pharmacy with FT Registered Pharmacist......................	3.3	9.1	37.2	85.4	98.9	98.7	100.0	100.0
Pharmacy with PT Registered Pharmacist......................	36.7	50.0	45.4	13.5	2.7	4.3	5.8	5.7
X-ray Therapy......................	2.5	3.9	14.8	43.3	70.8	82.0	93.5	93.7
Cobalt Therapy.....................	0.0	0.4	1.4	8.3	22.0	41.7	60.0	76.1
Radium Therapy....................	0.0	0.8	10.6	32.2	62.6	79.7	85.2	95.6
Radioisotope Facility...............	0.8	2.1	13.4	48.1	84.6	94.7	98.1	99.4
Histopathology Lab.................	2.5	8.6	30.4	73.9	92.8	97.7	98.1	98.1
Organ Bank........................	0.0	1.0	.7	2.4	4.0	9.0	4.5	23.9
Blood Bank........................	17.5	34.6	59.6	72.7	83.9	88.0	92.3	94.3
Electroencephalography............	0.8	4.1	12.0	36.7	69.6	87.7	96.1	98.1
Inhalation Therapy.................	9.2	21.4	44.4	76.2	90.9	96.3	100.0	98.7
Premature Nursery.................	5.8	13.2	29.1	48.3	68.1	83.3	87.7	89.9
Self-Care Unit......................	5.0	1.9	1.7	4.0	9.5	15.3	20.6	28.3
Extended Care Unit................	5.8	4.7	13.1	14.1	11.4	14.0	16.1	18.9
Inpatient Rental Dialysis...........	0.0	1.2	2.9	6.6	15.6	27.7	47.1	59.1
Outpatient Renal Dialysis..........	0.8	0.8	1.4	4.1	11.6	15.7	25.8	45.3
Physical Therapy...................	9.2	27.8	59.3	81.7	95.3	96.3	98.1	98.7
Occupational Therapy.............	1.7	2.5	5.1	12.1	24.5	39.0	52.9	76.7
Rehabilitation Inpatient Unit.......	0.8	2.9	3.1	7.7	14.0	22.3	29.0	52.8
Rehabilitation Outpatient Unit......	0.8	3.1	2.7	8.0	13.1	20.0	27.1	52.2
Psychiatric Inpatient Unit..........	0.0	1.4	2.7	9.7	23.5	45.0	56.8	74.8
Psychiatric Outpatient Unit.........	5.0	2.9	3.6	6.9	17.8	27.3	41.9	55.3
Psychiatric Partial Hospitalization...	1.7	1.4	1.9	5.1	10.8	14.0	20.6	34.6
Psychiatric Emergency Unit........	5.0	2.9	3.7	12.2	23.5	38.3	43.9	59.1
Psychiatric Foster and/or Home Care.............................	0.0	0.0	0.1	0.4	1.3	0.7	4.5	3.8
Social Work Department............	18.3	3.7	11.7	30.5	60.0	72.0	83.9	86.2
Family Planning....................	0.8	1.4	1.6	3.3	9.1	16.0	22.6	37.7
Home Care Department............	0.8	3.7	3.7	8.8	16.3	14.0	23.9	22.0
Hospital Auxiliary..................	56.7	68.1	81.9	88.1	93.2	95.0	94.2	95.0
Organized Outpatient Department..	43.3	21.0	22.1	29.0	46.5	65.3	74.8	84.9
Major Emergency..................	0.8	1.9	4.4	17.6	37.2	46.3	58.7	64.2
Basic Emergency..................	21.7	28.0	39.1	48.3	46.7	44.7	37.4	34.6
Provisional Emergency.............	50.8	59.9	47.4	29.1	14.6	6.3	3.2	0.6
Emergency Referral................	6.7	3.3	3.4	1.4	1.5	1.0	0.6	0.6
Percentage of Hospitals Having These Teaching Accreditations								
Cancer Program....................	0.0	0.4	3.7	9.9	27.6	41.5	53.2	64.5
Residency..........................	0.0	1.1	2.3	9.2	33.9	59.8	79.1	89.2
Internship..........................	0.0	0.0	0.1	4.1	27.6	55.1	75.9	89.2
Medical School Affiliation..........	0.0	0.2	0.9	5.3	10.8	21.9	41.1	58.4
Professional Nursing School........	0.0	0.0	0.5	8.2	28.9	47.8	58.9	62.0
Member of Council of Teaching	0.0	0.2	0.5	1.2	6.0	13.6	36.1	60.2

Source: American Hospital Association, *Hospitals,* Journal of the American Hospital Association, Guide Issue–Part 2, vol. 45, no. 15 (August 1, 1971), pp. 464, 480–84, 489.
    Reproduced with permission from "Trends in the Environment, the Economics, and the Organization of the Health Care System," a document prepared by Cambridge Research Institute, Inc., Cambridge, Massachusetts, for the New England Deaconess Hospital, Boston, Massachusetts (1972); p. 114.

EXHIBIT 2

PROPRIETARY HEALTH SYSTEMS, INC.
Illustrative Hospital Outpatient Services
Outpatient (Dispensary) Statistical Report

	Total Visits		
Clinics	*1970*	*1969*	*1968*
Medical			
Medical.........................	4,033	4,498	4,746
Diabetic........................	724	610	615
Arthritis........................	65	88	155
Dermatology and venereal.......	458	436	503
Cardiac—Adult..................	601	501	497
Cardiac—Child..................	61	36	35
Allergy.........................	2,183	2,224	1,853
Gastrointestinal.................	51	50	56
Podiatry........................	257	340	321
Hypertensive....................	163	162	118
Hypocholestermia................	14	16	37
Endocrine.......................	86	64	81
Neurology.......................	100	124	77
Phy. med. rehab.................	1,071	1,172	670
Surgery			
Surgery.........................	1,362	1,460	1,585
Urology.........................	477	442	562
Orthopedic......................	1,064	717	635
Eye.............................	151	320	302
Ear, nose and throat............	286	279	259
Vascular........................	24	18	16
Neurosurgery....................	—	1	—
Thoracic........................	—	2	11
Plastic reconstruction...........	78	78	131
Gynecology			
Gynecology......................	2,551	2,386	2,406
Family planning.................	865	597	268
Planned parenthood.............	3	2	154
Sterility—Adolescent gyn........	27	10	8
Obstetrics			
Obstetrics......................	2,588	3,137	2,729
Pediatrics			
Pediatrics......................	2,198	2,117	2,241
Well baby......................	989	960	1,066
Adolescent......................	193	179	187
Adolescent nutrition.............	96	16	45
Youth counseling................	—	4	22
Psychiatry			
Psychiatry......................	1,161	1,150	1,074
Speech.........................	238	312	253
Child guidance..................	349	266	371
Psychological testing............	84	63	65
Remedial reading...............	1,459	1,438	1,302
New patients....................	3,046	2,438	2,299
Old patients....................	4,208	5,042	5,100
Total Patients.............	7,254	7,480	7,399
Total Visits................	26,110	26,275	25,456

Source: Report of the New York Infirmary, for the years 1968–69–70.

three skilled care nursing centers, and a school of nursing. AM's sales in 1969 were $77.6 million, and in 1970 about $130 million. Per-share earnings jumped to about $0.95 in 1970 from $0.68 in 1969. American Medical Enterprises operated hospitals in California and Texas as well as medical laboratories and other services. In 1970, sales for these activities were $54.1 million, IAT $2.49 million, and per-share earnings $0.69. Hospital Corporation of America operated 33 acute-care hospitals, mostly in the Southeast. Sales in 1970 were $70.3 million, up from $55.1 million in 1969. During the same period, IAT increased from $3.3 million to $5.6 million, or from $0.73 to $0.93 per share.

More often, in recent years, the differences in clientele of the governmental, voluntary, and proprietary institutions had faded. Government institutions were accepting more Blue Cross and paying patients; the voluntaries found that with Medicare[1] and Medicaid the "charity" patient had largely disappeared; and the proprietaries served former "charity" patients (i.e., many Medicare and Medicaid patients).

Although these particular differences had blurred, the health system remained fragmented and operated on the basis of the most informal cooperation among the various autonomous providers, facilities, and financial intermediaries (e.g., insurance companies, Blue Cross/Blue Shield, etc.). Because of the absence of a "total" health care system and rising costs, several proposals relating to the provision of some kind of national health care program were advocated. These included: President Nixon's "National Health Insurance Partnership Act"; Senator Edward M. Kennedy's "Health Security Act"; the American Medical Association's "Health Insurance Assistance Act"; and the American Hospital Association's "Ameriplan." The Nixon and Kennedy plans advocated a reorganized health service delivery system and the creation of what were called health maintenance organizations (HMOs). Some authorities believed that if a federal program were passed, it would contain incentives for HMOs.

The most prominent example of the HMO concept in the United States was the Kaiser Permanente Medical Program, which had been started in the 1930s with the encouragement of the late Henry J. Kaiser. Established originally to provide Kaiser employees with low-cost, high-quality medical care, by 1970 the plan served two million subscribers (of which only 3 percent were Kaiser employees) and employed 2,000 physicians in 21 hospitals and 54 clinics. This nonprofit program was organized in three parts: The Kaiser Foundation Health Plan, Inc., was the administering organization, which enrolled subscribers and established service contracts with Permanente physician groups and the Kaiser hospitals; six inde-

---

[1] Medicare is a federal program providing hospital and medical insurance benefits for covered persons age 65 and over. Medicaid is a federally assisted state program providing medical assistance to the medically indigent.

pendent Permanente Medical Groups, each of which included practically all specialties (although no group was entirely self-sufficient); and the Kaiser Foundation Hospitals, which was a legally separate nonprofit corporation which owned, operated and managed hospitals, equipment, and services for inpatient and outpatient care. The program operated on a prepayment basis. Largely, but not totally self-contained, Kaiser hospitals were primarily staffed by Permanente physicians. In instances when a particular specialty was unavailable in a Permanente group, physicians used other community resources and medical schools.

THE FORMATION OF PROPRIETARY HEALTH SYSTEMS, INC.

Proprietary Health Systems, Inc., was founded in 1968 by a financial institution and a major insurance company that had a portfolio interest in investing in the health services industry. Ten patient-care facilities with an aggregate of 910 licensed beds were acquired during 1968, and numerous other facilities were acquired during 1969 and 1970.

"The rationale behind the creation of the corporation," observed one executive, "was that 'Health was a great field'. Acquisitions were done very much on that basis; it was a matter of 'let's buy it and don't bother me with the details.' Companies were up for grabs at that time and took the best offers they could find. The criteria applied in making purchases were (a) high quality—that is, they should be the best in their area, and (b) good earnings. On the whole the corporation made good buys, given the generally inflated prices of the time."

PHS's patient-care facilities were primarily nursing homes, otherwise known as convalescent hospitals, which provided skilled nursing, convalescent, and rehabilitative care, primarily to elderly inpatients. In April 1972, the company's 70 patient-care facilities had an aggregate of 7,600 beds licensed by applicable governmental authorities and, subject to staffing and other licensing requirements, could be licensed for an additional 150 beds. Under management's current operating policies, the number of licensed beds actually in operation varied from time to time. Of the company's 7,600 licensed beds, all but 300 were convalescent hospital beds, the balance being in two facilities for elderly persons not requiring nursing care. These latter facilities were located adjacent to or in the immediate vicinity of a convalescent hospital. The company also owned and operated a 60-unit residential apartment in New Mexico, which had an intercom system with a neighboring convalescent hospital owned by PHS. See Exhibit 3 for data on the size and location of PHS's facilities.

PHS incurred a substantial loss in 1970. Management attributed this to the rapidity of the company's acquisition program and to reimburse-

EXHIBIT 3

PROPRIETARY HEALTH SYSTEMS, INC.
List of Facilities Owned by PHS, Inc.

	Region	Number of Facilities	Number of Licensed Beds
I.	New England..............	22	2,681
II.	Midwest...................	6	621
III.	Northwest.................	21	1,916
IV.	Southwest.................	21	2,382
		70	7,600

ment problems in the patient-care industry caused by changes in government regulations and practice. "The concept of the corporation was good," noted one individual, "but the execution was weak. Nobody asked, 'How do we operate these?'."

ECF's, Rehabilitation Units, and Nursing Homes

"The health delivery business," said Ed Morgan, "can be visualized as a continuum which ranges from the acute-care hospital at one end, through the extended-care facility and the nursing home, to home health services at the other end. These segments are distinguished by the length of the patient's stay—which is shortest in the acute-care hospital and gets increasingly longer as one moves along the continuum. The segments are also distinguished by differentials in the cost per day per patient. The figures are about like this:

Type of Institution	Length of Stay	Approximate Cost per Day	Capital Construction Cost per Bed
Acute-care hospital...........	7–8 days	$85	$40–50,000
ECF..........................	20–40 days	$30	$12–14,000
Nursing home................	180–220 days	$15	$8,000
Residential care unit.........	360 days	$10	$5,000
Home service.................	—	$1–2	—

Extended-care facilities (ECFs), rehabilitation units, and nursing homes provided the kind of care required after a patient had passed the acute stages of an illness, or when he was too ill to take care of himself properly but did not need intensive medical treatment.[2]

---

[2] Information of ECFs, etc., in this and the following five paragraphs is largely based on "Trends in the Environment, The Economics and The Organization of the Health Care System," prepared by Cambridge Research Institute, Inc., Cambridge, Massachusetts, for the New England Deaconess Hospital, Boston, Massachusetts (1972) p. 95–97.

Extended-care facilities (ECFs), as defined by the American Hospital Association, provided physician services and continuous professional nursing supervision for patients who required inpatient care but who did not require the level of service associated with regular hospital inpatient services. ECFs were assuming an increasingly important place in the health care system. In 1967, there were 4,154 ECFs in the United States, with 290,893 beds. In 1969, 4,840 facilities were reported with over 341,000 beds. Some ECFs were owned or operated by hospitals; in 1970 nearly 15 percent of all A.H.A.–registered hospitals had extended-care units. It was reported that 71 percent of ECFs were for-profit institutions, 9 percent were government owned, and 20 percent were nonprofit, tax-exempt institutions.

Because ECFs could provide care at a lower cost per patient day, hospitals were encouraged to set up a special unit to provide extended care services to appropriate patients. The federal hospital construction program under the Hill-Burton Act required hospitals requesting funds to give assurance that an ECF would be provided which was structurally part of (or in the immediate vicinity of) the hospital, which had a transfer agreement with the hospital, or which was supervised by the hospital staff or had its own medical unit. Medicare, too, required that hospitals receiving Medicare reimbursements had at least a transfer agreement with an ECF. In 1968, 38 Blue Cross plans provided benefits in ECFs.

Rehabilitation inpatient units in hospitals provided coordinated multidisciplinary physical and restorative services. These units helped patients learn to cope with some new physical disability. In 1970, such units were reported in nearly 15 percent of all A.H.A.–registered hospitals, mostly hospitals with 500 or more beds.

Nursing homes typically provided housing and long-term care, primarily for the aged. Surgical services were not a principal function of these institutions, but most of them provided some level of nursing care. A few facilities were limited to the care of convalescent children or to providing services to mentally disturbed patients. However, it was estimated in 1969 that 88 percent of the residents in nursing homes and related facilities were at least 65 years of age.

The number of nursing home beds had grown rapidly. In 1961, there were 23,000 nursing homes, with 593,000 beds. By 1969 there were 19,000, with 944,000 beds (see Exhibit 4). The U.S. Department of Labor forecast 1.2 million nursing home beds by 1975, exceeding the number of beds in short-term hospitals. This was primarily a reflection of the changing age distribution of the population, but it also reflected changes in the reimbursement policies of insurance companies and government agencies.

Proprietary Health Systems' patient-care operations and facilities were subject to regulatory and licensing requirements of state and local authorities. Such authorities reviewed the safety, fitness, and adequacy of

EXHIBIT 4

PROPRIETARY HEALTH SYSTEMS, INC.
Growth in Nursing Homes and Related Facilities

	1961		1963		1967		1969	
	Units	Beds	Units	Beds	Units	Beds	Units	Beds
Nursing care homes[1]........	9,400	311,700	8,128	319,224	10,636	584,052	11,484	704,217
Personal care homes with nursing care[2].........	1,400	83,100	4,958	188,306	3,853	191,096	3,514	174,874
Personal care homes[3].......	9,700	124,000	2,927	48,962	4,396	66,787	3,792	63,532
Domicilary care homes[4].....	2,200	47,000	688	12,068	256	4,619	120	1,253
Nursing home units in hospitals.................	300	27,000	688	44,864	*	*	*	*
Total.................	23,000	592,800	17,189	613,864	19,141	846,554	18,910	943,876

Notes: If room and board are the only services provided by an establishment, it is excluded as a health facility.

* Included in "nursing care homes."

[1] A nursing care home is one in which at least 50 percent of the residents receive one or more nursing services, and where at least one registered nurse (RN) or licensed practical nurse (LPN) is employed 35 hours or more per week. Nursing services include nasal feeding, catheterization, irrigation, oxygen therapy, full bed bath, enema, hypodermic injection, intravenous injection, temperature–pulse–respiration, blood pressure, application of dressing or bandage, and bowel and bladder retraining.

[2] A personal care home with nursing care is one in which either (a) some of the residents but less than 50 percent receive nursing care, or (b) more than 50 percent of the residents receive nursing care but no RNs or LPNs were employed full time on the staff.

[3] A personal care home is one in which the facility routinely provides three or more personal services but no nursing service. Personal services include rub or massage service, or assistance with bathing, dressing, correspondence, or shopping, walking, or getting about, and eating.

[4] A domicilary care home is defined as one in which the facility routinely provides less than three of the personal services specified in the definition above and no nursing service. This type of facility provides a sheltered environment primarily to persons who are able to care for themselves.

Sources: U.S. Department of Health, Education and Welfare, Public Health Service, Health Services and Mental Health Administration, Health Resources Statistics, 1969, May 1970 pp. 237–243, 257–263; presented in "Trends in the Environment, the Economics, and the Organization of the Health Care System," prepared by Cambridge Research Institute, Inc., Cambridge, Massachusetts (1972), p. 98. Also, Health Resources Statistics, 1971 (May 1972), p. 320.

the facilities, equipment, personnel, and standards of care. Licenses were subject to annual renewal. These regulations were in addition to requirements and standards, which had to be met in order to qualify for payment under the Medicare and Medicaid programs.

PHS's facilities competed on a local and regional basis with other comparable facilities. It was intended that PHS facilities supplement rather than compete with acute care hospitals; however, such competition could develop, since some hospitals had indicated that they would expand into the convalescent care field. Competition also existed with nonprofit patient-care facilities, some or all of the financial requirements of which might be obtained from government grants or other sources not available to PHS.

Management and Operations in 1971

Unprofitable operations continued at PHS from 1970 into 1971. During 1971, however, new management was brought in and steps were taken to establish operations on a profitable basis.

The first major appointment occurred in June 1971 when Edward Morgan joined PHS as its president. Morgan had graduated from a well-known Eastern business school in the mid-1960s and had joined a medical supply and pharmaceutical company where he ran a market research and development group. He had been asked to look at opportunities in health care and got to learn a little about the health delivery system. "After a while, I got an entrepreneurial itch. I raised some money and acquired some ECFs and nursing homes. Later we merged with a larger company. I stayed with them about a year in order to make the 'earn out' that we had arranged, and then decided that I saw less personal opportunity staying within the corporation than I wanted. The opportunity at PHS came up and I took it."

Morgan brought with him a group of eight people who had been working with him in his previous two companies. (An organization chart for PHS is shown in Exhibit 5.) During the next few months there was a profit turn-around; the cash drain ceased and, in fact, PHS developed a positive cash flow. This was accomplished by about October 1971. The reasons for the turn-around involved cost reductions (a reduction in administrative overhead at the regional office level) and an increase in occupancy rates (accomplished through designing and promoting services).

EXHIBIT 5

PROPRIETARY HEALTH SYSTEMS, INC.
Organization Chart, May 1971

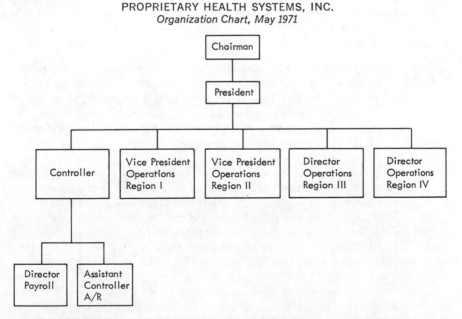

Note: Each hospital had an administrator. Groups of three or four hospitals in an area were under the responsibility of a district manager. Districts were then grouped under regional managers.

At the beginning of December 1971, Mark French joined PHS as chairman. French had previously been a manager in a national firm manufacturing processed foods. Several years earlier in this capacity, he had had some contact with the Kaiser medical care program. "I found that Kaiser was the only group that was willing to listen and to look at the question of feeding their patients and to criticize what they were presently doing. Also, they were way ahead of the others in the field—conceptually and in every other way." When the opportunity to move into a health delivery organization was offered to him he had readily accepted: "The possibility of developing an innovative health care organization is far more interesting to me than being in on the birth of soluble coffee. There is much more personal satisfaction—and an opportunity to make a tremendous contribution to mankind." "I think that you can also see," said Morgan "that French was an expert in one industry and can apply what he learned there to another business."

Operating Plan for 1972

Within three months of joining PHS, Morgan was engaged in leading his staff in preparing a budget for 1972. "The budget, operating and marketing plan we prepared contained the basic elements of what I wanted to do after my first few months here," said Morgan. These plans, in addition to cost and profit budgets, included specific plans for quality control, cost control, management control, expanding PHS's market share and its market, and a profit-sharing plan for managers. Each of these is discussed in turn in the following excerpts from a PHS management report prepared in March 1972.

> ***Quality Control.*** Our objectives are to provide quality patient care and service at a profit. In terms of return on equity, the profit budget for 1972 shows a return of 11.8 percent before taxes. Quality, of course, is more difficult to measure, and we have taken several steps to insure that the quality of our patient care and service is superior. In particular, we added in 1972 a director of nursing services, a director of dietary services, and a director of real estate.
>
> Each of these three functions plays an important role in maintaining and increasing the quality of our services. The director of dietary services, for example, is a qualified ADA-registered Dietitian. This function provides central diets and menus for all of our nursing centers that insure appropriate threapeutic foods for our patients. In addition, programs are being designed to create tastefully prepared foods that will be presented in an appetizing manner. The director of nursing services is a registered nurse, with experience in hospitals and nursing centers, and this function provides guidelines for nursing care and services in our facilities (for example, developing staffing patterns, medication routines, nurses training programs, and consistent charting routines). The director of real

estate can aid in maintaining and improving our physical plants (e.g., through development of standard housekeeping and maintenance programs).

In addition to the positions indicated above, each region contains one registered nurse who is designated as "Nurse Consultant" for that Region. As such, she is available for consultation and periodically makes inspection tours of the facilities within the region to evaluate the quality of patient care and services and to recommend corrective action.

Cost Control. Several programs have been initiated to control and/or reduce expenses:

1. A consulting group was retained to help lower and maintain our experience ratings for Unemployment Compensation. Our current rating averages close to 2.5 percent and we are projecting a 4 percent decrease, or a savings of $88,000.
2. A national utility consulting firm has been retained to help us control utility costs, which are running at an annual rate of $1 million.
3. The director of real estate, in addition to working with the utility consultants, is responsible for cost control and reduction in the following areas:
    a. Appealing all real estate and property tax rates or assessments.
    b. All capital expenditures.
    c. Repairs and maintenance in each facility.
4. The director of dietary services is responsible for developing menus that are costed at $"X" per patient day, as well as staffing patterns and procedures for lowering dietary personnel costs.
5. The director of nursing services is responsible for developing and recommending cost reductions and efficiencies in the area of nursing wages and supplies.
6. Timely reporting to administrators and other managers is a key in cost control, and we have provided detailed financial statements by the 15th of each month for the preceding month.

Management Controls. A new chart of accounts was introduced early in 1972 that is designed to give more accurate information than those used in the past. In January 1972, the first nursing centers began use of our own payroll system; the past custom of preparing payrolls through several banks or using a manual system is being phased out. This step provides greater control over payroll, which approximates 50 to 55 percent of our total costs. Finally, a weekly profit report has been developed that will provide more timely information than can be provided through the normal monthly financial statements.

Expanding Market Share. Patients, their families, and friends indicate during the admission process to our nursing centers that there are two general reasons they have selected us as opposed to our competitors: (1) referral by an "expert"; (2) personal choice and selection. Naturally, both the referral and the personal choice or selection are presumably made on the basis of whether our patient care and service is either reputed or observed to be of an appropriate quality. Since most sources of referral, as well as patients, their families and friends, are either not qualified to judge levels of patient care and service that are reasonably similar, or do not always take the time to do so (in the case of hospital social workers, for example), marketing through an indirect selling effort, a direct sales effort, and promotion or advertising can be particularly effective depending on size (rural versus city) and sophistication of the market. (See Exhibit 6.)

In addition to plans designed to increase our occupancy, several programs have begun to improve the profit mix of our centers. The private paying patient (as opposed to welfare or Medicaid) is the most profitable segment of our market. The private patient generally pays from $5 to $15 per day above the rates paid by welfare or Medicaid. Historically it has been considered somewhere in between "immoral and unprofessional" to provide anything but one level of service to nursing center patients. In the last six months, however, we have had some notable success in the following areas, and plan to extend these ideas further:

1. Selective menus (e.g., a choice between fish and roast beef) for patients willing to pay for them.
2. A "Pavilion" area in some of our centers where additional staffing can provide added personal services desired by these patients or their families.
3. Limousine Shopping Service.

EXHIBIT 6

PROPRIETARY HEALTH SYSTEMS INC.
Excerpts from PHS Report on Selected Marketing Activities

Indirect Selling programs are being implemented in all of our Centers. A Marketing Manual has been developed and its use is designed to accomplish two results: 1) Define Sources of Patient Referral by Priority or Importance; 2) Develop a routine schedule for visitation and/or contact. Each Marketing Manual contains a list of Patient Referral Sources that have proven to be beneficial across the country (e.g., physicians, Hospital Social Service Workers, Bank Trust Officers, Visiting Nurses Associations, etc.) and recent seminars in each Region have further attempted to educate our Administrators on the Sources of Patient Referral, who they are, and how to "sell" them. In all cases, senior and experienced management is reviewing every Marketing Manual with each Administrator to determine that the appropriate sources of patient referral have been correctly defined and scheduled for visitation.

The next step is to consummate the sale to our sources of patient referral and involved scheduled visitation on a frequent and repetitive basis. For example, a survey of 6 of our "best" Nursing Centers revealed that these Administrators were making less than two marketing contacts per week. None of these Administrators scheduled their visit in advance. A similar survey of five Nursing Centers with census problems showed that only one Administrator was making any marketing contacts at all!

Our *Direct Selling* effort occurs within each Nursing Center or

EXHIBIT 6 (*continued*)

wherever our Administrators have direct contact with a patient or a Decision-Maker for the patient. "The best salesman is a good product" has more validity in this area than others since a visit to our Nursing Center by a patient or his representative should result in a positive image of our quality patient care and service.

Some of the areas in which we are improving our Direct Selling effort include:

1. The administrator and Director of Nurses are now required to work every other weekend since this is a time when many Admission inquiries are made.

2. Administrators and Directors of Nursing are trained in the presentation of our facility, its patient care, service and, of course, how to close a sale—e.g., "When may we schedule your admission?"

3. Nurse Supervisors who have frequent contact with Admission inquiries (e.g., the Evening Nurse Supervisor) are also exposed to the correct procedures for handling an Admission Inquiry.

4. Follow-up on Admission Inquiries is being required of all Administrators until a final disposition—Admit or do not Admit—of each inquiry is made.

5. A reporting system is being developed to compare the number of Admissions to the number of inquiries so that the Administrator and his immediate superiors can react to unfavorable trends in the number of inquiries or the number of Admissions per inquiry.

We have also begun several other Promotional or Advertising programs which are divided into the categories of Direct Mail, Newspaper and Magazine Advertising and Direct and Indirect Selling Aids.

A) The primary thrust of our *Direct Mail* campaign revolves around a magazine that will be sent monthly to approximately 100 potential sources of patient referral for each of our Nursing Centers. This magazine is similar to the magazines found on the airlines and is paid for through advertising by our vendors (pharmacies, food suppliers, etc.) This magazine will be sent to physicians, hospitals and others who will probably place them in the Waiting Rooms and Reception Areas for public reading.

B) *Newspaper and Magazine* advertising is used in selective areas only. Some examples are:
1. County Medical Society Magazines.
2. Specialty magazines (See Exhibit 5 for an example).
3. Telephone Directory Advertising.

An important part of our newspaper advertising program is a continual flow of News Releases about activities at each of our Centers. For example, we are attempting to designate each of our Centers as a Polling Place, thus creating free publicity. We are offering our meeting rooms, to Clergy, Women's Clubs, Men's Clubs, etc., and making announcements of these meetings in the papers.

EXHIBIT 6 (*continued*)

C) *Direct and Indirect* Selling Aids include maps, post cards and Information Sheets that are used by our Administrators in making presentations to physicians, social workers, and other sources of patient referral. Brochures and other literature have been developed to provide Admission Inquiries with information about our centers.

Expanding the Market. Medicare Certification is perceived by the medical community and the lay public in general as being a positive selection criteria for Nursing Centers. We have requested and obtained Medicare Certification of 24 of our facilities which have not participated in the program in the past. These facilities plus the 20 already participating in the program are being publicized in all of our promotional materials, as well as in News Releases to the papers, as participating in the Medicare program. Personal letters have been sent also to physicians in each community involved.

Meetings with the Joint Commission on Accreditation of Hospitals, Extended Care Facilities, and Nursing Care Facilities have been held. Forty-five units have now been accredited and the remainder will be completed in three months. Certification by this body will be publicized accordingly. This step along with the recent Medicare Certification requests should result in an expansion of our market since we will qualify to render a higher level of patient care for the post-hospital, post-surgical patient.

Other specialty market areas are being investigated and/or utilized on a trial basis with the thought that an increased market from which to draw can help to increase occupancy. Additionally, many specialty medical markets can justify substantially higher prices and profit margins than the markets in which we currently operate. For example, some of these specialty programs include:

1. An Artificial Kidney Center established in Litchfield, Illinois, in conjunction with the Veterans Administration.
2. A proposal presented to St. Francis Hospital in Evanston, Illinois, to utilize a portion of one of our facilities as an Alcoholic Treatment Center.
3. Utilization of part of our center in Boston, Massachusetts, for light mental or psychiatric patients.
4. Negotiation of a national contract with the Veterans Administration for the treatment of permanently disabled war veterans.

Marketing Costs—Direct. The final major area in our Marketing Plan for 1972 was the cost and manpower segment; where appropriate we budgeted additional "Marketing" expenditures as follows:

EXHIBIT 6 *(concluded)*

1. Reception Coverage in the Administrators
   Absence for Marketing Calls and Activities........ $ 54,000
2. Promotional Literature and Selling Aids........... 29,000
3. Training—Sales and Marketing.................... 6,000
4. Added Travel and Entertainment Expense........ 15,000
5. Marketing Seminar Expense...................... 11,000
6. Added Personnel................................ 108,000
   Total.. $223,000

The "Added Personnel—$108,000" provides nine men (four in California, two in Washington, and three in New England) whose responsibilities will revolve around marketing our centers in major metropolitan areas. Specifically, these men will call on physicians offices, social workers, visiting nurses, retirement and senior citizens clubs, bank trust officers, and other sources of patient referral. Each of these men will report directly to the district manager who is in charge of 3–10 nursing centers.

Profit Incentives. Finally we established a profit-sharing plan. [Details of this are given in Exhibit 7.]

EXHIBIT 7

PROPRIETARY HEALTH SYSTEMS, INC.
Administrative Profit Sharing Plan

Based upon the premise that the responsibility and authority for operation of a Nursing Center is in the hands of the Administrator, this paper outlines a Profit Sharing Plan designed to reward those who accomplish profitability and patient care goals for their Nursing Center.

Each Nursing Center has as its objective to earn a profit and to render good patient care. The following list of rules will guide the implementation of the Profit Sharing Plan (PSP).

PSP Rules

1. Administrators and District Administrators are eligible for participation in the Profit Sharing Plan (PSP).

2. All PSP calculations will be made by the Controller based upon his audit of financial statements after all adjustments. It is anticipated that PSP Bonus checks will be mailed no later than three months after each audit.

3. PSP Bonus checks will be issued based upon financial audits by the Controller for the first and second six months of our Company's fiscal year. (For example, January–June and July–December.)

4. PSP Bonus Checks will be issued upon approval of the President and Regional Vice-President.

5. All PSP Bonus Checks will be charged as an expense to the Nursing Center's Financial Statements after earned, but not charged to the next six month period.

EXHIBIT 7 (continued)

6. The President and Regional Vice-President of the Company have the authority to deny any PSP Bonus Check for any reason.

7. At least one inspection will be made by an Officer each six months to determine compliance with established standards of quality necessary to maintain a high level of patient care and service. This inspection will result in an "Acceptable" or "Unacceptable" rating which will determine participation in the PSP. A copy of this inspection report will be sent to the Administrator, District Administrator, Regional Vice President or Director and President of the Company. The basis of this inspection will be guidelines established by the Joint Commission on Accreditation of Extended Care and Nursing Care Facilities.

8. ALL PSP Bonus Checks will be based upon the computerized monthly Profit and Loss Statement sent to the Nursing Center each month. EXCEPTION: See Rule 9.

9. Because some facilities rely heavily on Annual Cost Audits with Medicare or Medicaid, the Controller may recommend, and the President and Regional Vice-President may approve, that these PSP Bonus Checks be computed and paid on an Annual basis. You will be notified if your facility falls into this category.

10. Sample Calculations—See illustration 1 below.

1. *PSP Goal* will be established with each Administrator.
2. PSP Profits are defined as all profits* less Accounts Receivable (A/R) over 45 days old.
3. Administrators will receive 10 percent of all *PSP Profits* in excess of the *PSP Goals*.

Illustration 1

XYZ Nursing Center—100 Beds
January–June 1971
Profit Before Taxes.................... $31,000
A/R Over 45 Days..................... 1,000
PSP Goal............................ 20,000

PSP Profit = Profit Before Taxes less A/R over 45 days
= $31,000–$1,000 = $30,000

* * * * *

Administrators Profit Sharing Plan = (*PSP Profit* less *PSP Goal*) × 10%
= ($30,000–$20,000) × 10%
= $1,000

Assessment of Current Business Operations

The top management of PHS considered that a large chain of nursing care units had a number of potential advantages over a series of indi-

---

* Profit before Federal Income Taxes but after all other applicable State and Federal Taxes.

vidual, independent units and that this would be reflected in better services to patients and/or lower costs.

One PHS executive noted the advantages in marketing:

> In the area of marketing we have an advantage. By having accreditation with the Joint Commission and being certified for Medicare, the patient is assured of high standards and a broader scope of medical services. It is then possible to promote our name and gain regional or national credibility. We can go to insurance companies and corporations and make our service a part of their retirement benefit program—or we can sell our services to state and federal government agencies on a broad basis.
>
> The area of promotion or advertising, in fact, is particularly challenging—since the fundamental name of each nursing center is in question. At present each unit still bears the name it possessed when it was acquired by PHS. Should we rename them all? And if we should, should we use the Holiday Inn–type approach (e.g., PHS nursing centers, PHS medical centers, etc.)—or should we retain the good will of our existing names and use the auto industry approach (South Shore Ford or Jim Murdock Chevrolet)?

Another PHS executive pointed out what he believed to be some of the economic benefits of size:

> One thing is that one can have common specialists serving a number of units—e.g., inhalation, physical, occupational, or speech therapists.
>
> A chain of units also has some functional advantages over the "mom and pop" operations. People costs, for instance, account for half our expenditures. We can cut this down by introducing training programs (and using initially less skilled versus expensive, highly skilled people). We can develop job standardization. We can make comparisons of efficiency between our units—in both personnel and other areas. One area in which we have had comparisons is the question of dietary costs. Because of our size we can also arrange certain purchasing economies— such as the purchase of "X" thousand pounds of hamburger meat for a week's meals.

Future Expansion of Proprietary Health Systems, Inc.

The top management of PHS believed that there was "great fragmentation in the patient-care business. "It is essentially a "mom and pop" business," observed Morgan. In planning the future of PHS, Morgan saw a number of alternative possible ways in which the company might grow during the next few years. Morgan discussed some of these choices with Mark French in May 1972, and subsequently with the casewriter:

> Expansion would be easy through acquisition of additional facilities like our present properties or through construction of new units. These

would each be free standing units and PHS would be providing one portion of the health care delivery system. If we had the money, we could be a $500 million company in five years going this route.

The problems we see include, among other things, the possibility of government intervention in the health field. Also we would want to avoid doing the same thing that was done in the past—i.e., acquiring a lot of properties rapidly but not operating them profitably. We are in the process of equipping our organization to cope with this kind of task— but at present we are not staffed to do it.

An alternative approach would be vertical integration, i.e., expansion in the existing locations that we have. This would involve additional facilities that would be complementary to our present ones. This might include additional nursing-home beds, acute-care hospital beds, ECF beds, or home health care services which we would acquire or build. For example, in New Hampshire, we presently have an ECF, a basic nursing home, and a residential care unit. We plan to add acute beds, housing for the elderly, and an office building for physicians. We would then sell the community, employee groups, insurance companies, and others on contracting with us on a prepaid basis to provide all levels of health care to the community.

If we bought more facilities like our present properties, we would be buying franchises and additional locations whose value would appreciate. Secondly, we could become the biggest national chain much more rapidly. This last factor would give us considerable advantage in negotiating with a variety of agencies and would also offer us benefits of scale.

On the opposite side, the problem is that it would not take us towards our ultimate objective—which is to tie together all the elements of the health system. The reason for wanting to do this is that we believe that we can deliver better health care, more profitably, if we control the different levels of the delivery system; we will be able to ensure cost control and the most efficient utilization of each element of the delivery system. A second factor is that we believe that this is the area with the greatest profitability. The evidence for this is that we see that acute hospital care may cost $80 per day and an ECF may cost anything from $20 to $40 per day and there are considerable savings to be made by transferring patients into nursing home beds (at $15 per day) or even into a home situation (at $1 or 2 per day) where you can provide the patient with insulin shots on a home care basis. The point is that you can provide appropriate care for the patient, minimize costs for providing this care, and lower the prices to the patient, the government, or his insurance company. By contrast if you are on a fee-for-service basis (as opposed to a prepaid basis), you have the wrong incentives—your objective is to maintain the patient in the highest revenue producing part of the delivery system (e.g., the acute hospital). In this instance, the acute hospital is structured like a car dealership that only sells Cadillacs; in other words the customer has only one price range to choose from—and that is the highest in the field.

We also see the possibility of completely redesigning the structure of acute-care hospitals by building a surgical center which is exactly that—in other words a center with one or more surgical suites, adjacent to an ECF or nursing home type facility which can provide inpatient care for $15 to $30 per day. Acute hospitals, as they exist today are not functional in so far as efficient, low-cost delivery of health care.

Of course, vertical integration could involve either (a) developing other free standing units (unrelated to each other) on the present sites we have, or (b) developing a total HMO. A further question that we have to consider is: if we go this route, do we add just an acute-care facility—or should we add home care? What else should we add? Or alternatively should we contract with other HMO units to provide certain services?

In terms of direction, there is less expansion potential in acute care nationally because opportunities for acquisition are less. (For example, many of the "good" acquisitions have been made and religious and community groups are less inclined to "sell out" than an individual proprietor.) On the other hand there is a real opportunity to expand low-cost alternatives to acute-care facilities.

The Current Challenge: May 1972

PHS had a capital expenditures program of $7 million budgeted for 1972; about $2.5 million of this was to come out of equity. There had been little expansion during 1971 and early 1972, because ensuring profitable operations on a current basis was seen to be "the Number One short-term problem."

Nevertheless a number of opportunities for the acquisition of both acute-care hospitals and nursing homes were regularly brought to Ed Morgan's attention ("about a couple of hospital proposals and five to six nursing home proposals per month"). In early May 1972, for instance, it had been suggested to Morgan that PHS might want to consider purchasing a majority interest in Florida Nursing Centers, Inc., a company consisting of 35 nursing homes in 12 states with a capacity of 3,500 beds.

"We have to make decisions about these things all the time," said Morgan, "but we want to be sure, when we move, that it is the right direction. As I see it, we have about two years to show what we can do. Our major stockholder (a large insurance company) has a big stake in health care you have to bear in mind—so their interest in us is different from the interest an ITT would have in the field."

In mid-May 1972 Morgan and Mark French were reviewing the company's position. "We need to get more and better control of operations," said Morgan, "and we need to make our profit margin. [See Exhibit 8 for 1972 financial statements.] However, I guess I feel we have the ship under control—that improvements have been demonstrated. Certainly there are some organizational changes that we want to make [see Exhibit 9 for the organization chart established for 1972]. But the situation now is very different from what it was a year ago when there was a cash drain of $300,000 per month. Now there is a cash inflow of $300,000 per month." He went on to outline to French some of the alternatives PHS faced in planning its future growth. "I think we are going to have to face these strategic questions over the next few months, Mark, and I think we need to raise them now rather than wait until they hit us six months from now."

"I think you're right, Ed" said Mark French. "The issue we face is which segments of the health care business should we get into."

EXHIBIT 8

PROPRIETARY HEALTH SYSTEMS, INC.
1972 Operating Budget

	Millions of Dollars
Operating Revenue	
Patient care—private	11.6
Patient care—Medicare	1.9
Patient care—welfare	16.7
Total patient care	30.7
Miscellaneous	1.1
Total operating revenue	31.8
Contractual adjustments	(1.1)
Net operating revenue	30.7
Operating Expenses	
Nursing service	8.9
Employee benefits	2.5
Plant operations and maintenance	1.3
Dietary	3.5
Laundry	0.7
Housekeeping	0.9
Medical records and services	0.2
Social services	0.1
Activities	0.3
Administrative and general	3.4
Management	0.4
Total Departmental	22.2
Property and related	2.8
Depreciation and amortization	1.4
Interest Expense	1.7
Total Fixed	5.9
Total Operating Expense	28.1
Profit	2.6
Provision for Federal Income Tax	—
Profit—Net	2.6

EXHIBIT 8 (continued)

PROPRIETARY HEALTH SYSTEMS, INC.
Balance Sheet
December 31, 1971

Assets	$000s	Liabilities	$000s
Current Assets		**Current Liabilities**	
Cash....................................	1,004	Accounts payable—trade................	787
Accounts receivable—patients..........	3,762	Accrued payroll, interest, and taxes......	1,073
Reserve for doubtful accounts..........	(685)	Medicare current financing..............	108
Accounts receivable—others............	189	Other accrued liabilities................	627
Inventories............................	316	Current maturities of long-term debt.....	1,945
Prepaid accounts......................	503	Contractual liabilities—Medicare........	633
Total Current Assets...............	$ 5,090	Contractual liabilities—welfare..........	1,058
Property and Equipment		Total Current Liabilities.............	6,235
Land and land improvement...........	4,695	**Long-term Liabilities**	
Building and building improvement.....	38,872	Long-term debt.........................	39,575
Furniture and equipment...............	5,562	**Investment**	
Leasehold improvement................	340	Common stock..........................	5,327
Total................................	49,471	Paid-in capital.........................	16,463
Less accum. depr...................	4,011	Retain earnings (deficit)................	(5,274)
Net property.......................	45,459	Total Investment....................	16,515
Other Assets			
Notes receivable.......................	4,251		
Deposit—leases........................	338		
Lease acquisition costs (NET)..........	2,778		
Cost in excess of net assets............	4,109		
Other assets...........................	298		
Total Other Assets.................	11,775		
Total Assets......................	62,326	Total Liabilities and Capital.........	62,326

Note: Totals may not add exactly due to rounding.

EXHIBIT 9

PROPRIETARY HEALTH SYSTEMS, INC.
Organization Chart, May 1972

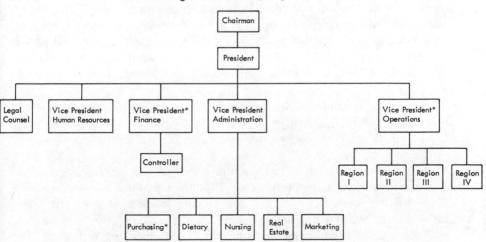

* The vice president of "operations" was due to start August 1972; other positions marked thus (*) were to be filled by December 1972. Meanwhile, purchasing was being handled on a regional basis.

3   *Hawaii Best Company (A)*

Gradually rising from his chair in his third-floor plush office overlooking Waikiki Beach in Honolulu, James Lind, President of Hawaii Best Company (HBC), greeted Charles Carson, Vice President and General Manager of the company's Islands Division, and invited him to take the seat across from his desk.

"Charlie, I am sure that something has gone wrong," he said as Carson remained standing. "You have many fine qualities—I was the one who recognized them when I promoted you to vice president—but I have been reviewing your progress these past few months and . . . and the results have not met our expectations."

Carson fidgeted at the window, watching the October morning across the harbor. His face reddened, his pulse quickened, and he waited for Lind to continue.

"The costs in your division are higher than budgeted, the morale is low, and your branch managers are unhappy with your stewardship," Lind said. "And your cooperation with Gil Harris has fallen short of satisfactory."

Carson grew angrier at the mention of Harris, a young aggressive man with a master's degree from a well-known eastern business school. Harris was a latecomer to HBC, but Carson knew that everyone was pleased with his performance.

"Charles, at the country club last week, I was speaking to one of our vendors. He intimated that your dealings with him had not been entirely clean. This is what hurts me the most.

"I know you are 49, that your son is only eight, that this is a difficult time for you and your family," Lind concluded as Carson stared out the window. "You have spent almost all your life in Hawaii; . . . it would be difficult for you to move to the mainland. It will be even harder for you to find a similar position in the Honolulu community. But I must ask for your resignation, and I will do my best to help you find a more suitable opportunity."

"Jim, I can't believe it," Carson finally replied. "It's just all wrong." He turned slowly from the window, his face blood-red.

"I have been with this company for ten years. I built this division. Sure, this year's results are not quite what you expect but my division is still the largest contributor to corporate profits. I'll bet your friend Gil has been telling you about the vendor deals. Well, it's a damned lie, and I won't stand for it! That boy will stop at nothing to grab power."

There was a long silence as Lind and Carson stared at opposite corners of the large office. "I will not resign," Carson suddenly declared, and he left the president's office coughing, his face flushed and his heart pounding.

Lind stood motionless as he watched the door close. He was uncertain about what to do; it never had occurred to him that Carson might refuse to resign. He decided to proceed as he had planned, but with one modification.

"Janice, please take a memo," he said to his secretary, and he dictated a note to Charles Carson informing him that his employment with HBC was terminated as of that afternoon, October 10, 1972.

After sending out a general release memo informing all division heads that Carson had resigned and that Joseph Ward, a promising young executive, presently employed as the manager of planning in the Operations Division, would assume the position of Acting General Manager of the Islands Division, Lind hurriedly left the office. He had less than an hour to catch the 12:30 plane, intending to visit each of the seven branch heads on the outer islands, to tell them about the change and their new Acting General Manager.

While Lind was having his memos sent out, Carson was trying to contact his previous boss and old friend, Roy North, past President of HBC and presently an influential member of the company's board of directors and its powerful executive committee. Carson intended to have the matter taken to the board for deliberation.

BACKGROUND

Mr. North was one of five members of the board's executive committee, which customarily approved the appointments, promotions, stock options

EXHIBIT 1

HAWAII BEST COMPANY (A)
Board of Directors—1972

| Name | Age, Place Most of Life Spent | Background | Current Activity | Previous Association in Years | | Number of Shares Represented |
				Industry	Company	
Choy, Eduardo	65, Hawaii	No academic degree; Financial	Entrepreneur; Corporate chairman; Banker	0	15 as director	3,000
Donahue, John	70, Hawaii	Engineer; Retired	Retired corporate executive of the company; Vice president of a property management company	40 with company	8 as director	500
Eichi, Ishi	40, Hawaii	Legal; Attorney	Practicing attorney	0	2 as director	0
Fields, J. B.*	54, Hawaii	M.B.A. (Harvard); Finance	Executive vice president of a very large multinational company headquartered in Honolulu	0	15 as director	2,500 + 4% owned by his company.
Fong, Charles	40, Hawaii	M.B.A. (Harvard); Finance	Executive vice president of a real estate development and investment firm	0	2 as director	500
Hanley, Don*	70, Hawaii	Secretary	Retired	19	19 as director	10,000

Name	Age / Origin	Field	Position	Years	Years as director	Shares
Johnson, T.†	48, Hawaii	Accounting	Corporate Treasurer of the Company	15	2 as director	1,000
Lind, James*†	53, Mainland U.S.A.	Engineer; Alumnus of Columbia Business School	Corporate president	28	2 as president and director	4,000
North, Roy*	56, Mainland and 16 years in Hawaii	Engineer; Financial analyst	Executive vice president of a conglomerate head-quartered in Honolulu	16	10 as director	1,500
Rusk, Dean*	52, Hawaii	Accounting and finance insurance; Alumnus of Harvard Business School	Executive vice president of a local large company operating in insurance, sugar, real estate, and merchandising, business	0	5 as director	0
Simon, A. F.*	65, Hawaii	Contractor; Entrepreneur	Corporate chairman and president; entrepreneur	0	20 as director	30,000
Vogel, Lawrence	63, Hawaii	Finance; Fiduciary	Corporate president; Fiduciary agent, represents a large local trust	0	10 as director	0

* Member of the board's executive committee.
† HBC employee.

and salary adjustments of personnel earning over $10,000. This included department heads, division managers, and vice presidents. The committee held at least one meeting a month, and these, like the regular monthly meetings of all 12 board members, were well-attended. (Exhibit 1 shows selected data about the directors).

Several of the directors were descendants or close friends of the founders of the Hawaii Best Company, but only James Lind and Thomas Johnson were HBC employees. Board members held 5 percent of outstanding stock; the rest was widely owned by the people and business concerns in Hawaii. No one outside the board represented more than 1 percent of the HBC stock.

In 1971, with $30 million in sales and an e.p.s. of $1, the Hawaii Best Company was a manufacturer and marketer of a special formula. The company was listed on the Pacific Coast stock exchange with 1 million shares outstanding which yielded a stable dividend of $1 per share over the last five years. It sold its line of special formula X to industrial, commercial and residential customers in the state of Hawaii. Its manufacturing facilities and three sales branches were strategically located in Honolulu, and seven other sales branches were spread over the outer islands. The company usually negotiated hard for its basic raw material K, used in the manufacture of special formula X, from its only locally available long-term supplier. Imports of the raw material were deemed uneconomical for HBC and a second source of local supply did not appear on the horizon.

The company also sold special formula Y, but only in the outer island branches and not in Honolulu. It was purchased in finished packaged form from several vendors within and outside the state of Hawaii, but the company was in no way involved in its manufacture.

Over the past five years the company's sales grew at an average annual rate of 4 percent, but its market share remained constant. Relative to the competition, HBC's profit performance had declined and, according to one competitor, "it was only through some 'creative' accounting that the company barely made its dividend in 1971."

HBC had two rivals in its industry: the larger company had annual sales of $60 million, the smaller sales of $15 million a year. It was a fiercely competitive industry, and special favors or discounts, although illegal, were sometimes granted to woo customers from another company. And customers were precious; just ten clients accounted for one-quarter of HBC sales.

HBC's ORGANIZATION STRUCTURE

Exhibit 2 shows HBC's skeletal organizational structure. The President, James Lind, was responsible to the board of directors. Thomas

Johnson, Vice President Finance and Secretary, and President James Lind regularly attended the monthly board meetings, and other vice presidents were also invited frequently to keep the board informed on matters of importance in the area of their specialty. According to Andrew Simon, Chairman of the board of directors, "This practice gives us an opportunity to know what we have underneath the first layer."

In addition to managing five divisions and attending to the normal duties of the president, Lind took a special interest in the negotiations involving labor contracts and purchasing of raw material K and special formula Y. The specific responsibility for negotiating labor contracts rested with the Vice President of Industrial Relations, John Wyle. Control of the purchase of raw material K lay with the Senior Vice President of Operations. The Vice President and General Manager, Islands Division, was responsible for buying special formula Y.

In all these negotiations, however, it was not uncommon for Johnson to get involved as well.

Among the corporate vice presidents in 1971, John Wyle, 51, had been the longest with the company. However, he had suffered two serious heart attacks since joining the company in 1945—one in 1959 and the other in 1968. According to the former HBC president North, "Wyle is the best industrial relations man we can find and he is a good personal friend of ours (their wives played cards together) but, frankly, his health concerns me and several of the directors."

Since joining the company in 1947 as a clerk, Thomas Johnson had risen to the position of Vice President Finance by 1968. In 1970 at the age of 46, he was elected to the company's board of directors at the suggestion of President Lind. Johnson had been actively under consideration for the presidency when Roy North vacated the position in December, 1969. One member of the selection committee put it this way: "Johnson is quite happy in his present position. He is a little lazy. He never wanted the top job."

Gil Harris, 33, joined the company in March, 1970 as Vice President for Marketing and General Manager of the Honolulu Division, responsible for the conduct and performance of the three Honolulu branches and for the company-wide market research, market planning and advertising campaigns.

As Vice President and General Manager of the Islands Division, Charles Carson had controlled the conduct and profit performance of all the branches in the state outside Honolulu. Carson also participated in the marketing decisions, such as advertising and promotions, and his division was charged a pro-rata share of expenses on the basis of divisional sales.

The Islands Division and the Honolulu Division were created by Lind in February 1970 after the sudden death of Vice President Sales Robert

EXHIBIT 2

HAWAII BEST COMPANY (A)
Organization Structure 1972

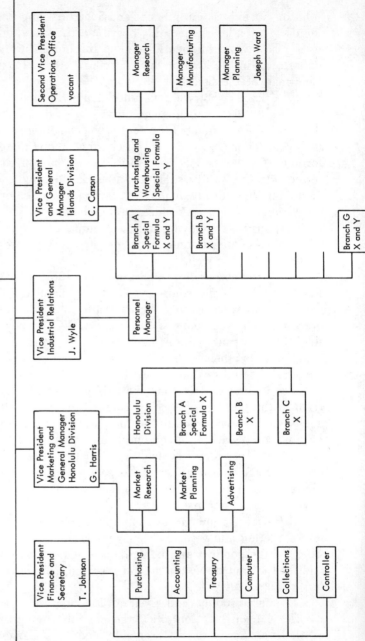

Gellerman, 46. Gellerman had been responsible for the company-wide sales and advertising throughout the state. Prior to the establishment of the two divisions, Lind consulted Chairman Simon, former HBC President North, and other members of the executive committee, and received their unanimous support. Also included in the restructuring were the functions of market planning and market research, which were consolidated under the new Vice President for Marketing and General Manager, Honolulu Division.

The position of Senior Vice President Operations had been vacant since May, 1970, when Lind asked for the resignation of the man who had held that office. The three managers within the division—manufacturing, planning, and research—had since been reporting directly to Lind. They constantly vied for the attentions of the president and the corporate vice presidents in the hope that one of them could assume the vice presidency. Three key members of the board were acquainted with Donald May, the research manager, but the other two were virtually unknown to the board.

Arrival of James Lind

On January 1, 1970, James Lind replaced Roy North as president of Hawaii Best Company when the latter left the company to become an Executive Vice President of a multinational conglomerate headquartered in Honolulu. North, under whose control HBC had prospered for seven years, recommended Lind for the presidency after an unfruitful search for a candidate within the company and the Hawaiian community. The board of directors accepted Lind, then a top executive in a trade association in New York, and he soon proved to be a man of integrity, dedication and charm.

Although the business community in Hawaii, according to some observers, was tight-knit and nearly impervious to outsiders, Lind was readily admitted and liked. The morale at HBC soared during the early months of his presidency, because he was a man who was both extraordinarily hardworking—he put in up to 70 hours a week—and "human." He was one of the best fund raisers for community projects in Hawaii.

Financially, however, the company was not performing well under Lind's leadership. Rising labor and material costs, and the combination of the inflationary spiral and the fierce competition put pressure on the profit margins. Lind began to make changes in key personnel in an effort to offset the problem.

In February, he promoted Charles Carson, a man who had been with the company for over eight years, to Vice President and General Manager of the newly created Islands Division.

Three months later he asked for the resignation of Frank Adams, Senior Vice President for Operations. Lind felt that Adams, after 27 years at HBC was "utterly lacking in an ability to negotiate for key raw materials," and brought his grievance to the board of directors. Before Adams was asked to resign, a severance package was worked out and approved by the board. Adams, then 53, was utterly shaken. He became an estimator for a local construction firm at one-quarter of his former salary. This was the first such severance in the history of the company and as one director put it: "The event was extremely painful; it left deep scars on us and our families."

Lind's final major organizational change was to bring in an old friend of his whom he hoped could develop new marketing strategies for the entire company. Gil Harris, from the Global Chemical Company of New York, was made Vice President for Marketing and General Manager of the newly formed Honolulu Division.

Lunch at the Club

"Jason, thank you for meeting me here, and for cancelling your other engagement to see me. I'm sorry, but I had to talk to you; something had happened that I think you should know about."

Charles Carson leaned heavily on the table in the restaurant of Honolulu's only country club. The man across from him curiously fingered the stem of his martini glass. Jason Fields, the executive vice president of the third largest international company based in Hawaii, was a busy and important man. An illustrious graduate of the Harvard Business School, Fields was one of the three most influential members of the company's board and its executive committee. Fields's employer controlled 4 percent of the HBC's outstanding stock. He did not have too much time to spend with Carson, his golf buddy and a VP of one of the two companies of which Fields was a director. (The other company was a major buyer from Carson's division at HBC).

"I'll try to be brief," Carson said. "Jim called me to his office this morning and asked me to submit my resignation. I refused. But before he left for his bloodsucking trip, he terminated my association with the company as of this afternoon."

Fields raised his eyes briefly.

"I control the company's three largest customers, you know," Carson continued. "I can easily take them to the competition. But he still has the gall to accuse me of taking a kickback, with absolutely no proof! I think Harris has put him up to it. He's been charging a substantial proportion of his division's expenses to my division. I have been arguing with him about these expenses during the last several weeks, and he finally told me he'd have my head if I went to Lind about it."

"Not even a note of thanks. Not even a mention of it to the board," Carson murmured. "I wonder how long the board will allow Lind to destroy the very people who built this company."

"I don't know what to do."

"Neither do I, Charlie," Fields answered. "I'm truly sorry to hear about this. This is strange. I had no idea this was even being considered. The executive committee met this morning and Jim, of course, was there, but this was never mentioned. I'd like to help in any way I can, Charlie. . . . All I can say is wait and see what happens at the next board meeting. It's scheduled for October 17.

"Well," said Carson, "I just hope the board takes this chance to finally straighten up the organization. Its relationship to the company, the delegation of responsibility, the criteria for employee evaluation—there are a lot of things that have remained garbled and unclear ever since Frank Adams was asked to resign. The morale of the executive staff is low. Earnings are not improving. Everyone is concerned about his own skin. Who will be axed?"

Lind's Turbulent Ride

Lind was deeply shaken over Carson's refusal to resign, and on the plane to Maui he tried to analyze the situation. He realized that he had made a mistake in promoting Carson a year and a half ago, although the psychological tests that he had had administered to all executives at the time pointed strongly to Carson as the man for the job. Lind remembered, too, the annual physical check-up the company executives were required to undergo, and recalled sadly the high blood pressure and excessive cholesterol level that Carson's exams revealed.

"I must stick to my guns," Lind mused. "I refuse to be blackmailed by the three powerful customers Charlie has in his pocket. I cannot let my authority be challenged, especially by a man I believe has taken kickbacks."

After a sleepless night, Lind telephoned Andrew Simon to inform him of Carson's resignation.

"Yes, Jim, Jason Fields called me yesterday to tell me," Simon relayed. "He was quite upset. And I saw Roy North at a cocktail party last night. He, too, knew about the event, and he appeared visibly disturbed. This is a sad situation. I am a little more than concerned, but you are the boss. We'll try to handle the matter appropriately at the board meeting next week."

Simon returned the receiver to the cradle thoughtfully. For the first time in his 20 years as chairman of the board, he felt that there was a conflict between the management of company affairs and the way he thought they ought to be managed.

Approaching 65, Simon was still active and healthy, and never missed a board meeting. He was once the caretaker president of HBC for one year in 1956. His deep concern for the company was reflected in the way he usually helped in its decision-making process—carefully—after long consideration and debate. He had discussed the matter of Adams' resignation privately first with Lind, then with the executive committee, and then with the entire board before Simon had been fully convinced that Adams should go. Similarly, he had spent long hours deciding on Lind's appointment, consulted extensively with several members of the board individually. Both Mr. and Mrs. Lind were interviewed thoroughly before the board selected him for the presidency.

4   Midway Foods Corporation (D₂ Revised)

In February 1958, Midway Foods Corporation produced three principal items: two packaged food products and its Midway brand of candy bar. In addition, it purchased from Sherwood & Co., Ltd., of England its Robin Hood brand of candy bar for resale in the American market. Since candy sales accounted for most of Midway's volume, the company was basically a competitor in the candy subdivision of the food industry. And since both bars utilized chocolate as a principal ingredient, in a more direct sense Midway was a competitor in the chocolate bar segment of the candy industry.

COMPANY HISTORY

During 1949, Midway Foods had gone into bankruptcy. When the present management purchased it, there had been no shipments for over eight months. At that time Midway occupied a decrepit factory building on Maxwell Street, a location immediately adjacent to Chicago's "flea market" where residents and peddlers sold or traded everything from fish and fur coats to buggy whips and rebuilt lawnmowers. Midway manufactured several food products under less than ideal conditions in a plant where it was extremely difficult to maintain even minimal sanitation standards. Its products were distributed in Cook County and surrounding areas through jobbers to a limited number of small retail accounts, and its Midway bar was known to local wholesalers for its poor quality, poor appearance, and a price fully equal to that of competing products. Because of the characteristics of its products, and also because the previous management had "robbed the trade" during the war when rationing

451

made that possible, Midway enjoyed singularly bad relations with the trade.

In the 1956–57 season, sales had passed the $6 million mark and were expected to exceed $7 million in 1957–58. The brand had been successfully launched throughout the Midwest, and had achieved some distribution on a nationwide basis. In the words of one industry source, "Midway not only has the goodwill of the trade, they have its respect." The company had moved to a five-story plant in Cicero, Illinois, increased employment to 100 people, and increased output of the Midway bar by more than 5,000 percent. The Midway bar was still below average in size, but had been considerably improved quality-wise so that it became average in the market. The product line had been reduced by the discontinuance of all but two of the packaged food items, and a second candy bar had been added—the Robin Hood bar.

Corporate Characteristics

During his months of field exploration the researcher listed a number of factors that seemed to him to be dominant in Midway operations.

One characteristic appeared to be management's adherence to its explicitly formulated concept of corporate purpose. While the long-range target was "to become one of the major companies in the American candy industry," there were four shorter-range purposes or missions. First, management wanted the company to achieve "scope," a size at which the Midway line would be an important one with its brokers, at which the company could support a certain minimum selling organization, and at which it could begin to achieve efficient use of television advertising. To implement this purpose, it was early company policy to aim for growth rather than profits and to plow all available funds into additional advertising to achieve increased sales. Second, Midway aimed to sell only nationally branded food, with "no one-shot deals, no subcontracting, and no unbranded items." Third, the company aimed to be a marketing company—a company that relied on its marketing skills for survival and growth, and one that would not take on any activities "for corollary reasons." People at all levels in the various departments seemed to understand and accept this concept of corporate purpose. Finally, the company wanted to accomplish these things without outside equity capital. Midway was privately held and intended to remain that way at least for the foreseeable future.

A second characteristic was management's readiness to take very sizable risks. Management stated that in order to go national as rapidly as possible the company had to spread its resources thin. "The risks in doing this are great, but so are the rewards," said Mr. Clark Kramer, president of Midway. To implement rapid expansion on limited resources, the marketing department prepared a budget which "has no fat in it for contingencies. If the marketing vice president[1] thinks we can get by on $4,000 for TV in Atlanta, that's all he asks for. If it rains, or the TV program is a flop, he has to come back for some more money," Mr. Kramer said. "I understand the risks involved and concur 100 percent in doing it this way. Any other way and we couldn't have grown the way we have."

A third characteristic was management's willingness and ability to make changes within the company and, in a more limited way, its initiative in influencing its competitive environment. This process of adaptation involved both destruction of existing systems and creation of new ones. Four examples, three internal and one external, were apparent to the researcher:

Internally, one example of this process was (1) the discarding of conventional record-keeping in favor of punched card data processing. Each sales invoice coming to the company was represented on a punched card, and subsequent accounting and statistical reports were prepared from the cards. (2) The manufacturing department had become adept at tearing down and rebuilding old machines for higher speed and more automated operation. (3) Finally, the company's organization had undergone considerable change, and numerous "less adaptable" people had been let go in the process.

As part of its influence on its environment, Midway had been instrumental in destroying the conventional concept of a candy broker. Management had insisted that brokers employ detail men to call on retail outlets. In the first years, Midway paid part of the cost of these men. While not new in the food industry, permanent detail men were almost nonexistent in the candy industry prior to 1953. In the succeeding years Midway had "persuaded" its brokers to hire detail men and had replaced brokers who would not be persuaded. By 1957 other candy companies were beginning to follow suit, and brokers all across the country were beginning to recognize the need to hire detail men in order to remain competitive.

Fourth, and more difficult to define, was a group of characteristics descriptive of the people who made up the management of Midway. Youth (the average age of the four top executives was 39.8 years), drive, hard work and long hours, quick thinking and decisive actions, willingness to experiment, and, finally, esprit de corps seemed to characterize the personnel of Midway. One of the vice presidents said: "Even the clerks can tell this company is going places—one of them comes in at 4 A.M. during the rush season to see that things are ready to go out when the trucks arrive."

Finally, on a more technical level, corporate marketing strategy ap-

---

[1] Mr. Milt Lombard.

peared to be clearly defined, and defined in terms which suited the company's position in the industry.

A Visit to Midway

Leaving Chicago's Midway airport, the researcher took a bus north along Cicero Avenue, the heart of Cicero, a once famous Chicago suburb situated on the "near west side." The bus passed several miles of combined residential and industrial buildings, including the Hawthorne plant of the Western Electric company, "automobile row," and several partially completed urban clearance and renewal projects. The researcher got off the bus, walked west through a "run-down" semi-industrial neighborhood, which adjoined a slum area known as one of Cicero's toughest, turned a corner and saw the familiar picture of a Midway bar, freshly painted on a high wooden fence. The fence enclosed a yard at one side of the factory, an old five-story building with a sign painted high on one wall reading, "Home of MIDWAY Foods." The researcher walked into the yard, passed the parked cars, the loading dock, a shed used for storage of old machines and miscellaneous junk, and through the main entrance into the shipping room. On the far side of the shipping room he waited for the only elevator to come down and the freight to be unloaded, and then he and a messenger rode to the fifth floor.

The elevator opened upon a long, narrow hallway which was partially blocked by a receptionist's desk and which led into the general office area. The researcher said good morning to the president's secretary, an attractive brunette whose desk was at the end of the hall. To his right were desks, filing cabinets, and the partitioned offices of two of the vice presidents; on his left was the president's office. After a few minutes' conversation with the secretary, the researcher knocked on the president's door and went in. Mr. Kramer looked up from his work and said, "Good morning, come on in."

The researcher put his papers on Mr. Kramer's desk, took off his coat, and sat down to enjoy the comforts of the spacious, air-conditioned office that was in striking contrast with the remainder of the plant and its surrounding environment. In addition to the window air conditioner, the well-appointed office contained a sofa, rug, and several chairs; a TV set; and a long, ultramodern desk, behind which sat Mr. Kramer in his swivel chair.

"What would you like to talk about today?" Mr. Kramer asked.

"First I'd like a little background on some of the changes during the past seven years."

"O.K. Let's go. Midway is an old company which prospered during the war and then went downhill into bankruptcy. It wasn't a going business when I bought it—a low-quality product, a small group of unskilled factory people, very poor trade relations, and a local distribution organization.

"We feel we have come quite a way since then. Sales have gone from about zero to over $6 million on Midway alone. We now have an adequate plant instead of the run-down one on Maxwell Street. And we have a second candy line, the Robin Hood brand which we market for Sherwood & Co. On that brand alone there has been considerable growth, over 150 percent since we became their marketing agents two years ago.

"A lot has changed. Milt Lombard has the factory in shape and running with reasonable efficiency. It's not like Maxwell Street where we used to have to set up the end of the production line in the street each day—and where Milt was sleeping in the factory when we went to operating a third shift. We now have national distribution on the Midway brand, and we are becoming one of the major television advertisers in our industry. Also, just this month we have added an administrative vice president to help us modernize our paper work and to increase our emphasis on profits. Hiring him was part of our plan to shift from 'phase one' to 'phase two.' "

"What do you mean, 'phase one' and 'phase two'?" the researcher asked.

"Phase one was growth. For the past seven years we have had one major objective, scope. We have been trying to expand sales, to achieve national scope. We weren't so interested in profits, because profits on small volume don't mean very much. In fact, going for scope has tended to keep our profits small; we have invested most of our gross margin in additional advertising.

"But now we are large enough to begin aiming for profits. We are calling it phase two of our development, and it will be to expand more slowly and begin to reap the profits of our advertising investments. We need the profits for two reasons: (1) we have to add to our capital resources in order to continue our expansion, and (2) we want to be sure we can run an $8 million business at a profit before we become an $80 million business."

"Does this shift mean you are going to be trying to operate at reduced risk from now on?"

"Exactly. Beginning with the 1958–59 season we will be aiming for a more conservative approach. Thus far we have gone all out to increase sales, and have taken the risks because we had to in order to achieve the necessary scope. And if something went wrong, we were small enough so that I could make up for it by not drawing salary or some such thing. Now we have reached a size where that is no longer the case.

"One other thing; to achieve growth with real stability we must diversify both within the candy industry and out into the food field. We want to begin this when we have a good opportunity, and also when we have achieved more depth in our organization."

Executive Personnel

As of mid–1959, Midway's executive organization was composed of the following personnel:

Mr. Clark Kramer	President
Mr. Hal Reiss	Marketing vice president
Mr. Andy Kallal	Sales vice president
Mr. Milt Lombard	Manufacturing vice president
Mr. Otto Lehman	Head of research and development
Mr. Ben Nagle	Administrative vice president

Management Meeting

At a general management meeting held on February 14, 1959, the discussion turned to Item No. 2 of the agenda, "title and salary review." The first person to be considered was Sam Painter, a member of the administrative department.

EXHIBIT 1

MIDWAY FOODS CORPORATION
Salary and Bonuses for Sam Painter

Year	Month	Weekly Pay	Bonuses
1956.................	July	$ 60	$ 30
	December		
1957.................	February	65	
	August	70	
	December		200
1958.................	January	75	
	March	80	
	April	90	
	August	100	100
	December		325
1959.................	February	120	

Midway management stated that Sam had been a controversial employee; some of his attitudes had been resented by fellow employees and by the executive group. Sam was 26 years old and had a high school diploma. Prior to employment at Midway he had been a dental technician. After six months with Midway, Sam had gone into the Army. Upon his release in 1956 he rejoined Midway at a salary of $60 a week. Changes in his salary since 1956 are shown in Exhibit 1.

C. KRAMER:[2] Now let's go on to Item No. 2.

B. NAGLE:[3] Well, this subject has been on a few agendas, but I think it now becomes more pointed. When Joe Rivers[4] left, Hal[5] made a suggestion

---

[2] Mr. Clark Kramer, president of Midway Foods.

[3] Mr. Ben Nagle, administrative vice president.

[4] Mr. Joe Rivers had been employed in the administrative department as Mr. Nagle's assistant. He had been encouraged to resign three months previously.

[5] Mr. Hal Reiss, marketing vice president.

that Joe not be replaced, that the job be abandoned, and that the various people who had reported to Joe report to me. Some months ago, we decided not to have a controller for the time being. We also agreed that this group would review any promotions of people who report directly to a vice president. [With the departure of Joe Rivers, Sam Painter reported directly to Mr. Nagle.] We agreed we should all review these people because their positions must, of necessity, become bigger and broader. And I would like to have a sense of direction on the staff we now have. Now I've taken one of these jobs which seems to be a debatable one—that's Sam Painter's—and let me read to you a job description which I prepared for background. "Sam Painter reports to the administrative vice president and at present he supervises one accounts receivable clerk, one credit clerk, three customer service clerks, and one warehouse inventory clerk. His basic functions are: responsibility for the proper administration of accounts receivable, cash receipts, credit limits, customer order processing, customer claims, freight claims on customer–into–warehouse shipments, warehouse inventory control, and intrawarehouse shipments."

Basically, he delegates responsibility and commensurate authority within a section for the effective execution of the foregoing functions. He is supposed to train and develop personnel under his jurisdiction for the assumption of more responsible duties. "His specific duties are as follows:

"(1) *Credit and collection.* Determines credit limits for new accounts, assumes responsibility for prompt collection of accounts receivable, and prepares monthly aging reports of overdue accounts receivable.

"(2) *Customer order processing.* He is responsible for seeing that the customers' orders and inquiries are promptly and efficiently processed. . . ."

H. REISS: Is this . . . do we have to go through this, Ben, with each one of these guys?

B. NAGLE: Yes, yes!

H. REISS: I don't think this is the function of this meeting.

B. NAGLE: Well, people ought to know what he does.

H. REISS: Fine. Whatever you want him to do, let him go ahead and do it, but I don't think we ought to be burdened with job descriptions in a meeting.

B. NAGLE: I was asked to prepare job descriptions. I'm doing what I was asked to do.

H. REISS: [to Mr. Kramer] Do you feel that this is the proper function of a meeting?

C. KRAMER: Did I ask you to prepare them?

B. NAGLE: Yes, sir.

C. KRAMER: Did I ask you to read them at the meeting?

B. NAGLE: You said to bring them in.

C. KRAMER: Yes, but I don't recall that I wanted them read, Ben. I don't know about the other fellows, but I can't digest it. I think it's not important, really.

B. NAGLE: I don't think you can discuss the scope of a man without knowing what he does.

H. REISS: What do you want to do with these people, Ben?

B. NAGLE: I want to know what management wants me to do with them.

H. REISS: Well, you're management. What do you want to do?

B. NAGLE: Well, to be specific, in my opinion Sam Painter has been a controversial personality for some time. The job he now performs is a responsible job. He has neither title nor proper salary for the job. The job calls for a title.

H. REISS: Of what?

B. NAGLE: Of something.

H. REISS: What?

B. NAGLE: As a "customer service supervisor," for instance, and "credit manager."

H. REISS: Why should the title be such a long one?

B. NAGLE: Well, he had to start in as credit manager.

H. REISS: Customer service supervisor would certainly cover credit.

C. KRAMER: Well, that's easy, Ben. If you want him to sign as credit manager, he can sign as credit manager, but his title doesn't have to be a hyphenated eight-word spread.

H. REISS: I understand customer service as covering all those areas.

C. KRAMER: How does he sign letters now?

B. NAGLE: Well, customer service, except . . .

C. KRAMER: Then it would be very simple to have him sign letters "Sam Painter, Customer Service Manager," wouldn't it?

B. NAGLE: Except that with the salary he's getting . . .

C. KRAMER: But mechanically it would be very simple. . . .

B. NAGLE: Well, letters of collection would be more normal if they had credit manager.

H. REISS: I kind of like the term customer service manager, Ben, instead of credit manager. When you really think of it, credit is one of the customer services. It's much more inclusive and I don't think it hits the customer quite so hard.

C. KRAMER: Not so much stigma to it.

H. REISS: That's right.

M. LOMBARD:[6] How old is this Sam?

H. REISS: I'd say about 26. Do you want to go into this, "When I was 26 . . ."

M. LOMBARD: No, I'm more concerned with the title in relation to what you think of his maturity. He may be doing the job. I have a fellow running Cicero now who is the acting plant manager.

B. NAGLE: I think——do you want my opinion? I think on an objective basis he does a very competent job, gets his work done, and is capable of growth. The only objection to him is what I would call on a subjective basis. His social attitudes might not be what we'd like; he might not be a type of personality we'd like to live with intimately. But a fact is a fact: He does a good job, and the question is do we want to live only with people we love or sometimes must there be someone in the pile that we don't love?

H. REISS: To add to what Ben says, I have found that among our outside people he is considered to be extremely valuable; he answers almost all their needs, does it promptly, and does it efficiently. And a lot of the correspondence that used to come into the sales department, well, about 90 percent of it, is

---

[6] Mr. Milt Lombard, manufacturing vice president.

now directed to Painter, which would certainly indicate the kind of confidence customers have in him.

C. KRAMER: What is he getting paid?

B. NAGLE: One other thing here. In the past two weeks I've had an opportunity to get down to the grass roots. I think he's done a very commendable job in the last six months in the area of human relations. The people who are subordinate to him, I think, are beginning to like him. He gets along with them. Six months ago the chronic complaint was that he was supercilious, was a wise little acre; but the people like him now, I've found.

C. KRAMER: You mean in two weeks you've suddenly changed from one opinion to another?

B. NAGLE: Me? No. I say I've had a chance to dig down and find out about this. People at his own level and at other department levels are not so antagonistic towards him as they were six months ago.

H. REISS: More important, I think almost everyone in the place that works with him respects his ability. I have a great deal of respect for his ability. One of the reasons people who work with him may dislike him is that he's a perfectionist. He demands good work from people. He has a great many personality problems; the prime one is his basic insecurity. I don't think we want to get into this at this particular juncture. The problem up for discussion is, Does Sam Painter deserve the title of customer service manager and the salary increase that goes with it? Is it that much of a promotion?

C. KRAMER: Milt, what's your opinion? Are you close enough to it to have any feeling?

M. LOMBARD: I don't have much to do with Sam. That's why I asked the question about his age and what you fellows think about his maturity. Is he mature enough to carry that title, whatever that title means? Will a promotion help him now, or will it hinder him? These are things you fellows can better. . . .

B. NAGLE: Well, that's what we're here for. He's wearing the robe. Shall we give him the mantle now? This is the problem we're going to be faced with right along with the development of a corporation with comparatively young executives. You're not going to hire 40-year-old guys for those kinds of jobs, or 35-year-old guys. This is going to be our pattern in the future. They're going to be around 25 and 27. Because of our age, we're not going to hire mature people.

H. REISS: Well, Sam's problem is a personality problem. He walks around as if he's the cock of the walk, and in the terminology of the street I think he could be classified as a wise guy, a punk.

B. NAGLE: Right.

M. LOMBARD: This is the point.

H. REISS: Wait a minute, Milt.

M. LOMBARD: I don't want to call him that because I don't have much to do with him.

H. REISS: You call a spade a spade.

M. LOMBARD: All right.

H. REISS: He tends to be arrogant, but when you pin it down it's his attitude rather than fact. Now I believe that you can change attitudes. I believe that people change with responsibility; they grow as they get additional responsibility. I believe that the guy should be rewarded for the work that he does. And if he can't overcome this, it isn't going to hurt him any more as customer service manager at a hundred and a quarter a week than it did as customer service department at a hundred a week. But if he can't overcome this, he's got to understand that this is as far as he goes.

C. KRAMER: I think that's not too significant from my point of view. What I'm interested in doesn't concern his present title or the title he will get at this meeting or the salary he will be raised to. I'm much more concerned with what type of man he is. I agree that as far as I know Sam is a real "hot shot." We just stumbled onto a really good man. He's a real worker, he's intelligent, and he's interested. There are only two things I have against Sam. Number one, I think he's an arrogant young punk. Number two, I don't like his views on segregation. Now, I can live in perfect happiness with a customer service manager who believes in segregation, but I could not live in happiness or work in happiness with a department head that believed in segregation. I just don't think this conforms enough with my own personal philosophy about life. And in case you're concerned here, I don't want to make a big thing over this, but I want us to think about this. Now, Sam is relatively young, it's true. I agree with you, Hal, that I think he can be changed. He was brought up in a blighted area and his background contains all the things that you would think would lead a guy to be just what Sam has become. So it's no surprise that he's become this. I think if we work with him we have a pretty good chance of getting him to understand some things, and to have a much healthier attitude towards life in general and business in particular. I'm in favor of taking this step, incidentally. But I would be very much against the next step unless Sam shows a distinct and specific change.

[Heated discussion]

H. REISS: I think we've blown this up out of all proportion.

C. KRAMER: Well, perhaps it seems that way, but it's important to me, Hal, because the Midway organization is very near and dear to me, and I'm concerned about the type of people in it. I say that being a great worker, an intelligent man, is not sufficient to cover up all things.

H. REISS: Clark, when you were 19—let's say your emotional development and maturation processes were at 19 what his will be at 27 or 28—when you were 19, did you ever get the urge to throw down to your seniors a provocative idea just to gain the center of attention?

C. KRAMER: I'm sure I must have, but I don't believe this is the case with Sam. I don't think we should discuss Sam's views on segregation or the reasons therefor. I've said that I believe he has these views.

H. REISS: But. . . .

C. KRAMER: We can discuss it later. But I also said that, if these are his true views, and if he doesn't change them, I don't think I can live at peace with him in the company. And if he goes further, as he will expect to go, and as we will expect him to go, then he must change his views. I don't believe in everyone in the company conforming to my views on everything or even anything except a few things, such as Mother, God, Country, and Integration, for example, and a few others. These I believe in as being the basic principles under which our country has existed and will exist. And if I don't believe in these things, then what's the use of it all, you see? And I don't want anybody in our company who is an opponent of what I consider to be these basic truths.

* * * * *

H. REISS: All I'm saying is that this is part of Sam, this attitude of challenging accepted ideas, challenging his superiors, challenging people with whom he works. We've either got to knock this attitude out of him or he's done in our company.

C. KRAMER: Let's not question the worth of his being provocative and stimulating and so forth. I'm merely trying to peer into the man to find out what is really there, and I'm saying that, as willing as I am to go along with this step, this is as far as I can go; and if it comes up again, as it surely will, and I feel that he has not changed basically and truly in this regard, you have my promise that he'll not go any further in our company.

B. NAGLE: What shall we call him, customer service manager or supervisor? Makes a big difference if you're going to start handing out manager or supervisor titles.

H. REISS: Well, which do you want?

B. NAGLE: I think supervisor is . . .

H. REISS: Is supervisor higher or lower?

B. NAGLE: Lower.

H. REISS: Lower. O.K.

C. KRAMER: I personally prefer manager. I don't feel strongly about either one, but it's a better word, I think.

B. NAGLE: You mean as manager, then we'll call him . . . It doesn't make any difference, the title.

C. KRAMER: Customer service manager is a title everybody understands, and so forth.

H. REISS: One more thing, while we're at it. What sort of salary bracket is this job? I don't see the need of going through this routine any time a man wants to be promoted within grade. . . .

C. KRAMER: Hal, we have agreed—at one of our first meetings we agreed—that any man that was being promoted in various departments into a position of being manager would be discussed at this meeting because all of us will have to live with him, and all of us have opinions about him; and in the absence of any formal job evaluation program the best way to evaluate these people would be just the four of us sitting around talking about them.

H. REISS: Well, then, suppose Ben wants to give him $10 in two more months. Does he come back to the group again for this?

C. KRAMER: No. That's not the point.

B. NAGLE: I don't want to create another Joe Rivers situation.

C. KRAMER: That's the thing I'm thinking about.

[Mr. B. Nagle proposed a 25 percent pay increase for Sam, from $100 a week to $125. After discussion it was agreed that a $20 boost immediately, with another $5 in six months, would seem more appropriate.]

5   *Consolidated Drugs, Inc.*

Mr. Richard Trucks had been transferred to the Syracuse (New York) division of Consolidated Drugs, Inc., in the first week of May 1952. At this time he was appointed sales manager of the Syracuse wholesale drug division. Formerly he had been an assistant to the vice president in charge of sales at the company's headquarters in New York.

At the month-end sales meeting on the last Friday of June 1952, Mr. Asa Bush, a salesman in one of the division's rural territories, informed Mr. Trucks that he wished to retire at the end of July when he reached his sixty-fifth birthday. Mr. Trucks was surprised by Mr. Bush's announcement because he had been informed by the division manager, Mr. B. D. Burton, that Mr. Bush had requested and received a deferment of retirement until he reached his sixty-sixth birthday in July 1953. The only explanation offered by Mr. Bush was that he had "changed his mind."

The retirement of Mr. Bush posed a problem for Mr. Trucks, in that he had to decide what to do about a successor to Mr. Bush's territory.

Background of the Syracuse Division

When Mr. Trucks became the divisional sales manager he was 29 years old. He had joined Consolidated (as the firm was known in trade circles) as a sales trainee after his graduation from Stanford University in 1946. During the next two years he worked as a salesman. In the fall of 1948 the sales manager of the company made Mr. Trucks one of his assistants. In this capacity Mr. Trucks helped the sales manager to arrange special sales promotions for the lines of different manufacturers.

Mr. Trucks's predecessor, Mr. John K. Martin, had served as divisional sales manager for 15 years before his death in April. "J. K." as Mr. Martin had been known, had worked as a salesman for the drug wholesale house that had been merged with Consolidated to become its Syracuse division. Although Mr. Trucks had made Mr. Martin's acquaintance in the course of business, he had not known Mr. Martin well. The salesmen often expressed their admiration and affection for Mr. Martin to the new sales manager. Several salesmen, in fact, made a point of telling Mr. Trucks that "Old J. K." knew every druggist in 12 counties by his first name. Mr. Martin had died of a heart attack while trout fishing with the president of the Syracuse Pharmacists' Association. The Syracuse division manager said that most of the druggists in town attended Mr. Martin's funeral.

The Syracuse division of Consolidated was one of 25 wholesale drug houses in the United States owned by the firm. Each division acted as a functionally autonomous unit having its own warehouse, sales department, buying department, and accounting department. The divisional manager was responsible for the performance of the unit he managed. There were, however, line functions performed by the regional and national offices that pertained directly to the individual departments. A district sales manager, for instance, was associated with a regional office in Albany for the purpose of implementing marketing policies established by the central office in New York.

As a service wholesaler, the Syracuse division sold to the retail drug trade a broad line of approximately 18,000 items. The line might well be described as consisting of everything sold through drugstores except fresh food, tobacco products, newspapers, and magazines. In the trading area of Syracuse, Consolidated competed with two other wholesalers; one of these carried substantially the same line of products; the other, a limited line of drug products.

The history of the Syracuse division had been that of a profitable family-owned wholesale drug house before its merger with Consolidated in 1928. The division had operated profitably since that date with the exception of three years during the 1930s, although it had not shown a profit on sales equal to the average for the other wholesale drug divisions of Consolidated. Since 1945, the annual net sales of the division had risen each year. But since its competitors did not announce their sales figures, it was impossible to ascertain whether this increase in sales represented a change in the competitive situation or merely a general trend of business volume in the Syracuse trading area. Mr. Martin had been of the opinion that the increase had been at the expense of competitors. The district drug sales manager, however, maintained that, since the trend of increase was less than that of other divisions in the northern New York region, the Syracuse division may have actually lost ground competitively. A new measuring technique for calculating the potential wholesale purchasing power of retail drugstores, which had been adopted shortly before Mr. Trucks's transfer, indicated that the share of the wholesale drug market controlled by the Syracuse division was below the median and below the mean for Consolidated divisions.

Only a few of the employees working in 1952 for the Syracuse division had also been employed by the predecessor company. Mr. Martin had been the only person in the executive echelon whose employment in the Syracuse division antedated the merger. Most of the executives and salesmen currently active in the organization had come into the organization either between 1933 and 1941 or after the end of World War II. Two salesmen, however, Mr. Bush and Mr. John Jameson, had worked for the predecessor company before the merger.

Of those who were employed as executives or salesmen before World War II, only Mr. B. D. Burton, the division manager, had a college degree, which he had earned at a local Y.M.C.A. night school. All the young men employed since 1946 were university or pharmacy college graduates. None of the younger men had been promoted when vacancies had occurred in the job of operations manager (who was in charge of the warehouse) and of merchandise manager (who supervised buying) in the Syracuse division; however, two of the younger men had been promoted to similar positions in other divisions when vacancies had occurred.

The Syracuse Division Sales Force

From the time that Mr. Trucks took over Mr. Martin's duties he had devoted four days a week to the task of traveling through each sales territory with the salesmen who covered it. He had, however, made no changes in the practices or procedures of the sales force. The first occasion on which Mr. Trucks was required to make a decision of other than routine nature was when Mr. Bush asked to be retired.

When Mr. Trucks took charge of the Syracuse division sales force, it consisted of nine salesmen and four trainees. Four of the salesmen, James Pepper, Michael Waller, Daniel Carmack, and Paul Smith, had joined the company under the sales training program for college graduates initiated in 1946. Concerning the other five salesmen, who had been with the company many years, Mr. Trucks was given the following information: Asa Bush and John Jameson were senior in terms of service to the others. John Dangler joined the company as a warehouse employee in 1928 when he was 19 and became a salesman in 1933. Homer Babbidge came to Consolidated as a salesman in 1933 when the wholesale drug firm for which he had previously worked went out of business. In 1952, Mr. Babbidge, who was then 48 years old, had been a wholesale drug salesman for 28 years. Russell Means at the age of 26 came to Consolidated in 1938 after working as a missionary salesman for a manufacturer. Mr. Means served as an officer in the Army Medical Corps during the war and was discharged as a captain in hospital administration in 1945. He returned to Consolidated immediately after his discharge.

The four trainees had graduated from colleges the preceding June. When Mr. Trucks arrived in Syracuse, these men were in the last phase of their 12 months' training program. The trainees were spending much of their time traveling with the salesmen. Mr. Trucks, who now had the full responsibility for training these men, believed that Mr. Martin had hired four trainees to cover an anticipated turnover both among the salesmen and among the trainees themselves, as well as to implement the New York head office's policy of getting more intensive coverage of each market area. The trainees, he understood, expected to receive territory assignments either in the Syracuse division or elsewhere on the completion of their training period.

Mr. Trucks had not seen very much of the salesmen. His acquaintance with them had been formed at the sales meetings and in traveling with them through their territories.

Mr. Trucks judged that Homer Babbidge was an easygoing, even-tempered person. He seemed to be very popular with the other salesmen and with his customers. Mr. Babbidge was proud of his two sons, one of whom was in high school and the other married, with a son named after Mr. Babbidge. Mr. Trucks thought that the salesman liked him, because Babbidge had commented to him sevreal times that his suggestions had been very helpful.

Asa Bush had not, in Mr. Trucks's opinion, been particularly friendly. Mr. Trucks had observed that Bush was well liked because of his good humor and friendly manner with everyone; however, Mr. Trucks had noticed that on a number of occasions Bush had intimated that his age and experience should cause the sales manager to defer to his judgment. Mr. Bush and his wife lived in the town of Oswego.

On June 4, 1952, Mr. Trucks had traveled with Mr. Bush, and they visited five of Mr. Bush's accounts. On a routine form for sales managers' reports on field work with salesmen, copies of which were filed with the district sales manager and the New York sales manager, Mr. Trucks made the following comments about Mr. Bush:

> *Points Requiring Attention:* Not using merchandising equipment; not following weekly sales plan. Pharmaceutical business going to competitors because of lack of interest. Too much time spent on idle chatter. Only shows druggist what "he thinks they will buy." Tends to sell easy items instead of profitable ones.
>
> *Steps Taken for Correction:* Explained shortcomings and demonstrated

how larger, more profitable orders could be obtained by following sales plan—did just that by getting the biggest order ever written for Carthage account.

Remarks: Old-time "personality." Should do terrific volume if trained on new merchandising techniques.

On a similar form made out by J. K. Martin on the basis of working with Mr. Bush on March 3, 1952, the following comments were made:

Points Requiring Attention: Not getting pharmaceutical business. Not following promotion plans.
Steps Taken for Correction: Told him about these things.
Remarks: Bush made this territory—can sell anything he sets his mind to—a real drummer—very popular with his customers.

Daniel Carmack, 29 years old, was the oldest of the group of salesmen who had passed through the formal sales training program. Mr. Trucks considered him earnest and conscientious. He had increased his sales each year. Although Mr. Trucks did not regard Carmack as being the "salesman type," he noted that Carmack had been fairly successful in the use of the merchandising techniques that Mr. Trucks was seeking to implement.

John Dangler handled a number of the big accounts in downtown Syracuse. Mr. Trucks believed that Dangler was an excellent salesman who considered himself "very smooth." Mr. Trucks had been surprised at the affront Dangler had taken when he had offered a few suggestions about the improvement of Dangler's selling technique. Mr. and Mrs. Dangler were good friends of the Burtons. The Danglers were social friends of merchandise and operations managers and their wives. Mr. Trucks suspected that Dangler had expected to be Mr. Martin's successor.

John Jameson seemed to Mr. Trucks to be an earnest and conscientious salesman. He had been amiable, though not cordial, toward Mr. Trucks. Mr. Trucks's report on calls on ten accounts on June 5, 1952, with Mr. Jameson contained the following statements.

Points Requiring Attention: Rushing calls. Gets want book and tries to sell case lots on wanted items. Carries all merchandising equipment but doesn't use it.
Steps Taken for Correction: Suggested change in routing; longer, better-planned calls; conducted presentation demonstration.
Remarks: Hardworking, conscientious, good salesman, but needs to be brought up to date on merchandising methods.

Mr. Martin's comments on observations of Mr. Jameson on March 4, 1952, reported on the same form, were as follows:

Points Requiring Attention: Uses the want book on the basis of most sales. Not pushing promotions.

Steps Taken for Correction: Discussed shortcomings.

Remarks: Jameson really knows how to sell—visits every customer each week. Hard worker—very loyal—even pushes goods with very low commission.

On the day Mr. Trucks had traveled with Jameson, the latter suggested that Mr. Trucks have dinner at the Jamesons' home. Mr. Trucks accepted the invitation, but at the end of the day Jameson took him to a restaurant in Watertown, explaining that he did not want to inconvenience his wife because his two daughters were home from college on vacation.

Russell Means had caused Mr. Trucks considerable concern. Means complained about sales management procedures, commission rates, the "lousy service of the warehouse people," and other such matters at sales meetings. Mr. Trucks believed that most of the complaints were founded in fact, but concluded that the matters were usually trivial, since the other salesmen did not complain about them. Mr. Trucks mentioned his difficulties with Means to Mr. Burton. Mr. Burton's comment was that Means had been very friendly with Mr. Martin. Means seemed to be quite popular with his customers.

James Pepper was, in Mr. Trucks's opinion, the most ambitious, aggressive, and argumentative salesman in the Syracuse division. He had been employed by the company since his graduation from the University of Rochester in 1948, first as a trainee and then as a salesman. Pepper had substantially increased the sales volume of the territory assigned to him. He had persuaded Mr. Martin to assign him six inactive hospital accounts in July 1950. Within six months Pepper made sales to these accounts in excess of $36,000. The other salesmen considered him "cocky" and a "big spender." Mr. Trucks thought his attitude was one of independence. If Pepper agreed with a sales plan, he worked hard to achieve its objectives, but if he did not agree, he did not cooperate at all. Mr. Trucks thought that he had been very successful in working with Pepper.

Paul Smith, who was 24 years old, impressed Mr. Trucks as being unsure of himself. Smith seemed to be confused and overworked. Mr. Trucks attributed this difficulty to Smith's trying to serve too many accounts in too large an area. Smith was very interested in Mr. Trucks's suggestions on improvement in his work. Mr. Trucks believed that he would improve in time with proper help. Smith had raised his sales to the point where he was on commission instead of salary in March 1952.

Michael Waller, 25 years of age, was the only salesman who worked on a salary. His sales volume was not sufficient to sustain an

income of $325 a month, which was the company minimum for sales-
men with more than one year's experience Waller was very apologetic
about being on a salary. Mr. Trucks believed that Waller's determina-
tion to "make good" would be realized because of the latter's conscien-
tiousness. When he had been assigned the territory two years before, it
had consisted largely of uncontacted accounts. The volume of sales had
tripled in the meantime. Mr. Trucks felt that Waller appreciated all the
help he was given and that in time Waller would be an excellent salesman.

Both Bush and Jameson earned about $2\frac{1}{8}$ percent of sales in commissions. The other salesmen all earned about $2\frac{1}{4}$ percent of sales as
commissions, except Pepper and Carmack who earned about $2\frac{3}{8}$ percent.
Mr. Trucks said that expense accounts amounted to about $\frac{3}{4}$ percent of
sales for both city and country salesmen. The differences in percentage
rates of commissions were explained by Mr. Trucks in terms of the differential commissions set by the company. Higher commission rates were
given on items the company wished to "push," such as pharmaceuticals
and calendar promotion items.

The trainees were something of an unknown quantity to Mr. Trucks.
He had training conferences with them in which he had thought they
had performed rather poorly. He believed that Mr. Martin had neglected the training of the new men. All four of them seemed to be good
prospects and were eager to be assigned territories, as they informed
Mr. Trucks as often as possible.

The turnover of the Syracuse division sales force had been very low
among the prewar salesmen. Six of the sales training program men had
left the division since 1947. Two of these men had been promoted to
department heads in other divisions, whereas four had left to work for
manufacturers. Because manufacturers valued salesmen with whole-
saling experience and competing wholesalers did not have training
programs for young men, there were many opportunities for a salesman
who desired to leave.

Sales Management

Since Mr. Trucks had become sales manager, he had devoted considerable thought to the problem of improving the sales performance
of the Syracuse division. He had accepted a transfer to the new job at
the urging of Mr. Cameron Crow, the vice president in charge of sales.
Mr. Trucks was one of a dozen young men whom Mr. Crow had brought
into the New York office since the end of World War II to work as assistants to the top sales executives. None of the young assistants had
remained in the New York office for more than three years, for Mr.
Crow made a policy of offering the young men field assignments so

that they could "show their stuff." Mr. Trucks believed that the sales performance of the Syracuse division could be bettered by an improved plan of sales management. He knew that the share of the Syracuse market for wholesale purchases of retail drugstores[1] held by Consolidated was only 19.5 percent as against a 48 percent share for some of the other divisions in their respective markets.

Mr. Crow, for whom Mr. Trucks worked immediately before his transfer, had focused his staff's attention upon the qualitative aspects of sales policy. Mr. Trucks had assisted Mr. Crow in implementing merchandising plans intended to utilize the salesmen's selling efforts in such a way as to minimize the handling cost of sales and maximize the gross margin.

The company encouraged the salesmen to use a threefold plan for increasing profitability:

1. Sales of larger average value per line of the order were encouraged because the cost of processing and filling each line of an order was practically constant;

2. Sales of larger total value were encouraged because the delivery cost for orders having a total weight between 20 and 100 pounds was practically constant;

3. Because some manufacturers offered margins considerably larger than others, sales of products carrying higher margins were encouraged. Salesmen's commissions varied with the margins available to Consolidated on the products they sold.

The executives of the company also sought to increase the effectiveness of Consolidated promotions by setting up a sales calendar. The sales calendar coordinated the activities of all Consolidated divisions so that during a given calendar period every account would be solicited for the sale of particular items yielding satisfactory profits. The type of activity represented by the sales calendar required that the salesmen in each division follow a pattern in selling to every individual account. The sales manager was responsible for coordinating the activities of his own salesmen.

The matter of selling patterns was largely the responsibility of the division sales manager. Mr. Trucks believed that his predecessor had never really accepted the changes that had taken place in the merchandising policy of the New York office.

Mr. Trucks had inherited from his predecessor a system of sales department records which had been carefully maintained. The national

---

[1] The potential wholesale sales for retail drugstores were calculated by the New York office market-analysis section. This market estimate, called the P.W.P.P. (potential wholesale purchasing power), was calculated for each county by adjusting retail drugstore sales to an estimate of the purchases of goods from wholesalers.

offices required each division to keep uniform sales and market-analysis records. During the period of Mr. Trucks's work in the New York office, he had developed a familiarity with the various uses for these records.

The basis of the sales and market-analysis record was the division trading area. The limits of the trading area were determined by the economics of selling costs, and the factors on which the costs were based were transportation costs of delivery and salesmen's traveling expenses. Mr. Trucks knew from his own experience that delineation of trading areas was influenced by tradition, geographic conditions, the number of salesmen, the number of calls a salesman could make, the estimated market potential, competition, and agreements with adjacent Consolidated divisions. The Syracuse division was bordered by the trading areas of Consolidated divisions located in Rochester and Albany on the east, south, and west; to the north was the Canadian border. A map of this division is included here in Exhibit 1.

Within the divisional trading area the market was broken into sales territories. Exhibit 2 includes data on salesmen's territory assignments; Exhibit 3 shows the salesmen's territories by counties; Exhibit 4 indicates estimated potential sales and sales by counties for various classification of customers. During the time since his arrival, Mr. Trucks had formed the opinion that the present salesmen's territories had been established without careful regard for the number of stores in the area, the sales potential, or the amount of traveling involved. Although Mr. Trucks had not yet studied any one territory carefully, he suspected all his salesmen of skimming the cream from many of their accounts because they did not have adequate time to do a thorough selling job in each store.

Mr. Trucks had been able to observe the performance records of other divisional sales managers while he worked in New York. He knew that some sales managers had achieved substantial improvements over the past performances of their divisions.

Sales Territories of Bush and Jameson

The territory that Mr. Bush covered included accounts scattered through small towns in four counties of the rural area northeast of Syracuse (see Exhibit 5). Mr. Bush had originally developed the accounts in the four-county area for the predecessor company. At the time he undertook this task the competing service wholesaler already had established a mail-order business with the rural druggists in this area. Mr. Bush had taken to the road in a Model-T Ford in 1922 to build up the sales in all four counties. He had been hired specifically for this job because he was a native of the area and an experienced "drummer."

Five years later Mr. John Jameson, a friend of Mr. Bush, became a

EXHIBIT 1

CONSOLIDATED DRUGS, INC.
Syracuse Division Trading Area

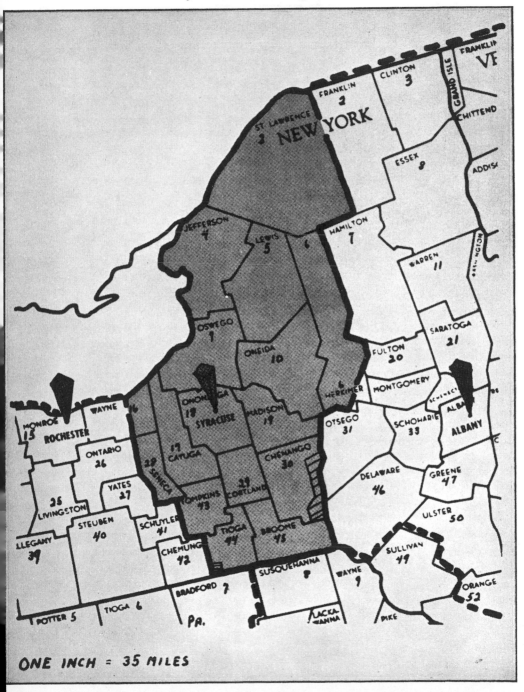

ONE INCH = 35 MILES

EXHIBIT 2

CONSOLIDATED DRUGS, INC.
Selected Data on Salesmen's Territory Assignments and Performance

Salesman	County	Sales, 1951*	Active Accounts	Estimated Potential† (000)	Assigned Accounts‡
Babbidge	Chenango....................	$ 20,634	4	$ 189	15
	Tompkins....................	63,226	9	388	19
	Tioga.......................	39,839	4	161	11
	Broome.....................	122,968	22	1,807	45
	Total..................	246,667	39	2,545	90
Bush	Jefferson....................	81,162	16	371	20
	Lewis.......................	28,798	8	87	11
	Oswego.....................	148,073	25	517	37
	Total..................	258,033	49	975	68
Carmack	Onondaga...................	76,339	14	297	14
	Madison....................	86,950	12	417	19
	Cortland....................	46,005	6	146	11
	Total..................	209,294	32	860	44
Dangler	Onondaga...................	252,051	33	743	44
	Total..................	252,051	33	743	44
Jameson	St. Lawrence................	136,058	25	364	32
	Jefferson....................	123,681	19	353	19
	Oswego.....................	1,091	1	200	1
	Total..................	260,830	45	917	52
Means	Onondaga...................	244,642	29	1,009	48
	Total..................	244,642	29	1,009	48
Pepper	Onondaga...................	212,691	28	500	29
	Total..................	212,691	28	500	29
Smith	Herkimer....................	48,530	10	312	19
	Oneida.....................	113,607	46	1,053	85
	Total..................	162,137	56	1,365	104
Waller	Wayne......................	22,675	4	103	5
	Cayuga.....................	70,598	14	312	18
	Seneca.....................	36,260	8	186	13
	Total..................	129,533	26	601	36
	Hospitals, Syracuse (Pepper)...................	$ 36,079			
	All others...................	$ 8,595			
	House accounts............	$ 76,622			
	Total division sales....	$2,197,174			

* This figure includes sales to chain and independent drugstores and to miscellaneous accounts, but does not include sales to hospitals.

† No potential is calculated for hospitals or miscellaneous sales. Where a county is divided among several salesmen, the potential-sales figure for each salesman is obtained by allocating the county potential in proportion to the *number* of drugstore accounts in that county assigned to that salesman.

‡ Includes hospitals and other recognized drug outlets in the territory.
Source: Company records.

EXHIBIT 3

CONSOLIDATED DRUGS, INC.
*Syracuse Division Salesmen's Territory Assignments
by Counties*

Code Number	County	Salesmen
1..........	St. Lawrence	Jameson
4..........	Jefferson	Bush, Jameson
5..........	Lewis	Bush
6..........	Herkimer	Smith
9..........	Oswego	Bush, Jameson
10..........	Oneida	Smith
16..........	Wayne	Waller
17..........	Cayuga	Waller
18..........	Onondaga	Means, Dangler, Pepper, Carmack
19..........	Madison	Carmack
28..........	Seneca	Waller
29..........	Cortland	Carmack
30..........	Chenango	Babbidge
43..........	Tompkins	Babbidge
44..........	Tioga	Babbidge
45..........	Broome	Babbidge

division salesman, and, at the suggestion of Mr. Bush, covered other accounts in the same four-county area. Mr. Jameson had been a salesman for a proprietary medicine firm before he joined the wholesale drug house. He was seven years younger than Mr. Bush. Since that time Mr. Jameson had serviced a number of accounts in the four-county area. The list of accounts that each of these men handled appears in Exhibits 6 and 7. Mr. Trucks noticed that the incomes which Messrs. Bush and Jameson had received from commissions were very stable over the years.

A Visit from Mr. Jameson

On the Wednesday morning following the June sales meeting, Mr. Trucks saw Mr. Jameson come in the front door of the Syracuse division offices. Although the salesman passed within 30 feet of Mr. Trucks' desk he did not appear to notice the sales manager. Mr. Jameson walked through the office area to the partitioned space where Mr. Burton's private office was located. Twenty minutes later Mr. Jameson emerged from the division manager's office and made his way to Mr. Trucks's desk.

"Hi there, young fellah!" he shouted as he approached.

"Howdy, Jack. Sit down and chat awhile," Mr. Trucks replied. "What got you out of bed so early?" he asked, knowing that the salesman must have risen at 6 o'clock to make the drive to Syracuse from his home in Watertown.

EXHIBIT 4

CONSOLIDATED DRUGS, INC.
Selected Data on Sales and Sales Potentials, by Counties

County	Code	Population	Percent	Chain and Independent Stores								Hospitals			Miscellaneous Sales (in thousands)
				Sold	Inactive Accounts	Accounts not Sold	Total	P.W.P.P. (in thousands)	Percent Area P.W.P.P.	Sales (in thousands)	Percent P.W.P.P.	Sold	Not Sold	Sales (in thousands)	
St. Lawrence...	1	99,400	7.0	19	2	5	26	$ 364	3.9	$ 107	29.4	2	4	$ 3	
Jefferson...	4	86,700	6.1	26	8	—	34	724	7.8	201	27.8	2	2	2	
Lewis...	5	22,800	1.6	8	—	—	8	87	0.0	29	33.1	—	1	—	
Herkimer...	6	46,800	3.3	10	6	1	17	312	3.3	49	15.6	—	2	—	
Oswego...	9	78,300	5.5	22	4	—	26	537	5.7	124	23.1	1	2	—	
Oneida...	10	226,000	15.9	46	14	12	72	1,053	11.3	111	10.5	—	13	—	
Wayne...	16	14,400	1.0	4	—	1	5	103	1.1	23	22.0	—	—	—	
Cayuga...	17	71,100	5.0	12	4	—	16	312	3.3	56	17.9	2	—	2	
Onondaga...	18	346,600	24.3	104	7	9	120	2,549	27.3	722	28.3	6	9	36	
Madison...	19	47,000	3.3	12	2	3	17	417	4.5	87	20.9	—	2	—	
Seneca...	28	29,700	2.1	6	1	3	10	186	2.0	28	15.1	2	1	2	
Cortland...	29	37,700	2.6	6	2	1	9	146	1.6	46	31.5	—	2	—	
Chenango...	30	39,900	2.8	4	2	6	12	189	2.0	21	10.9	—	3	—	
Tompkins...	43	60,200	4.2	9	1	4	14	388	4.2	63	16.3	—	5	—	
Tioga...	44	30,600	2.1	4	—	7	11	161	1.7	40	24.7	—	—	—	
Broome...	45	187,800	13.2	22	2	13	37	1,807	19.4	115	6.3	—	8	—	
Total....		1,425,000	100.0	314	55	65	434	$9,335	100.0			15	54		
Totals, 1951....		—	—							$1,819	19.5			$45	$334
Totals, 1950....		—	—							$1,659	18.6			$27	$256

Source: Company records.

EXHIBIT 5

CONSOLIDATED DRUGS, INC.
Counties Sold by Messr. Bush and Jameson

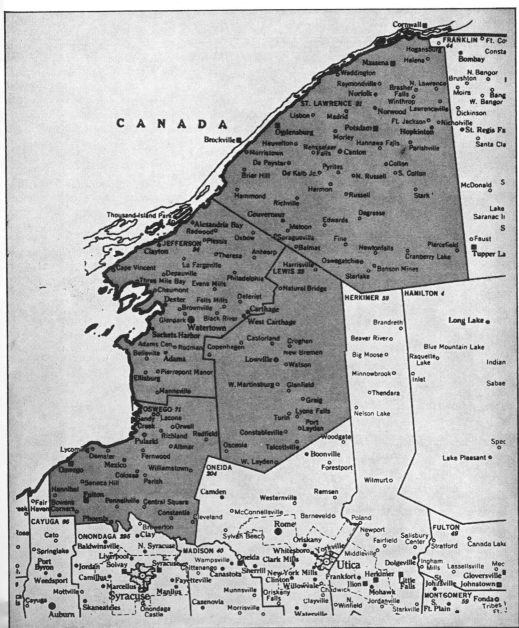

EXHIBIT 6

CONSOLIDATED DRUGS, INC.
Accounts Sold by Asa Bush, by Counties, with 1951 Purchases

Jefferson County:		Oswego County:	
Adams Center, D*.......	$ 1,986	Caloose, D*.............	$ 684
(Alexandria Bay, D.......	10,192)	Central Square, D.......	743
(Alexandria Bay, D.......	8,764)	Constantia, M..........	29
(Bellville, D..............	1,165	Cleveland, M...........	156
(Carthage, D.............	33,903)	(Fulton, D..............	6,051)
Chaumont, D.............	336	(Fulton, D..............	9,817)
(Clayton, D..............	5,901)	(Fulton, D..............	11,116)
(Clayton, D..............	9,113)	(Fulton, D..............	15,396)
Deferiet, D..............	205	Hannibal, D.............	1,558
Dexter, D................	6,481	Hastings, M.............	1,539
Ellisburg, D.............	131	Lacona, M..............	185
LaFargeville, D..........	290	Mexico, D..............	6,371
Plessis, D...............	490	Oswego, D..............	4,827
Redwood, M.............	60	(Oswego, D..............	8,307)
Rodman, D..............	1,787	(Oswego, D..............	9,641)
Sackets Harbor, D........	358	(Oswego, D..............	16,415)
County total.........	$81,162	(Oswego, D..............	17,593)
		(Oswego, D..............	8,982)
Lewis County:		Oswego, H..............	6
Beaver Falls, D*..........	$ 1,270	Parish, M...............	2,065
Croghan, D..............	8,199	Phoenix, D..............	3,895
Harrisville, D............	6,172	(Pulaski, D..............	3,501)
Lowville, D..............	7,896	(Pulaski, D..............	11,636)
Lowville, D..............	1,438	Sandy Creek, D.........	5,655
Lyons Falls, D...........	2,008	West Monroe, D........	1,911
Port Leyden, D..........	775		
Turin, M.................	1,040	County total........	$148,079
County total.........	$28,798		

Territory total.......................... $258,039
Increase over 1950....................... 0.9%

* D-Independent Drugstore; C-Chain Drugstore; M-Miscellaneous Account; H-Hospital.
Note: Accounts in parentheses are those indicated by Mr. Jameson as the ones he wanted.
Source: Company records.

Mr. Jameson squeezed his bulky frame into the armchair next to the desk. "It's a shame Asa is retiring," he said. "I never thought he could stand to give it up. I never knew anyone who enjoyed selling as much as Asa——'cept, maybe me." Mr. Jameson continued praising Mr. Bush and telling anecdotes that illustrated his point until Mr. Trucks began to wonder whether Mr. Jameson thought that the sales manager was biased in some way against the retiring salesman. Mr. Trucks recalled that he had made some critical remarks about Mr. Bush to Mr. Burton, but he could not recall any discussion of Mr. Bush's shortcomings with Mr. Bush himself or any of the other salesmen. Mr. Jameson ended his

EXHIBIT 7

CONSOLIDATED DRUGS, INC.
Accounts Sold by John Jameson, by Counties, with 1951 Purchases

St. Lawrence County:		Jefferson County:	
Canton, D*...............	$ 13,080	Adams, C*...............	$ 1,049
Edwards, D..............	672	Carthage, C..............	1,176
Edwards, M..............	1,885	Evans Mills, D...........	1,229
Gouverneur, D...........	226	Philadelphia, D..........	2,101
Gouverneur, D...........	9,383	Watertown, D............	16,782
Gouverneur, C...........	16,519	Watertown, D............	2,632
Heuvelton, D.............	108	Watertown, D............	4,889
Massena, D..............	11,259	Watertown, D............	17,041
Massena, D..............	3,397	Watertown, D............	10,262
Massena, C..............	2,448	Watertown, D............	14,622
Massena, C..............	2,225	Watertown, D............	21,249
Massena, H..............	38	Watertown, D............	12,791
Madrid, D................	1,432	Watertown, D............	5,388
Morristown, D...........	2,731	Watertown, D............	475
Norfolk, D...............	2,995	Watertown, D............	6,282
Norwood, D..............	3,139	Watertown, C............	2,019
Ogdensburg, D...........	8,090	Watertown, C............	3,318
Ogdensburg, D...........	22,555	Watertown, M............	378
Ogdensburg, D...........	7,203	Watertown, H............	70
Ogdensburg, D...........	3,380	Watertown, H............	2,009
Ogdensburg, M..........	149	Total county........	$125,760
Ogdensburg, H..........	2,653		
Potsdam, D..............	15,444	Oswego County:	
Potsdam, C..............	7,371	Pulaski, C................	$ 1,091
Rensselaer Falls, D......	367		
Total county........	$138,749		

Territory total..........................	$265,600
Increase over 1950......................	11.6%

* D-Independent Drugstore; C-Chain Drugstore; M-Miscellaneous Account; H-Hospital.
Source: Company records.

remarks by saying, "Old J. K., God rest his soul, always said that Asa was the best damn' wholesale drug salesman he had ever known."

There was a brief silence as Mr. Trucks did not realize that Mr. Jameson was finished. Finally Mr. Trucks said, "You know, Jack, I think we ought to have a testimonial dinner for Asa at the July sales meeting."

Mr. Jameson made no comment on Mr. Trucks's suggestion; instead, he went on to say, "None of these green trainees will ever be able to take Asa's place. Those druggists up there are old-timers. They would resent being high-pressured by some kid blown up to twice his size with college degrees. No sir! You've got to sell 'em right in those country stores."

Mr. Trucks did not believe that Mr. Jameson's opinion about the adaptability of the younger, college educated salesman was justified by the evidence available. He recalled that several of these men in country territories had done better on their May sales quotas than either Mr. Bush or Mr. Jameson. He was proud of his self-restraint when he commented, "Selling in a country territory is certainly different."

"That's right, Dick. I wanted to make sure you understood these things before I told you." Mr. Jameson was nervously massaging his double chin between his thumb and forefinger.

Mr. Trucks looked at him with a quizzical expression. "Told me what?"

"I have just been talking to Mr. Burton. Well, I was talking to him about an understanding between Asa and me. We always agreed that if anything should happen to the other, or he should retire, or something —well, we agreed that the one who remained should get to take over his choice of the other's accounts. We told J. K. about this and he said, 'Boys, what's O.K. by you is O.K. by me. You two developed that territory and you deserve to be rewarded for it.' Well, yes, sir, that's the way it was."

Without pausing, Mr. Jameson went on, "I just told Mr. Burton about it. He said that he remembered talking about the whole thing with J. K. 'Yes,' he said, 'Tell Trucks about it,' he said, 'Tell Trucks about it.' Asa and I went over his accounts on Sunday. I went over his list of accounts with him and checked the ones that I want. Here is the list with the accounts all checked off.[2] I already know nearly all the proprietors. You'll see that——"

"Wait a minute, Jack! Wait a minute!" Mr. Trucks interrupted. "You've lost me completely. In the first place, if there is any assignment of accounts to be made I'll do it. It will be done on a basis that is fair to the salesmen concerned and profitable to the company. You know that."

"Dick, I'm only asking for what is fair." Mr. Jameson's face was flushed. Mr. Trucks noticed that the man he had always believed to be deliberately confident and self-possessed was now so agitated that it was difficult for him to speak. "I don't want my territory chopped up and handed to some green kid!"

Mr. Trucks noticed that everybody in the office was now watching Mr. Jameson. "Calm down, Jack," he whispered to the salesman, indicating with a nod of his head that others were watching.

"Don't talk to me that way, you young squirt!" replied Mr. Jameson. "I don't care. A man with 25 years' service deserves some consideration!"

"You're absolutely right, Jack. You're absolutely right." As Mr. Trucks repeated his words Mr. Jameson settled back in his chair. The typewriters started clattering again.

---

[2] Mr. Jameson's selected accounts are the accounts in parentheses in Exhibit 6.

"Now, first of all, Jack," queried Mr. Trucks, as he tried to return the conversation to a friendly basis, "where did you get the idea that your territory was going to be 'chopped up'?"

"You said so yourself. You said it at the very first sales meeting when you made that speech about how you were going to boost sales in Syracuse." Mr. Jameson emphasized his words by pounding on the side of the desk with his Masonic ring.

Mr. Trucks reflected for a moment. He recalled giving a talk at his first sales meeting at the end of May entitled, "How We Can Do A Better Job for Consolidated." The speech was a restatement of the merchandising policy of the New York office. He had mentioned that getting more profitable business would require that a larger percentage of the total purchases of each account would have to come to Consolidated; that attaining a larger share of the business from each store would require more selling time in each store; and that greater concentration on each account would necessitate reorganization of the sales territories. He realized that his future plans did entail reorganization of the territories; he had not anticipated, however, any such reaction as Mr. Jameson's.

Finally, Mr. Trucks said, "I do plan to make some territorial changes —not right away—at least not until I have looked things over pretty darn carefully. Of course, you understand that our first duty is to make greater profits for the company. Some of our territories would be a great deal more profitable if they were organized and handled in a different manner."

"What are you going to do about Asa's territory?" asked Mr. Jameson.

"Well, I just haven't had a chance to study the situation yet," he replied. "If I could make the territory more profitable by reorganizing it, I guess that is what they would expect me to do." Since Mr. Trucks had not yet looked over the information about the territory, he was anxious not to commit himself to any course of action relating to it.

"What about the promises the company made to me about letting me choose the accounts I want?" the salesman asked.

"You don't mean the company's promise; you mean Mr. Martin's promise," Mr. Trucks corrected him.

"Well, if Mr. Martin wasn't 'the company' I don't see how you figure that you are!" Mr. Jameson's face resumed its flush.

"O.K., Jack. How about giving me a chance to look over the situation. You know that I want to do the right thing. Let me go over your list of the accounts you want. In a few days I can talk intelligently about the matter." Mr. Trucks felt that there was no point in carrying on the discussion.

"All right, Dick," said Mr. Jameson, rising. The two men walked toward the front entrance of the office. As they reached the top of the steps leading to the front door, Mr. Jameson turned to the sales manager and offered his hand, "Look, Dick. I'm sorry I got so mad. You just can't imagine what this means to me. I know you'll see it my way when you know the whole story." Mr. Jameson's voice sounded strained.

Mr. Trucks watched the older man leave. He felt embarrassed at the realization that Mr. Jameson's parting words had been overheard by several manufacturers' representatives standing nearby.

A Conversation with the Division Manager

Mr. Trucks decided to talk at once to Mr. Burton about his conversation with Mr. Jameson. He walked over to Mr. Burton's office. He hesitated in the doorway; Mr. Burton looked up and then indicated with a gesture that Mr. Trucks was to take a seat.

The sales manager sat down. He waited for Mr. Burton to speak. Mr. Burton was occupied for the moment with the problem of unwrapping a cigar. Mr. Trucks opened the conversation by saying, "Jack Jameson just stopped by to speak to me."

"Yeah?" said Mr. Burton, removing bitten flakes of tobacco from the end of his tongue.

"He said something about getting some of Asa Bush's accounts when Asa retires," Mr. Trucks said in a deliberately questioning manner.

"Yeah."

The sales manager continued, "Well, this idea of his was based on a promise that he said J. K. had made."

"Yeah. He told me that, too."

"Did Martin make such a promise?" Mr. Trucks inquired.

"Hell, I don't know. It sounds like him." He tilted back in his swivel chair.

"What shall I do about it?"

"Don't ask me; you're the sales manager." Mr. Burton paused, holding his cigar away from his lips as if he were about to speak. Just as Mr. Trucks was about to say something, Mr. Burton lurched forward to flick the ashes from his cigar into his ash tray. "Look here, Dick. I don't want any morale problems around here. You're the first of the 'wonder boys' to be put in charge of a department in this division. I don't want you to do anything to mess up the morale. We never had any morale problems when Martin was alive. We don't want anything like that in this division."

Mr. Trucks was momentarily bewildered. He knew by the way that Mr. Burton used the phrase "wonder boys" that he was referring to the college men who had been brought into the Syracuse division since the war.

Mr. Burton went on, "Why the devil did you tell the men that you were going to reassign the sales territories without even telling me?"

"But you were there when I said it."

"Said what?"

"Well, at my first sales meeting, that one of the ways we were going to get more business was to reorganize the sales territory," Mr. Trucks replied.

"I certainly don't remember anything like that. Dick, you gave a good inspirational talk, but I sure can't remember anything about reassigning territories."

"Actually, I just mentioned the reorganization of territories in passing," the sales manager smiled.

"I'll be damned. That sort of thing is always happening. Here everybody is frothing at the mouth about something that they think we are going to do and we haven't the slightest idea why they think we're going to do it. You know, the real reason Asa Bush asked to be retired instead of staying on as he planned was probably this fear of having his territory reorganized. Both he and Jameson know that their pension on retirement is based on their earnings in the last five years of active employment. Now that I think of it, three or four of the other salesmen have stopped in during the last couple of weeks to tell me what a fine job they were doing. They probably had this territory reassignment bogey on their minds."

Mr. Burton's cigar was no longer burning. He began groping under the papers on his desk for a match.

Mr. Trucks took advantage of this pause in the conversation. "Mr. Burton, I think there are some real advantages to be won by an adjustment of the sales territories. I think——"

"You still think that after today?" the division manager asked in a sarcastic tone.

"Why, yes! The profit we make on sales to an individual account is related closely to delivery expense. The larger the total proportion of the account's business we get, the more profit we make because the delivery expense remains more or less constant."

"Look, Dick. You college men always have everything all figured out with slide rules, but sometimes that doesn't count. Morale is the important thing. The salesmen won't stand for having their territories changed. I know that you have four trainees that you'd like to put out on territories. You put them out on parts of the territories belonging to some of the more experienced men—bam! God knows how many of our good salesmen would be left. Now, I've never had any trouble with sales force morale since I've been manager of this division. Old Martin, bless his soul, never let me down. He wasn't any damn' Ph.D., but, by golly, he could handle men. Don't get off on the wrong foot with the boys, Dick. With the labor situation in the warehouse being what it is,

I've just got too much on my mind. I don't want you to be creating more problems than I can handle. How 'bout it, boy!"

Mr. Burton ground out his half-smoked cigar, looking steadily at Mr. Trucks.

Mr. Trucks was upset because the division manager had imputed to him a lack of concern for morale problems. He had always thought of himself as being very considerate of the thoughts and feelings of others. He realized that at the moment his foremost desire was to get away from Mr. Burton.

Mr. Trucks rose from his chair saying, "Mr. Burton, you can count on me. I know you are right about this morale business."

"Atta boy," said the division manager. "It does us a lot of good to talk like this once in awhile. Now, you see if you can make peace with the salesmen. I want you to handle everything yourself."

"Well, thanks a lot," said the sales manager, as he backed out of the office door.

As he walked through the office after talking with Mr. Burton, he saw two manufacturers' representatives with whom he had appointments already seated near the receptionist's desk. His schedule of appointments that day did not permit him to do more than gather the material pertaining to the Jameson and Bush territories.

Mr. Trucks Goes Home

Mr. Trucks left the office shortly after five o'clock to drive to his home in a suburb of Syracuse. It was a particularly hot and humid day. Pre–Fourth-of-July traffic lengthened the drive by nearly 20 minutes. When he finally turned into his own driveway, he felt as though his skin were caked with grime and perspiration. He got out of the car and walked around the house to the terrace in the rear. Nancy, his wife, was sewing in a deck chair under the awning.

"Hello, Dick. You're late," she said, looking up with a smile.

"I know it. Even the traffic was bad today." He dropped his coat on a glass-topped table and sprawled out full length on the glider. "Honestly, I'm so exhausted and dirty that I am disgusted with myself."

"Bad day?"

"Awful. You just can't imagine how discouraging it is trying to get this job organized. You would think that it would be obvious to everybody that what ails the Syracuse division is the organization of the sales force," said Mr. Trucks, arranging a pillow under his head.

"I didn't realize that you thought anything was wrong with the Syracuse division."

"Well, what I mean is that we get only 20 percent of the potential wholesale business. If I could organize the salesforce my way—well,

God knows, maybe we could get 40 percent of the business. That is what the New York office watches for. The sales manager who increases his division's share of the market gets the promotions when they come along. I knew Mr. Crow transferred me to this division because he knew these possibilities existed."

"I don't understand. Is Mr. Crow still your boss, or is Mr. Burton?" asked his wife.

"Nancy, it's terribly discouraging. Mr. Burton is my boss, but I'll never get anywhere with Consolidated unless Mr. Crow and the other people in New York promote me."

"Don't you like Mr. Burton?"

"I had a run-in with him today."

"You didn't!" she said crossly as she laid her sewing aside.

Mr. Trucks had not anticipated this reaction. He gazed up at the awning as if he had not noticed his wife's intent expression. "We didn't argue particularly. He just——well, he doesn't know too much about sales management. He put his foot down on my plans to reorganize the territories."

"I can't understand why you would go and get yourself into a fight with your boss when you haven't been here even two months. We should never have bought this house!"

"Honestly, honey, I didn't have any fight. Everything is O.K. He just ——well, do you want me to be a divisional sales manager all my life?"

She smiled and said nothing.

He continued, "I'm sorry you married such a grouch, but I just get plain mad when somebody calls me a 'wonder boy.'"

"You're tired," she said sympathetically. "Why don't you go up and take a shower while I feed the children. We can have a drink and then eat our dinner whenever we feel like it. It's only meat loaf anyway."

"That sounds wonderful," he said, raising himself from his prone position.

An Unexpected Caller

Mr. Trucks had just stepped out of the shower when he heard his wife calling to him. "Dick, Jim Pepper is here to see you."

"Tell him I'll be down in just a minute. Give him a drink, Nancy."

As he dressed, Mr. Trucks wondered why the salesman had chosen the dinner hour to call. During the month since he had moved into his new home no salesman had ever dropped in uninvited.

When Mr. Trucks came downstairs, he found Mr. Pepper sitting on the living room couch with a Tom Collins in his hand.

"Hello, Jim," said Mr. Trucks crossing the room with his right hand extended. "You look as if you had had a hot day. Why don't you take off your coat? If we go out to the terrace, you may get a chance to cool off."

"Thanks, Dick," the visitor said as he moved out to the terrace. "I'm sorry to come barging in this way, but I thought it was important."

"Well, what's on your mind?" said Mr. Trucks as he sat down.

Mr. Pepper started to speak but hesitated as Mrs. Trucks came out of the door with two glasses in her hand. She handed one glass to Mr. Trucks, then excused herself, saying, "I think I better see if the children are all right."

After she had disappeared into the house, Mr. Pepper said, "I heard about what happened at the office today, so I thought I'd come over to tell you that we stand 100 percent behind you."

Mr. Trucks was perplexed by Mr. Pepper's words. He realized that the incident to which the salesman referred was probably his meeting with Mr. Jameson. Mr. Trucks said, "I'm not sure what you mean, Jim."

"I heard that you and Jameson had it out this morning about changing the sales territories,'" Mr. Pepper replied.

Mr. Trucks smiled. Two thoughts entered his mind. He was amused at the proportions that the brief conversation of that morning had assumed in the minds of so many people; but, at the same time, he was curious as to how Mr. Pepper, who had presumably been in the field selling, had heard about the incident so soon. Without hesitation he asked, "Where did you hear about this, Jim?"

"Jack Dangler told me! He was down at the warehouse with Homer Babbidge when I stopped off to pick up a special narcotics order for a customer. They are all excited about this territory business. Dangler said Jameson came out to his house at lunch time and told him about it. Everybody figured that you were going to change the territories when you started traveling around with each of the boys, especially after what you said at your first sales meeting."

"Well, the reason I went on the road with each of the men, Jim," said Mr. Trucks, "was so that I could learn more about their selling problems and, at the same time, meet the customers."

Mr. Pepper smiled, "Sure, but when you started filling out a rating sheet on each account, I couldn't help thinking you had some reason for it."

Mr. Trucks realized that the salesman had spoken with irony in his voice, but he thought it was better to let the matter pass as if he had not noticed it. Since he was planning to use the information he had gathered for reorganization of the sales territories, he decided that he would be frank with Mr. Pepper in order to find out what the young salesman's reaction might be on the question of territorial changes. He said, "Jim, I've thought a lot about making some changes in the territories——"

Mr. Pepper interrupted him, "That's terrific! I'm sure glad to hear that. I don't like to speak ill of the dead, but old Martin really gave the trainees the short end of the stick when he put us on territories. He either gave a man a territory of uncontacted accounts so he beat his head against a stone wall until he finally quit, and that is just what happened to two guys who trained with me; or else he gave him a territory where somebody had to be replaced, and where some of the best accounts had been handed over to one of the older salesmen. Well, I know for a fact that when I took over my territory from Rick Hunt, Jack Dangler and Rusty Means got 12 of Hunt's best accounts. And, damn it, I got more sales out of what was left than Hunt ever did, but Dangler and Means's total sales didn't go up at all. It took me awhile, but, by golly, I had the laugh at every sales meeting when our monthly sales figures were announced."

"Is that right?" said Mr. Trucks.

"Damn' right! And I wasn't the only one. That's why those old duffers are so down on the four of us that have come with the division since the war. We've beaten them at their own game."

"Do you think that Waller and Carmack and Smith feel the same way?" asked Mr. Trucks.

"Think, hell! I know it! That's all we ever talk about. If you reorganize those territories and give us back the accounts that Martin took away; you'll see some real sales records. Take, for example, the Medical Arts Pharmacy out by Mercy Hospital. Jack Dangler got that one away from my territory and he calls there only once a week. If I could get that one back, I'd get in there three times a week and get five times as much business."

Mr. Trucks had to raise his hands in a gesture of protest. "Don't you have enough accounts already, Jim, to keep you busy?"

"Dick, I spend 50 hours a week on the road and I love it; but I know damn' well that if I put some of the time I spend in 'two-by-four' stores into some of those big juicy accounts like Medical Arts Pharmacy, I'd do even more business."

Mr. Trucks commented, "I'm not particularly anxious to argue the point now, but if you start putting your time into Medical Arts Pharmacy, what's going to happen to your sales to the 'two-by-four' stores?"

The salesman replied, "Those druggists all know me. They'd go right on buying."

Mr. Trucks did not agree with Mr. Pepper, and he thought that the salesman realized this.

After a moment of silence, Mr. Pepper rose from his chair saying, "I'd better scoot home. My wife will be waiting for me with a rolling pin for being late, so I'd better get out before your wife gets at me with a skillet." Mr. Pepper laughed heartily at his own joke.

The two men walked around the house to Mr. Pepper's car. As the salesman climbed into the car, he said, "Dick, don't forget what I said—

Waller, Carmack, Smith, and I stand 100 percent behind you. You won't ever hear us talk about going over to a competitor!"

"Who's talking about that?" asked Mr. Trucks.

"Well," said Mr. Pepper as he started the motor and shifted into gear, "I don't want to tell tales out of school."

"Sure," Mr. Trucks said quickly. "I'm sorry I asked. So long, Jim. I'll see you soon."

Mr. Trucks watched the salesman back out of the driveway and drive away.

6   *Blow-Mold Packers, Inc.*

Seven months after taking his MBA degree with distinction at Stanford University, Mr. Harold Finer, CPA, decided to quit the academic world and to accept a standing invitation to join Blow-Mold Packers, Inc. (BMP), a fast-growing firm with some $36 million sales in the blow-molded plastic container business.[1] Finer's title would be that of assistant to the president, and his assignment, staff direction of the acquisition program on which BMP had recently embarked.

In joining BMP in January 1970, Finer was entering a firm with which he already felt himself familiar. As a second-year student, he had considered writing his research report on the company and had wound up exploring a business opportunity in which BMP's president was personally interested (the sale of inexpensive teaching machines). Then, on graduation, while deciding what to do next, Finer had spent some time with BMP at the president's invitation. "I accepted his offer," Finer said, "and for a month he paid my expenses while I wandered around listening and seeing what was happening."

At this time (June 1969), BMP included four divisions in the East, Midwest, and West, all in the same line of business. The Western division, with an old plant at San Jose, California, and a new one just about to start at nearby Sunnyvale, was the original BMP; the other three divisions (Mid-America, Eastern, and Blowco) were formerly independent, smaller concerns that had been acquired in 1967 and 1968. In an industry where transportation charges were a significant element in costs, the geographic dispersal provided by these widely

---

[1] Disguised industry.

separated plants was believed to give BMP a cost advantage and hence also a long-term sales advantage. In 1971, two of the acquired divisions were still being run by their original managements, and all were being run on a decentralized profit-center basis. Characteristically, both the divisional and the headquarters line executives had grown up with and in the industry. (See Exhibit 1 for a profile of top management personnel.)

EXHIBIT 1

BLOW-MOLD PACKERS, INC.
Management Personnel Data

Title	Name	Age	Education	Previous Job Experience
President............	Leo Hauptman	45	BS chemistry, Reed College	Research chemist—Gigantic Chemical Co. Vice president research—National Resin Co. Founder—BMP
Executive vice president and division manager, Eastern division............	Frank Silone	41	High school	Mechanic—Mid-America Plastics Co. Founder-president—Eastern Blow-Molding Co.
Division manager, Mid-America.......	J. E. Gardner	58	BS, ME, University of Kansas	Salesman Vice president—Mid-America Plastics Co. President—Mid-America Plastics Co.
Division manager, Blowco............	Frederick Winn	45	BA, Occidental College	Treasurer and vice president—Blowco
Division manager, Western	Donald Ferenzi	40	BA, CPA, City College, Los Angeles	Associate—Smith & Wesson, Certified Public Accountants Controller—BMP Treasurer—BMP
Vice president, R & D..............	Robert Quant	39	BS chemistry, University of Kansas	Chemist—Mid-America Packaging Vice president—Eastern-Molding Corp.
Treasurer............	Harold Finer	30	MBA, Stanford University	Associate—Mitch, Lynch & Smith, Certified Public Accountants Director—Corporate Development, BMP

Source: Casewriter's interviews.

At headquarters, reporting to BMP's president and founder, Mr. Leo Hauptman, age 45, were a few line executives and a newly hired staff. The exact role the staff should play had not yet been decided when Finer visited the company in the summer of 1969. As his contribution to solving this problem, Finer had suggested that each staff man should define his own objectives. "I noted that the new professionals had no specific tasks, and to compound this, everyone reported to Leo," Finer said. "We had no system of responsibility. After some discussions with me, Leo decided to get each of the corporate staff people to write up his own program of action, stating his priorities, problems, and a timetable. This led to BMP's 'red book' of goals."

While Finer saw some organizational problems during his first month's stay at BMP, looking back on this period as of April 1971, he said, "What I saw then was success!"

Past growth in sales and profits of roughly 50 percent a year from 1961 through 1969 had permitted BMP to make acquisitions through exchange of stock on a favorable basis. Although the first three companies acquired had brought dispersal rather than diversification, by 1969 BMP's president felt the time was ripe for invasion of new fields. Hence, at the time Finer joined the company, the search for acquisition prospects took him far away from blow molding. Examined were concerns in such diverse lines as baby foods, soap, wigs, and even plastic credit cards. Commenting on these prospects, Finer later said, "I was apprehensive of certain of the possible purchases on the grounds that there seemed little match between our company and the prospective acquisition, but it was difficult not to find Leo's enthusiasm contagious —even in the case of his most far-out ideas." As things turned out, however, none of them was purchased.

Midway through fiscal 1970, it became clear that BMP would not continue to enjoy the growth in sales and profits which had previously made financing acquisitions through exchange of stock both easy and profitable. (See Exhibits 2 and 3 for relevant financial statements.) Instead, sales appeared to be headed to a level 30 percent below budget, and profits to a level 35 percent below. Although Finer continued to look at a few prospects, he later explained, "I became unhappy selling something we didn't have. I knew we didn't have the professional management which I was trying to sell to the companies we were trying to acquire, and I was very unhappy trying to sell it. I decided that my attention should go elsewhere."

In line with this thinking, Finer began to spend his time increasingly in the treasurer's office on control problems. This was an area in which, as a CPA, Finer felt he could be of some help.

As fiscal 1970 soured, changes in organization were effected. Among the first were the creation of the post of executive vice president to co-

EXHIBIT 2

BLOW-MOLD PACKERS, INC.
Consolidated Balance Sheet as of September 30, 1970
(dollars in thousands)

Assets

Current:
Cash and marketable securities...........................	$ 965.6
Accounts receivable (net)................................	3,817.1
Inventories at lower of cost or market....................	2,274.5
Other..	150.9
Total Current Assets.................................	$ 7,208.1

Fixed:
Gross fixed assets.......................................	$ 7,107.8
Less: accumulated depreciation, etc......................	1,649.8
Net Fixed Assets.....................................	$ 5,458.0

Other:
Patents and copyrights (net).............................	6.4
Other..	151.3
Total Other Assets...................................	$ 157.7
Total Assets...	$12,823.8

Liabilities

Current:
Accounts payable..	$ 2,428.4
Accruals, including taxes payable........................	357.2
Current portion of long-term debt........................	202.6
Total Current Liabilities.............................	$ 2,988.4
Deferred federal income taxes............................	55.5
Long-term debt (less current portion).....................	3,439.6
Contingent deferred credit...............................	104.8
Total..	$ 3,599.9

Stockholders' equity
Common stock...	71.2
Capital in excess of par value and paid-in surplus........	4,410.8
Retained earnings.......................................	1,753.5
Total Stockholders' Equity............................	$ 6,235.5
Total Liabilities and Stockholders' Equity........	$12,823.8

Source: Company records.

ordinate manufacturing policies and the departure of the recently hired corporate sales manager, after his proposals for implementing sales centralization struck other managers as "unrealistic." As the fiscal year drew to its disappointing close in September, several additional changes were made. The corporate staff was disbanded, with five of 12 members leaving the company, and five, apart from Finer and a man in R&D, moving to divisional line positions. The company's treasurer, Mr. Don Ferenzi, was reassigned to head the Western division, where shakedown problems with the new Sunnyvale plant were causing continued cost and output problems. Into the vacated treasurer's position stepped Hal Finer. "I became treasurer," he said, "because Leo asked me to step in

EXHIBIT 3

BLOW–MOLD PACKERS, INC.
*Comparative Consolidated Statement of
Earnings for Years Ending September 30
(dollars in thousands)*

	1970	1969	1968
Net Sales....................................	$33,210.8	$36,640.4	$27,012.8
Cost of goods sold............................	30,557.0	33,432.3	24,452.4
Selling, general, and administrative expenses...	1,569.1	1,437.5	1,279.5
	$32,126.1	$34,869.8	$25,731.9
Operating income............................	$ 1,084.7	$ 1,770.6	$ 1,280.9
Other income................................	39.2	28.2	55.1
	$ 1,123.9	$ 1,798.8	$ 1,336.0
Other deductions............................	147.8	97.0	59.6
	$ 976.1	$ 1,701.8	$ 1,276.4
Special items*...............................	115.4	—	—
Income before federal income taxes...........	$ 860.7	$ 1,701.8	$ 1,276.4
Federal income taxes........................	235.1	764.5	585.5
Net earnings............................	$ 625.6	$ 937.3	$ 690.9

Percentage Breakdown

	1970	1969	1968
Net Sales....................................	100.0%	100.0%	100.0%
Cost of goods sold............................	92.0	91.3	90.5
Selling, general, and administrative expenses....	4.7	3.9	4.8
	96.7	95.2	95.3
Operating income............................	3.3	4.8	4.7
Other income................................	0.1	0.1	0.2
	3.4	4.9	4.9
Other deductions............................	0.5	0.3	0.2
	2.9	4.6	4.7
Special items*...............................	0.3	—	—
Income before federal income taxes...........	2.6	4.6	4.7
Federal income taxes........................	0.7	2.1	2.2
Net earnings............................	1.9	2.5	2.5

* Start-up costs on new plant plus loss on abandonment of old equipment.
Source: Company records.

on Don Ferenzi's departure to the Western division. I had a long-standing interest in control, so I thought I would try it."

Seven months after assuming his new post, against a backdrop of continued declines, Finer raised the issue of implementing the control proposals which he had previously put forward during his first half-year in office. In a memorandum titled, "Some Notes on BMP's Strategy and the Treasurer's Program," he drew attention to the fact that no action had yet been taken on 16 of some 40 suggestions that he and the president had made following their joint budget review of the four divisions early in fiscal 1971. Under the heading, "Taking It Seriously," Finer wrote as follows:

A management control system cannot work unless managers take it seriously. Essentially, this means that the president and his senior colleagues must find that the management control reports are useful and that they must then use these reports and the budget reviews as an important source of information as to what is happening in the company. . . . Top management's belief in the system must be made evident if other individuals are to be motivated to act in the way intended by the system.

Translating these rather philosophical observations into an actual record of our recent budget review only highlights the point at issue: viz. [the number of Presidential] requests for action as of the OCT./NOV. Budget Review in 1970 on which no action had been reported as of APRIL 1971—some six months later.[2]

In the pages that follow, data are provided regarding the environment in which Finer was trying to get his program implemented, as well as on this program itself. These data bear on BMP's leadership and organization, company activities, industry trends, the treasurer's program and its implementation in Finer's first six months, Finer's assessment of what had been accomplished to date and why progress had not been greater, and the steps that he proposed to be taken next.

BMP's Leadership and Organization

After founding his company in 1959, Mr. Hauptman indicated he had run it as a one-man show for a number of years. Later, he said, he had come to see the need for a more participative leadership style:

. . . When the company was started, it was purposely designed to function in an autocratic way. There was only one stockholder: me. There was no question about who was going to make a decision. I was answerable to no one but myself. This helped a lot during the early period. I'm sure that if someone had come and asked me why I made a particular decision, I might have thought twice and never accomplished anything.

During this period, the organization was completely subservient. I was able to handle all the tasks that involved decisions. Finally, it outgrew me, and we had to bring in some heavyweights. . . . Don Ferenzi, who is now over at Western, was one of the first such men that we brought in. He had his CPA so we couldn't call him a bookkeeper, and thus was born the controller's office.

From there on it has been one hell of a climb to get this group of characters to evolve into an organization. For a long time our only organization was me, meeting with someone else to solve a crisis.

---

[2] A following passage of the treasurer's "Notes" went on to summarize these neglected items. Eight were suggestions to the Western division, and are reproduced below as part of the Appendix.

Finally, after I joined the YPO[3] and got some managerial ideas, we decided to have a meeting and set down some objectives and goals for the company. Twelve of us went away and formulated some goals. At the second corporate meeting we had a psychologist who helped us to discuss our two-person relationships and the problems of delegation. Soon after that meeting we went public. . . . [Pointing to his attire] That's when I got my vest.

Besides the YPO, there were other influences on the evolution of the president's role-concept and the company structure. Mr. Hauptman continued his account of these as follows:

At the end of 1967 we started our program of acquisition, buying firms in the Midwest and East. Of course, the pattern of purchases we made gave us instant delegation of many responsibilities. But it hasn't solved many of our management problems. . . .

Then, too, Du Pont, as it does with many of its smaller customers, tried to help us to set up a rational set of procedures. Du Pont's help led us to develop our "red book" of organizational problems and goals.

I would say that throughout this period, our aim was to develop an organization like General Motors. That is, an organization with decentralized plants, centralized control, and creativity. General Motors's Sloan captures for me the essence of being a great manager.

* * * * *

I honestly believe Sloan had the proper approach: decentralized manufacturing, but with centralized centers for finance, research, sales, and technical services.[4]

President Hauptman went on to describe his own recent effort, in line with the General Motors model he admired, to run the several divisions of his company with the aid of a central headquarters staff. He also gave his views on why this scheme had failed:

Finally, something happened. I got on the kick of building a centralized corporate staff. We got personnel, sales, materials management, engineering, and corporate development staff people in here. You might even say we developed "instant corporitis."

What should have happened was for me to get all of those guys into a room and tell them what they were going to do. Instead, some of our old line people complained that superimposing a corporate staff would cause us to lose talent and versatility in our line divisions. The result was that we went on a decentralized basis with the staff acting as consultants.

Basically, the structure which we were working toward was sound. But we had a few unfortunate things happen. First, there were a few

---

[3] The Young Presidents' Organization, a group whose activities included conducting short-session management training programs.

[4] See Alfred P. Sloan, *My Years with General Motors* (Garden City, N.Y.: Doubleday & Co., Inc., 1964.)

guys on the staff who weren't congruent with corporate goals. They thought that the jungle warfare of office politics was the way to succeed. They were wrong. They are gone. Second, on top of the mismatch of people, we tried to do too much too fast. We had 14 or 15 highly paid and talented people running around without a true sense of direction. With the move to Sunnyvale and the new-plant problem there, we had to cut our goals down.

As to people in his company and his own role in relation to them, Mr. Hauptman's comments included the following:

> One of my main jobs is to protect the values of the organization.
> Our managers must develop the desire to learn. I think we have an interesting thing going here with our company!
> Our business requires creativity in sales and R&D.
> We have to get cross-fertilization through sharing of ideas and through crisscrossing people in the organization.
> Young guys have survived rather well in our organization; maybe they are more willing to listen than the older experts!
> Having personal help such as Hal Finer is useful. They run interference for me. They serve up material for me to make decisions.
> I think Hal is more concerned than I am that I get on with it and make a decision about the organization. I have to see how I think the organization should be five years hence.
> I think one of the terrible things about myself is my desire for involvement. I have to develop an impersonal approach eventually. I must develop a regularity and a rhythm.
> One of our major tasks currently is to get the right kind of information. We are developing an MIS[5] and we will get the information!
> You ask about rewards. In my opinion, once top management understands the information they will be getting, the information itself will be a major reward! It will be an important scorecard in the game.
> Of course, we will have to come up with an incentive pay scheme. Probably we will have to provide some form of stock incentive.
> The real question is, can we both make money and make people a little bit happier?

Managerial Responses.   Interviews with management personnel elicited many comments on BMP's organizational environment. Speaking of the president, Finer indicated that his strength lay in creativity rather than in decision implementation through his organization.

> I would say that Leo Hauptman, the president, is an intellectual who is capable of dealing with the problems of business at a high level of abstraction. He has a fantastic ability to conceptualize and to visualize new products and new applications. He knows philosophically where he wishes to go, and this is vitally important. But in some sense he tries to wave a magic wand when it comes to implementing the detailed pro-

---

[5] Management information system.

grams necessary to achieve his basic goals through the organization. For example, it is his policy to have a fresh flower on each secretary's desk each Monday morning. With the same type of motion which he makes to have this rather mundane task accomplished, he indicates that he wants to have responsibility accounting. The intentions are often widely separated from the implementation.

There is in the company a lack of systematic relationships. Almost all of the communications are informal and many of them obscure completely the nominal lines of authority.

As to the corporate staff, Finer furnished the following account of why it was hired and how:

About two years ago, Leo thought that he had the solution to some of the problems of the growth of the company. His solution was to "hire a corporate staff." He wanted to staff this organization with systems people. He hired these people out of a belief that the organization would be professionalized. He hoped that the professional education of the staff personnel would help by breathing into the organization some systematic relationships which were desirable in the old organization, but not obtainable.

It is interesting to note that the professionals were all interviewed by psychologists and not by line managers. Leo is oriented toward defining the individual rather than the problems. He doesn't want people around whom he can't understand as people.

Reporting his own early views on the corporate staff, Finer said he had seen it as a difficult assignment for both Leo and the professionals:

There was some question as to how professional were the professionals; there was the problem of bringing 12 staff people in on top of an already unsystematic organization, and there was therefore the increasingly worrisome query as to whether the transition could ever be consummated from entrepreneurial to professional. Thus the corporate staff could not possibly learn enough about the business to cope with the old-timers in the organization, and there was not enough of a management information system to give them the formal and numerical tools with which they could work.

Finer believed further that the effort to create a corporate staff, while not wrong in any absolute sense, could have been premature, in view of the importance of the growth and development of the line managers, whose role in the company was critical. In a memorandum drafted by Finer at the president's request and finalized and signed by the president under the title, "Ending 1970–1971 Strategy," this point was put as follows:

The failure of the corporate staff was in my opinion not a failure of concept so much as an overly ambitious *top* management program in circumstances where the company's *middle* management had not been adequately and formally developed at the corporate and divisional level. Thus the creation of the corporate staff was fated to be a premature attempt to bring centralization into being at a time when no systematic and detailed internal procedure for sales or manufacturing financial reporting was available, and at a time when the critical manufacturing problems of efficiency and quality were largely occurring within the local plant (and even line) organization.

While this experience does not diminish my belief in a long-term program to develop a corporate staff. . . . I do believe that at the present time we must emphasize internal management growth within . . . our existing corporate and divisional organization in circumstances where the facts indicate that this is where the problems are.

The idea that inexperience was a problem in the line as well as in the staff was also expressed by BMP's executive vice president, Frank Silone. This officer, who had entered the company through the recently acquired Eastern division of which he had been the founder-president, had the following to say:

We have got to find the right people to fill the boxes on the organization chart with a minimum amount of confusion. . . . It is unfortunate, but many of the people in responsible positions just don't know their own inadequacies. For example, we have supervisors who just don't know anything about the equipment. When something breaks down, they make sure that they are nowhere around so their own ignorance will not be exposed.

The managers just don't get involved. They let the decisions be left too far down in the organization. Our old corporate staff was unsuccessful because we had mechanical engineers who never had practical experience.

As to the staff, Silone believed that its members had not only been too inexperienced, they had also had a "wrong" conception of their role:

The old staff failed, but not because the divisions were unwilling to cooperate. There has never been a hesitancy among the general managers to work together with the staff people. I have heard that there was. This is foolish. The general managers have too much to do, and they don't have enough staff people within their own groups to accomplish the tasks.

What did happen was that we got staff groups who were inexperienced, ineffective, and hired for the wrong purpose. Starting with this base, the staff people came in to work on areas that had low priority. The general managers just didn't have time to support them. Unless they were going to work in areas that were important to the line people, they should just forget it.

Staff is a supporting function. They should do the things that the line managers don't have time to do or can't do for themselves.

Another headquarters executive expressed the view that what was needed throughout BMP was better communication and direction:

> Direction from a staff and from a corporate point of view has been almost negligible. In my experience, I have found that you can't have an organization without objectives, directives, reports, and instructions. There has to be communication, both up and down. The failure has been that no one person was available to monitor the organization and make sure that it was given direction.

BMP's Activities

Blow Molding. Blow molding was one of the most recent developments in plastic technology. Using a technique borrowed from the glass industry, the blow molders had developed a relatively inexpensive method of fabricating lightweight, inexpensive bottles, which could be lithographed directly or labeled with gummed labels. The major volume application for blow molding was initially detergent and bleach bottles, but new equipment had been developed to make possible larger products, such as automobile gasoline tanks, beer kegs, oil drums, etc. In addition, new formulations for the plastics had been developed, and these had been approved by the Food and Drug Administration (FDA) for use in food and drug containers. Other technical advances, such as the development of a clear, see-through plastic, had allowed the industry to compete successfully for some cosmetic business and other products where it was deemed desirable to have the contents visible.

The actual process of blow molding consists of blowing a thin balloon of molten thermoplastic material against the inside walls of a female mold and chilling it to a rigid solid. This technique offers extremely high production rates and low unit costs.

A typical line producing 32-ounce detergent containers could produce over 10,000 bottles per shift, with four persons employed directly in the fabrication of the bottles. Such an installation would require an investment of from $100,000 to $150,000. Industry sources indicated that additional lines could be added at a slightly lower cost owing to the overlapping of auxiliary equipment. In a completely automated operation such as BMP's, however, where all equipment was tied to a single blow molding machine, capital investment in the factory was roughly proportional to the number of lines required.

BMP was believed to be among the largest of the approximately 250 independent blow molders in the United States. In addition to this group of independents, however, there were approximately 330 blow molding plants which were integrated into the end user's operation, and another 50 blow molders which were owned by large manufacturers of resins.

The independent blow molders such as BMP were equipped to perform a variety of services for their customers. In addition to producing the package, BMP would accept contracts to fill the containers with the end product. In most cases BMP had to label the bottles produced either with paper labels, lithography, or therimage; to store the packages until needed by the marketer; and to make final shipment.

In some special cases where contamination danger was high or a particularly unusual resin was used, the customer supplied the resins employed in fabricating the bottles. In most cases, however, BMP assumed all responsibility for the purchase of raw materials. In addition, in those cases where BMP filled the bottles, it often purchased the materials for and compounded the customer's product. In either event, materials costs represented a high proportion of BMP's sales dollar, as was generally true in blow molding. On the average, BMP realized only 20 percent more sales income than it paid out in materials charges. With this breakdown of the company's sales dollar in mind, one executive stated, "We are really just a $7 million business. The other $29 million we take into sales is just dollars which we trade between our customers and our suppliers."

Product Lines.   The bottles which BMP produced were originally almost all for household items, such as detergents and bleaches. Later the company had taken advantage of new formulations to develop clear plastic bottles for shampoos, etc. With the acquisition of the Blowco Company, BMP had become an important supplier to pharmaceutical houses, its lightweight containers taking over a large share of the market for aspirin and stomach-pill bottles, etc. Because some Blowco customers supplied their own resins, materials costs were not so high a portion of total costs as they were in other BMP divisions. Gross margins, too, needed to be higher than in other divisions, to compensate for higher handling costs on the very large number of very small bottles, extra quality controls, and, in some cases, filling of the containers by Blowco.

Sales.   In terms of both product applications and customers, BMP's sales were highly concentrated. Thus the five highest-volume applications (bottles for like products of several customers) accounted for two-thirds of BMP's sales, with two applications alone accounting for one half. Similarly, the top 10 customers accounted for 45.6 percent of sales, with the top three accounting for 24.1 percent. The loss of one important customer who had purchased his own blow molding machines had been an important factor in the profit decline of 1970.

In an attempt to mitigate the risk of losing a large account, BMP's president and division managers were actively engaged in maintaining relationships with large current customers and in seeking new ones. For fiscal 1971, BMP had developed five new accounts which were budgeted to yield 16 percent of sales.

Besides seeking to attract new customers for established applications, BMP also sought to develop new applications and find customers to adopt them. Mr. Hauptman's personal record was a particularly strong one in this area. In the past his new product-application ideas had led to some of BMP's strongest sellers. Company-developed new applications were budgeted to yield 5.6 percent of total unit sales in 1971. Thus new customers and new applications were expected to contribute almost one fifth of sales in fiscal 1971.

Purchasing and Materials Management. Although materials costs were passed on, BMP had always sought to make effective use of its considerable purchasing power. Executives claimed and Finer agreed that the purchasing function was well handled, and that every possible advantage was being achieved through present procedures. Besides effective buying, BMP required effective inventory controls. From a sales standpoint it was critical for the company to have on hand materials for prompt delivery of rush orders.

Inventory and shipping requirements in turn placed a premium on efficient warehousing and materials handling. Overheads and indirect labor connected with this function were a charge on BMP and were grouped together as the materials management expense ($570,000 for the first six months of fiscal 1971).

Manufacturing. Among its four divisions BMP had six plants. These varied from one another in terms of product lines, facilities, and machinery, and so far no effort had been made to standardize their operations. Even within a single plant, variations in the yield of finished goods from raw materials were an important factor. Different resins employed affected yields considerably. In addition, heat, air pressure, and machine speed played important roles. More manageable, but important nonetheless, were operator errors, maintenance, and mechanical downtime.

In addition to other differences, BMP's divisions in fiscal 1971 had different ratios of capacity to sales. Thus, in the first half of the year two of the divisions were looking for more volume. One was oversold. And one, Western, was in the position of having actual sales in excess of rated capacity during the first quarter, while budgeted sales for the year as a whole would be insufficient to fill up the plant—should planned improvements in efficiency actually be achieved. At the end of the second quarter, however, Western's capacity expansion program was lagging behind schedule.

Western's first-half problem with capacity was associated with a problem of high costs. Both problems were, in turn, associated with the new plant at Sunnyvale which had been opened late in 1969. As to why this plant was still having trouble, Finer laid some blame on the way its design was planned. He said:

Leo believes in people. He let all of those who were potentially involved with the Sunnyvale plant help to design it. The result was that nobody was responsible. Many now are asking, "Who put the lines in an 'S' shape? Why did the costs jump so far?" We don't know the answers to these questions.

Although Western's cost problem at Sunnyvale attracted the most executive attention, Finer emphasized that this was not the only significant cost problem BMP had. Both direct labor and overheads were rising as a percentage of sales in other plants as well. Finer saw this upward movement as an important problem for a company performing a service function for large cost-conscious customers in an industry which, he felt, was becoming increasingly competitive.

Industry Trends

BMP's analysis of industry trends as of early 1971 was expressed in a report drafted by Finer and finalized by the president as part of a policy memorandum entitled, "Ending 1970–1971 Corporate Strategy." In part, this went as follows:

Whilst the demand for our products is increasing and whilst there is evidence for a growing acceptance of the custom molder's role, competition and consolidation amongst the various molders over the last few years have begun to rationalize a new structure for our industry in which only the most efficient will survive.

The Treasurer's Program

On assuming office, Finer realized that his approach to control was going to be different from that of his predecessor, Mr. Ferenzi, who was now head of the Western division. At least through the "good" year of 1969, Mr. Ferenzi had focused most of his attention on materials costs, since these were some 80 percent of the total. Mr. Ferenzi had also argued that BMP had no need for a standard cost system, or for cost records on the basis of which the relative efficiency of different line layouts and machines could be compared. Nor did Mr. Ferenzi believe it was worthwhile to try to keep track of the estimated profitability of different applications and package types and sizes. It was more important, he argued, to establish BMP in new fields as they developed than to seek to concentrate company efforts on fields with the highest current estimated payoff.

As far as imposing controls on the divisions was concerned, Mr. Ferenzi had collected reports on the basis of which, he believed, unfavorable trends could be spotted and help given. These reports were not standardized, he said, nor were divisional managers evaluated on the basis of their profit performance. Mr. Ferenzi was sure, however, that divisional managers acted like entrepreneurs and attempted to maximize profit.

In line with his belief that "only the most efficient" would survive as the blow molding industry was "rationalized," Finer had concluded that BMP's old system of controls would no longer suffice for 1971. In his previously cited "Notes," he informed the organization that these accounts "revealed very little about the performance of our factory managers" and "even less [about] our account executives." Furthermore, while the "old system was analytical to the extent that it revealed the profits by plant on a relative basis," any comparison that might be made was "subject to the obligation of the reader to exercise some judgment as to the impact of product mix on plant revenues and costs."

Finer's own program, in contrast with his predecessor's, called for measuring individual performance by a system of "responsibility accounting," for detailed budgets and budget reviews, for collection of additional data on variables "critical to the business," for an "integrated system of reports" designed to help implement the above objectives, and—as a longer-run goal—for development of standard costs, first on a product[6] and then on a process[7] basis.

Responsibility Accounting. The principle of holding executives accountable for their level of performance was one that Finer wished to see applied throughout the company, at least as far down as divisional departmental managers (e.g., divisional managers for sales, production, quality control, engineering, maintenance, etc.). What responsibility accounting was and why it was important, Finer explained to other members of the organization in his previously cited "Notes" as follows:

> For management control purposes, a responsibility accounting system is nothing more or less than a way of defining the job assigned to each manager in our organization by providing him with an explicit listing of all the costs and/or revenues for which he is responsible. . . . Each individual manager then knows precisely what his boss expects of him, and, more importantly, knows that . . . superlative efforts on his part will not pass unnoticed. . . .

Holding managers accountable, Finer continued, meant measuring their performance against some yardstick. Since nothing in BMP's old system of accounts adequately served this purpose, this yardstick would at first have to be a manager's best estimate of what he could accomplish. Speaking informally of this approach, Finer said, "It's not ana-

---

[6] All costs associated with the production of a particular size and shape of container.

[7] Costs collected by type of production activity, i.e., compounding, molding, labeling, etc. These would be useful in understanding the economics of the various parts of the production process.

lytical, but it seeks to record the promises which the managers make when they take over, and to see how they perform with regard to those promises." In his "Notes" he wrote, "The recommendation proposed here is . . . that a yardstick of good performance be for the time being the achievement of budgeted goals. A corollary of this policy is that managers who consistently fail to meet their promises must be replaced.

Budgets and Budget Reviews.   As Finer envisioned his control system, the "promises" the managers made as to what they hoped to achieve would be pulled together into divisional and corporate budgets. Both the targets set and the actual performance against target would be subject to periodic review. Finer would, of course, have a role in this process, along with the president.

Collection of Additional Data.   Besides collecting prime financial data for the operating budget and budget reviews, Finer envisioned integrating these data into statistics on critical variables. These variables Finer listed as follows:

1. Manufacturing capacity adjusted for standard downtime versus scheduled production.
2. Standard contribution by line hour by product and plant versus overhead by line hour by plant.
3. Standard contribution by account executive, product (old/new), and customer (old/new).
4. Aged finished goods, raw material, and accounts receivable/payable statistics.

An Integrated System of Accounts.   In line with his plans to initiate in BMP such new departures as responsibility accounting, numerical goals, and collection of more detailed data on variables critical to the business, Finer decided that one of his high-priority tasks was to prepare an integrated set of report forms on which managers would be asked to enter the kinds of information required. What would be in these reports, who would fill them out, and where they would be routed were among the issues to be decided.

Standard Costs.   Over the longer run, Finer knew he would not be satisfied with a budget that featured estimates based on "promises" from each manager reflecting what each "believed" he could accomplish. Finer thus looked forward to developing "analytical" standards, by which he meant standards derived from analysis of past experience. In line with this intention, standard costs would be developed in two phases, with "first priority" being given to the development of direct labor and direct material job costs, and "second priority" to process costs. To communicate to others in the company why such changes were needed in the accounting system, Finer included in his "Notes" the explanation reproduced as Exhibit 4.

EXHIBIT 4

BLOW-MOLD PACKERS, INC.
*Excerpts from the Treasurer's "Notes" Pertaining to the Need for an
Analytical Standard Cost System*

. . . The present policy of the treasurer's department . . . has as its
aim the establishment of an analytical system of accounting which will
yield a formal schedule of standard costs and/or standard revenues for
each of our managerial centers of responsibility and for each of our
products—and which will in this way supplement the system of responsibility accounting by adding to it such financial and statistical data as
will help our managers to analyze their performance as well as communicate it.

I. *First Priority—Job Costing:*

The earliest priority of this program is to set up an accounting system
which will determine and allocate the actual usage of raw materials and
direct labor by job and which will in this way:

1. Verify our *actual* raw material process costs on a monthly basis.
2. Refine the yardstick of good performance for 90 percent of our
   costs by:
   a. Enabling and encouraging operating improvements to be
      made (and demonstrated) on a job-by-job basis.
   b. Allowing valid comparisons of costs to be made on a product-
      by-product basis as between different plants and different
      time periods.
   c. Raising questions as to precisely where material wastage and
      poor labor utilization are occurring on particular products.
3. Refine the yardstick of good performance for all our account
   executives [salesmen] by creating a formal schedule of standard
   contribution dollars based on standard material and labor costs.
   In this way the company can break away from its overreliance on
   the fabricating fee concept (which in any event is contaminated
   with material price and usage variances) and instead reinforce
   the responsibility accounting concept which formalizes the sepa-
   ration between the sales (contribution) and the production (cost)
   functions.
4. Refine the sales strategy of the company by relating it to a formal
   monthly statement of product (as well as account executive)
   profitability.

II. *Second Priority—Process Costing:*

The second priority of this program is to correlate such a body of
financial and statistical data as will enable us to understand how costs
behave as a process (as opposed to a job) and how process inputs can be
optimally related to process outputs. This program seeks to help our
managers discover the relationships that lie behind economic variables
and, for example, seeks to show:

Exhibit 4 (*continued*)

1. How our "fixed" costs vary with output or investment decisions.
2. How standards of improvement can be created for our overhead cost centers.
3. How savings can be created *and traced* as a result of capital investment programs.
4. How the optimum use can be made of our productive capacity through rational sales contracts based on the financial history of given products and given customers.

Source: Treasurer's files.

Implementation of the Treasurer's Program

Looking back in April 1971, Finer recalled that he had first gone to work, informally and unofficially, in the treasurer's office during June of the previous year. "By September," he added, "I had a clear idea of what I wanted." Thus, when Finer became treasurer himself, he was able to move quickly to implement several parts of his program. Indeed, he had already been able, inspite of "some resistance," to get the idea of responsibility accounting accepted.

Finer's first official recommendation, made in October 1970, pertained to his goal of setting up a new integrated system of reports. Readied for presentation to the board when it convened for its December meeting was a 30-page black notebook, containing forms for the different reports that Finer saw as needed by various levels: i.e., by the board itself, by the president, by the executive vice president, by the general manager, and by the departmental managers of the divisions. Accompanying these forms was a short introduction explaining the various purposes they served, and a one-page diagram indicating where the data would be filled in and where each of the reports would be routed.

Besides for the first time introducing forms on which department heads in each division would record their budgeted and later their actual costs and revenues (if any), Finer made some changes in the operating statements used internally for purposes of control by the corporation and each of its divisions. These changes reflected Finer's conviction that "fabricating fees"—especially as computed in the past (i.e., sales less materials at net)—had received undue attention as measures of divisional performance. For one thing, Finer believed that divisions should be charged with materials not at *net* but at *gross* (the reason being that any trade discounts received were really a function of the whole corporation's size and ability to pay). For another thing, Finer believed that the important measure to watch was not just the fabricating fee, but the fabricating fee *minus* the direct labor costs apt to be incurred in making up each order. To the resulting figure, which he hoped to see used as an important measure of performance, Finer gave the title, "contribution from sales." In essence, the changes he proposed would affect divisional statements as follows:

Old	*New*
Sales	Sales
— Materials costs (net)	— Materials cost (gross)
= Fabricating fee	= Fabricating fee
— Direct labor costs	— Budgeted direct labor†
— Overheads	= Contribution from sales
— Corporate charges*	— Direct labor variance
= Profit before taxes	— Overheads
	= Profit before taxes

* No corporate charges would appear under the new setup, since cash discounts and other income would be set against the cost of the headquarters group.

† Figures would reflect management's estimates until standard costs could be developed on an analytical basis.

In addition to affecting the divisional reports by as much as $300,000, the proposed changes emphasized the importance of account executives by breaking out profitability by account executive as well as by plant. As Finer put it, "Plants do not generate sales; we must control the salesmen."

After the new report forms were devised, Finer's next major project, carried out in October and November, was his first divisional budget review. In company with Mr. Hauptman, he called on each general manager to examine and discuss each division's forecast for 1971. On returning from these trips, Finer drafted and the president finalized and signed a letter to each manager, summarizing the conclusions reached.

Besides being sent to the officers concerned, these letters were also bound in a black notebook for presentation to the board in December.

In each instance, these letters of review began with the assurance that any comments made, including any that would appear "critical," were made "in good faith" and with the "sole intent" of helping the manager "improve his role." There followed a review of the figures which the manager had submitted. Here attention was directed to any special problems which might reduce the profit below forecasted figures (e.g., inadequate sales in one division, inadequate capacity in another, the impact of downtime and quality control problems on predicted labor costs in a third). Following this analytical section, there came a section headed "Specific Actions to be Taken." Included in this were four to nine proposals per division, of which some comprised subsidiary steps. Winding up each letter was a group of exhibits. Most of these pertained to each division's problems and the actions recommended especially for it, but also included in each letter were the budgeted operating statements that had been presented by all four divisions. (Excerpts from the budget reviews of October–November 1970 are presented in the Appendix.)

The objective on which Finer indicated he had made least headway during his first six months in office was his project of developing standard job and process costs upon an analytical basis. In connection with this purpose, forms had been developed on which managers were asked to record their current cost estimates and their actual costs in detail, so that variances could be analyzed and more realistic standards developed. Managers, however, saw these forms—at least in their initial versions—as calling for more work than the information on them was worth. One divisional accountant put this point as follows:

> We are now on our third cost accounting program since Hal Finer became treasurer. We are gradually coming to an agreement and getting the program down to a level where there is a balance between the usefulness of the information and the time consumed in preparing it. Three months ago I couldn't handle all of the numbers we were supposed to be collecting. For each job we were being asked to collect far more information than we were capable of using. The detail which we were being asked to gather was far too great. No one could use it for every job. The materials quantity usage variances were not useful to me here, and no one in the factory knew how to use them. . . .

Another divisional executive, a manufacturing manager, indicated that he still believed that "feel" and a few figures were the only feasible guides to efficient operations in the kinds of business done by his plant:

> I don't find the new system particularly useful yet. As it becomes firmly entrenched and we develop some history and information, I am sure that it will be more useful to me. Right now I rely mainly on some of the numbers and estimates which I have collected to tell me how efficiently we are doing our job. I have been in the industry a long time. Experience plus a few numbers are still the best guide.
>
> The problem of this plant is that we make such a wide range of sizes that it is difficult to set numerical standards. Speed can vary all over the lot. You really have to sense the rhythm of the plant to know if things are slacking off or if they are running properly.

Lack of understanding and cooperation was also a problem, Finer indicated, in making the best use of a relatively high-cost computer ($100,000 a year) that had been installed at the beginning of 1970 in the Western division to account by skid for the actual movement of Western's materials. Western's general manager, Mr. Ferenzi, "does not know if he wants the computer with all its detail by location and skid," Finer said. Partly for this reason, data inputs into the computer were incomplete. On material used, for example, "The fact was that

30 percent of the pallet tickets were not getting up to the data-processing center." Under these circumstances, Finer continued, Mr. Ferenzi had decided to take the computer off calculating actual material costs altogether. "Instead, the decision was made to use the computer to calculate theoretical costs based on theoretical usage per the product bill of material. Right now it is just in the process of making these unreal pro formas."

Pursuing the computer issue further in his "Notes," Finer summarized his position as follows:

> . . . viewed historically Sunnyvale has become an increasingly worrisome force for those of us who are trying to create a corporate-wide system of direct material and labor job costing.
>
> The focus of our present problem centers on Sunnyvale's computer installation, and no doubt there is currently a feeling going around that the treasurer has turned into a data addict who spends his nights kneeling before a programmed prayer wheel in his search to become the electronic-age administrator that he far from looks. Nonetheless, it is true that the computer represents the only viable way to create a job costing system at the Western division, and it is also true that as yet Western's management has been unable to collect any accurate input for this system in spite of many detailed recommendations as to how this might be done. Put as briefly as possible . . . no progress has been made in correcting inaccurate inventories, maintaining accurate inventories, or in reconciling the various skid tickets which in total make up the material handling system and which in detail can provide the basis for a real-time actual materials cost system.

Assessment of Progress to Date

With April 1971 came Finer's second budget review and the first review in which he could compare actual achievements for a six-month period with the budgeted promises that he had asked the division heads to make at the beginning of the current fiscal year. This time, Finer's "Treasurer's Report" assumed the form of an assessment of progress to date. Starting with a rundown on profit prospects for fiscal 1971 as a whole, the review went on to analyze where first-half cost and income factors were getting out of line, not only with the optimistic forecasts made six months before, but also with the record of past achievements. There followed a section on the revised forecasts for the second half of the year, and then a discussion of the implications of these data for BMP's sales and manufacturing policy makers.

As to profit prospects for 1971 as a whole, Finer pointed out that these now appeared headed toward being only $58,000 after taxes—a net reduction of over 90 percent from what had been expected six months earlier.

Already first-half pre-tax operating profits for the four operating divisions combined were $628,000 below budget. This variance Finer traced to four major causes: $190,000 represented "standard contribution dollars" lost through the failure of BMP's manufacturing operations to provide capacity for budgeted volume; $152,000 represented "failure to achieve actual output at budgeted direct labor"; $211,000 represented failure to control overhead costs; and the remaining $74,000 was a variance caused by "failure of BMP corporate sales to deliver budgeted volume where manufacturing capacity was available." One of the graphs in the back of the report (see Exhibit 5) indicated in which divisions these four variances arose. Except in the case of inadequate sales volume, the Western division proved the major source of un-

EXHIBIT 5

BLOW-MOLD PACKERS, INC.
First-Half Variance Analysis, Divisional Performance,
Six Months Ending March 31, 1971

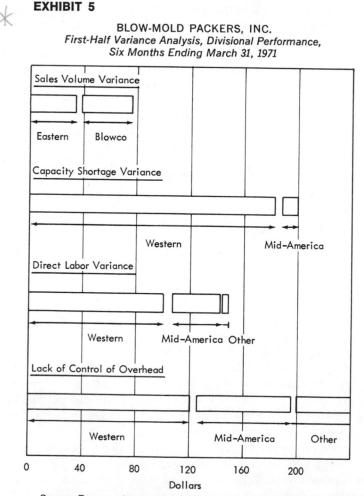

Source: Treasurer's report at the termination of the first half of fiscal 1971.

favorable actual-to-budgeted performance, with the Mid-America division also making significant additions to variances due to lack of direct labor and overhead controls.

Comparisons of divisional performance in 1971 with 1968 showed just how far the divisions had slipped since BMP's last really good year (see Table 1).

TABLE 1

Year	Western	Mid-America	Eastern	Blowco	Total
1968 pre-tax profit..............	$ 448	$197	$259	$165	$1,069
1971 pre-tax budgeted profit (loss)........................	(920)	47	44	205	(624)
Gap* 1968–71..................	($1,368)	($150)	($215)	$ 40	($1,693)

* Based on 1971 first-half actual results plus estimated second-half figures; excludes corporate income in both cases.

Back of these long-term profit declines lay the same difficulties in each division that the variance analyses had shown. Rising overheads were the most at fault in Western and Mid-America, while lower contribution from sales at Eastern reflected mainly a "sales famine." (For a graph of these relationships, see Exhibit 6. For detailed divisional operating statements for the first six months of 1971, see Exhibit 7.)

As to the division heads' revised forecasts for the last six months of 1971, Finer indicated he had made "an attempt to examine the validity of the operating assumptions" which lay behind the newly submitted figures. In this connection he pointed out that "Western has forecast an increase in monthly production rates exceeding, by over 50 percent, its best output performance of the current fiscal year, and at the same time has forecasted halting its long history of rapidly rising overhead costs." At Blowco, he noted, "Increases in overheads . . . are expected to halt in spite of declining excess capacity." Eastern and Mid-America, in contrast, were not at this time found to be expecting favorable reversals of past trends.

As to the implications of these data for sales and manufacturing policy makers, Finer argued that not industry trends, but BMP's own decisions seemed to be the root of the company's troubles:

> Although it is true that the packaging industry and specifically blow molding is getting more competitive, the preceding analysis shows that it is also true that BMP's deteriorating financial position is due as much to BMP's own decisions as it is to any decisions that have been made in the outside world. Thus, while on the one hand fabricating fees have generally held up, on the other hand, contribution dollars have fallen due to increased direct labor costs in the West, and pre-tax division costs

EXHIBIT 6

BLOW-MOLD PACKERS, INC.
Historical Analysis—Contribution and Overhead Trends, 1968–71

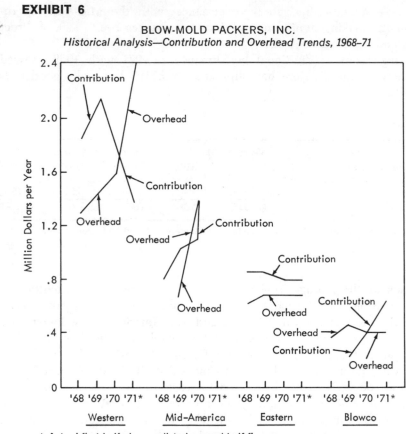

* Actual first-half plus predicted second-half figures.
Source: Treasurer's report as of the termination of the first half of fiscal 1971.

have risen due to dramatic increases in Western's and Mid-America's overhead burden.

To underscore the point that the company must now take remedial actions, Finer then pointed to the breakeven charts that he had prepared for the two divisions where excess overhead charges were a problem. If present cost-income assumptions were valid, Mid-America could do very little better than break even, even if it operated at 100 percent of its capacity. And Western would need to generate 40 percent more sales volume than its present contracts to achieve this same result. With expected losses at Western more than wiping out expected divisional profits elsewhere, BMP in 1971 would be dependent on its extradivisional or "corporate" income for the small profit that, overall, the company expected to show.

EXHIBIT 7

BLOW-MOLD PACKERS, INC.
Internal Operating Data, First Half of Fiscal 1971
(dollars in thousands)

	Western	Percent	Mid-America	Percent	Eastern	Percent	Blowco	Percent	Total	Percent
Sales	$5,730	100.0	$7,150	100.0	$3,161	100.0	$941	100.0	$16,982	100.0
Materials costs (gross)	4,638	81.0	6,000	83.9	2,565	81.1	498	52.9	13,701	80.7
Fabricating fee	1,092	19.0	1,150	16.1	596	18.9	443	47.1	3,281	19.3
Standard direct labor	501	8.7	422	5.9	125	4.0	144	15.3	1,192	7.0
Sales expenses	65	1.1	52	0.7	48	1.5	21	2.2	185	1.1
Contribution from sales	526	9.2	676	9.5	423	13.4	278	29.6	1,904	11.2
Operating expenses:*										
Manufacturing (including direct labor variance)†	722	12.6	434	6.1	247	7.8	135	14.3	1,539	9.1
Materials management	256	4.5	191	2.7	94	3.0	29	3.1	570	3.3
Administrative (plant)	143	2.5	50	0.7	71	2.2	30	3.1	293	1.7
Total Operating Expense	1,121	19.6	675	9.5	412	13.0	194	20.5	2,402	14.1
Operating income (loss)	(593)	(10.4)	—	—	11	0.4	83	8.9	(498)	(2.9)
Other income (loss) (net)	—	—	2	0.03	(27)	(0.9)	5	0.5	21	0.1
Divisional income (loss)	(593)	(10.4)	2	0.03	(16)	(0.5)	88	9.4	(519)	(3.0)
Corporate income									375	2.2
Pre-tax income									(144)	(0.8)
Provision for taxes (refund)									90	0.5
Profit (loss) after tax									(54)	(0.3)

* Included in operating expense were the following costs per division:

	Western	Mid-America	Eastern	Blowco
Indirect and labor	$332	$264	$140	$77
Other manufacturing	566	169	169	82

† Total direct labor variance = $152,100.

Note: Figures fail to add due to rounding.

Source: Treasurer's report at the termination of the first half of fiscal 1971.

Impediments to Progress

At about the same time as Finer wrote his midyear "Treasurer's Report," he wrote his previously quoted "Some Notes on BMP's Strategy and the Treasurer's Program." Here he posed the question why, in view of the profit decline that had started more than 12 months earlier, so little had been done to implement his past proposals for improving control.

Two answers came to mind: management's propensity for not "taking it seriously," and management's propensity to "blame it all on Sunnyvale." Finer called on top managers to set an example that would evidence its belief in controls. And he called on top managers to recognize also that BMP's problems went beyond a single plant:

> It is an easy and understandable feeling for BMP's top managers to become preoccupied with the dangers of Sunnyvale and to ascribe all their and our difficulties to this division's lack of success. And it is certainly true that Sunnyvale represents a critical step in the development of our company and a precipitous height from which to fall should this investment become mismanaged. At the same time it must be pointed out that the disappointing financial results of the company are due to a number of factors which are quite independent of Sunnyvale's management—and which include, amongst other trends:
>
> 1. Rapidly rising overhead costs at our Mid-America division.
> 2. Lack of either a sales strategy or a retrenchment program for our Eastern division.
> 3. Insufficient emphasis on cost control at our Blowco division.
> 4. Rapidly falling contribution from our sales volume dollar.
>
> The selective degree of inattention which is given to these problems is a dysfunctional force for the company and a demoralizing influence on the efforts of the treasurer's department to establish company-wide policies with regard to cost and revenue controls.

Proposed Steps

Both for BMP as an organization and for himself as treasurer, Finer in his "Treasurer's Report" and his "Notes" came up with several proposals as to what should be done next.

For the corporation, Finer's "Report" prescribed as follows:

> 1. Controls must be more stringently created and applied to BMP's present level of overhead expenditure ($5.5 million *budgeted* in 1971 versus $3.1 million actual 1968), and in this context it is recommended that as a first step no increase in overhead expenditure should be allowed without the authorization of either the president or the treasurer.
> 2. A decision must be made with regard to consolidating and expanding

BMP's Mid-America division, which is the fastest sales growth division in the company. The increased pre-tax operating profit potential of this division is substantial (up to $812,000 per annum at present fabricating fee rates, *if* manufacturing capacity here can be planned to equal expected sales levels).

3. Corporate sales must be given the priority responsibility of selling BMP's capacity on the East Coast. A 35 percent increase in unit sales produced by this division at current fabricating fee levels would add in excess of $312,000 to the pre-tax income of this division.
4. A definitive and integrated plan must be prepared for the president by corporate sales and Western's operating management to make some sense out of Sunnyvale.

For himself as treasurer, Finer set the following "goals for 1971":

1. To enforce the responsibility accounting system.
2. To establish direct material and labor job costing throughout the company.
3. To improve the budgetary process through the data supplied by 1 and 2.

As further elaborated in his "Notes," Finer's program of action was as follows:

It is the treasurer's belief that the president must increasingly be able to insist that the budgetary process is effectively carried out and that budgetary instructions are complied with, regardless of the rank or position of those involved. In addition it is the treasurer's position that the president will shortly have to lay down a policy with regard to the implementation of the various forms of analytical accounting that have been described in the preceding pages.

This program of action proposed by the treasurer's department is in support of these objectives and is as follows:

1. Use the May meeting to impress our managers that responsibility accounting and the budgetary process are to be taken seriously.
2. Hire a professional accountant to examine and report on monthly variances wherever and whenever they occur.
3. Use the May meeting to push for managerial programs which will aim to overcome Sunnyvale and non-Sunnyvale weaknesses alike.
4. Use James Albee . . . to implement a corporate-wide system for direct material and labor job costing *once* direction has been given by the president as to the nature of the program he requires here.
5. Conduct a financial budget review in August and September 1971, in preparation for the presentation of the fiscal 1972 budget to the president and the board of directors.

This has perhaps been yet another overelaborate attempt to state my belief that we must now set about strengthening our divisional management teams and strengthening the relationship and understanding between them and a simplified corporate organization which is geared toward financial control as the only viable prelude to greater manufacturing cost reductions, more profitable utilization of our plant capacities, and lusher incentives to those managers who can demonstrate performance excelling standard.

Though prescription is admittedly not the best method of working with others, it is the contention of this writer that we have yet to demonstrate that we can handle more complex approaches to the problem of administration.

Appendix: Blow-Mold Packers, Inc.

Excerpts from the 1971 Budget Review Letters of October and November 1970

(Drafted by Harold Finer, finalized and signed by Leo Hauptman)
　To Mr. Frederick Winn, General Manager, Blowco, Inc.

I.　*Review of 1971 Budget Submitted by Blowco, Inc.*

1.　*General Comments*
Exhibit A, attached . . . shows that Blowco fully expects to be the Company's second most profitable division in 1971. Specifically, the Blowco budget commits your division to a 100 percent increase in unit volume . . . with . . . little or no change in indirect expense forecasted. . . . The remainder of this section is directed toward examining the credibility of what is, at first sight, a most ambitious program.

2.　*Sales Forecasts*
a.　*Specific drop-outs and vulnerabilities*
. . . detailed examination of Blowco's sales forecasts reveals certain specific weaknesses in your unit volume program:
Of the total units forecast, some 20 percent already looked bad or doubtful.

✻　✻　✻　✻　✻

Of the remaining units, some 32 percent are attributable to the sale of . . . a product class still subject to technical and market uncertainties.

✻　✻　✻　✻　✻

. . . Orders for [the second most important product] have been canceled for the first quarter and . . . this whole program may yet suffer serious delay.

b. *Lack of overall sales program*

. . . There is in fact . . . a wide gap between Blowco's list of call priorities and what it, as a division:

Is able to achieve with the marketing resources budgeted for it—i.e., no increase in selling expenses in spite of a 100 percent increase in volume now forecasted . . . and

Has been able to achieve (and is forecasting) in terms of profits and production capabilities for our regular lines.

These gaps add an atmosphere of incredibility to an already sparsely laid out framework for both future marketing strategy and individual account-call and follow-up procedures.

3. *Production*

* * * * *

Lack of overall production program

Apart from the peaks and valleys indicated by your production plans for fiscal 1971, there seems to be a fundamental lack of production planning at Blowco—a lack of demand for systematic high levels of production at an optimum product mix.

To Mr. J. E. Gardner, General Manager, Mid-America.

I. *Review of 1971 Budget Submitted by Mid-America*

1. *General Comments*

. . . Mid-America expects to be the Company's least profitable division . . . in spite of the fact that volume is forecast to increase substantially and . . . that Mid-America can truly be said to have the most favorable product mix of any division in the Company. In view of the seriousness of this fact . . . I intend to devote much of the following . . . notes to examine exactly what is amiss at your division.

* * * * *

5. *Budgetary Practices*

* * * * *

As we discussed at the last Executive Operating Committee meeting, a budget is a commitment, and as such, it is neither optimistic nor pessimistic—rather, it is a realistic promise. . . . In this connection I was disappointed to learn that:

Your departmental budgets were not examined by you in sufficient detail to insure that each manager involved was committed to a plan congruent with the best interests of the company.

* * * * *

Your production capacity (which was overstated) does not in fact match with your sales program, and that quite apart from production capacity your real constraint may well prove to be warehouse space—an item which was not even referred to in your budget.

To Mr. Frank Silone, General Manager, Eastern Division.

I. *Review of 1971 Budget Submitted by Eastern*

1. *General Comments*
    . . . shows clearly that . . . Eastern is committed to improve its profit picture. . . . What . . . additionally throws credit on your shoulders are the facts that:

    You delegated the responsibility of preparing the budget. . . .

    Most of the numbers in the budget clearly emanated from the departmental managers who . . . generally took an active part in the budgetary process.

    Red-book objectives were prepared by each individual manager outlining a program of action for self and divisional improvement.

    Your budget contained realistic assumptions; and as such, could be contrasted with the budgets of the other divisions which have all been returned for numerical adjustments.

To Mr. Donald Ferenzi, General Manager, Western Division.

DEAR DON:

Subject: Western Division—Budget Review—28–30 November 1970

This memorandum stems from the discussions which we had last week and from some of the impressions that were reported to me by Frank Silone and Hal Finer. Although some of the comments which follow may appear critical, I would like to emphasize at once that this letter is written in good faith and that, in particular, I do not hold you responsible for the present condition of the Western Division. . . .

I. *Review of 1971 Budget Submitted by the Western Division*

1. *General Comments*
    . . . the Western Division presented a budget which reflected its commitment to be the most profitable division in the company. The remainder of this section of these notes is directed towards examining the validity of this commitment.

2. *Production*
    The briefest inspection of the Sunnyvale plant highlights the critical production problems of your division and the impact that these problems are likely to have on your financial results. Summarily, these problems may be listed as:

    a. Lack of line running time.
    b. Lack of organization.
    c. Lack of quality control effectiveness.
    d. A carryover of the San Jose housekeeping and safety culture.

    a. *Lack of Line Running Time*

* * * * *

... To be specific, in your Sunnyvale plant your current rate of line downtime is presently creating direct labor costs per thousand units of 80 percent above budget.

In your older plant, direct labor costs are currently costing 17 percent above budget.

... The numerical impact of this situation is likely to add $284,-000 to your direct labor costs—thereby ... making your division the lowest instead of the highest contributor to corporate profits.

b. *Lack of Organization*
... During our budget review you have seriously questioned the abilities of your

Assistant general manager	Warehouse manager
Quality control manager	M&E manager
Materials management manager	Resin manager
and your controller	

Quite apart from whether or not your feelings are justified, whilst these feelings exist ... they inhibit the establishment of an organization to cope with your two-plant operation and ... they also inhibit any rational attempt to analyze your indirect labor budget in terms of those responsible for its increase by $70,000. ...

c. *Lack of Quality Control Effectiveness*
... During the course of our budget review, it became apparent that your division is currently suffering from an outbreak of quality control problems. ... Perhaps even more disturbing ... is the fact that there appears to be no systematic reporting procedure ... by which you, as general manager, can estimate [the] physical and financial effects. ...

3. *Sales*
Of the unit sales increase forecast for the Western Division, 150 percent of the total were contributed by account executives outside of the division, leaving lost ground to be accounted for.

* * * * *

Finally, it should be noted that this lack of marketing aggressiveness arises in circumstances when 1970 was a poor year ... and where our new Sunnyvale plant may well be at 56 percent of capacity in the fourth quarter ... with its extremely high-cost overhead burden.

II. *Specific Action to Be Taken*
Don, as I have already indicated, I am trying to use this budget review, not as a destructive tool but as a constructive method of helping myself (and, I hope, you) to become a better manager. The following decisions are made for this reason only. ... Specifically, I want you to see to it that:
a. You become familiar with the economic and managerial assumptions

that lie behind every material figure in your budget by the time of the next budget review.

b.   Frank Silone is brought into an active role in order to help you stabilize the manufacturing organization within your division.

c.   You change your Sunnyvale direct labor budget figures to read their current actual rate in the first quarter, $2 less in the second, $2 less in the third, and $2 less in the fourth quarter—which will still be $2 above your present budget. Needless to say, I expect you to at least keep your manufacturing performance within these limits.°

d.   You submit a written report to Frank Silone and myself by January 1st recommending the form of organization you propose to adopt at San Jose and at Sunnyvale, and justifying the $70,000 increase in indirect labor charges that your division had budgeted for the coming year.°

e.   You prepare a written report to Frank Silone and myself by the end of the second quarter listing the merits and weaknesses of each key manager under your control. Each report should only be presented after discussing its contents with the individual manager concerned, and each report should be accompanied by a recommendation with regard to the manager's eligibility for future promotion and responsibility.°

At the risk of going into too much detail—but at the same time because I believe this topic is of the utmost importance—I will go further and suggest that you:

Spend between one and two hours a week with each of your key managers—using this time both to understand his point of view and to review specific situations which have arisen in his department during the course of the week.

Hold weekly staff meetings along the lines of your memorandum of November 15th.

Make no personnel changes without discussing them with Frank Silone and me.

Keep notes with regard to both the individual and the group meetings which you hold with your managers.

f.   You prepare a written report to Frank Silone and myself by the end of the second quarter showing your plans for the line at San Jose and giving economic justification for either transferring it to Sunnyvale or for the dual operation which will result from leaving it at San Jose. In the meantime, please see to it that the San Jose offices and quality control laboratory are cleaned up by the end of the current calendar year.°

g.   You create systematic records which account for the financial impact of ineffective quality control. In this regard, I shall want to see quality control statistics on a monthly basis along the lines requested by Mark Simon in connection with his responsibility accounting program.°

h.   You appoint a manager who will be responsible for housekeeping and safety procedures and who will have the authority to see that they are implemented.° In this connection, the manager appointed should:

Study our existing safety and housekeeping rules.°

Distribute the DuPont Safety Manual to key managers.°

° Starred entries denote actions that Finer stated were not yet implemented at the time of his second budget review during April 1971.

Devise some kind of competition and prize system which will encourage *all* our employees to participate fully in the program.°

j. You prepare a written report to Frank Silone and myself with regard to this up-coming Union negotiations.°

Whilst you are helping Frank Silone and me in this way, I will try to breathe some new life into our sales program. . . . In the meantime, I want to sincerely thank you for volunteering to help the company in a role which I know will mean plenty of personal anguish for you.

With kindest personal regards,
Leo Hauptman

7

John Adams

You know, if there is one topic I think we should spend more time talking about somewhere in the Harvard Business School curriculum, it is "company atmosphere." It exists everywhere, obviously, but it certainly is hard to get a very good impression of what it will be like in a company you are considering going to work for. It turned out to be much more important to me than I had ever anticipated, and I really wish we had spent more time thinking about what it is, what influences it, how to recognize it early, and what the choices open to you are in learning to live with it. I sure ran into problems of this sort when I went to work for Accutronics right after I got my MBA in 1967.

John Adams, Harvard Business School graduate of 1967, was discussing some of his experiences in his job of the preceding three years. Adams had resigned his position a few weeks before and was stopping over briefly in Boston to visit some old friends and classmates before proceeding to his new job in Florida.

Spring, 1967

Adams's first contact with Accutronics had been on a job interview trip in the spring of 1967, shortly before his graduation from the Harvard Business School.

Accutronics was a Denver-based company that had started with the development and manufacture of specialized microwave and radar components and was trying to build up competence in highly sophisticated electromechanical systems for military and space applications as well. The company was strongly oriented toward research and technology. It had grown very rapidly from sales of a few million dollars in the early

60s, when it had been founded by a small group of businessmen and university scientists, to about $35 million per year in 1967.

In reviewing the impressions he had formed of Accutronics on this brief 1967 visit, Adams commented as follows:

> I think what impressed me most about the company at that time was their strong commitment to growth and the emphasis they placed on individual ability and initiative in getting ahead. They really preached the virtues of competition. I must have been told a dozen times that they expected people to use their initiative and to take on responsibility for doing what needed to be done, and that as soon as you showed that you could handle the job, you would get more to do. They all said that there was simply too much opportunity for growth and too much to get done to worry about whether you would be infringing on someone else's private domain. In fact, the president had stated publicly that they were strongly committed to their policy of rapid growth, partly because this was necessary to provide enough career opportunities for the caliber of people they wanted in their organization.
>
> I was to go to work in a headquarters staff group, which reported to the executive vice president, a fellow named Mike Butler. He was aggressive and forward and seemed to be a real go-getter. My first meeting with him was in his home, and he just about stood me up against a wall and fired questions at me. He wanted direct answers, too, not these "on the other hand" statements. He hit me with technical questions about radar sets, inertial guidance, what I expected to earn in five years, how many hours a week I would be willing to work, and so on. I don't think he expected me to know the answers to a lot of the technical questions; I think he was more interested in seeing how I responded to that sort of cross-examination. After awhile he called another vice president and told him—just as brusquely—that he had a good man at his house and arranged another interview for me.
>
> Nobody was very specific as to exactly what I would be doing; they said they were much more interested in getting good men than fitting people in slots. Mike said the work at first would mostly be on special projects at headquarters and would also involve something he called "internal consulting," which meant working on problem areas in various parts of the company's operations. He said it would be an excellent chance to get around to various parts of the company and learn about their operations, and then after a few years to go out into one of the operating departments. He emphasized that they didn't want any career staff men, and that suited me fine.
>
> The job met a number of the criteria that were important to me. It seemed like an environment in which I could get ahead, mostly on the basis of my own ability and level of effort and performance, rather than on seniority or politics; in fact, Mike told me that the main reason they were able to make such good headway against the big companies was that they didn't waste their time with very many rules or procedures or in internal jockeying for position and bickering. I must admit that appealed

to me, because I've been in organizations where it has been very different.

The company was also growing very fast, with no slowdown in sight. They all seemed to have a real drive to make Accutronics into a major industrial company, rather than just something which would provide them with security and a comfortable income. It looked like a good chance to make use of both my engineering and business training, too—a real challenge to try to deal with both the scientific and commercial worlds within the company.

The salary offer was pretty good—$13,000, which was above the offers most of the fellows seemed to be getting[1]—but I did have a few higher offers elsewhere. It sounded like the kind of work I would really like, though, and I was sure that if I did a good job the advancement in both position and money would be enough to keep me happy. I thought it might even give me some experience which could be useful if I ever saved enough money to be able to strike out on my own some day, which is still a dim goal I have tucked away in the back of my mind.

Adams had financed his business school education by a combination of savings and student loans and had graduated in the top third of his class. He was characterized by several of his professors as being unusually mature and well balanced; one of the slightly older students with some working experience whom they could rely on for constructive and commonsense comments. According to several of his classmates, he was the sort of person that people found it easy to talk to and had been well liked and respected. One friend characterized him as ambitious and a hard worker, but also a "strong family man," and said that he tried to spend as much time with his wife and child as is possible while attending the Business School. Another spoke of him as having a strong competitive spirit, but with equally strong ideas about fair play and consideration for others. He was remembered as being active in section activities, particularly the intramural sports program.

Previous to attending the Harvard Business School, Adams had obtained a degree in electrical engineering at a western college, had worked for a large steel company for about a year, and had served as an officer in the Navy for two years. He had been active in sports while in high school and college, and had won several wrestling championships. He and his wife were both from the same medium-sized northwestern city.

Fall, 1967

In the fall of 1967, Adams wrote a few words to a classmate about his new job with Accutronics:

. . . As far as the job is concerned, things are going just great. I have worked on a number of interesting projects already and have learned a lot

---

[1] Average starting salary in 1967 for Harvard MBAs with an engineering degree was actually $12,000 (placement bureau records).

both about how the company works and about some problems I never gave much thought when I was at the B-School.

People certainly have a strong sense of identification with the company, as we used to call it so glibly, and I am beginning to see how it has come about. It does not come at all from what you could call a paternalistic attitude on the part of the company; it is completely different. I don't know what to call it; everyone is caught up in both the challenge and the reward of making the company grow. We have been doubling our sales every two or three years for a number of years, mostly through internal growth, and it looks like we will be able to keep that up for a while. There is no union out here, either; even the hourly employees seem to feel that they are a part of the team. The management tries to promote this feeling, of course, and they have done a good job of it.

They weren't fooling when they said the hours would be long! We don't get any overtime, of course, and I was amazed to find that people think nothing of working 60 hours a week regularly. I've worked over 80 hours a week for several weeks at a time, and if I had worked like that in the steel company I would have been carted off to the company headshrinker. Those hours are tough for the men with families, but I don't really mind it because this is such a dynamic and exciting place to be working. We have a congenial group in the department, and people seem willing to pitch in and get the job done. There are a number of us with MBAs in the department, and we all view this as a steppingstone for a better job out in the divisions.

One reason people work the way they do out here, I am sure, is that the officers themselves put in a fantastic work week. They built up the organization from nothing and it took a lot of work, and their level of effort just filters down in the organization. If your boss works long hours, you do too. Besides, I think most people feel they are in on the ground floor now, and that the rapid growth will generate enough promotions to make the present long hours worthwhile. . . .

One thing that was both surprising and rewarding was to find that the level of education of most of the management out here is so high. Most people in my office have MBAs from somewhere, and of course we have a lot of Ph.D.s in the sciences around here. This makes the competition tougher, but it also makes it a much more rewarding place to work. I was also surprised at the number and quality of job applicants that we have. We seem to be getting the reputation of a growth company in a growth industry, and a surprising number of people from all over the country who want to change jobs for one reason or another seem to be attracted to our situation. Part of the reason for our popularity may also be the living conditions out here; we both have found them very pleasant.

Fall, 1968

Adams wrote as follows about his first year at Accutronics:

. . . Work is still exciting and worthwhile; the pace hasn't slowed down at all and I feel I have learned a lot during the last year. I am still working on a variety of projects, just like when I started, but there are enough different things coming up constantly so that it by no means resembles a routine. I don't report directly to Walter Gorman (the department head) any more, though. We have expanded in this area a lot, and during the year two people with some previous experience were hired in above me. I must be the only member of the class of 1967 who has been "demoted" twice already and still likes his job! The company is still growing like a weed, though, so there are bound to be lots of opportunities opening up, even though people are brought in from the outside to fill some of them.

Nobody has left the department to ge elsewhere in the company yet, either, although the department is now about two and one-half years old. That worries me a bit, because I didn't come out here to be a staff man all my life. I think part of the reason may be that some of the operating divisions and departments seem to regard us as spies from a competitor rather than as someone working for the same company, but maybe this is natural. They have been used to doing things their own way, and besides, I guess we often do regard them as enemies in our efforts to justify the importance of our department by ferreting out inefficiencies and showing how we can save money for the company. You inevitably get involved in politics and see people doing some things in order to protect themselves or "get" somebody else, but I guess that happens everywhere.

Just like with any job there are some drawbacks, of course. We do work long hours, and not all of it is necessary. Walter tries to establish an atmosphere whereby you come in on Saturdays unless you have something special going on at home, rather than coming in only if there is something special going on at work. I think one of the ways he tried to do this was pretty funny. On a few Saturdays when I was not in he left a little note on my desk saying "see me." Each time when I talked with him on Monday morning, he said he got someone else to do it and implied I missed out on something worthwhile without saying what it was. I came in about 11 A.M. one Saturday and found a note on my desk, and so I went right over to ask about it. He was completely at a loss about it, because he had left it there only five minutes ago and there really was nothing that he wanted anyway! I still come in most Saturdays, though—it is simply expected, and most people do.

I now see that one of the reasons people work so hard is that there are a lot of what I would call "false crises," or deadlines which are shorter than they need to be just to get people to do more work. The president even stated at one of the regional management conferences that this was something he did deliberately in order to get more work out of his people, and I'm not so sure that I like that. But it does seem to accomplish his objective, even though people view it as something temporary.

I've gotten to understand the company a lot better during the past year, and I really give the management a great deal of credit for what they have been able to build up from virtually nothing. Lots of them are millionaires now, and the stock is still going up. I wish I had more money to put into it. And one of the most interesting things to me has been the insight you get into how the problems of a company change as it becomes larger, and how difficult it is for the management to change their behavior as the problems get too complicated to handle on the "personal" basis that worked so well during the earlier stages.

Summer, 1970

Back in Boston briefly while en route to his new job in Florida, Adams commented as follows about his recent career at Accutronics and his reasons for leaving:

I've now taken another job; I left Accutronics a few months ago. I had my ups and downs out there, but when I left things were going very well for me.

After my first year I was shifted around a lot. Our department sort of fell apart, mostly, I think, because of opposition from the divisions. I went through a great number of "reorganizations," but for the year before I left I was working as one of the two assistants to the operations vice president. I had several divisions assigned to me, and I was supposed to know everything that was going on in those divisions. Our total sales, by the way, were over the $100 million rate when I left, which will put us in *Fortune's* list of 500. Most of that was through internal growth, too, although we did buy several small companies.

I worked on all sorts of projects, and also sat in on a lot of top management meetings, including the monthly operating meetings involving the officers of the company and the division managers. Usually when my boss visited any of the divisions I was responsible for, I went along with him too.

It was great experience to see how things work at that level in such a large and dynamic company, and I wouldn't trade it for anything. I was making good money, too, and was well liked, I think, by the people I worked with. Several said to get in touch with them if I ever wanted to come back. They were certainly nice to me when I left, and I have a lot of friends there that I will call up and chat with if I ever get to Denver again.

I guess the main reason I left is that I just didn't like the atmosphere in the company as well as when I started. It seemed to me that too many people were spending too much of their time on things which had nothing to do with making a contribution to the company, and I didn't see how I could avoid it myself, even if only in self-defense. I saw too many people lose out because they didn't pay enough attention to the politics involved, and I just didn't find playing politics very satisfying. Besides, I don't think I'm very good at it.

I certainly was naive when I graduated from the Business School. I had been in the service and worked some before that, and I thought I knew how the world worked. When I went out to Accutronics I really thought that getting ahead would depend mostly on solving problems for the company better than anyone else, and one of the main reasons I went with them was that they seemed to be looking for someone with exactly my viewpoint. I now doubt that more than 10 percent of the reasons for promotions in most companies depend on this. I'm convinced that the surest way to go down the drain in most organizations is to spend your time solving problems better, rather than impressing the people who make the promotions.

I have never made any list to see what happened to the people who were sort of in my department, but it would be interesting to see what became of that group. There were several in the 25 to 35 age category in my general area at headquarters when I arrived, and we hired several more during the year. After the first year there were so many reorganizations that it would be impossible to keep track. As I remember it, this [Exhibit 1] would be the list of people, with a little bit on their backgrounds and what happened to them.

Don't let the title "staff assistant" worry you; it really doesn't describe either your work or your relative position in the department very well. It was just a catchall title that was used a lot in our department.

It scares me to look at what has happened to the relatively few men in my group who have stayed—without exception, I think it is fair to say that they have given up. They have decent jobs, and they do whatever they are told, no matter how foolish it seems. Lou DiSantis is the example that I feel the worst about because he and I came to be good friends, and our wives also saw a lot of each other. He came to Accutronics because he hadn't liked the work atmosphere in the two large companies he had worked for and thought he would find something completely different out here. He enjoyed it for a while and really felt that he was contributing, but by now he has had to compromise so many times that he just doesn't have any spark any more.

The last time we talked about this he said he had concluded that the key is "to keep your nose clean, don't take a strong stand on anything, and just draw your check." He knows that much of what he is doing is wasted effort, but the only way to get along is to do it. I know he makes over $25,000, and he said if anyone ever found out what he *really* contributes to the company he would be fired for sure.

Mitchell, who was sort of in my department but whom I didn't put on the list because he is a lot older, is another example of the same thing. One time when I was talking to him about this and told him how dissatisfied I was because of the things we do which obviously bear no relation to the main task of the company, he said I was taking it much too seriously. "I don't give a damn what I do," he said, "I just do what they want me to and draw my paycheck. That's the only way to get along." Well, he is in a tough spot because of his age and lack of marketable experience, and he also has a large family. I don't really blame him, but I never have to regard my job that way.

Maybe examples of some of the things that were going on will give you a better idea of why I left. The incident that stands out most vividly in my memory is something that happened about a year and a half ago. I was working for one of the corporate staff departments that reported

EXHIBIT 1

Department Roster

Name	Age in 1967	Education and Background	Brief Job Titles and Comments for 1967–70 Period
David Gordon*.....	27	MBA, Stanford	Staff assistant; left after one year
Andy Johnson*.....	27	MBA, Wharton	Staff assistant; left after 18 months
John Adams*......	27	MBA, Harvard Business School (H.B.S.)	Staff assistant; various jobs; left after three years
Kirk Spencer*......	28	MBA, H.B.S.	Staff assistant; left after 18 months
Frank Nolan........	28	MBA, Stanford	Staff assistant; assistant to marketing vice president; left after four and one-half years
Gene Farrell........	29	BA	Accounting staff; some supervisory (staff) positions
Bob Hartwell.......	31	BA	Systems and procedures work
Len Halstead.......	31	BA; CPA	Internal auditor
Ed Becker*.........	32	MBA, Columbia, formerly planning director for a division of a large company	Staff assistant; out for six months with nervous breakdown
Lou DiSantis*......	33	MBA, H.B.S., accounting and data-processing experience	Accounting systems specialist
Leo Hoyt...........	34	MBA, Michigan, former consultant	Staff assistant and internal consultant; left after three years
Ray Nelson........	35	MBA, H.B.S., former budget manager for a division of a large company	Budget analyst, financial analyst, left after three years

* Indicates personnel added during 1967–68.

to Walter Gorman, who in turn reported to Allen Lawson, one of the vice presidents at the time. Another department which also reported to Gorman did work which was related to ours, and I suppose these two departments could conceivably have been combined into one.

One day when George, our department head, was away on a trip, Fred, the head of the other department, called Andy[2] and me into his office. He closed the door, and then said that he was out to get George and wanted to know whether we were for or against him. If we were for him, he said we could help undermine George, and if we were against

---

[2] Andy Johnson, a co-worker. See department roster, Exhibit 1.

him, he would take care of us when he got control of George's department anyway.

Well, we never talked about *that* in school. We both said we didn't want to get involved in such power politics and got out of there as fast as possible. Andy and I discussed it, of course, but couldn't really decide what to do about it, aside from hoping the problem would go away. But when George came back from his trip, I decided that the best thing to do would be to tell him what Fred was up to so that he would at least be on his guard. I said I wanted to tell him something off the record, and he assured me that it would be completely personal and confidential between the two of us.

So, I told him what had happened. Before I had even finished, he stalked out of the office and left me standing there. He went straight to Allen Lawson without even bothering to look for Walter Gorman, and inside of two minutes I was in Al's office. A few minutes later a company lawyer came in also. I was ordered to tell them the story, Andy was brought in separately for his version; Walter was called in, Fred was called in, then we were all called in, and so on. This went on for days, and it soon became apparent that Al Lawson was trying to minimize the whole thing. Andy and I must have been asked a dozen times if perhaps Fred had been kidding. We were all asked what everyone else said, what they said someone else said, and so on. It was a first-class mess, and Andy and I came out of the worst. No action was taken against Fred, but Andy and I were clearly in Al's disfavor.

I had been at the company a little over a year at that time, and that was the first time I thought seriously about leaving. I'd be damned if I would quit under those circumstances, though; I never had been a quitter before and I didn't intend to quit then. What saved me was that I was picked up by Sam Merrill, who was the second in command in one of the divisions. I had worked with Sam on some projects previously, and we had gotten along fine. I worked for him about six months, and then his boss, the division manager, became the operations vice president, with responsibility for all of the company's operations. He took Sam along, and Sam took me along back to headquarters. This affair with Fred had blown over to some extent by then—Fred left the company a few months after it happened—but Al Lawson never did look me square in the eye again.

What really clinched it was when I found out, about a year after the incident, why Al had been so reluctant to have Fred placed in a bad light. I was told by a friend who left the company shortly after this had happened to Andy and me. It seems that Al had approached my friend with the suggestion that he act as an "informal source of information" for Al with respect to what was going on in Gorman's department, and my friend had turned it down. He suspected strongly that Fred had taken on the task, because "all of a sudden Fred's wife just couldn't keep from talking about how closely Al and her husband worked together." This would all have occurred shortly before our fiasco.

Another thing that I must admit made me feel both furious and very sad was when I found out that at least three people had asked Al Lawson, who was my "big boss" for a couple of years, if they could offer me a job in their divisions. I found this out when I went around to say goodbye to several of these people as I was leaving the company, and they mentioned that they were sorry I had never come to work with them. I never heard about the offers, even though two of them would have been clear promotions at the time.

There were other incidents, of course, which seemed important at the time but which are easy to forget. There were so many things going on that were directed at promoting the interests of some individual or department rather than the company interests. The great quantities of viewgraphs and reports that we generated were one example of this; most of them were never used for any purpose at all, and we knew it. Walter Gorman wanted them to impress Al Lawson, I guess, and I'm not sure why Al wanted them. Nobody that had any line authority paid the least bit of attention to them, as became completely clear during my last year when I was sitting in on operating meetings.

We even had cases of our computer people simulating results from the computer by using it as a typewriter. At one point the managment became enchanted with the idea of putting the entire operations of the company on a computer. The computer systems people had serious doubts about the feasibility of the project in relation to the resources and time available, but they were given the task and a completely unrealistic deadline anyway. Rather than say it couldn't be done, they pretended to meet the deadline by working out most of the figures on a desk calculator and printing the results on the computer. What do you suppose that does to your sense of "professional responsibility"?

It sounds amazing, but during one period even quitting became a real challenge. At one point the management came very suspicious about the possibility of persons taking confidential information from the company, either of a technical or commercial nature. There were some cases of individuals quitting and starting up competing companies in certain of the specialties they had been working in, but I guess that happens generally in a high-technology industry such as ours where the right idea or process is sufficient to attract all the financial backing you might need. Denver is full of such companies, and I guess Boston is too. As far as I know there were never any instances of people misusing commercial information, though, as opposed to the technical know-how they acquired.

Anyway, when Andy quit he left his letter of resignation, saying he was giving the customary 30-days' notice, on Gorman's desk one evening. The next morning he was met by Gorman, Al Lawson, and the company legal counsel as he came to work, and the four of them went to his desk and went through it, item by item. He was allowed to keep his personal papers, and was then asked to leave immediately. They said they preferred not to have anyone working there who was not happy with the company and that there was no point working any longer once he had given his notice.

This pattern was repeated with several people. They all got their pay for the next 30 days, of course, so that was not an issue. But it certainly is not a very nice atmosphere under which to leave a company, and it really made you wonder as to what sort of a reference you could expect from them in the future.

I don't think that sort of treatment of those who left the company was done with any ill intent or malice towards the people involved. It just seemed to be the natural outgrowth of the strong team spirit that the management tried to foster in the company and which they believed in themselves. They *really* believed there was an "Accutronics type," and the reaction was that if you didn't like it there you weren't an Accutronics type after all and didn't belong in the company. The fault was always seen as being in the individual rather than the system. There is some value to that kind of an approach, but I think they carried it too far. There were some periodic surveys made by teams of outside consultants to determine what people liked and didn't like about the company, but most of the results I ever saw looked like they pertained to some other company.

I don't want to give the impression that what happened in my group is normal at the company, because I don't really know that much about the atmosphere in the other areas, although I know the politics were not confined to our area. I knew lots of people who were very strong in their support of the company, and it certainly had an excellent public image. There was a high turnover of professional personnel—around 2½ percent per month—during the last year I was there, but part of that may have come from the fact that it looked like the growth would be slowing down to a more normal rate because of the leveling off of defense spending, and the opportunities in relation to the costs involved just wouldn't be as great as several years ago. Four of us from the Class of '67 went out there, though, mostly working in different areas, and I was the third to leave. I don't know if the fourth is still there or not.

Another thing that became obvious was that there was a big difference in the way people responded to what you might call the politics of the situation. I really think some people simply never realized what was going on. Of those who were aware of it, some "fought the system," some just accepted things the way they were, and some viewed it as a personal challenge and opportunity.

Frank Nolan was a wonderful example of the last type. He viewed it all as a big game and seemed to take genuine delight in finding out how things worked around the company so he could play the game better. He paid more attention to the informal things going on than anyone else that I knew of, and he also seemed to know more about what was going on in various parts of the company than anyone else. He always had a series of complicated explanations for what seemed like simple things, but in several cases I think he turned out to be right.

Just as an example of the kind of thing he paid attention to, I was told that when he first came with the company, which was a couple of years before I did, he made it a point to find out what colleges all of the top-management people had gone to, where they had first met, how they happened to join the company, what jobs they had had in the company, whom they seemed to be bringing along as proteges in the company, what social activities and clubs they were involved in, and so on. I guess information of that sort does help you to understand what is going on, but I have to admit that I don't like to think that those things are all that important, and I don't like to spend much of my time on them.

I became pretty good friends with Frank, and he was quite outspoken about a lot of things. We talked a lot about where the company was going and what the opportunities were likely to be for people like us within the company. He had been quite enthusiastic about the staff group that they were trying to build up, but after I had been there about six months he concluded that Walter Gorman, who was really his superior, was never going to make it into the top-management ranks. Frank attached a great deal of importance to working for someone on the way up in the company, and at that point he just about quit working for Walter. He didn't try to make any formal moves, he just managed to get started on some projects for Carl Lund, the marketing vice president, who he thought was going to move up. He took to working Lund's hours, which were a little different from ours, and simply told Walter that he was "on an important and confidential project for Lund," when Walter came to him with work. There were sparks for a while, but after a while Frank started working for Lund full time.

Frank based his conclusions about Walter on a whole lot of things— the progress the department was making and the reception we were getting out in the divisions, the apparent lack of strong backing of Walter by Lawson, Butler, and the rest of the officers, the fact that Walter and his wife had been at the company for over two years but were not on close social terms with anyone of consequence in the company, and a difference in dress and appearance. Gorman did look a bit like a gambling casino operator, and Frank felt there was a significant "All-American" bias in the management. He also felt that what our department was trying to do would not be seen as being as important to the company as either research, production, or marketing skills during the next several years.

Frank was right about Walter, by the way. About six months after this Walter was "reorganized" into a less important job, and a while later he left the company.

Frank also had a way of trying to trade information so that he always came out a little bit ahead in the exchange. He seemed to collect bits of information from all over that might make some sense when put together. Whenever he would volunteer some information to you, you could be sure that the main reason was he thought you had something that he needed. In a way he was trying to place himself in the center of the wheel, with bits and pieces of information flowing back and forth along the spokes but with him in the center, putting things together.

Although Frank and I got along very well, I noticed that he always managed to cover up whatever he was working on whenever I came in his office. Nobody else did that, and we all used to joke about it a bit. Frank tried to maintain the impression that he was always working on something confidential and important.

It is easy to find fault with any company, I suppose, and I hope I am not being too critical of Accutronics. Many people seemed to like it, so maybe there is such a thing as an Accutronics type, and I'm not it.

I can't pass my experience off as "bad management" on the part of the company, because it has been an enormous success story. I give a great deal of credit to the group of about six or eight who changed that company from an unknown with a few million dollars in sales in the early 60s to one of the outstanding growth companies of the past ten years, with a sales level which will bring it into the *Fortune* list of 500.

The growth may slow down, but they want to make it into a billion-dollar corporation in their lifetimes. They all started with nothing, they took big risks, they still work extremely hard, and it has paid off. Individually, they are worth anywhere from several million to over 50 million dollars in terms of the market value of their stock by now.

I am sure my viewpoint of what was happening in the company would be different if I were in their position, but I still think they overrate the value of their "modern management approach," which they honestly believe is ten years ahead of the rest of industry, and underemphasize the part that several virtual monopolies which resulted from outstanding technical and production breakthroughs have played in their success. I think a lot of us were misled by this when we were evaluating the company as a place to work. I know I assumed for quite a while that any company with such an outstanding growth record *must* be "well-managed," but the longer I was there the more convinced I became that the growth was due more to several critical technical breakthroughs than to exceptional management skills or approaches.

The management group is unquestionably smart and hard-working, and they built up the company by competing fiercely against some of the giants of industry. I suppose this is probably why they seek aggressive and ambitious people and encourage competition within the company to the extent that they do. But you don't compete against Lockheed Electronics or General Dynamics or Litton when you come to work for Accutronics now; you compete against people within the company. It is people versus people, not companies versus companies, and I think that makes a big difference. I don't think that the kind of competitive behavior which paid off extremely well for the company is necessarily what you should encourage at lower levels within the company, because I really think it results in a lot of wasted effort. Also, some good people probably have left the company for just the reasons I did.

I think most of the things I didn't like were the results of our widespread pyramidal form of organization, and a basic management philosophy that the best man will be the one that climbs the pyramid, regardless of the environment or the nature of the competition. It is ironic that this was one of the things about the company that appealed to me in the first first place. Their strong emphasis on competition and the "free enterprise" philosophy within the company made it seem like a place where I would have the greatest chance of getting ahead by my own abilities and work rather than by seniority or politics, and a place where I wouldn't be hemmed in by a lot of restrictions and formalized procedures.

I had lots of arguments about this with one of the personnel men that I knew quite well, and he was quite definite about the prevalence in top management of a strong belief that "the best man will get ahead, regardless of the environment." I kept asking him best man for *what,* and what about the need to cooperate within the company, to observe some kind of limits on the form of competition, and so on, but we never got anywhere. They oftentimes put several people or several departments on virtually the same tasks, for example, and made a practice of obscuring titles and responsibilities and then encouraging people to take on more responsibility if they could get away with it. They also did a great deal of reorganizing; the number of blue sheets that came around announcing changes in personnel or organizational structure was amazing.

I think that is just like offering a big prize to the winner of a boxing match and sending the referee home. You wouldn't have a boxing match following the Marquis of Queensberry rules for very long; you would have a street fight. Unless you restrict the grounds on which people are allowed to compete, I think that loose an approach to organization will lead to a lot of conflict and activities which are not good for the company and which may also be unpleasant for the people involved. I remember a quip of Harry Truman's with regard to the sometimes merciless criticism of public officials that "if you can't stand the heat get out of the kitchen." Maybe that is what I'm doing.

I have just accepted a job with a much smaller and highly technical company in the Cape Kennedy area. They sought me out and gave me a substantial salary increase, but the money is not the main reason I quit. I was making $20,000 a year at Accutronics, which was above most of the people who were roughly in my category out there and which I suppose is above what most of my classmates are making now. I just didn't like working there any longer because of some of the things I've mentioned to you.

I'm looking forward to the new job, both because of the challenges involved in the business as well as the financial opportunities for me. I also think that this management will be likely to keep things in check a little more within the company than was the case out at Accutronics. It's a tough balance to maintain, though—aggressive company behavior but a cooperative and satisfying working atmosphere. If I were just graduating and job hunting again, I sure would pay more attention to factors like this. Unless you fit in with the atmosphere you find in the company, you will either have to change yourself, quit, or be unhappy about it.

Part Three

Policy Formulation and Administration in Diversified Firms

1 CIBA-GEIGY Corporation (A)

In the spring of 1974 the top management of CIBA–GEIGY Corporation, the principal U.S. subsidiary of CIBA–GEIGY Limited (a publicly owned Swiss corporation), was impressed with the opportunities that a major acquisition program in the United States could bring the corporation as a whole. With the U.S. dollar undervalved relative to the Swiss franc and with prices on the New York Stock Exchange at a ten-year low, it appeared an opportune time to acquire U.S. companies at favorable prices. Officers of both the U.S. subsidiary and the Swiss parent hoped that reinvesting the U.S. cash flow in the United States would allow the U.S. subsidiary to repatriate dollars to the parent under more favorable conditions in the future.

Diversifying acquisitions were of particular interest to Mr. Don MacKinnon, a vice president of CIBA–GEIGY Corporation, who was pressing the case for corporate diversification in the United States. In his view, diversifying acquisitions could help open up new paths of growth for the U.S. subsidiary while providing a hedge against increasing R&D costs, which were limiting the company's traditional specialty chemicals business. In 1973, the parent company reported that the group's U.S. sales had increased only 4 percent in contrast to the worldwide average increase of 14 percent (measured in local currencies).

Mr. MacKinnon was interested in household products as one area of possible opportunity for CIBA-GEIGY. A recently formed Acquisitions Task Force under his direction had already identified Airwick Industries, Inc., as a possible acquisition candidate which could serve as an entree to the household market. However, since the task force had also identified attractive acquisition candidates in non-household areas, Mr. MacKinnon was not sure whether CIBA–GEIGY should, in general, attempt to move into household products. He also had some questions and reservations about Airwick Industries in particular.

The following cases describe both the choices facing Mr. MacKinnon and his colleagues in making their recommendations to the board of directors of CIBA–GEIGY Corporation and to the Swiss parent, and the context in which these choices had to be made. The (A) case will describe CIBA–GEIGY's historical background, present operations, organizational setting, corporate objectives, and diversification philosophy, for the purpose of gaining an understanding of the company's overall corporate strategy. The (B) case will describe Airwick Industries and the issues that CIBA–GEIGY'S management faced as they tried to decide whether or not to acquire this company.

Company Background

The creation of CIBA–GEIGY Corporation paralleled the merger of the two parent Swiss companies, CIBA AG and J. R. Geigy AG, in October 1970. In contrast with competitors in Germany, England, the United States, or Japan, which could bank on their home markets for between 40 percent and 70 percent of their business, CIBA and Geigy had practically no home market. Approximately 98 percent of their sales were outside Switzerland, and both firms had significant holdings in the United States. The merger of the parent companies inevitably brought the two U.S. subsidiaries together into one organization.

By 1973 the newly structured U.S. subsidiary accounted for almost one-fourth of the merged companies' total sales. U.S. sales were distributed among principal markets as shown below in Table 1.

CIBA–GEIGY's products were almost entirely specialty chemicals—patent-protected, high-technology products that had a specific purpose or filled a particular need. The company did not sell commodity chemicals like sulfuric acid or caustic soda or benzene.

Although CIBA–GEIGY Corporation did not issue public financial

TABLE 1

Breakdown of U.S. Sales, 1973

Line of Business	Percent of Total
Agrochemicals	41 %
Pharmaceuticals	28
Dyestuffs and chemicals	16
Plastics and additives	13
Madison Laboratories*	2

* Madison Laboratories sold such consumer specialties as breath spray, dental cream, and skin care products.

EXHIBIT 1

CIBA–GEIGY CORPORATION (A)
Worldwide Group Sales, 1973

Division	SFR M	Percent of Total Sales
Dyestuffs and Chemicals......................	SFR 2,047	24.5
Pharmaceuticals.............................	2,338	29.0
Agrochemicals...............................	1,673	20.5
Plastics and Additives.......................	1,433	17.8
Consumer Products..........................	246	3.0
Photographic Group..........................	417	5.2
Total..................................	SFR 8,154	100.0

statements, 1973 sales were described as being in excess of $550 million. The worldwide CIBA–GEIGY group, consisting of the Swiss parent and its 60 affiliated companies, had total sales of approximately $2.6 billion. This placed the group about number 14 among the world's chemical companies. Exhibits 1 and 2 give a breakdown of sales by product area and geographic area for the CIBA–GEIGY group of companies. Exhibit 3 presents the group's published financial statements for 1973. Exhibit 4 summarizes the top-management structure of the CIBA–GEIGY group of companies.

Current Operations

Headquartered in Ardsley, New York, CIBA–GEIGY Corporation had about 8,000 employees throughout the United States, most of whom were located at its principal facilities in New York, New Jersey, Alabama, Louisiana, Rhode Island, and North Carolina. The company's business was organized into four principal operating divisions:

The *Agricultural* division sold mainly pesticides, used by commercial farmers to improve crop yields by controlling weeds and insects. This

EXHIBIT 2

CIBA–GEIGY CORPORATION (A)
Geographical Distribution of Group Sales, 1973 (in percent)

Region	Percent of Total Sales
Europe...	51
E.E.C..	35
EFTA...	7
North America.................................	26
Latin America..................................	9
Asia..	9
Africa, Australia, and Oceania..................	5

EXHIBIT 3

CIBA-GEIGY CORPORATION (A)
Consolidated Summary of Group Financial Status
At December 31, 1973
(In millions of Swiss francs)

		December 31, 1973
Current assets		
Liquid funds...	1,493	
Receivables and other current assets.....................	2,234	
Stocks...	1,925	5,652
Less Current liabilities		
Suppliers...	432	
Banks..	945	
Other current liabilities, including provisions.............	1,281	2,658
Net current assets..		2,994
Long-term assets		
Interests in associated companies, and loans............	244	
Fixed assets...	6,326*	6,570
Total Net Current Assets and Long-term Assets............		9,564
Less Long-term liabilities		
Debenture loans...	375	
Other loans and long-term liabilities......................	958	1,332
Group equity..		8,232
Of which minority interests represent SFr.138m, at December 31, 1973		
Total Equity and Liabilities........................		12,222

* Current value. Use of acquisition value less appropriate depreciation would give a valuation of SFr. 3997m.
Source: 1973 annual report of CIBA-GEIGY Limited.

was the company's largest division. Its particular strength was in the sales of herbicides used to control weeds in cornfields. CIBA-GEIGY's pesticides business was in a solid number one position with 20 percent of the U.S. market.

The *Pharmaceuticals* division sold ethical pharmaceutical products through separate CIBA and GEIGY marketing organizations. Almost all of the division's products were prescription items, and they were advertised and promoted only to physicians, hospitals, and pharmacists, not to the general public. The division's most important group of products were those used to treat hypertension, arthritis, depression, and diabetes. In pharmaceuticals, CIBA-GEIGY was among the seven largest companies in the United States.

The *Plastics and Additives* division sold a wide range of products, including epoxy resins, polymer additives, pigments, and fiberglass reinforced epoxy pipe. It was estimated that the company was number two or three in epoxy resins and number one or two in reinforced plastic pipe in the United States.

The *Dyestuffs and Chemicals* division sold synthetic dyestuffs used in the textile, paper, and leather industries. It also sold a number of chemi-

EXHIBIT 4

CIBA–GEIGY CORPORATION (A)
Top-Management Structure of CIBA–GEIGY Limited Organization

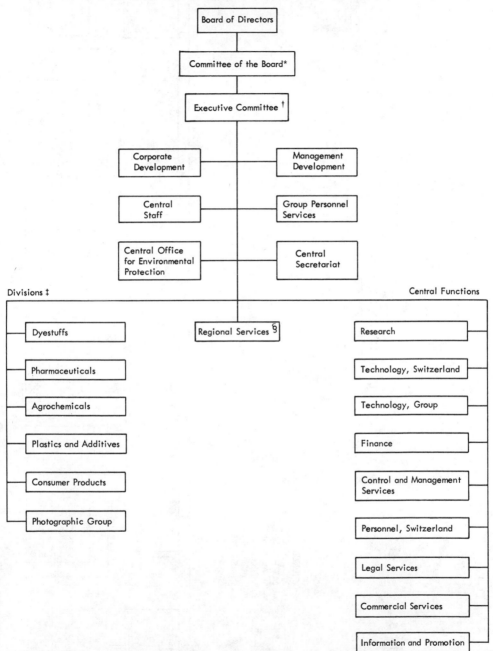

* Prepares the fundamental principles of business policy for consideration by the board, supervises business activity, sanctions investment projects in excess of 10 million Swiss francs, and deals with fundamental questions of personnel, investment, and financial policy.

† Responsible for the implementation of business policies approved by the board.

‡ Responsible for worldwide strategy in specific market sectors. Reviews specific product-market strategies of operating companies.

§ Monitors the group's investment in its 60 international affiliates. Reviews overall business plans of subsidiaries and parcels out sector strategies to group-level divisions for review.

EXHIBIT 5

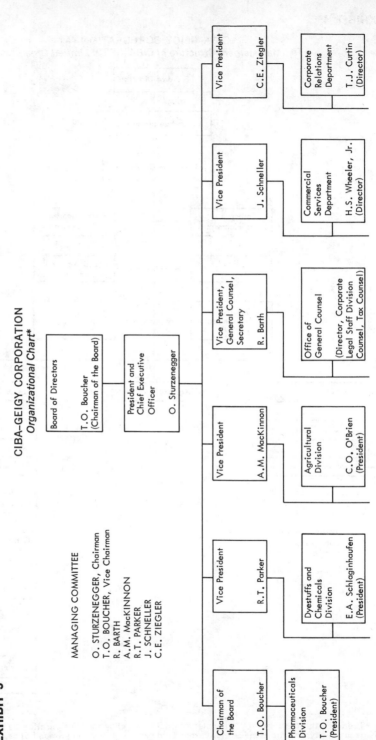

CIBA–GEIGY CORPORATION
Organizational Chart*

MANAGING COMMITTEE

O. STURZENEGGER, Chairman
T.O. BOUCHER, Vice Chairman
R. BARTH
A.M. MacKINNON
R.T. PARKER
J. SCHNELLER
C.E. ZIEGLER

Board of Directors

T.O. Boucher
(Chairman of the Board)

President and
Chief Executive
Officer

O. Sturzenegger

Chairman of
the Board

T.O. Boucher

Pharmaceuticals
Division

T.O. Boucher
(President)

Vice President

R.T. Parker

Dyestuffs and
Chemicals
Division

E.A. Schlaginhaufen
(President)

Vice President

A.M. MacKinnon

Agricultural
Division

C.O. O'Brien
(President)

Vice President,
General Counsel,
Secretary

R. Barth

Office of
General Counsel

(Director, Corporate
Legal Staff Division
Counsel, Tax Counsel)

Vice President

J. Schneller

Commercial
Services
Department

H.S. Wheeler, Jr.
(Director)

Vice President

C.E. Ziegler

Corporate
Relations
Department

T.J. Curtin
(Director)

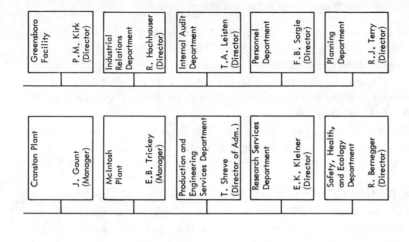
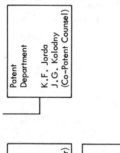
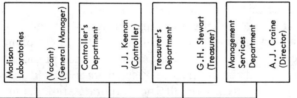

Plastics and Additives Division — H.W. Zussman (President)

Madison Laboratories — (Vacant) (General Manager)

- Controller's Department — J.J. Keenan (Controller)
- Treasurer's Department — G.H. Stewart (Treasurer)
- Management Services Department — A.J. Craine (Director)

Patent Department — K.F. Jorda, J.G. Kolodny (Co-Patent Counsel)

Cranston Plant — J. Gaunt (Manager)

- McIntosh Plant — E.B. Trickey (Manager)
- Production and Engineering Services Department — T. Shreve (Director of Adm.)
- Research Services Department — E.K. Kleiner (Director)
- Safety, Health, and Ecology Department — R. Bernegger (Director)

Greensboro Facility — P.M. Kirk (Director)

- Industrial Relations Department — R. Hochhauser (Director)
- Internal Audit Department — T.A. Leisten (Director)
- Personnel Department — F.B. Sorgie (Director)
- Planning Department — R.J. Terry (Director)

* This chart indicates lines of authority and is not indicative of position status.

cals used to assist in dyeing and in textile finishing processes. In addition, the division did a large business in florescent whiteners, which soap and detergent companies used in their products to improve the appearance of the wash. In dyestuffs, the company was number three in the U.S. market after Du Pont and Sandoz, and in florescent whiteners the company was number one.

In addition to these principal operating divisions, a small consumer specialties business was run through Madison Laboratories. It was not considered to be a successful operation by the top management of CIBA–GEIGY.

CIBA–GEIGY Corporation was managed by the corporate managing committee, consisting of the chairman of the board, the president, and the five corporate vice presidents. Each of the operating divisions had a division president, who reported to one of the corporate vice presidents. Each division president was backed up by a team of divisional vice presidents, who were responsible for such areas as marketing, production, research, and administration. The divisions were responsible for their own activities in all of these areas, but they were free to call upon the corporate staff for necessary services. Once their budgets had been submitted to the corporate managing committee and approved, the divisions had considerable freedom to operate within their budgets. In capital expenditures, however, all projects over $100,000 required the specific approval of the corporate managing committee.

Two of CIBA–GEIGY's larger plants, in Cranston, Rhode Island, and McIntosh, Alabama, served more than one division. In those plants the production activities were directed by the production vice presidents of the various divisions, but all the support services were managed by a corporate plant manager. The heads of all the corporate staff departments and corporate plants and facilities reported to one or another of the corporate vice presidents. Exhibit 5 presents the organization of CIBA–GEIGY in chart form.

CIBA–GEIGY's board of directors consisted of four company officers, four representatives from the Swiss parent company, and two outsiders.

Relationships with the Swiss Parent Company

In the area of research there was considerable dialogue and exchange of information between the parent company and its U.S. subsidiary. Since both the subsidiary and the parent company invested large amounts of money in research, it was critical that these efforts be carefully coordinated. Similarly, capital expenditures were closely coordinated with the parent company to assure that the worldwide production capacity remained in balance.

Cash flows to the parent company from CIBA–GEIGY Corporation was an important link between the two entities and took four forms. First, dividends were paid to the parent company on an annual basis. Second, the U.S. subsidiary paid a significant amount of money to the parent company as part of its share of the group research budget. Third, cash flowed to the parent company in connection with royalty agreements. Finally, a minimal amount of cash flowed to Switzerland in payment for purchases of intermediate and finished products.

A regional services department in Switzerland was responsible for monitoring the group's investment in its 60 international affiliates. In addition, product line or division managers in each of the affiliates maintained close contact with corresponding "divisions" at group headquarters. The influence of the headquarters divisions was reflected mainly through the planning system. The three-year plans of each subsidiary's divisions were reviewed with the corresponding division in Basle.

Corporate Objectives

CIBA–GEIGY Corporation's objectives were to continue to improve its long-term profits through new products derived from research and from acquisitions in related fields. As explained by Mr. MacKinnon:

> We wish to remain a very research-oriented organization with vigorous and ongoing internal growth. However, we also look to our acquisition program as a means of complementing this growth. I should emphasize that we have no interest in becoming a vast conglomerate. We are not making acquisitions merely to become bigger. We are interested only in those companies which would complement our current business or put us into related new business areas.

Mr. MacKinnon added that acquisitions would be financed primarily with CIBA–GEIGY Corporation's own cash flows. The company was willing to invest up to $250 million in new acquisitions. Of this amount $150 million was expected to come from U.S. sources.

CIBA–GEIGY's Acquisition Program

A first step in implementing the acquisition program was the creation of an Acquisitions Task Force in September 1973. This group was chaired by Mr. MacKinnon and included CIBA–GEIGY's general counsel, corporate secretary, director of corporate planning, and three staff executives from the corporate planning and treasury functions. These three staff executives functioned as full-time members of the task force, reporting to Mr. Robert Terry, the director of corporate planning.

The group initially had two major responsibilities: first, to establish basic criteria for any acquisitions CIBA–GEIGY might make, and second, to determine areas of acquisition interest.

A memorandum, spelling out acquisition criteria and areas of interest, was prepared by the task force and approved by the corporate managing committee. This set the overall guidelines for the acquisition search, and was distributed to leading investment banking firms and large commercial banks so that these organizations could refer potential acquisition candidates to CIBA-GEIGY. Exhibit 6 presents a copy of this memorandum.

EXHIBIT 6

CIBA–GEIGY CORPORATION (A)
Areas of Acquisition Interest and Consent Decree Provisions

CIBA–GEIGY is at present entering into a major acquisition program, and this memorandum sets forth our acquisition interests and also discusses those provisions of the Consent Decree which affect our interests.

Acquisition Criteria

In general, we are looking for acquisition candidates which meet the criteria listed below, and which might be available for cash. It is possible that in the case of a particularly attractive situation, we might be willing to take a major stock position offering the probability for a control position or full ownership at a later date.

1. The candidate should participate in growing markets.
2. The candidate should have a proprietary position in its markets.
3. The candidate's operations should be likely to be favorably affected by CIBA–GEIGY's know-how in the fields of research, development, manufacture, and marketing of complex synthetic organic chemicals.
4. The candidate's business should be product rather than service oriented.
5. The candidate should have sales of $50 million or more.
6. The candidate should earn a good gross profit margin on sales.
7. The candidate should have the potential to yield a return on investment of 10 percent or more.
8. The probable purchase price should not exceed $250 million.

Since CIBA–GEIGY's business in the United States approximates 25 percent of the worldwide sales, we are particularly interested in companies that would offer potential for substantial growth outside the U.S. through the efforts of our worldwide resources.

Consent Decree Provisions

Under the terms of the Consent Decree into which CIBA and Geigy entered at the time of their merger in 1970, CIBA–GEIGY Corporation

EXHIBIT 6 *(continued)*

and its parent company, for a period ending in September 1975, may not acquire "any other person engaged in the United States in any of the same lines of commerce" as CIBA–GEIGY Corporation, except upon 15 days prior notice to the Department of Justice. If within such 15 days prior the Justice Department requests information relating to the proposed transaction as authorized by the Antitrust Civil Process Act, then the transaction cannot be consummated until an additional period of 60 days after the company furnishes the information so requested to the Department of Justice.

Areas of Acquisition Interest

We are not interested at the present time in exploring totally new business areas. We have, however, been able to identify the following areas of growth which we wish to pursue:

1. The whole area of specialty chemicals is of interest to us. A definition of specialty chemicals would include among others, certain of the following characteristics:

    They are sold in moderate volumes, but at high per unit selling prices, at least two times raw material costs.

    They are usually sold under brand names, and are promoted to the end user based on performance specifications for what they do.

    They require a relatively high level of research and development, based on a knowledge of the customer's technology.

    Although gross profit margins typically run at least 50 percent of sales, heavy expenditures for marketing and research may yield only an average after tax margin on sales, but a high return on investment.

    The types of specialty chemicals we currently produce are listed in the previous section. Other types which could be of interest to us include such items as: specialty adhesives, biocides, moulding compounds, coatings, specialty cleaning products, flame retardants, intermediates for cosmetics, detergents, etc., chemicals for pretreating and finishing textiles, etc.

2. Proprietary pharmaceuticals and cosmetic and toiletry products.

3. Animal health products, including feed additives and veterinary products.

4. Proprietary household and garden products such as those marketed by S. C. Johnson.

5. Suppliers of products to the health care industry, including disposable hospital and medical products, diagnostic aids, dental, and optical supplies.

6. Products, processes and related services for the environmental industry, i.e., air, liquid, and solid waste treatment. It should be noted

EXHIBIT 6 (concluded)

that our interest in these areas is not in the equipment side, but our orientation is toward the chemicals and related services side.

7.   Photo chemicals and related products.

We have not included such items as seed breeding and food additives (principally flavors and fragrances), on the above list as our Agricultural Division has already conducted extensive studies in these areas using outside consultants, and has identified most of the candidates which might be of interest to us.

In addition to contacting investment banking firms and commercial banks, CIBA–GEIGY also screened 15 to 20 thousand companies. Working with Standard & Poor's and Moody's industrial directories, the task force first reviewed approximately 10,000 publicly owned companies, evaluating them in terms of their criteria for industry and growth. This manual screening was complemented by a computer review by industry, conducted for CIBA–GEIGY by a leading investment banking firm. The company also purchased the Dun & Bradstreet computer tapes, which allowed the task force to review another 8,000 additional companies, most of them privately owned.

At the same time as this massive screening was going on, the task force worked with all of the company's divisions to identify any companies or divisions of other companies in which they might have had an interest.

After several months of screening, about a hundred companies emerged as meeting CIBA–GEIGY's general criteria. The task force then prepared a two-page summary covering each of these organizations, for review by the corporate managing committee. It was from this group of a hundred companies that a final selection of six acquisition candidates was made.

2 CIBA-GEIGY Corporation (B)

In June 1974 the top management of CIBA–GEIGY Corporation was presented with a detailed task force report on Airwick Industries, Inc. CIBA–GEIGY had decided to concentrate its acquisition activities on six companies, and Airwick Industries was one of the six. While detailed reports were prepared from public sources on each of the six companies, a special Airwick Task Force from CIBA–GEIGY had actually interviewed key vice presidents at Airwick Industries. This unusual procedure reflected both CIBA–GEIGY's understanding that Airwick Industries may be looking for a merger partner and Airwick Industries' friendly disposition toward CIBA–GEIGY. For five years a French subsidiary of CIBA–GEIGY Limited had distributed Airwick products in France.

Based on this report and on publicly available information, Mr. Don MacKinnon and the Acquisitions Task Force had to decide whether or not to give their support to this potential acquisition. Since Mr. MacKinnon was the only executive at CIBA–GEIGY Corporation with extensive mergers and acquisitions experience, his opinion would be a highly respected input to the final decision. If it were decided to seek the acquisition of Airwick Industries, an overall plan had to be prepared, including a starting position and desired end position for negotiations with Airwick Industries' board of directors.

This case summarizes the basic substance of the Airwick Task Force report, along with the publicly available information on Airwick Industries. In addition, it presents the issues and questions raised by Mr. MacKinnon and the task force as they considered whether or not to proceed with this diversifying acquisition.

AIRWICK INDUSTRIES, INC.

Company Background

In the late 1930s, an independent researcher worked with a blind subject for four years in an attempt to discover the natural odor opposites of the most common indoor malodors. On the basis of this work, he was able to develop an odor counteractant formula made up of 125 components, including among other things, a group of green plant extracts. It was this combination product, called Airwick Liquid, which eventually formed the business base of Airwick Industries' predecessor company.

Until Airwick Liquid was developed, most odor control products simply masked or overpowered unpleasant odors with a strong and supposedly more pleasant aroma. Airwick Liquid was, therefore, unquestionably a salable product, but substantial resources were required to penetrate the postwar, home-centered market. To overcome the lack of financial resources, the responsibility for developing a sales force and distribution system was assigned to a national distributor, while the company, then known as Airkem, Inc., limited its marketing efforts to products for industrial, commercial, and institutional applications, and to exploring foreign markets.

By the mid-1950s domestic retail sales of Airwick began to sag under intense competitive pressure. Even a transfer of marketing rights to Lever Brothers could not reverse the sales deterioration. In 1963, the company purchased the Airwick name from Lever and began to market Airwick Liquid itself. The company spent a good deal of money promoting the product that year, which resulted in a net loss in 1963, but the sales stopped declining. The company was profitable through 1974, although development costs and promotion for new products penalized earnings growth in the late 1960s.

As of June 1974, the company's principal products consisted of odor counteracting air fresheners, together with a full line of sanitary maintenance items, such as disinfectants, cleaners, and insecticides containing odor counteraction features, and certain swimming pool products. These products were marketed through four operating segments.

1. Consumer—household products distributed through food brokers in the United States and Canada.
2. Institutional—commercial, institutional, industrial products distributed through franchised distributors and 14 company branch offices in the U.S. and Canada.
3. International—household, commercial, institutional, and industrial products marketed through distributors in more than 50 foreign countries.

4. Aquatic—swimming pool treatment chemicals and dispensers sold through distributors and dealers in the United States and Canada.

Table 1 shows the revenues and pretax income for each of the segments from 1969 through 1973.

The relative profitability of the principal segments of the company's business significantly changed beginning in 1971 due to three major factors: Consumer segment sales and margins increased sharply after 1970, reflecting (a) the completion of national distribution and the market acceptance of a new product, "Airwick Solid," in United States retail markets, and (b) manufacturing efficiencies resulting from integrated, higher volume production of this product within the company's plants; earnings of the Institutional segment declined, reflecting higher marketing expenses and increased costs of goods, warehousing, and transportation not offset by increases in selling prices; and International sales and margins increased, reflecting the broadening distribution and market acceptance of "Airwick Solid" in European retail markets.

Exhibits 1 and 2 present Airwick Industries' consolidated statement of earnings for the period 1969–73, and a balance sheet as of December 31, 1973.

Consumer Segment

The Airwick Consumer Brands Division marketed six products, three of them in the "air freshener" category. The three air fresheners—Airwick Solid, Airwick Liquid, and Airwick Spray—accounted for 97 percent of the division's net sales. The remaining 3 percent included On Guard, an automatically dispensed toilet bowl cleaner; Airwick Cat Litter Deodorant Spray; and a disinfectant spray. In 1973, all of Consumer division's profits were derived from Airwick Solid and Airwick Liquid.

The air freshener market had shown substantial growth in recent years with the bulk of the growth in the "solid" type of product. Table 2 summarizes the key sales trends for the 1970–73 period.

In addition to having experienced rapid growth, the air freshener market was highly competitive. Many manufacturers and distributors were trying to stake out a position in the market for room deodorants. A number of competitors were larger, better known, and financially stronger than Airwick Industries and were capable of expending large sums in advertising and promoting their products.

Airwick's major competitors included Bristol-Myers with its Renuzit brand; American Home Products with its Wizard brand; Home Products Corp. with Days-Ease; and S. C. Johnson & Company with Glade. In-

TABLE 1
Revenues and Pre-Tax Income for Major Operating Segments: 1969–73 (dollars in thousands)

	Consumer				Institutional				International				Aquatic			
	Revenues		Pre-tax		Revenues		Pre-tax		Revenues		Pre-tax		Revenues		Pre-tax	
1973........	$17,500	52%	$2,475	49%	$9,100	27%	$ 800	16%	$4,050	12%	$1,500	30%	$2,950	9%	$250	5%
1972........	14,251	51	2,090	55	8,117	29	429	11	2,920	11	1,047	28	2,485	9	221	6
1971........	11,066	50	1,222	47	7,048	32	615	23	1,895	8	590	22	2,158	10	203	8
1970........	6,785	43	(23)	—	6,380	40	931	69	1,294	8	386	29	1,468	9	58	4
1969........	4,606	37	(304)	—	5,835	46	1,210	86	1,022	8	310	22	1,118	9	193	14

EXHIBIT 1

CIBA–GEIGY CORPORATION (B)
Airwick Industries, Inc., and Subsidiaries
Consolidated Statement of Earnings

	Year Ended December 31				
	1969	1970	1971	1972	1973
Sales and other revenue					
Net sales.........................	$12,376,000	$15,724,000	$21,855,000	$27,307,000	$33,024,000
Other revenue...................	205,000	203,000	312,000	466,000	772,000
	12,581,000	15,927,000	22,167,000	27,773,000	33,796,000
Costs and other charges					
Cost of sales....................	5,120,000	6,755,000	9,495,000	11,236,000	13,778,000
Selling and administrative					
expenses......................	5,934,000	7,674,000	9,937,000	12,600,000	14,860,000
Interest expense					
Long-term debt................	53,000	45,000	46,000	47,000	59,000
Other.........................	23,000	61,000	24,000	4,000	45,000
Miscellaneous charges..........	42,000	40,000	35,000	98,000	71,000
	11,172,000	14,575,000	19,537,000	23,985,000	28,813,000
Earnings before income					
taxes....................	1,409,000	1,352,000	2,630,000	3,788,000	4,983,000
Income taxes......................	702,000	610,000	1,195,000	1,677,000	2,300,000
Net Earnings..............	$ 707,000	$ 742,000	$ 1,435,000	$ 2,111,000	$ 2,683,000
Average number of common shares					
outstanding (Note 1)............	3,062,344	3,070,512	3,204,658	3,399,252	3,457,290
Earnings per share of common					
stock (Note 1)...................	$0.23	$0.24	$0.45	$0.62	$0.78
Cash dividends declared on					
common stock (Note 2)..........	$0.08	$0.08	$0.09	$0.11	$0.15

Notes:
1. Earnings per share of common stock have been computed on the weighted average number of common shares outstanding in each year, after giving retroactive effect to the 3 for 2 stock split in 1972 and the 2 for 1 stock split and the reclassification on a share for share basis of Class A and Class B common stock for a single class of common stock in 1973 and retroactive adjustment for shares issued in 1972 in connection with the acquisition of King-Kratz Corporation in a pooling of interests (Note A-3 to Notes to Consolidated Financial Statements). Shares issuable under employee stock options and warrants are excluded from the weighted average number of shares in determining earnings per share on the basis that the dilutive effect is less than 3 percent.
2. Dividends per share of common stock have been computed on the number of shares outstanding at time of declaration, after giving retroactive effect to the changes described in Note 1. The pooled company paid no dividends.

tense competition developed in 1973 in the "solid" segment of the household air freshener market. While the market was expanding significantly, competitive products proliferated. American Home Products was a new entrant, and it was believed that Gillette was preparing to enter the market. Table 3 shows the share of market for the most recent four-week period ending March 15, 1974, in comparison with data for the comparable period in 1973. The averages for the past two years are also summarized.

As can be seen from Table 3, Renuzit had recently eclipsed Airwick as the number one brand (all forms combined). However, consumer

EXHIBIT 2

CIBA–GEIGY CORPORATION (B)
Airwick Industries, Inc., and Subsidiaries
Consolidated Balance Sheet
Year Ended December 31

Assets	1973	1972
Current Assets		
Cash...	$ 1,770,000	$ 1,683,000
Short-term investments—at cost which approximates market value...		993,000
Customers' receivables................................	3,747,000	3,101,000
Other receivables......................................	137,000	61,000
Inventories (Note A-4)		
Finished goods.......................................	2,379,000	1,313,000
Work in process......................................	393,000	180,000
Raw materials..	1,980,000	1,185,000
	4,752,000	2,678,000
Prepayments, advances, and other items...............	515,000	477,000
Total current assets...............................	10,921,000	8,993,000
Property, plant and equipment—at cost, less accumulated depreciation and amortization (Notes A-5 and D).......	5,187,000	3,038,000
Other assets		
Prepayments of obligations to former distributor, less amortization of $652,000 in 1973 and $569,000 in 1972 (Note A-6)..	351,000	433,000
Patents, trademarks and other, less amortization of $371,000 in 1973 and $334,000 in 1972 (Note A-6)..........	188,000	182,000
Prepaid pension costs (Note A-7).......................	470,000	500,000
Deferred charges and other............................	519,000	320,000
	1,528,000	1,435,000
	$17,636,000	$13,466,000

Liabilities	1973	1972
Current Liabilities		
Notes payable—bank (Note G)..........................	$ 870,000	$
Current maturities of long-term debt (Note E)...........	69,000	92,000
Accounts payable......................................	2,363,000	1,777,000
Accrued compensation and other expenses..............	759,000	538,000
Income taxes (Notes A-10 and F).......................	1,238,000	1,033,000
Total current liabilities............................	5,299,000	3,440,000
Long-term Debt (Note E)................................	511,000	609,000
Deferred income taxes (Notes A-9 and F).................	189,000	11,000
Commitments (Note G)		
Stockholders' equity (Notes H and I)		
Capital stock		
Preferred—authorized, 100,000 shares of $1 par value, none issued...	—	—
Common stock, par value $0.05—authorized, 6,000,000 shares; issued and outstanding, 3,464,942 shares in 1973 and 3,447,482 shares in 1972.....................	173,000	172,000
Additional contributed capital...........................	3,510,000	3,444,000
Retained earnings......................................	7,954,000	5,790,000
	11,637,000	9,406,000
	$17,636,000	$13,466,000

The accompanying notes are an integral part of this statement:

EXHIBIT 2 (continued)

Airwick Industries, Inc., and Subsidiaries
Notes to Consolidated Financial Statements
December 31, 1973 and 1972

Note A—Summary of Accounting Policies

A summary of the significant accounting policies consistently applied in the preparation of the accompanying consolidated financial statements follows:

1. Principles of Consolidation
   The consolidated financial statements include the accounts of the wholly-owned domestica and foreign subsidiaries and the accounts of King-Kratz Corporation acquired in 1972 in a pooling of interests transaction. Material intercompany amounts and transactions were eliminated in consolidation.

2. Foreign Currency Translation
   Current assets and current liabilities are translated at the rate of exchange in effect at the close of the period. Long-term assets are translated at the rates in effect at the dates those assets were acquired, and long-term liabilities are translated at the rates in effect at the dates these obligations were incurred. Exchange adjustments are charged or credited to income. The exchange adjustments resulted in an exchange gain of $36,000 for 1973 and an exchange loss of $52,000 for 1972. Revenue and expense accounts are translated at the average of exchange rates which were in effect during the year, except for depreciation and amortization which are translated at the rates of exchange which were in effect when the respective assets were acquired.

3. Pooling of interests
   On October 31, 1972, the Company acquired all of the issued and outstanding shares of King-Kratz Corporation by issuing 81,586 shares of its common stock.

4. Inventories
   Inventories are stated at the lower of cost or market; cost is determined using the first-in, first-out method.

5. Property, Plant, and Equipment
   Depreciation and amortization are provided for in amounts sufficient to relate the cost of depreciable assets to operations over their estimated service lives. The buildings are being depreciated on the double-declining balance and straight-line methods over a 45-year period. Other depreciable assets are depreciated generally on the straight-line method over periods ranging from two to 20 years. Leasehold improvements are amortized over the lives of the leases or the service lives of the improvements, whichever is shorter, on the straight-line basis.
   The Company capitalizes, for both financial reporting and tax purposes, leased equipment where the terms of the lease result in the creation of a material equity in the property accruing to the Company. The consolidated balance sheet reflects all such leased manufacturing equipment as assets and long-term obligations.

6. Amortization Policies
   Payments to a former distributor are being amortized on the straight-line basis to the expiration date of the agreement.
   The cost of marketing rights to a line of products is being amortized on the straight-line basis over the terms of the underlying agreements.
   The cost of patents and trademarks are capitalized and amortized to operations over their statutory lives. Amortization is computed on the straight-line method.
   Goodwill is amortized on a straight-line basis over a period of five years.

7. Pension Plans
   The Company has a pension plan covering substantially all of its full-time employees. It is the Company's policy to fund normal pension cost. A United Kingdom subsidiary also has a pension plan for its employees. As of January 1, 1972, the Company amended its pension plan which resulted in increased benefits to its employees. As a result of the amended plan, the Company has incurred past service cost which it has funded and is amortizing over a ten-year period. The changes in the pension plan had no significant effect on net earnings for 1972. The pension charges to income amounted to $152,000 each in 1973 and 1972.

8. Research and Development
   Costs incurred in the development of new products are charged to income as incurred.

9. Deferred Income Taxes
   Deferred income tax expense results from timing differences in the recognition of revenue and expense for tax and financial statement purposes.

10. Investment Tax Credits
    Investment tax credits are accounted for by the "flow-through" method. Under this method, credits are recognized as a reduction of income tax expense in the year the assets giving rise to the credit are placed in service.

Note B—Acquisition

On January 31, 1974, the Company acquired approximately 90 percent of the issued and outstanding common stock of Seablue Corporation, a corporation engaged in the manufacture, distribution and sale of swimming pool supplies and equipment for approximately $3,600,000 in cash in a transaction to be accounted for as a purchase. Further, the Company will offer to purchase the remaining 10 percent of the issued and outstanding common stock from the minority stockholders at the same terms offered the principal stockholders. If all of the remaining stockholders accept the offer, the Company's total purchase price will amount to approximately $4 million.

Note C—Foreign Operations

The following is a summary of the accounts of the foreign subsidiaries at December 31, 1973 and 1972:

EXHIBIT 2 (continued)

Airwick Industries, Inc., and Subsidiaries
Notes to Consolidated Financial Statements (continued)
December 31, 1973 and 1972

	1973	1972
Current assets............	$3,698,000	$3,021,000
Current liabilities.........	1,862,000	1,294,000
	1,836,000	1,727,000
Fixed assets, less accumu-		
lated depreciation and		
amortization............	109,000	86,000
Other assets..............	9,000	9,000
	1,954,000	1,822,000
Less		
Amounts due to parent		
company—net.........	221,000	160,000
Long-term debt..........	195,000	226,000
Deferred income taxes...	3,000	
	419,000	386,000
Net assets..........	$1,535,000	$1,436,000

The cumulative amount of undistributed earnings of foreign subsidiaries on which the parent company has not recognized United States income taxes amounted to approximately $1,500,000 and $1,400,000 at December 31, 1973 and 1972, respectively. During the year, the Company received dividends amounting to $1,297,000 from foreign subsidiaries.

It is the Company's practice to provide currently for taxes which will be payable upon remittance of foreign earnings to the parent company, based upon estimates of the amounts to be received in dividends.

Note D—Property, Plant, and Equipment
These assets are summarized as follows:

	1973	1972
Land.......................	$ 400,000	$ 221,000
Buildings and improvements.	2,365,000	1,537,000
Machinery and equipment...	3,705,000	2,238,000
Machinery under lease option		
agreement................	202,000	202,000
Leasehold improvements....	211,000	217,000
Construction in progress.....	68,000	
	6,951,000	4,415,000
Less accumulated deprecia-		
tion and amortization......	1,764,000	1,377,000
	$5,187,000	$3,038,000

Note E—Long-term Debt
This item comprises the following obligations:

	1973	1972
Mortgage loan—5⅞ percent, payable in monthly install- ments of $2,125 to 1985.......	$306,000	$332,000
Note payable—bank (interest rate ½ of 1 percent over mini- mum lending rate) repayable in installments of $50,000 in installments of $50,000 in 1975 and $145,000 in 1976..........	195,000	246,000
Other........................	117,000	182,000
	618,000	760,000
Less unamortized discount.....	(38,000)	(59,000)
	580,000	701,000
Less current maturities........	69,000	92,000
	$511,000	$609,000

The aggregate maturities of long-term debt are summarized as follows:

	1973	1972
1973............................	$	$121,000
1974............................	105,000	128,000
1975............................	107,000	61,000
1976............................	177,000	221,000
1977............................	25,000	25,000
1978............................	25,000	
Subsequent.....................	179,000	204,000
	$618,000	$760,000

Note F—Income Taxes
The Federal income tax returns of the parent company subsequent to 1969 are subject to review by the Internal Revenue Service. Income tax expense for the year ended December 31, 1973, is made up of the following components:

	U.S. Federal	Foreign Income tax	Foreign Taxes withheld at source	Total
Current tax ex- pense..	$1,125,000	$829,000	$168,000	$2,122,000
Deferred tax ex- pense..	175,000	3,000		178,000
	$1,300,000	$832,000	$168,000	$2,300,000

Income tax expense for the year ended December 31, 1972, is made up of the following components:

	U.S. Federal	Foreign	Total
Current tax expense..	$1,081,000	$596,000	$1,677,000

Deferred tax expense results from timing differences in the recognition of revenue and expense for tax and financial statement purposes. The sources of these differences in 1973 and the tax effect of each were as follows:

Excess of tax over book depreciation.....	$ 66,000
Computer development costs expensed on tax return and deferred on books....	59,000
Convention expenses expensed on tax return and deferred on books..........	41,000
Other timing differences..................	12,000
	$178,000

Note G—Commitments
The minimum rental commitments under all non-cancellable leases are as follows:

	1974	1975	1976
Plant facilities.........	$111,000	$107,000	$ 99,000
Equipment.............	88,000	87,000	87,000
Office facilities........	142,000	119,000	112,000
	$341,000	$313,000	$298,000

	1977	1978	1979 and beyond
Plant facilities.........	$ 88,000	$ 82,000	$303,000
Equipment.............	53,000		
Office facilities........	102,000	94,000	77,000
	$243,000	$176,000	$380,000

EXHIBIT 2 *(concluded)*

Airwick Industries, Inc., and Subsidiaries
Notes to Consolidated Financial Statements (continued)
December 31, 1973 and 1972

Some of the leases require the Company to pay for maintenance, taxes and insurance. Total rental expense amounted to $454,000 and $308,000 for 1973 and 1972, respectively.

At December 31, 1973, the Company had a credit line with a bank amounting to $2 million. The related short-term debt outstanding was $870,000 at an interest rate of 9¾ percent per annum. During January 1974, the credit line was increased to $6 million. The credit line can be withdrawn at the bank's option. There were no compensating balance arrangements at December 31, 1973, under the line of credit. However, there is an informal understanding that the Company maintain a principal operating account with the bank.

Note H—Stock Options and Warrants

Under qualified stock option plans as approved by the stockholders on May 25, 1966, and April 24, 1968, options may be granted officers and key employees of the parent company within ten years to purchase an aggregate of 120,000 shares of common stock under the 1966 plan and 90,000 shares of common stock under the 1968 plan. The option price must be not less than the fair market value of the stock on the date of grant. Options are exercisable after two years from the date of grant but not later than five years from such date.

Under a nonqualified stock option plan as approved by the stockholders on April 26, 1972, options may be granted to employees of the Company within ten years to purchase an aggregate of 198,000 shares of common stock. The option price must not be less than the fair market value of the stock on the date of the grant. Options are exercisable two years from the date of the grant but not later then ten years from such date.

Changes during 1973 under the plans were as follows:

	Shares		
	Reserved	Granted	Available
Balance—January 1, 1973..................	263,600	88,500	175,100
Granted...............		61,800	(61,800)
Cancelled.............		(5,500)	5,500
Exercised.............	(17,460)	(17,460)	
Balance—December 31, 1973..............	246,140	127,340	118,800
Option price range....		$4.813–$21.25	
Exercisable at December 31, 1973.........		30,540	

Changes during the 1972 under the plans were as follows:

	Shares		
	Reserved	Granted	Available
Balance—January 1, 1972..................	131,100	115,500	15,600
1972 plan..............	198,000		198,000
Granted...............		40,500	(40,500)
Cancelled.............		(6,000)	6,000
Exercised.............	(61,500)	(61,500)	
Balance—December 31, 1972..............	267,600	88,500	179,100
Option price range....		$4.813–$19.50	
Exercisable at December 31, 1972.........		45,000	

Note 1—Capital Stock

On April 26, 1972, the stockholders authorized the following changes in the capital structure:

(a) An increase in the authorized Class A common stock from 400,000 shares ($0.05 par value) to 600,000 shares ($0.05 par value).

(b) An increase in the authorized Class B common stock from 1,600,000 shares ($0.05 par value) to 2,400,000 shares ($0.05 par value).

(c) Both the Class A and Class B common stock outstanding were split on a 3 for 2 basis.

On January 24, 1973, the stockholders authorized the following changes in the capital structure:

(a) An increase in the authorized Class A common stock from 600,000 shares ($0.05 par value) to 1,200,000 shares ($0.05 par value).

(b) An increase in the authorized Class B common stock from 2,400,000 shares ($0.05 par value) to 4,800,000 shares ($0.05 par value).

(c) Both the Class A and Class B common stock outstanding were split on a 2 for 1 basis.

(d) Class A and Class B common stock were reclassified on a share for share basis for a single class of common stock.

Accordingly, retroactive effect has been given to the financial statements for the Company's 2 for 1 split in 1973 and for the reclassification on a share for share basis of Class A and Class B common stock into a single class of common stock.

To the Stockholders
Airwick Industries, Inc.

We have examined the consolidated balance sheet of Airwick Industries, Inc., and Subsidiaries as of December 31, 1973 and 1972, and the related consolidated statements of earnings, retained earnings, additional contributed capital, and changes in financial position for the years then ended. Our examination was made in accordance with generally accepted auditing standards, and accordingly included such tests of the accounting records and such other auditing procedures as we considered necessary in the circumstances. We have received reports of other auditors with respect to their examination of certain of the consolidated foreign subsidiaries whose assets and revenue constitute 19.9 percent and 14.9 percent, respectively, in 1973 and 20.8 percent and 13.8 percent, respectively, in 1972 of the corresponding consolidated totals. Insofar as our opinion expressed herein relates to amounts for certain of the foreign subsidiaries, it is based solely on the aforementioned reports of the other auditors.

In our opinion, based upon our examination and the aforementioned reports of other auditors, the consolidated financial statements referred to above present fairly the consolidated financial position of Airwick Industries, Inc. and Subsidiaries at December 31, 1973 and 1972, and the consolidated results of their operations and changes in financial position for the years then ended, in conformity with generally accepted accounting principles applied on a consistent basis.

Alexander Grant & Company
New York, New York
January 31, 1974

TABLE 2

Air Freshner Market Retail (dollars in thousands)

	Total Market		Solids		Aerosols		Liquids	
	Sales	% Change Prev. Yr.	Share of Total	% Change Prev. Yr.	Share of Total	% Change Prev. Yr.	Share of Total	% Change Prev. Yr.
1973........	$91,400	+34%	43%	+110%	34%	± 0%	23%	+9%
1972........	68,000	+16	27	+ 73	45	+ 9	28	+1
1971........	58,400	+13	19	+ 90	49	+22	32	+8
1970........	51,700	n.a.*	11	n.a.	55	n.a.	34	n.a.

* n.a. = not available.

research in the solid segment showed that Airwick had maintained strength with an extremely high 92 percent consumer intent to repurchase after trying the product.

In early 1974, Airwick was prepared to produce private label solid air fresheners for chain stores. The company had already signed production contracts with Grand Union, Purity, and Finast. A contract with A&P was about to be signed. Airwick managers predicted that the private label business would be as profitable as the existing Airwick Solid business on a per unit basis.

The idea behind Airwick's entrance into private labeling was to eliminate competition while gaining more factory volume for Airwick. In areas of the country where Airwick Solid had excellent distribution and was number one or a close number two, it was believed that when the

TABLE 3

Air Freshner Market Shares Food Stores (dollar basis)

	Four-Week Shares		Average— 52-Week Shares	
	Ending 3/16/73	Ending 3/15/74	Last 12 Mos.	Year Ago 12 Mos.
Airwick Liquid............................	4.5%	4.9%	4.4%	4.7%
Airwick Solid............................	19.1	17.0	16.1	18.7
Total Airwick......................	23.6%	21.9%	20.5%	23.4%
Renuzit Aerosol........................	6.7%	6.5%	6.8%	7.0%
Renuzit Solid..........................	11.8	21.6	17.0	10.3
Total Renuzit.....................	18.5%	28.1%	23.8%	17.3%
Wizard Aerosol.........................	10.7%	8.8%	10.3%	12.8%
Wizard Solid...........................	—	5.7	3.3	—
Wizard Wick...........................	2.3	1.9	2.3	2.6
Total Wizard.....................	13.0%	16.4%	15.9%	15.4%
Days-Ease Solid........................	5.5%	6.2%	7.5%	1.3%
Glase Aerosol..........................	20.1	9.8	15.0	17.6
All other Brands.......................	19.3	17.6	17.3	25.0

chain added the Airwick private brand to the shelf, the marginal number three or four brands would be taken off the shelf. In areas where Airwick Solid did not do as well, private branding was thought to be a way of getting in the store and protecting Airwick from competitors that also may be interested in doing private label work.

Despite Airwick's planned entrance into private labeling, the company had been notably unsuccessful in developing and introducing new products. In the past all new product introductions (Airwick Solid, Cat Litter Spray, On Guard, and the disinfectant spray) were formulas taken directly from products sold by the Institutional division. With the exception of Airwick Solid, they were all unsuccessful.

Airwick consumer products were sold through a system of 63 food brokers across the United States. These brokers were under the supervision of seven Airwick-employed regional managers who reported to the sales manager.

Due to the desperate situation in 1963 when the existing broker network was established, Airwick started and continued paying commissions at the rate of 7.5 percent. While there were many exceptions, the standard industry commission over the years was 5 percent.

Heavy advertising was an important part of Airwick's marketing program. Given the increased competition, it appeared that advertising expenditures would have to increase in order to maintain position against competing products.

Institutional Segment

The Airkem Institutional Division was responsible for two classes of products: commercial products and emergency odor removal products. Commercial products contributed substantially all of the division's sales and profits.

Commercial products included a semisolid odor counteractant trademarked "Solidaire," liquid and spray odor counteractants, odor-controlled insecticides, and sanitary maintenance items, such as disinfectants and detergents. The division also designed, manufactured, and sold equipment to dispense a number of these products and, in Canada, marketed a line of floor and carpet care equipment manufactured by another firm. Commercial products were used by institutions, such as hospitals, nursing homes, schools, and motels. Specialized odor-controlled formulations were sold for spray-system application in atmospheric control of odors emanating from factories and other industrial establishments.

Emergency odor removal products included counteractant formulations designed to remove or reduce certain odors, such as the odor of smoke from fire in residences, automobiles, and commercial and industrial establishments.

The division sold its products principally through about 55 franchised distributors that were responsible for sales in specified geographic areas in the United States and Canada. These distributors resold the products to the ultimate users, or in some cases used them in rendering services to their customers. The franchised distributors in the United States normally used the name "Airkem" in their trade styles.

The division also acted as its own distributor of Airkem products, and performed all the functions of a franchised distributor, through branch offices in 14 geographical areas, four of which were added in 1974. As compared to sales to distributors at the wholesale level, branch office sales direct to consumers produced higher revenues, but the start-up and staffing costs of the branches created higher operating expenses, which adversely affected the earnings of the Institutional division since 1971. In total, the branch offices accounted for 31 percent of the Institutional division's sales in 1973.

The division advertised the products trademarked "Airkem" nationally, principally through print media, and supplied distributors with merchandising aids and promotional literature. In Institutional markets, Airwick competed with many large and small firms. No one firm dominated the market.

The Institutional division competed in a growing market, which was estimated to be $500 million at the consumer dollar level or about $250 million in terms of factory dollars. There was very little data on the size and breakdown of the market since unlike the consumer segment of the business, there was no auditing information service like SAMI.

International Segment

Airwick's household products and some of its Institutional products were also marketed abroad. Marketing in Europe and other international markets was managed by Airkem (Export) Limited, a British subsidiary. This subsidiary accounted for about 97 percent of the sales and substantially all of the profits of the International segment. Its principal plant, located in Hitchin, England, manufactured Airwick concentrates. Marketing in Latin America, the Caribbean, and Taiwan was managed from the home office of the company.

In building up its European-based business, Airwick had adopted the policies of not participating in advertising expenditures (except for the U.K.), not interfering in local marketing issues (all major marketing decisions were left to the distributors), and not signing long-term contracts with distributors.

Pre-tax margins overseas were higher than at home because more expenses were assumed by the overseas distributors than by U.S. distributors. The plant at Hitchin produced the compounds and concentrates sold by the International segment, while the distributors did the finishing and packaging.

Competition in foreign markets was generally less intense than in the United States since odor counteractants and related products were relatively new. The potential for growth in Europe was considered particularly good. While past growth in the International segment was almost entirely due to Airwick Solid, further exploitation of the Airwick Solid concept and the systematic development of the Institutional markets provided a possible source of continued growth in the major E.E.C. countries.

Aquatic Segment

The Aquatic segment of the company was comprised of King-Kratz Corporation and Seablue Corporation. The King-Kratz Corporation, acquired by Airwick in October 1972, produced and marketed a line of chemicals and dispensers for water treatment in swimming pools. King-Kratz and its competitors purchased their basic ingredient, iso-cyanarate, from Monsanto and FMC, and then tableted and/or packaged the various products for sale. King-Kratz products were sold to companies engaged in distributing swimming pool supplies and equipment. These distributors sold to dealers who, in turn, sold or used the products in providing services to pool owners.

Seablue Corporation, acquired by Airwick in January 1974 for $4 million in cash, was a distributor of swimming pool equipment and supplies sold under the trademark "Seablue." It also manufactured and sold high-rate sand filters and diving stands. Seablue Corporation had sales and distribution centers in Atlanta, Baltimore, Charlotte, Cincinnati, Dallas, Houston, Kansas City, Memphis, Miami, and New Orleans, and sold to swimming pool builders swimming pool maintenance and service companies, and specialty stores. Prior to its acquisition by Airwick, Seablue Corporation was the largest customer of King-Kratz Corporation.

Swimming pool chemical needs were predicted to grow at 11 percent during the 1971–75 period. Approximately one-half of these requirements were expected to be in "in- and on-ground pools," with the remaining amount in above-ground pools. (Above-ground pools were the round ones usually found in backyards.)

King-Kratz had a strong position in the in-ground market. They were also strong in nonresidential pools. Growth in these segments was expected by management to continue, provided raw materials were available. However, to get a foothold in the above-ground segment, King-

Kratz would have to develop a home owner–oriented product line and get it into mass merchandisers. This, it was thought by management, would require additional financial and marketing resources.

In 1974, King-Kratz was attempting to "get closer to the dealer" and

EXHIBIT 3

SEABLUE CORPORATION

	Year Ended October 31,			Two Months Ended December 31, 1973
	1971	*1972*	*1973*	*(unaudited)*
Sales......................................	$5,431,475	$7,571,283	$9,575,479	$797,508
Less, cost of goods sold.................	4,081,843	5,702,997	7,155,008	651,030
Gross profit.............................	1,349,632	1,868,286	2,420,471	146,478
Less, selling expenses...................	264,288	360,806	446,611	52,919
Selling profit............................	1,085,344	1,507,480	1,973,860	93,559
Less, general and administrative expenses..............................	777,843	929,759	1,238,289	163,749
Operating profit (loss)....................	307,501	577,721	735,571	(70,190)
Add, Other Income:				
Discounts earned.....................	48,077	67,368	83,799	6,844
Interest income......................	—	4,283	124	89
Rental income........................	—	917	200	—
Currency exchange...................	—	—	14,148	—
Miscellaneous income...............	596	2,037	12,959	2,438
	48,673	74,605	111,230	9,371
Net profit (loss) before other deductions..	356,174	652,326	846,801	(60,819)
Less, Other Deductions				
Discounts allowed....................	52,717	71,701	105,206	10,013
Interest expense.....................	45,185	63,349	129,531	19,866
State income taxes...................	5,210	6,764	12,209	—
Rent expense........................	—	64	295	—
Currency exchange...................	—	(50)	—	(83)
Miscellaneous expense..............	—	—	(1,795)	2,048
	103,112	141,828	245,446	31,844
Net profit (loss) before federal income taxes and extraordinary charges.......	253,062	510,498	601,355	(92,663)
Less, federal income taxes—current.....	110,921	236,246	237,937	(44,989)
federal income taxes—deferred—....	—	—	15,688	1,039
	110,921	236,246	253,625	(43,950)
Net profit (loss) before extraordinary charges..............................	142,141	274,252	347,730	(48,713)
Less, extraordinary charges (write-off of worthless (investment).................	6,000	—	—	—
Net income (loss).......................	$ 136,141	$ 274,252	$ 347,730	$(48,713)
Net income (loss) per share:				
before extraordinary charges........	$2.41	$4.65	$5.89	$(0.83)
less, extraordinary charges..........	0.10	—	—	—
	$2.31	$4.65	$5.89	$(0.83)

to prepare for "going direct" in the near future. This modification in distribution policy was expected to result substantially in increased marketing expenses since the division would (1) pick up new customers to service, (2) be shipping more orders to more customers in smaller lots, and (3) have to spend more contact time with individual dealers.

Seablue's plans included adding products to their line of chemicals, which it purchased from outside suppliers, and diving boards, stands, and filters, which it manufactured. The company also envisioned backward integration by having King-Kratz manufacture more of their products, making more plastic parts themselves, and moving products back from Seablue to King-Kratz for national distribution. In 1974, Seablue was among the lowest performing profit centers in the company. Exhibit 3 shows Seablue's earnings statement for 1971–73.

Advertising

In 1974, Airwick advertised Airwick Solid and Airwick Liquid on a national basis. It advertised On Guard and the Cat Litter Spray in

TABLE 4

Top Five Advertisers in Deodorizer and Air Freshener Market: January–June 1974

Brand	Advertising Dollars (in thousands)
Renuzit	$1,883.1
Airwick	1,615.2
Wizard	1,594.7
Days–Ease	917.3
Glade	708.9

Source: LNA Multi-Media Report Service, Vol. 2, No. 2.

certain selected markets. It also advertised the products trademarked "Airkem" nationally, and supplied distributors with merchandising aids and promotional literature.

Though Airwick was a leading advertiser in the air freshener market, the company could not spend as heavily on advertising as some of the companies with which it competed.

Table 4 shows the total advertising expenditures for the leading marketers of deodorizers and air fresheners during the first six months of 1974.

Manufacturing

In the United States, Airwick manufactured its formulas at its Carlstadt, New Jersey, plant by compounding essential oils, aromatic chemicals, and emulsifying agents. The formulas were then blended with other ingredients and packaged into finished products at Carlstadt and at a second manufacturing facility at St. Peters, Missouri. The company also manufactured plastic packaging components. The King-Kratz products were processed at the company's Missouri plant. Swimming pool filters and diving stands were manufactured at the Seablue Corporation plant in Richardson, Texas.

In Canada, Airwick had in the past subcontracted the manufacture and packaging of most products. In June 1974, the company commenced direct production of some products at a newly leased Canadian facility, and anticipated that most products would be in production at that facility by the end of 1974. The company's British subsidiary manufactured the formulas at its plant in Hitchin, England, which were then transferred to independent distributors to be packaged as finished products and sold under Airwick's trademarks. In Latin America and the Caribbean most of the products were imported in finished form from the United States.

Most of the raw materials used by Airwick were regular articles of commerce and had been historically available in sufficient quantities for its manufacturing operations. However, since the latter part of 1973, the company experienced industry-wide shortages of some basic chemical components, including chlorine and disinfectant chemicals. These shortages limited the company's ability to expand sales and production in its Institutional and Aquatic marketing segments.

Research and Development

Airwick's research and development program was primarily directed toward the development of new products and the improvement of present products. Theoretical studies were conducted relative to release mechanisms for odor control products and odor perception, counteraction, and measurement. Company engineers designed and developed dispensing units, and designed and maintained molds used for forming containers, for the company's products. The research and development department was responsible for quality control and package design for the company's products, and also furnished technical assistance to the field sales organization.

There were 38 employees in this department in 1974, of whom 26 held degrees in chemistry, biology, or engineering. Expenditures for company-sponsored research and development were approximately

$418,000, $488,000, and $629,000 during 1971, 1972, and 1973, respectively, and $671,000 was budgeted for 1974.

ASSESSMENT OF AIRWICK ACQUISITION

Conclusions and Recommendations of the Airwick Task Force

After two weeks of interviewing and analysis, the Airwick Task Force concluded that if CIBA-GEIGY had a strategic interest in entering the household products business, Airwick could be an attractive way of doing it—assuming the price was not excessive.

The detailed findings of the Airwick Task Force included the following points:

1. Airwick is a profitable company whose earnings may have temporarily plateaued due to severe competition in the Consumer segment of their business.
2. Competition in the Consumer segment of the business will definitely restrict growth and reduce profitability of this segment in the immediate years ahead. Indeed, without a more carefully prepared marketing plan, a well-conceived new products program, and additional advertising expenditures, it will be difficult to achieve an increase in sales of much more than 5–6 percent annually.
3. The Institutional segment of Airwick (Airkem Institutional Division) is in excellent shape. They have good management, good products, and a good marketing program. They participate in a large, fractured market where the leading competitor is estimated to have only 8 percent share of the market as compared to an estimated 5 percent for Airwick. There is good potential for this division.
4. The International segment appears to be a profitable part of Airwick in terms of contribution as a percent of revenues. Current growth rates can most likely be maintained.
5. While the Aquatic segment appears to be healthy, it does not appear to be the kind of business that would normally be attractive for CIBA–GEIGY.
6. Airwick's present financial position is difficult because of a need for cash. At year-end 1973, the company had only a minimum of debt outstanding, but as of May 7, 1974 it had $8 million in short-term loans outstanding paying prime interest rates. The cash shortage seems to have been caused by the recent acquisition of the Seablue Corporation for $4 million in cash; the necessity of building inventories for the Aquatic segment of the business, which is

seasonal; and the turndown in Airwick's Consumer business over the last nine months.

7. Production is relatively simple and efficient. While the new St. Peters plant is impressive, the Carlstadt, New Jersey, plant is overcrowded and needs immediate relief.

8. The research and development activity appears to be suffering from underfunding and a lack of direction.

9. Airwick appears to be highly people oriented. The president addresses a substantial number of employees by their first name and seems to know a great deal about them. This personal attention is reflected in their benefit programs which appear to compare favorably with those of CIBA–GEIGY.

10. Potential synergisms:

   a. Madison Laboratories has personnel with marketing skills which may help Airwick; Airwick has the sales organization which Madison Laboratories lacks.

   b. CIBA–GEIGY has money which Airwick needs to grow.

   c. CIBA–GEIGY has available space and equipment which may be useful to Airwick.

   d. CIBA–GEIGY's chemical ability and research facilities could improve Airwick's products and provide Airwick with a better research and development effort with little increase in incremental costs.

   e. CIBA–GEIGY's Agricultural Division has products which could be marketed by Airwick.

11. A savings of $1 million in Airwick's overhead could be achieved which would add to the return of any contemplated investment in Airwick.

Questions Raised by Mr. MacKinnon and the Acquisitions Task Force

Despite the conclusions of the Airwick Task Force, Mr. MacKinnon and the Acquisitions Task Force were concerned by several unresolved questions. For a start, it had not yet been firmly decided whether or not CIBA–GEIGY Corporation should be in the household products business. Neither was it clear that Airwick Industries was the best vehicle for developing a position in this business if, indeed, it was decided that household products was an appropriate field for CIBA–GEIGY Corporation. In addition, there was concern as to how to go about valuing a company whose major division was in a deteriorating competitive position. Linked to this concern was uncertainty over the appropriate negotiating strategy for a company like Airwick. Finally, assuming that Airwick could be acquired for the "right" price, it was not clear how this multinational business would fit into the geographic-based management structure of the CIBA–GEIGY group of companies.

These questions had special importance in the spring of 1974 since CIBA–GEIGY was just completing a tender offer for a majority of the shares of a hybrid seed company and was holding discussions with two other acquisition candidates complementing other areas of CIBA–GEIGY's business. While these diversifying acquisitions, if consummated, would not eliminate the possibility of further acquisitions, there was concern that post-merger problems would consume more top-management time and corporate funds than currently expected.

Household Products. Prior to the merger of CIBA and GEIGY, policy in both companies vacillated with respect to consumer products. After the merger, the group decided that consumer product markets should be considered an appropriate area for growth. Household products, lawn and garden products, and toiletries were targeted as prime opportunity areas. However, each local subsidiary had the freedom to decide for itself whether or not it was worthwhile entering any of these consumer market segments.

The potential acquisition of Airwick posed a "fish or cut bait" decision for CIBA–GEIGY with respect to consumer products, in general, and household products, specifically. In fact, CIBA–GEIGY was seriously considering divesting the small Madison Laboratories Division which was having a great deal of difficulty selling toiletries, developed for the most part in Switzerland, in the U.S. market. Madison had annual sales in the $8–$9 million range, and was only breaking even at the contribution to corporate overhead level. By the time the Airwick acquisition study was presented, CIBA–GEIGY had already held three sets of discussions with companies interested in acquiring Madison.

In analyzing both Madison and Airwick, an important question was whether research, product quality, and strong patents—CIBA–GEIGY's special strengths—were relevant to their long-run success. Superficial features often played an important role in such products, and this could offend the Swiss business philosophy. Consideration had to be given to the fact that advertising budgets could reduce profits for several years, and that this, too, might not be satisfactory. Finally, there was only limited management experience in the consumer products area.

At the same time, the Swiss parent had a small research program going in the household odor area, and several European subsidiaries were participants in the Institutional cleaning market.

Assessment of Airwick. Mr. MacKinnon and the Acquisitions Task Force agreed with the Airwick Task Force that the Institutional segment of Airwick had good potential and might be able to provide an outlet for some CIBA–GEIGY products handled by the Agricultural division. On the other hand, the domestic Consumer segment was an area of concern. Airwick's sales projections seemed unrealistically optimistic, but there was no way of revising these estimates on any scientific basis under the current press of events. Furthermore, it was suspected that Airwick might have to develop a catch-up advertising program since the company had fallen behind the competition in this area. Finally, the softening U.S. economy was not an encouraging environment for nonessential consumer goods.

Even the attractive European market for Airwick's consumer products posed a troublesome dilemma. What would Airwick gain if it built the market abroad, only to see the big consumer products companies in Europe buying into the new market with "me-too" products at a lower price?

Airwick's Aquatic operations were another concern. While they represented one-third of Airwick Industries' total sales, CIBA–GEIGY had already decided on its own against going into this business. Both the president and chairman of Airwick had indicated to Mr. MacKinnon that neither a spin-off of this business to Airwick shareholders nor a straight sale of the division would be acceptable to them. Since they controlled over 30 percent of the outstanding shares between them, their wishes in the matter had to be considered carefully.

Valuation and Negotiating Strategy.   The valuation issue was complicated not only by the deteriorating competitive position of Airwick's Consumer Brands Division, but also by the difficulty in establishing a value for discrete parts of Airwick's business. Joint use of assets by the several divisions made asset-based analysis highly tenuous.

Recent movement in Airwick's stock price complicated both the valuation and negotiating tasks. As a practical fact, Mr. MacKinnon knew that CIBA–GEIGY Corporation would have to pay Airwick shareholders a premium over market value. But on what basis should this premium be figured? During the first quarter of 1974 the price of Airwick's shares held steady around the $8 level. However, as both parties were preparing to enter final negotiations, the price of Airwick's shares ran up to about $10 per share. Since Airwick was being actively courted by other potential acquirors, Mr. MacKinnon suspected that news of potential merger negotiations had somehow leaked to the financial community. The resulting problem was what price would be required for the Airwick shareholders to feel they were receiving a substantial enough premium to support the acquisition. Exhibit 4 shows the price range of Airwick's common stock through the second quarter of 1974. It also shows the number of unexercised options held by Airwick's officers and directors.

While CIBA–GEIGY had decided that a tender offer would be the most appropriate acquisition vehicle in this case, several management issues had to be resolved before such an offer could be made to the

EXHIBIT 4

CIBA–GEIGY CORPORATION (B)
Price Range of Airwick's Common Stock*

	High	Low
1972:		
First quarter..........................	$14.28	$ 9.12
Second quarter.......................	21.88	13.78
Third quarter..........................	24.81	17.50
Fourth quarter.......................	23.38	18.68
1973:		
First quarter..........................	23.63	14.13
Second quarter.......................	19.38	13.38
Third quarter..........................	24.38	15.88
Fourth quarter.......................	23.88	8.50
1974:		
First quarter..........................	11.00	6.50
Second quarter.......................	13.00	6.00

* Adjusted to reflect a 3 for 2 stock split in May 1972 and a 2 for 1 stock split in February 1973.

Unexercised Options, All Directors and Officers, April 4, 1974
Number of shares......................... 97,300
Average option price...................... $6.89

public. Airwick Industries had a stock option and bonus program for its management employees, while CIBA–GEIGY Corporation did not have stock options. There was thus a question about how to handle the stock options and whether or not to continue the Airwick bonus program if Airwick were merged with CIBA–GEIGY. In addition, since CIBA–GEIGY Corporation had never written management contracts with its key employees, a decision was needed as to what to do if such contracts were requested during the negotiations.

Organizational Issues. A final question of concern was how to integrate Airwick Industries into the CIBA–GEIGY management structure, if it were acquired. Under current arrangements, consumer product companies normally reported to country-based subsidiaries of CIBA–GEIGY Limited. Thus, consumer product companies in France reported to CIBA–GEIGY (France). This arrangement presented problems in the Airwick case, since the company had a major International segment operated from England. If current patterns were followed, Airkem (Export) Ltd. would have to be separated to some extent from the U.S. operations. This arrangement, it was feared, might lead to a decreased commitment on the part of Airwick's domestic managers to international development.

An alternate arrangement would be for the CIBA–GEIGY Corporation to assume direct responsibility for Airwick's worldwide operations.

This posed difficult questions, too. How could you take direct business responsibility away from France for Airwick's French business when they have done such a good job for Airwick on a distributor basis in the past? What kind of commitment to Airwick products could you expect from French managers if everything were to be directed from New York?

A final alternative was to have Airwick report directly to Switzerland. This however, would involve a major break in CIBA–GEIGY's worldwide operating philosophy.

3

CML Group, Inc.

In early January, 1971, John Morgan, general manager of Hood Sail-makers, Inc., the world's largest and most prestigious manufacturer of sails for big ocean racing yachts, was trying to make a final decision on whether to recommend to Hood's board of directors that $314,000 be requested for the establishment of a sailcloth weaving mill in Ireland. Hood had been a wholly owned subsidiary of the CML Group since February of 1970 but still operated with its own board of directors.[1] The project, even if recommended, would require approval by CML Group management, however, because of its size and nature. Hood was but one of the four recent acquisitions in the "leisure time" field that made up the CML Group, a company which had attained an annual sales volume of over $11 million in its first year and a half of operations.

In Mr. Morgan's opinion, several factors favored the investment. It represented a 13 percent after-tax return (based on cash flow) for the division, substantially better than Hood was making on its present asset base. Perhaps more importantly, both Ted Hood, founder and current president of the division, and his father, R. S. Hood, an influential Hood board member and general manager of the Hood cloth manufacturing operation, were in favor of the project, as they both felt that it would significantly enhance the long-run competitive position of the company and was therefore an important strategic move.

Mr. Morgan recognized that going ahead with the investment presented certain difficulties, however, and that several of these were of particular concern to CML corporate management. Most significant was

---

[1] Hood's board included five members, three chosen by the Hood family and two by CML.

571

Hood's sales and profits slump during fiscal 1970, when earnings had dropped about 30 percent from their peak year level. Though profitability was considerably better in the current year, sales had not risen appreciably above the prior year. As Hood had doubled its weaving capacity in 1968, only about 50 percent of existing weaving capacity was currently being utilized. Under such circumstances, corporate management's reluctance to invest in substantially increased capacity for Hood was understandable, especially in view of opportunities to invest in other divisions. Corporate management also questioned Hood's ability to take on a major new commitment in light of the many pressing issues already demanding management time and energy. Secrecy surrounding Hood's unique weaving process presented a further problem. All Hood sailcloth was currently woven in the very closely guarded Marblehead facility. A second mill naturally increased Hood's risk of exposure. Finally, uncertainties such as future tariff levels, fluctuation in domestic demand, and possible competitive moves and reactions complicated the economic analysis.

Since Mr. Morgan had joined Hood as general manager only nine months earlier and had no prior experience in the industry, he recognized that he was still in a transition period with regard to learning an entirely new business and establishing his own position within the company. Several factors made it important to come to some decision on the Irish project fairly soon, however. Although the Industrial Development Authority (IDA) of the Irish government had agreed to supply as a nonrepayable grant $266,000 of the $580,000 total funds required, Hood had already requested several extensions of the original deadline for purchasing land and commencing construction. While Mr. Morgan felt that a further extension could probably be obtained, he sensed that an increasingly wide credibility gap was developing on the part of IDA over Hood's real intentions in Ireland. In addition, preliminary planning for the Irish facility, which had already cost Hood about $20,000 since early 1969, was currently being funded by Hood at the rate of $1,000 per month in retainer fees and travel expenses. Further delay was therefore both risky and expensive.

CML GROUP DEVELOPMENT

In May 1969, Charles Leighton, Robert Todd, and Sam Frederick[2] resigned from the Willard Corporation, a large diversified manufactur-

---

[2] *Charles Leighton* (36 in 1971); M.B.A., Harvard Business School, 1960; product line manager, Mine Safety Appliances Corporation, 1963–64; instructor in management of new enterprises at the Harvard Business School, 1964–65; Group vice president, Willard Corporation Leisure Time Group, 1965–69.

Robert Tod (32); M.B.A., Harvard Business School, 1967; project engineer,

ing company which had grown largely by acquisition, in order to establish their own company in the leisure time field.

Mr. Leighton had joined Willard in 1965 as group officer in charge of three divisions (a jewelry manufacturer and two boat manufacturers) with total sales of $7 million per year. Throughout the next four years internal growth and six acquisitions had raised the sales of the renamed "Leisure Time Group" to about $70 million; profits grew at about 25 percent per year during this period. By the time Mr. Leighton and his colleagues left the Willard Corporation in 1969 their group was one of the largest, most profitable, and most rapidly growing groups in the company, which then had sales of several hundred million dollars.

In the spring of 1969, Mr. Leighton described the original objectives of CML as follows in a short pamphlet prepared for prospective investors:[3]

> We want to build an organization devoted to self-expression and individual creativity for profit. Basically, we intend to use the skills demonstrated by our success at Willard to build our own diversified company in the leisure time field. Our plan is to acquire companies and to operate them on a decentralized basis so that chief executives of acquired companies retain full authority for management of their business, with us at the corporate level providing supplementary assistance in the form of long-range planning help, marketing and manufacturing consultation, accounting, and, most importantly, strong financial control and support. We are looking for companies with top-quality product lines and excellent trade names in businesses where management experience and creativity are more important to success than bricks and mortar. Companies we'll be interested in will generally have been founded by men with great creativity from a product standpoint, but who basically dislike the administrative burdens of running a growing business. A key element of our strategy is therefore to provide administrative assistance to these companies, thereby freeing up more of an owner-manager's time for the really creative things he's most interested in. Another key aspect is motivation. We plan to acquire companies only on an earn-out basis so that the owner-manager is fully motivated to realize the growth and profit potential which we feel are in the business when we buy it.
>
> From a financial standpoint our objectives are the following: growth in corporate earnings per share of at least 20 percent per year, a pretax return on CML's investment in acquired companies of at least 20 percent, and a 12½ percent annual profit growth of acquired companies.

Hooker Chemical, January–September 1967; Group operations manager, Willard Corporation Leisure Time Group, 1967–69.

Sam Frederick (36); M.B.A., Columbia, 1962; accounting with Arthur Andersen & Co., 1962–68; Group controller, Willard Corporation Leisure Time Group, 1968–69.

[3] See Exhibit 1 for further discussion of objectives appearing in CML's first annual report.

With these objectives in mind CML's co-founders established the new company in early June 1969. Two million dollars of outside equity funds were raised in just ten days by selling 50 percent of the company to 18 large investors.[4] The best known of these was a major national foundation which invested $400,000 in the company, choosing CML Group for one of its first attempts to invest in new ventures. The four co-founders paid a total of $40,000 for the remaining 50 percent of the equity.[5] Mr. Leighton described as follows the relative ease with which outside equity funds were obtained despite the unfavorable economic climate prevailing at the time:

> At that time, we hadn't made any attempt yet to negotiate with prospective acquisitions, so we couldn't talk specific companies to financial backers. Despite this, we felt we had several things to offer. First, we represented a team whose combined skills balanced out any individual weaknesses. I've always maintained that covering yourself on weaknesses is far more important than having outstanding but spotty strengths. Second, we had a very good four-year track record at Willard. Third, we had a concept of management which we had spelled out in detail in a recent *Harvard Business Review* article and which had already proved itself at Willard. Finally, we had two very influential men behind us. One was my father-in-law, Dan Smith,[6] who provided invaluable advice and experience. Homer Luther was the other. At 29 he was already an extremely successful and influential investment manager. I had met him in 1964 while he was an MBA student at Harvard. We got to know each other as a result of a Creative Marketing study he made of the product line I handled at Mine Safety Appliances. We had kept in touch off and on since then, and after we decided to leave Willard we called him, since he had told me that if we ever needed money we should come to him. His introductions to potential investors and his assistance in general were invaluable. Dan Smith and Homer also became substantial investors in CML, and both are very active directors of the company.

EXHIBIT 1

CML GROUP, INC.
Excerpt from a Letter to the Stockholders, July 30, 1970

To Our Stockholders:

A little over a year ago, the CML Group, Inc., was founded on the premise that a variety of new skills will be needed for business success

---

[4] A total of 800 shares of convertible preference stock (convertible on a 1 for 1 basis) and 3,200 shares of common stock were sold to outside investors for $500 per share. As no investment banking fees were paid, total cost of the issue was only $364.

[5] A total of 4,000 shares of common stock were sold to the four co-founders at $10 per share.

[6] Dan T. Smith, Professor Emeritus of Finance, Harvard Business School.

EXHIBIT 1 (*continued*)

in the 1970s. The ability to provide an environment which would encourage creative product development and innovative marketing will become a key success factor. Our previous business experience led us to believe that the orientation of business toward individual creativity could attract imaginative entrepreneurs and result in a high rate of profitable growth. Of course, financial control, production, and the other customary management skills will remain critical to the success of any business.

The "leisure-time" industry is the best candidate for the implementation of this theory because it contains a number of very creative people who founded companies with interesting products. As a result of increasing discretionary income in all levels of society, this industry also has a high growth rate. It was decided to group several of these companies into one corporation emphasizing performance and quality.

Widespread equity ownership among the managers of the companies would provide strong motivation for capital growth and act as a measure of their common success. The creative leaders could become even more productive by delegating their administrative burdens and financial problems to qualified persons. An active corporate management team would be able to introduce modern control systems and other management tools to support long-term growth. The diversity of experience and skills of the CML management team would be an advantage in this effort. Accordingly, the CML Group was incorporated in June of 1969.

The principal objectives of the Group were established at the outset as follows:

First of all, the Group would seek several outstanding "leisure-time" companies to provide a base for business operations. At the same time, the Group would keep itself in a strong financial position. Bank relationships would be developed and lines of credit established. A pattern would be established for the integration of new members into the Group; this would include the strengthening of autonomous management whenever necessary and the introduction of an extensive, but easily administered control system.

Secondly, the Group would begin immediately to prepare itself for a public offering of its stock at the most favorable opportunity in the next few years. Improved marketability of the Group's common stock would provide a better tool for use in attracting additional companies and employees and would improve the original subscribers' return on their capital investment. The Group determined that a high rate growth in sales and profits of each company after joining the Group would be the most important factor in valuing the Group's stock at the time of public sale. Also important would be a record of making prudent acquisitions.

Ultimately and most importantly, the Group would begin to build for the long term. The desired environment would be developed slowly to ensure that creativity and innovation became permanent

EXHIBIT 1 *(concluded)*

characteristics of the Group. The best management teams take time to form, particularly when business practices are considered a complement to innovation and art rather than the dominant force. The control systems would have to be structured so that the effect of changes within and without the business could easily be assessed and recognized.

Source: A letter to the stockholders appearing in CML Group, Inc.'s, July 31, 1970, annual report.

Acquired Businesses

Exhibit 2 shows CML's balance sheet as of July 31, 1969, shortly after registration of the new company and before any acquisitions had been made, and as of July 31, 1970, following one year of operations. During its first year CML acquired four companies and reported fiscal 1970 sales of approximately $11 million (see Exhibit 3 for the first year's operating results). Terms of purchase for acquired companies appear in Exhibit 4. A brief account of each acquired company follows.

Boston Whaler, Inc.   Boston Whaler, CML's largest division, was estimated to be the tenth largest U.S. manufacturer of outboard boats. CML's 1970 annual report described this division as follows:

> The first company to join the CML Group was Boston Whaler, Inc., of Rockland, Massachusetts, in September, 1969. Their principal product is the Boston Whaler outboard motor boat. A 30 percent interest in Boston Whaler Bearcat, Inc., manufacturer of nonpolluting 4-cycle outboard engines, was acquired at the same time. Dick Fisher, the chairman of Boston Whaler, has been instrumental in the founding of several companies requiring a high level of technical skill. The creativity and innovative talents of Mr. Fisher made this company particularly attractive as the first member of the Group.
>
> The Boston Whaler meets the high quality criteria of the Group. [A well-known consumer report] has rated Boston Whaler as the most outstanding outboard boat produced in the United States. The boats are easily identified by their distinctive and functional shape and a well-regarded trademark. Boston Whalers are made of a monolithic casting of plastic foam with a smooth molded fiberglass "crust" on both sides. This construction causes the Boston Whaler to be extremely durable, and unsinkable. No other boat manufacturing company has developed the technical skills needed to build a comparable product.
>
> An asset with long-term growth implications is the Boston Whaler marketing organization. There are eight sales representatives whose principal products are the Boston Whaler and Bearcat engines. More than 700 dealers are located throughout the world. The dealers are known to be the most reputable in the industry. Obviously, other prod-

EXHIBIT 2

CML GROUP, INC.
Consolidated Balance Sheet as of July 31, 1969 and 1970
(thousands of dollars)

Assets	1969	1970
Current assets		
Cash..	$ 242	$ 731
Short-term commercial paper....................	1,787	—
Net receivables.................................	—	1,217
Inventories......................................	—	2,433
Prepaid expenses...............................	14	109
Total current assets..........................	$2,042	$4,490
Property, plant, and equipment (net)..............	3	2,143
Investments and other assets		
Investments.....................................	—	876
Excess of cost over net book value of		
acquisitions...................................	—	1,959
Other assets....................................	7	137
Total Assets................................	$2,052	$9,604
Liabilities and Stockholders' Equity		
Total Current Liabilities............................	$ 14	$2,545
Long-term debt....................................	—	3,424
Subordinated convertible debenture...............	—	498
Stockholders' equity*		
Preference stock (par value $.10.................	1	1
Common stock (par value $.10)..................	1	1
Capital in excess of par.........................	2,038	2,771
Retained earnings..............................	(2)	364
Total Equity...................................	$2,038	$3,137
Total Liabilities and Equity.................	$2,052	$9,604

* Stockholders' equity information:

Source of Equity	Number of Shares Outstanding		
	Convertible Preference	Common	
	Nonfounders	Non-founders	Founders
Sold during June 1969..............	800 (Series A)	3,200	4,000
Exchanged to acquire Boston Whaler...........................	1,000 (Series B)		
Exchanged to acquire Hood Sailmakers......................	4,600 (Series C)		
Sold during summer of 1970.........		920	
Total outstanding as of 7–31–70.....................	6,400	4,120	4,000

Series A ranks on a parity with common stock with respect to voting and dividend privileges. May be converted by holder into common stock at any time on a share-for-share basis. May be redeemed by CML any time after September 30, 1971, at the original selling price ($500 per share).

Series B ranks on a parity with common stock with respect to voting privileges. Receives a preferential annual dividend of $10 per share. See footnote in Exhibit 4 for conversion privileges.

Series C ranks on a parity with common shares with respect to voting and dividend privileges. See footnote in Exhibit 4 for conversion privileges.

Source: Company records for 1969; annual report for 1970. Errors are due to rounding.

ucts can be sold through this system as they are developed or acquired by Boston Whaler.

During the current fiscal year, Boston Whaler has introduced a new product, the "Outrage," a larger outboard boat with a new and distinctive hull configuration. A patent application is pending to cover the boat design. It is expected that the boat will have a pronounced effect on the design of larger outboard boats.

Major programs now under way in cost savings, manufacturing efficiency, and overhead reductions are expected to improve profitability to a level in excess of all previous years.

Despite modest volume and profit declines during 1970, Boston Whaler's long-term sales growth was expected to run somewhat above the 8 percent average for the industry. In addition, significant profit increases at current sales levels were expected reasonably quickly through improving margins. These had consistently run well under half the

EXHIBIT 3

CML GROUP, INC.
*Consolidated Statement of Income and Retained Earnings
for the Year Ended July 31, 1970
(thousands of dollars)*

Net sales..		$11,109
Less costs and expenses		
Cost of goods sold................................	$7,943	
General, selling, and administrative..............	2,553	10,496
Income from operations......................		613
Interest expense (net)...........................		190
Income before income taxes..................		423
Provision for income taxes*.....................		217
Net income ($21.25 per share)†...............		206
Deficit, beginning of year........................		(2)
Retained earnings of pooled companies..........		161
Retained earnings, end of year..................		$ 365

* Represents a reserve against future income tax payments. No income taxes were paid in 1970. Income for tax purposes had been reduced to zero as a result of:
  a) A tax loss carryforward in connection with a relatively minor portion of one subsidiary's business spun off at the time of acquisition.
  b) Amortization charges in connection with certain assets revalued for tax purposes at the time of acquisition.
  † The annual report comments as follows upon earnings per share: Net income per common share and common equivalent share is based on the 9,675 weighted average number of shares outstanding. For purposes of computing net income per common share, the convertible preference shares—Series A, B, and C— are considered to be common stock equivalents. The weighted average number of common and common equivalent shares assume conversion of the Series A on a share-for-share basis and the Series B and C on the basis of the number of shares issuable at the last sales price of common stock and the current level of income affecting the conversion rate of these securities.
  The 7 percent subordinated convertible debentures and stock options are not included in the net income per share computations, as their effect is not dilutive.
  Source: 1970 annual report.

EXHIBIT 4

CML GROUP, INC.
Terms of Payment for Companies Acquired

Accounting Treatment	Name of Company	Acquisition Date	Original Payment in Shares of CML Stock		Original Payment in Cash and Notes (thousands of dollars)		Additional Earn-out (thousands of dollars)	
			Common	Convertible Preference	Cash	Notes	Minimum	Maximum
Pooling.........	Boston Whaler	9/30/69	250	1,000			$ 500*	$2,975*
Pooling.........	Hood Sailmakers	2/25/70	400	4,600			1,600†	5,000†
Purchase........	Carroll Reed	10/1/70			$700	$ 600	400‡	400‡
Purchase........	Mason & Sullivan	5/1/70			450	1,050	1,100‡	1,100‡

* Represents conversion value of 1,000 shares of convertible preference stock. Conversion value is contingent upon the earnings of Boston Whaler, Inc., for the period beginning 8/1/69 and ending 7/31/74, and on the market price of CML's common stock at the time of conversion.
† Represents conversion value of 4,600 shares of convertible preference stock. Conversion value is contingent upon the earnings of Hood Sailmakers, Inc., for the period beginning 8/1/70 and ending 7/31/75, and on the market price of CML's common stock at the time of conversion.
‡ Additional cash amount payable through 1974 contingent upon achievement of certain earnings by the purchased company.
Source: 1970 annual report.

level of Willard's outboard runabout divisions of equivalent size, which CML management knew well from their previous experience.

Carroll Reed Ski Shops.   This division was described as follows in CML's 1970 annual report:

> The [Carroll Reed] Ski Shops, which joined the Group in October 1969, are a series of retail stores and a national mail-order business headquartered in North Conway, New Hampshire.
>
> The business was founded by Carroll Reed in 1936 to service the burgeoning ski areas in northern New England. Mr. Reed's creative merchandising skills are the principal reason for the store's development into one of the country's best-known ski shops. The company has become known for its its extremely high quality merchandise, excellent service, and unique "country store" style that appeals to both men and women.
>
> In the early spring, an Executive Vice President [and General Manager] was employed by Mr. Reed. The new individual has had significant merchandising experience and will be of value in the day-to-day management of the business. This new management depth will better allow Mr. Reed to concentrate on the future expansion of the business. The Group believes that the company employees are a major asset who provide an excellent foundation for future growth.
>
> During the fiscal year, the mail-order handling systems were substantially improved by the construction of a 6,000 square foot addition in North Conway for order processing and additional storage space. The order processing was improved by introducing computerized equipment on a limited basis. A new ski shop of approximately 4,000 square feet is about to open in Simsbury, Connecticut, as the first in a planned program of store expansion.
>
> Three residents of the northern New England area have been elected to the Board of Directors of Carroll Reed Ski Shops, Inc., and participate actively in the long-term planning for the business. They are Tom Corcoran [M.B.A., Harvard Business School, 1959], a former Olympic skier and President of Waterville Valley ski area; Malcolm McNair, Professor Emeritus of Retailing at Harvard Business School, and Leon Gorman, President of L. L. Bean, Inc., in Freeport, Maine.
>
> Growth opportunities exist for Carroll Reed Ski Shops in the gradual expansion of the retail store business. The mail-order business can be further expanded without significant addition of facilities or personnel. Carroll Reed Ski Shops also provides a vantage point to study several fast-growing sectors of the leisure time industry.

Mr. Reed had played a leading role as one of the early pioneers in recreational skiing in this country and had opened the first U.S. ski lift and school, headed by world-famous Hans Schneider, in Jackson, New Hampshire, in the early 1930s. Several years later he sold his interest in the ski area and founded Carroll Reed Ski Shops (CRSS) in nearby

North Conway. Not long after joining CML Mr. Reed described CRSS's success over the years to the casewriter, as follows:

> When my wife and I began this business in 1936 we had no idea it would ever grow to what it has become. We simply did not want to go back to Boston, liked the Conway area very much, and felt we could make a living here in this kind of business by treating customers well so that they would stop in and buy something from us the next time they passed through the area. I feel that many of our customers have come to feel a personal closeness to Kay and me and like the way we do business, and that this is what has brought them back over the years. It's this personal touch, a certain integrity in what we stand for in each transaction, that gives us something special to offer. This is the main basis on which we are able to compete with large city stores selling much the same type of merchandise as we do.

During the summer of 1970, Mr. Tod made the following observations about CRSS:

> Carroll Reed has a number of important strengths. Most important are its reputation, based upon the quality and style of the items sold; its interesting, well-laid-out store in North Conway, which accounts for nearly half of total sales; its masculine image, despite the fact that 70 percent of all merchandise sold is for women; and the courteous, service-oriented manner of its retail people. They have unusually capable people with exceptionally high employee morale compared to others in their industry.
>
> Carroll Reed's mailing list for catalogue sales, which account for about half of total sales, is another valuable asset. Average order size is nearly four times that of the mail-order industry as a whole, and about double that for small specialty houses like Carroll Reed. Another strength is Carroll's wide delegation of buying responsibility to six buyers. In most operations of their size, the top man tries to do all the buying himself.
>
> The division's primary weakness, however, is its geographical dependence on one region—North Conway. This is alleviated somewhat by a couple of factors. Catalogue sales reach a customer group scattered across the country. Even retail sales are not confined to North Conway residents. Because of its location as both a winter and summer resort, North Conway draws large numbers throughout the year from all over New England and Middle Atlantic states. Partly as a result of these factors their product line has shifted significantly from almost 100 percent ski equipment in the early years to an increasing percentage of primarily women's fashion sportswear, and now less than one-third of their volume is ski related.
>
> Another weakness is their dependence on one retail outlet for selling marked-down merchandise from the catalog business. This problem is

particularly pressing because of the current push to expand catalogue sales. Retail outlets are needed to dispose of unsold merchandise at the end of the catalogue season. The current procedure is to turn much of this over to the discount basement of a large downtown Boston department store at about 17% of Carroll Reed's retail price.[7]

Mr. Tod felt there were several additional areas of CRSS's operation in need of some strengthening, including internal controls (such as inventory and catalog order processing) and market knowledge in the mail-order area. He thought that an expansion of mail-order sales was CRSS's greatest opportunity for profit growth. The second major retail store, which was being planned for Simsbury, Connecticut, would provide both a non–New Hampshire retail outlet and an additional retail outlet for the resulting increase in markdowns.

Mason & Sullivan Company.   CML's 1970 annual report described this division as follows:

> The projected growth rate for the hobby sector is among the highest of the "leisure time" market because of early retirement and a renewed interest in hand work. The Group entered one of the fastest growing segments of the industry when Mason & Sullivan of Osterville, Massachusetts, joined in June. This business sells clocks, barometers, and music boxes in kit form and by mail.
>
> The founder, Ed Lebo, purchases the working parts of the various items in Europe. Wood, metal trim, and other parts are purchased from numerous suppliers in the New England area. Because the designs are largely antique reproductions with hand-crafted movements, there is virtually no model obsolescence.
>
> The company has two unique assets. It has a high quality reputation among woodworking hobbyists throughout the United States and Canada; it also has established relationships with craftsmen-suppliers in Austria, Germany, Switzerland, and England.
>
> Shortly after Mason & Sullivan joined the Group, the former chief executive of a large mail-order house was employed as Vice President and General Manager to assist in the day-to-day operations of the business. Efforts are being made to introduce control and information systems to support future profitable growth.
>
> Mr. Lebo plans to expand the product line to include other related items.

Hood Sailmakers, Inc.   By any index, Hood was clearly the leading supplier of sails for large ocean yachts (over 40 feet in length), commanding over 50 percent of the U.S. market. Exhibit 5 shows the text of a *Yachting* magazine article describing the company and its products.

---

[7] Approximately 10 percent (at retail valuation) of total sales were made at markdown prices.

EXHIBIT 5

CML GROUP, INC.
A Reprint from Yachting, *September 1970*

Ted Hood: Sailmaker to the Twelves
by B. D. Burrill

"They are the ultimate teaching and testing ground as far as we're concerned. A Twelve is under sail as much in three months as the average cruising boat in five years." Speaking was Frederick E. "Ted" Hood, the 43-year-old Marblehead, Mass., sailmaker who has made more sails for 12-Meter yachts than any man alive. And perhaps no man in the years since 1958, with the possible exception of Olin Stephens, has contributed more to keeping the America's Cup firmly bolted in the New York YC's trophy room than this genius of boat speed. During these years a small sailmaking operation that started in 1950 has grown into one of the world's largest, to a great extent as a result of the success his 12-Meter sails have enjoyed.

Ted Hood's involvement with the America's Cup and 12-Meter boats began in 1958 when he served in the cockpit of *Vim* during her brilliant bid to become the Cup defender. He served as an advisor to skipper Bus Mosbacher on sail trim and tactics, and generally made himself useful where help was needed. One day, when working on a coffee grinder, he somehow managed to loosen the bolted-down winch—Ted would be a good man aboard any boat on the basis of his physical strength alone.

Hood got his chance to make sails for *Vim* after her owner, the late Capt. Jack Matthews, had seen the sails he produced for the 5.5-Meter *Quixotic*, a Ray Hunt design built and sailed by Ted, which narrowly missed becoming the 1956 U.S. Olympic representative. In spite of a DSQ in the next to last race, *Quixotic* had only to beat one boat in the final race to win the trials. Well up in the fleet on the final leg, the main halyard shackle unaccountably opened, the sail came down, and she finished last. So Ted's first experience with Meter boats wasn't very happy. But he also made sails for *Easterner* and *Weatherly* in 1958 and two famous red-top spinnakers borrowed from *Vim*, "Big Harry" and "Little Harry," were used by *Columbia* in her successful defense of the Cup.

In 1962 Ted designed and made just about everything except the hull and winches for *Nefertiti* which was the last boat eliminated in the trials by *Weatherly*, which had Bus Mosbacher at the helm. All of the Twelves, including the Australian challenger *Gretel*, used Hood sails that summer. *Gretel*, in fact, used a mainsail made in 1957 for *Vim* in the race she won over *Weatherly* in '62. This would seem ultimate proof of a theory which Ted still believes strongly, particularly with respect to mainsails, that good sails get better with age if they receive proper care. A Dacron sail develops a certain "set" much like the old cotton sails. After a few years the fabric has settled down and stretch is gone.

EXHIBIT 5 (continued)

One anecdote of the '62 campaign bears repeating. Just before the final trial races between *Weatherly* and *Nefertiti,* Ted Hood spent a whole day, at Mosbacher's request, on the rival Twelve making sure her sails were the best possible. Some sails even went off to Marblehead for recutting and were rushed back in time to be used against him. Some of *Nefy's* crew felt this hurt their chances, but it's a mark of the man that he only wanted to win over the best possible boat, and he'd rather have been beaten by *Weatherly* than the Aussies. Hood now doubts that he'd ever again have the time to get involved in designing and campaigning a Twelve, business being what it is.

Not long after the '62 defense, the New York YC's Trustees passed a resolution interpreting the Cup's Deed of Gift to mean that challengers not only had to be designed and built in the challenging country but that gear and sails should come from there too. This has effectively cut off the challenging nations from Hood sails but they continue to order them from Marblehead as yardsticks. Many of the early pictures of the French trial horse *Chancegger* showed a lovely Hood main with one lower panel of a distinctly different color. Obviously the section had been removed for testing the Hood-woven cloth which continues to be one of the secrets of any Hood sail.

Hood sailmakers now have lofts in Canada, England, France, Australia, and New Zealand. And while a challenging Twelve from any one of these countries would be allowed to have sails made at the local Hood loft, they cannot use the fabric produced in Marblehead. Largely due to the great success of the English loft, there is a plan afoot to weave Hood cloth in Ireland. If this ever reaches fulfillment, the sail gap will almost certainly be narrowed.

Back in 1964, with future challenges in mind, the Australians sent their top sailmaker, the late Joe Pearce, to spend a year with Hood, and he became a top assistant. With Ted preoccupied by a second unsuccessful attempt with *Nefertiti,* Pearce became the man who dealt with the sails for the defender, *Constellation,* during the trials. Pearce may have learned quite a bit about the cut, but said his boss, "we didn't tell him much about the cloth."

Following this, and until his untimely death, Joe Pearce became the Hood sailmaker in Australia. He made *Dame Pattie's* sails in 1967 but by mutual agreement there was no communication with Marblehead on the subject of 12-Meter sails. The same arrangement applies with Peter Cole, the present Aussie Hood sailmaker, who has supplied the motive power for *Gretel II.* The Hood loft in France, newest of the foreign operations, has not been involved in Baron Bich's undertaking.

Although nearly all of the technical improvements and lessons learned are applicable to Hood's normal business of making sails for cruising/racing yachts, there are some special problems and differences in making sails for the Twelves. To begin with, a 12-Meter has a ¾ foretriangle rig (the maximum allowable under the rule) while most boats today

EXHIBIT 5 (continued)

have masthead rigs. Mainsails must be fitted to masts and booms that are designed to bend to a far greater degree than on any cruising boat. Spinnakers are not made to the maximum size the 12-Meter rule permits —experience has shown time and again that shape is more important than sheer size when it comes to making a Twelve go downwind. Nevertheless, a maximum 'chute is made every Cup summer just to be sure that the theory still holds.

In preparing for a Cup summer, the Hood loft is looking for ways to make their sails lighter, smoother and stronger. The Twelves put tremendous strains on their sails and it is essential that they be strong and durable. But still, to save weight, less provision is made to prevent chafing than in a normal sail. As to the weight of sailcloth, there is continuous research into ways of making it lighter but still strong enough to retain its shape-holding ability. This work comes under the supervision of Ted's father, Steadman, known to everybody as "The Professor," who has done much over the years to insure the success of his son's business. The Professor's research is continuous and he says that progress is slow. But the following table on mainsail cloth weights used by the Twelves would seem to belie this claim:

Year	Weight
1958	14–oz.
1962	12–oz.
1964	10–oz.
1967	7.5–oz.
1970	6.9–oz. (or slightly less)

One characteristic of every U.S. defender since 1958 has been a tendency to hobby-horse less than her rival in the seas off Newport. While hull design is all important in this respect, there is little doubt that lightweight sails—weight saved up high where it really counts— have also contributed significantly to this advantage.

One recent development of Hood research that has reached a sufficiently advanced stage to be used on 12-Meter sails this summer is the Hood Ring, a replacement for the large hand-worked grommets in the corners of sails. Hood Rings have proved to be almost twice as strong as the best hand-sewn equivalent even though they are considerably lighter in weight. Hood Rings are inserted by special high-pressure hydraulic tooling and now there is virtually no handwork in a typical Hood clew since roping has also been eliminated.

Other new wrinkles in 12-Meter sails this season include Cunningham holes for draft control in both genoas and mainsails. The latter have Cunninghams along the foot as well as the luff. When this was written, experimental zippers (two of them, side-by-side) seemed to have proved their worth as a further means of draft control along the luffs of main-

EXHIBIT 5 (*concluded*)

sails. Hood and others have been using foot zippers on mainsails for many years. This year's lightest polypropylene spinnaker cloth is even lighter than *Intrepid's* much talked-about Floater of '67, but The Professor won't say by how much. Mainsail headboards are now made of titanium for the ultimate in strength without weight.

Valiant and *Heritage* have the recently developed Hood Sea Stay, a hollow grooved rod in which the genoa luff is hoisted. This item eliminates hanks as well as the space between headstay and sail, thereby significantly reducing turbulence at the leading edge.

In perfecting 12-Meter sails, spinnakers and jibs are recut often. There has been a definite trend among U.S. Cup sailors toward working for perfection with the sails at hand rather than ordering one after another and trying to decide which of the lot is best, as was popular until 1964. *Intrepid*, for example, went through the entire '67 campaign with only two mainsails in her inventory. Hood has had great luck in making mainsails right the first time and thus virtually eliminating recutting. The 7.5-oz. main *Intrepid* used most only had one seam let out near the head. *Valiant's* first Hood main had not been touched, at least through the Preliminary Trials. Ted points out that owners often will get him out to look at sails believing they need to be recut when what is really needed may be a proper knowledge of how to adjust luff and sheet tension or how tight to carry a leech line. Hood personnel spend long hours discussing and demonstrating adjustment techniques to 12-Meter crews.

The problem is trying to find enough time to satisfy everybody. There can be little doubt that over the long haul Ted Hood's success in making 12-Meter sails has meant much to his business, even though it is now quite a small part of the total. But one of the ironies of a Cup summer for Hood is that much less other work comes in. Many owners apparently feel that the loft will be too busy with the Twelves to pay much attention to them. This is not true—a 12-Meter sail goes through the same manufacturing process as any other. But what is certainly true is that what started as a bedroom sail repair business during college years would never have grown to be the international enterprise it is today had Ted Hood not become sailmaker to the Twelves.

Source: Article appearing in the September, 1970, issue of *Yachting* magazine.

Some of the reasons behind the company's success were discussed in CML's 1970 annual report:

> In every major ocean race of recent years, the winning boats (including *Intrepid* in the recent America's Cup Race) have consistently used Hood Sails. When Hood Sailmakers of Marblehead, Massachusetts, joined the Group in February [1970], the Group became a very im-

portant factor in the marine accessories segment of the "leisure time" industry.

The business was started by Ted Hood as a hobby when he was a boy. Now there are sail lofts in Massachusetts, California, Canada, England, France, New Zealand, and Australia. The company weaves and finishes its own cloth in mills in Massachusetts, and, as such, it is the only fully integrated sailmaker in the world. Hood Yacht Systems, a division of Hood Sailmakers, manufactures masts, rigging, and specialty marine hardware.

The principal asset of the company is its technological and inventive skill. No other sailcloth maker has the technical ability to make such light yet strong cloth without the use of plastic resins. These innovative skills have also been applied in the design of sails and the manufacture of specialty marine hardware.

During the year, an entirely new style of sailcloth was introduced for use in the America's Cup. The company also began to extrude its own fibers for use in its "Floater" spinnaker cloths. The "Sea Stay" style of rod rigging became commercially available. Sail lofts were opened in France and California. A new [Executive] Vice President and General Manager was employed to give additional depth in administration and production management.

Additional lofts are planned in the United States and substantial sales growth is expected in the foreign markets. New marine accessory products are being developed for Hood Yacht Systems.

Competition for Hood came mainly from dozens of small local manufacturers, which generally had strong market coverage in particular regions of the country only. Hood in fact had itself been established in the late 1930s as a strictly local loft supplying the Marblehead market. Over the years it had grown both nationally and internationally to its current position of preeminence. Mr. Morgan, the new division general manager, described the company's success as follows:

> Hood's success can be attributed to a couple of factors. The most important of course is Ted Hood himself. Ted is a soft-spoken, modest kind of guy with an amazing knowledge of sailing and racing. He exudes confidence. What an ocean racer wants most from a sailmaker Ted Hood can supply in abundance . . . expert consultation in sail design and individual help in getting the best out of sails once they're made. Since the CML merger much of Ted's administrative load has been reduced and he now spends much more of his time testing new designs and out working with customers. Not only is this the kind of thing he enjoys most, but it's where Ted's time is most valuable to the company.
>
> Hood Sailcloth is also a key competitive factor. Hood has a real product edge as the only U.S. sailmaker with its own weaving capability. In a very closely guarded process here in Marblehead we produce a tight-weave cloth of unusual lightness and strength. In fact, many in

racing circles attribute *Intrepid's* victory over Australia's *Gretel* in the 1970 America's Cup Race at least in part to the fact that *Intrepid's* sails [using Hood cloth] weighed about half those of *Gretel.*

Hood sails were sold by five salaried salesmen and Mr. Hood himself through a variety of channels: direct to sailors (about half) and to dealers, naval architects, yacht builders, and the federal government. Hood competed only slightly in areas other than the large yacht market.

CML'S OPERATING PHILOSOPHY AND POLICIES

Hood's Irish investment was being considered in the context of an intricate set of relationships between CML and its divisions. According to Mr. Leighton, these relationships typically began taking shape even prior to acquisition itself and were strongly affected by personal factors:

> It would have been very difficult to have acquired any of our companies without our personal interest in their products. Bob Tod, for instance, is a great hydroplane enthusiast and for a time even held the U.S. Class B hydroplane speed record. This, together with our outboard boat experience at Willard, made it much easier to approach Dick Fisher about joining us. My own sailing background gave us some immediate rapport with Ted Hood. Ted and I had even competed once in the 1956 New England Men's Sailing Championships. I had come in second behind Ted, who went on to win the U.S. Men's Championships that year. All of us in the group are skiers, so Carroll Reed's business was not completely foreign to us. Learning Carroll Reed's mail-order business in turn provided a background for rapport with Ed Lebo when we first approached him about selling Mason & Sullivan.

Mr. Leighton considered preacquisition discussions to be extremely important because they provided an opportunity for both parties to get to know each other. This involved both discovering the owner-manager's underlying needs and aspirations and outlining clearly for him what joining CML would mean in terms of policies, procedures, authority and responsibility relationships, management changes, etc. This "foundation building" period was considered of prime importance because it paved the way for changes to be made after acquisition. According to Mr. Leighton, only by letting an owner-manager know beforehand what changes to expect could a transition be made smoothly. He commented:

> Most companies in our industry can benefit substantially from association with a larger, more sophisticated firm such as CML. We can provide capital and management know-how usually not available to a small company. We provide a vehicle for taking a small company public at favorable values and minimum expense. We can also provide a valuable environment for the top man in these companies. The independent businessman typically feels alone and would like someone to recognize his achievements and exchange ideas. His board of directors (if he has

one) usually is not made up of professional managers who can give real guidance. He has no one to turn to for advice on a continuing basis. Therefore, he is typically a very lonely man under extreme pressure from long hours, and surrounded by subordinates he may not wish to confide in. About the only persons around to motivate and console him are his wife, banker, and accountant, and they may not be close enough to the business to do this effectively.

Countering this strong need for association is, of course, an equally strong need for autonomy. This creates an antagonism of forces which inevitably causes an owner anxiety during early stages of discussion with us. He has normally spent years building up his business and wants to make sure he'll remain in control after acquisition. Our big initial job is to subdue these anxieties. For this reason we deliberately don't talk price or even ask for financial statements during early contacts. Instead, we try to get to know his business, his problems, his personality. We explain to him in detail what life will be like with us and exactly what changes in his operation he can expect. The whole emphasis is one of building up trust and understanding. At some point along the way he inevitably brings out his financial statements to show us. As a result of our emphasis on mutual understanding, we are less apt to get involved in a bidding match than if we were to negotiate mainly on a price basis.

According to Mr. Leighton, the acquisition process itself had varied considerably among companies acquired so far:

One of our companies first came to us about joining CML. Another I had heard might be available. I simply phoned the president and set up a meeting to talk. For a third company we had to make overtures over a number of months before we finally got anywhere. Another acquisition came to us in an interesting way. Last spring an acquaintance of mine and the former president of a medium-sized mail-order company phoned to say that he had a company he wanted to buy personally, but that the purchase price was above his financial means, and he wondered whether CML might like to buy it in partnership with him. We liked the company so much we bought it outright and put him in as general manager, with the former owner's concurrence, of course. This route is one we may use more frequently both for hiring new managers and acquiring new companies. I had a very qualified fellow in here not long ago who said he wanted to work for us. I told him we simply didn't have an opening at present, but that if he could bring us an attractive company we might acquire it and with the owner's approval put him in as general manager with attractive financial alternatives. He's working on one right now.

The Corporate Office

In January 1971, CML's corporate office consisted of four officers. Mr. Leighton, chairman of the board, focused mainly on relationships external to operations, concentrating primarily on new acquisitions, investor relations, and the raising of new capital. Mr. Tod, president, spent an estimated 90 percent of his time working directly with divisions and was the corporate officer immediately responsible for operations. Mr. Chaffee,[8] treasurer, worked closely with divisional controllers in preparing accounting statements and various management studies, such as cost-volume relationships, product mix contribution analyses, etc. He also handled company-wide cash control, auditor relations, tax form preparation, and corporate office accounting. Management felt that the existing four-man corporate staff was sufficient to handle expected growth for the next three or four years, with perhaps the addition of a financial controller to share some of Mr. Chaffee's current responsibilities.

Since July 1970, borrowing and cash receipts for the entire corporation had been consolidated at the corporate level. Divisions could therefore no longer borrow on their own or build up their own cash balances; all funds passed through central CML accounts. Each division paid (or received) interest on funds received from (or advanced to) CML. Apart from interest payments there were no corporate charges.

Financial Control

Mr. Tod commented as follows on the company's philosophy regarding divisional autonomy:

> We want to give divisions their heads and let them make their own decisions within the broad policy constraints set at the corporate level. This much autonomy is workable only in the presence of complete, accurate, timely information on operations. Such data come in several forms. Prior to the beginning of our fiscal year each division submits three forecasts: monthly profit and loss for each of the following 12 months, end-of-month balance sheets for each of the following 12 months, and an annual capital budget showing forecasted expenditures by month. As the year proceeds, forecasts are compared on a monthly basis with actual operating figures.
>
> In addition to strictly accounting data we receive a number of key indicators from divisions on a monthly basis. These are vital measures of each division's performance. For instance, from one division I get catalogue and retail sales and open-to-buy figures. For another I get bookings (orders), shipments, and discount levels for both dealer and

---

[8] Philip Chaffee (32): BS, University of Vermont, 1962; Financial Management Program, 1962–65, and then traveling audit staff, 1965–67, of the General Electric Company; manager of corporate auditing, ITEK Corporation, 1968–70. Mr. Chaffee had joined CML as controller in June, 1970, and had assumed Mr. Frederick's duties as treasurer upon the latter's resignation in December 1970.

direct sales, while another supplies order backlog, production, and inventory figures in addition to about six or eight others. For one division I look hardest at advertising response figures. Any variances are discussed in detail at regular meetings with division managements. Meetings are summarized in memo form and then sent back to divisions. If divisions don't agree with opinions or decisions stated in these memos they are supposed to let me know right away. With this system I feel we have about as tight a control system as we could get without our actually making the decisions ourselves.

Part of the reason for the emphasis on close control, Mr. Tod explained, stemmed from a desire to avoid an experience CML management had had at Willard. One of their divisions that had been reporting adequate profits for several years had suddenly shown considerable red ink following an examination of inventories which had precipitated large writedowns. This situation had come as a complete surprise to both group and division management, and in management's opinion was simply the result of inadequate controls.

Mr. Leighton offered the following comments on operating control:

> We have two main operating policies: "No closets to hide in" and "No surprises." Together they spell full decentralization of operations *except for* financial information flows. If things go wrong in a division, division management has nowhere to hide because we've given them complete authority and responsibility for their operations. On the other hand, if things go well they take the bows. We don't want surprises either good or bad from divisions, and we try to ensure this by getting complete and frequent information on operations.

Division controllers were considered an important link in providing information flow from divisions to the corporate level, and CML had inherited what corporate management considered to be experienced men within three of the acquired companies. (The fourth required only a part-time bookkeeper.) Two of these men were CPA's, while the third was an M.B.A. from the Tuck School at Dartmouth. All had extensive backgrounds in either public or corporate accounting.

Divisional General Managers

Another important ingredient to CML's operating strategy was the division general manager. Professionally trained, experienced general managers had been hired to complement all four division presidents, partially relieving them of administrative duties and thereby giving them more time to do what they were best at. While several of the general managers hired so far were still quite new to the company, Mr. Tod felt that they were already proving to be valuable additions to the divisions.[9] He stated that one of the most significant ways in which CML could benefit an acquired company was by recruiting for it people who would not normally be attracted to small companies, which often offered little opportunity for equity participation and promotion. Compensation of general managers was tied to earnings growth formulas similar to those of owner-managers, and involved liberal cash bonus and stock option possibilities based on performance. The relationship of a division general manager to an owner-manager was determined partly by this congruence of compensation interests, partly by the fact that each general manager had been selected by the owner-manager of the division involved from among several candidates prescreened by CML management, and partly by the understanding that the owner-manager ultimately had final say on all decisions affecting a division and in fact could fire the general manager if it became apparent that the two could not work together. All these arrangements had, of course, been discussed at length with owner-managers during the "foundation setting" stage preceding acquisition. All four general managers hired so far were still with the company in January 1971.

Financial controls and other influences ushered in by CML appeared to have caused some changes within acquired companies. Middle management personnel from various divisions described some of these as follows:

> It's not at all like it used to be around here. [The owner-manager] had always been an easygoing guy running the business pretty much on a day-to-day basis. I liked this myself. It suited my style. Unfortunately, all this is changing now. Things are becoming much more systematic and "big business" around here. We're feeling this most in cost reduction and in sales promotion, but every one is feeling it to a certain extent. I don't think this will cause people to quit, though. Most of the workers are very unskilled and easy to train, so they aren't likely to do much better elsewhere. Most of the management people are like

---

[9] *Fred Snow* (35), executive vice president and general manager of Carroll Reed Ski Shops since March 1970; AB, Babson College, 1958; salesman, sales manager, promotions manager, and marketing vice president of Fieldcrest Company, 1959–70.

John Morgan (33), executive vice president and general manager of Hood Sailmakers, Inc., since April 1970; Princeton, electrical engineering, 1959; MBA, Harvard, 1966; prior to joining Hood, had had a number of technical and management positions at General Electric Company over a 10-year period.

Bob Lavery (49), vice president and general manager of Mason & Sullivan Company since July 1970; BS, Kansas State College, 1940; 25 years' experience in catalog sales, first with Montgomery Ward and more recently with a successful medium-sized mail-order firm where he had been president since 1961.

Dave Wilson (33), vice president and general manager of Boston Whaler, Inc., since January 1971; Cambridge, England, chemical engineering, 1961; MBA, Harvard, 1968; had worked for six years as a process engineer with a major U.S. chemical company, and since 1968 as president of a Canadian manufacturing concern where he had achieved profitable operations of the company for the first time since 1960.

me. They've come here because they love [boating, sailing, skiing] and will stick it out because they love the sport.

❖ ❖ ❖ ❖ ❖

[The new general manager] is a good man. We had about nine different men around here doing his job before he came. He made a tenth, but because he has just a little more finesse plus the authority of the job behind him things have been running much more smoothly around here since he came. I'm not sure, though, that any of the other nine couldn't have done just as well if they had been given the position.

❖ ❖ ❖ ❖ ❖

I think people are happier and things are running more smoothly since we joined CML. Previously, it was hard to get big decisions made. Problems would frequently just float along without ever being resolved. This was frustrating. [The new general manager] is the kind of guy who looks at the facts and comes to a decision on them. This has made life easier for all of us.

Mr. Tod's Role

An additional important corporate link with divisions was provided by Mr. Tod himself. Mr. Tod tried to visit each division at least once every two weeks, and to spend not less than 50 percent of his time physically on site with division personnel. These visits enabled him to participate on an ongoing basis in divisional developments. According to Mr. Tod, discussion during these visits ranged over every aspect of a division's business: pricing policy, marketing strategy, expansion requirements, personnel problems, production scheduling, and so on. He stated:

> It's hard to generalize about this relationship because it's so different in each specific instance. How I deal with a division depends upon the division involved, its key man, its employees, its particular problems, and so forth. One division president, for instance, is constantly after me to spend more time with him and his people. Until recently another division has been quite reluctant to seek any help.
>
> There do seem to be certain patterns, however. When a new division first comes on board, Charlie and I try to schedule a luncheon for all its employees at which we introduce ourselves and discuss CML and our plans for the division. We deliberately wait two or three weeks after original announcement of the acquisition before having this luncheon in order to let division personnel get used to the idea prior to meeting us. During this period, we intentionally stay away from the division; this helps convey the impression that we don't intend to meddle too much in divisional operations. Before the luncheon meeting, Charlie and I try to learn as much as we can about the 12 or 15 key people in the division. We feel this is useful for getting to know a new division better and for establishing relationships with its key people.

While the above described the usual procedure, not every acquisition had had an initiation luncheon. One division president had objected to the custom so no luncheon had been held for that division.

Because, in principle, divisions operated relatively autonomously, Mr. Tod felt his influence upon operations was based less on exerting direct authority than on the confidence and respect he inspired as a manager. He commented on this situation to the casewriter as follows:

> The influence I can exert comes in preparation, really. I must have intimate knowledge of the business of each division, and must have the numbers involved in any particular situation at my fingertips. This means doing my homework. Otherwise, division people won't listen. They may pay lip service, but they'll make their own decisions in the final analysis. Of course, if they do, they'll have to live with them.
>
> I have to be able to understand our divisions' businesses as well as division presidents themselves in order to do my job. I think I will be able to continue to do this as we expand the number of divisions. Keep in mind that all our divisions are in the leisure time industry and in many ways aren't really that different from one another. Our two mail-order businesses have a number of similarities, for example. The same is true, though to a lesser extent, of our two marine divisions.
>
> I realize I have to walk a fine line most of the time between supervisor and boss, consultant, and advisor. The key to this role of course is working with people, and the key to that is flexibility . . . listening to people, getting to know their capabilities, and correctly evaluating their judgments. All this of course requires intimate knowledge of the facts of specific situations. Again, doing your homework is essential!

When asked to comment upon the kinds of divisional situations he became involved in, apart from those involving routine financial control, Mr. Tod replied that these could be best classified according to the role he played in the development or solution of each. He saw himself playing several roles, but primarily those of:

1. Management consultant
2. Management recruiter
3. Participant in key decisions

Mr. Tod described several situations as examples of each.

1. Management Consultant. This role typically involved the collection and analysis of information in such a way that it shed light on some important aspect of a division's operation. Mr. Tod described several instances in which he had played this role.

Consumer Analysis. Dick Fisher, himself an avid fisherman, had deliberately designed the Boston Whaler for the fisherman's every need. As a result, the product combined the general advantages of stability, maneuverability, unsinkability, safety, and performance with specific fishing-oriented features, such as a built-in bait box and a rack for fishing rods. Given this background and orientation, the company naturally directed advertising toward fishermen. Soon after acquisition Mr. Tod began to question whether such an orientation was really justified, however. He commented on this situation as follows:

> Working closely with the Boston Whaler sales organization during the months following acquisition, I came increasingly to feel that a significant percentage of Whaler owners were using the boat for family and recreational in addition to strictly fishing purposes. If this were true, I felt that Boston Whaler advertising copy should reflect the fact. One problem was that there wasn't really much product-in-use data available within the division. During my visits there I had plenty of opportunity to discuss my feelings, though, and suggested from time to time that a customer survey might be made to get a better feel for who bought Whalers and just how the boats were used. It took a while before anything happened, but gradually people began to get interested. During this period I spent quite a lot of time with the division advertising manager talking about what information might be helpful and how it might be obtaned. After a while he began putting together a questionnaire, and we discussed this and revised it several times. Finally, by September [1970] a completed questionnaire was mailed out to about 400 customers. Responses have shown a significant family recreational clientele, and recent ad copy is already beginning to reflect this.

Winter Catalog Program. Mail-order catalogs of one division had traditionally been published and mailed twice a year. The winter catalog consisted of 32 pages; the spring catalog, typically a less ambitious project, contained 24 pages. Each had a total mailing of several hundred thousand copies.

A review of catalog sales in past years had convinced Mr. Tod that an expansion of the spring catalog, in terms of pages, items, or mailings, or any combination of the three, could add to profits substantially. To demonstrate this he reconstructed from divisional accounting data a detailed analysis of the company's catalog experience to date, showing how past changes in pages, items, and mailings had affected volume, tying in enough cost data to provide estimates of profitability. This analysis indicated an optimum mix consisting of a 10 percent increase in total items offered, an increase in the number of pages from 24 to 32, and a continuance of mailings at their former level.

Getting the division to implement this increase was another matter, however. Mr. Tod commented:

> Division personnel just didn't feel there was enough time to produce the eight additional pages before the deadline for mailings. It took a little pushing on our part to get this through, but eventually the division made it. I was able to help a little on a bottleneck situation involving

page layout. By setting up a very simple PERT chart with deadlines for the various activities involved, I was able to persuade division personnel to farm out certain layout functions. As it turned out, by following the PERT chart, the catalogue was completed three days before the mailing deadline. Partly as a result of the page increase, profits from the 1970 Spring Catalogue were about $50,000 higher than the previous year.

The division president had the following to say about this situation:

> I didn't feel we were geared up at the time to handle the increased volume. One reason I sold to CML was to get their professional help in solving some of our internal systems problems like order processing and inventory control. We haven't had too much help on this so far, however. The increase in catalogue volume before straightening out these problems inevitably caused some foul-ups with customers. I'm a little afraid that this kind of thing may undercut some of the goodwill and close personal contact with customers we've worked so hard to build over the years.

2. Management Recruiter.   A second corporate role vis-à-vis divisions in which Mr. Leighton and Mr. Tod appeared to be equally active was that of management recruiter. Mr. Leighton described this role as follows:

> In talking with prospective acquisitions we typically find that the presidents really don't enjoy what they're doing. They have to be concerned with banking relations, accounting, marketing, production, and sales, but what they really want to do is develop more and better products.

To reduce the administrative load on division presidents, CML had helped recruit general managers for all four divisions, leaving the final hiring decision in the hands of division presidents themselves.

Mr. Leighton added:

> We try to get division presidents to hire a man who will complement them. Generally, we try to get an M.B.A. who's been out and gotten six or seven years' experience. We would rather go out and pay someone in his early 30s a lot of money because he has tremendous potential and good background than to get someone with less experience more cheaply or someone with more experience but with less potential.
>
> We want the man that every company wants. We spend as much time trying to meet and recruit a man as we do a company. For example, we went night and day after John Morgan.

Mr. Morgan had graduated from Princeton in 1959 with a degree in electrical engineering and had joined the General Electric Company shortly afterwards. He worked there until 1964 in a number of technical and supervisory positions, including foreman of shop operations and project supervisor for the transfer of products from United States to European factories. Mr. Morgan then entered the Harvard Business School, graduating as a Baker Scholar with High Distinction in 1966. Following graduation Mr. Morgan returned to G.E., where he subsequently held positions as manager of business planning, manager of marketing administration (both at the division level), and finally as manager of resource planning for a $600 million product group. He resigned in the spring of 1970 to become general manager of Hood Sailmakers.

Mr. Leighton commented as follows on the process of recruiting a Hood general manager:

> We had heard some very good things about John from his professors at Harvard. The feedback we got about his work at G.E. was also excellent. We heard that he was considered one of their most able young men. We decided that if he was that good, we would like him to join our team, so we went after him.

Mr. Morgan offered the following remarks on this situation:

> I really hadn't been thinking of leaving G.E. when Bob and Charlie approached me. I had recently been promoted for the third time since leaving the Business School in 1966. I was getting all the right signals from higher management, and I felt I was on the way up.
>
> I think what really appealed to me in CML's offer was the opportunity to build something on my own. Financially I'm at about the same level as at G.E. Of course there's a possibility of building some equity here, but the risks are great also. Over the long run G.E. probably offered about as good an opportunity for building a personal estate. What I couldn't resist about the Hood offer was the excitement of working in a small operation where I could really influence the future of the company.

3. Participant in Key Decisions. A third important role played by corporate management was that of participant in key decisions facing divisions. Mr. Tod offered the following as an example of the kind of decision he typically became involved in.

Production Cutback. During the third quarter of fiscal 1970, Mr. Tod and one division president had held quite different opinions over what constituted a wise production level for the division. Each side claimed a good case for its position. Division management argued that sales for January and February had been well ahead of forecast, indicating that another good year was in the making. Corporate management feared that trends in the general economy might significantly reduce fourth-quarter shipments and was urging sizable production cutbacks. Mr. Tod was unsuccessful in getting division management to accept his view, however, and production continued at high levels throughout the first three quarters.

Mr. Tod noted:

> I made my voice heard, but I couldn't convince anyone to follow me. In fact, I'm not sure whether if I'd been in the division's shoes I would have cut production myself, given the demoralizing impact this has on a division if high sales eventually materialize. From our standpoint, however, the risk of overproduction seemed sizable, and we were advocating a path of prudence.
>
> As it turned out, an unexpected stock market slide caused May and June sales to drop well below forecast. Inventories rose substantially as a result, requiring much more CML financing than originally budgeted. The division became dependent on us because it had to ask for additional financing to carry inventory. This puts us in a good position to exert our influence. At our urging, the division is reducing next year's forecast well below the level originally planned. In addition, it is making contingency plans to cover a further sales drop next year, and is cutting overhead substantially.

Hood's Irish Project

Corporate management's involvement in Hood's Irish weaving mill project constituted yet a further example of its role as participant in key decisions facing divisions.

Hood's organization had grown rapidly in recent years. As recently as early 1967, production facilities had been limited to one weaving and one sail-making facility, both located at Marblehead, and all sales (already 30 percent foreign in 1967) had been made by Mr. Hood and three sales consultants working out of Marblehead. To reduce tariff expenses on sails shipped abroad and to give better service to foreign customers, Hood had begun setting up foreign lofts, first in England (1967) and later in France, New Zealand, Australia, and Canada. In the United States a West Coast loft had been opened during this period, and the Marblehead weaving capacity had been nearly doubled. This expansion had naturally been accompanied by an increase in the number of Hood employees, from a total of about 165 in 1967, all located in Marblehead, to approximately 300 by 1971, 175 in the United States and 125 abroad. The organization had also become increasingly complex, as evidenced by Mr. Morgan's sketch appearing as Exhibit 6.

The concept of a European-based weaving mill had originated in 1968 with the manager of the newly established English loft, which paid a 20 percent tariff on all sailcloth imported from Marblehead. Hood's interest in a European mill naturally increased with the opening of additional foreign lofts in 1968 and 1969, since duties on the sailcloth they imported ranged as high as 35 percent in France and 31 percent

EXHIBIT 6

CML GROUP, INC.
Organization Chart of Hood Sailmakers, Inc.

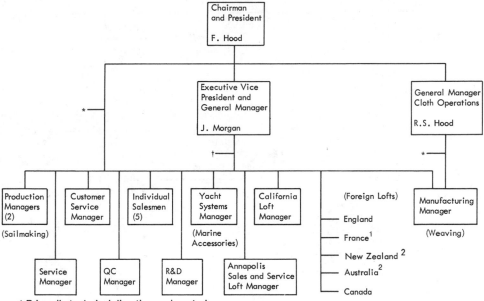

* Primarily technical direction and control.
† Primarily administrative direction and control.
[1] Owned 80 percent by Hood Sailmakers, 20 percent by the loft general manager.
[2] Owned 50 percent by Hood Sailmakers, 50 percent by the loft general manager.
Source: Sketch prepared by John Morgan, general manager of Hood Sailmakers, in early January 1971.

in Australia. The ad valorem value of cloth represented approximately 25 percent of the final selling price of Hood sails; import tariffs therefore constituted a significant percentage of each foreign sales dollar: from 5 percent in England to more than 8 percent in Australia and France.

Because of increasing pressure from the managers of foreign lofts, Mr. Hood in early 1969 hired a brother-in-law of the English loft manager to begin site studies for a European mill. The desirability of an Irish site soon became evident because the Republic of Ireland's inclusion in the British Commonwealth permitted tariff-free export to all Commonwealth countries, because the Irish government offered to underwrite 50 percent of capital costs for the new facility and to waive all tax on profits earned in Ireland, and because of low labor rates in Ireland. By August 1970, the Irish Development Authority (IDA) had agreed to fund $266,000 of the total $554,000 fixed capital required by the project, and quotes for the necessary equipment were already being solicited.

EXHIBIT 7

CML GROUP, INC.
Capital Requirements for Irish Weaving Mill
(thousands of dollars)

	Total Cost	Sources of Funds	
		IDA Grant	CML
Land.................................	$ 8.4	$ 4.2	$ 4.2
Building..............................	216.0	108.0	108.0
Equipment............................	329.6	154.1	175.5
Working capital (net)*................	26.0	0.0	26.0
Total funds required...........	$580.0	$266.3	$313.7

After-Tax Cash Flow Savings Resulting from Transferring to Ireland All Weaving of Cloth Sold Outside the United States
(thousands of dollars)

	1971	1972	1973	1974	1975
Cash flow increase resulting from decreases in:					
Tariffs...............................	$ 16	$ 18	$ 20	$ 23	$ 27
Variable costs of manufacture.......	56	63	65	83	96
U.S. corporation profit taxes........	74	85	87	110	128
Subtotal..........................	$146	$166	$172	$216	$251
Cash flow decrease resulting from an increase in:					
Fixed cost of manufacture†.........	98	97	96	96	96
Net cash flow increase (net cash flow savings)............	$ 48	$ 69	$ 76	$120	$155

Note: Discounted Cash Flow Return on $314,000 Investment = 13 percent
* Net of working capital freed in the United States as a result of moving a portion of the weaving operation to Ireland.
† Excludes depreciation.
Source: Company records.

As shown in detail in Exhibit 7, the project called for a total investment of $580,000. Mr. Morgan calculated that the cash flow savings resulting from the new mill (shown in the lower half of Exhibit 7) represented a 13 percent after tax return on CML's $314,000 investment in the project. Cash flow savings were expected in three areas:

1. Elimination of tariffs on cloth currently woven in Marblehead and shipped to lofts in Commonwealth countries.
2. A reduction in variable cost of manufacture arising mainly from lower labor rates in Ireland.
3. A reduction in U.S. corporate profits tax arising because the Marblehead mill would suffer a significant loss of contribution margin (approximately 40 percent) as a result of moving production to Ireland. The resulting reduction in profits reported in the United States would reduce U.S. taxes on corporate profits.

The only recurring cash outflow resulting from the investment arose from an increase in fixed manufacturing expenses. While no reduction in Marblehead's fixed expenses was expected despite the 40 percent reduction in through-put, Ireland would itself incur $98,000 of additional fixed costs (after depreciation).

Mr. Morgan offered the following comments on the Irish project:

> From my standpoint, the big advantage of the project is strictly financial . . . the 13 percent after tax return it represents for us. There are minor strategic advantages, of course. The investment will protect our positions in England and France, where duties have pushed prices about as high as they can go. If duties should go even higher, which we feel could happen, we might be pushed out of these markets if we are still shipping cloth from Marblehead.

Hood's board of directors was scheduled to meet on January 15 to decide on a recommendation with regard to the Irish investment. Mr. Tod saw three alternatives open to the board: (1) dropping the project outright, (2) going ahead with it full speed, or (3) delaying it until Hood's domestic market improved. The more he considered the many factors involved, the more he came to favor the third alternative. First, cash inflows were relatively small during early years of the project. They would therefore not significantly contribute to the earnings track record CML hoped to establish prior to going public in 1972. Second, the tax status of profits earned in Ireland raised a complex set of questions including (1) whether or not future investors would be evaluating CML's earnings on a before-tax or an after-tax basis, (2) future cash needs in Europe providing a use for profits earned abroad, (3) difficulties and costs associated with eventual repatriation of profits earned abroad, and (4) possible legal complications arising from the fact that earn-out for former Hood owners was based on before-tax rather than after-tax profits. Third, Hood was showing a somewhat lower return on the funds currently being advanced by CML[10] than some of the other divisions of the company. Therefore, while Hood profits had improved somewhat in recent months, the division had not yet entirely demonstrated an ability to achieve its full profit potential. Fourth, the continued slump in domestic sales had reduced Hood's Marblehead operation to 50 percent of capacity. This made a sizable investment in additional capacity difficult to justify. Fifth, and most important, Hood management was already spread extremely thin over a great number of activities and did not appear to have the time and energy at present to take on a major new commitment.

There were, of course, disadvantages to delay. The IDA grant might

---

[10] Totaling $800,000 in early January 1971.

be lost. Hood funds and management energy would be expended just maintaining status quo on the project. The Hoods themselves, concerned with the long-run competitive advantages of the investment and eager to get under way, might be disappointed.

Mr. Tod commented on his position as follows:

> I just feel we can get a quicker pay-out by putting our money in other areas . . . expanding one company's product line, for instance, or improving another company's sales organization.

Mr. Leighton offered the following comments:

> I think over the long run it makes sense for Hood to begin weaving abroad. It's a question of timing, really. With sales down, plus an overcapacity situation, I'm afraid of what the Irish investment will do to Hood's current profit picture. In addition, I wonder whether at this point in time Hood has enough management time and energy to take on something like this. A start-up situation is never easy.

ACHIEVEMENTS TO DATE: FUTURE PROBLEMS AND OPPORTUNITIES

Hood's Irish investment was under consideration just 18 months after the formation of CML and 15 months since its first acquisition in September 1969. Mr. Leighton had the following to say about CML's achievements to date and the problems and opportunities facing the company in the months to come:

> Progress so far has been excellent. Three out of four companies will show significant profit increases this year over last—20 percent or more. In the case of one division profits will fall somewhat, but mainly because we are deliberately scheduling manufacturing below breakeven in order to work off excess inventory built up last year. Fiscal '72 should bring a big profit increase for this division.
>
> As for further acquisitions, the biggest constraint at this point is pressure on Bob Tod. Right now, for instance, we are looking at three companies as possible acquisitions this spring. All are out of state and only one is in New England. This is quite different from our existing divisions, which are all easily accessible from Boston. The big question on further acquisitions becomes how many companies one man can handle at once. This depends, of course, on how spread out they are geographically, and on the quality of division management. If our divisions can more or less run themselves, we can spread Bob a lot thinner. The real key to further growth then becomes the development of good management teams within divisions, and this in turn depends heavily on the quality of people we can bring into CML Group companies. As a matter of fact, after acquiring our fourth company last July we completely stopped all acquisition search and spent six months

just looking for people. Now that general managers have been installed in all divisions and we've got four really good division management teams, we're back looking at acquisitions again.

There are other ways of easing the pressure on Bob, of course. One would be to limit acquisitions to businesses very similar to existing divisions. This would reduce the learning effort required at our level. Another would be to eventually develop several Bob Tods as group vice presidents for our three main areas: marine, sporting equipment and related accessories, and hobby crafts. An advantage of this would be the increased promotion opportunities it would open to new employees now being brought into the company. A disadvantage is that it would necessarily reduce the tremendous fun and personal involvement we are now having with our companies. How we go on this is a personal decision we'll have to make at some point. A third possibility would be to bring new companies in under existing divisions.

A long-term objective is to take CML public sometime after the fall of 1972. This would provide the three full years of audited operations required by the SEC. We'd like a major "quality" brokerage firm to handle the public offering, and want a large enough offering in our shares to provide for after-market trading. To achieve this we feel we will need from $750,000 to $1 million in after-tax profits.

As far as we're concerned, the current economic downturn couldn't have been timed better. It has pushed us to trim dead weight in divisions to a point where they are now lean and hungry. When the economy finally turns around we should be in a position to show attractive internal earnings increases. This of course is the real key to the long-run success of CML Group: Our ability to show earnings per share increases through internal growth rather than through newly acquired earnings. Stated another way, we believe that our future success will depend far more on our ability to successfully manage than on our ability to successfully acquire.

4   Fuqua Industries (A)

In February 1973, Mr. J. B. Fuqua, chairman of the board of Fuqua
Industries, was preparing for a meeting with Mr. Carl L. Patrick, Fuqua's
president, Mr. Ted Davis, controller, and Mr. Kay Slayden, vice president–operations. Several months before, Mr. Slayden had recommended
that Fuqua sell its Trojan Seed subsidiary and Messrs. Fuqua and
Patrick had agreed with Mr. Slayden's evaluation. Although Trojan had
an extremely good record of sales and profit growth, Mr. Slayden had
argued that the subsidiary was requiring too much cash to finance its
growth and that Trojan's appetite for capital was likely to continue in
the future. Mr. Slayden had also argued that Fuqua's investment in
agribusiness could earn a higher return in Fuqua's recreation subsidiaries.
In recent weeks, however, Ted Davis had raised some objections to the
divestiture. Mr. Davis pointed out that in terms of return on sales,
Trojan was Fuqua's fourth most profitable subsidiary and that, since
Trojan had proprietary products in the hybrid corn seed business, it
would not be wise to sell Trojan at a time when agribusiness was becoming somewhat of a glamor industry.

As Mr. Fuqua prepared for the meeting where a final decision would
be reached, he reflected on Fuqua's previous experience with divestitures.
Divestitures were nothing new to Fuqua Industries. Several subsidiaries
had been sold in recent years, and Mr. Fuqua often stated that he
viewed divestitures as a part of Fuqua's overall strategy "to maximize
shareholders' wealth":

> Selling a company takes more courage than buying one. We think
> that management should be realistic and objective in its employment of
> corporate resources and funds. Managements of public companies do

stockholders a disservice when sentimental attachment to inadequate management or unprofitable ventures takes precedence over good business judgment.

What bothered Mr. Fuqua the most about Trojan was the large amount of capital that it required:

> There are two types of businesses—cash cows and cash hogs. You can operate and grow your cash cows, but each day you can also milk them. Cash hogs are different and have to be fed continually. What you do with a hog is feed him to a certain point and then send him to slaughter.

Mr. Fuqua wondered if the time hadn't come to sell the Trojan Seed Company.

FUQUA INDUSTRIES

In 1965, J. B. Fuqua acquired a controlling interest in the Natco Corporation. Natco's stock was listed on the New York Stock Exchange and the company's principal business was tile manufacturing. In recent years, Natco had been operating at a loss and its stock had been selling at below book value. Upon gaining control of Natco, Mr. Fuqua made a few fundamental changes in the business and soon it was generating profits. The company was renamed Fuqua Industries, Inc., and became the base for an aggressive series of acquisitions. By 1968, the Natco division had been sold and Fuqua's subsidiaries had grown to include recreation, transportation, shelter, and agribusiness companies. From 1965 to 1969, sales of the company grew from $14 million to over $300 million, and net income went from a loss to a $10.5 million profit. By the end of 1972, sales had topped $430 million and net income was over $18 million. (See Exhibits 1, 2, and 3 for more detailed financial information.)

J. B. Fuqua

J. B. Fuqua, 54, was the embodiment of the Great American Dream. Mr. Fuqua was raised on a Virginia tobacco farm and never received any formal education beyond a high school diploma. At the age of 21, Mr. Fuqua moved to Augusta, Georgia, and quickly became manager and subsequently owner of a local radio station. He later became the owner of Augusta's first television station and had a variety of other business dealings throughout the State of Georgia.

Besides his business achievements, Mr. Fuqua was also active in politics and served three terms in the Georgia House and one in the State Senate. He also served as chairman of the Senate Banking Com-

EXHIBIT 1

FUQUA INDUSTRIES (A)
Financial Highlights

Comparative Income Statement (dollars in thousands)	1967	1968	1969	1970	1971	1972	Forecast 1973
Net Sales (restated for poolings).......	221,686	252,026	333,464	339,308	358,783	433,960	484,000
% Increase from prior year.............		13.7	32.3	1.8	5.7	21.0	11.5
Net sales (as reported).................	60,175	223,863	324,190	327,837	352,363	433,960	484,000
%Increase from prior year.............		272.0	44.8	1.1	7.5	23.2	11.5
Pre-tax operating income (restated)....	15,199	21,777	27,636	22,139	26,452	35,475	42,400
% Increase from prior year.............		43.3	26.9	(19.9)	19.5	29.1	19.5
Pre-tax operating income (as reported).	6,633	19,102	26,303	21,213	26,701	35,475	42,400
% Increase from prior year.............		189.0	37.7	(19.4)	25.9	32.9	19.7
Net operating income (restated for poolings)...........................	8,156	10,847	13,970	11,109	13,493	18,069	21,400
% Increase from prior year.............		33.0	28.8	(20.5)	21.5	33.9	18.4
Net operating income (as reported).....	3,591	9,156	13,262	10,666	13,620	18,069	21,400
% Increase from prior year.............		156.0	44.8	(19.6)	27.7	32.7	18.4
Income tax % of pre-tax income........	46.3	50.2	49.5	50.2	49.0	49.1	49.5
Earnings per Share (dollars)							
Net operating income (primary)........	0.96	1.27	1.68	1.31	1.53	1.87	2.09
Net operating income (fully diluted)....	0.93	1.24	1.65	1.30	1.39	1.81	2.09
Comparative Balance Sheet (as reported, dollars in thousands)							
Current assets........................	22,179	61,419	108,221	115,750	133,598	161,772	
Net working capital....................	13,627	18,990	40,117	55,309	57,621	62,936	
Plant, property, and equipment—net...	15,708	54,774	78,716	84,669	97,252	130,376	
Total assets...........................	49,682	159,539	246,462	269,562	308,203	370,296	
Long-term debt.......................	9,654	48,004	85,012	102,927	103,649	112,937	
Net worth (equity).....................	30,897	65,741	87,625	97,503	117,614	146,803	
Debt/equity ratio.....................	24/76	42/58	49/51	51/49	47/53	43/57	
Performance measurements (as reported)							
Asset turnover (sales per ending asset dollar).......	1.21	1.50	1.32	1.22	1.14	1.17	
Return on Sales (Net operating income as percent of sales).............................	5.97%	4.09%	4.09%	3.25%	3.87%	4.16%	
Return on Assets Asset turnover × return on sales.....	7.22%	5.73%	5.40%	3.97%	4.41%	4.87%	
Leverage Factor Asset dollars per equity dollars.......	1.61	2.43	2.81	2.76	2.62	2.52	
Return on Shareholders' Equity (Net operating income as percent of equity)...........................	11.6%	13.9%	15.2%	11.0%	11.6%	12.3%	
Plant, Property, and Equipment (dollars in thousands) Additions—net of disposals (as reported)......................	3,118	10,017	31,205	16,906	24,843	24,179	24,000
Provision for depreciation (as reported)......................	1,759	7,906	9,797	10,953	12,610	15,041	17,700
Shares and Shareholders Average number of common shares and common equivalent shares (thousands)							
—Primary........................	7,694	7,840	8,027	8,151	8,551	9,424	10,000
—Fully diluted....................	7,903	8,208	8,477	8,189	9,747	9,823	10,000
Number of common shareholders of record (year end)...................	2,771	5,939	7,323	11,038	13,897	15,122	

EXHIBIT 2

FUQUA INDUSTRIES (A)
Statement of Consolidated Income

	Thousands of Dollars Except per Share Amounts	
	1972	1971
Net Sales and Revenues.............................	$433,960	$358,783
Costs and Expenses:		
Cost of products sold or services rendered...........	333,753	276,574
Selling, administrative expenses, etc.................	55,242	47,751
Interest expense...................................	9,490	8,006
Total costs and expenses.......................	398,485	332,331
Income before taxes and extraordinary items..........	35,475	26,452
Taxes on income...................................	17,406	12,959
Income Before Extraordinary Items (net operating income)...	18,069	13,493
Extraordinary Items (loss from the sale of a business less applicable income taxes)......................	—	(3,500)
Net income....................................	$ 18,069	$ 9,993
Earnings per Common Share and Common Equivalent Share		
Income before extraordinary items..................	$1.87	$1.53
Extraordinary items...............................	—	(0.41)
Net Income....................................	$1.87	$1.12
Earnings per Common Share—assuming full dilution		
Income before extraordinary items..................	$1.81	$1.39
Extraordinary items...............................	—	(0.36)
Net Income....................................	$1.81	$1.03

mittee and the State Democratic Committee. Mr. Fuqua was a close friend of Carl Sanders, Georgia's former governor and currently a member of Fuqua's board of directors and executive committee.

In 1965, Mr. Fuqua decided that he wanted to build a major public company. Mr. Fuqua pointed out that in developing Fuqua Industries he had first developed a strategy:

> My strategy was to build a major public company by acquiring existing profitable businesses, which had been developed by other people, and getting proven management along with these companies. My theory was that buying profits would be faster and less risky than growing our own profits.

J. B. Fuqua was extremely knowledgeable in business and finance, and was also innovative in his business practices. For example, in late 1972, Fuqua Industries issued a preliminary 1972 annual report that contained unaudited figures for 1972 and a forecast of 1973 earnings.

EXHIBIT 3

FUQUA INDUSTRIES (A)
Consolidated Balance Sheet

	Thousands of Dollars	
Assets	*1972*	*1971*
Current Assets		
Cash..	$ 7,469	$ 13,707
Receivables......................................	56,546	46,119
Inventories......................................	93,052	76,009
Prepaid expenses................................	4,705	4,015
Total Current Assets.........................	161,772	139,850
Notes Receivable and Other Assets..................	35,333	34,303
Property, plant, and equipment		
Land..	16,030	8,427
Buildings and improvements.......................	71,382	51,725
Machinery, equipment, and vehicles................	110,225	99,757
Allowance for depreciation (deduction)..............	(67,261)	(60,725)
Net carrying value............................	130,376	99,184
Motor carrier and broadcast operating rights...........	18,364	18,497
Excess of cost over net assets of businesses		
acquired...	24,451	23,177
Total assets.................................	$370,296	$315,011
Liabilities		
Current Liabilities		
Accounts payable and accrued expenses...........	$ 49,809	$ 45,824
Federal and state income taxes.....................	18,657	3,673
Notes payable and current portion of long-		
term debt.......................................	30,370	30,939
Total Current Liabilities........................	98,836	80,436
Deferred Income Taxes.............................	11,720	9,052
Long-term Debt		
Parent...	42,052	31,383
Subsidiaries....................................	33,044	28,833
Subordinated Debt.................................	37,841	45,548
Stockholders' Equity		
Preferred stocks...................................	$ 2,697	$ 3,479
Common stock.....................................	9,740	8,533
Additional capital.................................	60,760	43,316
Retained earnings.................................	73,606	64,431
Total Stockholders' Equity.....................	146,803	119,759
Total Liabilities and Stockholders' Equity......	$370,296	$315,011

Mr. Fuqua also listed his phone number in letters to shareholders, soliciting their comments.

Acquisitions

By 1968, Fuqua Industries had acquired 14 major businesses. The largest of these was the Interstate Motor Freight System. Mr. Fuqua explained why he acquired Interstate:

Our plan called for building a strong base of earnings in businesses that generate a high cash flow. Transportation and Interstate, in particular, was such a business.

Although Interstate was Fuqua's largest single subsidiary, the recreation subsidiaries comprised the largest portion (47 percent) of Fuqua's 1968 sales. In addition to transportation and recreation, Fuqua owned companies in shelter (17 percent of sales), and agribusiness (7 percent of sales). These four groups provided the base for Fuqua's subsequent growth, and from 1969 to 1972 nine acquisitions and three divestitures were completed (see Exhibit 4).

In acquiring companies, Fuqua had several criteria:

1. Stay in basic industries.
2. Buy growth-minded companies with a good track record.
3. Stay away from "glamor" fields or businesses requiring high technology.
4. Keep the subsidiary intact and let them run their own show.
5. Buy no business which competed in the low-price end of its market.

Indeed Fuqua's acquisitions had stayed very close to these criteria. For example, of the 20 subsidiaries in operation at the end of 1972, 16 were still run by the management team that had sold the business.

Most of Fuqua's early acquisitions were made for an exchange of stock. Recently more acquisitions were being made on a cash basis.

Besides its acquisitions, Fuqua had also disposed of three subsidiary businesses. This was seen as a part of the overall strategy to maximize shareholders' wealth, and also as a reflection of Mr. Fuqua's belief that "the first loss is the least loss" and that "management's time, capital, and risk can better be put into other businesses than in trying to prove that you didn't make a mistake." The three divestitures—Ward Manufacturing, Varco Pruden, and Career Enterprises—had all been operating at a loss and management felt that divestiture and reinvestment of capital in other businesses made more sense than trying to turn the businesses around.

Subsidiary Operations

At the end of 1972, Fuqua was involved in the four previously mentioned product groups. Table 1 presents summary data on these businesses.

Recreation Subsidiaries

Fuqua's recreation subsidiaries accounted for almost half of Fuqua's total sales and 57 percent of operating income, and management indi-

EXHIBIT 4

FUQUA INDUSTRIES (A)
Aquisitions and Divestures (1969–72)

Date of Acquisition (Divestiture)	Former Name (Location)	Business Description	Accounting Method
1969..................	Trojan Seed Company (Olivia, Minnesota)	Hybrid corn seed. Sales, 1968: $4.8 million. Net income, 1968: $92,000.	Pooling
1969..................	Career Enterprises, Inc. (St. Petersburg, Florida)	Adult education schools. Sales, 1968: $2.1 million. Net income, 1968: $179,000.	Pooling
1969..................	Haft–Gaines Co. (Fort Lauderdale, Florida)	Land development; developing of Inverrary in southern Florida. Sales, 1968: $5.9 million. Net income, 1968: $337,000.	Pooling
1970..................	Anderson & Thompson Ski Co. (Seattle, Washington)	Manufacturer and distributor of ski equipment. Sales, 1969: $6.3 million. Net income, 1969: $242,000.	Pooling
(1970).................	Ward Manufacturing Co. (Hamilton, Ohio)	Camping trailer and mobile camping equipment. Net income, 1969: ($459,000).	Assets sold at a loss of $4.1 million.
1971..................	Arizona Valley Development Co. (Phoenix, Arizona)	Land development. Major project is the development of 3,500 acres in Arizona City. Sales, 1970: $5.1 million. Net income, 1970: $474,000.	Pooling
1971..................	Hutch Sporting Goods, Inc. (Cincinnati, Ohio)	Football, baseball, and basketball equipment. Sales, 1971: $4.3 million. Net income, 1971: $546,000.	Purchase
1971..................	Gilcrease Hills Development Corporation (Tulsa, Oklahoma)	Land development. Major project is a planned community in Tulsa.	Acquired a 50 percent interest

(1971)..........	Varco Pruden, Inc. (Pine Bluff, Arkansas)	Construction and erection of metal buildings. Net income, 1970: $33,000.	Sold at a loss of $1.2 million
(1971)..........	Career Enterprises, Inc. (St. Petersburg, Florida)	Adult education schools. Net income, 1971: $420,000.	Sold at a loss of $6.7 million
1972..........	Ajay Enterprises, Inc. (Delavan, Wisconsin)	Manufacturer and distributor of golf, bowling, and billiard equipment. Sales, 1971: $14.2 million. Net income, 1971: $382,000.	Pooling
1972..........	Gulf States Theatres, Inc. (New Orleans, Louisiana)	Operates motion picture theatres in the South and Southwest. Sales, 1971: $9.9 million. Net income, 1971: $493,000.	Purchase

Amount paid for acquisitions:
Poolings: Acquired for 1,446,918 shares of common stock valued at $36.4 million, and 661,480 contingent shares valued at $11.8 million.
Purchases: Acquired for $6.9 million in cash, $12.2 million in notes, and 102,000 shares of common stock valued at $2.1 million.

TABLE 1

Sales and Earnings by Product Group

Sales and Revenues	1967	1967 % of Total	1968	1969	1970	1971	1972	1972 % of Total	1973 Fore-cast
Recreation									
Snowmobiles and lawn-mowers	$ 13.9	6%	$ 21.1	$ 30.8	$ 36.8	$ 45.7	$ 56.4	13%	$ 68.0
Sporting goods	15.9	7	19.8	24.1	28.3	31.4	39.1	9	39.0
Marine products	38.4	18	49.7	49.4	29.6	34.0	42.4	10	48.0
Entertainment	23.9	11	23.8	23.9	26.4	25.9	37.2	9	45.0
Photographic finishing	14.1	7	16.9	19.5	17.9	17.8	21.8	5	23.0
Total recreation	106.2	49	131.3	147.7	139.0	154.8	196.9	46	223.0
Transportation	66.3	31	71.1	96.9	112.6	130.5	140.7	32	147.0
Shelter	25.8	12	29.4	36.8	36.4	36.9	58.4	13	74.0
Agribusiness	18.0	8	20.8	20.7	28.8	32.9	38.0	9	40.0
Total continuing operations (1)	216.3	100.0	252.6	302.2	316.8	355.1	434.0	100.0	484.0
Add: discontinued operations	42.2		40.3	42.1	28.0	5.0	—		—
Less: restatements of businesses purchased	36.8		40.9	10.8	5.5	1.3	—		—
Total sales and revenues	$221.7		$252.0	$333.5	$339.3	$358.8	$434.0		$484.0

Earnings	1967	1967 % of Total	1968	1969	1970	1971	1972	1972 % of Total	Compound Annual Growth Rate %	1973 Fore-cast
Recreation										
Snowmobiles and lawn-mowers	$ 2.4	14%	$ 4.7	$ 5.8	$ 6.2	$ 7.3	$ 9.9	22%	32%	$11.4
Sporting goods	1.1	7	2.0	2.9	3.2	3.1	4.0	9	30	4.1
Marine products	1.0	6	3.6	3.3	0.3	0.6	3.3	7	27	4.5
Entertainment	2.5	16	3.2	4.5	4.2	4.5	6.2	14	16	6.8
Photographic finishing	1.6	10	1.8	1.4	1.0	1.7	2.4	5	9	2.9
Total recreation	8.6	55	15.3	17.9	14.9	17.2	25.8	57	24	29.7
Transportation	3.6	23	4.3	6.0	4.5	9.2	10.0	22	23	10.0
Shelter	0.3	2	2.0	5.9	5.2	4.2	2.8	6	56	5.5
Agribusiness	3.1	20	3.0	1.5	3.1	5.3	6.8	15	17	6.9
Total continuing operations (1)	15.6	100.0	24.6	31.3	27.7	35.9	45.4	100%	23%	52.1
Add: discontinued operations	1.7		1.6	0.5	1.6	(0.8)	(0.1)		—	—
Less: unallocated corporate expenses and corporate interest	0.9		1.7	3.9	6.2	7.9	9.8		—	9.7
Less: restatements of businesses purchased	1.2		2.7	0.3	1.0	0.2	—		—	—
Income before income taxes	15.2		21.8	27.6	22.1	27.0	35.5		19	42.4
Income taxes	7.0		11.0	13.6	11.0	13.5	17.4		—	21.0
Net operating income	$ 8.2		$10.8	$14.0	$11.1	$13.5	$18.1		17%	$21.4

(1) Includes all continuing companies for all periods, regardless of date of acquisition, except that Gulf States Theatres is included only for the periods since June 1, 1972.
Source: 1972 Annual report.

cated that Fuqua's position in recreation was likely to increase in the future. Management cited government statistics that illustrated the growth of expenditures on recreation activities, and pointed out that the increasing level of affluence plus the pressures of urban life were making recreation businesses an excellent growth opportunity.

Fuqua's recreation subsidiaries were involved in a wide variety of activities. Pacemaker Corporation and Thunderbird Products Corporation produced pleasure boats ranging in size from 15 to 63 feet in length. During the 1970–71 recession, sales and earnings of the boating companies declined substantially, but 1972 saw a dramatic turnaround. Fuqua's involvement in marine products also included Yarbrough Manufacturing, which was the largest manufacturer of boat trailers in the United States.

McDonough Power Equipment, Inc., manufactured the "Snapper" and "Comet" lawnmowers. McDonough's sales and profits had increased in each of the last ten years and the company emphasized innovative products that competed in the premium end of the power lawnmower market. Scorpion, Inc., was the fourth largest manufacturer of snowmobiles in the United States. Spotty snow conditions in 1971 and 1972 had resulted in lower earnings for Scorpion, and a shakedown was reported throughout the snowmobile industry. Management felt, however, that companies like Scorpion would eventually dominate the industry.

Through its Ajay Enterprises, A & T Ski, and Hutch Sporting Goods subsidiaries, Fuqua was also a major producer and distributor of skiing, baseball, football, basketball, boxing, bowling, billiards, and golfing equipment. These products were sold in retail outlets throughout the United States.

Fuqua's recreation activities also extended to entertainment and photofinishing. Martin and Gulf States Theatres operated over 250 motion picture theatres primarily in the South and Southwest, and Fuqua also owned three ABC television affiliates and three AM radio stations. Colorcraft Corporation operated primarily in the Eastern half of the United States and offered photo-finishing services to drug stores, camera stores, and other retailers.

Transportation

Fuqua's involvement in transportation consisted of the Interstate Motor Freight System and its Canadian subsidiary, the Direct System. By the end of 1972 these companies served over 34,000 miles of certified routes in the United States and Canada. Although the trucking industry was subject to substantial Interstate Commerce Commission regulation, Interstate had more than doubled sales and earnings since its acquisition in 1967. J. B. Fuqua pointed out that Interstate was one of the "cash cows" that was needed to maintain the overall Fuqua strategy.

Shelter and Agribusiness

Fuqua's shelter and agribusiness subsidiaries accounted for about 20 percent of 1972 sales and earnings. In real estate, Fuqua's subsidiaries were involved in the development of the Inverrary and Arizona City planned communities. Fuqua Homes manufactured mobile homes in 14 plants throughout the United States.

Agribusiness represented the smallest portion of Fuqua's total sales, but the return on investment and sales was termed "excellent." The Stormor Company was a large manufacturer of grain drying and storage bins. Rome Industries manufactured land clearing and specialized agricultural and construction equipment primarily for use on Caterpillar tractors. Rome had a long history of profitable operations, but the business was described as extremely cyclical. The Trojan Seed Company had a worldwide reputation for its advanced hybrid corn seed products, and since 1967 sales and pre-tax income had increased four- and five-fold respectively.

COMPANY OPERATIONS AND STRATEGY

As Fuqua Industries had grown from a tile manufacturer to a $400 million company, a distinctive management style and philosophy had developed. In many instances, this philosophy reflected the ideas of J. B. Fuqua; but there was also a common theme to the concepts expressed by other corporate officers. The quotes, below, were made by various corporate officers and are representative of the philosophy and thinking of Fuqua's top executives.

❄   ❄   ❄   ❄   ❄

We believe in Alfred Sloan's concept that the prime responsibility of a public company is to maximize shareholders' wealth. Our job is to keep our funds where they can earn a high return for our shareholders.

American industry is burdened with bad divisions that no one has the guts to sell, and with managements that are afraid to make decisions.

Cash is a liability, not an asset. A well-run company shouldn't have any cash.

Our subsidiaries can run themselves and don't need a lot of people looking over their shoulders.

We write very few memos and prefer to meet in groups to discuss things.

We can move fast on acquisitions because we are familiar with the industry [recreation] and know what we want.

Each position here [corporate office] is a function of the person in it.

We don't have an organization chart. Mr. Fuqua doesn't believe in them.

❄   ❄   ❄   ❄   ❄

Corporate Office

Fuqua's corporate office was located on the 38th floor of a large bank building in downtown Atlanta. Only 17 professionals and officers worked at the corporate office. The small size of the staff was cited as a strength and there were no plans to expand the staff. In general, Fuqua preferred to resolve any problems with face-to-face discussions. As a result, corporate executives travelled a great deal and, on an average day, about half of the corporate staff would be out of town.

Control.   The controller's office was Fuqua's major corporate office function and consisted of Ted Davis, controller, and six assistant and group controllers. On a monthly basis, the controller's office received profit and loss statements, balance sheets, and flow of funds statements that were supplemented with a commentary prepared by the subsidiary. Although the chief financial officer in each subsidiary reported to the subsidiary president, there was an indirect link between these officers and the corporate controller's office, and any discrepancies or questions were usually handled by the group controller and the subsidiary's financial officer.

Fuqua operated on an annual budget and each subsidiary prepared a preliminary budget in October. The budgets included the usual financial data plus a list of major expenditures and a narrative prepared by the presidents. Fuqua executives commented that the budgeting process was more than a forecasting exercise, and included a "total evaluation of the company, the industry, and environmental factors."

The preliminary budgets were usually reviewed in early December at a meeting of the subsidiary management, Carl Patrick, the corporate controller, the group controller, and the vice president for operations. A final budget was due in corporate headquarters by early February.

Fuqua's management was extremely proud of their budgeting system and emphasized the scope and realism of the budgets. One result of this confidence in the budgets was the decision at the end of 1972 to publish unaudited 1972 figures and a forecast of 1973 results by major product groups. Management felt that the budgets provided a realistic basis for the forecasts and, since the budgets were revised each quarter, shareholders could be notified of any substantial changes in the forecast.

Fuqua had no formal long-range or five-year planning system, and management felt that in their types of businesses 18 months was a long time horizon. One corporate officer commented that "a good book for people interested in five-year planning is *Future Shock*."

Finance.   All borrowings were done on central basis, with advances made to the subsidiaries as funds were needed. Excess cash generated by the subsidiaries was sent to Fuqua. Each subsidiary had a corporate account on which interest was charged to the subsidiary or could be

EXHIBIT 5

FUQUA INDUSTRIES (A)
Biographical Data on Corporate Executives

Name	Position	Age	Years with Company	Employment Prior to Company
J. B. Fuqua...............	Chairman of the board, chief executive officer	54	8	
C. L. Patrick.............	President, chief operating officer	54	3	Chairman and president of Martin Theatres (Fuqua subsidiary)
Lawrence Klamon........	Senior vice president, general counsel	36	5½	Cravath, Swaine, & Moore (NYC): associate
Kay Slayden.............	Vice president–operations	39	1½	Teledyne Brown Engineering: vice president
Jay Farish...............	Vice president–acquisitions	44	3½	Diversified Products Group: vice president and general manager
Robert Prather..........	Vice president–acquisitions	28	3	—
Robert Spencer..........	Vice president–insurance	47	5½	Polaris Corp.: insurance manager
Keith Johnson...........	Treasurer	30	½	Citizens Southern Bank: trust and tax officer
Ted Davis...............	Controller	33	2	Touche, Ross & Co.: senior consultant
Jim Bahin...............	Group controller	28	½	Arthur Young & Co.: senior consultant
Hugh Carey.............	Group controller	28	½	Touche, Ross & Co.: consultant
Chuck Cansler..........	Group controller	28	2	Ernst & Ernst: senior accountant
Dan Shepherd...........	Operations manager	33	½	Mattel, Inc.: director of operations
Rob Berman.............	Operations manager	29	½	West Point Pepperal: operations
Elliot Fisch.............	Financial analyst	24	5	—

earned from advances to Fuqua. The interest rate applied to the corporate account was close to the current prime lending rate, and interest expense or income was reflected in each subsidiaries' pre-tax income.

Since 1967, Fuqua had substantially increased its long-term debt and the debt to equity ratio of about 1.0 was planned to continue.

Prior to 1969, Fuqua had followed a policy of paying cash dividends. This was a hold over from the old Natco management. In 1969, this policy was changed and dividends consisted of a 2 percent stock dividend plus ½₀ of a 1980 Warrant for each share of common stock. From 1970 to 1972, 2 percent stock dividends were paid. Management did not expect to pay cash dividends in the near future.

Operations. Fuqua's subsidiaries were given a great deal of autonomy in running their businesses and all of the subsidiary presidents reported to Carl Patrick. Mr. Patrick had been appointed president in February 1970 after serving as president of Fuqua's Martin Theatre subsidiary. Mr. Patrick's predecessor, E. D. Kenna, had attempted to institute a group vice president function at Fuqua, but Mr. Patrick preferred to have all of the subsidiaries reporting directly to him:

> As a former subsidiary president, I think that I'm a little more sensitive to the needs of our presidents. These are highly motivated, entrepreneurial managers and when they have a problem they want to talk to the top man.

Although operations were viewed as a subsidiary responsibility, a small (two-man) operations staff operated out of corporate headquarters. Mr. Kay Slayden, vice president–operations, stated that most of his time was spent at subsidiaries that needed assistance and that his job was mostly one of a "trouble-shooter." Mr. Slayden felt that in the future operations would receive increased emphasis at Fuqua.

Current Situation

In early 1973, Fuqua's management was pleased with 1972's record levels of sales and earnings and was confident that the 1973 earnings per share forecast of $2.09 could be reached. Management was concerned, however, that the stock market was not responding to Fuqua's excellent 1972 performance and overall growth since 1967. By February 1973, Fuqua's common stock was selling at about $15, or 8 times earnings. Table 2, traces the price of Fuqua's common stock.

Although Fuqua had no acquisitions planned in the immediate future, it was expected that acquisitions would be made in the recreation area during 1973. Of course, the low stock price greatly affected the types of

TABLE 2

Fuqua Industries Common Stock Price

Year	High	Low
1967	32	12
1968	41	26
1969	46	27
1970	32	7
1971	26	13
1972	28	16

transactions that could be arranged, and cash purchases would eventually be limited by Fuqua's debt capacity.

THE TROJAN SEED COMPANY

In 1969, Fuqua Industries acquired the Trojan Seed Company for 143,000 shares of common stock valued at $5.4 million. In addition, 158,000 contingent shares of Fuqua common stock were to be issued to Trojan's management in July 1973. Table 3 contains a summary of Trojan's performance since 1967. As can be seen in the table, Trojan had grown substantially since its acquisition, and pre-tax income as a percentage of sales was at a near record high. Nevertheless, 1972 was not a good year for the corn seed business as acres of corn planted declined by almost 20 percent. Trojan's sales in 1972 were about the same as in 1971, but the amount of seed in inventory increased by over $2 million. These large investments in inventory and the increases in plant and equipment had the effect of greatly increasing Fuqua's investment in the subsidiary. By the end of 1972, Fuqua had advanced Trojan $16.7 million, or about half of Fuqua's advances to all of its other subsidiaries combined.

TABLE 3

Trojan Financial Data (dollars in thousands)

	Sales	Pre-Tax	Percent of Income	Receivables	Inventory	Fixed Assets	Corporate Account
1967*	$ 3,916	$ 554	14.7%	$ 294	$ 724	$ 600	$ —
1968*	4,847	269	5.5	768	1,655	2,100	—
1969	8,026	(292)	—	1,915	3,998	2,400	5,628
1970	14,441	545	3.8	2,929	10,042	2,700	8,792
1971	17,084	3,007	17.6	3,280	14,429	4,800	11,372
1972	17,166	2,713	15.8	5,787	16,566	4,900	16,764

* Not owned by Fuqua Industries.

Description of Business

The Trojan Seed Company was the fourth largest producer and developer of hybrid corn seeds behind DeKalb, Pioneer, and Funk. Trojan was the only company of the top four dealing exclusively in hybrid corn seeds. Exhibit 6 presents additional financial data on the DeKalb and Pioneer Seed companies.

The great majority of the corn produced from Trojan seed was used as feed for cattle and swine. Although the demand for beef and pork had grown at only about 6 percent in recent years, demand was expected to increase as the per capita consumption of meat throughout the world rose. Although Trojan only sold its corn seed in the United States, world markets were seen as having tremendous potential.

In 1968, Trojan was the first company to develop a "high lysine" corn. This seed produced corn containing twice as much protein as regular corn. This meant that cattle and swine could eat more corn and less protein supplement in their daily diet, further enlarging the domestic demand for its seed. Because of the proprietary nature of its product, Trojan's seed sold at about 15 percent higher than the market prices. Since the cost of seed was a small portion of the farmer's total expenses, management felt that the higher price did not contract demand, but rather emphasized the higher quality of Trojan's seeds.

Marketing and Distribution

Until its acquisition by Fuqua, Trojan had concentrated its distribution in the northern portion of the Corn Belt. After the acquisition, the dealer network grew to over 3,000 dealers and Trojan seed was sold throughout the 11 Corn Belt states.

In order to offer the best possible product to a particular customer, Trojan dealers marketed 54 different hybrid seeds. Trojan's sales force and dealers were offered a wide variety of bonuses and incentives to increase sales, and management felt that these incentives had been instrumental in the rapid expansion of Trojan's business.

Production and Processing

The production and processing of hybrid corn seeds required substantial investments in drying stations and inventory. Inventory planning was extremely difficult, and was complicated not only by the need to forecast demand eighteen months in advance, but also by such uncertain variables as weather conditions and the Federal Feed Grain Program.

The hybrid corn seeds that were sold to the farmer required seven

EXHIBIT 6

FUQUA INDUSTRIES (A)
Financial Summary of Selected Hybrid Corn Companies

Year	Sales ($000)	Pre-Tax Income ($000)	Pre-Tax Income (%)	Inventory ($000)	Sales/Inv.	Return on Assets (%)	Per Share Data		
							Earnings	Dividends	Price Range
DeKalb AgResearch Inc.†									
1972	$149,100	$29,600	19.9%	$28,700	5.2	7.1%	$1.25	$0.09	58-15
1971	147,400	25,000	17.0	17,600	8.4	n.a.†	1.07	0.09	28-15
1970	114,000	18,400	16.1	21,200	5.4	n.a.	0.75	0.08	16-6
1969	98,100	14,200	14.5	19,600	5.0	n.a.	0.58	0.08	n.a.
Pioneer Hi-Bred International, Inc.‡									
1972	$ 82,000	$13,400	16.3%	$27,900	2.9	9.3%	$0.63	$0.14	n.a.
1971	75,600	8,600	11.4	22,600	3.3	6.6	0.42	0.11	n.a.
1970	71,600	13,300	18.6	21,500	3.3	10.4	0.66	0.15	n.a.
1969	57,200	7,500	13.1	23,000	2.5	6.3	0.34	0.11	n.a.

* Approximately 40 percent of sales were of hybrid corn seeds.
† n.a. = not available.
‡ Approximately 65 percent of sales were of hybrid corn seeds. Pioneer was privately held until mid-1973.

generations to be developed. The first six generations were grown in a little over two years at research nurseries in Hawaii and Florida. Usually in February, Trojan would contract independent farmers to plant adjacent rows of male and female sixth generation seed. In the fall, the seventh generation corn would be sold to Trojan, and during the winter the seed would be dried and stored and then sold the next year. The uncertainties of seventh generation seed yield and final demand were usually absorbed in high levels of seventh generation seed inventories as seed could be stored for five or more years without deterioration.

Two examples illustrate the complexity of the inventory management problem. In February, management had to contract to plant a specific number of acres of sixth generation seed and agree to purchase all of the seventh generation corn seed that was produced. Of course, the yield of the sixth generation seed was uncertain. A low yield combined with high demand the following year for seventh generation corn seed could leave a company with insufficient inventory to meet demand. To avoid this risk, a larger number of sixth generation acres could be contracted. But if the yield on the sixth generation corn was exceptionally large, and if demand for seventh generation seed declined the following year, the company would be left with a substantial inventory of seventh generation seed.

After the Fuqua acquisition, Trojan expanded its storage and drying capabilities to eight facilities throughout the Corn Belt. Management felt that current capacity could support annual volume of up to $40 million and no additional storage facilities were planned.

Research

Trojan was a research-oriented company and its staff of 60 researchers, employed in six research centers, was recognized as among the industry's best. To illustrate the intensity of Trojan's research effort, in 1972 Trojan tested over 3,700 new hybrid seeds. Only four of these were judged worthy of commercial distribution. Trojan's management felt that research provided Trojan with a significant competitive advantage and was determined to maintain the company's research emphasis.

Management

Trojan's top management consisted of Robert Mills, president, and Ira Keeshin, chief financial officer. Mills and Keeshin had sold Trojan to Fuqua and remained with the company after the acquisition.

Robert Mills's background had been in marketing. Mills was described as having "the typical enthusiasm of any good salesman." Ira Keeshin was described as a more "level-headed" financial type, and Fuqua's management was pleased that Mr. Keeshin could "balance" Mr. Mills's enthusiasm. Management personnel in research, production, and marketing were all described as excellent.

THE DIVESTITURE DECISION

As early as October 1972, Kay Slayden had become concerned with the situation at Trojan. Mr. Slayden explained:

> Although Trojan accounted for only 4 percent of our sales and 6 percent of profits, it had about 50 percent of the advances from Fuqua. What concerned me even more was that as Trojan continued to grow, the situation was likely to get even worse.

As Mr. Slayden reviewed the final 1972 figures for Trojan, he was again convinced of his original assessment. Mr. Slayden also felt that the Trojan divestiture should be considered as part of an overall strategy of getting out of agribusiness and redeploying those assets in the recreation area.

At the end of 1972, a decision had been reached to sell Fuqua's farm equipment subsidiary, Rome Industries. Although Rome had been operating at a substantial profit, Fuqua's management felt that the business had only moderate growth potential in a highly cyclical industry. By February 1973, serious negotiations were under way to sell Rome and Mr. Slayden argued that the Rome divestiture offered even more reasons to sell Trojan.

As the principal opponent to the Trojan divestiture, Ted Davis was concerned that Fuqua was going to be selling Trojan at just the time that Fuqua could begin to benefit from its extensive investments in the subsidiary. Also, current forecasts were expecting 1973 to be a record year for corn production and the long-term outlook for the seed business was excellent. As Mr. Davis prepared for the meeting on the divestiture, he calculated the figures shown in Table 4. Mr. Davis felt that the 7.1

TABLE 4

Ted Davis' Trojan ROI Calculation

	Thousands of Dollars
Average Fuqua advances—1972	$15,250
Initial investment (143,000 shares at $38)	5,434
Contingent shares (158,000 shares at $20) to be paid July 1973	3,160
Total investment (at market)	$23,844
1972 net income (adjusted for Fuqua interest)	$ 1,690
Return on investment	7.1%

percent after-tax return on investment was adequate, and that the ROI would increase in the future as Trojan's earnings improved and as Fuqua's investment in the subsidiary gradually declined.

DIVESTITURE ALTERNATIVES

Kay Slayden listed five potential buyers of the business:

1. The current management
2. The public
3. A food cooperative
4. Pfizer, Inc.
5. Another pharmaceutical or chemical company

Given Trojan's profitable record and future potential, Kay Slayden hoped to sell Trojan for substantially more than its book value. Since Fuqua would want to sell the business on an immediate cash basis, Mr. Slayden strongly doubted if Messrs. Mills and Keeshin could raise the necessary cash. Also, since Mills and Keeshin didn't know of Fuqua's interest in selling Trojan, Mr. Slayden was uncertain as to how they would react.

A public offering of Trojan stock seemed like an attractive alternative. Currently, other hybrid seed companies were selling at about 30 times earnings on the over-the-counter markets and a spin-off could enable Fuqua to maintain an interest in Trojan. Exhibit 7 shows some figures prepared by Mr. Slayden to determine the effect of various divestiture alternatives.

If Fuqua were to sell Trojan to the public, Mr. Slayden thought that Fuqua's Stormor subsidiary could also be included in the offering. Since Stormor would be Fuqua's only remaining agribusiness company, it would make sense for Fuqua to divest of all of its agribusiness holdings.

There were some reservations, however, on a public offering. Mr. Slayden was not sure that Fuqua would want to sell Stormor since the subsidiary was extremely profitable and also was one of Fuqua's "cash cows." An alternative was to include Stormor in Fuqua's shelter group of subsidiaries—and only spin-off Trojan. Mr. Slayden also was uncertain if Fuqua would be able to retrieve its advances to Trojan if a public offering were made. A final uncertainty was the price the public would be willing to pay for Trojan. Mr. Slayden had heard that the Pioneer Seed Company was planning on going public during the summer, so he was somewhat concerned that the market could become "glutted" with seed companies.

Another alternative was to sell Trojan to a food cooperative. Since food cooperatives were not operated for a profit, writing off good will on a purchase would not be a problem for a cooperative. Although Mr.

EXHIBIT 7

FUQUA INDUSTRIES (A)
Divestiture Alternatives

	Spinning Off Trojan to Public with P.E. of 20			Combining Trojan and Stormer and Spinning Off to Public at P.E. of 18			Selling Trojan to Pfizer at P.E. of 14	Selling Trojan to Hercules at P.E. of 17
Cash to Fuqua (000)	40%	80%	100%	40%	80%	100%		
Gross from sale	8,178	16,356	20,445	12,267	24,534	30,668	20,566	24,973
Tax on gain	1,853	3,707	4,634	2,328	4,655	5,819	4,670	5,992
Net from sale	6,325	12,649	15,811	9,939	19,879	24,849	15,896	18,981
Cash available from corporate account	15,000	15,000	15,000	11,026	11,026	11,026	15,000	15,000
Total available cash	21,325	27,649	30,811	20,965	30,905	35,875	30,896	33,981
Effect on future earnings/share if total freed-up cash is used to reduce bank debt								
Loss of subsidiary earnings	$ (578)	$ (1,155)	$ (1,444)	$ (1,029)	$ (2,058)	$ (2,572)	$ (1,444)	$ (1,444)
Savings on interest	746	968	1,078	734	1,082	1,256	1,081	1,189
Net gain/(loss) in earnings	168	(187)	(366)	(295)	(976)	(1,316)	(363)	(255)
Net gain/(loss) per share	0.02	(0.02)	(0.04)	(0.03)	(0.10)	(0.13)	(0.04)	(0.03)
Effect on future earnings/share if total freed-up cash is used to purchase Fuqua stock at $20/Share								
Loss of subsidiary earnings	$ (578)	$ (1,155)	$ (1,444)	$ (1,029)	$ (2,058)	$ (2,572)	$ (1,444)	$ (1,444)
Loss of interest income from subsidiary	(525)	(525)	(525)	(386)	(386)	(386)	(525)	(525)
Adjusted income for 1973	19,797	19,220	18,931	19,485	18,456	17,921	18,931	18,931
Purchased shares	1,066,250	1,382,460	1,540,575	1,048,250	1,545,254	1,793,784	1,544,810	1,699,055
Adjusted shares outstanding	8,933,750	8,617,540	8,459,425	8,951,750	8,454,746	8,206,216	8,455,190	8,300,945
Adjusted earnings/share	$2.21	$2.23	$2.24	$2.18	$2.18	$2.19	$2.24	$2.28
Net gain/(loss) per share	0.12	0.14	0.15	0.09	0.09	0.10	0.15	0.19

Slayden hadn't contacted any cooperatives, he thought that hybrid seed could be a logical extension of their business, and that many of the larger cooperatives would have the resources to buy Trojan.

The most promising prospect in February 1973 seemed to be the giant pharmaceutical company, Pfizer, Inc. By chance, Pfizer had contacted Fuqua in December to ask if Trojan could be bought. Pfizer already did a substantial business in animal medicine and serums and was anxious to extend its product line to include hybrid seeds. As a worldwide company, Pfizer was also in a position to take advantage of Trojan's potential in foreign markets.

Kay Slayden had already held preliminary discussions with Pfizer, but was somewhat discouraged. Mr. Slayden said that during the discussions he was outnumbered by 100 to 1 and that every issue seemed to require a new team of Pfizer staff specialists. Mr. Slayden feared that negotiations with Pfizer could drag on indefinitely. Also Pfizer had asked to visit Trojan's facilities and to meet Trojan's management. Mr. Slayden knew that this confronted him with the problem of how to tell Mills and Keeshin that Trojan was for sale.

The negotiations with Pfizer had suggested that other pharmaceutical or chemical companies might also be interested in extending their product line into hybrid seeds. Mr. Slayden had already contacted the Hercules Chemical Company, but Hercules wasn't sure if it would be willing to repay Fuqua's advances to Trojan. After talking with Hercules, Mr. Slayden thought that Trojan would be a better fit for a pharmaceutical company that was selling animal medicine than a chemical company whose major agribusiness product was fertilizers.

As Kay Slayden thought about selling Trojan, he wondered if he should continue to negotiate exclusively with Pfizer or if there was anything to be gained in finding other parties interested in purchasing Trojan.

5

Fuqua Industries (C)

As Ted Davis, formerly controller and now vice president–operations of Fuqua Industries, entered his office on December 26, 1973, he noticed a message on his desk—"Mr. Fuqua and Mr. Patrick would like to see you at 10:00 o'clock." Ted knew that the meeting was to decide if Fuqua should sell its Scorpion snowmobile subsidiary. Since Fuqua's fiscal year ended on December 31, Davis was also aware that a firm decision to sell Scorpion would have to be made in the next five days if Scorpion were to be reported as a discontinued business in 1973.

Largely due to the energy crisis and a second bad snow year, snowmobile sales were at a virtual standstill, and by the end of November Scorpion had already lost $2.9 million. Davis expected a year-end after-tax loss of about $3.5 million. The loss would reduce Fuqua's earnings per share by about 30¢ and would also cause a year-to-year decline in the overall earnings of Fuqua's recreation group. The sale of the Trojan Seed Company earlier in the year had resulted in a gain of over $15 million, and a loss on the sale of Scorpion (estimated at about $10 million) could be offset by the Trojan profit. If Scorpion were sold, Davis estimated that Fuqua's earnings from continuing operations could be within one or two cents of the $2.09 1973 earnings forecast, and that earnings of the recreation group would show an increase of about 20 percent.

While Davis recognized that the arguments for selling Scorpion were convincing, he had been impressed with Scorpion's business and management. In Davis's opinion, Scorpion could recover from its current problems and was in a good position to benefit from the current industry shakedown. Just before the Christmas holidays, J. B. Fuqua had commented to Davis that if Fuqua Industries were not a public company Scorpion was the type of company that he would want to keep.

Fuqua Industries—1973[1]

Except for the problems with Scorpion and a declining stock price, 1973 had been a good year for Fuqua Industries. Excluding Scorpion, sales and earnings of all the product groups were close to or above forecast and earnings per share for the first nine months were $1.97, compared with $1.17 for the same period in 1972. Fuqua had discontinued its agribusiness operations (Stormor, which manufactured grain storage bins was reclassified in the shelter group), and acquired four additional recreation subsidiaries (see Exhibit 1). All four of the acquisitions were made for cash, and Fuqua was also in the final stages of negotiating the purchase for $4.3 million in cash and notes of the Ebonite Corporation, a major manufacturer of bowling balls.

Despite this impressive record, Fuqua's common stock declined throughout the year. The stock market had been depressed throughout

EXHIBIT 1

FUQUA INDUSTRIES (C)
Acquisitions—1973

Date of Acquisition	Former Name (location)	Business Description	Accounting Method
1973	Columbus Cycle & Supply Co., Inc. (Columbus, Ohio)	Distributor of bicycles and bicycle parts and accessories. Sales, 1972: $18.6 million. Net income, 1972: $896,000.	Purchase
1973	Hendel Manufacturing Company	Manufacturer of tennis apparel. Sales, 1972: $2.5 million. Net income, 1972: $142,000.	Purchase
1973	Wheelsport Distributing Company (Portland, Oregon)	Distributor of motorcycle accessories. Sales, 1972: $4.1 million. Net income, 1972: $374,000.	Purchase
1973	Signa Corporation (Decatur, Indiana)	Manufacturer of small boats. Sales, 1972: $3.3 million. Net income, 1972: $214,500.	Purchase
1974 (to be consummated within the next few weeks.)	Ebonite Corporation	Manufacturer of bowling balls. Sales, 1973: $7.2 million. Net income, 1973: $655,000.	Purchase

Amount paid for 1973 acquisitions: Approximately $21 million in cash and notes.

---

[1] A more complete description of Fuqua Industries can be found in Fuqua Industries (A).

1973, but Fuqua's decline from $20 at the beginning of the year to a low of $6 by December was greater than the stock market indices.

One result of the low stock price was that Fuqua's common stock had been trading below its book value, and in August the company offered to exchange up to 2 million shares of common stock for 9½ percent subordinated debentures, with principal due in 1998. The exchange rate was $15 face amount of debentures for each share of common stock that in August was selling for about $10 a share. The offering resulted in over 1.2 million shares being exchanged for the subordinated debt.

Fuqua's management explained that although the exchange offering increased the company's long-term debt, the reduction in shares outstanding would have a substantial impact on per share earnings. Preliminary forecasts for 1974 indicated an 18 percent forecasted increase in profits would result in a 31 percent increase in earnings per share.

SCORPION, INC.

In 1968, Fuqua Industries acquired Scorpion, Inc., (formerly named Trail-A-Sled) for 194,000 shares of common stock valued at $8.5 million. At the time of the acquisition, Fuqua described snowmobiling as "the fastest growing winter sport in North America." Table 1 contains a summary of industry data and Scorpion's performance since 1968.

As can be seen in the table Scorpion grew at substantial rates until 1972, when spotty snow conditions greatly contracted demand. The lower than planned sales for Scorpion also resulted in high inventory levels and increased advances from Fuqua. Although 1973 was also marked by poor snow conditions, it was the energy crisis that had virtually put the snowmobile industry at a standstill. For the 11 months ending November 30, 1973, Scorpion sales were $6.4 million below budget and losses of $2.9 million had already been reported. (See Exhibits 2 and 3 for recent financial statements.)

Description of the Business

Scorpion, Inc., was the fourth largest producer of snowmobiles in the United States. Until the 1972 and 1973 slowdowns, the industry had been marked by a large number of producers and rapid growth. Recently many of the marginal companies had gone out of business and other companies were reportedly for sale or on the verge of bankruptcy. Table 2 lists the market share and status of the major snowmobile manufacturers.

Scorpion produced ten models of snowmobiles that were available in a variety of colors and styles. Scorpion did not compete in the low-price end of the market, and their snowmobiles were known for their

TABLE 1

Snowmobile Industry and Scorpion Data

	Industry		Scorpion Income Statement			Scorpion Balance Sheet			
	Unit Shipments	Unit Retail Sales	Sales ($000)	Pre-Tax Income ($000)	Pre-Tax Income (%)	Receivables ($000)	Inventory ($000)	Fixed Assets ($000)	Corporate Account ($000)
1968*	100,000	85,000	8,067	1,923	23.8%	689	1,978	658	—
1969	200,000	255,000	11,810	1,221	10.3%	1,653	2,807	1,339	2,281
1970	480,000	425,000	14,684	784	5.3%	2,216	4,184	1,668	3,669
1971	565,000	495,000	19,385	1,234	6.4%	1,380	3,389	2,168	3,223
1972	595,000	460,000	20,347	713	8.5%	1,512	7,162	2,496	6,928

* Not owned by Fuqua Industries.

EXHIBIT 2

FUQUA INDUSTRIES (C)
Scorpion, Inc., Profit and Loss
11 Months Ending November 30, 1973
(final three dollar-digits omitted)

	1973		1972
	Actual	*Budget*	*Actual*
Net sales............................	$ 6,760	$13,127	$16,824
Cost of sales.........................	5,663	9,801	13,034
Gross profit......................	$ 1,097	$ 3,326	$ 3,790
Selling G & A........................	3,579	$ 2,887	3,100
Interest expense......................	778	818	340
Other Expense.......................	2,377	138	350
Pre-tax income (Loss)...........	$(5,637)	$ (517)	$ 273
Taxes on income.....................	$(2,706)	(248)	142
Net Income (Loss)..............	$(2,931)	$ (269)	$ 131

quality, endurance, safety, and reliability. Scorpion did not produce a "speed sled," which often resulted in dealers taking on a second sled line to complement Scorpion's rugged, family-style sleds.

Although its snowmobiles were sold throughout the United States, a major portion of sales were generated in the upper Midwest. At the end of 1972, Scorpion had 15 independent and two company owned dis-

EXHIBIT 3

FUQUA INDUSTRIES (C)
Scorpion, Inc., Balance Sheet
11 Months Ending Nov. 30, 1973
(final three dollar-digits omitted)

	1973		1972
	Actual	*Budget*	*Actual*
Cash..	$ (79)	$ 50	$ (99)
Receivables—net................................	9,058	5,151	1,588
Inventory.......................................	9,210	4,481	9,771
Prepaid items...................................	13	6	41
Current assets.............................	$18,202	$ 9,688	$11,301
Other assets......................................	12		44
Fixed Assets—Net...............................	2,242	2,097	2,570
Total Assets...............................	$20,456	$11,885	$13,915
Accounts payable and accruals....................	$ 1,801	$ 1,458	$ 1,991
Accrued income taxes payable...................	<491>	<15>	503
Current portion of long-term Debt................	$ 13	78	21
Current liabilities................................	$ 1,323	$ 1,521	$ 2,515
Long-term debt..................................	53	45	124
Deferred taxes...................................	101	101	81
Fuqua corporate account........................	18,843	8,983	8,367
Stockholder's equity.............................	136	1,235	2,828
Total Liabilities and Stockholders' Equity...	$20,456	$11,885	$13,925

TABLE 2

Snowmobile Manufacturers

Name	Market Share Percentage	Status
Ski-Doo	30%	Will stay
Arctic Cat	25	May be acquired
Polaris	11	Will stay (Textron owned)
Scorpion	7	Unknown
Sno-Jet	7	Will stay (Glastron owned)
Yamaha	6	Will stay
Rupp	6	May drop out

tributors. The two company owned distributors accounted for 24 percent of sales and future plans called for a larger number of company owned distributors, particularly as Scorpion intensified its efforts outside of the upper Midwest.

Scorpion operated a 180,000 sq. ft. manufacturing facility at its headquarters in Crosby, Minnesota. The company was one of the few manufacturers to make all the major parts of the snowmobile, including molding of rubber parts. Extensive engineering efforts were also made and new models were introduced annually.

Management

After its acquisition by Fuqua in 1968, two of Scorpion's three original founders remained in active management. Later these men left Scorpion and in early 1973 Harvey Paulson was hired as head of Scorpion.

Harvey Paulson was described as a professional manager with an impressive record in manufacturing and engineering at the Bernzomatic Company of Toronto, Canada. Paulson had been vice president and member of Bernzomatic's board of directors. During his six years there, the company moved from a $4 million loss to a $1.6 million profit. In fact, Paulson's ability had been cited as a major reason not to sell Scorpion.

THE DIVESTITURE DECISION

The major reason for selling Scorpion was that the time required for a recovery of the snowmobile industry and Scorpion was considered so long, and the investment required so large, that the funds could be put to better use by investing in other businesses.

Fuqua executives estimated that by the end of the year Scorpion's after-tax losses would be around $3.5 million. Due to a substantial increase in receivables and inventories, Fuqua's advances to Scorpion were forecasted to be about $17 million. With such a substantial loss, Fuqua's earnings per share were expected to be about 30¢ a share lower because of Scorpion. Table 3 shows the impact of Scorpion on the earnings of the recreation group.

TABLE 3

Recreation Earnings (amounts in millions)

	1972 Actual	1973 Forecast	1974 Forecast
With Scorpion..................	$29.4	$27.5	$31.7
Without Scorpion..............	28.5	33.7	33.5

Although there was no question that keeping Scorpion would have a substantial negative effect on 1973 earnings, some members of management argued that the long-term outlook justified retention of the business. For example, Rob Berman, a member of Ted Davis's operations staff, estimated that Scorpion would probably lose $1 million (pre-tax) in 1974 and could break even in 1975. Berman felt that after Scorpion reached a breakeven level in 1975 that the subsidiary had substantial growth opportunities.

Keith Johnson, treasurer, was also concerned about the proposed divestiture. Johnson recognized the 1972 to 1973 recreation earnings decline, but pointed out that a 1973 to 1974 comparison would be much more favorable if Scorpion were held. Johnson thought that it would be unrealistic for Fuqua to assume that they could receive any more than $9 million to $10 million for their $17 million investment in Scorpion. Johnson also thought that the Scorpion divestiture could result in an overall loss on the disposal of businesses. Exhibit 4 compares Fuqua's

EXHIBIT 4

FUQUA INDUSTRIES (C)
Earnings per Share 1967–72

	From Continuing Operations	After Extraordinary Items*
1972............................	1.62	1.85
1971............................	1.23	1.10
1970............................	1.02	1.20
1969............................	1.52	1.46
1968............................	1.06	1.07
1967............................	0.83	0.90

* Includes such items as gain (loss) from operations of discontinued operations and gain (loss) on disposal of businesses.
Note: Income from continuing operations is restated for prior years to exclude the gains (losses) of discontinued operations.

EXHIBIT 5

FUQUA INDUSTRIES (C)
Gains (Losses) of Discontinued Businesses (1973)
(final three dollar-digits omitted)

Company	Income (Loss) from Operations*	Gain (Loss) on Disposal
Trojan Seed Company.............................	$1,706	$15,260
Rome Industries.................................	743	273
Gilcrease Hills Development......................	(465)	(2,998)
Fuqua Communites, Inc..........................	(330)	(1,374)
Ward Manufacturing (additional loss since divestiture in 1969)........................	—	(2,784)
Total...	$1,654	$ 8,377
Less applicable income taxes....................	(810)	(4,104)
Net..	$ 844	$ 4,273

* Refers to gains or losses on the operation of the business prior to its disposition.

historical earnings performance before other extraordinary charges. Exhibit 5 indicates the gains and losses on dispositions that had already occurred in 1973.

Divestiture Alternatives

Ted Davis was sympathetic to the arguments for keeping Scorpion and also felt that Harvey Paulson had the ability to make Scorpion a major snowmobile company. Davis realized, however, that the long-term outlook for snowmobiles was still uncertain and that J. B. Fuqua would question if all the management time spent on Scorpion would really be justified.

Davis knew that J. B. Fuqua had contacted several larger companies about buying Scorpion, but Davis questioned just how quickly and how good a deal could be negotiated with a larger company. The chances of selling Scorpion to another snowmobile company was even lower, since most of Scorpion's competitors were in even worse financial condition than Scorpion. In fact, several of Scorpion's competitors had already approached Fuqua about the possibility of Fuqua acquiring them. Nevertheless for the 10:00 o'clock meeting, Ted Davis hoped to be able to propose other prospective buyers for Scorpion.

If a decision to sell Scorpion were made and a prospective buyer could be located, Ted Davis knew that he would also have to outline the type of deal Fuqua should seek in any negotiations. As a first step Ted Davis had prepared the figures shown as Exhibit 6. Although Ted felt that these figures could help in determining an appropriate purchase price for Scorpion, he knew that the exhibit did not address the type of deal he should structure.

EXHIBIT 6

FUQUA INDUSTRIES (C)
Divestiture Alternatives
1973 Reported Earnings

| | Retain Scorpion | | Divest Scorpion* | | | | | |
| | | | Sell for $5 million | | Sell for $10 million | | Sell for $15 million | |
After-Tax Items†	($000)	Per Share	($000)	Per Share	($000)	Per Share	($000)	Per Share
Income from continuing operations‡	$16,789	$1.73	$20,289	$2.10	$20,289	$2.10	$20,289	$2.10
Income from discontinued operations§	844	0.09	844	0.09	844	0.09	844	0.09
Gains from other disposition§	4,273	0.45	4,273	0.45	4,273	0.45	4,273	0.45
Subtotal	$21,906	$2.27	$25,406	$2.64	$25,406	$2.64	$25,406	$2.64
(Loss) from Scorpion's operations	—	—	(3,500)	(0.37)	(3,500)	(0.37)	(3,500)	(0.37)
(Loss) on Scorpion disposition	—	—	(6,150)	(0.65)	(3,570)	(0.38)	(1,020)	(0.11)
Net Income	$21,906	$2.27	$15,756	$1.62	$18,336	$1.89	$20,886	$2.16

* Assumes Fuqua's year-end investment in Scorpion to be $17 million.
† Assumes 49 percent tax rate.
‡ Average shares outstanding in 1973 were 9,448,863. Preference dividends of $446,000 are subtracted from continuing operations before computing per share figure.
§ See Exhibit 5.

6   Sybron Corporation (E)

BACKGROUND

Sybron in 1954 was an old, reasonably profitable company (Pfaudler) with a 70 percent market share of a cyclical, slow-growth, and technologically vulnerable industry (glass-lined steel tanks for the chemical and process industries). They were concerned about their future (only $16 million in sales, limited internal growth opportunites, and attractive balance sheet and cash flow), but rather than accept a "friendly takeover" by General Dynamics at a substantial premium, they decided to strike out on their own to build a growth company.

Sixteen years and many acquisitions later, Sybron consisted of 25 domestic and 25 international divisions, with sales over $300 million. The stock price had increased by a factor of 13 during the period, and was eight times more than it would have been if the original General Dynamics merger offer had been accepted. During the last five years earnings per share had been relatively flat, however, and the stock price had suffered in the 1968 market break.

Donald Gaudion, who was a young vice president of sales for Pfaudler in 1954, was the principal proponent of the growth strategy and the president of the company since the mid-50s. As of 1970, the principal products of Sybron, with percentage of total sales and profits, respectively, were:

1. *Instruments*—24 percent, 19 percent—third largest U.S. manufacturer (Taylor Instrument Division), also four foreign divisions;
2. *Health*—41 percent, 37 percent—a major factor in dental equipment and supplies, also in hospital products;

EXHIBIT 1

SYBRON CORPORATION (E)
Historical Financial Data*
(per share amounts)

	1954	'55	'56	'57	'58	'59	'60	'61	'62	'63	'64	'65	'66	'67	'68	'69	'70
Net sales..............	16	14	18	39	33	38	51	50	51	54	59	134	165	187	265	300	333
Net income (A.T.)........	0.7	0.6	0.9	1.5	1.4	1.7	2.0	2.1	2.2	2.3	2.9	8.0	10.5	12.4	14.8	16.7	16.1
Income per share (A.T.)...	0.34	0.30	0.44	0.48	0.44	0.52	0.59	0.61	0.64	0.66	0.84	1.15	1.30	1.44	1.35	1.45	1.38
Long-term debt..........	1	1	1	1	2	3	3	3	8	6	6	12	10	17	28	54	60
Common equity..........	8	8	9	14	15	17	18	20	21	23	25	59	72	87	124	134	140
Approx. price range of stock..............	1-3	2-3	3-4	3-5	4-5	5-6	5-9	9-18	7-13	9-10	10-15	12-17	18-26	20-42	32-44	27-38	20-45
	$32 (3/31/71)																

* Source: Financial data for Sybron are as reported in annual reports of Sybron Corporation and its successor companies, without retroactive restatement for pooling of interest of acquired companies. Per share amounts have been adjusted to reflect all subsequent stock dividends and splits. All dollar figures are in millions except for per share figures which are in dollars.

3. *Process, water, and waste treatment equipment*—23 percent, 27 percent—of sales; and
4. *Specialty chemicals*—12 percent, 17 percent—most profitable and fastest growing segment.

Operations outside the United States accounted for 35 percent of Sybron's total worldwide sales of $378 million.

This case focuses on a number of issues currently considered by Mr. Gaudion, the president, to be of importance to the long-run growth and profitability of the company.

> Of course I have to concern myself with the current operations and performance of our divisions, but I cannot afford to let the daily and seemingly more pressing problems divert too much of my time from broader and longer-term issues. Unfortunately, the current problems and issues have a way of continually intruding on the time of any executive, for the very good reason that there are usually people directly concerned with the problems and pressing for their resolution. Nobody is beating down my door to get a resolution of what Sybron should aspire to for the year 2000, though, so I have to make sure I devote sufficient attention to such issues myself, as well as get others interested in them.
>
> Perhaps the best way to explain to you the issues I am most concerned with is to give you some discussion memoranda I have written during the past year. I simply distributed these to our corporate executives and our division managers in the hopes they would stimulate their thinking. Perhaps we should provide for some more systematic attention to defining these issues, establishing some priorities for attacking them, and coming to some conclusions about them, but we have not done that as yet.

Three of Mr. Gaudion's memoranda are reproduced (with minor deletions) below. They deal principally with three interrelated questions:

a. What growth goals should the company establish?
b. What businesses should the company seek to be in?
c. How much coordination and integration of businesses should be attempted?

As may be seen, Mr. Gaudion was becoming more and more convinced that size was beginning to bring significant disadvantages as well as advantages, and that many other larger companies seemingly had not found a very effective way to deal with these disadvantages.

EXHIBIT 2

SYBRON CORPORATION (E)

"The Seventies—The Case for no Biggerness"
Donald A. Gaudion
February 4, 1970

Almost two decades ago (1954) we wrote an outline of some of the advantages of corporate size, entitled "The Case for Bigness." Among other things it was proposed that several Rochester companies band together to avoid being taken over by the conglomerators and raiders of the Fifties. At that time most of us were in the $10 to $15 million category. In the ensuing period we have followed this policy with the result that we are now in the $350 million size, with a five year plan

taking us to the half billion mark, even without any sizable acquisitions. The question is now, should we continue our aggressive, though highly selective, acquisition program? Or should we stick to largely internal development, with perhaps an even more selective policy of a very limited number of "niche-fillers." (Basically, the purchase of "product lines" that supplement eixsting product lines?) It should be clearly stated, contrary to the title of this paper, that this internal development would be expected to generate a 10 percent to 15 percent per share annually *earnings* growth. We are *not* building a case for 'no biggerness" in earnings.

We have largely achieved the element of bigness outlined in the 1954 report. We have a NYSE listed stock rapidly achieving investment status. We have minimized our capital goods cyclical image, diversified our fields of interest to where market and product obsolescence is not likely to have significant impact, built an organization of generalists and specialists in depth, developed over $100 million of volume overseas, with solid organizations in the "developed" areas and at least skeleton organizations in the LDCs (less developed countries). Furthermore, we have built the necessary team to analyze, screen, negotiate and operate a multinational, multidivisional organization that currently numbers over 50 segments.

Analysis of our acquisition program will indicate that the earnings growth rate of our acquisitions exceeds that of the base companies from which we began. In other words, we have successfully "boot-strapped" our way into areas of higher growth. With "minimum disruption" of the basic momentum of the companies we merged, we have developed dynamic management teams at the divisional level. The budgetary, long-range planning, manpower inventory, goal setting performance reviews, reporting and control disciplines have been instituted and continue to develop.

Then why not let the program continue to develop, adding additional divisions and further diversification as long as they meet our increasingly stringent requirements?

EXHIBIT 2 *(continued)*

Basically, we are now concerned with the problems of "giganticism."

First, let's look at the case histories of some of the giants. The "blue chips" of the pre–1950 era, such as the motors, the large chemicals (duPont, Monsanto, Dow, Carbide, Cyanamid, etc.), AT&T did pretty well with earnings growth in the decade following World War II. But somewhere around 1957–58 they began to soften and their performance in the Sixties has been dismal. The conglomerators of the Fifties, such as General Dynamics, Brunswick, GPE, AMF, etc., developed massive cases of indigestion during the Sixties even though some of them, such as Brunswick (based on leisure time and health), seemed to be soundly conceived. They would now be termed "concept" stocks.

As we all know, these painful problems of indigestion were no deterrent to the merger and acquisition trend in the Sixties as companies like Litton, Gulf and Western, Kidde, Teledyne, Whittaker, "Automatic" Sprinkler, LTV, and dozens of others sprang up. And with the magic of PE multiple leverage (as long as massive doses of new leverage were added) they looked like the "wave of the future." With their multi-market diversification, decentralized global operations they were predicted to be best able to cope with our rapidly changing world. Yet, following mysteriously similar timing to those of the Fifties, they all fell out of bed in the last couple of years of the Sixties.

Let me quickly say at this point that *I* believe most of them *will* survive and they will go on into the Seventies being basically sound companies with good growth in volume. But what I am concerned about is their *earnings* growth rate. We know that much of their earnings growth during the Sixties was due to financial leverage rather than "internal" development. That cannot go on due to its non-recurring nature and what I believe will be relatively permanent higher interest rates. And, as will be discussed later, I am concerned about the diminishing rate of return brought on due to the management problems of size alone. So, history seems to indicate that the "billion dollar club" is made up of affluent members as far as volume of sales and stability are concerned. *But* the club lapel pins showing the PE multiples are not going to be worn nearly as proudly since the rate of earnings growth will be lower than the "lean and hungry" bourgeoisie trying to get into the club.

Why, with all the prestige of size, can't they outdistance their smaller rivals in earnings growth rate?

Obviously, the answer is complex. I believe it is a blend of the management problems of size combined with the government pressures to prevent monopoly.

I can quickly dispose of the government factor by saying that if we had true laissez-faire, size via monopoly *would* be unbeatable. General Motors and AT&T, for example, *would* run out their competition and then raise prices to whatever extent necessary to give them the optimum

EXHIBIT 2 (*continued*)

---

and necessary earnings growth rate and stock price. We have long since passed the point of questioning government regulation of monopoly, and now only try to keep it reasonably livable and then try to adapt to it. We then address ourselves to the question of management of the billion dollar plus corporation. Obviously, the billion dollar bench mark is symbolic—it may be high or it may be low, depending, probably, on the complexity of the product line. But somewhere in this range the problems of keeping a profit-conscious organization become increasingly difficult. It will be noted, I have said "increasingly difficult" and *not* "impossible." Perhaps by spelling out and analyzing some of the reasons for failure, the organizational techniques for correcting these problems may be devised.

Simple arithmetic, or "the trees don't grow to the sky" theories, account for much of the problem. The dynamic new company, *if it survives babyhood*, is likely to be "lean and hungry," has a small group of highly motivated, entrepreneurial people, probably has a strong, authoritarian leadership, ruthlessly eliminates people who do not contribute in an above average way to its objectives, has few communications problems since the group is small. But, of course, it also has a *much* higher degree of risks as the people who play the "new issue" game know.

By decentralized (almost fragmented) divisional management we have *tried* to keep alive the entrepreneurial spirit of these small companies and yet add the stability and attributes of size—"The Case for Bigness." By and large, we have achieved much of this objective in our development to date and our growth rate in earnings per share *has* been substantially above average, as outlined in the beginning of this report. And, although the figure seems to be difficult to come by, not over a quarter (and perhaps less) of our 10–15 percent compounded earnings growth rate has come about through "Chinese money"—acquisition leverage in the first year of merger.

The problem of size seems to center around motivation and communications. Movement alone breeds excitement and attracts the type of management that likes a fast-moving, fluid (almost chaotic) atmosphere. "Success breeds success." So we have been blessed with an ability to hire and keep the profit-oriented, entrepreneurial types. In many cases we have acquired companies that are still being managed by the entrepreneur who fought them up from scratch.

Then, from a motivation point of view, why change course? For one reason, as the number of these units increases the percentage contribution of the single unit to the total becomes automatically smaller and, therefore, the management gets an increasing feeling that they have little to do with overall performance. Yet their stock options, bonus, etc., are tied strongly to corporate performance. Why not tie then to divisional performance? Then we develop even greater fragmentation than we

EXHIBIT 2 (*continued*)

---

have now, *no* synergism (although there isn't much now) and essentially become a closed-end investment trust.

Closely allied to this element is the averaging down problem. Ideally *all* of the divisions would end up every year exactly on the corporate target for return on assets employed, earnings growth rate, etc. Actually it is a spectrum with rather wide variation. Theoretically, we would chop off, in one way or another, all those below the corporate norm. In a large sense, we try to do this by building the weaklings up. If performance shows no chance of meeting the norm it will be eliminated but this takes time. In the meantime the high performers tend to be demotivated.

Another aspect of motivation has to do with "executive perks," capital expenditures, paper work, corporate airplanes, etc. How do these all get lumped together? When one division gets a brand new plant, or has a new fringe benefit, or a new control procedure, others want it. Yes, controls *are* in effect to make sure that every item is checked out in terms of its effect on profit, but paper controls are a poor substitute for the "hard-driving, penny-pinching manager." And also who knows when the "h–d–p–p* manager" is "milking" the operation—showing excellent short-run performance but leaving a shell to his successor. This type of subjective evaluation is always the source of much disagreement in the company. "Quantitative" analysis we have. But how do we do on "qualitative" analysis? It probably takes a decade to *really* arrive at a provable qualitative judgment on many of these factors. And by then we may be in catastrophic trouble.

Again, the problem of span of control. The man at the top of the pyramid is finally responsible for making these qualitative, subjective judgments. Over how large an organization can he do this successfully?

This leads into the question of communications. The airplane has facilitated the man-to-man confrontations around the world necessary to make such judgments and to make sure the "party line" is understood, with all of its refinements and innuendoes. But the human body has not been improved enough to maintain such a schedule without wearing out at an early age. And we must hire only bachelors or risk ending up with broken family lives throughout the company.

Trying to pulse the point of diminishing returns is extremely difficult. Perhaps that statement in itself indicates we are beyond it? I hope not. But there are red flags, or at least yellow ones, flying here and there in the organization. And, if nothing else, we should devise a control mechanism which will gauge this point. How serious are our communications and motivation problems? Are the measurable advantages of size and momentum continuing to offset the known deteriorating entrepre-

---

* Hard-driving, penny-pinching.

EXHIBIT 2 (concluded)

---

neurial spirit? In the final analysis, a slowing of the EPS growth rate is the certain signal. I don't want to be around when that signal flashes!

In the meantime (and in order *not* to end on a dismal note) we *must* continue to explore new techniques of organization, motivation, and control. This, again, requires a never-ending search for innovative people. It also necessitates continuing study of the experience of others. So far, the innovations of people like Jimmy Ling (e.g., spinning off segments of the whole in order to motivate their managers) have not looked too exciting. Perhaps we can devise some better ones.

In the meantime, I feel no great urge to rush into membership in the billion dollar club except through internal growth and very carefully "screened niche-fillers."

EXHIBIT 3

SYBRON CORPORATION (E)

"The Seventies—Can We Repeal the Law of the S Curve?"
Donald A. Gaudion
February 23, 1970

We are all familiar with the almost inexorable law of the S curve as it applies to the life cycle of a new product. The new product is usually slow to get started but as it gains market acceptance its volume growth speeds up. Then as competitors find an attractive market they copy it, work around its patents, and begin to tap the lucrative market. The product growth curve begins to shoulder off and, if there are no improvements, eventually goes into a decline. The trick, of course, is to either constantly improve the product ahead of competition or bring out other new products that are in the base of the S curve phase of development.

In earlier memos on "The Seventies," we have implied that corporate growth tends to follow the same pattern—at least, perhaps, growth in earnings per share, if not volume. As we tried to get at the reason for this we felt it revolved around motivation of management and communications, rather than anything more fundamental since theoretically a fully decentralized divisional operation should be essentially the same as an independent small company.

Since we were talking mostly about *earnings growth rates,* as opposed to volume growth, let's analyze another interesting element. John Kenneth Galbraith, in his *New Industrial State,* makes a very plausible case for the fact that *big* business had already, in cooperation with *big* government and *big* labor, taken over society, with the implication that it could do whatever it wishes. If this is so, why can't big business develop an earnings growth rate that will give it the 25 plus PE multiple necessary to keep its capital cost in line?

EXHIBIT 3 *(continued)*

As summarized in "Business and The Consumer," * this reasons "that the American economy consists of two quite different economic systems:

> "The 'entrepreneurial economy' of over 11 million enterprises, largely controlled by owners and working in a competitive system to 'maximize profits' which will accrue to these owners; and,

> "A 'mega-economy' of a few hundred super-corporations dominating the whole economy and all aspects of our lives and shaping a future in which the whole society must live."

> "Under this view, the two economic systems are totally different: the competitive one, virtually helpless in a marketplace which it cannot greatly influence or control—and threatened by government, labor, competitors, and the whims of consumers; while the mega-economy is controlled by a bureaucratic and managerial group—referred to as 'the technostructure'—which seeks power along with profits.

> "Galbraith and his followers claim that the latter system generally has been successful in creating an autonomous area of such power that it can plan its own prices, production, and growth and has either neutralized or allied with the government, its competitors and outside financiers, so that it can pass higher costs, including taxes and wages, and even the burden of dividends on to the public by raising prices."

If we look at the post World War II period of vastly increased costs for such items as wages, a variety of fringes such as pension costs, which alone now equal 10 percent or more of the payroll, Blue Cross, constantly rising Social Security taxes, etc., all of which are ground into increasing material costs, it would seem that industry *has* been capable of "passing these costs on to the consumer." In effect, industry, in the case of increased local, state and federal taxes, is just the collection agent for the government and, I believe, probably a more efficient one than many of others involved in the intricate system of amassing the 38 to 40 percent of the gross national product being used to run our governments. So, as long as these taxes (and other costs), are being assessed equally to all competitors they eventually *are* passed along in the form of higher prices.

Then, coming back again to our fundamental question, why have the *shareholders* of these "mega-corporations" *not* fared well? As we know, the after-tax profits of industry tend to average out around 5 percent of the sales price. In an "average" company, therefore, an increase in prices of 1 percent (assuming, for the moment, other costs remain the same) would increase after-tax profits by ½ percent which, of course, is a 10

* U.S. Chamber of Commerce.

EXHIBIT 3 *(continued)*

percent increase in earnings. A 2 percent increase in prices equals a 20 percent increase in earnings, etc.

The only point of this exercise is to dramatize the fact that a very small (compared to our inflationary price increases of recent years) increase in prices would make a great increase in percentage earnings. Parenthetically, as all Sybron people know, it is one of the baffling phenomenon of large companies *to me* to know how we will take in some $350 million this year on the basis of thousands of different pricing decisions in over 50 different autonomous divisions and end up in December each year worrying about meeting or missing budget by a few cents per share, each after-tax cent of which equals a little over $100,000 (1¢ on 11 million shares). It would appear that we *are* able to pass on all of our cost increases on a *very precise* basis!!

This ability to pass on increased costs *has* been true of all of the "megacorporations," the "blue chip" companies that we discussed in earlier memos. None of them, to my knowledge, has gone bankrupt. Most of them have shown average earnings. Few have cut dividends. They just haven't grown at above average rates.

Then let's talk about the *cost* of capital as opposed to the costs of wages, materials, taxes, etc. We are seeing interest costs practically doubling in a very short span of years. We are also witnessing companies increasing their debt-equity ratios. Since this is a fixed cost ground into the profit and loss statement before taxes, I predict the mega-corporations will pass it on to their customers in the form of higher prices. It therefore becomes just another contributor to the inflationary cycle. There *will* be loud screaming about the cost-profit squeeze and it *will* take time but eventually it will be recognized as a relatively permanent cost increase, that we're not going back to 4–5 percent interest rates, and it will be built into costs.

If the increased cost of debt is about to be recognized and built into the cost-price system, why not the increased profits needed to maintain the equity market, the price of the stock? As we all know, traditionally profit (or loss) is what is left over after all the bills have been paid. Therefore, return on the shareholders equity has *not* been considered a "cost" such as interest on debt.

What I believe has happened is that the "professional management" (as opposed to entrepreneurial owner-managers) have tended to forget the stockholder in their financial control systems. Thus, they have passed on fantastic cost increases in wages, materials, taxes, etc. (or in the case of the large chemical companies had such volume and productivity increases that they could hold prices and still absorb inflationary costs), *but* they have *not* worried enough about the amount left over for the shareholder.

EXHIBIT 3 *(continued)*

Many factors have contributed to this, a few of which can be mentioned. The government jaw-boning against "inordinate" profits of the business giants has made them feel self-righteous in "passing on our productivity increases to our customers in the form of lower prices, if possible."

Admittedly in a highly competitive economy with costs going up, price increases are hard to fight through. It is much easier to explain the necessity for increases "to cover the higher cost of labor" or "the higher cost of interest," etc. than to argue for the necessity for "higher profits." Profit is still a scare word. *But* it is interesting to note that, as we said earlier, few, if any, of the giants have gone bankrupt. They *have* passed on enough costs to remain afloat.

"Professional management" salaries are set generally on the basis of the size of the company rather than on its PE multiple. Thus, the personal incentive, whether it is at the sales and manufacturing manager level or at the top management level, is on volume rather than profit.

In addition to the tangible fringes, the "psychic" income of being in the management of a corporate giant that is a "household word" is important to many people. Their leadership is called for in a variety of non-corporate functions. They are large buyers of goods and services, they give employment to thousands and they get a feeling they are making large contributions to the welfare of mankind by creating masses of material goods.

Cutting through all of this negative thinking to a positive conclusion, then, I believe we may see a change *forced* on the mega-corporations in the Seventies. They may be *forced* into giving the shareholders a higher priority in their allocation of resources.

I cannot *really* believe that an industry like the chemical industry, which when I was graduated from business school in 1938 was *the* glamour industry, will be content with its 10 PE multiple instead of its traditional 20 to 30, or more. Granted all of its "commodity product" pricing problems, its management and employee motivation problems, its government pressures, it will still be driven by the necessity of getting capital for its 10 to 15 percent compounded annual volume growth needs. And, if Dow, duPont, Monsanto, Cyanamid, Carbide, etc., start grinding a better profit growth record into their prices (and as we saw earlier, it is a small percentage versus the cost increases they have recovered), the public will have to pay. So I believe a change in their management thinking may be in the cards for the Seventies or else the management will be fired by the shareholders.

Translated into policy for Sybron, I believe we must continue our efforts to obtain, or maintain, preeminence in our present fields of effort in spite of the problems of size. We must do this with internal develop-

EXHIBIT 3 *(concluded)*

ment and through "niche-filling" acquisitions *that enhance* our *proprietary positions.*

My hang-ups with this course of action revolve around management techniques and organization for self-renewal and, in turn, motivation and communications as we get larger. Also, of course, the definition of "niche-fillers" and "enhancement of proprietary position" as opposed to further diversification and size for the sake of size. As we move out into "higher technology," for example, in the health or instrumentation fields are we enhancing our proprietary position or diversifying further? This becomes even fuzzier as we look at our chemical business. These are the policies that we must continue to refine as we plan our way into the Seventies.

EXHIBIT 4

SYBRON CORPORATION (E)

"The Seventies—The Illusory Search for Perpetual Above Average Growth in Earnings per Share"

Donald A. Gaudion
February 10, 1970

Is it inevitable that a corporation must eventually return to an average trend line growth rate? Or can it perpetually stay above average if it maintains an above average management team that continually moves the company into new areas as the environment changes?

First, as we have frequently pointed out, the obvious, but frequently overlooked, difference is between the management of a diversified company and the management of a diversified investment portfolio. The portfolio manager can quickly buy and sell into new industries, and companies within those industries, as the outlook for them changes. The management of a diversified company cannot quickly buy and sell divisions of the company as there are changes in the external environment. We must, of necessity, be into them for the longer pull.

Therefore, as we analyze an industry for long-term growth potential we are talking about "what we want to look like as a company in the year 2000." We have to avoid "Wall Street Fads," or situations that are obviously catch-up. And this avoidance of catch-up situations is extremely complex.

We are not talking about such easily identified fad situations as hula-hoops or other consumer promotions. They are at one end of the fad spectrum. What we are concerned about is the life expectancy of more fundamental markets.

For example, there is unquestionably a large accumulated market vacuum to be filled in such areas as pollution and health care, to use

EXHIBIT 4 (*continued*)

a couple in which Sybron has a vital interest. We identified the pollution problem in the middle Fifties and merged with the leading company at that time, Permutit. Our experience in the ensuing period has not been reassuring even though recognition of the problem has grown tremendously. More recently we have cast our lot with "health care." When will that really take off and how long will it take to catch up in hospital building? Or has it already passed its peak as the public rebels at the skyrocketing cost of health care?

As this point we have to remind ourselves that we are primarily concerned with growth in earnings per share. This adds an additional complication to the growth equation. Plastics development in the chemical industry is our favorite example of a high technology, effective new product introduction, 15 percent compounded annual unit volume growth rate situation which developed into a "commodity priced" product with no growth in earnings per share.

We have seen similar, but less spectacular, developments in consumer fields such as black-and-white TV, then a hiatus and finally a rapid growth in color TV, the timing of which baffled the consumer research experts. During the past couple of decades we have watched Wall Street move in and out of atomic power, various elements of electronics, (e.g., transistors, printed circuits, etc.), air transport, office machines, public utilities, and dozens of other "waves of the future." It is extremely difficult to find a situation that over a long period of time will exceed the basic rate of growth in population and this may be slowing down.

But then we have the Xeroids, the unique "one product" developments that quickly capture a new market with a patented technological and/or marketing break-through. Xerox, Polaroid, Technicon, IBM, Avon Products fall into this category. During the Fifties we dreamed of such a potentiality. Our management approach to it has been to search the world for new ideas in our fields and "crap shoot" with a certain amount of money in their development (always keeping the amount gambled in manageable proportions to our earning power so that it did not sink the ship). Our record with Nuclear Safeguard, Fluoridator, Audiac, high temperature coatings and many others of lesser significance has not been impressive to say the least. Cyberail is, of course, our largest current gamble and the returns are not yet in. I visualize no great change in our policy of continually searching out this type of opportunity. However, I feel that we should continue to discount the effect of this on our future and look upon any success as merely "velvet."

To try to determine a growth vehicle that will carry over several decades, rather than a few years, requires a much more fundamental analysis, in my opinion. Flexible, above average, "far-seeing," globally oriented management is really the *only* answer. And, as we have frequently pointed out, they must be trained to "live out into the future" rather than be hung up with the myths of the past.

EXHIBIT 4 (concluded)

Somewhat parenthetically, this is why I believe in our current efforts to build "social orientation" into our management team. I believe this type of mind is the one capable of riding with the tumult of our revolutionary world changes and hopefully keeping ahead of them (or at least abreast of them since even this may be above average). The precise, methodical, make-no-mistakes type of mentality will probably get overwhelmed in the speed of change. Controlled entrepreneurs will survive. Apart from the need for genius management, are we able to make any generalizations at all to guide us in this illusory search for "perpetual" above average earnings per share growth?

Part Four

Corporate Response to
Social Change

1   *Albert Manufacturing Company*

The Albert Manufacturing Company was founded in 1938 to produce various machined and fabricated components for industrial users. Shortly after the start of World War II the company began to make mechanical and hydraulic assemblies for aircraft. This part of the business grew and in April 1947 was set up as a separate division. To house operations the company leased a newly constructed plant in Wichita, Kansas, with 1.2 million square feet of floor space. By the end of 1954 sales of the Wichita division were running at about $120 million annually. The division had approximately 1,200 employees.

Early in January, 1955, Mr. Henderson, works manager of the Wichita division and a vice president of the Albert Company, called Mr. Paul Bellows to his office. Bellows was purchasing agent for the division. Henderson told Bellows he had just received a telephone call from the manager of the local office of the Federal Bureau of Investigation. The manager informed him that an investigation then in progress by the FBI had brought to light information involving certain of the division's buyers. Henderson said he had arranged for the investigators to visit the division the following morning. He asked Bellows to receive them and to keep him informed as to developments.

The next day Mr. Arnold Rand and Mr. Peter Thomas, FBI agents, called on Bellows. Mr. Ralph Nance, assistant purchasing agent, was also at the meeting. After a brief exchange of pleasantries the following discussion took place:

BELLOWS: As you can well imagine Nance and I are very curious about this matter. We have not mentioned it to anyone but we have speculated between ourselves as to the nature of the thing. What's the story?

RAND: Well, I guess I ought to go back to last fall. We were conducting an investigation on placement of government contracts at the P. B. Blake Company on the north side of town. After several weeks and rather by accident, Pete Thomas was interviewing a witness who was a buyer in Blake's purchasing department. The fellow confessed to having accepted a $4,500 bribe from a local tool supplier. Later we verified that he had received the money from the company he named. The supplier involved has gone on record that the money was a personal loan from their salesman and was to have been repaid. However, the buyer involved did not support this contention. The buyer turned state witness and gave us several other instances of similar occurrences, but they were not as serious—at least there wasn't as much money involved.

NANCE: Where is the tie-in with the Albert Company?

RAND: This buyer has made a sworn statement that he knows three of your buyers have also been accepting expensive gifts and perhaps being bought off as he was. . . .

THOMAS: Bellows, this thing is nebulous as hell. We don't have much to go on, but there are enough basic implications that we think these three buyers of yours may well be tarred with the same brush.

RAND: I'd like to tell you about a fishing trip that our informant was on. He stated—and we have verified this—that he was one of 12 guests at an upstate fishing lodge over a three-day weekend. The whole bunch were flown up to this lodge, spent the weekend in substantial style and returned. All expenses were paid by the supplier. Now get this—your three buyers were there along with the chief tool designer and two manufacturing engineers from Albert. It was at this occasion that our informant states he learned of the arrangements, shall we say, between the supplier and your buyers.

BELLOWS: What can we do to get this thing off the ground? What can we do to help clear this thing up?

RAND: We would like to examine your records to see who placed orders with the specific company mentioned in the charge and two other companies also implicated. Then we think that sworn statements will be taken. After that if there are any concrete leads we will conduct an investigation outside the company to ascertain if the individuals have increased bank balances, are living beyond their means, and stuff like that. . . .

THOMAS: There is one thing that bothers us. We don't have jurisdiction.

BELLOWS: What do you mean jurisdiction?

THOMAS: At the P. B. Blake Company we could investigate because they held prime contracts from the government. You don't, and therefore we can't come in and do the same kind of thing.

BELLOWS: Could you if we asked you to?

THOMAS: That would take care of the matter completely.

BELLOWS: Well, that settles that. We are asking you now and will give you whatever you need in the way of an official request. Now then, when and how will you start the ball rolling?

RAND: In about three days if you can be ready for us. If possible, we would like to use a private office because of the secrecy necessary until we know where we are. We will also need personnel records, purchase order files, and a lot of other things.

BELLOWS: We will be ready for you. Let me say now I am more concerned than you are and want this cleaned up one way or the other as quickly as possible but with a minimum of disruption of the purchasing department. However, even if we have got to shake this department up hard, I will give you every support. Nance, get things organized to take care of this. Don't tell anyone what is going on until we decide the time is right . . . explain the presence of strangers by, well let them be headquarters auditors or something. Gentlemen, Ralph Nance will be your contact and will personally make all the necessary arrangements. Again, I want to assure you that you have our cooperation. Tell me, who are the vendors in question?

RAND: The Supreme Engineering Company is the firm specifically mentioned in the allegation. The other two are Superior Tool and Die, Inc., and Allied Tool Company.

NANCE: Thanks, you can be assured that things will be set up for you.

Mr. Bellows was especially concerned about this investigation because he had given special emphasis to a strict code of ethical conduct with suppliers since he had assumed his current assignment. The departmental policy was that no employee was to accept any gift or courtesy that he was not in a position to reciprocate. In a variety of ways Bellows had tried to get this standard of conduct understood and accepted by all those in the department. The topic was frequently discussed at weekly meetings with purchasing supervisors. All male employees of the department had attended a company school where one of the subjects discussed was the company policy on bribery. The issue had been discussed at the monthly dinner meetings held for male employees of the purchasing department. Bellows had authorized his buyers to make a fairly liberal use of expense accounts so that they could reciprocate in buying lunches, and so on, for suppliers' representatives and not feel under any obligation to them. He knew that some of the production and engineering employees had accepted Christmas gifts and entertainment from suppliers, but he had believed that his buyers had been completely honest in dealings with suppliers.

The Wichita division was highly specialized in that it made only a limited line of small gear trains, landing gear assemblies, hydraulic pumps and actuators, and certain fabricated assemblies. The vast bulk of the more or less common components needed were obtained from subcontractors. In 1954, the purchasing department had paid slightly over $55 million to subcontractors, or about half of the total sales of the division.

Buyers for the division were divided into groups, each headed by a senior buyer. These groups were organized along product lines, each being responsible for purchasing items that fell within a broad classification. A service group typed purchase orders, maintained the files, expedited orders that were overdue, and performed other functions of a clerical or routine nature. The entire purchasing department employed 128 people.

The flow of work into the department was in the form of requisitions that specified the items required and the date they should be available. A requisition was first processed by a member of the service group, who entered it in a master log and then routed it to the proper buying group. The assistant buyer for the group, upon receipt of a requisition, determined what previous suppliers had furnished the item. Any specifications that applied were pulled out together with the blueprint of the part. Then invitations to quote were sent out to approved sources or, if there was only one source, the supplier's representatives were contacted for negotiation. After a supplier had been selected, the assistant buyer filled in on the requisition the supplier's name and the price per unit. Certain other details also were added, such as the storeroom that was to receive the goods, discount terms, shipping point, and so forth. The requisition then was passed on to the appropriate buyer.

In most of the groups the effective control in selection of suppliers was in the hands of the buyers. However, in all groups every requisition had to be signed by a senior buyer. At this stage it went back to the service group. The necessary number of copies were typed, hecto masters for receiving and accounting were prepared, the facsimile signature of the purchasing agent was applied, and copies were mailed to the vendor. The requisition had been transformed from a request to purchase into a contract with a supplier.

About a week after the FBI agents started their investigation, Nance and Thomas discussed progress made during the preliminary stage. Thomas stated that he thought matters were progressing extremely slowly but that things should speed up in the near future. He and Rand had screened all the purchase orders placed by the division with the three suppliers in question during the past six months. All the orders had been for some type of tooling, primarily for tool repair work. All had been placed by the three buyers named in the original complaint.

Thomas gave Nance the following summary of the findings of the purchase order review:

1. All 1,976 purchase orders were initialed by the senior buyer for tools, Mr. Clinton Boles. The buyers that actually handled the orders and the distribution of orders among the suppliers in question were:

	Superior	Supreme	Allied	Total
Adolph Stimmer (assistant buyer)	622	257	48	927
John Lippen (buyer)	73	159	0	232
John Ruppert (assistant buyer)	280	531	6	817

2. While only 54 purchase orders were placed with Allied, the total dollar value of these orders was $86,409. The dollar value for

Superior Tool and Die was $234,765, and for Supreme Engineering it was $303,040.

3. Among the orders were three, all placed with Supreme, which radically increased in price during the period of manufacture. The original quoted prices for these orders were $257.75, $1,166.00, and $2,500.00. The final prices on the orders, as authorized by change notices to the purchase orders, were $1,186.50, $3,775.00, and $4,996.00.[1]

Nance had intimate knowledge of tool buying and of the tool buying group. He at one time had been responsible for buying tools at the home plant of the Albert Company, and Stimmer then had been an assistant buyer reporting to him. Any tool supplier usually could build a new tool. Quotations of delivery and price could be readily obtained by furnishing the supplier with blueprints and specifications. Repair of tools was an entirely different matter. It was necessary for someone from the tool firm to inspect the tool requiring repair before submitting a quotation. Time was important because the tool generally was needed for production of a scheduled part. Therefore, repair jobs were often placed on an advise price basis; that is, the supplier would take the tool and after completing his inspection at his plant would submit a price. The buyer then would judge whether or not this price was fair. If he decided it was too high, he either negotiated a new price or moved the tool to another supplier.

The tool buying group, unlike the other buying groups, dealt in general with small firms. A relatively low capital investment was required to start a tool shop and there were many local tool makers that were highly specialized and extremely small, sometimes employing no more than four or five men. Adequate credit and other information was difficult to obtain for these small firms.

About two weeks after they began their investigation, Thomas and Rand told Nance they were going to interview, under oath, Stimmer, Lippen, Ruppert, and Boles. They further stated that they wanted to discuss the progress made to date with Bellows and Nance as soon as they had had time to weigh the statements of the men. Nance suggested they meet the following afternoon. Rand and Thomas agreed.

The next afternoon Rand, Thomas, Nance, and Bellows gathered in Bellows' office. Rand opened the meeting.

RAND: Guess you will be surprised to learn that we are ending the investigation.

---

[1] During the manufacture of tools, design changes often become necessary or desirable. Such changes sometimes cause revisions in the delivered prices. Change notices also may tempt the supplier, particularly one who deliberately quoted under his costs to get an order, to demand an exorbitant price increase. This practice is frowned on by reputable tool vendors but is sometimes resorted to by marginal producers.

BELLOWS: You're all through already?

RAND: That's right. We have been unable to uncover any concrete evidence. We must have proof and, while there is no lack of suspicious circumstances, we just can't pin down anything definite.

BELLOWS: You can't come out here, tear into everything, arouse considerable doubt in our minds, and then pull out. We want these men either nailed to the cross or exonerated—is this too much to ask?

NANCE: I thought you were making satisfactory progress.

THOMAS: Paul, you must realize we work for a boss, too. He gave us almost five weeks to firm the investigation up. We just can't do it. There is a lot of smoke but no fire that we can find. So we want to give you everything we have and, if you come across some new evidence later on, we promise to give you all the help we can. That's all there is to it. We're sorry it turned out this way but. . . .

NANCE: Tell us what the score is now before we discuss this aspect further.

RAND: OK. First, Lippen is clean. He was recently transferred out of the tool group and actually was in the group only three weeks during the period of time the alleged offense took place. Both Stimmer and Ruppert absolutely deny the charge. They admit close knowledge of the suppliers but were rather evasive on the question of entertainment. Stimmer stated he was at the fishing party I mentioned to you earlier. Ruppert says he doesn't associate with salesmen outside of the office.

THOMAS: I handled the outside investigation. We went over every phase of Stimmer's and Ruppert's personal affairs—bank accounts, recent large purchases, standard of living, and so forth. Both are clean insofar as concrete evidence is concerned, but there is considerable doubt in my mind as to whether these guys are on the level. Stimmer lives well but not too far over the level he could support on his income. Ruppert took a very expensive vacation last year—two weeks in Florida at a fancy hotel. I believe a supplier paid a large part of the bills while he was there, but again I have no proof.

RAND: I think you should also know that we have checked the suppliers very carefully, too. I have tried to determine the expense account entries on the salesmen's reports turned into the companies. You realize that a company is in a box with the Internal Revenue if we catch it falsifying expenses. Again nothing conclusive, but, Paul, you should know that these companies all have substantial entries listing entertaining your people. I believe your name was even listed a few times.

BELLOWS: If you could check all of the 2,200 suppliers we do business with, I bet you will find my name quite often. Needless to say, I don't even know many of the salesmen, but a purchasing agent's name on the sales report for a lunch impresses the sales manager—and who is going to check to find the salesman is doing a little padding?

RAND: That is undoubtedly true, but there were still many of Albert's personnel on the statements. I was surprised that people outside of the purchasing department were mentioned freely. However, there was nothing to implicate Stimmer or Ruppert.

THOMAS: Well, what else can we say? We have a lot of suspicion that Stimmer and Ruppert are, at best, pretty close to these suppliers. Boles, of

EXHIBIT 1

THE ALBERT MANUFACTURING COMPANY—Wichita Division
Organization Chart—Purchasing Department

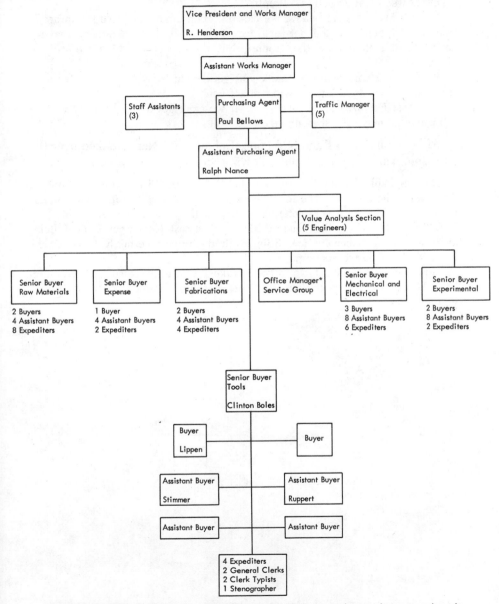

* Equal in classification to senior buyer. There were 18 clerks, typists, and stenographers in the service group out of a total of 43 for the entire purchasing department.

course, could be involved in this thing too. We didn't get around to checking his personal affairs as closely as the others, but I don't think he is completely out from under, from what little we have been able to determine.

BELLOWS: What do you say, Ralph?

NANCE: Well, I don't believe we can do much more. We have the information and can be on the lookout for future indications. It is regrettable that we can't run this thing into the ground, but there isn't anything we can do about it.

BELLOWS: Then I want to thank you gentlemen for your help so far and, if we do uncover anything, we will contact you.

THOMAS: Feel free to do that—even if we can't get out right away we can tell you what move you should make.

After Thomas and Rand had gone, Bellows and Nance talked over the situation. Nance expressed the following views.

NANCE: Paul, I'm not sure what I should do, but I'll tell you one thing: I don't want these guys in the tool group any longer. I've got to have a senior buyer that I can trust completely and buyers that are above reproach.

This whole mess is like shadow boxing. Just last November I rated Boles as ready for advancement and Stimmer and Ruppert certainly have always been considered as competent.

However, as I see it I have to got to take action to make sure the situation is under control and guarantee this kind of thing doesn't happen again. Do you agree?

2 Corporate Performace and Private Criticism—Campaign GM Rounds I and II

Early in February 1970, the world's biggest automaker found itself under attack from a small, just-hatched, nonprofit corporation founded in Washington, D.C., by a group of mostly young lawyers. Called the Project for Corporate Responsibility, this fledgling venture announced that its first move would be a "Campaign to Make General Motors Responsible." Round I of this Campaign was fought in 1970; Round II in 1971. As of the end of the second battle, it was still too early to say whether the challengers would be in the ring again for Round III.

In seeking to change GM's corporate life style and values, the campaigners undertook to work from within, albeit from a very small base of operation. Thus, their initial act was to purchase 12 shares of GM stock—out of some 287.5 million shares outstanding. Small as it was, this investment would allow the Project to place proposals on the GM proxy statement—provided management either raised no objection or its objection was overruled by the SEC.

Besides this contingent right to bring its propositions to a stockholder vote via the proxy machinery, the Campaign arsenal started with only one heavy gun: This was a promise of support from Ralph Nader, the nation's best-known advocate of consumers' causes. For Nader, GM was an old adversary. In 1965 he had published a book, *Unsafe at Any Speed*, dedicated to the thesis that built-in deficiencies of automotive design were to blame for a high percentage of highway accidents. Singled out for particular criticism was a GM car, the strong-selling, rear-engine Corvair. Despite a colorful, muckraking style, this book might well have proved a "sleeper" had not someone at GM, reportedly without top management's knowledge, placed a "tail" on

Nader, thus providing him with the basis for a celebrated $26 million lawsuit for invasion of privacy. The resulting publicity sent *Unsafe at Any Speed* onto the best-seller list, launched Nader on an influential career, helped to bring about the passage in 1966 of the first federal automotive safety legislation, and helped also to send GM's Corvair, after a few declining years, into oblivion in 1969.

Nader's promise to introduce Campaign GM to the press[1] assured it of a wide publicity. Some of what might be called the campaign's underlying social philosophy was spelled out in his briefing as follows:

> Corporations, [Nader] said, produce, process, and market most of the nation's goods and services and constitute a power grid that shapes the actions of men in both private and public sectors. Yet, he added, far less is known about the actual operations of the giant corporations than any other institution in America, including the national security agencies. . . . [But] corporate imprints are reflecting themselves in growing violence to our air, water, and soil environments, in imbalanced consumer and producer technologies that harm their users and dehumanize their operators, in the colossal waste and depreciation of consumer goods and services and in the Moloch-like devouring of a society's resources to the detriment of sane and human allocation of these resources to meet the needs of all the people by superior distribution and innovation.
>
> According to Nader, the choice for citizens is one of either suffering increasing corporate predation or bringing about an "accountability of corporate power to the people" by gaining access to company information, asserting an effective voice in company policies, and insisting on remedies for unjust treatment.[2]

Insofar as size was a measure of corporate capacity for doing either harm or good, GM was an obvious target:

> GM's officers are in truth the princelings of a private superstate. Operating worldwide, GM last year had 794,000 employees and gross revenues of $24,300,000,000, a sum greater than the revenues of any government except that of the United States and that of the Soviet Union. In essence, what Campaign GM seeks to do is to call into question the "legitimacy" of management's near monopoly on corporate power.[3]

---

[1] Nader did not himself join the campaign because of his pending suit against the company. In August 1970, this suit, then reduced to $17 million, was settled out of court for $425,000, the largest award of its type ever made. Adding sting to the humiliation he had inflicted, Nader promptly announced that his net proceeds would be used to monitor GM's future behavior from a social responsibility point of view. See *New York Times*, August 17, 1970.

[2] Luther J. Carter, "Campaign GM: Corporation Critics Seek Support of Universities," *Science*, April 24, 1970, p. 452.

[3] Carter, p. 453.

Round I Proposals

On its February 7 launching date, the campaign sponsored only three demands for inclusion in GM's proxy statement. As summarized by *Business Week*, these were as follows:

> Amend the certificate of incorporation to put GM on record as limiting its business purposes to those consistent with the public's health and safety.
>
> Expand the board from 24 to 27 members to make room for three representatives of the public interest. [The Campaign's] choices are former White House consumer affairs adviser Betty Furness, prominent biologist Rene Dubos, and the Reverend Channing Phillips, president of the Housing Development Corp. in Washington, D.C.
>
> Require management to set up a shareholders' committee to watchdog the public impact of GM decisions and determine its proper role in society.[4]

Before GM could decide how to respond, these three demands were expanded into nine, the additions pertaining to car crash resistance, vehicle emissions, warranty provisions, pollution from manufacturing plants, GM support for public transportation, and opportunities for black employment (Exhibit 1).

GM's reaction, some three weeks later, was to opt for excluding the entire list, a decision which it backed by a 70-page letter and 320 pages of appendices. Accompanied by this dossier, the dispute then went to the SEC for settlement under the agency's guidelines. At that time these guidelines stated that a management could exclude a shareholder's proposal if (1) it was "not a proper subject for action by security holders" under the laws of the company's state of incorporation; if (2) it asked management to act on matters relating to the day-to-day conduct of the business; or if (3) it clearly was "submitted primarily for the purpose of promoting general economic, political, racial, religious, social, or similar causes."[5] Applying this last test, the SEC ruled out all of the campaign proposals except Resolutions II and III, and on Resolution III the wording of the full text had to be amended to allow GM (1) "to restrict the funds allocated to the Stockholders' Committee to reasonable amounts as determined by the Board of Directors"; and (2) "to restrict information to be made available to the Committee to areas which the Board of Directors does not deem privileged for business or competitive reasons."

Had the campaigners been unable to devise any proposal capable of

---

[4] "Nader's Pitch to GM Stockholders," *Business Week*, February 14, 1970, p. 30.

[5] For a critical discussion of controversial features in these guidelines, see "Proxy Rule 14a–8: Omission of Shareholder Proposals," *Harvard Law Review*, Vol. 84 (1971), pp. 700–28, and Donald E. Schwartz, "The Public-Interest Proxy Contest: Reflections on Campaign GM," *Michigan Law Review*, Vol. 69 (1971), pp. 430–54.

EXHIBIT 1

Campaign GM: Rounds I and II

Campaign GM's Original Round I Proposals

I. RESOLVED: That the Board of Directors amend . . . the Certificate of incorporation by adding the following language: . . . none of the [corporate] purposes . . . shall be implemented in a manner which is detrimental to the public health, safety or welfare, or in a manner which violates any law of the United States or of any state in which the Corporation does business.

II. RESOLVED: That . . . the By-Laws of the Corporation be amended to read as follows: The business of the Corporation shall be managed by a board of 27 [instead of 24].

III. RESOLVED:

1. There be esablished the General Motors Shareholders Committee for Corporate Responsibility.

2. The Committee for Corporate Responsibility shall consist of no less than 15 and no more than 25 persons to be appointed by a representative of the Board of Directors, a representative of the Campaign to Make General Motors Responsible, and a representative of United Auto Workers, acting by majority vote. The members of the Committee shall be chosen to represent the following: General Motors management, the United Auto Workers, environmental and conservation groups, consumers, the academic community, civil rights organizations, labor, the scientific community, religious and social service organizations, and small shareholders.

3. The Committee for Corporate Responsibility shall prepare a report and make recommendations to the shareholders with respect to the role of the corporation in modern society and how to achieve a proper balance between the rights and interests of shareholders, employees, consumers and the general public. The Committee shall specifically examine, among other things,

A. The Corporation's past and present efforts to produce an automobile which:

1. Is non-polluting.
2. Reduces the potentiality for accidents.
3. Reduces personal injury resulting from accidents.
4. Reduces property damage resulting from accidents.
5. Reduces the costs of repair and maintenance whether from accidents or extended use.

B. The extent to which the Corporation's policies toward suppliers, employees, consumers and dealers are contributing to the goals of providing safe and reliable products.

C. The extent to which the Corporation's past and present efforts have contributed to a sound national transportation policy and an effective low cost mass transportation system.

EXHIBIT 1 *(continued)*

D. The manner in which the Corporation has used its vast economic power to contribute to the social welfare of the nation.

E. The manner by which the participation of diverse sectors of society in corporate decision-making can be increased including nomination and election of directors and selection of members of the Board of Directors.

4. The Committee's report shall be distributed to the shareholders and to the public no later than March 31, 1971. The Committee shall be authorized to employ staff members in the performance of its duties. The Board of Directors shall appropriate to the Committee all sums necessary to accomplish its tasks, including compensation to its members and staff. The Committee shall have the power to obtain any information from the Corporation and its employees as deemed relevant by the Committee.

IV. RESOLVED: That General Motors announce and act upon a commitment to a greatly increased role for public mass transportation —by rail, by bus, and by methods yet to be developed.

V. RESOLVED: That, by January 1, 1974, all General Motors vehicles are designed so as to be capable of being crash-tested—front, rear, and side—against a solid barrier at 60 miles per hour, without causing any harm to passengers wearing shoulder restraints.

VI. RESOLVED: First, that General Motors support and commit whatever funds and manpower are necessary to comply with the vehicle emission standards recently recommended by the National Air Pollution Control Administration for the 1973 model year; and to comply with these standards before 1973 if in the course of developing the emission controls this is shown to be technologically feasible. Second, that General Motors commit itself to an extensive research program (with an annual budget as large as its present advertising budget of about a quarter billion dollars) on the long-range effects on health and the environment of all those contaminants released into the air by automobiles which are not now regulated by the government. These would include, but not be limited to, asbestos and particulate matter from tires. The results of this research would be periodically published.

VII. RESOLVED: That first, the warranty for all General Motors cars and trucks produced after January 1, 1971, be written to incorporate the following:

1. General Motors warrants that the vehicle is fit for normal and anticipated uses for a period of five years or 50,000 miles, whichever occurs first.

2. General Motors will bear the cost of remedying any defects in manufacture or workmanship whenever or wherever they appear, for the life of the vehicle. Neither time nor mileage limita-

EXHIBIT 1 (concluded)

tion nor exclusions of successive purchasers nor other limitations shall apply with respect to such defects.

3. General Motors accepts responsibility for loss of use of vehicle, loss of time, and all other incidental and consequential personal injuries shown to have resulted from such defects.

Second, General Motors raise its reimbursement rates to dealers on warranty work, making them competitive with other repair work.

VIII. RESOLVED: That General Motors undertake to monitor daily the in-plant air contaminants and other environmental hazards to which employees are exposed in each plant owned or operated by General Motors; that the Corporation report weekly the results of its monitoring to a safety committee of employees in each plant; that if such monitoring discloses a danger to the health or safety of workers in any plant, or in any part of a plant, the Corporation shall take immediate steps to eliminate such hazard; and that no employee shall be required to work in the affected area so long as the hazard exists.

IX. RESOLVED: That General Motors take immediate and effective action to allot a fair proportion of its franchised new car dealerships to minority owners; furthermore, that General Motors act to increase significantly the proportion of minority employees in managerial and other skilled positions.

Source: The Project for Corporate Responsibility.

passing the SEC screen, they could still have mounted at least a hit-and-run raid on GM by going to the annual meeting and making their suggestions from the floor, rather than by getting them on the proxy statement. Indeed, a floor confrontation was all that had occurred in the pioneering drive made in 1967 to mobilize stockholder support of corporate social reform. Masterminded by Saul Alinsky, this drive had been directed at Eastman Kodak, where a civil rights organization bought a few shares of stock and then appeared at the annual meeting to accuse the company brass of not employing enough black workers. Although the dissidents had mustered only a few thousand shares—mostly church-controlled—out of Kodak's 161 million, in the end the company had stepped up its minority hiring.

Reflecting this success, the Kodak precedent was being followed in 1970 at several companies besides GM. Affected among others were Honeywell, American Telephone, General Electric, Boeing, Commonwealth Edison, United Aircraft, and Gulf Oil.[6]

---

[6] Robert W. Dietsch, "Whose Business Is Business?" *New Republic*, April 25, 1970.

Round I Tactics and Countertactics

Besides outlining the rationale for Campaign GM in his introductory speech to the press, Nader also indicated where the campaign would seek for allies:

> "It will go to institutions that own GM stock," Mr. Nader [said], "and, if they decline to respond, to the constituents of those institutions who will be contacted."
>
> "The campaign will reach to the universities and their students and faculty, to the banks and their depositors and fiduciaries, to churches and their congregations, to insurance companies and their policyholders, to union and company pension funds and their membership and to other investors," he said.[7]

Of the possible alliances mentioned in this list, the universities soon became the campaigners' principal objective for reasons one observer identified as follows:

> The corporate responsibility issue arises at a time when university students, who remain in a continuing state of ferment, seem especially susceptible to arguments for corporate reform. Fairly or not, large corporations are identified by many students with the Pentagon and the Vietnam War; Dow Chemical and its napalm contract (which Dow no longer has) have provided students with a symbolic target. And, this year, environmental problems are a major concern on campus and Campaign GM offers students an outlet for their desire to strike a blow against pollution.
>
> *   *   *   *   *
>
> In Campaign GM, students seem to have found an ingenious alternative to staging sit-ins and picketing corporate recruiters as a means of prodding the giants of industry to move faster in reconciling profit objectives with the requirements of a humane society and a clean, healthful environment.[8]

Although attempting to use students and sympathetic faculty members to sway the trustees, boards, and regents who controlled the universities' stock, the campaigners readily admitted that this tactic, no matter how successful, could not suffice to assure victory in the vote at GM's annual meeting. The largest university holding, that of MIT, was only 291,000 GM shares, and the combined investment of all educational institutions was under 10 percent or so of GM stock. Under these circumstances, reporters were eager to know what the campaigners expected to accomplish. Replying to this query, one of the project's principal sponsors, Mr. Geoffrey Cowan, reportedly predicted that the

---

[7] *New York Times*, February 8, 1970.

[8] Carter, pp. 452 ff.

attempt to force socially conscious behavior on corporations might prove, "like the first lunch counter sit-ins," the start of "a whole new movement."[9]

Along with the campaigners and neutral observers, GM knew that its attackers could not win at the polls.[10] Nevertheless, having lost the skirmish about the proxy statement, the company had to decide whether to continue its active resistance, and, if so, what kind of posture —defensive or offensive—to adopt, as well as how much effort to devote to rounding up supporters, and where and how to proselytize.

How the company would answer these questions quickly emerged from a letter and a booklet, *GM's Record of Progress*, which the company had sent, along with its proxy, to all shareholders. The letter said in part,

> General Motors believes the purpose of this proposed committee is to harass the corporation and its management and to promote the particular social and economic views of the sponsors.
>
> If General Motors is to fulfill its responsibilities in the future, it must continue to prosper and grow. Indeed, the corporation can only discharge its obligations to society if it continues to be a profitable investment for its stockholders.

GM's booklet accused the campaign of misrepresenting the company's record. Far from being "against" greater automotive safety, low-cost mass transit, effective automotive emission controls, and social welfare, the company claimed to be "working diligently in all these areas—and more" and to have established an "excellent record of responsible progress."[11] The rest of the booklet's 21 single-column pages were devoted to spelling out in some detail just what the record to date had accomplished.

Besides documenting its past progress in the social sphere, GM took several new steps in the brief span of weeks between the start of the campaign on February 7 and the annual meeting on May 22:

1. In February 1970, GM joined with Ford in expressing a willingness to produce engines capable of using lead-free gasoline, thus lowering certain types of pollution. The company said this change should be effected on 1971 cars.
2. In March 1970, GM agreed to sponsor a new Minority Enterprise Small Business Investment Company (MESBIC) to provide low-cost loans to minority businesses.

---

[9] *New York Times*, February 22, 1970.

[10] According to one authority on proxy battles, "Even a 10% or 15% vote against management would be unheard of for a shareholder's proposal." *Business Week*, p. 30.

[11] General Motors Corporations, *GM's Record of Progress* (1970), p. 20.

3. In March–April, 1970, GM announced the coming introduction of a low-priced exhaust cleaner for pre-1966 cars, the unit to be available at least in California within a few months.
4. In March 1970, GM set the fall of 1971 as the date for the availability of relatively low-emission turbine-powered trucks and buses.
5. In March 1970, GM offered ten oil companies the use of 27 modified GM cars in order to speed the introduction of nonleaded gasoline.

In addition to reporting these new steps as they occurred, GM took special pains to place the whole story of its record of progress before the public press. As one newspaperman informed his readers, "An all-day program has been scheduled for April 16 to provide reporters, many of whom will be covering the annual shareholders' meeting, with General Motors' efforts . . . past, present and future . . . to curb industrial air and water pollution," etc. Commented one observer, "Some, or even all of this seems somehow to suggest overkill. There is little evidence in corporate history to indicate that socioeconomic issues tend to get much attention in actual proxy voting."[12]

In contrast to its efforts to reach stockholders and the general public, GM did relatively little—or relatively little that was reported—to carry its story to the campuses. Whatever quiet contacts GM may have sought with university trustees, it sought little contact with the faculties and students who were its detractors' principal allies. One notable exception occurred at MIT, where in mid-April the company agreed to send two spokesmen to "debate" a representative of Campaign GM. Selected for this mission were the company's treasurer and its director of emission control. Sticking closely to the line which the company had plotted in *GM's Record of Progress,* the former first charged the campaign with distortion, then listed all the areas in which GM claimed to have made social advances. Thereafter he turned the podium over to GM's second speaker for a much longer and more detailed presentation on the technical topic of emissions control. There followed what the *Boston Globe* described as "some tough and frequently hostile questions" bearing on the makeup of GM's board, the percentage of investment in social projects, the pace at which safety and antipollution advances were adopted in the absence of outside legislative pressure, the number of GM's nonwhite dealers, and how much lobbying the company had done to get government funds for public transportation. After the question-and-answer period, GM's representatives departed, leaving the field to the campaign spokesman, Mr. Joseph Onek, a young lawyer. His remarks, reported at length in *The Harvard Crimson* (Exhibit 2), encapsulated the criticisms which the campaigners hoped that

---

[12] *Christian Science Monitor,* April 15, 1970.

EXHIBIT 2

Campaign GM: Rounds I and II

Remarks on Behalf of Campaign GM, Round I, by Mr. Joseph Onek, MIT, April 13, 1970

MR. ONEK: We are campaigning to Make GM Responsible. Obviously then, we believe that GM is now behaving irresponsibly. And the record bears us out.

Pollution Control

Let us look first at the question of air pollution. It has been estimated that GM vehicles and plants are responsible for 35 percent of the nation's air pollution by tonnage. Yet for years, GM refused even to acknowledge that the automobile and air pollution were related.

This issue was already raised by GM. You saw the slides and the charts.* Everything was California models first and the rest of the nation afterwards. Why is that?

Well, it is true that the problem in California was somewhat worse, but certainly there were severe problems throughout the nation, particularly in New York. Why weren't controls applied to New York models until years later? The answer is quite simple. GM wasn't responding to legislation requiring it to act.

In addition, none of those devices they put on involved a new scientific breakthrough. They were old processes, old devices that could have been put on years before. It was a question of a little more money and GM wasn't ready to spend it until they were finally forced to.

And it is significant that even today, when GM recognizes the problem and purports to be concerned about it, that General Motors is spending only $15 million a year on anti-pollution research while it is spending $250 million a year on advertising.

Misleading Accounts

Instead of action, GM provides misleading accounts of what it has accomplished. In its Annual Report, and in the recent full-page ads it took out in the *Times,* GM states that its 1970 cars, as equipped for California use, reduced hydrocarbon emissions by 80 percent. But this figure is based on tests made on finely tuned cars which were just off the assembly line.

What General Motors did not say is that the Department of Health, Education, and Welfare tests demonstrate that once the 1970 cars have been on the road a while, as many as four-fifths of them fail to meet the standards which GM claims to have met.† This is an example of GM's commitment to honesty and to pollution control. We have asked the Securities and Exchange Commission to require GM to recall this mis-

---

* The reference here is to the previous remarks by one of GM's representatives, who discussed the company's progress in the area of emissions control.
† Auto makers have argued that declining efficiency indicates inadequate maintenance.

EXHIBIT 2 (*continued*)

---

leading statement about pollution control efforts. And if SEC does not take action, we intend to appeal to the courts.

Safety

GM's record in automobile safety is equally poor. Fifty-five thousand Americans die in automobile accidents each year, more than have died in the entire Vietnam war. GM has done little to prevent this blood-letting. It delayed for years before installing seat belts and collapsible steering wheels. Nor does it appear interested in constructing a truly crash-proof car.

In 1963, a GM safety engineer wrote that it was impossible to protect against injury in collision at 30 miles per hour. Now, just seven years later, the National Highway Safety Bureau has already tested successfully a prototype vehicle that can withstand impacts at 47 miles per hour, without injury to passengers wearing a normal shoulder belt. I think it is a disgrace and a tragedy that this prototype had to be developed by the Federal Government rather than by the automobile industry.

Another aspect of the auto safety picture is the high cost of property damage of even very minor accidents. . . .

Racial Disaster

General Motors' record in the field of racial justice is a disaster. There are 13,000 GM dealers in this country. Seven, only seven, are black. And even in blue-collar employment, GM has consistently lagged behind Ford and Chrysler.

For the sake of fairness, I should add that ever since those riots in Detroit, GM has been doing much better in the racial area. But I always thought that we were trying to build a society where progress can be made without the need for riots and killing.

Mass Transit

The mass transit issue involves both air pollution and racial justice. The lack of mass transit in this country has clogged our cities with polluting automobiles, has driven white men's roads through black men's homes, and has deprived blacks of access to the new jobs in the suburbs. And GM is a charter member of the powerful highway lobby which has fought for years to prevent federal funding of mass transit programs.

Let's get back to what GM said earlier about going on record for mass transit. They have always been on record for mass transit as long as the money isn't funded.

The big controversy in the mass transit area for the last ten years has been what is going to be done with the federal highway trust fund. Millions of dollars have been set aside for national defense highways. . . . Can't we take some of those highway funds which are already there and use them to build monorails, bus lines, or some other forms of transportation?

EXHIBIT 2 (continued)

And the answer of General Motors and the automobile manufacturers' association has been no—thou shalt not touch money from the highway trust fund. Therefore there have been no new funds appropriated for mass transit because most of the people who want more mass transit thought that money should come out of the highway trust fund.

Warranties

If I had more time, I would talk about automobile warranties, an area where the performance of GM and other manufacturers has been strongly condemned by the Federal Trade Commission. I have a feeling, however, that many of you have sufficient first-hand experience with that problem.

In short, then, GM is a corporation which has acted irresponsibly in many areas of vital concern. We at Campaign GM contend that shareholders can and should do something about the record of the company they own. We have proposed two resolutions which we believe would have a significant impact.

First, we have proposed the addition of three new members to the GM Board of Directors.

Special Interests?

GM strongly opposes our candidates for the Board. It says that they represent "special interests." It is significant that GM now has on its Board directors of oil companies, banks, and insurance companies. Apparently oil companies and banks are not "special interests." Only consumers and blacks are.

We recognize that the election of three public interest board members, although significant, is not the be-all and end-all. So we have proposed the establishment of a Committee on Corporate Responsibility to examine not only GM's performance in the problem areas I have already described, but also the structural changes which may be needed to make GM responsible.

GM opposes this proposal, even though the Commission's recommendations would be advisory only. The reason is obvious. GM does not want independent and respected experts examining what it has done and what it could be doing for society. It does not wish to have its closed and archaic decision-making process exposed and challenged.

Resolution Change

I recognize that an MIT General Assembly Task Force‡ recommended that MIT abstain on this proposal because it felt that even though the need for a Committee on Corporate Responsibility was manifest, the method of selecting Committee members was inadequate.§

We at Campaign GM had a great deal of trouble determining what

‡ One of the bodies at MIT that studied Campaign GM's proposals and advised the Executive Committee of the MIT Corporation how to vote.
§ See Exhibit 1, Resolution III.

EXHIBIT 2 *(concluded)*

the selection process should be. We did not want to leave the matter entirely in GM's hands and we could not think of groups other than the UAW and Campaign GM with sufficient knowledge and interest to participate in the selection process.

I would like to make two announcements, however. First, Campaign GM is ready to provide MIT and other shareholders with a list of types of persons we would nominate for the Committee on Corporate Responsibility.

Second, we at Campaign GM will gladly relinquish our role in the selection process, if a better process is suggested. The Committee on Corporate Responsibility is too important to be jettisoned simply because of the difficulties in selecting its members.

We believe that every responsible shareholder should support our proposals.

Source: *Harvard Crimson,* April 24, 1970.

MIT and other institutions would consider when voting their GM stock. He ended with a plea for university involvement:

> In closing, I would like to say only this. In the last decade we have been made painfully aware of the shortcomings in our society—our racism, our excessive reliance on military force, our rape of the environment. Naturally, therefore, some of the leading institutions in our society are being challenged and attacked.
>
> Some of the attacks take the most primitive forms—bombing and killing. We are following a different route. We are using reasoned argument and legal process, the very methods which our major institutions say they respect. And many Americans will be watching to see how these institutions respond.[13]

Denouement of Round I at the Annual Meeting

Not until the voting at the annual meeting would it be clear exactly how many votes Campaign GM Round I would have won. Some strange bedfellows had, however, declared their commitment to the cause. These included a number of colleges: Tufts (9,300 shares), Brown (4,700), and Amherst (37,000 for at least one proposal). Still other colleges would at least abstain—an action that was counted as a moral victory. This contingent comprised Yale (86,000), Williams (21,000), Stanford (24,000), Swarthmore (2,200), and Rockefeller University (63,000). The absence of MIT and Harvard from these lists was a special dis-

---

[13] "Is It a Kandy-Kolored Streamline Baby or a Safe, Non-Polluting Motor Vehicle?" *Harvard Crimson,* April 24, 1970.

appointment to Campaign GM, but the governing committee of MIT had at least indicated that it would formally ask the company to concern itself with socially desirable goals.[14] Similarly, a number of other large colleges and foundations, though supporting management, had "also cautioned that they might not do so the next time around." Most notable of these was the Rockefeller Foundation, which had castigated GM for its " 'defensive and negative attitude' toward its critics."[15] Besides these sources, more announced support would come from such scattered quarters as U.S. Senator Hart (315 shares); the New York City Pension Fund; the new chief of the United Auto Workers (UAW), who had come to the annual meeting to speak on behalf of the shareholders' committee—disclosure proposal; and, most quixotically, the son of GM's senior board member—Mr. Stewart R. Mott (2,000 shares). Another well-known figure in the campaign corner was Mr. Robert Townsend of *Up the Organization* fame. At a pep rally just before the meeting, he echoed a favorite campaign theme by telling his hearers how soon GM could build a clean car if only the company would divert to this purpose $200 million of the $240 million annually spent on advertising.

At 2:00 P.M., when GM's Chairman James M. Roche gavelled the annual meeting to order, it had already attracted an overflow crowd of some 3,000 people. Present along with the Campaigners and Middle America were what the *New Yorker* called the familiar *"enfants terribles* of the annual meeting circuit." These included Mr. Louis Gilbert, champion of cumulative voting, and—wearing a paper money hat and a gilded gadfly pin—Mrs. Wilma Soss, champion of limits on executive pay. "Warming up" in another corner was Mrs. Evelyn Y. Davis "in white tights and a black bathing suit, with a sash reading 'Miss Air Pollution' across her chest." Less familiar were a peace movement chairman and a Nobel laureate who had come to "sneak in" a nomination to the GM board for the younger Mott, supported by speeches against the war in Vietnam.

Planned and unplanned scenes with all these actors took several hours, and then attention turned to the first campaign proposal. A "footloose correspondent" sent by the *New Yorker* described what happened next:

> It was 5:06 P.M. before the proposal on the Shareholders' Committee came up formally. Whether by calculation or not, the chairman had managed things so adroitly that much of the audience was by then im-

---

[14] This Committee included four academic administrators (three *ex officio*), the physician-in-chief of a research hospital, three company presidents, a corporate board chairman, a former executive vice president, and a retired corporate director. See *MIT Institute Report*, Special Supplement, May 22, 1970.

[15] "Businessmen in the News: James M. Roche," *Fortune*, June 1970, p. 31.

patient to go home. Betty Furness got the floor, and had barely opened her mouth when she yielded graciously to a challenge from Mrs. Soss. Then Mrs. Davis—without anybody's yielding to her—broke in. Soon another lady shareholder was recognized and was allowed to deliver a rambling tirade against Ralph Nader, and even to suggest, if I understood her correctly, that if Nader's youthful followers would stop drinking and taking drugs there would be fewer splendid General Motors cars involved in accidents. Not long after she finally braked herself, a male stockholder told Mr. Roche that by repeatedly calling upon certain predictable fillibusterers in the room he was in effect conducting a filibuster himself. . . . Shortly thereafter, discussion was closed and a vote on the Shareholders' Committee was taken.[16]

When the vote was finally counted on both campaign proposals, management had won handily, as shown in Table 1.

TABLE 1

Proposal	Number of Shareholders for	Number of Shares for	Percentage of Shares for
Shareholders' committee............	61,794	6,361,299	2.73%
Three additional directors..........	53,495	5,691,130	2.44%

Undaunted by this count, a spokesman for the campaign first complimented GM's top officer on "the courtesy and stamina he had displayed" in chairing the day's tumultuous proceedings, then added, "Mr. Roche, we look forward to seeing you next year."[17]

GM Under the Gun

In picking GM for the two-time target of an effort to make U.S. corporations more "responsible," the campaigners had selected the world's largest auto maker and one of the world's largest companies. Despite its blue-chip status, however, GM was beset by a wide range of conventional business problems. Not just social critics, but dealers, customers, investors, labor, government agencies, and competition all posed difficulties calling for managerial attention. The following list of company problems is drawn from press notices for only 15 months through 1971's first quarter:

1. In January 1970, reflecting a growing unrest over car sales felt to be subsidized, car dealers threatened to take the four major auto companies to court over discounts made to large fleet buyers. Re-

---

[16] E. J. Kahn, Jr., "Our Footloose Correspondents—We Look Forward to Seeing You Next Year," *New Yorker,* June 20, 1970, pp. 40–51.

[17] Kahn, Jr.

sponding in May, the "Big Three" auto makers halted these allowances—and by year's end found themselves defendants in antitrust suits filed by eight states and several cities, charging a conspiracy to eliminate competition in sales of government fleets.

2. In February 1970, in the wake of past complaints from customers, dealers, and the FTC over defects and warranties, the company told a Nixon aide that inspectors had been put into all plants. A few days later, Chairman Roche was reported as blaming auto workers for the industry's quality woes.

3. In April 1970, owing allegedly to slumping sales and rising costs, the Big Three reported their worst first quarter since the 1958 recession. In GM's case the drop was 33.4 percent in earnings, and it followed an 11-year low in profit margins for 1969. Investors responded with a "pasting" for automotive stocks.

4. In June 1970, canvassing ways to cut costs, GM and Ford were reputedly mulling the purchase of Japanese steel, currently making well-publicized inroads against hard-pressed domestic suppliers.

5. In July 1970, hoping to control the net costs of the new contract soon to be worked out between the auto makers and labor, GM's Chairman Roche charged that the UAW had "shirked its obligations," and he reiterated an April demand for greater productivity and efficiency.

6. In August, predicting the "rout" of foreign-made autos by Detroit's upcoming minicars, GM's Chevrolet Division made ready to introduce its own contender, the "Vega," at a price still undisclosed. When the announcement came, the price was so high ($2,091) that analysts questioned the dent on import sales, and leading import makers announced themselves "unafraid." Two days later, Ford set the price on its "Pinto" minicar to undercut the Vega by $172.

7. Early in September, Nader charged GM with having "lied" about company data that showed Corvair to be unsafe. Repudiating this charge the next day, the firm called this attack "false and vitriolic" and offered the U.S. Secretary of Transportation any information desired. Evidence from both sides was later turned over to the National Highway Safety Bureau, which indicated in November that Corvairs tipped over and that carbon monoxide emission was a problem, but which reportedly did not support Nader to the extent he had hoped.

8. In mid-September, contract negotiations having broken down, the UAW selected GM as the sole target of a strike which turned out to last at least ten weeks in GM's U.S. plants and 14 weeks in Canada. Strike results for the company included a half-year loss of $210 million, a 64 percent decline in yearly earnings, omission of bonuses

FIGURE 1

Cost of GM Strike

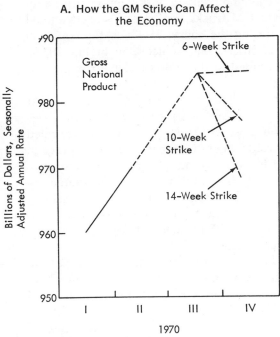

A. How the GM Strike Can Affect the Economy

B. Estimated Daily Cost of the GM Strike

$14 million	in wages of 403,000-plus workers in United States and Canada
$90 million	in lost sales of 26,000 cars and trucks in United States and Canada
$40 million	in payments to suppliers
$20 million	in taxes related to sales, but not including state, local, and federal income taxes

Source: *Business Week*, November 7, 1970, p. 19.

Note: Data from Wharton econometric model, University of Pennsylvania.
Source: *Business Week*, October 3, 1970, p. 18.

for top executives,[18] omission of the customary extra year-end dividend, and bids by Ford and Chrysler to lure customers away.

9. Late in November, GM's strike was settled by a contract giving labor gains estimated at 30 percent over the next three years. Besides setting an at least mildly inflationary wage-and-benefit pattern, the strike had reportedly cost Michigan's economy $4 million a week in revenue losses, and it had cost the federal government a $1.4 billion drop from GM's 1969 income tax. National social costs were also high, as suggested by the charts in Figure 1.

10. Late in November, following the labor settlement, GM added an average of $24 to its 1971 model prices, bringing the increase from 1970 to a total of 6.9 percent.

11. In November, maintaining a position it had adopted the previous year, GM refused to agree that the wheels on some 200,000 of its

[18] In 1968, bonuses and salaries for 63 top officers and directors had been respectively $4.9 million and $9.9 million. In 1969, parallel figures for 67 recipients were $5.6 million and $9.4 million.

trucks were defective, and, in the first such action of its kind, the company was ordered to institute a recall on a nonvoluntary basis. This action followed a Nader intervention and a ten-month study of possible safety defects in GM trucks and buses by the National Highway Safety Bureau, during the course of which the company had voluntarily recalled almost 47,000 vehicles, including 19,000 school buses. GM promptly filed in the courts to have the government's order set aside.

12. In December, Nader reported that the break-up of Ford and GM had been recommended by agents of the Justice Department.

13. In February 1971, the annual report for the previous year revealed that GM's profit from foreign operations had fallen 26 percent, despite a rise of 8 percent in overseas sales. Strikes in Britain were a major cause, with some of the problem being contributed by Peruvian government decrees which forced termination of assembly in that nation. Even so, GM's nondomestic operations contributed $377 million to the U.S. balance of payments, bringing the post–World War II total to $12.3 billion.

14. Making up a sales backlog from the strike, GM's sales pattern through 1971's first quarter was very strong—but still difficult to interpret. Overall, analysts wondered if domestic minicars had "flopped." According to *The Value Line* for April 16, "The introduction of U.S.-built subcompacts. . . failed to stem the tide of imports which continue to post new records."[19] Worse still, relatively low-margin minicars were eating into large-car sales; thus "the home-grown small cars . . . appear to have realized Detroit's worst nightmare."

Over the longer run, down-turns in earnings (Exhibit 3) and certain unfavorable trends in sales caused some observers to wonder if "mighty GM" could be faltering:

> There are many who say GM's engine has been missing badly in recent years. Once, the race between Chevrolet and Ford was strictly no contest, with Chevy regularly winding up the year leading by more than 300,000 cars. Last year the lead was under 200,000 and for the first six months of this year, Chevy leads by about 80,000. GM has been noticeably tardy in recognizing some emerging market segments. Ford's Mustang had the sporty car market to itself for 2½ years before GM countered with the Camaro. Cynics wonder if GM has missed the market on occasion because the world a GM executive sees from his pinnacle can be distorted. Says a man who once was close to the pinnacle: "The

---

[19] According to a GM speaker at the Harvard Business School, GM regarded the "competitive threat of the foreign car manufacturers as the principal most important determinant of the American industry's future prosperity." *Harbus News*, April 15, 1971.

EXHIBIT 3

Campaign GM: Rounds I and II
GM Financial Data
(dollars in millions)
A. Selected GM Financial Trends, 1965–70

	1965	1966	1967	1968	1969	1970	Estimated 1971*
Assets.....................	$11,479	$12,213	$13,273	$14,010	$14,820	$14,174	—
Sales......................	20,734	20,209	20,026	22,755	24,295	18,752	$27,800
Operating margin (%).......	21.6%	18.7%	18.0%	18.1%	16.7%	7.9%	15.0%
Working capital.............	$ 3,685	$ 3,606	$ 4,006	$ 4,230	$ 4,352	$ 3,011	$ 3,480
Net plant..................	4,617	5,130	5,330	5,438	5,645	6,396	6,500
Net worth.................	8,030	8,514	9,048	9,548	10,021	9,680	10,250
Net income...............	2,126	1,793	1,627	1,732	1,711	609	1,870
Earnings/net worth (%)....	26.5%	21.1%	18.0%	18.1%	17.1%	6.3%	18.0%
Earnings/sales (%).........	10.2	8.9	8.1	7.6	7.0	3.2	—
Average annual PE ratio (%).................	13.8	13.3	14.3	13.5	12.9	3.8	—

* Estimated by *The Value Line.*

B. Growth Rates per Share, Annually Compounded

	Ten Years	Five Years	Three Years	1969
Sales...................	7.9%	7.4%	6.4%	6.8%
Net income............	6.9	–0.3	–1.5	–1.2

Source: *The Value Line,* April 16, 1971, p. 131, and General Motors annual reports.

top executives tend to be too isolated from what goes in the market place."[20]

Round II Campaign Proposals and Concurrent Pressures

True to the promise given at the annual meeting in May, Round II of Campaign GM was initiated the next November. This time, only three demands were made (Exhibit 4), all of which reached the proxy statement:[21] As summarized by the *Wall Street Journal,* these demands were as follows:

---

[20] "Mighty GM Faces Its Critics," *Business Week,* July 11, 1970, p. 72.

[21] Since the previous year, the path to inclusion had become easier following a successful court challenge to an SEC ruling based on its social issues guideline. This challenge had come from shareholders in Dow, who had asked the D.C. Court of Appeals to overrule an agency decision supporting Dow management's resistance to an antinapalm resolution. After the court had remanded this issue to the SEC for a more formal finding so that "the bases for its decision" could "appear clearly on the record," many resolutions on behalf of social issues found their way onto 1971 proxy statements. Meanwhile the SEC had asked for a ruling from the Supreme Court on the adequacy of its procedures, claiming that these had to be informal to enable it to cope expeditiously with the growing volume of its work.

A "proposal on shareholder democracy" that would require GM to list on its proxy statement for next year's annual meeting all candidates nominated by nonmanagement stockholders. In the past, GM has listed only the management slate on its proxy.

A "proposal on constituent democracy" that would require GM to allow three groups—GM employees, purchasers of new GM vehicles, and GM auto dealers—to each nominate a director candidate. The three candidates thus selected would be voted on by all shareholders.

A "proposal on disclosure" that would require GM to publish in its annual report specific facts and figures regarding its progress on auto-pollution control, auto safety and minority hiring.[22]

Besides having to contend with Nader's friends in Campaign GM, the company concurrently had to contend with other challenges sponsored or abetted by Nader. Thus GM, along with other corporations, could be affected by at least three of Nader's prime reformist schemes: one a plan for breaking up monopolies and oligopolies, another a Code for Professional Integrity, and the third a Federal Incorporation Act. Of these, the first would operate by setting ceilings on market share. The second would encourage and protect engineers and other professionals in business in reporting what they believed to be "illegal, hazardous or unconscionable" behavior by their employers. The third would, among other things, broaden the requirements for corporate disclosures and would even "pierce the corporate veil" to make officers personally responsible for acts which currently resulted only in indictments of the corporation. As a precedent for this idea, Nader pointed out that brokers could be suspended by the SEC for violating the securities law. He continued: "Suppose you suspend the president of General Motors for six months. He would be crawling up the wall, wondering who's going to usurp his power. It's a tremendous built-in deterrent. . . . Another idea would be suspending advertising."[23]

GM, along with the whole auto industry, would be affected by Washington's increasingly rigorous climate of legislation and regulation, a climate which Nader had helped as much as anyone to create (Exhibit 5). Spurred on in part by critics who suspected all regulators of a flaccid backbone and all industry of needless foot-dragging, units such as the National Highway Traffic Safety Administration (NHTSA) and the Environmental Protection Agency (EPA) were making demands in 1970 and 1971 that, according to the auto industry, were "unattainable" within the time-frame specified. One dispute erupted

---

[22] *Wall Street Journal,* November 20, 1970. Besides the three Campaign resolutions, GM's proxy statement bore five others. Four came from such familiar critics as Mr. Gilbert, Mrs. Soss, and Mrs. Davis and bore on such relatively mundane matters as the locus of GM's annual meeting. The other, from a missionary unit of the Episcopal Church, sought to end GM's manufacturing in South Africa.

[23] *New York Times,* January 24, 1971.

EXHIBIT 4

Campaign GM: Rounds I and II

Summary of Campaign GM's 1971 Proxy Proposals with Campaign and Company Comments

Proposal 1: On Shareholder Democracy

Proxies are solicited in support of an amendment to the by-laws that will provide a process for shareholder nomination and election of Directors.

The stockholder has submitted the following statement in support of such resolution:

Reasons: "This proposal would, for the first time, give shareholders a real choice in the selection of Directors. Under the present system the only candidate shareholders have any opportunity to consider are management's nominees. This proposal would permit shareholder nominees for Director to be listed on General Motors' proxy, so that all the shareholders would have a chance to consider nominees for Director in addition to those proposed by management. The proxy would in effect become a ballot giving shareholders a choice among opposing nominees."

The Board of Directors favors a vote AGAINST this resolution for the following reasons:

The adoption of this Proposal would place the stockholders of General Motors at a serious disadvantage. In the opinion of the Board of Directors, it would not be in the best interest of those stockholders who look forward to the continued success of General Motors.

A corporation's board of directors should be a group of qualified individuals dedicated to the business success of the company and the interests of its stockholders and the public as they relate to the corporation. Directors should not have any commitment or interest in conflict with those of the corporation and its stockholders. To provide such a board, General Motors, like other companies, presents in its proxy statement a slate of nominees for directors that it recommends for election by the stockholders at their annual meeting.

If a group of stockholders wishes to propose an alternative slate, or even a partial slate, corporate procedures are already available which permit these stockholders to solicit proxies. . . .

*   *   *   *   *

This represents an attempt to secure the benefit of the Corporation's proxy solicitation facilities by groups of stockholders who have not demonstrated that they have broad stockholder support. These facilities would be theirs to use without cost. But the cost would be borne by GM stockholders.

The proposal would permit director candidates to be placed on the Corporation's proxy by only 1/100th of 1 percent (0.01 percent) of the 1,300,000 General Motors stockholders, or by the owners of ½ of one-thousandth of 1 percent (0.0005 percent) of General Motors 286,000,000 shares of stock.

EXHIBIT 4 (continued)

. . . Continuity of a successful Board of Directors is of utmost importance. The proposal would substitute an intentionally cumbersome procedure designed to permit small groups with little stake in the company's success to force the entire body of stockholders to vote on candidates that these groups might choose on the basis of their own interests. This is more than a proposal to experiment as it is a proposal to discard procedures that have contributed to the economic success of General Motors and to the economic well-being of its stockholders.

Proposal 2: On Constituent Democracy

Proxies are solicited in support of an amendment to the Corporation's by-laws that would allow for constituent participation in the selection of Directors. . . .

The proposal on Constituent Democracy would provide that regardless of the size of the Board of Directors, three of the Directors would be nominated by constituent groups of employees (including nonunion employees), consumers, and dealers. One Director would be nominated by each constituency. It is contemplated that this number would be a small minority on the Board of Directors.

The stockholder has submitted the following statement in support of such resolution:

Reasons: "This amendment recognizes the need to broaden the decision-making base of the Corporation by adding to the Board persons chosen by groups who have a vital interest in the Corporation's affairs. Employees, dealers and consumers are unable at present to influence significantly the policies of the Corporation. The Corporation will better serve the interests of the larger community if these groups can participate intimately in decision-making. At the same time, the shareholders' ultimate ownership right to choose Directors is maintained since they can veto absolutely any candidate."

The Board of Directors favors a vote AGAINST this resolution for the following reasons:

This proposal goes a step beyond the Stockholder Proposal Number[1]. It would provide for the nomination of three directors by groups that are not stockholders. These nominees would be chosen in a kind of "popularity contest" among loosely defined groups. In size these groups could range from some 20,000 in the case of GM dealers 115 countries to 800,000 in the case of GM employees throughout the world and up to 30,000,000 in the case of users of GM cars, trucks, and buses in all parts of the world. There would be no real means of verifying the eligibility of those voting.

The proposal would require General Motors to poll the members of each of these three groups to determine their nominees. . . . This proposal is hopelessly impractical. No reliable poll of these groups could be conducted without setting up voting procedures as elaborate as the

EXHIBIT 4 (continued)

election processes of some of our States. Under the Project's proposal, the expense of conducting such polls would be borne by all the stockholders. It would be considerable; the cost and effort incident to the polling of 800,000 employees and of as many as 30,000,000 "GM consumers" on a world-wide basis would be prohibitive.°

The proposal ignores the fact that each member of the Board of Directors is charged by law with representing *all* of its stockholders. It seems inevitable that directors elected under this proposal would soon find themselves in a conflict of interest. They would be divided between their allegiance to the group which nominated them—the dealers, employees or consumers—and the entire body of stockholders to whom each director has a legal responsibility.

The basic purpose and underlying philosophy of the proposal are wrong. The Board of Directors of a corporation in the United States is neither a political institution nor a legislative body. It consists of representatives elected by the stockholders to run the business on their behalf with due regard to the legitimate rights and interests of the stockholders, employees, dealers, customers, and the public at large.

Each of the three groups which would select nominees under this proposal has existing channels of communication and representation which have operated well for many years. . . .

Proposal 3: For Disclosure on Minority-Hiring, Air-Pollution, and Auto-Safety Policies

Proxies are solicited in support of a proposal to require the Corporation to disclose in its annual report data in three areas of immense concern to shareholders and the public: air-pollution control, auto safety, and minority hiring and franchising.

The purpose of this proposal is to provide information that is currently not available to shareholders in order that they may accurately evaluate the performance of management in meeting public responsibilities in these areas.

The stockholder has submitted the following statement in support of such resolution:

Reasons: "Shareholders have both the right and the responsibility to be concerned about the policies of the Corporation which affect the community. Shareholders require information about the Corporation's activities and its policies in order to assess their adequacy. The proposal would require management to furnish to the shareholders in the annual report the minimum information needed in three key areas of concern to the Corporation and its shareholders: minority hiring, pollution, and safety. Unless this information is furnished, the shareholders would be prevented from carrying out their proper role as owners."

The Board of Directors favors a vote AGAINST this resolution for the following reasons:

EXHIBIT 4 *(concluded)*

General Motors in its annual reports, its quarterly reports, its special mailings to stockholders, and its numerous formal statements to the press has an enviable record of open disclosure to its stockholders and the public generally. Detailed information is also filed with city, state, and Federal agencies. These filings are available to those having a legitimate interest in them. The final decisions as to matters to be included in stockholder reports, the degree of detail and the timing of the information should be determined by those charged with the successful operation of the company. The degree of success they have achieved over the years is evidenced by the many awards General Motors has won for the excellence of its reporting.

✧   ✧   ✧   ✧   ✧

While the proposal would permit omission of information if a competitive disadvantage would result, the Board of Directors would be required to demonstrate "clear and compelling reasons" for any such omission. The question of what facts or circumstances might constitute "clear and compelling reasons" is clearly one on which there can be—and undoubtedly would be—disagreement. This could lead to protracted argument and even to expensive litigation.

---

* According to one expert in the field of stockholder solicitation, it might cost GM as much as $100 million a year to carry out the consumer portion of this proposal alone. *Wall Street Journal,* May 12, 1971.

Source: Summary statements of the Campaign resolutions from the Project on Corporate Responsibility, *Campaign GM: Round II Proxy Statement* (Washington, D.C., November 19, 1970), pp. 5, 8, 11; supporting and opposing statements from General Motors Corporation, *Proxy Statement,* April 5, 1971.

EXHIBIT 5

Campaign GM: Rounds I and II

Meet Ralph Nader

Within three years of authoring *Unsafe at Any Speed,* Nader had been credited with providing most of the impetus for major federal legislation on auto safety and meat inspection codes. His crusades and his life style continued to capture attention in the press. The following excerpts are from a write-up in *Newsweek.*

EVERYMAN'S LOBBYIST AND HIS CONSUMER CRUSADE

Diseased fish, higher auto prices, dental X-rays, tires—you name it. Ralph Nader was upset about it last week. As Everyman's self-appointed lobbyist in Washington, the lanky, sallow-faced lawyer raced through six eighteen-hour days, propelled by a fine sense of what his admirers call "controlled outrage" and his detractors describe as "fanaticism."

✧   ✧   ✧   ✧   ✧

EXHIBIT 5 (*continued*)

The possibles for Nader have grown infinitely since he achieved his sudden fame in auto safety. Critics complain that he is too "emotional," too "vindictive." But his charges and denunciations now command head-lines at home and abroad, and a simple letter of inquiry from Nader to a Federal agency or industrial firm gets immediate attention.

❖ ❖ ❖ ❖ ❖

To finance his crusade, Nader currently has only his own resources—and by the standards of most of Washington's lobbyists, they would support perhaps one medium-size cocktail party at the Shoreham. . . . He couldn't care less for material things; his wardrobe numbers four suits, he eats in cut-rate cafeterias and he owns no car.

An ascetic? Obviously. But Ralph Nader's principal quality . . . is a well-honed sense of society's shortcomings and a practical view of how [to deal with them]. He summed up his own view of his special mission in a recent interview with *Newsweek* correspondents in Washington:

"I'm not really a reformer; so many reformers leave a lot to be de-sired. A dreamer? No, I've got to be practical. But the real question is [not] why I'm doing what I'm doing but why so many people don't care. What we do about corporate air and water pollution, corporate soil and food contamination, corporate-bred trauma on the highways, corpo-rate inflationary pricing, corporate misallocation of resources and corpo-rate dominance over state, local and Federal agencies—to suggest a few issues—will decide the quality of our lives." Then, in the very next breath, Nader denied he is either anti-business or convinced that busi-nessmen themselves are evil.

"It's a disservice to view this as a threat to the private-enterprise economy or to big business," he insisted. "It's just the opposite. It is an attempt to preserve the free-enterprise economy by making the market work better; an attempt to preserve the democratic control of technology by giving government a role in the decision-making process as to how much or how little 'safety' products must contain."

Source: "Everyman's Lobbyist," *Newsweek*, January 22, 1967, pp. 65–72.

over a government demand that car occupants be protected by airbags as a form of "passive restraint" (i.e., one requiring no positive human action) as early as 1973. Another storm broke over emission control requirements, when standards for 1975 as proposed by the Department of Health, Education, and Welfare were suddenly replaced within about two weeks by much stiffer standards from the EPA, which GM felt it could not meet, as shown in Table 2. Still another source of friction was the bumper code. Here the auto makers won an adjustment. Whereas NHTSA had at first suggested that both front and rear bumpers

TABLE 2

Automotive Exhaust Emission Requirements for 1975 as a Percent Reduction from Uncontrolled Levels

Constituent	Today	HEW Proposal (February 10, 1970)	EPA Proposal (February 26, 1970)
Hydrocarbons..................	80%	95%	97%
Carbon monoxide..............	69	86	96
Oxides of nitrogen..............	33*	83	90†

* California only.
† For 1976.
Source: General Motors, *Progress in Areas of Public Concern* (February 1971), p. 8.

be able to protect cars from damage in 5-mile-an-hour crashes by the 1973 model year, the rear-bumper requirement was later reduced to 2.5 miles an hour.[24]

Given the high pitch of public interest in safety and ecology during the start of the 1970's, the evolution of government standards and industry's reaction to them attracted considerable coverage in the press.

Round II Campaign Tactics

Whereas Round I of Campaign GM had won considerable press attention for its proselytizing on the campuses, Round II earned more coverage for seeking the support of financial institutions. The *New York Times* reported on evolving versions of this tactic, one account going as follows:

> The Project on Corporate Responsibility asked the nation's 12 largest mutual funds today to adopt a whole new standard for their investment decisions, under which the funds would consider corporate policies in two areas of social policy before investing. . . .
> . . . These were environmental policies and minority hiring. . . .
> The project itself did not attempt to dictate standards of good corporate behavior in these areas. Instead, it asked the funds and the [Investment Company Institute] to adopt standards of their own.
>
> ❉   ❉   ❉   ❉   ❉
>
> The project . . . suggested that the institute and industry leaders consult with church groups, minorities, environmental and other organizations in formulating the code.
> The project's letters represent the first time that the mutual fund industry, on a broad basis, has been asked to formulate investment policies that would take social policies of companies into account. Individual funds have previously been approached on specific issues, such

---

[24] *Wall Street Journal*, April 15, 1971.

as the campaigns to bring issues before the General Motors shareholders' meetings.[25]

According to an earlier story, the campaign had written to the 350 largest mutual funds, asking them to vote their GM shares on the basis of a shareholder poll—or, if a poll would be too expensive, on the basis of a 5 percent sampling. At the same time, the campaign had also written to the major brokerage firms holding customers' stock in "street names." These brokers were warned that, in the campaign's opinion, they could not legally vote their stock without instructions from the beneficial owners. Commented the *New York Times*, "This argument appears to be disputed."[26]

GM's Round II Counteroffensive

Forewarned well ahead of time, GM's management had ample chance to reconsider, if it wished, the tactics it had followed during Round I. A well-known apostle of conservatism, Milton Friedman, had recently penned a widely read statement attacking the position of corporation critics. Published under the title, "The Social Responsibility of Business Is to Increase Its Profits,"[27] this statement could have furnished GM some ammunition. Some observers, moreover, were eager to see the company assume a more aggressive posture. For example, the *Wall Street Journal* gave space on its editorial page to a long article by Jeffrey St. John titled, "Memo to GM: Why Not Fight Back?"[28]

In the event, GM undertook a countercampaign composed of (1) statements outlining the company's attitude toward the profit/social obligations issue, (2) enumeration of past achievements in the area of social responsibility, and (3) stepped-up action in the social sphere.

Among the spokesmen who undertook to enunciate what might be called GM's philosophic position was Chairman Roche. He made two major statements on this topic, one in a booklet distributed to a wide audience including all GM stockholders, the other to an urban executive club. In the first of these statements, Roche wrote in part as follows:

> Every executive must recognize that social progress throughout the nation in the long run is beneficial to his business. The modern business-man and his company are expected to engage in activities that are be-

---

[25] *New York Times*, April 21, 1971.

[26] *New York Times*, April 14, 1971.

[27] *New York Times Magazine*, September 13, 1970, p. 122 ff. (Reprinted with permission as a case by the Harvard Business School under the number 3–371–106/AM/P320.)

[28] May 21, 1971. Mr. St. John was identified as a columnist and radio–TV commentator and as the moderator of the business segment of the "Today" show.

yond the traditional concerns of a business. People and institutions still invest in a business with the expectation of earning a return. . . . Therefore profit must always be a primary concern. But now it is more widely recognized that profits and social progress must go hand in hand.

The corporate executive, therefore, must balance the responsibilities of the corporations to various publics. At General Motors, for example, we have responsibilities to our customers, to our employees, to our dealers, to our suppliers, as well as to our stockholders. We are anxious to live up to the expectations of each. . . .

❖ ❖ ❖ ❖ ❖

This corporation and every other must serve the society in which it operates. GM responds to society's expectations. When society in the competitive marketplace demands a different automobile, we try to make it. When society, through the various groups to which we are responsible, asks us to involve ourselves more in national problems, we attempt to do so.

However, we do not believe that corporations are the best equipped to answer every social problem. Corporations should take leadership only where they are best qualified. Other institutions—colleges, churches, government—all have a role to play. General Motors is determined to do its full share in meeting its obligations to society—alone where we are best able, together with other elements of society where that is more effective.

We want to know what you think of all this. As long as you as a stockholder express your will, General Motors will continue to respond. . . . If you are impressed with some of the progress you are seeing today, then some satisfaction belongs to you. If, on the other hand, you think we should follow other directions and have constructive suggestions, we hope you will give us the benefit of your counsel and support.[29]

Mr. Roche's other major statement was given before the Executive Club of Chicago. As characterized by the *Wall Street Journal,* this speech was "one of the toughest attacks ever made on corporate critics by GM."[30] Commenting, Nader called it "unvarnished GM, a massive display of GM's malignancies."[31] A campaign spokesman simply said, "He's flipped his lid."[32]

After charging unnamed critics with threatening the entire free enterprise system, impugning America's reputation, and creating an unfairly negative picture of U.S. business, Mr. Roche went on in part as follows:

---

[29] General Motors Corporation, *Progress in Areas of Social Concern* (February 1971), p. 33.

[30] March 26, 1971.

[31] *Business Week,* April 10, 1971, p. 101.

[32] *Wall Street Journal,* March 26, 1971.

An Adversary Culture

Corporate responsibility is a catchword of the adversary culture that is so evident today. If something is wrong with American society, blame business. Business did not create discrimination in America, but business is expected to eliminate it. Business did not bring about the deterioration of our cities, but business is expected to rebuild them. Business did not create poverty and hunger in our land, but business is expected to eliminate them.

As citizens and Americans, we heartily endorse all these objectives. . . . But every thoughtful American must face the fact that new aspirations entail new costs.

* * * * *

The Contributions of Business

Business does its job when it provides useful jobs at high wages, when it provides useful products at fair prices, when it provides economic growth that produces taxes for government and earnings for stockholders. These are the long-standing responsibilities of business. Their fulfillment by American business over two centuries has made our America what it is. It is an achievement to be proud of—an achievement to talk about.

Earlier, I said we must be ready to accept change. And business today is expected to respond to the new aspirations of the society it serves. This broad public expectation must be recognized, and these new challenges must be accepted. The costs of many are not prohibitive. . . . However, in other areas, for example in the control of pollution, costs are usually substantial. To the extent that they cannot be absorbed, they will raise the price of the product and in turn the overall level of prices in our economy.

Aspirations and Their Cost

As a nation we must be mature enough to face up to the costs involved in meeting our new aspirations. It can mean a weakened competitive position in the world. It can mean higher prices for the consumer, and higher taxes for the citizens. This no dire forecast. This is already a fact.

* * * * *

It is not enough that management should be aware of what benefits —and what costs—are involved in fulfilling social objectives. The owners of American business . . . must make the ultimate decision.

In the end, management must be responsive to the wishes of the stockholders. Management is obliged to inform stockholders as to the problems and short-term costs as well as the potential long-range benefits of a greater and more direct involvement in social objectives. Then, management must abide by the owners' decision.[33]

The documents that in 1971 undertook to tell the story of GM's achievements in the social sphere included both the annual report and a much expanded version of the previous year's *GM's Record of Progress.* Titled *Progress in Areas of Public Concern,* the new booklet dealt with such topics as automotive safety, emission and pollution control, urban transportation, abandoned car disposal, minority opportunities, etc. (For excerpts, see Exhibit 6). Like the earlier *Record of Progress, Progress in Areas of Public Concern* not only went to all GM stockholders but also provided the theme for a conference just before the annual meeting. Invited this time, among others, was a group of prominent educators and representatives of foundations and investment institutions. By special invitation of Mrs. Roche, key campaigners were invited, too.

In the area of action, GM's countercampaign got under way well before Round II started. Although Nader indicated that most of what was done was, in his opinion, simply "cosmetic," and a campaign spokesman saw GM's actions as aimed at "destroying our credibility,"[34] the press gave these moves extensive coverage, as indicated by the following list, mostly based on reports in the *Wall Street Journal:*

1. From June through November 1970, GM negotiated purchase of the German-patented Wankel rotary-type engine, in the expectation that with further development the Wankel could prove the eventual answer to auto pollution. Investment was put at $50 million.
2. In June, 1970, GM planned to start a model project in a small Michigan city to retrieve junked and abandoned cars; usable materials were to go to foundries, in an effort to demonstrate the economic feasibility of the sponsored system.
3. In June, 1970, GM took on a $1 million government contract to design safety cars.
4. In July, 1970, GM reported that a two-months' test-marketing project revealed car owners were reluctant to pay $20 for kits to curb used-car pollution.

---

[33] James M. Roche, *Address before the Executive Club of Chicago,* 1971, pp. 9–12. Regarding the cost point raised by Mr. Roche, one study reported, "Auto men now say that pollution and safety hardware already ordered will slap as much as $500 onto the price tag of a new car by 1975, and other proposals under discussion could raise the total to $1,000." This estimate has been disputed by Mr. Douglas Toms, head of NHSTA. "He has told the industry, 'I am confident that you can build a safe car for the same price that you can build a dangerous one.'" See "The Crash Program That Is Changing Detroit," *Business Week,* February 27, 1971, pp. 78–84.

[34] "A Black Director Pushes Reforms at GM," *Business Week,* April 10, 1971, p. 101.

EXHIBIT 6

Campaign GM: Rounds I and II

Excerpts from General Motors Corporation,
Progress in Areas of Public Concern*

Automotive Emission Control

Behind much of the problem are two basic misconceptions: first, that most of the air pollution problem is caused by the automobile; and, second, that the automotive industry, and particularly General Motors, is doing nothing. . . . Both of these are grossly in error.

First, let's look at the air pollution problem in the United States and the role of the automobile. Figure 2 shows estimates by the Federal government as to atmospheric tonnages of various pollutants—hydrocarbons, carbon monoxide, oxides of nitrogen, oxides of sulfur and particulate matter.

Unfortunately, using only the weight of pollutants is somewhat misleading. It doesn't illustrate the real picture of the air pollution problem —particularly as it relates to human health and plant life. Figure 3 shows that when both the total tonnage and health concern issues are considered, transportation is responsible for less than 10 percent of the total U.S. air pollution problem for the 1968 calendar year.

Let's look now at the second popular misconception: that we have done nothing to correct this contribution to the nation's air pollution. Just what has been done to minimize automotive emissions? Figure 9 illustrates what has happened to the total automotive hydrocarbon contri-

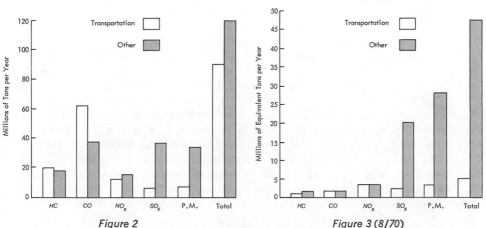

U.S. Air Pollution on A Weight Basis
H.E.W. Data for 1968

U.S. Air Pollution on A Relative Effect Basis
Pollutant Weights Adjusted to Same Effect
Level as for Particulate Matter

Figure 2 *Figure 3 (8/70)*

* Deletions not indicated. The original booklet contained 49 pages, 8″ × 11″ in size.

EXHIBIT 6 *(continued)*

bution to the atmosphere. Until about 1966, this contribution rose steadily. This would have continued if no control equipment had been added. As shown by the two lower curves, however, this trend was arrested because of the control systems on new cars. Figure 10 shows the same information for the carbon monoxide situation. These curves are graphic demonstrations of why GM believes we will take the automobile out of the air pollution problem for this decade.

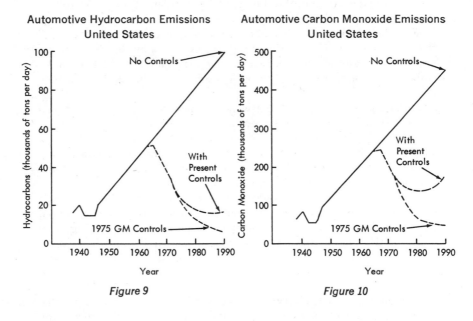

Figure 9

Figure 10

* * * * *

Industrial Pollution Control

Briefly, I would like to trace the trend of legislative concern, give you a report on General Motors' policies and progress, and suggest where we are headed.

In water pollution control the first permanent Federal legislation was not enacted until 1956. This law was amended in 1961, 1965, and 1970. The first Federal legislation concerned exclusively with air pollution was enacted in 1955. By today's standards it was only a token effort. It was not until the enactment of the 1967 Air Quality Act that the issues of industrial air pollution were met head-on. The point that I wish to make is this: In spite of the emotion, impatience, and criticism directed at industry and its pollution control programs, the fact remains that meaningful criteria and guidelines have been established only within the past four to six years.

EXHIBIT 6 (*continued*)

General Motors recognized the significance of Corporation-wide industrial pollution control in 1946.

Since 1947, we have installed more than 100 water pollution control facilities at our operations in the United States and Canada. Our record, I feel, is outstanding in industry.

GM's industrial air pollution control program in the past has shown similar progress. It has been directed primarily at the removal of dust from our power plants and foundry operations, which has been considered the major problem by industry and the regulating agencies.

The last decade has seen about a tenfold increase in capital expenditures to control plant pollution.

Urban Transportation

In planning the transportation of the future, our objective should be a system which has the proper balance between private transportation and high quality, convenient and flexible public transportation. And that balance will differ from city to city.

* * * * *

General Motors—both as a responsible corporate citizen and for obvious business reasons—has a vital stake in promoting improved transportation systems for metropolitan areas. In fact efficient, balanced transportation systems are necessary to the long-range success of our major product—the automobile. It is important that we help to minimize the problems created by the automobile so that it can continue to operate as a useful and necessary part of the urban environment. And this is what we are attempting to do. Let me discuss some of our work in this field.

One of the most promising systems developed by General Motors is called Metro-Mode. Buses would enter an exclusive lane on the freeway —and travel at 60- or 70-miles-per-hour to downtown destinations. The real questions, of course, are: Will such a system work? How many passengers can be transported? GM conducted a research project to get answers. Using platoons of 12 buses each, this study showed that a capacity of 27,000 passengers could be transported in each lane per hour.

Two other concepts were developed in special studies for the U.S. Department of Housing and Urban Development. One is the Network Cab, designed to provide improved mobility in the downtown areas. Another proposal is Dial-A-Bus. In this case the proposed service would be provided by small, 10- to 15-passenger buses summoned by telephone as with a taxicab, but on a share-the-ride basis to reduce the fare. Our studies indicate that [this system] would operate more effectively in cities of about 200,000 population with the proper population density.

EXHIBIT 6 (continued)

This could apply to perhaps 100 cities—such as Lansing, Michigan; Rochester, New York; and Cambridge, Massachusetts.

❋　❋　❋　❋　❋

Minority Opportunities

For many years, our policy, like those of other large companies, [was] one of nondiscrimination. However, in recent years we made a significant shift. We chose no longer just to be against discrimination. We chose instead to work actively to assure equal opportunity.

New programs have produced encouraging results. In 1965, about 67,000 of our 593,000 employees were from minority groups. This was 11.2 percent. Today, General Motors is the largest private employer of minority Americans. At the end of 1970, GM employed more than 92,000 minority Americans in the United States. This was 15.3 percent of GM's total employment.

To help recruit, we follow a number of approaches. We write every year to [educational] institutions seeking referrals of minority graduates. General Motors was one of the first major corporations to recruit actively on the campuses of predominantly Negro colleges.

In 1967, Pontiac Motor Division launched a program to provide jobs for the hard-core unemployed. The experiences [thus] gained proved useful when, in April 1968, General Motors began participation in the JOBS program of the National Alliance of Businessmen—a nationwide effort to hire the hard-core unemployed.

Since these programs were started, General Motors, up to the end of 1969, had hired 45,132 so-called hard-core unemployed. Nearly 21,000 of these—46.5 percent—were still on the job, a percentage only slightly less than that of other employees hired during the same period. During 1970, however, declining auto sales made it necessary for General Motors, like other companies, to lay off many employees. About 3,500 —one-sixth—of the 21,000 former hard-core unemployed had to be laid off in 1970. The remaining 17,500 continued to work. However, all with seniority have recall rights.

Some will point out that, while the overall percentage of our minority employment is relatively high, a disproportionate number are in hourly rather than salaried jobs. There is no denying this.

But we must recognize that every job at General Motors is a good job. The typical hourly employee, the man who assembles our cars, earns more than $12,000 a year with normal overtime.

Hiring, however, is only half the task. Giving disadvantaged workers equal opportunity to advance is the other part. To attain this objective, we engage in other programs to qualify our employees for advancement. Partly as a result, the number of minority workers among journeymen, apprentices, and employees-in-training for skilled trades has risen to nearly 2,300—a 50 percent increase—in three years.

EXHIBIT 6 (*continued*)

General Motors works for greater economic equality in other ways than employment. We have several activities by which we assist minority enterprise.

General Motors has 65 automotive dealers who are minority Americans, including 12 blacks. In addition, 160 other minority businessmen sell and service General Motors products throughout the United States. A year ago we had only seven automobile dealers who were black, and a year before only two.

We regard the growth from two to 12 as a measure of our progress. But we also consider the fact that there are still so few—in spite of our efforts—as a measure of the difficulty we face. Even a small dealership is a good-sized business in most communities. It is a high-risk, intensely competitive business, and clearly not for the inexperienced manager.

To overcome these obstacles, General Motors is making intensive efforts to locate potential new dealers. We are also encouraging our dealers to place promising individuals in their businesses so they can acquire the experience and background that may qualify them for dealerships. Where a qualified applicant may lack sufficient capital, General motors stands ready to join in the enterprise through capital investment.

We encourage minority enterprise in other ways as well. Last year, we formed a Minority Enterprise Small Business Investment Company—MESBIC. MESBICs provide low-interest funds together with managerial help and technical assistance to small minority-owned businesses. Ours was the seventh MESBIC to be formed. GM has committed an investment of $1 million to this venture.

Since 1969 General Motors has been depositing in minority-owned banks. This year we will maintain $5 million in 32 banks as part of a governmental program that is seeking total deposits of $65 million from private industry, and $35 million from government.

General Motors is also providing interest-free loans to two non-profit corporations acquiring land for low-cost housing projects. The first loan is for up to $1.1 million. The second is for up to $1 million.

Automotive Safety

At General Motors, we are committed to the advancement of safety through sound engineering. We have demonstrated this commitment by introducing safety features whenever they have reached production stage, often in advance of our competitors.

The GM Safety Research and Development Laboratory [dedicated in 1968] probably is the most extensive facility of its kind in the industry. Here we have the great variety of equipment necessary to conduct tests that ultimately provide data leading to safety improvements.

The result of utilizing safety test devices is that we have GM cars that are second to none in overall safety. Our energy-absorbing steering column, for example, has much greater performance than required by Federal safety standards, and its success in real-life accidents has been

EXHIBIT 6 *(concluded)*

well documented. Present instrument panels, seat backs and other interior components also are much superior than minimum standard requirements, and are performing very well in real life.

The improvements we have made in the vehicle thus far have not interfered with normal usage of the vehicle. However, it is becoming an increasingly difficult challenge to continue adding major vehicle improvements without affecting vehicle utility.

The great majority of safety work we do here at the Laboratory is directed primarily at occupant protection. The rest of the Proving Ground, with its 85 miles of varied road systems, tests and evaluates the performance, durability and reliability of our vehicles so that they can enable the driver to avoid accidents, if at all possible.

✿   ✿   ✿   ✿   ✿

Closing Remarks

This whole meeting was concerned with the need we at General Motors recognize to do better—to build even safer cars, to clean up the environment, to promote minority opportunity, to work for better mass transportation, to do all that is expected of us.

We are determined to do all these things—not only to benefit our customers, not only to benefit our stockholders—but to benefit the whole of society.

Source: GM, *Progress in Areas of Public Concern,* a booklet based on a conference held in February 1970, at the GM Proving Ground, Milford, Michigan, "for a group of prominent educators and representatives of foundations and investment institutions."

5. In August 1970, GM created a Public Policy Committee of five non-officer members of its board, charged with making sure that the company was meeting rising expectations in matters of broad national concern.

6. In September 1970, GM announced plans to install catalytic converters on some 1973 models and hoped that this device to control emissions could be included on all 1975 cars. (These hopes were later reported as having been overoptimistic.)

7. In November 1970, GM was reported to have devised a 90 percent effective way to cut fumes from coal-fired power plants.

8. In December 1970, GM reported that nearly $160 million out of $1.1 billion planned capital expenditures for 1971 would go for air-pollution control, for a 7 percent increase over 1970.

9. In January 1971, GM appointed its first black to its board. He was activist Leon H. Sullivan, Philadelphia pastor, sponsor of self-help programs and advocate of black business. Indicating that his main concern was improving the position of blacks in America, Sullivan set three-year targets for GM: (1) 50 new black dealers; (2) 1,000 black executives moving up the ladder; and (3) inner-city training centers for mechanics, capable of

handling 5,000 trainees a year. "My role is an expression of my ministry," he said. "When I'm not effective I'll resign."[35]

10. In January 1971, GM undertook to make deposits of $5 million in banks owned by minorities.
11. In February, GM went outside the fold to find an environment chief and appointed Professor Ernest S. Starkman of the University of California at Berkeley to a clean-air post.
12. In February 1971, unfolding a new national program to mollify critics of quality, GM announced that dealers would be paid to inspect and fix new cars on their lots.
13. In February 1971, GM established an advisory panel of six "top" scientists to study the environmental effects of products.
14. In February 1971, GM's annual report announced the following expenditures.

| | Budget (in millions) | |
	1970	1971
For control of automotive emissions and development of alternative power sources.........................	$119	$124
For air and water pollution from GM plants............	35	64

Dilemma for Money Managers and Colleges

Regardless of how many votes it would garner in the test at GM's annual meeting, the campaign and the issues it raised were reportedly taken seriously by both important financial institutions and important universities. Making up their minds how to vote—and even how to reach a decision—posed a real dilemma.

According to a survey of "money managers" conducted by the *Wall Street Journal*, the management companies in charge of the Putnam and Wellington Funds both created special committees to review the year's crop of social-action proxies. Putnam's included the management company's chairman, among others, and the well-known scientist Vannevar Bush. Similarly, the executive vice president of the First National City Bank reported, "Every proposal, no matter how humble, is given attention at the highest level." An official at the Chase Manhattan Bank expressed an often stated view that it was becoming easy to vote against management on social issues while basing that decision on investment implications. "A company that continues to pollute the air may not be around very long," he said.[36]

Taking an approach approved by the campaigners, the Dreyfus

[35] *Business Week*, p. 103. (Whereas the campaigners reportedly characterized other GM actions as "window dressing," Nader himself acknowledged his approval of the Sullivan appointment.)

[36] *Wall Street Journal*, April 28, 1971.

Corporation undertook to poll the holders of one of its smaller funds on how it should vote the GM shares held in this fund's portfolio.[37] Of wider impact, the SEC ruled in response to a dispute that a fund management company had to include on its proxy statement a shareholder proposal that, if ratified, would require the management company to consider the social policies of corporations before investing in their stock.[38] Indeed, one small management company even announced formation of a "Social Dimensions Fund" to invest in companies that would "contribute to society beyond satisfaction of basic material needs and the traditional goal of maximizing profit to the exclusion of all other ends."[39]

At the universities, many hard questions were posed initially by Campaign GM; these turned out to have far-reaching implications on which serious study was needed. For example, did it really matter how the college stock was voted, given the fact that the largest university holding (MIT's) was only 291,000 shares and that all educational institutions together held only 10 percent or so of GM's stock. If the college vote did matter, could the trustees properly ignore their student and faculty constituencies and vote only their own conscience, whatever this might be? If so, did GM deserve to be reprimanded, or had it been unfairly singled out, and was the economic system threatened by attacks on so prestigious a company? Even if the goals of the campaign merited respect, did an overriding obligation exist to vote the university's shares in whatever way would bring the maximum financial support for its primary goals of teaching and research? If, on the other hand, social values should be protected, could Campaign GM be treated as an isolated case, or was a long-term policy needed to cover all investment decisions? If the college did recognize a basic, long-term obligation to share financial choice in the light of social considerations, what limits and what scope should this obligation have, what guidelines should be followed, what extra costs incurred, and what administrative structure should be created to implement this policy?

After all, as a Harvard University committee observed (apropos of the idea of screening corporations for responsibility prior to making an investment), "Sophisticated criteria are likely to require elaborate machinery for gathering and processing information. Relatively simple low-cost machinery could cause the University to make decisions that are both intellectually and ethically shabby."[40]

---

[37] Ibid.

[38] *New York Times,* May 11, 1971.

[39] "A Fund That Bets on Social Progress," *Business Week,* May 1, 1971, p. 29.

[40] Harvard University Committee on Governance, *Harvard and Money,* cited in the *Report of the Committee on University Relations with Corporate Enterprise* (H.B.S. Professor R. W. Austin, chairman), *Harvard University Gazette,* March 5, 1971, p. 4.

Round II Outcome

Looking to the outcome of Round II about three weeks before the decision, *Business Week* reminded its readers that something important was riding on the vote count, even though that something was not the question of which side was sure to be declared the winner:

> The key question is whether Campaign GM—or any other dissident proposals—can win 3 percent of the shareholders' vote. If not, SEC rules allow management to keep the proposals off the proxy statement for three years. And that could stall the inchoate drive for reform through proxy power.[41]

Going into the meeting on May 22, campaign sponsors predicted they would get at least this meaningful 3 percent vote. Known supporters in the campaign corner included some colleges (Antioch, Bryn Mawr, and Vassar); the College Equities Retirement Fund, an organization with $1.5 billion in assets and 750,000 GM shares;[42] and the First Pennsylvania Banking & Trust Co., the largest bank in Philadelphia. Some time earlier First Pennsylvania had reportedly "stunned GM and the banking community" by declaring its intention to vote for at least one of the campaign's three proposals—that pertaining to disclosure through the annual report of what GM was doing to minimize pollution, to maximize minority employment, and to increase the safety of its cars. Although the Carnegie Fund would support GM, the Rockefeller Fund planned to abstain on at least two of the campaign resolutions.[43]

Given this encouragement, campaign workers were "clearly surprised" as well as disappointed by the vote when it came. Management had won a "smashing victory." The campaign's three proposals, faring worse than in the year before, got only 1.11 percent to 2.36 percent of the shares voted. Conceding their dismay, members of the campaign board now also reportedly "questioned the efficacy of their effort to force social change on the corporation through its shareholders." Said the campaign chairman, "We are going to have to reassess the kind of strategies we pursue in the future."[44]

---

[41] "The Moral Power of Shareholders," *Business Week*, May 1, 1971, p. 78.

[42] Characteristically, funds did not make their decisions public, but the Dreyfus Corporation did disclose that the poll of shareholders in its Leverage Fund resulted in a verdict favorable to GM. See *Wall Street Journal*, May 21, 1971.

[43] *Business Week*, May 1, 1971; *Boston Globe*, May 18, 1971; *Wall Street Journal*, May 19, 1971.

[44] *Wall Street Journal*, May 22, 1971.

Mt. Auburn was a busy Cambridge street. Mixed with a heavy flow of commercial traffic were bicyclists, motorcyclists, and hordes of small foreign cars jousting with an infrequent standard size model as traffic inched its way forward to Central Square. Joggers were there, too, but in a minority position. And the pedestrian flow was heavy. Almost universally young, the passers-by walked with a bounce that often sent long hair flying in the wind. Legs and faces tended to be unshaven. Clothing was simple: smocks, or T-shirts, army surplus rucksacks, colorful headbands or hats of Humphrey Bogart fame, blue jeans and sandals or hiking boots were the order of the day. The researcher was reminded that the metropolitan Boston area was a youth center heavily influenced by large numbers of young people who studied or worked there, or who merely drifted in and out.[1]

A loud exhaust backfire from a blue Porsche—a student with patched jeans of bright and varied hue—provided the last insight to the Mt. Auburn Street scene. "Porsche and Patches" mused the researcher as he turned and entered the door marked "The Real Paper." Coming into the ground-floor area, his first impression was that the area was too small for the ten desks and numerous people working there. The main room was often a maelstrom of phone calls, shouts, advertising personnel walking back and forth, and a steady stream of visitors coming to place classified advertisements with Ellen Paul, the staff person in charge of that activity.

On one side of the main door a bicycle was stored; on the left wall a bulletin board hosted a series of announcements: a lost cat, flea market sales, advertisements for the City Dance Theater, numerous plays, and The 100 Flowers Bookstore. Ellen's dog, Martha, padded around the room seeking attention, occasionally barking but never committing any grave social errors. To the left was the receptionist Cyndi Robbins, wearing a flannel shirt, blue jeans, and sandals. Social pleasantries completed, she commented, "It is a hassling job with the phone and so many visitors, but I like it here—the people, the experience, and the atmosphere."

Looking to the back of the room, the researcher noticed a man (later identified as the comptroller, Howard Garsh) sweeping the floor and stacking telephone reminder slips in a cabinet. Cyndi's directions to the publisher's office sent the researcher to the back of the main room, where

---

[1] At a later date, the researcher obtained some population data on two- and four-year colleges, degree granting technical-trade institutes and universities located in the New England area. There were over 35 of these institutions in metropolitan Boston, with approximately 130,000 students; approximately 120 schools in Massachusetts, with approximately 320,000 students; and 250 in New England, with approximately 600,000 students (of which 2,262 were primarily students of religion). He was intrigued with the academic program for one of the schools: "The Institute of Anatomy, Sanitary Science and Embalming."

EXHIBIT 1

THE REAL PAPER, INC.
*Statement of Income for the Year
Ended April 26, 1974, and the Eight Months
Ended April 27, 1973*

	1974	1973
Net sales.	$995,793	$462,557
Other income.	2,675	269
	$998,468	$462,826
Costs and Expenses		
Cost of publication.	$618,802	$273,468
Selling, general and administrative expenses.	304,674	135,738
Interest expense.	372	124
Total costs and expenses.	$923,848	$409,330
Net income from operations, before provision for federal income tax.	$ 74,620	$ 53,496
Provision for federal income tax.	1,092	2,100
Net Income.	$ 73,528	$ 51,396
Retained earnings, beginning of period.	51,396	—
Retained earnings, end of period.	$124,924	$ 51,396
Net income per common share, based on the weighted average number of shares outstanding at the end of the year, which was 2,800 shares in 1974 and 3,300 shares in 1973.	$ 26.26	$ 15.57

the publisher and the advertising sales director shared a small office, furnished in the same spartan manner as the remainder of the office.

In a brief meeting the researcher explained his general interest in the alternative newspaper industry and his specific interest in the *Real Paper*. Both Rob Rotner and the researcher agreed there were opportunities for learning in the development of a cast history on the *Real Paper*. Later, after consultation with other staff members, Bob welcomed the researcher to the group and agreed to collaborate on the project. (See Exhibits 1, 2, and 3.)

EXHIBIT 2

THE REAL PAPER, INC.
*Balance Sheet
April 26, 1974, and April 27, 1973*

Assets		
Current assets.	$161,812	$88,812
Fixed assets.	6,220	2,223
Other assets.	7,606	1,407
Total assets.	$175,638	$92,442
Liabilities and Stockholders' Equity		
Current liabilities.	$ 48,507	$37,320
Stockholders' equity.	127,131	$55,122
Total Liabilities and Stockholders' Equity.	$175,638	$92,442

EXHIBIT 3

THE REAL PAPER, INC.

Cost Breakdown (provided by Howard Garsh)

	Cost	Percent
Printing, composition, trucking, and circulation..........	$368,515	37
Salaries—editorial, circulation, art, free-lance editorial (including bonus).....................................	217,147	22
Salaries—sales, accounting, and clerical.................	125,613	12
Selling, general, and administrative expenses............	212,001	21
Net profit before tax (note: bonus totalled 4%)...........	74,620	8

HISTORY OF THE *REAL PAPER* AND ITS COMPETITION

Early interviews with staff members highlighted the need to study the intertwined history of the *Real Paper* and its primary local competitor, the *Boston Phoenix.*

The story seemed to begin in September 1965, when *Boston After Dark* (*B.A.D.*) was born, in a spirit of entrepreneurialism, as a special center-fold supplement to the *Harbus,* the Harvard Business School student paper. *Boston After Dark* was meant to be a student's guide to Greater Boston's arts and entertainment world. As a "freebie" its distribution soon expanded to other Boston campus locations. In 1970, Stephen Mindich, a Boston University graduate and former art critic and advertising salesman for *B.A.D.,* purchased the paper. His early and major innovation was to add politically oriented news to *B.A.D's* coverage of arts and entertainment.

The second critical historical event was the founding, in October of 1969, of the *Cambridge Phoenix* by a 26-year-old Vietnam veteran as an "alternative" newspaper for the Boston area. The Phoenix statement of purpose indicated that it "was conceived with the discovery that Boston, the intellectual, artistic, and economic center of New England was a journalistic vacuum." Within a year, the undercapitalized *Phoenix* was bought by Richard Missner, a 26-year-old M.B.A. Throughout 1970 and 1971, brisk competition developed between the *Phoenix* and *B.A.D.*

Fusion magazine, commenting on the competitive situation noted:

> . . . local college students had a twin forum in which to see their revolutionary outrage expressed. . . . Horror stories of government murder and graft ran alongside reviews and advertisements for films and rock performances that created for viewers a fantasy world of glamorous sex and violence. . . . Needless to say, both writers and readers were college-educated, white and middle class, reveling in self-righteousness as they defended people they rarely met, attacking the economic system while enjoying some of the most extravagant luxuries it could provide. Boston's weeklies provided access to the many valuable varieties of this lifestyle, as well as the impression that it was profound.

The *Phoenix*, however, soon began to develop major operating and financial problems. Its financial backer withdrew and the staff of the *Phoenix* became increasingly disgruntled with Missner, his leadership style, and his vision of what the paper should be. Once, holding up a copy of the *Wall Street Journal*, Missner indicated editorial changes he wanted made.

On May 2, 1972, the *Phoenix* staff agreed to form a union in support of a popular, just-fired editor-in-chief, whom Missner had planned to replace with a former advertising executive. A strike, a series of confrontations and negotiations ensued. By the end of the month, compromises were effected and the union was officially recognized. Chuck Fager, one of the union leaders and a current member of the *Real Paper* staff commented on the strike and the effect it had:

> It was really a surprise that we unionized. Sort of WHAM! There it was. People in every department had gripes of their own. . . . So we went out. As a result of the strike, we went through a proletarianization. For instance, we noticed the mailman. Well, he saw our picket signs and he refused to cross the line. Management had to go down to the post office to get their mail. We hadn't seen things from this perspective. . . . But once we were out, our jobs were on the line; we stood to lose everything. . . . But it was fun too. We were working together in a way that we had not worked before—making signs, picketing, and cooking food.

T.R.P. was "born" on July 31, 1972. The *Boston Globe*[2] reported this event as follows:

> On July 27, in a 2 P.M. memo, he [Missner] informs all Phoenix staffers to get out by 5 o'clock. The paper, it seems, has been sold to none other than B.A.D.'s Stephen Mindich for a figure Mindich claims to be $320,000. Outraged at Missner's move, they met outside their locked offices and decided to publish their own newspaper by working without pay. It hits the streets on July 31, and it is called The Real Paper. On the same day, the new Boston Phoenix, with a second section called Boston After Dark, appears.

Born into a field of competitive entrepreneurs, yet itself a creature of communal militance, the *Real Paper*'s trials were not yet over. For the first four weeks investors were sought, but to no avail. Chuck Fager said, "The most serious was the *New York Magazine*, but they weren't certain as to how willing we would be to respond to management policy. They were quite right to question that."

Walter Harrison[3] recalled some of the sacrifices of that period:

> We worked virtually 24 hours a day. The financial sacrifices were great. We all started collecting unemployment compensation. People

---

[2] *Boston Globe—Globe Supplement,* June 9, 1974, p. 11.

[3] Assistant to the publisher.

donated phones and office space. We had meetings virtually every night. For the first two weeks with donations and sales we just broke even.

Then, by the fourth week, having found no backers, but having established the viability of their new enterprise, Fager said, "A decision was reached. We had a meeting. Everyone wrote down on little cards what they had to have in order to keep going. Rotner presented a financial statement. And we found that we could cover salaries. Suddenly we had the option of independence and almost everyone was willing to take it. Why have a backer if you don't need one?"

One hundred shares of stock were issued to each employee in lieu of back pay. Corporate and administrative positions were filled by elections. According to Fager, "We had the equivalent of $50,000 to $100,000 of capital in our momentum, i.e., free press coverage, willing advertisers, and hawker and reader willingness to buy."

The early months of the new association were rewarding, if not in a financial, certainly in a communal sense.

The biggest change, some of the staff members say, has been the new atmosphere. Paul Solman, the *Real Paper*'s editor, says: "Having our paper shot out from under us may have been the best thing that ever happened. Coming over here and starting a new paper and running it ourselves, we've set a real precedent. Before this, 'democracy in the newsroom' has always had the clinker that one guy owns the paper, and you can't really tell the people what to do with their own money. But we've gotten rid of the clinker now."

Joe Klein, another writer, says that there is a greater feeling of participation at the paper by all of its staff. "I've never felt as close to the whole process of something I've worked on. I've never been so interested in the business side of the paper. . . . Everybody talks about how much like a family it is here."[4]

In the intervening year and one-half, staff attention was turned to consolidating and expanding *T.R.P.*'s position. Advertisers and readers gained confidence in the *Real Paper* as evidenced by its substantial growth in revenues and circulation. And, as would be expected, operational policies and practices were modified and personnel came and left. In 1974, the *Real Paper* was a well-recognized Cambridge phenomenon.

THE ALTERNATIVE NEWSPAPER INDUSTRY

Various members of its staff characterized the *Real Paper* as an alternative newspaper. Local newspaper columnists had, on occasion, described the *Real Paper* and the *Boston Phoenix* as "underground

---

[4] *Nation*, April 23, 1973, page 531.

press" or "counter-culture" papers. Some news distributors interviewed referred to them as "radical sheets" or "sex papers for freaks."

With circulation in the tens of thousands and distribution via hundreds of news outlets, the term "underground" seemed inappropriate to the researcher. If the *Real Paper* and the *Boston Phoenix* were alternative papers, alternative to what? What were the key, current developments? A survey of literature available in libraries and observations by industry members provided some limited information and insight.

Although the alternative weekly was often referred to as "a paper," the genre suited more a magazine than a newspaper model. It assumed a readership that obtained its basic news from other sources, such as daily newspapers, radio, or television. The alternative press typically serviced one or two specialized segments of a larger reader market, for example, a politically liberal or youth subcommunity. Most of the large and thriving alternative papers were located in large cities or near large college campuses.

In 1972, the Underground Press Syndicate estimated that there were 300 regularly published "underground papers" in the United States, with a combined readership of 20 million. The UPS also estimated that one in three persons in the 15-to-30 age bracket were regularly exposed to underground publications.

The model for the alternative newspaper was judged by many observers to be the *Los Angeles Free Press*. That paper, founded in 1964, was described by the Underground Press Syndicate as:

> . . . in basic ways demonstrably different from all predecessors. First, the Los Angeles Free Press was specifically designed for a mass, though specialized, audience; second, it was in a format inexpensive to produce, simple to learn, yet with high readability, creativity, general appeal and possibilities for development and refinement; third, it was economically self-supporting and self-spreading—it was successful; fourth, it was both hip and radical (the same thing, as we now know); and fifth, it was part of a people's movement and remained a part because it was, in general, operated in a communistic style.

Paul Solman, editor of *T.R.P.*, commenting on the history of the industry and current trends noted:

> . . . the rise of the underground press in the 1960s was concurrent with the rise of "The Movement" in this country. They were not so much businesses as they were political organizations. The relative inexpensiveness of offset printing enabled these organizations to turn to printed media. There was little stability and a great deal of manpower turnover within these organizations. Then as The Movement began to wane, these enterprises waned. The inheritor of these underground publications is the contemporary Alternative Press. It features the same format— offset tabloid—and many of the same people. But there was a dramatic

transition in becoming a stable Alternative Press. This involved a commitment to becoming an ongoing business institution. It meant accepting responsibility, getting away from drug cartoons and sex stuff, avoiding the utter tripe we used to get, and making a transition from being purely political—and using language like "pig" and "Amerikka"—to doing something more than just indulging your political biases.

Change and evolution appeared to be very much a part not only of the alternative but also of the wider newspaper industry scene. That industry was the tenth largest American industry in terms of revenues ($5.5 billion in 1972) and the fifth largest employer (380,500 in 1972). Some 75 percent of that revenue came from advertising—local retail, classified, and national; the latter category appeared to be diminishing somewhat in terms of importance.

Economically the industry had to bear the cost of high capital investment characteristic of many manufacturing operations, as well as the relatively high labor cost of many service organizations. Efforts to improve profits, described as marginal by some investment houses, depended on the newspapers' abilities to deal with distribution problems, antiquated production facilities, and a continuing rise in the cost of newsprint. The latter item has habitually made up 25–30 percent of the revenue dollar. Cost of Canadian newsprint had gone up 20 percent in 1973 and further major increases, as well as shortages, were expected to occur in 1974. Some papers had adopted a strategy of diversification into related communication areas as a "solution" to these problems.

THE *REAL PAPER* AND THE *FREE PAPER*

The *Real Paper* "book," as it was referred to by its staff, was an unstapled and folded collection of newsprint pages, typically 50 to 60 in number, in tabloid format. The front page usually featured *T.R.P.*'s logo as well as a multicolored graphic design, which related to one of the feature articles in that issue. Titles or references to other stories were also highlighted on the front page.

In describing the paper's content, *T.R.P.*'s editorial department distinguished between "the front of the book" and "the back of the book." The front of the book section accounted for the first 20 to 25 pages. It typically included several long feature articles, human-interest articles —for example, an attempt by girls to enter the all-male Boston Little League baseball competition—and a number of shorter news or political items. In addition, there were four regular features: Letters to the Editor; "Short Takes," a news column; a political cartoon; and Burt Solomon's "Cambridge Report," a column covering the political and cultural life of Cambridge.

Paul Solman, the editor, indicated that two to three "compelling" front of the book feature articles were the key to his editorial composition of the paper. A random sampling of some of these articles, from the spring of 1974 issues, follows: "The Great Commuter Race. Bikes Beat Cars and MBTA by a Wheel"; "TV Guide to Impeachment"; "The Behavior Mod Squad. Clockwork prisons: Brainwashing Saga Continues"; "A Shopper's Guide to Confession. What You Have to Know to Get the Best Deal on Penance"; "Have You Been Swindled? Nuclear Disaster Strikes Plymouth: A Shocking Scenario for the Future"; "The Death and Resurrection of the Black Panthers"; "The Strange CIA Past of Deputy Mayor Robert Kiley"; and "Prostitutes in Boston." It was evident, from a review of the titles listed on the front cover of these same editions, that feature and news articles ranged from local and national to international topics and touched on a variety of cultural and political topics.

Letters to the Editor made interesting reading in their own right and often created a dialogue between readers and staff that gave continuity to the weekly issues of *T.R.P.* The letters printed were usually only a fraction of those received. A random survey indicated letters from a variety of well-known personalities (Daniel Ellsberg) to unknown readers; from Boston College and MIT professors to AWOL American soldiers living in Sweden. Most of the letters printed appeared to be from students, or the young in age or spirit living in the metropolitan Boston area. Correspondents' addresses, however, indicated readers in each of the New England states.

The second regular front of the book item, "Short Takes," in the words of its compiler Craig Unger, "tries to get six or seven news items which I think are most interesting, amusing, and politically significant that get the least media play. It has very broad limits ranging from local news to international news. About two-thirds to three-quarters are of a political nature, and the rest are amusing."

The back of the book section accounted for approximately 60 percent of *T.R.P.*'s pages. It featured a number of regular departments, such as commentary and reviews on theater, cinema, music, and art; and "Local Color" by Henry Armetta, a column about the metropolitan Boston's entertainment field; plus a back page calendar for the upcoming week, which listed events of artistic interest in the Cambridge–Boston area. The staff of *T.R.P.* believes that its coverage of arts and entertainment, particularly the music field, was excellent and customers interviewed by the researchers tended to support that conclusion.

A substantial section of the back of the book was devoted to listings and classified advertisements. The researcher's random sample of approximately 100 purchasers of *T.R.P.* indicated that the Listings and

Classified sections were extremely popular. Listings provided an accurate and thorough calendar of well-known artistic events, as well as information on a host of lesser publicized activities, many of which were available at no or minimum cost. The film rating service gave staff evaluations of each film on a scale of worthless to masterpieces.

The classified pages' popularity was readily understandable to the researcher. They seemed to be an open-door communicating device among the many subgroup cultures in the community. This section had its own language system—the researcher was a WM–24–Stu (can you translate?). The advertisements or notices were a potpourri of every known youth interest or need. There were advertisements for jobs, apartments, and where to get advice about drugs, pregnancy, V.D., and low-blood-sugar problems; Personals—"Sarah from Newton—why did you walk out on me?"; leads on where to buy a wide range of products, inquiries for pen pals—often from prisoners; and a variety of travel and educational opportunities were presented (see Table 1).

And if the reader wanted new relationships, they came offered in group packages from "encounter" to "philosophic" discussion meetings. If one wanted individual companionship it came in a variety of formats: male–female, male–male and female–female.

TABLE 1

THE REAL PAPER, INC.
Representative Classified Advertisements

WARM, sincere attractive WJM. Pisces, 29, dislikes dating bars and phony people, would like to meet warm, sincere, affectionate, cuddly slightly mesugah WJF 18–30, short and pretty, with long hair, for lasting relationship. White CF, PO Box _____ Framingham, Mass. 01701

WHITE Male 25 Walpole Prisoner wants letters & visits from young women I'm 6' tall weigh 160 blond hair blue eyes. Real Box 749

TALL dark and sane. Are you still out there? Sorry didn't get in touch. Please send phone number or suggest meetings. Let's get it together this time. Patricia Box 750

I'M a young woman planning to bring former hillside farm in Western Mass. to long lost fullness. Educated, intelligent, willful, crazy, occasionally impossible, but often spontaneous, loving, energetic, able, funny, practical. Smoke insanely and visions a joy to me. Physically attractive, but so what? Want to feel the isness of things but that takes time and living. Want to make a home for friends to visit when in need of love, slowness, wholeness, rest, healing. Box 728.

WM 27 grad student, warm, aware, seeks female to enjoy the intoxication of spring with. I like tennis, books, nature, hiking, beautiful sex, politics, playing guitar. Let's get together. Real Paper Box 752.

ONE well-adjusted woman wanted to share sunny spacious, furnished 2-bedroom apartment in North End for summer. $100/month rent. Please call Joan at _____

Bob Williams, *T.R.P.*'s advertising manager commented on the importance of the listing and classified sections in an interview with a *Nation* writer.[5]

> The real reasons our paper or *B.A.D.* are essential to the lives of the people who read them are the classified ads and the listings. Around here, people move around a lot, a couple of times a year at least. Things change hands all the time. Apartments, stereos, TVs, cars, sex. There has to be a way for the things and the people to get together. Let's face it, Boston is one big party, with 350,000 kids looking for something to do. So the film listings, and the listings in general, are a big selling point. These things are the spine of the paper—the writers give it a competitive edge.

The *Free Paper* edition of *T.R.P.* was similar to *T.R.P.* in most respects. In any given week there were some differences in editorial content because of a post office ruling that price preferences given one reader over another must be accompanied by a minimum 20 percent content difference. The post office also required that a certain percentage of a paper's circulation must be paid to obtain second-class mailing privileges. Circulation of the *Free Paper*, since it was distributed to school living and dining halls, varied with the local student population, dropping during vacation periods.

Supplements to *T.R.P.* and the *Free Paper* were added to the regular editions about once each month. Jeff Albertson, newly assigned supplements editor, felt that the frequency of supplements would increase in the fall of 1974. Supplements were similar to the regular book in format and design. However, each was typically organized around one theme, such as buying guides to high-fidelity equipment, camping equipment, etc. Articles on the theme were prepared and advertisers with a particular interest in that field were sought.

The Metropolitan Boston Competitive Situation

In addition to several dozen weekly suburban newspapers covering their local scenes, three standard daily and two major weekly alternative newspapers were published in Boston. The daily newspapers included the *Christian Science Monitor*, whose masthead declared it to be "An International Daily Newspaper," and whose principal circulation was outside of metropolitan Boston.

The second paper, the *Boston Herald-American*, owned by the Hearst Corporation, was a recent merger of the *Herald-Traveler*, which had circulation strength in the suburbs, and the *Record-American* with "blue collar" readership in Boston. An industry observer described it as

---

[5] *Nation*, April 23, p. 533.

an "independent, conservative, Republican paper. It's probably losing a lot of money. There is a rumor that Mr. Mindich is considering launching a major Boston daily, contingent upon future plans of the *Boston Herald American*."

The *Boston Globe* was the largest of the three standard papers in circulation and was financially the most successful (net income of $3 million on $90 million in revenues in 1972). Local journalists conceded the *Globe's* competitive aggressiveness, citing its use of specialists covering such topics as urban renewal, mental health, affairs of the elderly, and the women's movement. One observer described the *Globe* as a paper "which serves the liberal educational community well and the City of Boston with less enthusiasm. The *Globe* espouses its liberal causes stridently and rarely hesitates to show a bias in its reporting."

In attempting to gain information about the alternative newspaper competitive situation, the researcher visited a dozen newsstands in the Greater Boston area. Clearly the leaders in this race were *T.R.P.* and the *Boston Phoenix*. But the customer had a variety of papers from which to make a selection depending upon his or her particular mix of reading interests. Larger newsstands typically carried, at a minimum, three other nonlocal alternative papers: the *Village Voice*, the *Free Press*, and *Rolling Stone*. The *Village Voice* (weekly price 35¢, 125 pages, over 150,000 circulation) was owned by *New York Magazine;* its masthead stated that it was "The Weekly Newspaper of New York." The *Voice* had an East Coast and national distribution pattern. Its content was focused on a wide range of local New York and national political issues and personalities; it had major, in-depth coverage of art, music, and the theater. As a member of the Audit Bureau of Circulation its advertisers included prominent local and national firms.

The *Los Angeles Free Press* (weekly, 35¢, about 40 pages, circulation 150,000) also had achieved regional and national distribution. Its coverage included politics, the arts, and a 20-page classified "sex" insert— literally a cornucopia of erotica. In contrast to the more academic style of the *Voice* (an interview with three African female jurists and an analysis of Shakespearean Theater), the *Freep's* editorial style seemed to the researcher to be sensational and its word system and headlines were strident in character.

The *Rolling Stone's* (biweekly, 75¢, over 100 pages, circulation 300,000) content was heavily built around popular music and the entertainment world, with some political coverage, e.g., an interview with Jane Fonda on her latest visit to North Vietnam. While both the *Voice* and *Rolling Stone* carried classified advertisements, these tended to down play sex themes and products.

A Boston newsdealer mentioned the *Texas Monthly* as a prototype of recent entries in the field. *Newsweek* magazine reported that it sold for $1, "has taken provocative looks at the inner workings of the state's highway lobby, banks, law firms and daily newspapers, dismissing the latter 'as strikingly weak and ineffectual.' The *Texas Monthly* received the prestigious 1974 National Magazine Award for Specialized Journalism."[6] "*Ramparts*, of course," the newsdealer said, "has been around a long time and there are a batch of others of the same cast."

In metropolitan Boston, *T.R.P.*'s primary competitor was the *Boston Phoenix*. Both papers were similar in format and price, both were published weekly, both used the same distribution methods—although with different emphasis—and both had free school editions.

Differences were also apparent to the researcher. The *Phoenix* was a larger book—often over 80 pages compared with *T.R.P.*'s 50- to 60-page editions. The larger *Phoenix* was divided into two distinct subparts: the *Phoenix* and its insert, *Boston After Dark*—the Arts and Entertainment section. The *Phoenix* enjoyed a larger circulation; industry estimates ranged from 80,000 to 110,000, with approximately 40,000 being the free edition. The *Phoenix* appeared to the researcher to enjoy a wider range of local and national advertisers than did *T.R.P.* In terms of visual appearance, the *Phoenix* appeared to be more crowded and less willing to use open space to lead the reader's eye around a page than did *T.R.P.*

The researcher wanted to obtain data on why a customer purchased *T.R.P.* versus the *Phoenix* and what was the market for these two papers. A random survey of purchasers by the researcher obtained limited information. Most could not make explicit their preference for one paper over the other. *T.R.P.* customers often mentioned "better Cambridge coverage," "more liberal," "easier to read," while *Phoenix* purchasers stressed "red hot classifieds" and "*B.A.D.* is the best guide." (See Exhibit 4.)

In reviewing this competitive situation between the *Real Paper* and the *Phoenix*, a *Boston Globe* writer commented:[7]

> The two papers continue in the image of advocacy journalism planted firmly left of center and sprinkled with occasional muckraking. But while in days past they overlapped on stories, they almost never do today. In fact, except for arts coverage—particularly music—you can browse through two issues of the same week and not see two pieces about the same thing. What you will find is that the *Phoenix*, reflecting its publisher's little-subdued dream to become a force in the community, concerns itself more with the news of the day, dealing with many of the same subjects and events as the city's dailies. "We've made a shift to respond to news happenings," says Miller. "We want to be topical." The *Real Paper*, on the other hand, seems to be moving more and more towards becoming a weekly magazine, opting for stylized

---

[6] *Newsweek,* June 17, 1974, page 29.

[7] *Boston Globe—Sunday Supplement,* June 9, 1974, page 7.

EXHIBIT 4

THE REAL PAPER, INC.
Comparison of Article Content of the Real Paper *versus the* Boston Phoenix

	Real Paper		Boston Phoenix	
Category	Number of Articles	Percent	Number of Articles	Percent
International events or politics...........	2	1.7	5	2.8
Art, movies, books, TV, dance............	32	26.7	59	33.0
Exposés.................................	5	4.2	1	0.5
Rock music, other types of music, album review columns.......................	15	12.5	32	17.9
Local events/politics....................	21	17.5	34	19.0
Counterculture, e.g., communes, drugs, etc..............................	1	0.8	2	1.1
National events/politics.................	9	7.5	20	11.2
Movements, including prison reform, women's, and gay......................	9	7.5	4	2.3
Sports..................................	2	1.7	14	7.8
Miscellaneous, including food, "Local Color," travel, tax information..........	24	20.0	8	4.5
Totals...........................	120	100.1	179	100.1

Source: These data were prepared by Kim Panushka of *T.R.P.* staff. She surveyed eight issues of each paper for the months of March and April 1974. The total number of major feature articles for *T.R.P.* was 120; for the *Boston Phoenix*, 179. Excluded were regular columns from staff writers.

features and columns rather than news reporting. Part of the reason for this is undoubtedly the *Real Paper's* constituency, which is more Cambridge-oriented than that of the *Phoenix*. . . .

What was the market for the two publications? Bob Williams, advertising manager for *T.R.P.*, gave one specific definition.[8]

In Boston you have 350,000 young people, under 30, within 2.5 square miles of space. You don't find a concentration like that anywhere in the country except Boston. It's a unique market. These kids spend around $40 million or $50 million a year.

Dennis Hale, staff writer for the *Nation* magazine, gave a more general comment.

So the New Journalism is not so much "new" as it is specific in its choice of audience. For the most part that audience consists of young, white, relatively affluent college students, graduates and dropouts. Like newspaper readers everywhere, these people have a set of opinions, of whose truth they are fairly certain, and they do not enjoy seeing these opinions challenged in print. At least, not too often. And the editors of "underground" and "alternative" papers are as sensitive as editors everywhere to the outer limits of their readers' tolerance.

---

[8] "Prospects for the Alternative Press," *Nation*, April 23, 1973, page 533.

Over a period of months, the researcher observed *T.R.P.*'s operations and interviewed a substantial number of its staff. Early in his research, he studied the production process, the financial and accounting systems, the circulation department, and the advertising sales activity. As the research progressed he then worked with the editorial area. A summary of this information follows.

Production

Getting the "book" out each week was a central activity at *T.R.P.* As in any daily or weekly publishing operation, this activity was characterized by speed, deadlines, coordination of a host of detail and people, and the ever-present last-minute changes.

The production of *T.R.P.* basically involved the laying out and printing of five types of copy within the time constraint of weekly publication, and the size constraint of how large a paper could be profitably published. This process could be summarized around six stages of production.

First, the various "copy traffic controllers" accumulated the five kinds of copy: editorial, advertising, art, classified, and listings. Each controller determined the space required for his or her copy and relayed that information to the layout editor.

Second, on Thursday, as the accumulation of copy was drawing to a close, the comptroller, managing editor, and advertising sales director met to determine the number of pages in the book. The comptroller would project the week's profit and loss statement under varying assumptions about advertising, density, and number of pages in the book.

Third, the layout editor was informed as to the number of pages to be published as well as about additions or deletions to copy. He then proceeded to allocate sections of each page of the book to various kinds of copy. This involved the use of a "paste-up board," a full-scale representation of a page.

Fourth, the paste-up boards were transferred to the composition shop. Here copy, which had been typed in even columns, was physically pasted onto the paste-up boards, which were photographed and the resulting negatives developed. These negatives, along with the negatives of copy photographs—called "halftones"—were combined by taping them together.

Fifth, the final negatives were taken to the printing plant where printing plates were made and the paper was printed on a webb offset press. It took about three hours to print an edition of 50,000 papers.

Sixth, on Saturday morning the newsstand distributors picked up papers from the printing plant for distribution to newsstands on Sunday. The hawker edition was distributed at 5:30 A.M. Monday mornings to hawkers. Subscription copies were addressed and mailed on Saturday for delivery to the post office on Monday.

Production of the *Free Paper* followed on Monday, when editorial people altered the layout boards and changed the front page design to conform to the required 20 percent content difference regulation. The paper was printed that same day and delivered to college campuses on Tuesday.

Neither composition nor printing facilities were owned by *T.R.P.*, and that work was subcontracted to local, independent firms. "Both of those operations would require substantial capital investments in equipment," Howard Garsh explained.

Control

The comptroller's office consisted of two people, Howard Garsh, the comptroller, and Stanley Korytko, the bookkeeper.

One day, while walking into 10–B Mt. Auburn with the researcher, Howard said, "I don't see how you can do this study without some reference to the figures. Let'd talk for a few minutes?" The researcher and Garsh walked upstairs, through a small office and into a connecting closet that served as Garsh's "cubbyhole," as offices were referred to at *T.R.P.* Garsh proceeded to search for papers in his files and in the clutter on his desk.

A lot of what I do here deals with keeping track of the company's financial status, either projected or actual. Accordingly, there are several tools I use, the weekly P & L projection according to various book size assumptions, the monthly profit and loss statement, and the semi-annual cash and operating budget projections. These budgets tend to be conservative, pessimistic, and possibly just a little extreme. That is, we overestimate expenses and underestimate income just so we don't get cocky and overextend ourselves.

Our auditor says he's never seen such beautiful papers. That's partly because we don't just make broad assumptions of percentage increases, but instead get down to the real arithmetic of it. For instance, the budget is based on Bob Williams' projection of revenue from display[9] advertising since that's the source of about 80 percent of our revenue. We ask for the most reasonable, honest estimate that doesn't pull the figures out of the air. He talks to the salesmen, looks at the economy, and maybe talks to some advertisers. And his estimate is usually conservative. As you can see from this. Remember, his projections were made one year ago.

---

[9] Regular advertisements from commercial customers, as opposed to classified advertising, e.g., notices of apartments for rent.

April 5, 1974	Budgeted $12,000	April 19, 1974	Budgeted $12,000
	Billed 14,500		Billed 14,000
(including a $2,000 ad insert)		(including a $2,000 ad insert)	
April 12, 1974	Budgeted $12,000	April 26, 1974	Budgeted $12,000
	Billed 12,500		Billed 15,000

Our bread and butter is accounts receivable. We stay right on top of them. Our credit allowances are 30 days net. And we allocate 4 percent of revenue to bad debt although experience shows at 1 percent is sufficient.

And we virtually have no accounts payable. Other than salaries, our major expenses are printing, composition, subscriber service, mailing, trucking, and editorial free-lance payments. We've never been in a position to keep any of them waiting. Certainly every account is paid within 30 days. There are reasons for this: first, we want a top Dun and Bradstreet rating, a reputation of being a good company to do business with, a company that pays its bills. Right now our D&B rating is two. D&B told us that all it would take to get a number one is for us to be in business a little longer. Second, we have the money so why not pay it, so we try to help them out by paying on the spot.

The main reason why you'll find differences between actual and projected is in the economics of each week's book, that is the number of pages and ad density. In order to consider those very issues in our weekly business planning, I project the weekly P&L based on assumptions about number of pages and ad density. We like to see about a $2,000 profit and not more than 55 percent ad density. Within those parameters we come to a decision about the number of pages in the book and transmit that decision to the layout editor, who plans the book accordingly.

The economics of our operation greatly affect our performance. For instance, profitability increases very rapidly with an increase in ad density. As past weekly projections have shown, most of our costs are fixed, e.g., mailing, trucking, sales expense, art expense. The only variable costs we have are composition, which really varies only slightly, editorial free-lance, which varies because nonstaff articles are used as editorial copy if we opt for a larger book. Printing costs, which increase by about $1,500 for every eight-page increase we make, and salesmen's commissions (10 percent of collections), which vary with billing but not by size of paper.

For instance, assuming a 56-page paper is average, we will probably spend a total of $20,000, most of which will be on fixed type costs. Typically we will get $2,800 from circulation revenue, and $3,000 from classified advertising, and that means we'd need about $14,000 from display advertising to break even. Usually the salesmen can bring in some last-minute advertising if we think we're running low. But there's a danger in thinking you can cram a lot of advertising into a book, because too much doesn't look good. So it can cause a problem: At what ad density do you decide you have to increase the size of the paper? And is increasing the size of the paper economically profitable? Anything over that $14,000 is gravy until we have to increase the book size. And increases come only in jumps of eight pages. Because each jump costs about $1,500, only one full page of ads (worth about $640) never justifies a book increase of eight pages. But what is the cutoff? I don't know.

The special supplements are pure gravy. The profit margin varies between 20 percent and 50 percent because the regular kinds of expenses are charged against the regular edition, and so that supplement must only cover its incidental printing, composition, editorial freelance, artwork, and mailing expenses.

Garsh's responsibilities also included relationships with the First National Bank of Boston. That bank, since *T.R.P*'s founding, had financed all major capital needs of the organization.

Circulation Department

Kevin Dawkins, who had joined *T.R.P.* in January of 1973, had just been put in charge of circulation activities.

T.R.P. was distributed through four channels: newsstands, hawkers, subscription, and controlled circulation—i.e., free distribution. The percentage breakdown of distribution channels in 1974 was newsstands 30 percent, hawkers 14 percent, subscription 4 percent, and controlled 52 percent. In 1972, Kevin pointed out, the newsstand and hawker percentages had been reversed with hawkers selling over 30 percent and newsstands roughly 15 percent of *T.R.P.* circulation.

Controlled circulation of the *Free Paper* goes to "every conceivable college from here to Worcester, Mass." A formula of one copy per four students was used, and never were more than 50,000 copies distributed. Dawkins commented, "It's gravy. It boosts our circulation which entitles us to boost our advertising rates. Besides, the audience is captive. This edition builds reading habits which can extend to higher newsstand sales. In college towns, though, if we miss delivery to the school for some reason, newsstand sales stay about the same. Sometimes I think the markets are separate."

As for newsstand circulation, two-thirds occurred within Route 128 (metropolitan Boston), and one-third beyond. *T.R.P.* worked through one distributor, Greater Boston Distributors, Inc., within the Route 128 area. Greater Boston had over 800 outlets including the Union News outlets in subways, railroad stations, and Logan Airport.

T.R.P. was sold at 75 percent of these newsstands. Money was paid only for copies sold. The price to the distributor was 12¢; he sold it to the independent newsstand operators for 19¢, and the newsstand price was 25¢. Greater Boston handled between 1,500 and 2,000 titles, among which were the most profitable in the country. Dawkins felt that *T.R.P.* should be at more newsstands, and be featured more prominently.

Newsstand relationships beyond Route 128 were handled through independent distributors. The newsstand circulation area extended as far to the west as Holyoke–Springfield, Massachusetts, as far east as Portland, Maine, and as far south as Providence, Rhode Island. The objective here was to penetrate outlying markets by first reaching college communities and communal areas.

Hawker relationships were one of Kevin's responsibilities. Hawkers were independent operators who bought a paper for 5¢ and sold it for 25¢ on busy street corners throughout Greater Boston.

> In 1970, 200 hawkers used to sell almost 40,000 copies of the *Old Cambridge Phoenix;* now we have 100 hawkers selling 15,000 copies of *T.R.P.* We used to have 75 hawkers in Boston alone—now there are only 45. There is a very high turnover here but we have a hard core of about 50 old-timers.
>
> The papers are trucked to a number of distribution points in Boston and Cambridge. The hawkers buy the papers for cash, but if someone is in a rough way we will front him or her for ten or 20 copies. They can turn unsold copies in the next week for new papers. All hawkers sell both our paper and the *Phoenix.*
>
> The typical hawker is the kind of person you would see at a rock and roll concert: long hair, T-shirt, blue jeans, and sandals. They are street people and they keep us anchored to that community.
>
> They do pretty well. Richie on the Boston University Bridge must make $80 from *T.R.P.* and the same from the *Phoenix* in a couple of days. Other hawkers can make $100 in two days and some people living in a group setup can clear $25–$30 in two days and they can live on that.
>
> And they have their codes too: the oldest one in seniority gets to take the best corner, although the old-timers have the territory well staked out. We don't even know some of their real names. One of them calls himself King Kong. They don't want to have any tax records.
>
> I'm trying to push hawker sales. We are advertising in *T.R.P.* and I'm preparing posters to put up around the city. Hawkers are great publicity for us, standing at each street corner and practically putting the paper through your car window. Everyone can see that front page, whereas on the newsstands we are buried. I'm trying to extend hawking to the suburbs by promoting hawking through guidance counselors.
>
> They are street people—that community is important to us. And I don't think the *Phoenix* really wants to use them; they aren't sophisticated enough. The *Phoenix,* you know, has hired two former *Herald-American* pros for their circulation department.

Subscriptions had been an increasingly expensive channel of distribution to service. The paper was physically distributed by Hub Mail, Inc.

The cost per paper per subscription was about 22¢, making it the least economic of all channels. Since the mailing service refused to operate on weekends, a mailed paper arrives at its earliest on Tuesday, whereas *T.R.P.* was delivered to newsstands on Sundays. The one redeeming feature about subscription sales, Kevin noted, was that *T.R.P.* gets "the money up front." Kevin intended to eliminate the discount that subscribers get by subscribing (raising the price from $10 to $13 per year) in an attempt to cover cost increases, and he hoped to negotiate a new mailing agreement which would have the paper in the mail on Saturday and delivered by Monday.

Kevin had growth in *T.R.P.* circulation as one of his primary goals. He was assisted in this program by a "road man" who visited newsstand owners to "sell" them on the advantages of carrying *T.R.P.*

> We are one of Greater Boston's top ten best selling accounts. They formerly had sort of a monopoly and weren't aggressive. Terrible things happen to people when they have power. But they are getting competition now and that helps us. We are considering selling papers via machines located in grocery stores.
>
> Our toughest competition is the *Phoenix*. They are supposed to have 110,000 circulation and their revenues are twice ours—they up their ad density and charge higher advertising rates than we do. But we will catch up with them! Within one year we will be bigger! I get excited about this! Walter Harrison (the former circulation director) has suggested to me that we experiment with a home delivery system.

In the spring of 1974 Bob Williams began to advocate broadcast media promotion as a means of building *T.R.P.*'s visibility and consumer demand. Except for development costs, it was anticipated that the program would operate largely through reciprocal advertising, with commercial radio and television broadcasters.

Kevin concluded:

> I want us to get recognition; we put out the best paper in the country and I know because I am in touch with lots of them. Our problem is we just aren't taken as seriously as we should be. We want to be an important part of the Cambridge–Boston community in the near future. We want people to use *T.R.P.* as more than just reading material. We want to serve as "the reference" for what goes on here. We want it to be an important part of their lives.

Advertising Sales Department

The advertising sales department was concerned with selling display and classified advertising, and comprised five display salespeople, one classified salesperson, Linda Martin (the advertising traffic controller), and Bob Williams, the department director. Advertising sales accounted for approximately 80 percent of the revenue of *T.R.P.*

Talking about *T.R.P.'s* advertising market, Williams said:

> There are basically two levels of advertisers we're concerned with. The first group is people who have clubs, restaurants, concert tours, Army–Navy stores, clothing, bookstores, record stores—all the people who sell mainly to college students. These people came in right away. They really had to. They need papers like ours as much as we need them. The second level is the larger companies—GM, stereo companies, Jordan Marsh, and the other big clothing stores, which don't have an immediate relation between advertising money spent and dollars earned. With these people, it's only a matter of time.[10]

There was no formal system of account assignment, since Williams believed that a strict delineation of "turf" was not healthy. Nevertheless, each salesperson seemed to have specialized in one way or another. For example, one salesman, Steve Cummings, concentrated in cameras, symphony, sex, and religion, e.g., Boston Symphony Orchestra, adult bookstores, Indian Gurus, and meditation movements. The four most important industries for advertising revenue were stereo components, liquor, phonograph records, and cameras.

The approach each salesman used was individualized. Price bargaining was allowed which "makes selling tougher," Bob commented. "Otherwise, it is just stating standard rates." A sense of flexibility, of tailoring to the advertiser's needs, seemed to the researcher to be a dominant theme in the advertising efforts of *T.R.P.* In two instances, the researcher observed that Williams was willing to bend contractual agreements or trade advertising for the specific products of the business. "It's those little guys we've got to help. They're where our future lies." *T.R.P.'s* advertisers were primarily Boston firms but about 15 percent of display advertisements were placed by national firms.

It seemed to Bob Williams that the *T.R.P.* advertising staff sold access to a special kind of consumer—a youthful, liberal, student market. But "hard" and reliable data was limited. A 1974 company-financed survey of approximately 300 purchasers of *T.R.P.* (*Free Paper* customers were not canvassed) provided the following profile: Average age 23.7; sex 55 percent male and 45 percent female; 87 percent had some college education and 47 percent were college graduates; 24 percent were professional-technical personnel, 23 percent full-time students, 12 percent unemployed, 11 percent clerical, 10 percent blue collar, 5 percent sales, 4 percent managerial, 1 percent housewives, and 10 percent miscellaneous. Thirty-six percent of the papers were sold in Boston, 32 percent

---

[10] *Nation*, April 23, 1973, page 533.

in Cambridge, 5 percent in Brookline, 3 percent in Newton, 3 percent in Somerville, and the remainder scattered in other Boston suburbs.

T.R.P.'s advertising charges were geared to its circulation rate base of 90,000 copies per week. Rates for display advertisements were $14 per column inch, or $1,120 for a full page. Discounts were given for continuity of placement: 13 weeks—10 percent, 26 weeks—15 percent, and 52 weeks—20 percent. Classified advertisements were $1.90 per line.

> In terms of rates we want to get between $11.00 and $11.50 per thousand readers and stay about 50¢ per thousand under the *Phoenix*. The more specialized your market is, the higher you can charge. Publications get $2 to $3 per thousand for a very general audience, to $5 to $6 for a somewhat specialized audience, up to $30 to $40 for a very specialized group.
>
> We don't cut our stated rates in the summer even though with school vacations, our free circulation drops, but we do make deals. Many of our advertisers are on yearly contract (a total of two-thirds of *T.R.P.* advertisers were on some kind of contractual basis)—they get more power in the fall and winter than in the summer but it balances out. In this business, one-half your customers don't even know what your circulation is; they are only interested in how much response the advertisement gets, and we have a very loyal readership.
>
> With-free copies, we don't go above 52 percent at the top; Bob Rotner makes that decision. Free circulation is good but it makes things a bit more fluffy—particularly for A.B.C.[11] counts. It makes it harder for you to really prove your circulation.

Some of the problems Williams noted were the business community's lack of respect for *T.R.P.* and the staff's prohibition of certain kinds of advertising. With regard to the former, Williams noted that some advertisers regularly abuse credit terms, and said, "People don't respect us the first time around. They think we're just a weak underground paper. Meanwhile, the staff prohibits cigarette advertising because it felt that it was detrimental to the paper's image, but that means a loss of revenue."

As for the future, Williams doubted that *T.R.P.* should follow the *Phoenix* to pursue suburban advertisers. He noted that the *Phoenix* was his roughest competition.

> I don't think the future is necessarily there. There is a 50 percent bad-debt ratio on advertising beyond Route 128,[12] mostly motorcycle places, bars, and so on. The people who read *T.R.P.* and shop are here

---

[11] Audit Bureau of Circulation, an agency which attested to the circulation figures of newspapers and magazines.

[12] A belt highway, approximately 12 miles west of the central city. Route 128 tended to be a dividing line between the more developed suburbs of Boston and the less developed, higher status suburbs of the city.

in town. We sell our circulation and a kind of readership. It would be foolish not to exploit it here. The *Phoenix* is entering the suburbs and doesn't have the circulation to back it up. That will hurt alternative weeklies in general. Furthermore, we're still thrashing around editorially. It would have been unwise to move until we get that straightened out. Finally, we are best sold to small and medium-sized businesses; and they are most cencentrated here in town.

The trick is to get local advertisers to transfer ad money from radio to print and more particularly, *T.R.P.* There are about 50 stations in this area, and ten of them program directly for the youth market. We do some reciprocal advertising with them now.

I love music and have a hi-fi set. The reality of Boston is that there is an important radio market here. If the company were interested, and it isn't, we could go into partnership with one of these stations. It would provide a great new combination for us. Bob Rotner once thought we should go into the newsstand distribution business.

By 1975–76, if my plans work out, we should be in a position to enter the suburbs. I am shooting for advertising sales this year of $1.5 million.

Editorial

Editorial offices were located on the second floor at 10–B Mt. Auburn Street. The physical layout consisted of a main room (about one-fourth the size of the first floor) and two closet-size offices at the far end; one of the latter also served as a hallway to the back porch. Paul Solman (editor) and Tim Friedman (managing editor) were technically assigned this space, but all members of the department seemed to participate in its use. Jeff Albertson's (the associate publisher) desk was next to Tom's office.

The main room contained five desks, two tables, filing cabinets, and all of the usual paraphernalia of an editorial operation. A chair, with one of its casters off, occupied the center of the room. "We bought all of this equipment secondhand," Paula Childs noted. "We sure scrimp around here. Howard buys us discard, advertising promotion pencils but no pens. But we are getting more space in the basement here—that should help a lot."

The researcher agreed that space was needed. Even in a summer lull period, editorial personnel flowed in and out and often there were not enough available desks and chairs. The room had a used and noncleaned look with papers on the floor and boxes of editorial supplies stacked in every conceivable place. A number of bulletin boards seemed to be a part of the communication system, telling Peter to get a photo at 10:30 and noting that a free-lance writer wanted his check right away—"He is flat broke." Office decor consisted of wall-sized pictures of Katherine

Hepburn, *et al.*, and advertisements for concerts and artistic events; a somewhat tired and dehydrated plant provided the final touch.

The researcher sought to capture the office tone. Clearly busyness was the order of the day, with editorial personnel constantly using the multiple phones and the limited desk space. Friendliness was another factor. Martha, the receptionist, seemed unflappable despite the constant barrage of questions and calls with which she was confronted. There was an air of informality. Standard dress seemed to be T-shirts, shorts, and sandals; it made the first floor look almost "Establishment."

Editorial proved to be a complex part of *T.R.P.* scene to "paint" for the reader. After several abortive attempts the researcher finally decided to look first at "who was in the area and what did they do," next at the "organization and leadership of the work," and finally at *T.R.P.*'s "editorial posture."

T.R.P.'s masthead (July) carried the names of 54 individuals, 32 of whom were listed under "Editorial." Of those names, Paul Solman commented, "14 are full-time personnel, eight are part-time members who regularly contribute, and ten are free-lance or irregular contributors to the book."

The editorial staff tended to specialize by function. On the "support" side, Paul and Tom were assisted by Jan Freeman (copy editor) and Paula Childs (listings and general editorial person), and general assistance to the entire group was given by Peter Southwick (photos) and recently "on board" Bruce Weinberg (production manager).

On the "creative" side the situation was more complicated since most staffers handled multiple assignments. The largest number worked primarily on "back of the book" material—the arts and entertainment section and, in addition, contributed regular columns used throughout the entire paper. The smallest number of full-time masthead personnel were involved with the development of feature stories. "When we came over from the *Phoenix* we had six full-time feature writers," Paul said. "Until recently we had four, but Joe Klein just left to go with *Rolling Stone* at twice what we could pay, and Ed Zuckerman is going back to journalism school. We need to hire another two writers; we're short-handed."

In addition to back of the book and feature writers there were a number of individuals (often part-timers) who specialized in writing a political or news column or, as in the case of Omar White, created a political cartoon. In addition to masthead personnel, there was a pool of free-lance writers who, on occasion, submitted articles to *T.R.P.* Boston seemed to attract a large number of writers, many of whom could not find, or did not want, a regular organizational relationship.

The editorial group was responsible for the creation and processing of copy with copy coming from staff columnists, staff feature writers, solicited manuscripts from free-lancers, and unsolicited manuscripts. This

EXHIBIT 5

THE REAL PAPER, INC.
Masthead—July 17, 1974

Real Paper

EDITORIAL
PAUL SOLMAN, EDITOR
TOM FRIEDMAN, MANAGING EDITOR
HENRY ARMETTA
HARPER BARNES
BO BURLINGHAM
STUART BYRON
PAULA CHILDS
STEPHEN DAVIS
CHUCK FAGER
JAN FREEMAN
ARTHUR FRIEDMAN
RUSSELL GERSTEN
ANITA HARRIS
JOE HUNT
JAMES ISAACS
JOE KLEIN, NEWS EDITOR
ANDREW KOPKIND
CHUCK KRAEMER
JON LANDAU
KAY LARSON
JON LIPSKY
DAVE MARSH
JIM MILLER
LILITH MOON
ARNIE REISMAN
LAURA SHAPIRO
BURT SOLOMON
PETER SOUTHWICK, PHOTOGRAPHER
CRAIG UNGER
BRUCE WEINBERG, PRODUCTION
DAVID OMAR WHITE
ED ZUCKERMAN

ADVERTISING
ROBERT WILLIAMS, DIRECTOR
JONATHAN BANNER
STEVE CUMMINGS
MIKE FORMAN
LINDA MARTIN
DONALD MONACK
ELLEN PAUL
RICHARD REITMAN
DICK YOUSOUFIAN

ART
RONN CAMPISI, DIRECTOR
DAVID BROWN
PAT MEARS
REBECCA WELZ

CIRCULATION
KEVIN DAWKINS, DIRECTOR
DON CUMMINGS
CYNDI ROBBINS
MIKE ZEGEL

BUSINESS
HOWARD GARSH, COMPTROLLER
STANLEY KORYTKO
WALTER HARRISON, ASST. TO THE
PUBLISHER
JEFF ALBERTSON, ASSOC. PUBLISHER
ROBERT ROTNER, PUBLISHER

Metropolitan Boston's Weekly Journal of News, Opinion and the Arts. Address all correspondence to the Real Paper, 10B Mt. Auburn St., Cambridge, Mass. 02138. Telephones: Editorial and Art, 492-8101; Advertising, Circulation and Business, 492-1650. Second-class postage paid at Boston, Mass. Published weekly by The Real Paper, 10B Mt. Auburn St., Cambridge, Mass. 02138.
Unsolicited manuscripts should be addressed to Jan Freeman and must be accompanied by stamped self-addressed envelope. Photographs should be submitted to Jeff Albertson, Photo Editor.
Subscription rates: 1 year, $10.00; 2 years, $18.00.

Printing by Arlington Offset

JULY 17, 1974   Vol. 3, No. 29

editorial activity, Tom commented, was organized along the back and front of the book lines.

> Jim Miller is our music editor and Stuart Byron is our film editor. They, along with Art Friedman, our regular theater columnist, and Kay Larson, our art columnist, hand me back of the book material each week. The back of the book tends to run itself, but Paul is looking for a back of the book editor. Both of us are front of the book oriented, and a good deal more of the budget goes into the front than the back of the book.

All staff members, with whom the researcher spoke, indicated that Paul was the central person in the process of generating or reviewing story concepts, interesting and assigning writers to develop those stories, and finally nurturing and reviewing the resultant manuscript as it evolved. It seemed to the researcher that this was an extremely personal and intuitive process, difficult for all involved to articulate and yet critical for *T.R.P.'s* success.

At a regular Friday morning meeting the editorial staffers gathered with Paul in an informal session to review the copy program. Story ideas were reviewed, modified, or discarded in a free-flowing meeting with staffers sitting on the floor and Paul, his chair tilted against the wall, leading the discussion.

Paul's primary operating pattern, however, seemed to be on an individual-to-individual basis. He often began the process of copy creation by talking with a writer about an idea. "At any given time I expect I am working on 50 story ideas of which five may actually come to print. I work at home two days a week because I can concentrate better there and handle the writers more effectively by telephone."

The researcher appreciated the latter comment since Paul's office routine could be described as frenetic. He was constantly on the phone, answering questions, reviewing edit problems with Tom or working with a writer. Paul's informal style and personal warmth made it easy for all to approach him and he seemed always to be "in conference" outside the office building, on the stairs, or even walking through the office. "When do you get time to reflect?" the researcher asked. Paul smiled, "It's tough."

With full-time, front of the book personnel, Paul's primary function seemed to be reviewing story ideas that they brought to him. With part-time and free-lance writers, Paul seemed to play a more active role in initiating concepts, but he also reviewed their suggestions and manuscripts. He had a wide acquaintanceship in the Boston community and seemed to the researcher to have knowledge about and interest in a wide range of topics and institutions.

> I handle all of the free-lance work. It is a shifting group of people. Some work for other outfits, some are teachers, some have a cause, most

need money—it's hard to make a living free-lancing. We pay them $75 for a short thousand-word story, $250 for a feature article or part thereof. Once in the judge and court system story, where a lot of research work was needed, we paid $600. But we negotiate with each; the budget puts on real limits.

Jan Freeman in commenting on copy development said:

> Paul's job is to think up ideas and then assign them to either regular or free-lance writers, although usually the regular staff generates their own ideas. It is a very difficult job and I suspect the ratio of ideas to finished stories is about 15 to one. The process depends a lot upon who is available and whether or not they are interested.
>
> A lot of what Paul wants to do this fall is to make the paper more useful. Tom would probably want more news stories of a political bent. Everyone's ideal would be to do more apartment rental agency stories. Did you read that? They are a real rip-off and take money under false circumstances. We did a lot of research on them. It was both an exposé and a news story.
>
> I want us to do more stories like that or the one in this week's issue on airline safety—more consumer-oriented pieces—but they take lots of time. We should do more local investigatives, like the article on the coroner's office in Boston's City Hall. We should do stories that make a real difference—a protest that demands a response.
>
> And we need more middle of the book material—material between the arts and listings and the political and news and feature stories at the front. We need think pieces, like the story in the *New York Times Magazine* section. A woman in an apartment house was robbed—bound and gagged. What was it like? What were her fears? Did she behave bravely enough? This was a special story and a woman wrote it from a woman's point of view. We need more material on ideas and people. I suggested to Paul that we do an article on people living together—roommates or lovers—or whatever. It should be funny and yet factual. These aren't news stories—they are people and idea combinations. And we should do more on scientists and science articles—the article in the *New York Times* on "black holes" in space is a good example.

Tom, who had joined *T.R.P.* in November of 1973, had as his prime objective introducing more organization into the editorial process. He felt progress had been made in this area and, by July, lead feature articles had been planned and were in process for the next five months.

> It was in my own self-interest to get some planning going—things were frantic here when I first came. I wish we had more full-time feature writers; we need at least three now. It would make my job easier. You get to know the regulars and how to work with them; they have to produce. But it isn't as cost effective. People don't have story ideas regularly every week, and so there are bound to be slow times when we won't get stories.

Both Paul and Tom spoke highly of the caliber of *T.R.P.*'s editorial staff, and conversations with other Boston journalists confirmed that evaluation. Some staffers had achieved awards, national publicity, and peer recognition from the wider journalistic field.

In trying to pin down *T.R.P.*'s current editorial style and format, the researcher talked with various members of the staff. Tom Friedman reflected, "Partially it's form—longer paragraphs and in-depth analysis. Partially it's an emphasis on the human dimension. We just don't feed them information; we create an ambience whereby the reader can relate to the event. We give them more than historical background, we give them more than information—we get to the basic reasons."

Joe Klein, who had received several journalist awards, contrasted *T.R.P.*'s and the *Phoenix*'s editorial style.

> Our style strives for both a sense of immediacy and perspective. Our copy is written more dramatically. We're also much more careful. We want to write the definitive story on the subject. Paul and I talk it out and decide what the story should be; it has to have a larger focus than just what happened last week; we take specific incidents and show how they reflect on institutions. I don't see that happening with any other publication in town.

Paul Solman commented:

> Our major articles, in contrast to the *Phoenix,* are long—we do in-depth reporting. Our feature article on selling the Encyclopaedia Britannica was a good example. The writer actually sold Britannicas. We want to be able to help people see why they behave as they do. Why does a blue collar making $14,000 spend 800 bucks on a set of encyclopaedias? Or our article on the hearing aid racket is another good example. We want to be at the cutting edge—what is really going on in that business. We want to answer questions. We want the truth. But the budget limits us; we are small and they are larger. We can't compete with them in terms of coverage.
>
> The development of a pool of feature article ideas is fairly random, he continued. A lot depends on what I read or hear from friends. We get lots of suggestions from people outside the staff. And one of my critical inputs is to gather staff who can contribute ideas. I have a sense of balance for the make-up of the paper but I don't have a specific formula for a certain amount of political, or human interest, or exposé material in any issue or any month.

Chuck Fager, one of the original staffers, reflected, "We have an ephemeral editorial policy now. Writers just stream in and out. The *Phoenix* does a better job of covering Boston and the State House than we do. But any differences between the *Phoenix* and us now is more individual writer style than editorial strategy."

An Evolving Editorial Posture

In the summer of 1974, the researcher noted, the topic of future editorial direction was the object of considerable discussion, not only within the editorial staff but within the paper at large. Paula Childs commented:

> We're not covering events enough—issues that deal with people's daily lives. We're not covering what's happening with rent control, what's happening in the ecology movement, what's happening in the neighborhoods—that kind of stuff. Also, I think we're too Cambridge-oriented. Our strongest following is Cambridge. We cover Cambridge things to a much greater extent than Boston. And I think that that's one of the reasons why people on the other side of the river continue to pick up the *Phoenix* instead of *T.R.P.*

Howard Garsh believed "more hard investigative reporting should be our first priority now." Walter Harrison wanted more emphasis on quality editorial work. Tom Friedman commented feelingly, "I want to have more impact on people's lives. My basic attitude is deep distrust of the people who run our country and our businesses. Some staffers want more emphasis on entertainment; some just want more people to buy it. I want the people to get the information they wouldn't get otherwise. I want more investigations. I want to work on an investigative paper, not just a successful operation. I'm trying to hold on to my sense of moral outrage."

Bob Rotner, from his perspective, saw two approaches to future editorial direction. "The edit people want witty headlines. The business people want headlines that sell. The edit people feel the paper ought to be political, serve the left. The business people see it as the ultimate guide to Boston, serving the consumer element. I want it to do more investigative reporting."

Paul Solman reflected not only on near-term and future editorial direction, but plans to get there, noting:

> We are planning some minor modifications for the fall. We will have two long feature stories and a larger number of shorter stories that will provide more information in readable form. And we will expand the number of vignettes from New York City and Washington events. One of the latter might be an interview with the aide of a congressman.
>
> And we're trying to figure out what we want the paper to be. The paper is essentially a reflection of the people here and they are not homogeneous. But in the longer run, we're working toward a personality for this paper that is intelligent, political, which I mean to say politically progressive, interesting to people, compelling, and well written.
>
> We're not real close now, but we're making progress. Our effort now is oriented to four activities. First, we simply want to get more

copy available for our use. Copy can always be edited and rewritten. So getting the basic fund is important. This means asking more of our staff people, as well as really pursuing the free-lance sources. This also means we will have to pay higher rates than competitors, pay for research, and make appeals to the really good people based on prestige, personal ties, and even convenience.

Second, we want to tie down regular contributors—good writers who may not be on the staff but can be relied on for quality stuff. We want to create a circle of regular free-lancers.

Third, we have to fight the tendency to diffuse our efforts. Accordingly, we created the position of managing editor which will free me from the day-to-day operational problems.

Fourth, we want to run two or three solid articles per week in the front page of the book that are smart and fascinating.

Success for most people is to be big and powerful. I don't have a specific vision of *T.R.P.* and success, but I want it to be something that serves the people. I want us to be a wing of society—out there after the bad gals and guys. Yet I want it to be entertaining too, for literate people. And I want it to be instructive to the public.

LOOKING AHEAD

The former *Cambridge Phoenix* and *T.R.P.* had been organized and had their early operating years during a period of major societal and youth unrest. Campus stories headlined strikes, riots, and "take-overs," while on the wider scene, the counter-culture movement was in full bloom.

Reporters of the mid-70s youth movement indicated that much of the past turbulence seemed to have disappeared. While the president of Ohio University did resign in June of 1974, citing "the mindless destructive events of the past week," most college campuses seemed quiet and the counter-culture movement had, in many observers judgments, "plateaued."

The transition from activism to a more restrained protest pattern was captured for the researcher in Sara Davidson's article on the Symbionese Liberation Army. She interviewed Dan Siegel, a well-known participant in the 1969 Berkeley disturbances about his changing career and life style.

> Siegel is 28, an attractive, modest-looking young man in a sports shirt and slacks. In 1969, when he was student-body president at Berkeley, he gave a speech that sent thousands surging down Telegraph Avenue to reclaim People's Park. Boy Dylan was singing from speaker vans: "You can have your cake and eat it, too."
>
> Siegel says he no longer had "the illusion that revolution will be easy or that a few gallant people can do it. Winning the hearts and minds of tens of thousands of people—that's what making revolution is about."

He walks toward the courthouse where he is preparing a test case in which the community is suing the district attorney, and he says that it's funny but in some ways, he feels old.[13]

Given these changes, as well as major developments in the wider environment, the researcher wondered what, if any, impact these forces would have on the future plans of *T.R.P.* He raised the question of future direction with Paula Childs. She commented:

> I'd like to see this paper eventually be able to own its own composition shop as well as its own printing company. I'd like to see this company own its own other media resources, like its own radio station. And I'd like to see the paper get to a large enough size that we can be covering the things we should be covering. You know. Right now we're in a tug-of-war between whether to be more like a magazine, or whether to be more like a newspaper. Right now, we're much more like a magazine than a newspaper.

Joe Klein, a former staff member, added:

> From here I'd like to see us grow in several ways. First, I want us to develop a broader base of readers and not be read by just street people and hippies. This would mean expanding into older neighborhoods and suburbs, as well as becoming more and more frequently read downtown. I want it to have impact. Furthermore, and I guess this is a second point, I want us to expand beyond Boston to a regional and even national scope. I want us to have as many readers outside of Boston as the *Village Voice* has outside New York. And third, I want us to become an alternative for top-notch daily journalists.

Bo Burlingham, another staff writer, asked:

> Have we reached the end of our growth with this format? It has worked so well. And the answer is so important because it affects so many things. Who do we hire? Young kids just out of college and ask them for a full-time commitment? Or, do we hire older more experienced part-timers who can work here—and write the book they always really wanted to create?
>
> It raises questions as to who our audience is—is it Cambridge, Boston, New England, or ——? How we work with that influences Howard's financing plans and Bob Williams' advertising programs. And questions, too, need to be asked editorially. Should we go on primarily with feature stories about current causes or events or institutions? There are lots of reasons why we should. They take less resources and time and are less risky. Or do we become an investigative journal? That's really rough. It takes lots of money and time to do well and it's risky.

Jan Freeman reminisced:

---

[13] *New York Times Magazine,* June 2, 1974, page 44.

So much of what we are, is what we were—a collection of people who grew up in the late 60s and who, by luck, got into an organization that we like and where we can do what we want.

Our audience is like us—it's growing up! It's no longer the 60s. Our audience isn't clear any more—it is a mixture. Paul knows this. We know we can't just do what we do best. We never have been a doctrinaire leftist paper—we have sort of been, as I told you—a newspaper-magazine. But what's next?

A *Boston Globe* reporter, Nathan Cobb, raised the question of future direction with various members of *T.R.P.* and the *Phoenix* staff. He commented:

Times change. *T.R.P.*, having achieved financial success, wonders where to go. "It's much less clear now what we should be doing than it used to be," says Paul Solman. "It used to be automatic. You didn't have to think about what you did because there was a counter-culture not being covered by anyone else. Now we're asking what kinds of things we can provide that no one else can."

✿   ✿   ✿   ✿   ✿

One suspects, though, that the two papers really are still viewed as a legitimate journalistic alternative by the fading remnants of the "youth culture." But out in the great beyond, out in those suburbs where folks are easing into their 30s and 40s, each may indeed be viewed as just another newspaper. "The dailies are getting more like us and we're getting more like the dailies," says Joe Klein of *T.R.P.*, an experienced and professional newsperson. "And that's all right with me. I'd like to see *T.R.P.* on every doorstep."

Bob Rotner, publisher, in talking with the researcher about his job and responsibilities as publisher, noted:

But to plan the future of the paper, and to make sure that just because the paper is successful now, it doesn't mean that it's going to be successful in a year or two, and there are certain things happening in the city and the country which need to be understood. We're not making ourselves obsolete. . . . What I hope I can do now is to make the decisions about the future by going to the appropriate places and finding out what is going to happen in the future, and then to make sure *T.R.P.* is going in the direction it needs to go, so that it doesn't have to worry about the future.